A Dostoevskii Companion

Texts and Contexts

D1617199

Cultural Syllabus

Series Editor

MARK LIPOVETSKY

(University of Colorado Boulder)

ACADEMIC
STUDIES
PRESS

A Dostoevskii Companion

Texts and Contexts

EDITED BY
KATHERINE BOWERS, CONNOR DOAK,
AND KATE HOLLAND

Boston
2018

Library of Congress Cataloging-in-Publication Data

Names: Bowers, Katherine, editor. | Doak, Connor, editor. | Holland, Kate, editor. | Container of (expression): Dostoyevsky, Fyodor, 1821-1881. Works. English Selections. (Bowers, Doak, and Holland)

Title: A Dostoevskii companion: texts and contexts / edited by Katherine Bowers, Connor Doak, and Kate Holland.

Description: Boston : Academic Studies Press, 2018. | Series: Cultural syllabus | Includes bibliographical references and index.

Identifiers: LCCN 2018023270 (print) | LCCN 2018027113 (ebook) | ISBN 9781618117281 (ebook) | ISBN 9781618117267 (hardcover : alk. paper) | ISBN 9781618117274 (pbk. : alk. paper)

Subjects: LCSH: Dostoyevsky, Fyodor, 1821-1881—Miscellanea. | Dostoyevsky, Fyodor, 1821-1881—Criticism and interpretation. | Dostoyevsky, Fyodor, 1821-1881—Correspondence. | Dostoyevsky, Fyodor, 1821-1881—Aesthetics. | Dostoyevsky, Fyodor, 1821-1881—Themes, motives.

Classification: LCC PG3328 (ebook) | LCC PG3328 .D6394 2018 (print) | DDC 891.73/3—dc23

LC record available at https://lccn.loc.gov/2018023270

Book design by Kryon Publishing Services (P) Ltd.
www.kryonpublishing.com

On the cover: *Reader of Dostoevsky*, by Emil Filla, 1907 (Oil on canvas, 98.5 × 80 cm)

Published by Academic Studies Press
28 Montfern Avenue
Brighton, MA 02135, USA
press@academicstudiespress.com
www.academicstudiespress.com

Table of Contents

Acknowledgments

This project has been a significant undertaking, and we are indebted to a number of people and institutions for their help, support, and advice.

A major debt of gratitude is owed to the wonderful graduate research assistants, without whom we would likely still be tracking down permissions and scanning documents! Anton Nonin organized nearly all the permissions we required, helped with scanning and OCRing texts, and also masterfully translated a number of Russian texts that appear in the volume. Kristina McGuirk and Hanna Murray also helped significantly with locating texts, scanning and editing. We send them all a massive thank you.

When we began working on the volume, we were glad to receive invaluable advice, suggestions, and encouragement from a number of Dostoevskii scholars. We thank all those who answered our request to share their Dostoevskii class syllabi, which proved immeasurably helpful as we began to plan the volume. We acknowledge, with thanks, the contributions of Carol Apollonio, Deborah Martinsen, Robin Feuer Miller, William Mills Todd, III, and Sarah J. Young who met with us to share their suggestions for improving our first plan for the volume. We are also especially grateful to those scholars and institutions that allowed us to reproduce copyrighted material without charge, purely for the love of Dostoevskii. In particular, we thank Robert Louis Jackson, Igor' Volgin, Vladimir Zakharov, and *Yale Review* for this support.

The volume originated as part of the *"Crime and Punishment* at 150" project, which was made possible through support from the Social Sciences and Humanities Research Council of Canada. Additional funding was provided by the Faculty of Arts and Department of Central, Eastern, and Northern European Studies at the University of British Columbia, and Academic Studies Press.

Finally, we are grateful to Academic Studies Press for their enthusiasm for and support of the volume, in particular Mark Lipovetsky, who gave us helpful structural suggestions; our first editor, Faith Wilson Stein, with whom we began the project; and her successor, Oleh Kotsyuba, who concluded it with us.

We hope that you find this volume as useful and interesting as we have found working on it to be.

How to Use this Book

Fedor Dostoevskii's popularity and relevance as a writer have not dwindled over time. Indeed, as Rowan Williams points out, the subjects of Dostoevskii's fiction—from absent fathers and child abuse to terrorism and the nature of national identity—are the quintessential anxieties of the twenty-first century.[1] *Crime and Punishment* remains the embarkation point for many readers setting out to discover Russian literature, and students remain fascinated by Raskol'nikov's Theory of Great Men, intrigued by the Underground Man's sardonic ramblings, and awed by their encounter with the Devil in *Brothers Karamazov*.

Though courses focused on a single author are not as common as they once were, a class simply titled "Dostoevskii" can still attract substantial enrollments. His writing also figures heavily in survey courses that cover nineteenth-century Russian literature, and his works regularly show up in surveys of the European novel, as well as classes on "Great Books," as one might expect. However, as disciplinary boundaries become more porous, Dostoevskii increasingly features in syllabi in other fields. Students might encounter "Notes from Underground" in a philosophy class, *Demons* in political science, *The Idiot* in divinity school, or *Brothers Karamazov* in an advanced seminar on Law and Literature, to give but a few examples. Such variety would not come as a shock to the author, a polymath who rejected the idea of art for art's sake and whose own fiction unabashedly tackled social, political, and theological questions. Therefore, although *A Dostoevskii Companion: Texts and Contexts* is written primarily from the perspective of literary studies, we hope that this collection will speak to those interested in Dostoevskii as a thinker as well as a writer.

The book is divided into three parts. The first part, Biography and Context, opens with a chapter on the early Dostoevskii, supplying background

---

1   Rowan Williams, *Dostoevsky: Language, Faith and Fiction* (London: Continuum, 2008), 1.

on the author and setting his work in the context of influences from Russian and European writing in the mid-nineteenth century. The second chapter, on "Dostoevskii and His Contemporaries," focuses on his place in the nineteenth-century Russian canon, with an emphasis on comparative approaches with Lev Tolstoi and Ivan Turgenev, the other two leading writers of his day.

The second part, Poetics, begins with a chapter on "Aesthetics," explores Dostoevskii's conception of what art and literature should be, notions of beauty in his work, and his idiosyncratic stance on the fraught question of Realism. "Characters," the longest chapter in the whole volume, consists primarily of secondary literature on Dostoevskii's most intriguing personages from Makar Devushkin to Alesha Karamazov. "The Novel" takes a broader look at the form and structure of Dostoevskii's novels, exploring their genesis through the writer's notebooks, and how narrative voice, plot, and time operate in his work. "From Journalism to Fiction" looks at Dostoevskii as a writer whose works not only incorporated both fiction and nonfiction, but often challenged the distinction between these two modes of writing, especially in his *A Writer's Diary*.

Finally, the third section, "Themes," concentrates on the content of Dostoevskii's writing, and looks explicitly at some of the social, political, and theological issues that he addresses. "Captivity, Free Will, and Utopia" brings together three interlinked themes in his oeuvre, beginning with his fictionalization of his own experience in prison, *Notes from the House of the Dead*, addressing his critique of socialist utopian thinking and yet recognizing that his ideas of universal brotherhood still carried a utopian urge. "Others" charts Dostoevskii's changing—and often problematic—representations of ethnic and religious minority groups, such as Jews and Muslims, while also examining his attitude towards women at a time when the "woman question" was at the forefront of political debate. "Russia" investigates the question of national identity in Dostoevskii's writing, particularly the apparent contradiction between the imperfect, historical Russia in which he lived and the idealized, holy Russia that he longed for. The final chapter, "God," examines the vital role that religion plays in Dostoevskii's works, looking at how the Bible and the Christian tradition inform his work, but also giving voice to more skeptical critics who have provided alternative readings.

We hope that the tripartite division—"Biography and Context," "Poetics," "Themes"—will help guide the reader, but we understand that it is an impossible task to separate these three entirely. Dostoevskii's biography inevitably contributed to both his philosophical views and the form of his writing, as the "Captivity, Free Will, and Utopia" section shows, connecting his time in prison in Siberia with his emphasis on the importance of free will. Moreover, the form and content of Dostoevskii's novels must be studied together: Gary Saul Morson has argued that the very form of Dostoevskii's novels reflected his philosophical indeterminism. Indeed, some of the most challenging perspectives in Dostoevskii criticism have come from scholars who have sought to reconcile the writer and the thinker. How could the exponent of universal love who penned *Brothers Karamazov* also have written the antisemitic tracts in *A Writer's Diary*?

Like the rest of the Cultural Syllabus series, this book is aimed primarily at undergraduate students, although we anticipate that it may also be of interest to the general reader with a knowledge of Dostoevskii. It is intended as a sourcebook for those who have already read at least some of the writer's stories and novels. Instructors may choose to assign particular excerpts, although we hope the volume is user-friendly enough for students to dip into themselves. Each chapter comprises a mixture of sources, ranging from Dostoevskii's own letters and journalism, to reviews of his work from his contemporaries, to seminal treatments of the writer by major figures such as the religious philosopher Nikolai Berdiaev and the literary theorist Mikhail Bakhtin, to some of the best current criticism on Dostoevskii from our own time. We have deliberately chosen to include a range of critical voices, many of which dissent from one another and some of which are rather hostile to Dostoevskii—though all of them think he is worth writing about! As editors, we try to contextualize each of these excerpts briefly in a short introduction to each chapter, but we purposefully refrain from providing our own critical judgments. We believe it is the students' job to do that thinking for themselves. For those looking to go further, each chapter includes a list of suggested further reading; we have sought to avoid duplication here, but many of the suggested works could be listed in several different chapters.

We deliberately chose not to organize this volume work by work, with one chapter on *Crime and Punishment*, another on *The Idiot*, and so on. One reason is that there already exist multiple series that do precisely that: the Northwestern Critical Companions, for instance, or Bloom's Guides. More importantly, however, we wanted to encourage readers to make connections between texts and perhaps spark a desire for students to read something new. For example, the "Russia" chapter includes readings on *Notes from the House of the Dead*, "The Peasant Marei," and *Demons*, not the most commonly assigned texts for undergraduates. However, the issues around national identity raised here will be relevant to students reading, say, *Crime and Punishment*, and it will encourage these readers to think beyond the particular text they are currently studying.

Finally, we would stress that we realize that this volume cannot provide encyclopedic coverage of Dostoevskii's life and times. Most university libraries will already have a copy of Kenneth Lantz's *The Dostoevsky Encyclopedia*, an excellent point of reference to begin research.[2] Several recommended biographies are also available, from Joseph Frank's five-volume magnum opus to the more accessible offerings by Konstantin Mochul'skii or Robert Bird.[3] Another invaluable resource is Deborah Martinsen and Olga Maiorova's *Dostoevsky in Context*, which provides superb coverage of a range of topics on the literary and historical contexts of Dostoevskii's Russia.[4] Rounding out these recommendations, *The Cambridge Companion to Dostoevskii*, edited by W. J. Leatherbarrow, offers a series of introductory essays on key topics in Dostoevskii criticism.[5] Our hope is that students will use *A Dostoevskii Companion* alongside these existing works, but that our volume will allow students the satisfaction of working with a variety of primary and secondary sources to form their own opinions and arguments about the classic Russian writer.

---

2   Kenneth Lantz, *The Dostoevsky Encyclopedia* (Westport, CT: Greenwood Press, 2004).

3   Konstantin Mochulsky, *Dostoevsky: His Life and Work*, trans. Michael A. Minihan (Princeton, NJ: Princeton University Press, 1971); Robert Bird, *Fyodor Dostoevsky* (London: Reaktion Books, 2012).

4   Deborah A. Martinsen and Olga Maiorova, eds., *Dostoevsky in Context* (Cambridge: Cambridge University Press, 2015).

5   W. J. Leatherbarrow, ed., *The Cambridge Companion to Dostoevskii* (Cambridge: Cambridge University Press, 2002).

Note on Translation, Transliteration, and Referencing

Our volume is intended primarily for Anglophone readers, and we assume no knowledge of the Russian language. As such, all the Dostoevskii texts and much of the secondary literature in this volume are presented in English translation. As editors, we wish to acknowledge the generations of translators whose work we have excerpted here. Too often their labor is invisible. Moreover, we would point out to our readers that any encounter with Dostoevskii in English is always mediated through translation; that is, translation shapes how we understand and interpret Dostoevskii. Thankfully, Dostoevskii has been well served by translators, with new versions of major works like *Crime and Punishment* still appearing at regular intervals in the twenty-first century. While each reader will have his or her favorite translation, many instructors find it rewarding to bring a variety of translations into the classroom and discuss the different variants with students. Even for students without knowledge of Russian, this exercise can make visible the work of translators and the decisions they make, while also showing the multiplicity of possible meanings and interpretations inherent within a Dostoevskii text.

While we encourage instructors to experiment with multiple translations in the classroom, we also wanted to provide as much consistency for the reader as possible within this volume. Therefore, when we include excerpts from Dostoevskii's own works, we most often use the Constance Garnett translations, which remain generally reliable and nearly all volumes have the significant advantage of being out of copyright.

In the contemporary criticism reproduced here, most scholars refer to the Russian texts of Dostoevskii, usually relying on the standard scholarly edition: F. M. Dostoevskii, *Polnoe sobranie sochinenii v tridtsati tomakh*, 30 vols. (Leningrad: Nauka, 1972–90). Rather than repeat this full reference multiple times, we use the abbreviation PSS throughout the book to refer to this edition.

As for transliteration, we have chosen to use the Modified Library of Congress system for transliteration (Dostoevskii, not Dostoevsky; Gogol', not Gogol), again for reasons of consistency. The exception is in bibliographic references in footnotes and the lists of further reading; here it is necessary to reproduce the exact title of published works, such as Richard Peace's *Dostoyevsky: An Examination of the Major Novels*. Where possible, we have standardized the referencing throughout the volume to accord with the *Chicago Manual of Style* to provide consistency for the reader and updated the spelling to American English.

Timeline of Dostoevskii's Life and Works

1821   Dostoevskii is born November 11 (October 30, old style) in Moscow.

1825   Serial publication of Pushkin's novel *Eugene Onegin* begins.

1825   Decembrist uprising in St. Petersburg.

1828   Tolstoi born.

1831   Dostoevskii and his brother attend school in Moscow (until 1836).

1836   Publication of Chaadaev's "First Philosophical Letter"; publication of Dickens's *Sketches by Boz*.

1837   Pushkin dies in a duel; Dostoevskii's mother dies of tuberculosis and the Dostoevskii brothers are sent to a St. Petersburg boarding school.

1838   Dostoevskii enters military engineering school in St. Petersburg.

1839   Dostoevskii's father is killed (allegedly murdered by his own serfs).

1841   Dostoevskii obtains a military commission; he begins experimenting with writing historical dramas à la Schiller and Pushkin (now-lost titles include *Maria Stuart* and *Boris Godunov*).

1842   Gogol''s *Dead Souls*, part 1 is published.

1843   Dostoevskii passes his final engineering examinations, translates Balzac's *Eugénie Grandet*.

1844   Dostoevskii resigns his commission in the army and embarks on a literary career; he translates George Sand's *La dernière Aldini*, finishes *Poor Folk* in November.

1845   *Poor Folk* is well received by critics; Dostoevskii enters literary society.

1846   *Poor Folk* and *The Double* are published; *The Double* receives negative critical reviews.

1847   Dostoevskii writes for the *St. Petersburg Gazette*; first signs of epilepsy.

1848   Marx writes "The Communist Manifesto."

1849   Dostoevskii begins work on *Netochka Nezvanova*; the novel remains unfinished when Dostoevskii is arrested for his membership in the Petrashevskii Circle; Dostoevskii is sentenced to death. The sentence is commuted at the last moment and he is sent to penal servitude in Siberia.

1850   Dostoevskii arrives at the prison in Omsk.

1851   The Crystal Palace is erected in Hyde Park for the Great Exhibition.

1852   Gogol' burns the second part of *Dead Souls* and dies.

1853   The Crimean War begins; Dostoevskii begins to experience periodic epileptic seizures.

1854   Dostoevskii is released from prison; begins his forced military service at Semipalatinsk; meets his future wife.

1855   Nicholas I dies; Alexander II ascends the throne.

1857   Dostoevskii marries Mariia Dmitrievna Isaeva; he publishes "The Little Hero," which he wrote while in prison in 1849.

1858   Dostoevskii begins writing again; writes *The Village of Stepanchikovo* and *Uncle's Dream*.

1859   Dostoevskii leaves the military; returns to St. Petersburg after ten years of exile. Darwin publishes *The Origin of Species*.

1860   Dostoevskii writes *Notes from the House of the Dead* and *The Insulted and Injured*; he joins his brother in editing the literary journal *Time*.

1861   Emancipation of the serfs; the first two parts of Turgenev's *Fathers and Sons* are published.

1862   Dostoevskii goes abroad for the first time, visits England, France, and Switzerland; meets Gertsen in London.

1863   Chernyshevskii's *What Is to Be Done?* is published. Dostoevskii publishes *Winter Notes on Summer Impressions*. Dostoevskii travels abroad again and begins an affair with Apollinariia Suslova.

1864   The Dostoevskii brothers found the journal *The Epoch* after *Time* is dissolved. Dostoevskii's wife dies in April and his older brother, Mikhail, in July. Dostoevskii works on *Notes from Underground*. Tolstoi publishes the first part of *War and Peace*.

1865   *Epoch* goes bankrupt and shuts down. Dostoevskii leaves Russia to escape his debts. Suslova rejects his proposal; Dostoevskii settles in Wiesbaden where he falls into gambling; he writes *Crime and Punishment*.

1866   Karakozov attempts to assassinate Alexander II. Dostoevskii returns to Russia, writes *The Gambler*, and meets Anna Grigor'evna Snitkina. *Crime and Punishment* is published.

1867   Marries Anna Grigor'evna; they settle in Dresden to escape his debts in Russia. The Umetskii trial takes place in St. Petersburg that fall.

1868   A daughter, Sofiia, is born, but dies several months later. *The Idiot* is serialized; the Dostoevskiis move to Italy.

1869   A daughter, Liubov, is born; the family moves to Dresden.

1870   Lenin is born; Dickens dies.

1871   Dostoevskii gives up gambling. A son, Fedor, is born in St. Petersburg. *Demons* is serialized.

1873   Dostoevskii becomes editor of *The Citizen* journal (resigns 1874).

1874   Dostoevskii is arrested and imprisoned again for censorship offenses. Dostoevskii travels to Bad Ems seeking a cure for emphysema. Dostoevskii travels to Staraia Russa for the first time.

1875   *The Adolescent* is published. A son, Aleksei, is born. Dostoevskii again travels to Bad Ems for his ailment.

1876   Dostoevskii begins publishing *A Writer's Diary* in *The Citizen*.

1877   The Russo-Turkish War breaks out; Tolstoi publishes *Anna Karenina*.

1878   Dostoevskii's son, Aleksei, dies; Dostoevskii begins work on *Brothers Karamazov*.

1880   *Brothers Karamazov* is published. Dostoevskii gives his "Pushkin Speech" at the unveiling of the Pushkin monument in Moscow; returns to Staraia Russa.

1881   Dostoevskii dies on February 9 (January 28, old style) and is buried in the Aleksandr Nevskii lavra in St. Petersburg. Alexander II assassinated March 13 (March 1, old style)

Part One

Biography and Context

CHAPTER 1

The Early Dostoevskii

This volume begins with a chapter on Fedor Dostoevskii's early literary career, from his student days in the early 1840s to his arrest, trial, and mock execution in 1849. Although ostensibly in the capital to attend engineering school, Dostoevskii and his brother Mikhail devoted themselves to literary pursuits. In *A Writer's Diary*, Dostoevskii recalls, "We passionately believed something, and though we both perfectly knew what was needed for the mathematics exam, we dreamed only about poetry and poets." The passion Dostoevskii felt was a product of his reading habits during this time, which heavily influenced his art and outlook.

During this period, Dostoevskii produced several translations of French and German works, three novellas (*Poor Folk*, *The Double*, *The Landlady*), ten stories (which include shorter works like "A Weak Heart" as well as longer ones like "White Nights"), and an unfinished novel, *Netochka Nezvanova*. These early works demonstrate Dostoevskii's preoccupation with the romantic concept of the "lofty and beautiful," which later would be ironized by Underground Man; during this period, however, Dostoevskii's engagement with these ideas was sincere and intense.

This chapter is organized around the way the early Dostoevskii shaped the later Dostoevskii. To this end, the chapter begins with an excerpt from Robert Bird's biography *Fyodor Dostoevsky*. Bird's opening discussion focuses not on the events of the 1840s, but on Dostoevskii's literary influences and aspirations, and the way these were shaped by the events of the 1840s. For Dostoevskii during this period, art was life.

The chapter includes a selection from the works that the young Dostoevskii was reading. Earlier writers like Jean-Jacques Rousseau (1712–78), Friedrich Schiller (1775–1805), and Ann Radcliffe (1764–1823) appear alongside

Dostoevskii's contemporaries, including Nikolai Gogol' (1809–52), Honoré de Balzac (1799–1850), and Charles Dickens (1812–70). Interested students might also seek out works by Eugène Sue (1804–57) and George Sand (1804–76), two of Dostoevskii's favorite writers that do not appear here. The excerpts that are included give a taste of the kind of literature that inspired young Dostoevskii as well as address common themes such as poverty, sentimentality, human value and dignity, and love. Throughout these works, individual freedom is valued, and human dignity championed.

Excerpts from Dostoevskii's own writing that appear in the chapter include an exchange of letters from his first novel, the epistolary *Poor Folk* (1846), and the first encounter between hero and heroine in "White Nights" (1848). These two passages readily demonstrate the connections between Dostoevskii's early writing and the works that influenced him. *Poor Folk* launched Dostoevskii's career—its depiction of the downtrodden urban poor impressed the literati of the day, including poet Nikolai Nekrasov and critic Vissarion Belinskii. In *Poor Folk,* in the correspondence between its heroes, we see the individual on display in all his mundane pettiness; yet, despite degradation and humiliation, Makar Devushkin and Varvara Alekseevna preserve their humanity, acting with compassion towards each other. "White Nights" tells of a romantic "Dreamer," a famous Dostoevskian character type, and his encounters with Nasten'ka, a young girl. The Petersburg setting comes to life, and here Dostoevskii was demonstrably influenced by both the sublime landscapes of Radcliffe and the physiological descriptions of Sue and Balzac.

During the 1840s, Dostoevskii lived in a world of "lofty and beautiful" words and ideas—ideas were life, but they could be dangerous too. The failed Decembrist uprising in 1825 had ushered in the reactionary conservative regime of Nicholas I, who instituted widespread state censorship. Despite—or because of—this repression of literature, art, and particularly the written word, was seen as a tool that could speak the truth to the people; this was a view held by the literary critic Belinskii, a major shaper of Russian letters during the period. Included here is Belinskii's "Letter to Gogol'" (1847), a publicly circulated letter that openly called for the abolishment of serfdom. In the letter Belinskii berates Gogol' for failing to live up to this vision of authorial "truth" in his latest book, and for propagating conservative views that are morally repugnant. The written word wielded power, and authorities banned Belinskii's "Letter." This letter would also play a role in Dostoevskii's arrest in 1849; his crimes, detailed in his official sentence, included possessing a copy of Belinskii's "Letter to Gogol'," reading it aloud, and passing it on for copying.

In the 1840s, Dostoevskii had become involved with the Petrashevskii Circle, a group of writers and artists that included political thinkers. Throughout his trial, Dostoevskii maintained that his involvement in the group was apolitical, and the trial document records Dostoevskii's assertion that "If the wish for a better future is liberalism, then he, Dostoevskii, is a freethinker as much as anyone else who believes in his right as a citizen" who "wishes nothing but good for his country, and carries within himself love for his motherland." Despite these passionate words, Dostoevskii was sentenced to death. At the last moment his sentence was commuted to penal servitude in Siberia, a cruel preplanned component of the punishment and a harrowing experience that proved intensely important for Dostoevskii's writing, as explored in Chapter 7.

The final document in this chapter is a letter from Dostoevskii to his brother Mikhail discussing the mock execution. This near-death experience changed Dostoevskii's course as a writer as it set him on a path leading definitively away from romantic themes. Filled with a newfound love of life, he recounts to his brother, "Life is a gift, life is happiness, every minute could be a century of happiness."

Further Reading

Allen, Elizabeth Cheresh, ed. *Before They Were Titans: Essays on the Early Works of Dostoevsky and Tolstoy*. Boston, MA: Academic Studies Press, 2015.

Frank, Joseph. *Dostoevsky: The Seeds of Revolt, 1821–1849*. Princeton, NJ: Princeton University Press, 1976.

Knapp, Liza. *Dostoevsky as Reformer: The Petrashevsky Case*. Ann Arbor, MI: Ardis Publishers, 1987.

Sekirin, Peter. *The Dostoevsky Archive: Firsthand Accounts of the Novelist from Contemporaries' Memoirs and Rare Periodicals*. Jefferson, NC: McFarland and Company Inc., 1997.

Terras, Victor. *The Young Dostoevsky, 1846–1849; a Critical Study*. The Hague: Mouton Publishers, 1969.

A Noble Vocation (2012)*

Robert Bird

*Y*ou are to provide concise and clear explanations according to the strict truth to the
questions offered here by the imperially sanctioned Investigative Commission:
*1) What is your name, patronymic and surname; what is your age; what faith; and
have you fulfilled the rites prescribed by religion at the proper time?*
Fedor, son of Mikhail Dostoevskii, 27 years of age, GrecoRussian Orthodox.
The rites prescribed by religion I have fulfilled at the proper time.
2) Who are your parents, and where are they if they are alive?
My father was a military doctor, Collegiate Councilor Dostoevskii. My mother
was of the merchant estate. Both are deceased.
*3) Where were you educated, at whose expense and when did you complete your
education?*
I was educated at the Main College of Engineering at my own expense.
I completed my education upon graduating from the officer course of the Main
College of Engineering in 1843.
*4) Do you serve, and if so, when did you enter the service, what position do you
occupy and what rank are you? Also, have you previously been under investigation
or on trial, and if so, then what exactly?*
I entered active service upon graduating the highest officer course of the
Main College of Engineering in 1843 at the drafting office of the Engineering
Department. I resigned in 1844 at the rank of lieutenant. I have never previously
been on trial or under investigation.
*5) Do you have property or capital, and if not, then what means did you possess for
maintaining and housing yourself and your family, if you have one?*

At my parents' death, together with my entire remaining family, I inherited an estate numbering 100 souls in Tula province. But in 1845, with the mutual agreement of my relatives, I renounced my portion of the estate for a one-time payout of money. At the present time I have neither property nor capital. I earn my living by literary work, which is how I have existed up to now.

6) With whom have you had close acquaintance and frequent relations?

Completely open relations I have had with no one, apart from my brother, the retired engineer sub-lieutenant Mikhail Dostoevskii . . .

Thus, under interrogation on June 8, 1849, did Fedor Dostoevskii describe his background and character. He was born on October 30, 1821 (11 November according to the Gregorian calendar) into a family that claimed an ancient noble lineage but had, in recent generations, occupied more humble stations in the regimented society of the Russian Empire. His grandfather was probably a parish priest in Ukraine, possibly in the Eastern Rite Catholic Church. Dostoevskii's father served in Moscow as a doctor at a hospital for the poor—the same hospital where Dostoevskii was born; he gradually ascended the service ranks of society and was granted noble status in 1828. In 1831 the family was able to purchase a country estate: Darovoe (meaning "given for free") in Tula province, with 100 peasants, including 40 male serfs. In 1832 the estate burned to the ground, leading to a tangle of mortgages and other debts. Legal wrangling over the legacies of his parents and the Kumanins, his aunt and uncle on his mother's side, would provide a constant source of stress during Dostoevskii's life, perhaps even playing a role in the attack that killed him at the age of 59, on January 28, 1881.

Seven children made it into adulthood; Fedor was the second of four boys. In 1837, soon after their mother's death, Fedor traveled with his beloved elder brother Mikhail (born 1820) to St. Petersburg, where together they prepared for the entrance exams for the Main Engineering School. Mikhail was not accepted, but Fedor passed his exams brilliantly. A lack of clout prevented him from winning a scholarship and left him reliant on his supportive but impoverished father. He became renowned for his studious ways, earning the monastic nickname "brother Photius." He completed his studies in 1843 with the rank of sub-lieutenant and entered the engineering corps in St. Petersburg.

By this time the Dostoevskii siblings had also lost their father, who died in June 1839 in circumstances that remain unclear; he either suffered an apoplectic fit or was beaten to death by the peasants on the family estate. It should be said that, regardless of the circumstances, and despite Sigmund Freud's imaginative reconstruction, it would not seem that Fedor felt at all responsible for his father's death and there is little trace of lasting trauma in his letters and autobiographical notes. Fedor was left at the mercy of guardians, including generous Kumanins and the officious Petr Karpenin, who became executor of the Dostoevskii estate after marrying Fedor's sister Varvara in 1840. Though they continued to support him in his studies, his relatives had little inclination to indulge his carefree attitude to money and his fantastic schemes for his future.

From early on Dostoevskii's financial problems were exacerbated by his wholehearted immersion in the imaginary realms opened up by poetry, drama and fiction. He later recalled seeing Friedrich Schiller's *The Robbers* at about the age of ten. In 1835 the family had subscribed to *Biblioteka dlia chteniia* (Library for Reading), which published everything from Pushkin to Balzac and George Sand.[1] On a trip to the Trinity St. Sergius Monastery in May 1837 Fedor and Mikhail regaled their aunt with a "mass" of poems learned by heart.[2] Years later he would recall a journey made that same month to the capital, together with Mikhail and their father:

> My brother and I were rushing into our new life, dreaming about something so frightfully strongly, about everything 'beautiful and lofty'—at that time this word was still fresh and was spoken without irony. And how many such beautiful words there were in circulation at the time! We passionately believed something, and though we both perfectly knew what was needed for the mathematics exam, we dreamed only about poetry and poets. My brother wrote poems, three or so poems every day, even on the road, while I constantly composed in my mind a novel based on Venetian life. (PSS 22:27)

In his first years in St. Petersburg, Dostoevskii wrote two dramas (*Mary Stuart* and *Boris Godunov*, both lost) and tried his hand at translating his favorite French authors, Eugène Sue (1804–1857) and Honoré de Balzac (1799–1850); his translation of Balzac's *Eugénie Grandet* (1833) was published in a journal in 1844. He confessed to his brother that he was completing a novel

---

1 EDS: The *Library for Reading* (1834–1865) was the first Russian "thick journal," a monthly compendium of literary texts that published serialized novels as well as short prose, poetry, and journalistic writing. By the time Dostoevskii launched his writing career in the 1840s, thick journals were the most common publication model. For more information, see Deborah A. Martinsen, ed., *Literary Journals in Imperial Russia* (Cambridge: Cambridge University Press, 1998).

2 Andrei Dostoevskii, *Vospominaniia* (Moscow: Agraf, 1999), 70, 80–81.

"the length of *Eugénie Grandet*."[3] Already at this time Dostoevskii conceived of fiction as a powerful force for personal and social liberation, if also a source of risk.

Tired of parades and ceremonial displays before the emperor, in August 1844 Dostoevskii resigned his commission. The lack of a constant income led Dostoevskii to request that he be paid his inheritance in a lump sum of 500 rubles, with 500 more to be paid in installments. His relatives were shocked at how cheaply he rated his inheritance, but they acceded to his request; it was advantageous to them. There are competing accounts of the circumstances that led to Dostoevskii's resignation from the engineering corps. There was at the time a rumor that he was asked to resign when the emperor noticed that a draft Dostoevskii made for a fortress lacked a front gate. This rumor not only fed on Dostoevskii's absent-mindedness but on his emotional insularity. It is the first hint of the claustrophobic images of imprisonment that soon came to pervade Dostoevskii's fictions, halfway between Piranesi and Escher.[4]

Having selected the new vocation of the professional writer, for the rest of his life Dostoevskii would try to make it compensate for his compromised birthright.[5] Writing in 1877 to a fourteen-year-old, Dostoevskii recalled that he had been intent on a literary career from the age of sixteen: "in my soul there was a kind of flame in which I believed, though I was not too concerned with what would come of it."[6] At the same time, Dostoevskii stressed,

> *my* infatuation [with a literary career] did not distract me at all from holding a realistic view of life, and though I was a poet, not an engineer, I was always one of the top students at the engineering school until the very last year; then I served, and though I knew that sooner or later I would leave the service, *for the while* I did not see anything in *my social* occupations that was too irreconcilably hostile to my future; on the contrary, I firmly believed that the future still would be mine and that I *alone* was its master.[7]

---

3 PSS 28/1: 100.

4 EDS: Giovanni Battista Piranesi (1720–78) and M. C. Escher (1898–1972) created art that visualized spaces of captivity and claustrophobia. Piranesi did a series of engravings focused on imaginary prisons, while many of Escher's works are rooms or environments that defy spatial logic.

5 William Mills Todd, III, "Dostoevskii as a Professional Writer," in *The Cambridge Companion to Dostoevskii*, ed. W. J. Leatherbarrow (Cambridge: Cambridge University Press, 2002), 66–92.

6 PSS 29/2: 156.

7 PSS 29/2: 157.

The confidence granted by his poetic vocation gave him the means for dealing with such traumas as the death of his parents. Reflecting upon it, Dostoevskii wrote to his brother in 1839:

> My soul is beyond my former tempestuous impulses. It is entirely serene, like the heart of a man who conceals a profound mystery. Man is a mystery. One has to solve it, and if you spend all your life solving it you won't be able to say that you've wasted your time. I am occupied with this mystery because I want to be a man [...] I think there is no ascetic holier than the poet. How can one commit one's ecstasy to paper? The soul always conceals more than it can express in words, colors or sounds.[8]

From his earliest surviving letters on, Dostoevskii always signed with his full name (F. Dostoevskii or Fedor Dostoevskii), even when writing to his family and closest friends. He was fashioning himself as an author.

Though his impudence and inconstancy strained his relations with family and colleagues, Dostoevskii appears almost to have cultivated these stresses as major sources of his fiction, most directly of the novel *Poor Folk*, the first draft of which he completed about a year after resigning his commission. The novel, like almost all of Dostoevskii's writing, is a study of the forces that constrain human freedom, both exterior forces such as money and power, and interior ones like illness and sexual desire. Moreover, Dostoevskii immediately set about questioning the very distinction between two realms, showing how subjective experience becomes objectified in material objects of desire and fear, and vice versa. However, like most of Dostoevskii's fiction, *Poor Folk* also revealed his belief in the power of fiction to redeem the world by manifesting an imaginative realm in which freedom is—or, at least, can be—sovereign [...]

The novel's mixed reception revealed that, as an author, Dostoevskii was also hermetically sealed in his own imagination. One witty critic complained:

> The novel has no form and is based completely on details so tiringly monotonous that it invokes a tedium the likes of which we have never experienced before. The details in the novel are like a meal in which instead of soup one is given sugar bonbons, and instead of beef,

---

8 PSS 28/1: 63.

sauce, stew, and dessert—sugar bonbons. It might be sweet, it might be useful, but only in the sense in which sweetshop apprentices are allowed to gorge themselves in order to inspire disgust for sugary sweets.[9]

Others found the sentimentalism quite powerful. Upon reading *Poor Folk* in manuscript, Nikolai Nekrasov (1821–1877), a leading poet and publisher of the day, rushed to meet the author in the middle of the night—a Petersburg white night in which the sun dips just below the horizon for a fleeting couple of hours. His enthusiasm was shared by Vissarion Belinskii (1811–1848), the leading critic and trendsetter. The novel was published in Nekrasov's almanac in 1846 and as a separate edition in 1847. By that time the adulation of Nekrasov and Belinskii had already been diluted by their dismay at Dostoevskii's puzzling follow-up novel *The Double*, which was published in Andrei Kraevskii's journal *Otechestvennye zapiski* (*Notes of the Fatherland*) in February 1846; but this consternation was hopefully dismissed. The future of Russian literature—and with it, to a large degree, of Russian civil society—seemed to rest with his talented, socially committed pen. By 1848 Dostoevskii was on course to achieve the cultural legitimacy and financial independence he so craved.

The European revolutions of 1848 found Russia in a state of severe cultural depression, fostered by the paranoid regime of Emperor Nicholas I. Nicholas had acceded to power in the midst of the Decembrist revolt of 1825, led by educated officers hankering for constitutional reform. After suppressing the revolt, Nicholas prohibited many forms of public discourse and instituted vigilant censorship over the rest. Philosophy as a subject was banned at the universities. When Petr Chaadaev (1794–1856) sneaked his "First Philosophical Letter" past the censors in 1836, he was declared mad and kept under house arrest.

Chaadaev's argument in this letter was that Russia was a blank space without any history or other redeeming features:

> At first brutal barbarism, then crude superstition, then cruel and humiliating foreign domination, the spirit of which was later inherited by our national rulers —such is the sad history of our youth. We had none of that exuberant activity, of the fervent turmoil of the moral forces of nations [. . .] There are no charming remembrances, no graceful images

---

9 N. G. Goncharova, *F. M. Dostoevskii v zerkalakh grafiki i kritiki* (Moscow: Sovladenie, 2005), 161.

in the people's memory; our national tradition is devoid of any powerful teaching.[10]

Chaadaev's argument struck at the heart of both traditional Russian culture, centered on Orthodox Christianity, and of the modernizing and Europeanizing project that Peter the Great had embarked upon at the turn of the eighteenth century [. . .] The traumas of modernization and the constraints on their open public discussion made imaginative art and literature a means not only of measuring historical change, but also of modulating it for educated individuals. By the late eighteenth century a vibrant poetry and, increasingly, fiction had arisen and had come to perform many of the functions accorded to philosophy and political theory in the contemporary European societies on which Russian was modeling itself. Aleksandr Pushkin (1799–1837) and Nikolai Gogol' (1809–1851) were two of the first individuals who were able to exist as professional writers. Moreover, artistic and literary criticism became unusually important as a venue for public discourse. Critic Vissarion Belinskii, in particular, became a major conduit for philosophical idealism and political radicalism. This was the milieu into which Dostoevskii gained entry with his *Poor Folk*.

Dostoevskii's letter to his brother Mikhail of March 24, 1845 shows how intently he plotted his entrance onto the stage of Russian literature. Fearing that censors and editors would delay *Poor Folk*, Dostoevskii considered publishing it himself:

> To publish oneself means to thrust one's chest forwards, and if the work is good, it will not only hold its own, but will redeem me from subjection to debt and give me food.
>
> And now about food! You know, brother, that in this respect I am left to my own powers. But come what may, however dire my circumstances, I have pledged to bear up and not take commissions. Commissions will crush and destroy everything. I want each of my works to be distinctly good. Look at Pushkin and Gogol'. They didn't write much, but monuments await both. And now Gogol' gets 1,000 rubles in silver for each signature [about twenty pages], while Pushkin, as you know, sold each line for ten rubles. But then their glory was paid for by years of penury and starvation [. . .] [11]

10 Peter Yakovlevich Chaadayev, *Philosophical Letters and Apology of a Madman*, trans. Mary-Varvara Zeldin (Knoxville, TN: University of Tennessee Press, 1969), 35–36.

11 PSS 28/1:106–7.

Dostoevskii's ambition became legend [. . .] His credo, expressed in a letter to Mikhail from November 26, 1846, was to attain

> an independent position [. . .] work for Holy Art, sacred work, pure, in the simplicity of my heart which has never before shuddered and moved as it does now before all the new images which are being created in my soul. Brother, I am being reborn not only morally, but also physically.[12]

[. . .] [F]rom the very beginning Dostoevskii was caught in the tension between the nobility of his aims and the limitations of his immediate position.

The tension is captured in the word *fantaziia*, which for Dostoevskii meant both liberating imagination and debilitating illusion. He consistently defined his own artistic method as "fantastic realism," which looks beyond surface reality to the forces that animate human action. After embarking on his vocation Dostoevskii quickly became aware of the dangers attending such a complete immersion in fiction, writing to his brother at the beginning of 1847:

> You see, the more we have of spirit and inner content, the better our corner [of the world] and our life. Of course, it is terrifying to think of the dissonance, the imbalance, which society represents for us. The *outer* must be balanced with the *inner*. Otherwise, in the absence of outer phenomena, the inner will attain dangerous ascendancy. Nerves and imagination [*fantaziia*] will take up too much space in one's being.[13]

It was increasingly obvious to him, however, that he was far from balanced:

> I recall that you once told me that my behavior with you excludes mutual equality. My beloved. This was utterly unjust. But I have such a mean, repulsive character [. . .] My nerves are not obeying me at these moments. I am ridiculous and disgusting, and therefore always suffer from unjust opinions about me. They say I am stale and heartless [. . .] But soon you will read *Netochka Nezvanova*. This will be a confession, like *Goliadkin*,[14] although in another tone and kind [. . .] My pen is ruled by a spring of inspiration that flows straight from my soul.[15]

---

12 PSS 28/1:134.
13 PSS 28/1:137–38.
14 EDS: The hero of *The Double*.
15 PSS 28/1:139.

Throughout his first works, then, Dostoevskii wrote in order to heal the perceived split between private and public, personal and artistic selves, learning to write sincerely but with objective effect [...]

Life, Dostoevskii was coming to believe, is the informing of reality with the imagination and memory. One cannot be true to real life, he suggests, without considering the effects of the imaginary. Even if images fail to have an impact, our memory of the image, the ideal, remains as a pledge of its realization in the future [...]

Already in his earliest works Dostoevskii deployed a riotous idiom that drew philosophical terminology and urban slang into a veritable whirlpool of language. His humor frequently verging upon hysteria, Dostoevskii seems at times almost in the thrall of his own verbal inventiveness, boasting about the neologisms (many derived from slang) he introduced to the Russian language. His characters are drawn in their speech no less than in their physical and intellectual profiles. Each is defined by his or her struggle to "achieve syntax" without compromising their individuality.

As an artist Dostoevskii has sometimes been accused of carelessness and inconsistency, especially when compared to the regal calm of Tolstoi and the majestic grace of Turgenev. (He frequently felt oppressed by the comparison to his noble competitors.) Nonetheless, from his earliest writings Dostoevskii deployed a consistent and precise terminology to mark his central concerns, including the crucial trio of terms: face/person (*litso*), fantasy/imagination (*fantaziia*) and impressions (*vpechatlenie*). In 1874, at the beginning of his work on *The Adolescent*, Dostoevskii provided a precise statement of his method:

> In order to write a novel one must first secure *one* or *several* powerful impressions that the author's heart has really experienced. *This is the task of the poet*. Out of this impression develops a theme, a plan, a measured whole [*stroinoe tseloe*]. *This is the task of the artist*, although the artist and poet help each other [...] in both cases.[16]

As Konstantin Barsht points out, one senses Dostoevskii's architectural training in his emphasis on *planning* and *measure* as the tasks of the artist: "The oblong page of a 'note book' was for Dostoevskii the four-dimensional 'chronotope' of the future work."[17] Only through artistry can the

---

16 PSS 16:10.
17 Konstantin Barsht, *Risunki v rukopisiakh Dostoevskogo* (St. Petersburg: Formika, 1996), 187.

work create effects in the physical world commensurate to the imaginary ("poetic") conception.

The story "Mr. Prokharchin" in particular illustrates how Dostoevskii was thinking about fictional forms as a physical body capable of creating effects in the world beyond the projection of a spectral healing image. One of the literary fashions was for "physiological sketches," which were documentary essays analyzing prominent types of city life. Dostoevskii was obviously eager to absorb impressions from contemporary reality, but he refused to stop at their mere documentation. Instead he focused on the states of mind of his world's denizens and experimented with literary forms capable of capturing them. In both senses he thought physiologically. This is not to say that he was always successful. Of his "Mr. Prokharchin," Dostoevskii wrote to his brother on 17 September 1846: "Prokharchin is horribly disfigured in a sensitive place. Everything vivid has disappeared. There remains only the skeleton."[18]

Despite his success Dostoevskii's correspondence continued to consist largely of requests for money: promises to repay money already borrowed and increasingly delusional get-rich-quick schemes in which he tried to involve his brothers, relatives and friends. It is beyond doubt that he was usually broke but, given his literary earnings and the generosity of those around him, one has to wonder what he did with the sums he earned. Some of his friends suggested that he was unreasonably generous and easily taken advantage of. Such view might receive confirmation from the unthinking charity of characters in his novels, from Ivan Petrovich in *The Insulted and the Injured* to Raskol'nikov in *Crime and Punishment*. As in so many cases, however, it's difficult to know whether Dostoevskii was describing himself or whether his readers simply extrapolated about him from his creations. More plausible is the link between Dostoevskii's constant financial difficulties and the nervous complaint from which he suffered and which contributed to his overexcited state of mind, which is described by contemporaries as impressionability and hyperbolism. He later recalled that in 1847–9 he had suffered from an illness of the digestive tract that at times caused "moral and emotional distress": "A man [with this illness] is infected by infinite mistrust and ends up imagining himself sick with all possible sicknesses,"[19] [. . .] By the time of his arrest Dostoevskii was comparing his struggle with creditors to Laocoön's with the serpents.[20]

---

18 PSS 28/1:126.
19 PSS 30/1:203.
20 PSS 28/1:155.

The analogy to Laocoön is equally apt for Dostoevskii's struggles to develop fictional forms capable of dealing with modernity without succumbing to its hazards. Dostoevskii's most important early works—*Poor Folk, The Double* and *White Nights*—all lament the disfigurement of society and of the individual psyche under the pressures of modern life. The main characters seek a healing image, most often in young women they see but can never possess either as body or as image. *Poor Folk* and *White Nights* provide pledges of a healing image that can be retained in memory, but there appears to be no antidote for the abandonment, disfigurement and even imprisonment that the fleeting image leaves in its wake. The aesthetic creed that emerges in Dostoevskii's early writings recognizes the origin of artistic images in the imagination but insists on the need for them to receive full incarnation in reality. Thus the artist, for Dostoevskii, ideally serves as medium for the communication of socially constructive affect. How precisely to live up to this role was a question that tortured Dostoevskii throughout his life.

The Ribbon Theft Incident from *Confessions* (1789)*

Jean-Jacques Rousseau

Would I had finished what I have to say of my living at Madame de Vercellis's. Though my situation apparently remained the same, I did not leave her house as I had entered it: I carried with me the long and painful remembrance of a crime; an insupportable weight of remorse which yet hangs on my conscience, and whose bitter recollection, far from weakening, during a period of forty years, seems to gather strength as I grow old. Who would believe that a childish fault should be productive of such melancholy consequences? But it is for the more than probable effects that my heart cannot be consoled. I have, perhaps, caused an amiable, honest, estimable girl, who surely merited a better fate than myself, to perish with shame and misery.

Though it is very difficult to break up housekeeping without confusion, and the loss of some property; yet such was the fidelity of the domestics, and the vigilance of M. and Madam Lorenzy, that no article of the inventory was found wanting; in short, nothing was missing but a pink and silver ribbon, which had been worn, and belonged to Mademoiselle Pontal. Though several things of more value were in my reach, this ribbon alone tempted me, and accordingly I stole it. As I took no great pains to conceal the bauble, it was soon discovered; they immediately insisted on knowing from whence I had taken it; this perplexed me—I hesitated, and at length said, with confusion, that Marion gave it me.

Marion was a young Mauriennese, and had been cook to Madam de Vercellis ever since she left off giving entertainments, for being sensible she had

---

*   From *The Confessions of Jean-Jacques Rousseau* (London: Reeves & Turner, 1861), 69–71.

more need of good broths than fine ragouts, she had discharged her former one. Marion was not only pretty, but had that freshness of color only to be found among the mountains, and above all, an air of modesty and sweetness, which made it impossible to see her without affection; she was besides a good girl, virtuous, and of such strict fidelity, that every one was surprised at hearing her named. They had not less confidence in me, and judged it necessary to certify which of us was the thief. Marion was sent for; a great number of people were present, among whom was the Count de la Roque: she arrives; they show her the ribbon; I accuse her boldly; she remains confused and speechless, casting a look on me that would have disarmed a demon, but which my barbarous heart resisted. At length, she denied it with firmness, but without anger, exhorting me to return to myself, and not injure an innocent girl who had never wronged me. With infernal impudence, I confirmed my accusation, and to her face maintained she had given me the ribbon: on which, the poor girl, bursting into tears, said these words—"Ah, Rousseau! I thought you a good disposition—you render me very unhappy, but I would not be in your situation." She continued to defend herself with as much innocence as firmness, but without uttering the least invective against me. Her moderation, compared to my positive tone, did her an injury; as it did not appear natural to suppose, on one side such diabolical assurance; on the other, such angelic mildness. The affair could not be absolutely decided, but the presumption was in my favor; and the Count de la Roque, in sending us both away, contented himself with saying, "The conscience of the guilty would revenge the innocent." His prediction was true, and is being daily verified.

I am ignorant what became of the victim of my calumny, but there is little probability of her having been able to place herself agreeably after this, as she labored under an imputation cruel to her character in every respect. The theft was a trifle, yet it was a theft, and, what was worse, employed to seduce a boy; while the lie and obstinacy left nothing to hope from a person in whom so many vices were united. I do not even look on the misery and disgrace in which I plunged her as the greatest evil: who knows, at her age, whither contempt and disregarded innocence might have led her? – Alas! if remorse for having made her unhappy is insupportable, what must I have suffered at the thought of rendering her even worse than myself. The cruel remembrance of this transaction, sometimes so troubles and disorders me, that, in my disturbed slumbers, I imagine I see this poor girl enter and reproach me with my crime, as though I had committed it but yesterday. While in easy tranquil circumstances, I was less miserable on this account, but, during a troubled agitated life, it has robbed me of the sweet consolation of persecuted innocence, and made me woefully experience, what, I think, I have remarked in some of my works, that remorse sleeps in the calm sunshine of prosperity, but wakes amid the storms of adversity. I could never take on me to discharge my heart of this weight in the bosom of a friend; nor could the closest intimacy ever encourage me to it, even with Madam de Warrens; all I could do, was to own I had to accuse myself of an atrocious crime, but never said in what it consisted. The weight, therefore, has remained heavy on my conscience to this day; and I can truly own the desire of relieving myself, in some measure, from it, contributed greatly to the resolution of writing my Confessions.

A Son's Revenge from *The Robbers* (1781)*

Friedrich Schiller

KARL. Locks, bolts, and bars, away! It must come out. Now, for the first time, come to my aid, thief-craft! (He opens the grated iron door with, house-breaking tools. An OLD MAN, reduced to a skeleton, comes up from below.)

THE OLD MAN. Mercy on a poor wretch! Mercy!

KARL (starts back in terror). That is my father's voice!

OLD MOOR. I thank thee, merciful Heaven! The hour of deliverance has arrived.

KARL. Shade of the aged Moor! What has disturbed thee in thy grave? Has thy soul left this earth charged with some foul crime that bars the gates of Paradise against thee? Say?—I will have masses read, to send thy wandering spirit to its home [. . .] Or comest thou, at my request, to reveal to me the mysteries of eternity? Speak, thou! speak! I am not the man to blanch with fear!

OLD MOOR. I am not a spirit. Touch me—I live but oh! A life indeed of misery! [. . .]

KARL. Heaven and earth! Who has done this?

OLD MOOR. Curse him not! 'Tis my son, Franz, who did this.

KARL. Franz? Franz? Oh, eternal chaos! [. . .]

---

* Extracts from Act IV, Scene 5 of *The Robbers: A Tragedy* from *The Works of Friedrich Schiller. Early Dramas and Romances*, trans. Henry G. Bohn (London: H. G. Bohn, 1849), 103–7.

OLD MOOR. I lay upon a sick bed, and had scarcely begun to recover a little strength, after a dangerous illness, when a man was brought to me, who pretended that my first-born had fallen in battle. He brought a sword stained with his blood, and his last farewell— and said that my curse had driven him into battle, and death, and despair.

KARL (turning away in violent agitation). The light breaks in upon me!

OLD MOOR. Hear me on! I fainted at the dreadful news. They must have thought me dead; for, when I recovered my senses, I was already in my coffin, shrouded like a corpse. I scratched against the lid. It was opened—'twas in the dead of night— my son Franz stood before me— "What!" said he, with a tremendous voice, "wilt thou then live forever?"—and with this he slammed-to the lid of the coffin. The thunder of these words bereft me of my senses; when I awoke again, I felt that the coffin was in motion, and being borne on wheels. At last it was opened —I found myself at the entrance of this dungeon—my son stood before me, and the man, too, who had brought me the bloody sword from Karl. I fell at my son's feet, and ten times I embraced his knees, and wept, and conjured, and supplicated, but the supplications of a father reached not his flinty heart. "Down with the old carcass!" said he, with a voice of thunder, "he has lived too long;"—and I was thrust down without mercy, and my son Franz closed the door upon Me.

KARL. Impossible!—impossible! Your memory or senses deceive you.

OLD MOOR. Oh, that it were so! But hear me on, and restrain your rage! There I lay for twenty hours, and not a soul cared for my misery. No human footstep treads this solitary wild, for 'tis commonly believed that the ghosts of my ancestors drag clanking chains through these ruins, and chant their funeral dirge at the hour of midnight. At last I heard the door creak again on its hinges; this man opened it, and brought me bread and water. He told me that I had been condemned to die of hunger, and that his life was in danger should it be discovered that he fed me. Thus has my miserable existence been till now sustained

[…]

KARL. Enough! Rise! [...] Ye lazy unfeeling sleepers! Up! Will none of you awake? (He fires a pistol over their heads.)

THE ROBBERS (starting up). Ho! hallo! hallo! what is the matter?

KARL. Has not that tale shaken you out of your sleep? [...] see here! The laws of the world have become mere dice-play; the bonds of nature are burst asunder; the Demon of Discord has broken loose, and stalks abroad triumphant! the Son has slain his Father! [...] Slain! [...] No, that is too mild a term! A son has a thousand-fold broken his own father on the wheel,—impaled, racked, flayed him alive!—but all these words are too feeble to express what would make sin itself blush and cannibals shudder. For ages, no devil ever conceived a deed so horrible. His own father!—but see, see him! He has fainted away! His own father—the son—into this dungeon—cold— naked—hungry—athirst—Oh! See, I pray you, see!—'tis my own father, in very truth it is.

THE ROBBERS (surround the old man). Your father? Yours?

SCHWEITZER (approaches him reverently, and falls on his knees before him). Father of my captain! Let me kiss thy feet! My dagger is at thy command.

KARL. Revenge, revenge, revenge! Thou horribly injured, profaned old man! Thus, from this moment, and forever, I rend in twain all ties of fraternity. (He rends his garment from top to bottom.) Here, in the face of heaven, I curse him—curse every drop of blood which flows in his veins! Hear me, O moon and stars! And thou black canopy of night, that lookest down upon this horror! Hear me, thrice terrible avenger. Thou who reignest above yon pallid orb, who sittest an avenger and a judge above the stars, and dartest thy fiery bolts through darkness on the head of guilt! Behold me on my knees behold me raise this hand aloft in the gloom of night— and hear my oath—and may nature vomit me forth as some horrible abortion from out the circle of her works if I break that oath! Here I swear that I will never more greet the light of day, till the blood of that foul parricide, spilt upon this stone, reeks in misty vapor towards heaven. (He rises.)

ROBBERS. 'Tis a deed of hell! After this, who shall call us villains? No! by all the dragons of darkness we never have done anything half so horrible.

KARL. True! and by all the fearful groans of those whom your daggers have dispatched—of those who on that terrible day were consumed by fire, or crushed by the falling tower—no thought of murder or rapine shall be harbored in your breast, till every man among you has dyed his garments scarlet in this monster's blood. It never, I should think, entered your dreams, that it would fall to your lot to execute the great decrees of heaven? The tangled web of our destiny is unraveled! Today, today, an invisible power has ennobled our craft! Worship Him who has called you to this high destiny, who has conducted you hither, and deemed ye worthy to be the terrible angels of his inscrutable judgments! Uncover your heads! Bow down and kiss the dust, and rise up sanctified. (They kneel.)

First Glimpse of Udolpho (1794)*

At length, the travelers began to ascend among the Apennines. The immense pine forests, which, at that period, overhung these mountains, and between which the road wound, excluded all view but of the cliffs aspiring above, except, that, now and then, an opening through the dark woods allowed the eye a momentary glimpse of the country below. The gloom of these shades, their solitary silence, except when the breeze swept over their summits, the tremendous precipices of the mountains, that came partially to the eye, each assisted to raise the solemnity of Emily's feelings into awe; she saw only images of gloomy grandeur, or of dreadful sublimity, around her; other images, equally gloomy and equally terrible, gleamed on her imagination. She was going she scarcely knew whither, under the dominion of a person, from whose arbitrary disposition she had already suffered so much, to marry, perhaps, a man who possessed neither her affection, or esteem; or to endure, beyond the hope of succor, whatever punishment revenge, and that Italian revenge, might dictate [...] From the deep solitudes, into which she was immerging, and from the gloomy castle, of which she had heard some mysterious hints, her sick heart recoiled in despair, and she experienced, that, though her mind was already occupied by peculiar distress, it was still alive to the influence of new and local circumstance; why else did she shudder at the idea of this desolate castle? [...]

At length, they reached a little plain, where the drivers stopped to rest the mules, whence a scene of such extent and magnificence opened below

---

* From Ann Radcliffe, *The Mysteries of Udolpho*, vol. 2 (London: G. G. and J. Robinson, 1794), 164–70.

[...] Emily lost, for a moment, her sorrows, in the immensity of nature. Beyond the amphitheater of mountains that stretched below, whose tops appeared as numerous almost, as the waves of the sea, and whose feet were concealed by the forests—extended the *campagna* of Italy, where cities and rivers, and woods and all the glow of cultivation were mingled in gay confusion. [...]

From this sublime scene the travellers continued to ascend among the pines, till they entered a narrow pass of the mountains, which shut out every feature of the distant country, and, in its stead, exhibited only tremendous crags, impending over the road, where no vestige of humanity, or even of vegetation, appeared [...] This pass, which led into the heart of the Apennine, at length opened to day, and a scene of mountains stretched in long perspective, as wild as any the travellers had yet passed. Still vast pine-forests hung upon their base, and crowned the ridgy precipice, that rose perpendicularly from the vale, while, above, the rolling mists caught the sunbeams, and touched their cliffs with all the magical coloring of light and shade. The scene seemed perpetually changing, and its features to assume new forms, as the winding road brought them to the eye in different attitudes; while the shifting vapors, now partially concealing their minuter beauties and now illuminating them with splendid tints, assisted the illusions of the sight [...]

Towards the close of day, the road wound into a deep valley. Mountains, whose shaggy steeps appeared to be inaccessible, almost surrounded it. To the east, a vista opened, that exhibited the Apennines in their darkest horrors; and the long perspective of retiring summits, rising over each other, their ridges clothed with pines, exhibited a stronger image of grandeur, than any that Emily had yet seen. The sun had just sunk below the top of the mountains she was descending, whose long shadow stretched athwart the valley, but his sloping rays, shooting through an opening of the cliffs, touched with a yellow gleam the summits of the forest, that hung upon the opposite steeps, and streamed in full splendor upon the towers and battlements of a castle, that spread its extensive ramparts along the brow of a precipice above. The splendor of these illumined objects was heightened by the contrasted shade, which involved the valley below.

"There," said Montoni, speaking for the first time in several hours, "is Udolpho."

The House of Monsieur Grandet in *Eugénie Grandet* (1833)*

Honoré de Balzac

There are houses in certain provincial towns whose aspect inspires melancholy, akin to that called forth by somber cloisters, dreary moorlands, or the desolation of ruins. Within these houses there is, perhaps, the silence of the cloister, the barrenness of moors, the skeleton of ruins; life and movement are so stagnant there that a stranger might think them uninhabited, were it not that he encounters suddenly the pale, cold glance of a motionless person, whose half-monastic face peers beyond the window-casing at the sound of an unaccustomed step.

Such elements of sadness formed the physiognomy, as it were, of a dwelling house in Saumur, which stands at the end of the steep street leading to the chateau in the upper part of the town. This street—now little frequented, hot in summer, cold in winter, dark in certain sections—is remarkable for the resonance of its little pebbly pavement, always clean and dry, for the narrowness of its tortuous road-way, for the peaceful stillness of its houses, which belong to the Old town and are over-topped by the ramparts [. . .]

It is difficult to pass these houses without admiring the enormous oaken beams, their ends carved into fantastic figures, which crown with a black bas-relief the lower floor of most of them. In one place these transverse timbers are covered with slate and mark a bluish line along the frail wall of a dwelling

---

* Excerpted from Honoré de Balzac, *Eugénie Grandet*, trans. Katharine Prescott Wormeley (Boston: Little, Brown, 1902), 1–6.

covered by a roof *en colombage*[1] which bends beneath the weight of years, and whose rotting shingles are twisted by the alternate action of sun and rain. In another place blackened, worn-out window sills, with delicate sculptures now scarcely discernible, seem too weak to bear the brown clay pots from which springs the hearts-ease or the rose bush of some poor working-woman [...]

Next to a tottering house with roughly plastered walls, where an artisan enshrines his tools, rises the mansion of a country gentleman, on the stone arch of which above the door vestiges of armorial bearings may still be seen, battered by the many revolutions that have shaken France since 1789. In this hilly street the ground floors of the merchants are neither shops nor warehouses; lovers of the Middle Ages will here find the *ouvrouère*[2] of our forefathers in all its naive simplicity. These low rooms, which have no shop frontage, no show windows, in fact no glass at all, are deep and dark and without interior or exterior decoration. Their doors open in two parts, each roughly iron bound; the upper half is fastened back within the room, the lower half, fitted with a spring bell, swings continually to and fro. Air and light reach the damp den within, either through the upper half of the door, or through an open space between the ceiling and a low front wall, breast-high, which is closed by solid shutters that are taken down every morning, put up every evening, and held in place by heavy iron bars.

This wall serves as a counter for the merchandise. No delusive display is there; only samples of the business, whatever it may chance to be—such, for instance, as three or four tubs full of codfish and salt, a few bundles of sailcloth, cordage, copper wire hanging from the joists above, iron hoops for casks ranged along the wall, or a few pieces of cloth upon the shelves. Enter. A neat girl, glowing with youth, wearing a white kerchief, her arms red and bare, drops her knitting and calls her father or her mother, one of whom comes forward and sells you what you want, phlegmatically, civilly, or arrogantly, according to his or her individual character, whether it be a matter of two sous' or twenty thousand francs' worth of merchandise [...]

On Saturdays after midday, in the fine season, not one sou's worth of merchandise can be bought from these worthy traders. Each has his vineyard, his enclosure of fields, and all spend two days in the country. This being foreseen, and purchases, sales, and profits provided for, the merchants have ten or twelve hours to spend in parties of pleasure, in making observations, in

---

1   EDS: A half-timbered house.
2   EDS: This is a term for a workshop.

criticisms, and in continual spying. A housewife cannot buy a partridge without the neighbors asking the husband if it were cooked to a turn. A young girl never puts her head near a window that she is not seen by idling groups in the street. Consciences are held in the light; and the houses, dark, silent, impenetrable as they seem, hide no mysteries. Life is almost wholly in the open air; every household sits at its own threshold, breakfasts, dines, and quarrels there. No one can pass along the street without being examined; in fact formerly, when a stranger entered a provincial town he was bantered and made game of from door to door [. . .]

The ancient mansions of the old town of Saumur are at the top of this hilly street, and were formerly occupied by the nobility of the neighborhood. The melancholy dwelling where the events of the following history took place is one of these mansions, venerable relics of a century in which men and things bore the characteristics of simplicity which French manners and customs are losing day by day. Follow the windings of the picturesque thoroughfare, whose irregularities awaken recollections that plunge the mind mechanically into reverie, and you will see a somewhat dark recess, in the center of which is hidden the door of the house of Monsieur Grandet.

Little Nell in The Old Curiosity Shop (1841)*

Charles Dickens

When we reached the door, the child setting down the candle, turned to say good night and raised her face to kiss me. Then she ran to the old man, who folded her in his arms and bade God bless her.

"Sleep soundly, Nell," he said in a low voice, "and angels guard thy bed! Do not forget thy prayers, my sweet."

"No, indeed," answered the child fervently, "they make me feel so happy!"

"That's well; I know they do; they should," said the old man. "Bless thee a hundred times! Early in the morning I shall be home."

"You'll not ring twice," returned the child. "The bell wakes me, even in the middle of a dream."

With this, they separated. The child opened the door (now guarded by a shutter which I had heard the boy put up before he left the house) and with another farewell whose clear and tender note I have recalled a thousand times, held it until we had passed out. The old man paused a moment while it was gently closed and fastened on the inside, and satisfied that this was done, walked on at a slow pace. At the street-corner he stopped, and regarding me with a troubled countenance said that our ways were widely different and that he must take his leave. I would have spoken, but summoning up more alacrity than might have been expected in one of his appearance, he hurried away [...]

---

* From Charles Dickens, *The Old Curiosity Shop. A Tale* (London: Chapman and Hall, 1841), 45–47.

I remained standing on the spot where he had left me, unwilling to depart, and yet unknowing why I should loiter there. I looked wistfully into the street we had lately quitted, and after a time directed my steps that way. I passed and repassed the house, and stopped and listened at the door; all was dark, and silent as the grave.

Yet I lingered about, and could not tear myself away, thinking of all possible harm that might happen to the child—of fires and robberies and even murder—and feeling as if some evil must ensue if I turned my back upon the place. The closing of a door or window in the street brought me before the curiosity-dealer's once more; I crossed the road and looked up at the house to assure myself that the noise had not come from there. No, it was black, cold, and lifeless as before.

There were few passengers astir; the street was sad and dismal, and pretty well my own. A few stragglers from the theaters hurried by, and now and then I turned aside to avoid some noisy drunkard as he reeled homewards, but these interruptions were not frequent and soon ceased. The clocks struck one. Still I paced up and down, promising myself that every time should be the last, and breaking faith with myself on some new plea as often as I did so.

The more I thought of what the old man had said, and of his looks and bearing, the less I could account for what I had seen and heard. I had a strong misgiving that his nightly absence was for no good purpose. I had only come to know the fact through the innocence of the child, and though the old man was by at the time, and saw my undisguised surprise, he had preserved a strange mystery upon the subject and offered no word of explanation. These reflections naturally recalled again more strongly than before his haggard face, his wandering manner, his restless anxious looks. His affection for the child might not be inconsistent with villainy of the worst kind; even that very affection was in itself an extraordinary contradiction, or how could he leave her thus? Disposed as I was to think badly of him, I never doubted that his love for her was real. I could not admit the thought, remembering what had passed between us, and the tone of voice in which he had called her by her name.

"Stay here of course," the child had said in answer to my question, "I always do!" What could take him from home by night, and every night! I called up all the strange tales I had ever heard of dark and secret deeds committed in great towns and escaping detection for a long series of years; wild as many of these stories were, I could not find one adapted to this mystery, which only became the more impenetrable, in proportion as I sought to solve it.

Occupied with such thoughts as these, and a crowd of others all tending to the same point, I continued to pace the street for two long hours; at length the rain began to descend heavily, and then over-powered by fatigue though no less interested than I had been at first, I engaged the nearest coach and so got home. A cheerful fire was blazing on the hearth, the lamp burnt brightly, my clock received me with its old familiar welcome; everything was quiet, warm and cheering, and in happy contrast to the gloom and darkness I had quitted.

But all that night, waking or in my sleep, the same thoughts recurred and the same images retained possession of my brain. I had ever before me the old dark murky rooms—the gaunt suits of mail with their ghostly silent air—the faces all awry, grinning from wood and stone—the dust and rust and worm that lives in wood—and alone in the midst of all this lumber and decay and ugly age, the beautiful child in her gentle slumber, smiling through her light and sunny dreams.

The Overcoat (1842)*

Nikolai Gogol'

In St. Petersburg all those who draw a salary of four hundred rubles or thereabouts have a terrible enemy in our northern cold, although some assert that it is very good for the health. About nine o'clock in the morning, when the clerks of the various departments betake themselves to their offices, the cold nips their noses so vigorously that most of them are quite bewildered. If at this time even high officials so suffer from the severity of the cold in their own persons that the tears come into their eyes, what must be the sufferings of the titular councilors, whose means do not allow of their protecting themselves against the rigor of winter? [. . .]

For some time Akakii Akakievich had been feeling on his back and shoulders very sharp twinges of pain, although he ran as fast as possible from his dwelling to the office. After well considering the matter, he came to the conclusion that these were due to the imperfections of his cloak. In his room he examined it carefully, and discovered that in two or three places it had become so thin as to be quite transparent, and that the lining was much torn.

This cloak had been for a long time the standing object of jests on the part of Akakii's merciless colleagues. They had even robbed it of the noble name of "cloak," and called it a cowl. It certainly presented a remarkable appearance. Every year the collar had grown smaller, for every year the poor titular councilor had taken a piece of it away in order to repair some other part of the cloak; and these repairs did not look as if they had been done by the skilled hand of a tailor. They had been executed in a very clumsy way and looked remarkably ugly. After Akakii Akakievich had ended his melancholy examination, he said to himself that he must certainly take his cloak to Petrovich the tailor [. . .]

---

* From Nicholas Gogol', "The Mantle," in *The Mantle and Other Stories*, trans. Claud Field (New York: Frederick A. Stokes Co., 1916), 29–36.

Akakii Akakievich accordingly betook himself to the tailor's attic. He reached it by a dark, dirty, damp staircase, from which, as in all the inhabited houses of the poorer class in St. Petersburg, exhaled an effluvia of spirits vexatious to nose and eyes alike. As the titular councilor climbed these slippery stairs, he calculated what sum Petrovich could reasonably ask for repairing his cloak, and determined only to give him a ruble.

The door of the tailor's flat stood open in order to provide an outlet for the clouds of smoke, which rolled from the kitchen, where Petrovich's wife was just then cooking fish. Akakii, his eyes smarting, passed through the kitchen without her seeing him, and entered the room where the tailor sat on a large, roughly made, wooden table, his legs crossed like those of a Turkish pasha, and, as is the custom of tailors, with bare feet. What first arrested attention, when one approached him, was his thumbnail, which was a little misshapen but as hard and strong as the shell of a tortoise. Round his neck were hung several skeins of thread, and on his knees lay a tattered coat. For some minutes he had been trying in vain to thread his needle. He was first of all angry with the gathering darkness, then with the thread.

"Why the deuce won't you go in, you worthless scoundrel!" he exclaimed.

Akakii saw at once that he had come at an inopportune moment. He wished he had found Petrovich at a more favorable time, when he was enjoying himself—when, as his wife expressed it, he was having a substantial ration of brandy. At such times the tailor was extraordinarily ready to meet his customer's proposals with bows and gratitude to boot. Sometimes indeed his wife interfered in the transaction, and declared that he was drunk and promised to do the work at much too low a price; but if the customer paid a trifle more, the matter was settled.

Unfortunately for the titular councilor, Petrovich had just now not yet touched the brandy flask. At such moments he was hard, obstinate, and ready to demand an exorbitant price.

Akakii foresaw this danger, and would gladly have turned back again, but it was already too late. The tailor's single eye—for he was one-eyed—had already noticed him, and Akakii Akakievich murmured involuntarily "Good day, Petrovich."

"Welcome, sir," answered the tailor, and fastened his glance on the titular councilor's hand to see what he had in it.

"I come just—merely—in order—I want—" […]

"What do you want, sir?" asked Petrovich, scrutinizing him from top to toe with a searching look, and contemplating his collar, sleeves, coat, buttons—in short his whole uniform, although he knew them all very well, having made them himself [...]

Then Akakii answered, stammering as usual, "I want—Petrovich—this cloak—you see—it is still quite good, only a little dusty—and therefore it looks a little old. It is, however, still quite new, only that it is worn a little—there in the back and here in the shoulder—and there are three quite little splits. You see it is hardly worth talking about; it can be thoroughly repaired in a few minutes."

Petrovich took the unfortunate cloak, spread it on the table, contemplated it in silence, and shook his head. Then he stretched his hand towards the windowsill for his snuffbox, a round one with the portrait of a general on the lid. I do not know whose portrait it was, for it had been accidentally injured, and the ingenious tailor had gummed a piece of paper over it.

After Petrovich had taken a pinch of snuff, he examined the cloak again, held it to the light, and once more shook his head. Then he examined the lining, took a second pinch of snuff, and at last exclaimed, "No! That is a wretched rag! It is beyond repair!"

At these words Akakii's courage fell [...]

"There is nothing more to be done with it; it is completely worn out. It would be better if you made yourself foot bandages out of it for the winter; they are warmer than stockings. It was the Germans who invented stockings for their own profit." Petrovich never lost an opportunity of having a hit at the Germans. "You must certainly buy a new cloak," he added.

"A new cloak?" exclaimed Akakii Akakievich, and it grew dark before his eyes. The tailor's workroom seemed to go round with him, and the only object he could clearly distinguish was the paper-patched general's portrait on the tailor's snuffbox. "A new cloak!" he murmured, as though half asleep. "But I have no money [...] Petrovich, I adjure you!" said Akakii Akakievich in an imploring tone, no longer hearing nor wishing to hear the tailor's words, "try to make this cloak last me a little longer."

"No, it would be a useless waste of time and work."

After this answer, Akakii departed, feeling quite crushed; while Petrovich, with his lips firmly pursed up, feeling pleased with himself for his firmness and brave defense of the art of tailoring, remained sitting on the table.

Poor Folk (1846)*

Fedor Dostoevskii

"O Varvara Alekseevna, I am undone—we are both of us undone! Both of us are lost beyond recall! Everything is ruined—my reputation, my self-respect, all that I have in the world! And you as much as I. Never shall we retrieve what we have lost. I—I have brought you to this pass, for I have become an outcast, my darling. Everywhere I am laughed at and despised. Even my landlady has taken to abusing me. Today she overwhelmed me with shrill reproaches, and abased me to the level of a hearth-brush. And last night, when I was in Rataziaev's rooms, one of his friends began to read a scribbled note which I had written to you, and then inadvertently pulled out of my pocket. Oh beloved, what laughter there arose at the recital! How those scoundrels mocked and derided you and myself! I walked up to them and accused Rataziaev of breaking faith. I said that he had played the traitor. But he only replied that I had been the betrayer in the case, by indulging in various amours [. . .] and now I am in a worse plight even than a tramp who has lost his passport. How misfortunes are heaping themselves upon me! I am lost—I am lost forever!

M. D."

August 13

"MY BELOVED MAKAR ALEKSEEVICH,—It is true that misfortune is following upon misfortune. I myself scarcely know what to do. Yet, no matter how you may be faring, you must not look for help from me, for only today I burned my left hand with the iron! At one and the same moment I dropped the iron, made a mistake in my work, and burned myself! So now I can no longer work. Also, these three days past, Fedora has been ailing. My anxiety

---

*   Extracts from Fyodor Dostoyevsky, *Poor Folk*, in *Poor Folk & The Gambler*, trans. C. J. Hogarth (Toronto and London: J. M. Dent, 1915), 98–103.

is becoming positively torturous. Nevertheless, I send you thirty kopecks—almost the last coins that I have left to me, much as I should have liked to have helped you more when you are so much in need. I feel vexed to the point of weeping. Goodbye, dear friend of mine. You will bring me much comfort if only you will come and see me today.

V. D."

August 14

"What is the matter with you, Makar Alekseevich? Surely you cannot fear the Lord God as you ought to do? You are not only driving me to distraction but also ruining yourself with this eternal solicitude for your reputation. You are a man of honor, nobility of character, and self-respect, as everyone knows; yet, at any moment, you are ready to die with shame! Surely you should have more consideration for your grey hairs. No, the fear of God has departed from you. Fedora has told you that it is out of my power to render you any more help. See, therefore, to what a pass you have brought me! Probably you think it is nothing to me that you should behave so badly; probably you do not realize what you have made me suffer. I dare not set foot on the staircase here, for if I do so I am stared at, and pointed at, and spoken about in the most horrible manner. Yes, it is even said of me that I am "united to a drunkard." What a thing to hear! And whenever you are brought home drunk, folk say, "They are carrying in that clerk." THAT is not the proper way to make me help you. I swear that I MUST leave this place, and go and get work as a cook or a laundress. It is impossible for me to stay here. Long ago I wrote and asked you to come and see me, yet you have not come. Truly my tears and prayers must mean NOTHING to you, Makar Alekseevich! Whence, too, did you get the money for your debauchery? For the love of God be more careful of yourself, or you will be ruined. How shameful, how abominable of you! [. . .] For God's sake beloved, do not ruin both yourself and me. I live for you alone; it is for your sake alone that I am still here. Be your better self once more—the self, which still can remain firm in the face of misfortune. Poverty is no crime; always remember that. After all, why should we despair? Our present difficulties will pass away, and God will right us. Only be brave. I send you twenty kopecks for the purchase of some tobacco or anything else that you need; but, for the love of heaven, do not spend the money foolishly. Come you and see me soon; come without fail. Perhaps you may be ashamed to meet me, as you were before, but you NEED not feel like that—such shame would be misplaced. Only do bring with you sincere repentance and trust in God, who orders all things for the best.

V. D."

August 21

"MY DEAR AND KIND VARVARA ALEKSEEVNA,—I feel that I am guilty, I feel that I have sinned against you. Yet also I feel, from what you say, that it is no use for me so to feel. Even before I had sinned I felt as I do now; but I gave way to despair, and the more so as recognized my fault. Darling, I am not cruel or hardhearted. To rend your little soul would be the act of a bloodthirsty tiger, whereas I have the heart of a sheep. You yourself know that I am not addicted to bloodthirstiness, and therefore that I cannot really be guilty of the fault in question, seeing that neither my mind nor my heart have participated in it.

Nor can I understand wherein the guilt lies. To me it is all a mystery. When you sent me those thirty kopecks, and thereafter those twenty kopecks, my heart sank within me as I looked at the poor little money. To think that though you had burned your hand, and would soon be hungry, you could write to me that I was to buy tobacco! What was I to do? Remorselessly to rob you, an orphan, as any brigand might do? I felt greatly depressed, dearest. That is to say, persuaded that I should never do any good with my life, and that I was inferior even to the sole of my own boot, I took it into my head that it was absurd for me to aspire at all—rather, that I ought to account myself a disgrace and an abomination. Once a man has lost his self-respect, and has decided to abjure his better qualities and human dignity, he falls headlong, and cannot choose but do so. It is decreed of fate, and therefore I am not guilty in this respect [...]

I know how beholden to you I am. As soon as ever I got to know you I began both to realize myself and to love you; for until you came into my life I had been a lonely man—I had been, as it were, asleep rather than alive. In former days my rascally colleagues used to tell me that I was unfit even to be seen; in fact, they so disliked me that at length I began to dislike myself, for, being frequently told that I was stupid, I began to believe that I really was so. But the instant that YOU came into my life, you lightened the dark places in it; you lightened both my heart and my soul. Gradually, I gained rest of spirit, until I had come to see that I was no worse than other men, and that, though I had neither style nor brilliancy nor polish, I was still a MAN as regards my thoughts and feelings. But now, alas! pursued and scorned of fate, I have again allowed myself to abjure my own dignity. Oppressed of misfortune, I have lost my courage. Here is my confession to you, dearest. With tears I beseech you not to inquire further into the matter, for my heart is breaking, and life has grown indeed hard and bitter for me—Beloved, I offer you my respect, and remain ever your faithful friend,

MAKAR DEVUSHKIN."

First Night from "White Nights" (1848)*

Fedor Dostoevskii

It was a wonderful night, such a night as is only possible when we are young, dear reader. The sky was so starry, so bright that, looking at it, one could not help asking oneself whether ill-humored and capricious people could live under such a sky. That is a youthful question too, dear reader, very youthful, but may the Lord put it more frequently into your heart! Speaking of capricious and ill-humored people, I cannot help recalling my moral condition all that day. From early morning I had been oppressed by a strange despondency. It suddenly seemed to me that I was lonely, that every one was forsaking me and going away from me. Of course, any one is entitled to ask who "every one" was. For though I had been living almost eight years in Petersburg I had hardly an acquaintance. But what did I want with acquaintances? I was acquainted with all Petersburg as it was; that was why I felt as though they were all deserting me when all Petersburg packed up and went to its summer villa. I felt afraid of being left alone, and for three whole days I wandered about the town in profound dejection, not knowing what to do with myself. Whether I walked in the Nevskii, went to the Gardens or sauntered on the embankment, there was not one face of those I had been accustomed to meet at the same time and place all the year. They, of course, do not know me, but I know them. I know them intimately, I have almost made a study of their faces, and am delighted when they are gay, and downcast when they are under a cloud.

---

* From Fyodor Dostoevsky, "White Nights," in *White Nights and Other Stories*, trans. Constance Garnett (New York: The Macmillan Company, 1918), 1, 4–7.

There is something inexpressibly touching in nature round Petersburg, when at the approach of spring she puts forth all her might, all the powers bestowed on her by Heaven, when she breaks into leaf, decks herself out and spangles herself with flowers. . . . Somehow I cannot help being reminded of a frail, consumptive girl, at whom one sometimes looks with compassion, sometimes with sympathetic love, whom sometimes one simply does not notice; though suddenly in one instant she becomes, as though by chance, inexplicably lovely and exquisite, and, impressed and intoxicated, one cannot help asking oneself what power made those sad, pensive eyes flash with such fire? What summoned the blood to those pale, wan cheeks? What bathed with passion those soft features? What set that bosom heaving? What so suddenly called strength, life and beauty into the poor girl's face, making it gleam with such a smile, kindle with such bright, sparkling laughter? You look round, you seek for some one, you conjecture. . . . But the moment passes, and next day you meet, maybe, the same pensive and preoccupied look as before, the same pale face, the same meek and timid movements, and even signs of remorse, traces of a "mortal anguish and regret for the fleeting distraction." . . . And you grieve that the momentary beauty has faded so soon never to return, that it flashed upon you so treacherously, so vainly, grieve because you had not even time to love her. . . .

And yet my night was better than my day! This was how it happened.

I came back to the town very late, and it had struck ten as I was going towards my lodgings. My way lay along the canal embankment, where at that hour you never meet a soul. It is true that I live in a very remote part of the town. I walked along singing, for when I am happy I am always humming to myself like every happy man who has no friend or acquaintance with whom to share his joy. Suddenly I had a most unexpected adventure.

Leaning on the canal railing stood a woman with her elbows on the rail, she was apparently looking with great attention at the muddy water of the canal. She was wearing a very charming yellow hat and a jaunty little black mantle. "She's a girl, and I am sure she is dark," I thought. She did not seem to hear my footsteps, and did not even stir when I passed by with bated breath and loudly throbbing heart.

"Strange," I thought; "she must be deeply absorbed in something," and all at once I stopped as though petrified. I heard a muffled sob. Yes! I was not mistaken, the girl was crying, and a minute later I heard sob after sob. Good Heavens! My heart sank. And timid as I was with women, yet this was such a moment! I turned, took a step towards her, and should certainly have pronounced the word "Madam!" if I had not known that that exclamation has been uttered a thousand times in every Russian society novel. It was only that reflection stopped me. But while I was seeking for a word, the girl came to herself, looked round, started, cast down her eyes and slipped by me along the embankment. I at once followed her; but she, divining this, left the embankment, crossed the road and walked along the pavement. I dared not cross the street after her. My heart was fluttering like a captured bird [...].

"Why are you trembling?"

"Oh, you are right at the first guess!" I answered, delighted that my girl had intelligence; that is never out of place in company with beauty. "Yes, from the first glance you have guessed the sort of man you have to do with [...] I am shy with women, I am agitated, I don't deny it, [...] I am in some alarm now. It's like a dream, and I never guessed even in my sleep that I should ever talk with any woman."

"What? Really?"

"Yes; if my arm trembles, it is because it has never been held by a pretty little hand like yours. I am a complete stranger to women; that is, I have never been used to them. You see, I am alone . . . [...] You will make me," I said, breathless with delight, "lose my timidity, and then farewell to all my chances. . . ."

"Chances! What chances—of what? That's not so nice."

"I beg your pardon, I am sorry, it was a slip of the tongue; but how can you expect one at such a moment to have no desire. . . ."

"To be liked, eh?"

"Well, yes; but do, for goodness' sake, be kind. Think what I am! Here, I am twenty-six and I have never seen any one. How can I speak well, tactfully, and to the point? It will seem better to you when I have told you everything openly. . . . I don't know how to be silent when my heart is speaking. Well, never mind. . . . Believe me, not one woman, never, never! No acquaintance of any sort! And I do nothing but dream every day that at last I shall meet some one. Oh, if only you knew how often I have been in love in that way. . . ."

"How? With whom?"

"Why, with no one, with an ideal, with the one I dream of in my sleep. [...] "

Letter to Gogol' (1847)*

Vissarion Belinskii

You are only partly right in regarding my article as that of an angered man: that epithet is too mild and inadequate to express the state to which I was reduced on reading your book.[1] But you are entirely wrong in ascribing that state to your indeed none too flattering references to the admirers of your talent. No, there was a more important reason for this. One could endure an outraged sense of self-esteem, and I should have had sense enough to let the matter pass in silence were that the whole gist of the matter; but one cannot endure an outraged sense of truth and human dignity; one cannot keep silent when lies and immorality are preached as truth and virtue under the guise of religion and the protection of the knout.

Yes, I loved you with all the passion with which a man, bound by ties of blood to his native country, can love its hope, its honor, its glory, one of its great leaders on the path toward consciousness, development, and progress. And you had sound reason for losing your equanimity at least momentarily when you forfeited that love. I say that not because I believe my love to be an adequate reward for a great talent, but because I do not represent a single person in this respect but a multitude of men, most of whom neither you nor I have ever set eyes on, and who, in their turn, have never set eyes on you. I find myself at a loss to give you an adequate idea of the indignation your book has aroused in all noble hearts, and of the wild shouts of joy that were set up on its appearance by all your enemies, both the non-literary—the Chichikovs, the

---

* Extracts from V. G. Belinsky, "Letter to N. V. Gogol'," in *Selected Philosophical Works* (Moscow: Foreign Languages Publishing House, 1948), 503–10. Belinskii wrote the "Letter to N. V. Gogol'" in response to opinions Gogol' expressed in *Selected Passages from Correspondence with Friends* (1846).

1 EDS: Belinskii refers to Gogol''s book *Selected Passages from Correspondence with Friends* (1847).

Nozdrevs, and the mayors[2] . . . and by the literary, whose names are well known to you. You see yourself that even those people who are of one mind with your book have disowned it. Even if it had been written as a result of deep and sincere conviction, it could not have created any impression on the public other than the one it did [. . .] Nor is that in any way surprising; what is surprising is that you find it surprising. I believe that is so because your profound knowledge of Russia is only that of an artist, but not of a thinker, whose role you have so ineffectually tried to play in your fantastic book. Not that you are not a thinker, but that you have been accustomed for so many years to look at Russia from your *beautiful far-away*[3]; and who does not know that there is nothing easier than seeing things from a distance the way we want to see them; for in that *beautiful far-away* you live a life that is entirely alien to it; you live in and within yourself or within a circle of the same mentality as your own that is powerless to resist your influence on it. Therefore you failed to realize that Russia sees her salvation not in mysticism or asceticism or pietism, but in the successes of civilization, enlightenment, and humanity. What she needs is not sermons (she has heard enough of them!) or prayers (she has repeated them too often!), but the awakening in the people of a sense of their human dignity lost for so many centuries amid dirt and refuse; she needs rights and laws conforming not to the preaching of the church but to common sense and justice, and their strictest possible observance. Instead of which she presents the dire spectacle of a country where men traffic in men, without even having the excuse so insidiously exploited by the American plantation owners who claim that the Negro is not a man; [. . .] a country where there are not only no guarantees for individuality, honor and property, but even no police order, and where there is nothing but vast corporations of official thieves and robbers of various descriptions. The most vital national problems in Russia today are the abolition of serfdom and corporal punishment and the strictest possible observance of at least those laws that already exist. [. . .]

Such are the problems that prey on the mind of Russia in her apathetic slumber! And at such a time a great writer, whose astonishingly artistic and deeply truthful works have so powerfully contributed toward Russia's awareness of herself, enabling her as they did to take a look at herself as though in a mirror—publishes a book in which he teaches the barbarian landowner to

---

2   EDS: These are unsavory characters from Gogol's, novel *Dead Souls*, Part I (1842).

3   EDS: Gogol' had been living and traveling abroad, with short intermissions, for more than a decade when Belinskii wrote the letter in July 1847.

make still greater profits out of the peasants and to abuse them still more in the name of Christ and Church [...] And would you expect me not to become indignant? [...] Why, if you had made an attempt on my life I could not have hated you more than I do for these disgraceful lines [...] And after this, you expect people to believe the sincerity of your book's intent! No! Had you really been inspired by the truth of Christ and not by the teaching of the devil you would certainly have written something entirely different in your new book. You would have told the landowner that since his peasants are his brethren in Christ, and since a brother cannot be a slave to his brother, he should either give them their freedom or, at least, allow them to enjoy the fruits of their own labor to their greatest possible benefit, realizing, as he does, in the depths of his own conscience, the false relationship in which he stands toward them [...]

Proponent of the knout, apostle of ignorance, champion of obscurantism and Stygian darkness, panegyrist of Tartar morals – what are you about! Look beneath your feet – you are standing on the brink of an abyss! [...] That you base such teaching on the Orthodox Church I can understand: it has always served as the prop of the knout and the servant of despotism; but why have you mixed Christ up in it? What have you found in common between Him and any church, least of all the Orthodox Church? He was the first to bring to people the teaching of freedom, equality, and brotherhood and to set the seal of truth to that teaching by martyrdom. And *this* teaching was men's *salvation* only until it became organized in the Church and took the principle of Orthodoxy for its foundation. The Church, on the other hand, was a hierarchy, consequently a champion of inequality, a flatterer of authority, an enemy and persecutor of brotherhood among men – and so it has remained to this day. But the meaning of Christ's message has been revealed by the philosophical movement of the preceding century. And that is why a man like Voltaire who stamped out the fires of fanaticism and ignorance in Europe by ridicule, is, of course, more the son of Christ, flesh of his flesh and bone of his bone, than all your priests, bishops, metropolitans, and patriarchs – Eastern or Western. Do you really mean to say you do not know that! Now it is not even a novelty to a schoolboy . . . Hence, can it be that you, the author of The Inspector General and Dead Souls, have in all sincerity, from the bottom of your heart, sung a hymn to the nefarious Russian clergy whom you rank immeasurably higher than the Catholic clergy? Let us assume that you do not know that the latter had once been something, while the former had never been anything but a servant and slave of the secular powers; but do you really mean to say you do not know that our clergy is held in universal contempt by Russian society and the Russian people? About whom do the Russian people tell dirty stories? Of the priest, the priest's wife, the priest's daughter, and the priest's farm hand. Does not the priest in Russia represent the embodiment of gluttony, avarice, servility, and shamelessness for all Russians? Do you mean to say that you do not know all this? Strange! According to you the Russian people is the most religious in the world. That is a lie! The basis of religiousness is pietism, reverence, fear of God. Whereas the Russian man utters the name of the Lord while scratching himself somewhere. He says of the icon: *If it works, pray to it; if it doesn't, it's good for covering pots.*

Take a closer look and you will see that it is by nature a profoundly atheistic people. It still retains a good deal of superstition, but not a trace of religiousness. Superstition passes with the advances of civilization, but religiousness often keeps company with them too; we have a living example of this in France, where even today there are many sincere Catholics among enlightened and educated men, and where many people who have rejected Christianity still cling stubbornly to some sort of god. The Russian people is different; mystic exaltation is not in its nature; it has too much common sense, a too lucid and positive mind, and therein, perhaps, lies the vastness of its historic destinies in the future. Religiousness has not even taken root among the clergy in it, since a few isolated and exceptional personalities distinguished for such cold ascetic contemplation prove nothing. But the majority of our clergy has always been distinguished for their fat bellies, scholastic pedantry, and savage ignorance. It is a shame to accuse it of religious intolerance and fanaticism; instead it could be praised for exemplary indifference in matters of faith. Religiosity among us appeared only in the schismatic sects who formed such a contrast in spirit to the mass of the people and who were numerically so insignificant in comparison with it.

I shall not expatiate on your panegyric to the affectionate relations existing between the Russian people and its lords and masters. I shall say point-blank that panegyric has met sympathy nowhere and has lowered you even in the eyes of people who in other respects are very close to you in their views. As far as I am concerned, I leave it to your conscience to admire the divine beauty of the autocracy (it is both safe and profitable), but continue to admire it judiciously from your *beautiful far-away:* at close quarters it is not so attractive, and not so safe . . . I would remark but this: when a European, especially a Catholic, is seized with religious ardor he becomes a denouncer of iniquitous authority, similar to the Hebrew prophets who denounced the iniquities of the great ones of the earth. We do quite the contrary: no sooner is a person (even a reputable person) afflicted with the malady that is known to psychiatrists as *religiosa mania* than he begins to burn more incense to the earthly god than to the heavenly one, and so overshoots the mark in doing so that the former would fain reward him for his slavish zeal did he not perceive that he would thereby be compromising himself in society's eyes. . . . What a rogue our fellow the Russian is! [. . .]

You, as far as I can see, you do not properly understand the Russian public. Its character is determined by the condition of Russian society in which fresh forces are seething and struggling for expression; but weighed down by heavy oppression, and finding no outlet, they induce merely dejection, weariness, and apathy. Only literature, despite the Tartar censorship, shows signs of life and progressive movement. That is why the title of writer is held in such esteem among us; that is why literary success is easy among us even for a writer of little talent. The title of poet and writer has long since eclipsed the tinsel of epaulets and gaudy uniforms. And that especially explains why every so-called liberal tendency, however poor in talent, is rewarded by universal notice, and why the popularity of great talents that sincerely or insincerely give themselves to the service of orthodoxy, autocracy, and nationality declines so quickly [. . .] And here the public is right, for it looks upon Russian writers as its only leaders, defenders, and saviors against Russian autocracy, orthodoxy, and nationality, and therefore, while always prepared to forgive a writer a bad book, will never forgive him a pernicious book. This shows how much fresh and healthy intuition, albeit still in embryo, is latent in our society, and this likewise proves that it has a future. If you love Russia, rejoice with me at the failure of your book! [. . .]

I would tell you, not without a certain feeling of self-satisfaction, that I believe I know the Russian public a little. Your book alarmed me by the possibility of its exercising a bad influence on the government and the censorship, but not on the public. When it was rumored in St. Petersburg that the government intended to publish your book in many thousands of copies and to sell it at an extremely low price, my friends grew despondent; but I told them then and there that the book, despite everything, would have no success and that it would soon be forgotten. In fact it is now better remembered for the articles that have been written about it than for the book itself. Yes, the Russian has a deep, though still undeveloped, instinct for truth.

Three Documents from the Petrashevskii Trial (1849)*

Summary of the Defendant's Testimony

Dostoevskii explained that he had never had a close relationship with Petrashevskii,[1] although he visited him on Fridays, just as Petrashevskii, in turn, would visit him. It was one of those acquaintanceships that he did not value very much, as he did not share many similarities in character or ideas with Petrashevskii; and, in visiting Petrashevskii quite rarely, he only maintained the relationship to the extent required by common courtesy. He never saw a reason to sever the relationship; and moreover, he was curious about Petrashevskii's Friday gatherings, not for the sake of Petrashevskii, but to meet some people there whom he saw quite rarely and whom he liked. Last winter, from September on, he, Dostoevskii, had been at Petrashevskii's no more than eight times. He was always struck by the peculiarity of Petrashevskii's character, and would often hear the opinion that Petrashevskii had more intelligence than reason. Petrashevskii was a man who constantly fussed around, read a lot, respected the Fourier system[2] (which he studied in detail), and paid particular attention to jurisprudence. All in all, he, Dostoevskii, respected Petrashevskii and considered him to be an honest and noble man. It is difficult to say that Petrashevskii, seen as a political man, had a particular system of judgement or took any particular view of political events. As far as he, Dostoevskii,

---

* The three documents have been translated from the original Russian by Anton Nonin and appear here under a Creative Commons BY-ND 4.0 license.

1 EDS: M. V. Petrashevskii (1821–66). From 1844 until his arrest in 1849 Petrashevskii held weekly gatherings at his home during which young intellectuals would socialize and use his library.

2 EDS: The "Fourier system" refers to the theories of French socialist utopian thinker Charles Fourier (1772–1837).

could tell, Petrashevskii's views were consistent only in regards to the Fourier system, which, Dostoevskii believed, prevented him from seeing things in any original way. However, he, Dostoevskii, said assuredly that Petrashevskii was nowhere near considering the immediate implementation of Fourier's system in our everyday lives. The group that gathered at Petrashevskii's on Fridays consisted, according to Dostoevskii, of close friends or old acquaintances; although sometimes new faces would appear; as far as he could tell, that happened quite rarely. At Petrashevskii's gathering, he, Dostoevskii, never saw any unity, any movement or common goal, and could decidedly say that you wouldn't have been able to meet three people there who would agree on any point, in any given subject.

Therefore, there were arguments within the group, constant conflicts and disagreements over opinions; and he, Dostoevskii, took part in some of the arguments. He spoke at Petrashevskii's three times: twice about literature and once about a subject that in no way was political—"About personality and human egoism"—and he does not recall that there was anything free-thinking or political about his words. If the wish for a better future is liberalism, then he, Dostoevskii, is a freethinker as much as anyone else who believes in his right as a citizen, and wishes nothing but good for his country, and carries within himself love for his motherland, and the knowledge that he would never harm it.

"If I am being accused," says Dostoevskii, "of talking about politics, about the West, about censorship, etc.—who doesn't think and talk about these issues in our time? What did I study for, why is my curiosity piqued by scholarship, if I don't have the right to speak my mind or disagree with an opinion that is considered to be authoritarian? You can't conclude from this that I am a freethinker and an opponent of monarchy—quite the opposite, for me there is nothing more ludicrous than the idea of republican rule in Russia, and everyone who knows me is aware of my thoughts on the subject. I did lament the existence of censorship and its unreasonable strictness because I felt that a misunderstanding had taken place, causing the difficult situation for literature to which I referred earlier. It saddened me that today, the calling of a writer is debased by dark suspicions, and that, before a writer even begins to write, the censorship sees him as an enemy of the government, and begins to review his manuscript with obvious prejudice."

He, Dostoevskii, read "The Correspondence Between Belinskii and Gogol'", on one of the evenings at Petrashevskii's, but there was nothing in his judgment of the text, nor even in the tone of his voice or in his gestures to indicate a predilection for either of the correspondents. Belinskii's letter is written too strangely to evoke sympathy; it is replete with oaths, written with bile, and therefore turns the heart against it.

He, Dostoevskii, knew Belinskii quite well; therefore, for him, Belinskii's correspondence with Gogol' represents a remarkable literary monument. As for him, Dostoevskii, he literally disagrees with every single exaggeration included in the letter, and he would never read it in order to present it as an example to be followed; but now he understands that he shouldn't have read this letter out loud.

As for the question of whether there was a secret conspiracy at Petrashevskii's gatherings, when he recalls the mishmash of ideas and characters at Petrashevskii's gatherings, as well as the arguments on the brink of animosity—"I can positively say that it a conspiracy would be impossible in that chaos."

In conclusion, Dostoevskii added "that he decidedly cannot say anything about Petrashevskii as a Fourierist-distributor and that, in this regard, Dostoevskii is only aware of Petrashevskii's scholarly convictions. Petrashevskii never revealed any of his plans or instructions, and he, Dostoevskii, is decidedly unaware if Petrashevskii even had any."

The Sentence of the Military-Judicial Commission

The Military Court finds the defendant Dostoevskii guilty: that he, upon receiving, in March of this year, from Moscow, from the nobleman Pleshcheev (a defendant), a copy of the criminal letter written by the writer Belinskii, read that letter at gatherings, first at the defendant Durov's home, then at the defendant Petrashevskii's home, and, finally, passed it on for copying to the defendant Mombelli. Dostoevskii was present at the defendant Speshnev's home during the reading of the outrageous work by Lieutenant Grigor'ev titled "Soldiers' Conversation." Therefore, the Military Court sentences him, the retired engineer-lieutenant Dostoevskii, for failure to report the distribution of the writer Belinskii's letter,[3] which contained criminal content against religion and government, and the malicious work of Lieutenant Grigor'ev—to be deprived of, on the basis of the Code of Military Decrees, P. V, Bk. 1, Art. 142, 144, 169, 170, 172, 174, 176, 177 and 178, of all ranks, of all rights to estate, and to be subjected to the death penalty by firing squad.

---

3 EDS: This refers to Belinskii's "Letter to Gogol'."

The Imperial Plan for Executing the Sentence Against the Convicted Conspirators[4]

On the Semenovskii Parade Square, across the middle of the earthworks, three stakes are to be erected at an elevation of one yard. No pits are to be dug.

Next to them are to be arranged, one battalion each, the Life Guards of the Regiment of Chasseurs and the Moscow Regiment, and a division from the Life Guard Cavalry Grenadiers Regiment.

On December 22, this year, at 9 o'clock in the morning, the criminals are to be brought in carriages. In front of and behind the convoy, one platoon is to be situated on each side from the St. Petersburg Division of Gendarmes. The convoy is to proceed at a trot from the fortress, across the Neva, onto the Gagarin Pier, along the embankment to the Arsenal, along the Liteinyi and Vladimirovskii Avenues, onto the Semenovskii Parade Square.

One mounted Gendarme is to remain on each side of each carriage. Ahead of each convoy will be one mounted Drill Adjutant.

The criminals are to be brought right up to the troops. Upon exiting the carriages, they are to be met by a priest, in a funeral garment, with a cross and the Holy Gospel, surrounded by the convoy. The prisoners will be escorted past the troops, stopping across from the center of the troops.

Once the criminals stand before the troops, sergeants and sub-officers are to be called into the center and commanded to present arms. The drummers are to sound three drum rolls. The verdict, according to statute, is to be read.

After the reading, it is commanded to slope arms, the sergeants and sub-officers are to take their places, and, to the beat of the drum, the ceremony is to be conducted. The uniforms are to be removed from the noblemen; the swords are to be broken above their heads (that is, for those who are sentenced to hard labor). Then long white shirts are to be put on the criminals (do not remove Lieutenant Palm's uniform, do not break the sword over him, and do not dress him in a long shirt). The priest gives his blessing and leaves. To the stakes the following criminals are to be brought: Petrashevskii, Mombelli, and Grigor'ev with their eyes covered. After tying the criminals to the stakes, fifteen privates are to approach at a distance of fifteen feet, accompanied by sub-officers, with loaded rifles. The rest of the criminals are to be left by the escorts.

After this, the Imperial Ratification is to be carried out.

---

4 EDS: This document demonstrates that the mock execution was planned in advance as part of the punishment.

After this, the criminals are to be dressed in warm clothes. Petrashevskii is to be put in shackles, and, accompanied by a gendarme and a courier, taken directly away. The rest of the criminals are to be returned to the fortress and sent away according to special orders.

All the general orders for the transportation of the criminals from the fortress, and for the performance of the execution ceremony, and their departure from the site of the pronouncement of the sentence, are to be placed under the personal responsibility of the St. Petersburg Commandant.

His Majesty wishes the execution of the Imperial Ratification to be performed personally by General Adjutant Sumarokov.

General Adjutant on duty at His Majesty's Headquarters Ignat'ev.

The Mock Execution Letter to Mikhail Dostoevskii, December 22, 1849*

Fedor Dostoevskii

December 22, 1849. Peter and Paul Fortress.

Brother, my dear friend! Everything has been decided! I have been sentenced to four years of labor in a fortress (Orenburg, I think), and then to the ranks. Today, December 22, we were taken to Semenovskii Square. There, we were read the death sentence, were allowed to kiss the cross, had sabers broken over our heads, and were dressed in our death clothes (white shirts). Then, three of us were stood at the pole for execution. I was sixth in line – we were called three at a time, therefore I was in the second party, and I had no more than a minute to live. I remembered you, brother, and your family; in that last minute, you and only you were on my mind, and only then did I realize how much I love you, my dear brother! I managed to embrace Pleshcheev and Durov who were nearby, and said farewell to them. Finally, a retreat was sounded, the ones who were tied up to the pole were brought back, and the pronouncement was read that his Imperial Majesty had granted us life. Then the real sentences followed. Only Pal'm was pardoned. He kept his rank and was sent to the army.

I have just been told, my dear brother, that today or tomorrow we will begin our journey. I asked to see you. But I was told that it is impossible, and I'm only allowed to write you this letter, to which, hurry and reply

---

* Translated from the original Russian by Anton Nonin, redacted by the editors. This translation appears here under a Creative Commons BY-ND 4.0 license.

as soon as possible. I'm afraid that somehow you have learned of our sentence (to death). From the carriage window when we were driven to Semenovskii Square, I saw a horde of people; maybe the news had already reached you and you suffered for me. Now you will feel better for me. Brother! I did not whimper and did not lose heart. Life is everywhere, life is within us, and not on the outside. There will be people near me, and to be a human among people and remain a human forever in any misfortune, not to become despondent and collapse—that is the point of life and its goal. I realized that. This idea has entered my flesh and blood. Yes, it's the truth! That head—the one that created, lived a higher life of art, that realized and grew accustomed to the high demands of the spirit—that head has been cut off from my shoulders. The memory remains, as well as the yet unmaterialized images in my head. They will torture me, truly! But what will also remain in me is the heart and the same flesh and blood that can love, and suffer, and desire, and remember that this is, nevertheless, life! *On voit le soleil!*[1] Well, farewell, brother! Do not grieve for me!

Now, regarding the arrangement of my material possessions: the books (the Bible remains with me), and a few pages of my manuscripts (drafts of plays, a novel, and the finished novella *Children's Fable*) were confiscated and will be handed, possibly, to you. My coat and old shirt I leave as well, and you may send for them. Now, brother, I am faced with what will likely be a long journey to prison. I need money. Dear brother, if you receive this letter, and if it is possible to find any amount of money, then send it right away. I now need money more than air (because of the special circumstance). Also send a few lines from yourself. Then, if the Moscow money comes through—make an effort for me and do not abandon me . . . Well, that is all! There is still debt, what can be done about it?! Kiss your wife and children. Remind them of me; do everything you can so they don't forget me. Perhaps we'll meet sometime? Brother, take care of yourself and your family, live quietly and predictably. Think about the future of your children . . . Live positively.

Never before have such abundant and healthy reserves of spiritual life surged in me as they do now. Will the body endure? I do not know. I'm departing unhealthy; I have jaundice. But whatever may be!

---

1 EDS: Dostoevskii quotes Victor Hugo's *The Last Day of a Condemned Man* (1829). In Hugo's novella this line comes as the condemned man fantasizes about a commutation of his sentence, observing that a convict is someone who "still walks, comes and goes, and sees the sun [*cela voit le soleil*]." Dostoevskii has altered the line slightly to read "*On voit le soleil!*" or "He sees the sun," which here carries a double meaning.

Brother! I have experienced so much in life that little is left that could scare me. Whatever will be, will be! [. . .] And maybe we'll see each other again, brother. Take care of yourself, survive, for God's sake, until we meet. Maybe one day we'll embrace each other and recall our early golden times, our youth and our hopes, which I, at this moment, tear out of my heart with blood, and bury.

Will I never pick up a pen again? I think that in four years, it will be possible. I will send you everything that I will write, if I write anything. My God! So many images, cast out, created by me will die, fade away in my head, or spread like poison in my blood! Yes, if writing is forbidden, I will perish. I would rather have fifteen years of imprisonment with a pen in my hand.

Write me frequently, write with details, write more, exhaustively. Expatiate, in every letter, on family details, the minutiae, don't forget that. It will give me hope and life. If only you knew how rejuvenating it was to receive your letters here in my cell. These two and a half months (the last ones), when correspondence was forbidden, tormented me. I was unwell. The fact that you sometimes did not send me money worried me sick: you yourself were in dire need! Once again, kiss your children; their sweet faces never leave my mind. Ah! I hope they will be happy! Be happy, you too, brother, be happy!

But do not grieve about me, for God's sake, do not grieve! Know that I was not despondent, that hope did not leave me. In four years my life will be easier. I will be a common soldier—not a prisoner anymore, and remember that I will embrace you some day. After all, I was already close to death today, and lived for three quarters of an hour with that thought—I was close to the final moment—and still I live!

And if someone remembers me with ill will, or if I had a quarrel with someone, if I left a bad taste in someone's mouth—tell them to forget it all if you chance to meet them. There is no bile and anger in my soul, I so wish to love and embrace someone from the past at this moment. I experienced that joy today when I bid farewell to my dear ones before death. I thought at that moment that the news of my execution would kill you. But now rest assured, I still live, and will live with the thought of one day embracing you. This is the only thought on my mind now [. . .]

Whenever I look at the past I think of how time was wasted, how much of it was lost in delusions, mistakes, idleness, the inability to live; how I didn't value it, how often I sinned against my heart and my spirit—my heart bleeds. Life is a gift, life is happiness, every minute could be a century of happiness.

Si jeunesse savait![2] Now, changing my life, I am reborn in a new form. Brother! I swear to you that I will not lose hope and I will keep my spirit and my heart in purity. I will be reborn for the best. That is all my hope, all my solace [...]

Well, farewell, farewell, brother! I embrace you tightly, kiss you hard. Remember me without pain in your heart. Do not grieve, please, do not grieve about me! In my very next letter I will write you about my life. Remember what I told you: consider your life, do not waste it, don't waste it, arrange your fate, think about the children. When, oh when, will I see you! [...]

Farewell, once again farewell! Farewell everyone!...

Your F. Dostoevskii

---

2   EDS: Here Dostoevskii refers to an epigram that appears in Henri Estienne's *Les Prémices* (1594). The full phrase reads: "*Si jeunesse savait, si vieillesse pouvait!*" ("If youth but knew, if old age but could!")

CHAPTER 2

Dostoevskii and His Contemporaries

This chapter explores Dostoevskii's place in the literary history of his era. A series of reviews and letters charts his often-troubled relationships with the other leading writers of his day, while a selection of excerpts from modern criticism illustrates the variety of critical approaches that scholars use when comparing nineteenth-century writers. All the great novelists of the second half of the nineteenth-century—among them Dostoevskii, Lev Tolstoi (1828–1910), and Ivan Turgenev (1813–83)—addressed similar "accursed" questions: the meaning of life in an increasingly secular and modern world; Russia's national identity and the country's relationship to the West; the nature of human beings and why social and political reforms succeed or fail. Yet these authors came to different answers to these questions; moreover, their novelistic styles differ radically. This chapter provides the foundations for a comparative study of Dostoevskii and the other writers of his time, and the rest of the book will return to the figures and personalities presented here as we explore both Dostoevskii's artistic methods and his ideas in more depth in the context of his era.

As we saw in the first chapter, Dostoevskii's literary début, *Poor Folk*, met with great acclaim from Belinskii and his circle, who believed that art should be judged based on its ability to reflect social reality critically and accurately. However, *The Double* (1846), published on the heels of *Poor Folk*, produced a much more ambivalent reaction, in part because it included a fantastic element: the hero, Goliadkin, encounters his own double and the story follows the tragicomic misadventures that unfold between them. This chapter begins with Belinskii's mixed review of *The Double*, which, while praising the author's "creative talent and depth of thought," concedes that St. Petersburg readers have found the story "insufferably long and therefore terribly boring." A more sympathetic review by the critic Valerian Maikov (1823–46) is also provided; Maikov notes that the novella mixes profound psychological analysis with a peculiarly Dostoevskian "mystical glint." This remark holds true for the novels that Dostoevskii wrote later in life, and anticipates his famous statement that he is not a psychologist but a "realist in a higher sense." Valerian Maikov died young, but his brother, the poet Apollon (1821–97), would become a friend and important ally of Dostoevskii throughout the politically turbulent years of the 1860s and 1870s.

During this period, Dostoevskii's strong Christian faith and Russian messianism meant that he had few natural allies among the intelligentsia, who increasingly moved left politically and embraced a philosophical materialism that Dostoevskii railed against. His debate with radical thinkers such as the novelist and philosopher Nikolai Chernyshevskii (1828–89) is recorded in Chapter 7. However, he even fell out with moderate liberals, such as his former friend Turgenev, whose Westernizing sympathies alienated Dostoevskii. With typical sardonic humor, Dostoevskii, visiting Turgenev in Germany, advised him to purchase a telescope if he wanted to continue writing about Russia from afar. Turgenev's dispute with Dostoevskii is recorded here through Dostoevskii's letters to Apollon Maikov and the philosopher Nikolai Strakhov (1828–71). The quarrel continued by means of fiction, as we see in Dostoevskii's portrait of the writer Karmazinov in *Demons* (1871–72), a thinly veiled caricature of Turgenev, reproduced here alongside a response from Turgenev.

Turgenev famously called Dostoevskii the Russian Sade, and was troubled by his emphasis on the darker aspects of human nature: the propensity for evil, violence, and sadism shown in his works. The radical populist Nikolai Mikhailovskii (1842–1904) takes up that theme in his study of Dostoevskii titled *A Cruel Talent* (1882), an excerpt of which is reproduced here. "No one in Russian literature," writes Mikhailovskii, "has analyzed the sensations of a wolf devouring a sheep with such thoroughness, such depth, one might say with such love, as Dostoevskii." The label "cruel talent" has stuck to Dostoevskii, and the problem of whether and how his depictions of cruelty might be reconciled with his vision of Christian love remains a crucial one for critics even now. Might Dostoevskii—as Blake said of Milton—be of the Devil's party without knowing it?

Surprisingly, Dostoevskii and Tolstoi—the two giant novelists who wrote contemporaneously—never actually met. Although the two men shared a skepticism of the radical intelligentsia, they had different temperaments, contrasting novelistic styles, and eventually developed political outlooks that were poles apart. The two men did read and comment on each other's work, often producing idiosyncratic interpretations captured here in Dostoevskii's review of *Anna Karenina* (1873–77) and Tolstoi's comments on the psychology of

Raskol'nikov in *Crime and Punishment* (1866). Subsequently, the paradigm of comparing Tolstoi and Dostoevskii's thought and art has proved enormously productive for critics. One of the first studies in this vein is *L. Tolstoi and Dostoevskii* (1900–1902) by Dmitrii Merezhkovskii (1866–1941), an excerpt of which is reproduced here, whereas Robert Louis Jackson's 1993 essay "The Root and the Flower" compares Dostoevskii and Turgenev. Despite the two writers' quarrel and the obvious differences between their novelistic approaches, Jackson finds intriguing convergences in their work.

Further Reading

Fanger, Donald. *Dostoevsky and Romantic Realism*. Cambridge, MA: Harvard University Press, 1965.

Jackson, Robert Louis. *Dialogues with Dostoevsky: The Overwhelming Questions*. Stanford, CA: Stanford University Press, 1993.

Kliger, Ilya. *The Narrative Shape of Truth: Veridiction in Modern European Literature*. University Park: The Pennsylvania State University Press, 2011.

Orwin, Donna Tussing. *Consequences of Consciousness: Turgenev, Tolstoy and Dostoevsky*. Stanford, CA: Stanford University Press, 2007.

Rosenshield, Gary. *Challenging the Bard. Dostoevsky and Pushkin, a Study of Literary Relationship*. Madison: University of Wisconsin Press, 2013.

Seduro, Vladimir. *Dostoyevski in Russian Literary Criticism*. New York: Columbia University Press, 1957.

Steiner, George. *Tolstoy or Dostoevsky: An Essay in the Old Criticism*. 2nd ed. New Haven, CT: Yale University Press, 1996.

A Review of *The Double* (1846)*

Vissarion Belinskii

The hero of the novel, Mr. Goliadkin, is one of those thin-skinned, obsessively ambitious people whom one can meet in the lowest and middle classes of our society. It always seems to him that he is insulted either by words, or looks, or gestures, that there are machinations and schemes are plotted against him everywhere. It is all the more amusing that neither his capital, nor his rank, nor his status, nor intelligence, nor abilities can evoke envy in anyone. He is neither smart nor stupid, neither rich nor poor, very kind and has a meek character to the point of weakness. He would not have such a bad life, but his unhealthy touchiness and suspicious quality of his character are a black demon in his life, who will turn his existence to hell. If one would look around, one would see so many Mr. Goliadkins, either poor or rich, smart and stupid! Mr. Goliadkin is overjoyed just from the thought of his virtue, which consists of him not wearing a mask, of the fact that he does not scheme, that he acts openly and follows a straight path. Even at the beginning of the novel, in his conversation with Dr. Krest'ian Ivanovich, it is not difficult to realize that Mr. Goliadkin is mentally disturbed. And so, the hero of the novel is insane. The idea is bold and is executed by the author with wonderful skill! [. . .] Anyone for whom mysteries of art are accessible can at the first glance see that there is more creative talent and depth of thought in *The Double* than in *Poor Folk*. But at the same time, an almost unanimous voice of St. Petersburg readers decided that this novel is insufferably long and therefore terribly boring, from which it follows that the praises for the author were groundless, and there is nothing extraordinary about his talent! Is such a conclusion just? Without beating around the bush, we'll say that on the one hand, it's a faulty statement, but on the other hand, there is a basis to it, as there is always one in judgments of a mob that doesn't understand itself.

---

* First published in *Otechestvennye zapiski* [Notes of the Fatherland] 45, no. 3 (1846). This excerpt has been translated by Anton Nonin and appears here under a Creative Commons BY-ND 4.0 license.

Thoughts on
The Double (1847)*

Valerian Maikov

In *The Double*, Dostoevskii's manner and his love for psychological analysis found full expression and originality. In this work, he has so deeply reached into the human soul, so unflinchingly and fervently gazed into the innermost machinations of human emotions, thoughts, and affairs, that the impression received from reading *The Double* can be compared to the impression of a man of inquisitive mind who infiltrates the chemical composition of matter. It is strange: what could possibly be more pragmatic than a chemical gaze at reality, however, the world, seen through that gaze, always appears to a human to be enveloped in some kind of mystical light. From what we ourselves have experienced and what we can conclude about impressions of the majority of Dostoevskii's admirers, in his psychological studies, there is always that mystical glint that is inherent in the reflection of deeply analyzed reality. *The Double* unwraps the anatomy of the soul that is dying from the realization of the fragmentation of private interests in a well-organized society. Recall that poor, sickly vain Goliadkin, who is constantly driven by fear of losing his composure in front of someone else, but at the same time, constantly self-destructing even before his rascal servant Petrushka, and constantly agreeing to give up his needs and individuality, as long as he keeps his rights. Recall that the slightest activity in nature seems to him as an evil sign of the conspiracy of enemies of all kinds, enemies who have dedicated themselves fully

---

First published as part of a longer essay, "Nechto o russkoi literature v 1846 g.," in *Otechestvennye zapiski* [Notes of the Fatherland] 50, no. 1 (1847). This excerpt has been translated by Anton Nonin and appears here under a Creative Commons BY-ND 4.0 license.

to cause him harm, who keep a watchful eye on his unlucky person, and who tenaciously, without rest, sabotage his paltry interests. Recall all that and ask yourself, is there nothing of Goliadkin in you? Something that you would never confess, but something that is explainable by the wonderful harmony that reigns in human society . . . However, if you were bored while reading *The Double*, there is nothing surprising about it, despite it being impossible not to sympathize with Goliadkin: not everyone can tolerate analysis. Was it so long ago when Lermontov's analysis stuck a thorn in many people's sides? Was it so long ago when an intolerable element was seen in Pushkin's poetry?

The Row with Turgenev: Letter to Apollon Maikov, August 16, 1867*

I kept putting off my visit to Turgenev still, eventually I had to call. I went about noon, and found him at breakfast. I'll tell you frankly—I never really liked that man. The worst of it is that since 1857, at Wiesbaden, I've owed him 50 talers (which even to-day I haven't yet paid back!). I can't stand the aristocratic and Pharisaical sort of way he embraces one, and offers his cheek to be kissed. He puts on monstrous airs; but my bitterest complaint against him is his book *Smoke*. He told me himself that the leading idea, the point at issue, in that book, is this: "If Russia were destroyed by an earthquake and vanished from the globe, it would mean no loss to humanity—it would not even be noticed." He declared to me that that was his fundamental view of Russia. I found him in irritable mood; it was on account of the failure of *Smoke*. I must tell you that at the time the full details of that failure were unknown to me. I *had* heard by letter of Strakhov's article in the *Notes of the Fatherland*, but I didn't know that they had torn him to pieces in all the other papers as well, and that in Moscow, at a club, I believe, people had collected signatures to a protest against *Smoke*. He told me that himself. Frankly, I never could have imagined that anyone could so naively and clumsily display all the wounds in his vanity, as Turgenev did that day; and these people go about boasting that they are atheists. He told me that he was an

---

* From *Letters of Fyodor Michailovitch Dostoevsky to His Family and Friends*, trans. Ethel Colburn Mayne (New York: Macmillan, 1917), 115–19.

uncompromising atheist. My God! It is to Deism that we owe the Savior—that is to say, the conception of a man so noble that one cannot grasp it without a sense of awe a conception of which one cannot doubt that it represents the undying ideal of mankind. And what do we owe to these gentry—Turgenev, Gertsen, Utin, Chernyshevskii? In place of that loftiest divine beauty on which they spit, we behold in them such ugly vanity, such unashamed susceptibility, such ludicrous arrogance, that it is simply impossible to guess what it is that they hope for, and who shall take them as guides. He frightfully abused Russia and the Russians. But I have noticed this: all those Liberals and Progressives who derive chiefly from Belinskii's school, find their pleasure and satisfaction in abusing Russia. The difference is that the adherents of Chernyshevskii merely abuse, and in so many words desire that Russia should disappear from the face of the earth (*that*, first of all!). But the others declare, in the same breath, that *they love Russia*. And yet they hate everything that is native to the soil, they delight in caricaturing it, and were one to oppose them with some fact that they could not explain away or caricature—any fact with which they were obliged to reckon—they would, I believe, be profoundly unhappy, annoyed, even distraught. And I've noticed that Turgenev—and for that matter all who live long abroad—have no conception of the true facts (though they do read the newspapers), and have so utterly lost all affection and understanding for Russia that even those quite ordinary matters which in Russia the very Nihilists no longer deny, but only as it were caricature after their manner—*these* fellows cannot so much as grasp. Amongst other things he told me that we are bound to crawl in the dust before the Germans, that there is but one universal and irrefutable way—that of civilization, and that all attempts to create an independent Russian culture are nothing but folly and pigheadedness. He said that he was writing a long article against the Russophiles and Slavophiles. I advised him to order a telescope from Paris for his better convenience. "What do you mean?" he asked. "The distance is somewhat great," I replied; "Direct the telescope on Russia, and then you will be able to observe us; otherwise you can't really see anything at all." He flew into a rage. When I saw him so angry, I said with well-simulated naiveté: "Really I should never have supposed that all the articles derogatory to your new novel could have discomposed you to this extent; by God, the thing's not worth getting so angry about. Come, spit upon it all!" "I'm not in the least discomposed. What are you thinking of?" he answered, getting red. I interrupted him, and turned the talk to personal and domestic matters. Before going away, I brought forth, as if quite casually and without any particular object, all the hatred that these three months have accumulated in me against the Germans. "Do you know what swindlers and rogues they are here? Truly, the common people are much more evil and dishonest here than they are with us; and that they are stupider there can be no doubt. You are always talking of civilization; with what has your 'civilization' endowed the Germans, and wherein do they surpass us?" He turned pale (it is no exaggeration), and said: "In speaking thus, you insult me personally. You know quite well that I have definitely settled here, that I consider myself a German and not a Russian, and am proud of it." I answered: "Although I have read your *Smoke*, and have just talked with you for a whole hour, I could never have imagined that you would say such a thing. Forgive me, therefore, if I *have* insulted you."

Then we took leave of one another very politely, and I promised myself that I would never again cross Turgenev's threshold. The next day, Turgenev came at exactly ten o'clock in the morning to my abode, and left his card with the landlady. But as I had told him the day before that I never saw anyone till noon, and that we usually slept till eleven, I naturally took his ten o'clock call as a hint that he doesn't wish to see any more of me. During the whole seven weeks, I saw him only once more, at the railway station. We looked at one another, but no greeting passed. The animosity with which I speak of Turgenev, and the insults we offered one another, will perhaps strike you unpleasantly. But, by God, I can do no other; he offended me too deeply with his amazing views. Personally, I really feel little affected, though his uppity manners are quite disagreeable enough in themselves; but I simply can't stand by and listen when a traitor who, if he chose, could be of service to his country, abuses Russia in the way he does. His tail-wagging to the Germans, and his hatred for the Russians, I had noticed already four years ago. But his present rage and fury against Russia arises solely, *solely*, from the failure of *Smoke*, and from the fact that Russia has dared refuse to hail him as a genius. It is nothing but vanity, and therefore all the more repulsive.

The Caricature of Turgenev in *Demons* (1872)*

Fedor Dostoevskii

There was a feeling in the hall that something was wrong again. Let me state to begin with that I have the deepest reverence for genius, but why do our geniuses in the decline of their illustrious years behave sometimes exactly like little boys? What though he was Karmazinov, and came forward with as much dignity as five *Kammerherrs* rolled into one?[1] How could he expect to keep an audience like ours listening for a whole hour to a single paper? I have observed, in fact, that however big a genius a man may be, he can't monopolize the attention of an audience at a frivolous literary matinée for more than twenty minutes with impunity. The entrance of the great writer was received, indeed, with the utmost respect: even the severest elderly men showed signs of approval and interest, and the ladies even displayed some enthusiasm. The applause was brief, however, and somehow uncertain and not unanimous. Yet there was no unseemly behavior in the back rows, until Karmazinov began to speak, not that anything very bad followed then, but only a sort of misunderstanding. I have mentioned already that he had rather a shrill voice, almost feminine in fact, and at the same time a genuinely aristocratic lisp. He had hardly articulated a few words when someone had the effrontery to laugh aloud—probably some ignorant simpleton who knew nothing of the world, and was congenitally disposed to laughter. But there was nothing like a hostile demonstration; on the contrary people said "sh-h!" and the offender was crushed. But Mr. Karmazinov, with an affected air

---

* Excerpted from *The Possessed*, trans. Constance Garnett (London: Heinemann, 1913), 445–50.

1 EDS: *Kammerherr*, literally "chamberlain," was a courtier's rank in the eighteenth century; by the nineteenth century, it had become an honorary rank.

and intonation, announced that "at first he had declined absolutely to read." (Much need there was to mention it!) "There are some lines which come so deeply from the heart that it is impossible to utter them aloud, so that these holy things cannot be laid before the public"—(Why lay them then?)—"but as he had been begged to do so, he was doing so, and as he was, moreover, laying down his pen forever, and had sworn to write no more, he had written this last farewell; and as he had sworn never, on any inducement, to read anything in public," and so on, and so on, all in that style.

[...]

Of course it did not end without trouble; but the worst of it was that it was his own doing. People had for some time begun shuffling their feet, blowing their noses, coughing, and doing everything that people do when a lecturer, whoever he may be, keeps an audience for longer than twenty minutes at a literary matinée. But the genius noticed nothing of all this. He went on lisping and mumbling, without giving a thought to the audience, so that everyone began to wonder. Suddenly in a back row a solitary but loud voice was heard:

"Good Lord, what nonsense!"

The exclamation escaped involuntarily, and I am sure was not intended as a demonstration. The man was simply worn out. But Mr. Karmazinov stopped, looked sarcastically at the audience, and suddenly lisped with the deportment of an aggrieved kammerherr.

"I'm afraid I've been boring you dreadfully, gentlemen?"

That was his blunder, that he was the first to speak; for provoking an answer in this way he gave an opening for the rabble to speak, too, and even legitimately, so to say, while if he had restrained himself, people would have gone on blowing their noses and it would have passed off somehow. Perhaps he expected applause in response to his question, but there was no sound of applause; on the contrary, everyone seemed to subside and shrink back in dismay.

"You never did see Ancus Marcius, that's all brag," cried a voice that sounded full of irritation and even nervous exhaustion.

"Just so," another voice agreed at once. "There are no such things as ghosts nowadays, nothing but natural science. Look it up in a scientific book."

"Gentlemen, there was nothing I expected less than such objections," said Karmazinov, extremely surprised. The great genius had completely lost touch with his Fatherland in Karlsruhe.

"Nowadays it's outrageous to say that the world stands on three fishes," a young lady snapped out suddenly. "You can't have gone down to the hermit's cave, Karmazinov. And who talks about hermits nowadays?"

"Gentlemen, what surprises me most of all is that you take it all so seriously. However . . . however, you are perfectly right. No one has greater respect for truth and realism than I have . . ."

Though he smiled ironically he was tremendously overcome. His face seemed to express: "I am not the sort of man you think, I am on your side, only praise me, praise me more, as much as possible, I like it extremely . . ."

"Gentlemen," he cried, completely mortified at last, "I see that my poor poem is quite out of place here. And, indeed, I am out of place here myself, I think."

"You threw at the crow and you hit the cow," some fool, probably drunk, shouted at the top of his voice, and of course no notice ought to have been taken of him. It is true there was a sound of disrespectful laughter.

"A cow, you say?" Karmazinov caught it up at once, his voice grew shriller and shriller. "As for crows and cows, gentlemen, I will refrain. I've too much respect for any audience to permit myself comparisons, however harmless; but I did think . . ."

"You'd better be careful, sir," someone shouted from a back row.

"But I had supposed that laying aside my pen and saying farewell to my readers, I should be heard . . ."

"No, no, we want to hear you, we want to," a few voices from the front row plucked up spirit to exclaim at last.

"Read, read!" several enthusiastic ladies' voices chimed in, and at last there was an outburst of applause, sparse and feeble, it is true.

"Believe me, Karmazinov, everyone looks on it as an honor . . ." the marshal's wife herself could not resist saying.

"Mr. Karmazinov!" cried a fresh young voice in the back of the hall suddenly. It was the voice of a very young teacher from the district school who had only lately come among us, an excellent young man, quiet and gentlemanly. He stood up in his place. "Mr. Karmazinov, if I had the happiness to fall in love as you have described to us, I really shouldn't refer to my love in an article intended for public reading . . ." He flushed red all over.

"Ladies and gentlemen," cried Karmazinov, "I have finished. I will omit the end and withdraw. Only allow me to read the six last lines:

"Yes, dear reader, farewell!" he began at once from the manuscript without sitting down again in his chair. "Farewell, reader; I do not greatly insist on our parting friends; what need to trouble you, indeed. You may abuse me, abuse me as you will if it affords you any satisfaction. But best of all if we forget one another for ever. And if you all, readers, were suddenly so kind as to fall on your knees and begin begging me with tears, 'Write, oh, write for us, Karmazinov—for the sake of Russia, for the sake of posterity, to win laurels,' even then I would answer you, thanking you, of course, with every courtesy, 'No, we've had enough of one another, dear fellow-countrymen, merci! It's time we took our separate ways!' Merci, merci, merci!"

Karmazinov bowed ceremoniously, and, as red as though he had been cooked, retired behind the scenes.

"Nobody would go down on their knees; a wild idea!"

"What conceit!"

"That's only humor," someone more reasonable suggested.

"Spare me your humor."

"I call it impudence, gentlemen!"

"Well, he's finished now, anyway!"

"Ech, what a dull show!"

Reaction to *Demons*: Letter to Mariia Miliutina, December 3, 1872*

Ivan Turgenev

My Dear Mariia Ageevna, I thank you from my heart for the friendly feelings which dictated your last letter. I was not in the least surprised by Dostoevskii's proceeding: he began to hate me when we were both young and at the commencement of our literary activities, although I did nothing to call forth that hatred. But unreasoned passions are, it is said, the strongest and most persistent of all. Dostoevskii has permitted himself something worse than a parody: he has shown me, under the mask of Karmazinov, as a secret partisan of Nechaev.[1] It is worthy of remark that he selected for this parody the only story which I published in the journal at one time conducted by him a story for which he overwhelmed me in his letters with thanks and praise. I still have his letters. It would certainly be rather amusing to make them public now. But he knows that I shall never do so. I am sorry that he should use his undoubtedly great talent for the satisfaction of such unlovely feelings; evidently he does not himself prize his gifts very highly, since he degrades them to a pamphlet.

---

*   From *Letters of Fyodor Michailovitch Dostoevsky to his Family and Friends*, trans. Ethel Colburn Mayne (New York: Macmillan, 1917), 316.

1   EDS: Sergei Nechaev (1847–82) was a revolutionary terrorist associated with the Nihilist movement; he was the prototype for Petr Verkhovenskii in Dostoevskii's *Demons*.

"Landowner's Literature": Letter to Nikolai Strakhov, May 18, 1871*

D id I really write you nothing about your article on Turgenev? I read it, as I read all your writings, with great delight, but at the same time with some degree of vexation. Once you had admitted that Turgenev has lost grasp, that he has no idea what to say about certain manifestations of Russian life (he jeers at them, every one), you were bound to admit as well that his artistic powers are at ebb in his recent work for it could not be otherwise. But on the contrary you hold that his recent work is on the same level with his earlier. Can both statements be accepted? Possibly I am myself mistaken (not in my judgment of Turgenev, but in my interpretation of your article). Perhaps you have merely expressed yourself confusedly . . . Know this: all that school is no more than "Landowner's Literature." And that kind of literature has said all it had to say (particularly well in the case of Lev Tolstoi). It has spoken its last word, and is exempt from further duty. A new school that may take its place is still to come; we have not had time to produce it. The Reshetnikovs have said nothing.[1] Nevertheless, the works of a Reshetnikov demonstrate the necessity for a new note in literature, which shall replace that of the landed proprietors however repellently such a writer expresses himself.

---

* From *Letters of Fyodor Michailovitch Dostoevsky to His Family and Friends*, trans. Ethel Colburn Mayne (New York: Macmillan, 1917), 209–10.

1 EDS: *Reshetnikovs* refers to socially and politically committed writers who believed literature should expose the plight of the poor. Dostoevskii's term comes from Fedor Reshetnikov (1841–71), an exponent of the school.

Thoughts on
Anna Karenina (1877)*

Fedor Dostoevskii

The idea behind *Anna Karenina,* of course, is nothing new or unheard of in Russia. Instead of this novel we could, of course, show Europe the source—Pushkin himself, that is—as the strongest, most vivid and most incontestable proof of the independence of the Russian genius and its rights to a great, worldwide, pan-human and all-unifying significance in the future. (Alas, no matter how we tried to show them that, Europe will not read our writers for a long time yet; and if Europe does begin to read them, the Europeans will not be able to understand and appreciate them for a long time. Indeed, they are utterly unable to appreciate our writers, not because of insufficient capacity, but because for them we are an entirely different world, just as if we had come down from the moon so that it is difficult for them even to admit the fact that we exist. All this I know, and I speak of "showing Europe" only in the sense of our own conviction of our right to independence vis-à-vis Europe.) Nevertheless, *Anna Karenina* is perfection as a work of art that appeared at just the right moment and as a work to which nothing in the European literatures of this era can compare; and, in the second place, the novel's idea also contains something of ours, something truly *our own,* namely that very thing which constitutes our distinctness from the European world, the thing which constitutes our "new word," or at least its beginnings—just the kind of word one cannot hear in Europe, yet one that Europe still so badly needs, despite all her pride.

* Excerpt from Fyodor Dostoevsky, *A Writer's Diary, Volume 2: 1877–1881,* trans. Kenneth Lantz (Evanston, IL: Northwestern University Press, 1994), 1069–72. Copyright © 1994 by Northwestern University Press. Published 1994. All rights reserved.

I cannot embark upon literary criticism here and will say only a few things. *Anna Karenina* expresses a view of human guilt and transgression. People are shown living under abnormal conditions. Evil existed before they did. Caught up in a whirl of falsities, people transgress and are doomed to destruction. As you can see, it is one of the oldest and most popular of European themes. But how is such a problem solved in Europe? Generally in Europe there are two ways of solving it. Solution number one: the law has been given, recorded, formulated, and put together through the course of millennia. Good and evil have been defined and weighed, their extent and degree have been determined historically by humanity's wise men, by unceasing work on the human soul, and by working out, in a very scientific manner, the extent of the forces that unite people in a society. One is commanded to follow this elaborated code of laws blindly. He who does not follow it, he who transgresses, pays with his freedom, his property, or his life; he pays literally and cruelly. "I know," says their civilization, "that this is blind and cruel and impossible, since we are not able to work out the ultimate formula for humanity while we are still at the midpoint of its journey; but since we have no other solution, it follows that we must hold to that which is written, and hold to it literally and cruelly. Without it, things would be even worse. At the same time, despite all the abnormality and absurdity of the structure we call our great European civilization, let the forces of the human spirit remain healthy and intact; let society not be shaken in its faith that it is moving toward perfection; let no one dare think that the idea of the beautiful and sublime has been obscured, that the concepts of good and evil are being distorted and twisted, that convention is constantly taking the place of the healthy norm, that simplicity and naturalness are perishing as they are crushed by a constant accumulation of lies!"

The second solution is the reverse: "Since society is arranged in an abnormal manner, one cannot demand that human entities be responsible for the consequences of their actions. Therefore, the criminal is not responsible, and crime at present does not exist. In order to put an end to crime and human guilt we must put an end to the abnormality of society and its structure. Since curing the ills in the existing order of things is a long and hopeless process, and the medicines needed have not even been found, it follows that the whole society must be destroyed and the old order swept away with a broom, as it were. Then we can begin it all anew, on different principles as yet unknown but which, nevertheless, can be no worse than those of the present order; on the contrary, they offer many chances of success. Our main hope is in science." And so this is the second solution: they wait for the future ant heap and in the meantime will wet the earth with blood. The world of western Europe offers no other solutions for guilt and human transgression.

The Russian author's view of guilt and transgression recognizes that no ant heap, no triumph of the "fourth estate," no abolition of poverty, no organization of labor will save humanity from abnormality and, consequently, from guilt and transgression. This is expressed in a monumental psychological elaboration of the human soul, with awesome depth and force and with a realism of artistic portrayal unprecedented among us. It is clear and intelligible to the point of obviousness that evil lies deeper in human beings than our socialist-physicians suppose; that no social structure will eliminate evil; that the human soul will remain as it always has been; that abnormality and sin arise from that soul itself; and, finally, that the laws of the human soul are still so little known, so obscure to science, so undefined, and so mysterious, that there are not and cannot be either physicians or *final* judges; but there is He who says: "Vengeance is mine, I will repay."[1] He alone knows *all* the mystery of this world and the final destiny of man. Humans themselves still cannot venture to decide anything with pride in infallibility; the times and the seasons for that have not yet arrived. The human judge himself ought to know that he is not the final judge; that he himself is a sinner; that the measure and the scales in his hands will be an absurdity *if* he, holding that measure and scales, does not himself submit to the law of the yet unsolved mystery and turn to the only solution—to Mercy and Love. And so that man might not perish in despair and ignorance of his path and destiny, of his conviction of evil's mysterious and fateful inevitability, he has been shown a way out. This the poet has brilliantly shown in a masterful scene in the novel's penultimate part, in the scene of the heroine's mortal illness, when the transgressors and enemies are suddenly transformed into higher beings, into brothers who have forgiven one another everything, into beings who, through mutual forgiveness, have cast off lies, guilt, and crime and thereby at once have absolved themselves with full awareness of their right to absolution.[2] But later, at the end of the novel, we have a gloomy and terrible picture of the full degeneration of a human spirit; this we follow step by step through the depiction of that compelling state in which evil, having taken possession of a human being, trammels his every movement and paralyzes every effort toward resistance, every thought, every wish to struggle with the darkness that falls upon the soul;

---

1   Deuteronomy 32:35, Romans 12:19—and, of course, the epigraph to *Anna Karenina*.

2   Dostoevskii errs here. The scene in which Karenin and Vronskii are reconciled at Anna's sickbed occurs, not in Part 7, but in Part 4, Chapter 17.

deliberately, eagerly, with a passion for vengeance, the soul accepts the darkness instead of the light.[3] In this picture there is such a profound lesson for the human judge, for the one who holds the measure and the scales, that he will naturally exclaim in fear and perplexity, "No, vengeance is not always mine, and it is not always for me to repay." And the human judge will not cruelly charge the grievously fallen criminal with having scorned the light of the age-old solution and with having *deliberately* rejected it. He will not, at least, cling to the letter of the law . . .

If we have literary works of such power of thought and execution, then why can we not *eventually* have *our own* science as well, and our own economic and social solutions? Why does Europe refuse us our independence, *our own* word? These are questions that cannot help but be asked. It would be absurd to suppose that nature has endowed us only with literary talents. All the other things are a matter of history, circumstances, and the conditions of the time. Our own homegrown Europeans, at least, ought to be thinking this way while they await the judgment of the European Europeans.

---

3   The scene leading up to and including Anna's suicide, Part 7, Chapters 23–31.

Tiny Alterations of Consciousness (1890)*

Lev Tolstoi

[The artist] Briullov one day corrected a pupil's study. The pupil, having glanced at the altered drawing, exclaimed: "Why, you only touched it a tiny bit, but it is quite another thing." Briullov replied: "Art begins where the tiny bit begins."

That saying is strikingly true not only of art but of all life. One may say that true life begins where the tiny bit begins—where what seem to us minute and infinitely small alterations take place. True life is not lived where great external changes take place—where people move about, clash, fight, and slay one another—it is lived only where these tiny, tiny, infinitesimally small changes occur.

Raskol'nikov did not live his true life when he murdered the old woman or her sister. When murdering the old woman herself, and still more when murdering her sister, he did not live his true life, but acted like a machine, doing what he could not help doing—discharging the cartridge with which he had long been loaded. One old woman was killed, another stood before him, the axe was in his hand.

Raskol'nikov lived his true life not when he met the old woman's sister, but at the time when he had not yet killed any old woman, nor entered a stranger's lodging with intent to kill, nor held the axe in his hand, nor had the loop in his overcoat by which the axe hung.

He lived his true life when he was lying on the sofa in his room, deliberating not at all about the old woman, nor even as to whether it is or is not

* Excerpts from "Why do Men Stupefy Themselves?" in Leo Tolstoy, *Essays and Letters*, trans. Aylmer Maude (London: Grant Richards, 1903), 28–30.

permissible at the will of one man to wipe from the face of the earth another, unnecessary and harmful, man, but whether he ought to live in Petersburg or not, whether he ought to accept money from his mother or not, and on other questions not at all relating to the old woman.

And then—in that region quite independent of animal activities—the question whether he would or would not kill the old woman was decided.

That question was decided—not when, having killed one old woman, he stood before another, axe in hand—but when he was doing nothing and was only thinking, when only his consciousness was active: and in that consciousness tiny, tiny alterations were taking place.

It is at such times that one needs the greatest clearness of mind to decide correctly the questions that have arisen, and it is just then that one glass of beer, or one cigarette, may prevent the solution of the question, may postpone the decision, stifle the voice of conscience and prompt a decision of the question in favor of the lower, animal nature—as was the case with Raskol'nikov.

Tiny, tiny alterations—but on them depend the most immense and terrible consequences. Many material changes may result from what happens when a man has taken a decision and begun to act: houses, riches, and people's bodies may perish, but nothing more important can happen than what was hidden in the man's consciousness. The limits of what can happen are set by consciousness.

And boundless results of unimaginable importance may follow from most minute alterations occurring in the domain of consciousness.

Do not let it be supposed that what I am saying has anything to do with the question of free will or determinism. Discussion on that question is superfluous for my purpose, or for any other for that matter.

Without deciding the question whether a man can, or cannot, act as he wishes (a question in my opinion not correctly stated), I am merely saying that since human activity is conditioned by infinitesimal alterations in consciousness, it follows (no matter whether we admit the existence of free will or not) that we must pay particular attention to the condition in which these minute alterations take place, just as one must be specially attentive to the condition of scales on which other things are to be weighed.

We must, as far as it depends on us, try to put ourselves and others in conditions which will not disturb the clearness and delicacy of thought necessary for the correct working of conscience, and must not act in the contrary manner—trying to hinder and confuse the work of conscience by the use of stupefying substances.

For man is a spiritual as well as an animal being. He may be moved by things that influence his spiritual nature, or by things that influence his animal nature, as a clock may be moved by its hands or by its main wheel. And just as it is best to regulate the movement of a clock by means of its inner mechanism, so a man—oneself or another—is best regulated by means of his consciousness. And as with a clock one has to take special care of that part by means of which one can best move the inner mechanism, so with a man one must take special care of the cleanness and clearness of consciousness which is the thing that best moves the whole man.

To doubt this is impossible; everyone knows it. But a need to deceive oneself arises. People are not as anxious that consciousness should work correctly as they are that it should seem to them that what they are doing is right, and they deliberately make use of substances that disturb the proper working of their consciousness.

From *A Cruel Talent* (1882)*

Nikolai Mikhailovskii

B ut enough of this nonsense about Dostoevskii's role as the spiritual leader of the Russian people and as a prophet. This nonsense was worth noting, but it is not worthwhile getting involved in a detailed refutation. Dostoevskii is simply a great and original writer who merits careful study, and who is of enormous literary interest. It is only in this way that we will study him.

Right after Dostoevskii's death we offered the reader a brief description of the literary physiognomy of the deceased, proposing in time to return to a more detailed elaboration of certain details. In passing, it was mentioned that three causes drew Dostoevskii to the ardent exaltation of suffering, with which he finished: a respect for the existing general order, the yearning for a personal homily, and *the cruelty of talent*. We propose to the reader now to deal with the last trait. The second and third volumes of the complete collection of Dostoevskii's works afford an excellent occasion for this. They contain short novellas, and stories, several of which most readers hardly even remember, but which are nonetheless of great interest in understanding Dostoevskii. In the second volume we find: *Poor Folk, The Double,* "Mr. Prokharchin," "A Novel in Nine Letters," "The Landlady," "A Weak Heart," "The Wife of Another and Husband Under the Bed," *White Nights, Netochka Nezvanova,* and "The Little Hero"; in the third volume we find: "Uncle's Dream," *The Village of Stepanchikovo and its Inhabitants,* "A Nasty Joke," *Winter Notes on Summer Impressions, Notes from*

---

* Excerpted from Nikolai K. Mikhailovsky, *A Cruel Talent,* trans. Spencer Cadmus (Ann Arbor, MI: Ardis, 1978), 10–13. Copyright © 1978. Published in 1978 by Ardis Pubishers, Peter Mayer Publishers, Inc. www.overlookpress.com/ardis.html. All rights reserved. The text has been modified slightly with permission of Overlook Press: transliteration and bibliographic style have been updated to match the rest of the volume.

the Underground, "The Crocodile, or An Unusual Happening at the Arcade," and *The Gambler*. All of these are works of greatly differing artistic value and greatly differing fame. Who does not know *Poor Folk*? But it is unlikely that many have read, for example, "The Wife of Another and the Husband Under the Bed." And in all fairness they were perfectly right not to read it, the story is a poor one. But for our purposes this insignificant story may be very useful and important. In these trifles Dostoevskii all the same remains Dostoevskii, with all the strengths and weaknesses of his talent and his thought. In them, these old trifles, one can find the rudiments of all of Dostoevskii's later images, pictures, ideas, artistic and logical devices. And it would be most interesting to complete this operation in full, from beginning to end, that is, to trace the entire, as it were, literary embryology, so to speak, of Dostoevskii. But we will not undertake that task and will look only at those features of the novellas and stories of the second and third volumes, which justify the title of this article: a cruel talent.

To begin with, it must be noted that cruelty and torture always preoccupied Dostoevskii, and they did so precisely for their attractiveness, for the sensuality which torture seems to contain. A large number of at times extremely subtle observations are scattered throughout his minor novellas and stories. Examples of them have been quoted in our epigraphs. The mere extraction of them could fill entire pages; especially if we were to lift them not only from Dostoevskii's early trifles, but also from his later works, when there flashed in his creative imagination the image of Stavrogin (*Demons*), who "asserted that he did not see any difference between the beauty of some sensual brutal thing and any deed whatsoever, even if it was the sacrifice of a life for humanity, that he found at both poles a coincidence of beauty, an equal of enjoyment." However, below as well, without even touching upon Dostoevskii's latest and major works, we will see excellent specimens of the understanding interest which he placed in his depictions of tormenting acts and cruel feelings. Of course, the artist for that matter is an artist in order to be interested and to understand: to him "the star book is clear," with him "speaks the sea wave."[1] And although in the star book hardly anything is written about cruelty, torture, and spite, and the sea wave does not speak about them, yet once these things exist and play an important role in human life, the artist must be interested in them and understand them. Must, however, is slightly too strong. Plato sent away from his ideal republic the poet "who was especially skilled in imitation

---

1   Cited from Evgenii Baratynskii's romantic poem, "On the Death of Goethe."

and capable of assuming many different forms." Plato understood the greatness of such an artist and proposed adorning him with garlands and anointing him with myrrh, but in spite of the famed versatility of the classical spirit, sent him out of the republic on grounds of "the incompatibility of several callings in one person." We, of course, would not require such narrowness and specialization of poetic work. On the contrary, the more diverse he is and the more strings of the human soul he touches, the more we value him. But we cannot require that the poet depict with the same force and truthfulness the sensations of a wolf devouring a sheep and of a sheep being devoured by a wolf. One of these two situations is closer and more interesting to him, which must affect his work.

I have hit upon an example suitable for its clarity, and I believe that no one in Russian literature has analyzed the sensations of a wolf devouring a sheep with such thoroughness, such depth, one might say with such love, as Dostoevskii—if it were only possible in fact to speak of having a loving attitude towards a wolf's feelings. And he was very little preoccupied with the elementary, crude sorts of wolf's feelings, simple hunger, for example. No, he dug into the very heart of the wolf's soul, seeking there subtle, complex things—not the simple satisfaction of appetite, but precisely the sensuality of spite and cruelty. This specialty of Dostoevskii's is too striking to go unnoticed. But in spite of the fact that Dostoevskii gave many great and valuable things in the sphere of this specialty of his, he seems to contradict somewhat another feature which is especially characteristic of Dostoevskii's works. Dwelling on our metaphor, someone else might perhaps say that Dostoevskii, on the contrary, dealt in great detail with the study of the feelings of a sheep being devoured by a wolf; after all, he is the author of *The House of the Dead*, he is the singer of *The Insulted and the Injured*, he so ably sought out the best, loftiest feelings where no one even suspected their existence. All of this is correct and was even more correct many years ago, when the evaluation of Dostoevskii was first cast in the form which prevails to this day. But taking into consideration Dostoevskii's entire literary career, we will have to draw the conclusion that he simply liked to torment the sheep with the wolf, and that during the first half of his career he was particularly interested in the sheep, while in the second half, in the wolf. But there was no very radical change here. Dostoevskii did not burn what he worshipped, and did not worship what he burned. His interests and the special features of his talent simply underwent a gradual change; what had previously been first and foremost became secondary, and vice versa. In his own time Dobroliubov was correct in speaking about the relative weakness of Dostoevskii's talent and about the "humanistic" bent of his artistic intuition.[2] But even then there already existed marked inclinations towards great but cruel talent which later developed so magnificently. The second and third volumes of the complete collection of Dostoevskii's works best attest to this fact.

They are a complete, carefully chosen menagerie, a complete nursery of wolves of different breeds, the owner of which hardly even shows off his valuable collection, and all the more so does not think of deriving a direct benefit from it; he knows his business so precisely and likes it so much that the study of the wolf's temperament is for him self-sufficing; he deliberately baits his animals, shows them a sheep, a piece of bloody meat, beats them with a hunting crop and a red-hot iron, in order to examine some detail of their viciousness and cruelty—to see for himself and, of course, to show his audience.

---

2   EDS: Nikolai Dobroliubov (1836–61) was a radical critic who attacked Dostoevskii's art and aesthetics. Dostoevskii's article "Mr. —bov and the Question of Art" provided a critical response to Dobroliubov, see Chapter 3.

Tolstoi and Dostoevskii (1902)*

Dmitrii Merezhkovskii

If in the literature of all ages and nations we wished to find the artist most contrary to Tolstoi we should have to point to Dostoevskii. I say contrary, but not remote, not alien; for often they come in contact, like extremes that meet.

The "heroes" of Tolstoi, as we have seen, are not so much heroes as victims. In them the human individuality, without being perfected to the full, is swallowed up in the elements. And as there is not a single heroic will ruling over all, so there is not one uniting tragic action: there are only separate tragic *nodi* and situations the separate waves which rise and fall in purposeless motion, not guided by a current within, but only by external forces. The fabric of the work, like the fabric of humanity itself, apparently begins nowhere and ends nowhere. With Dostoevskii there is throughout a human personality carried to the extremes of individuality, drawing and developing from the dark animal roots to the last radiant summits of spirituality. Throughout there is the conflict of heroic will with the element of moral duty and conscience, as in Raskol'nikov; with that of passion, refined, deliberate, as in Svidrigailov and Versilov; in conflict with the will of the people, the State, the polity, as in Petr Verkhovenskii, Stavrogin, and Shatov; and lastly in conflict with metaphysical and religious mystery, as in Ivan Karamazov, Prince Myshkin, and Kirillov. Passing through the furnace of these conflicts,

---

* Excerpted from Dmitri Merejkowski, *Tolstoi as Man and Artist with an Essay on Dostoïevski* (Westminster: Archibald Constable & Co., 1902). The translation has been slightly edited to ensure clarity and consistency with the rest of the volume.

the fire of enflaming passions and still more enflaming will, the kernel of human individuality, the inward ego, remains undissolved and is laid bare. "I am bound to display self-will," says Kirillov in *Demons*, to whom suicide, which seems the limit of self-abnegation, is in fact the highest pitch of the assertion of his personality, the limit of "self-will." All Dostoevskii's heroes might say the same. For the last time they oppose themselves to the elements that are swallowing them up, and still assert their ego, their individuality and self-will, when their end is at hand. In this sense even the Christian resignation of the Idiot, of Alesha, and old Zosima is an insuperable resistance to evil forces about them; submission to God's will, but not to man's, that is the inversion of "self-will." The martyr dying for his belief, his truth, his God, is also a "hero": he asserts his inward liberty against outward tyranny, and so of course "displays self-will."

In accordance with the predominance of heroic struggle the principal works of Dostoevskii are in reality not novels nor epics, but tragedies.

War and Peace and *Anna Karenina*, on the other hand, are really novels, original epics. Here, as we have seen, the artistic center of gravity is not in the dialogue between the characters, but in the telling of the story; not in what they say, but in what is said of them; not in what we hear with our ears, but in what we see with our eyes.

With Dostoevskii, on the contrary, the narrative portion is secondary and subservient to the construction of the whole work. And this is apparent at the first glance; the story, written always in one and the same hasty, sometimes clearly neglected language, is now wearisomely drawn out and involved, heaped with details; now too concise and compact. The story is not quite a text, but, as it were, small writing in brackets, notes on the drama, explaining the time and place of the action, the events that have gone before, the surroundings and exterior of the characters; it is the setting up of the scenery, the indispensable theatrical paraphernalia—when the characters come on and begin to speak then at length the piece begins. All Dostoevskii's artistic power is concentrated in his dialogue: it is in the dialogue that all is revealed and unrevealed. There is not in all contemporary literature a writer equal to him for mastery of dialogue.

Levin uses just the same language as Pierre Bezukhov or Prince Andrei, Vronskii or Pozdnyshev: Anna Karenina the same phrases as Dolly, Kitty, or Natasha. If we did not know who was talking, we should not be able to distinguish one person from another by the language, the sound of the voice, as it were, with our eyes shut. True, there is in Tolstoi a difference between the language of the common folk and the gentry, but this is not external or personal, but merely internal and according to class. In its essence the language of all the characters in Tolstoi is the same, or all but the same: it is colloquial parlance, as it were the sound of the voice of Lev himself, whether in gentleman's or peasant's dress. And merely for this reason we overlook the fact that in his works it is not what the characters *say* that matters, *but how they are silent*, or else groan, howl, roar, yell, or grunt: it is not their human words that matter, but their half-animal, inarticulate sounds, or ejaculations—as in Prince Andrei's delirium "i titi-titi-titi," or the bleating of Vronskii over the dead horse, or the sobbing of Anatole over his own amputated leg. The repetition of the same vowels, a—o—u, seems sufficient to express the most complex, terrible, heart-rending, mental and bodily emotions.

In Dostoevskii it is impossible not to recognize the personage speaking, at once, at the first words uttered. In the scarcely Russian, strange, involved talk of the Nihilist Kirillov we feel something superior, grating, unpleasant, prophetic, and yet painful, strained, and recalling attacks of epilepsy and so too in the simple, truly national speech of "holy" Prince Myshkin. Fedor Karamazov, suddenly getting quite animated and ingurgitating, addresses his sons thus:

> Heigh, you, children, bairns, little sucking pigs, for me—all my life through—there were no such thing as touch-me-nots. Even old maids, in them sometimes you would make valuable discoveries if you only made them open their eyes. A beggar woman, and a touch-me-not: it is necessary at the first go off to astonish—that is the way to deal with them. You must astonish 'em to ecstasy, to compunction, to shame that such a gentleman has fallen in love with such a slut as she.

Here we see the heart of the old man, but also his fat, shaking, Adam's apple, and his moist, thin lips; the tiny, shamelessly piercing eyes, and his whole savage figure the figure of an old Roman of the times of the decadence. When we learn that on a packet of money, sealed and tied with ribbon, there was also written in his own hand "for my angel Grushen'ka, if she wishes to come," and that three days later he added "and the little darling," he suddenly stands before us wholly as if alive. We could not explain how, or why, but we feel that in this belated "and the little darling" we have caught some subtle, sensual wrinkle on his face, which make us feel physically uncomfortable, like the contact of a revolting insect, a huge spider, or daddy-long-legs. It is only a word, but it holds flesh and blood. It is of course imaginary, but it is almost impossible to believe it is *merely* imaginary. It is just that last little touch which makes the portrait too lifelike, as if the painter, going beyond the bounds of his art, had created a portrait which is ever on the point of stirring and coming out of the frame like a specter or a ghost.

In this way Dostoevskii has no need to describe the appearance of his characters, for by their peculiar form of language and tones of voices they themselves depict, not only their thoughts and feelings, but their faces and bodies. In Tolstoi's case, it is the movements and gestures of the external body that reveal the inner state of the soul; they often transform his characters' most paltry words, or even incomprehensible sounds or silences, into something significant. Tolstoi works from the body to the soul, from the external to the internal. Dostoevskii achieves an equally clear image of the body, but he works the other way round. From the internal he arrives at the external, from the mental at the physical, from the rational and human we guess at the instinctive and animal. With Tolstoi we hear because we see; with Dostoevskii we see because we hear.

Not merely his mastery of dialogue, but other characteristics of his method bring Dostoevskii near to the current of great tragic art. At times it seems as if he only did not write tragedy because the outward form of epic narration, that of the novel, was by chance the prevailing one in the literature of his day, and also because there was no tragic stage worthy of him, and what is more, no spectators worthy of him. Tragedy is, of course, composed only by the creative powers of artist and audience; it is necessary that the public, too, should have the tragic faculty in order that tragedy may really be engendered.

Involuntarily and naturally Dostoevskii becomes subject to that inevitable law of the stage which the new drama has so thoughtlessly abandoned, under the influence of Shakespeare, and by so doing undermined at the root the tragic action. It is the law of the three unities, time, place, and action, which gives, in my opinion, such incomparable power, as against anything in modern literature, to the creations of the Greek drama. In the works of Tolstoi there always, sooner or later, comes a moment when the reader finally forgets the main action of the story and the fate of the principal characters. How Prince Andrei dies, or how Nikolai Rostov courses hares, how Kitty bears children, or Levin does his mowing, are to us so important and interesting that we lose sight of Napoleon and Alexander I, Anna, and Vronskii. It is even more interesting, more important to us at that moment whether Rostov runs down his hare than whether Napoleon wins the battle of Borodino. In any case we feel no impatience, we are in no hurry to learn the ultimate fate of these persons. We are ready to wait, and have our attention distracted as much as the author likes. We no longer see the shore, and have ceased to think of the destination of our voyage. As in every true epic there is nothing unimportant; everything is equally important, equally leading. In every drop there is the same salt taste, the same chemical composition of water as in the whole sea. Every atom of life moves according to the same laws as worlds and constellations.

Raskol'nikov kills an old woman to prove to himself that he is already "on the wrong side of good and evil," that he is not "a shuddering creature," but a "lord of creation." But Raskol'nikov in Dostoevskii's conception is fated to learn that he is wrong, that he has killed, not "a principle," but an old woman, has not "gone beyond," but merely wished to do so. And when he realizes this he is bound to turn faint, to get frightened, to get out in the square and, falling on his knees, to confess before the crowd. And it is precisely to this extreme point, to this one last moment in the action of the story, that everything is directed, gathers itself up and gravitates; to this tragic catastrophe everything tends, as towards a cataract the course of a river long confined by rocks. Here there cannot, should not be, and really is not, anything collateral or extraneous, arresting or diverting the attention from the main action. The events follow one another ever more and more rapidly, chase one another ever more unrestrainedly, crowd together, are heaped on each other, but in reality subordinated to the main single object, and are crammed in the greatest possible number into the least possible space of time. If Dostoevskii has any rivals they are not of the present day, but in ancient literature the creators of Orestes and Oedipus: I mean in this art of gradual tension, accumulation, increase, and alarming concentration of dramatic action.

"How well I remember the hapless day," the hero of *The Adolescent* cries wonderingly; "it always seems as if all these surprises and unforeseen mishaps conspired together and were showered all at once on my head from some cornucopia." "It was a day of surprises," remarks the narrator of *Demons*, "a day of untying of old knots and tying of new, sharp elucidations, and still worse confusions. In a word, it was a day when astounding events happened together." And so it is in all his stories everywhere that infernal "cornucopia," from which are poured on the heads of the heroes unexpected tragedies. When we finish the first part of *The Idiot*—fifteen chapters—so many events have taken place, so many situations have been placed before us, in which are entangled the threads of the most varied human destinies, and passions and consciences have been laid bare, that it would seem that long years had passed since the beginning of the story: in reality it is only a day, twelve hours from morning to evening. The boundless picture of the world's history which is enfolded in *The Brothers Karamazov* is condensed, if we do not count the intervals between the acts, into a few days. But even in one day, in one hour, and that almost on one and the same spot—between a certain seat in the Pavlovskii Park and the Terminus, between Garden Street and Haymarket Square—the heroes of Dostoevskii pass through experiences which ordinary mortals do not taste in a lifetime.

Raskol'nikov is standing on the staircase, outside the door of the old woman pawnbroker. "He looked round for the last time, pulled himself together, drew himself up, and once more tried the axe on the lock. 'Shall I not wait a little longer, till my heart ceases to throb?' But his heart did not cease. On the contrary, as if to spite him, it beat harder and harder. *And he scarcely felt the presence of the rest of his body.*"

To all the heroes of Dostoevskii there comes the moment when they cease "to feel their bodies." They are not beings without flesh and blood, not ghosts. We know well what sort of body they *had*, when they still felt its presence. But the highest ascent, the greatest tension of mental existence, the most burning passions—not of the heart and the emotions, but of the mind, the will, and the conscience—give them this divorce from the body, a sort of supernatural lightness, wingedness, and spiritualization of the flesh. They have the very "spiritual, ethereal bodies," of which St. Paul spoke. These are the men who are not suffocated by flesh and blood, or the Tolstoyan "human bubble." It seems as if, at times, they were bodily invisible, only their intense souls could be seen.

"We look at you and say, 'She has the face of a kind sister,'" says the Idiot, describing the beauty of a certain woman. It is curious to compare these instantaneous, supersensual descriptions of Dostoevskii with those of Tolstoi for instance, the figure of Anna Karenina, so full of deep-seated sensuality; the living souls of Dostoevskii with the overgrown beef of Tolstoi. All Dostoevskii's heroes live, thanks to his higher spirituality, an incredibly rapid, tenfold accelerated life: with all of them, as with Raskol'nikov, "the heart beats harder and harder and harder." They do not walk like ordinary mortals, but fly; and in the intoxication of this flight fly into the abyss.

In the agitation of the waves we feel the increasing nearness of the whirlpool.

The Root and the Flower: Dostoevskii and Turgenev (1993)*

Robert Louis Jackson

There is a trivial yet touching note connected with Turgenev's last hours in Bougival, France. According to a Russian eyewitness at the deathbed, Turgenev's delirium began when he started to speak in Russian, which most of those around him, of course, did not understand: "Proshchaite, moi milye, moi belesovatye" (Farewell, my dear ones, my dimly fading ones), Turgenev reportedly said; whereupon everybody asked: "Qu'est ce qu'il dit, qu'est ce qu'il dit?" (What's he saying, what's he saying?)[1] Now Turgenev, both in his lifetime and for a good while afterward, enjoyed an extraordinary esteem among general readers and literary cognoscenti. But there came a moment in the late nineteenth and early twentieth centuries when Turgenev's readers, like those Frenchmen at his deathbed, began to ask: "Qu'est ce qu'il dit, qu'est ce qu'il dit?" They no longer understood him.

The difficulty lay not only in the special character of Turgenev's art, its unique features, but also in the fact that a whole epoch had begun to break, anxiously yet decisively, with a whole vision, or perhaps one should say illusion,

* Excerpted from Robert Louis Jackson, *Dialogues with Dostoevsky: The Overwhelming Questions* (Stanford: Stanford University Press, 1993), 162–64, 172–73, 176–84, 186–87. Some of the footnotes have been cut. This piece was originally published as Robert Louis Jackson, "The Root and the Flower, Dostoevsky and Turgenev: A Comparative Esthetic," *Yale Review* 63 (Winter 1974): 228–51. It appears here with permission from *Yale Review*.

1 V. V. Vereshchagin, *Ocherki, nabroski, vospominaniia* (St. Petersburg: Tip. Ministerstva putei soobshcheniia A. Benke, 1883), 141.

of life and art. Not without reason has the novelistic universe of Dostoevskii been linked with this break. "Dostoevskii was the crisis of culture," the Russian philosopher Nikolai Berdiaev maintains at the end of his study of Dostoevskii's metaphysical thought. Though himself "a supreme manifestation of Russian culture, its summit," though leaving us an incomparable spiritual legacy, Dostoevskii's work, or "creative image," gave expression to the "Russian dislike of middle culture." "The crisis of culture," Berdiaev insists, "reveals itself in a longing to escape from the middle course into some sort of all-resolving end. There is an apocalyptic tendency in the crisis of culture. It is present in Nietzsche and it is present in the highest degree in Dostoevskii."[2] This apocalyptic tendency in Dostoevskii—the concomitant, no doubt, of a "maximalism" in all areas of his life and personality—was not only uncharacteristic of Turgenev, but alien to him as a man and artist.

Dmitrii N. Merezhkovskii was perhaps the first to suggest that the question of culture, of measure and of beauty ("the measure of all measures," as he put it), underlay the "Turgenev question," at least in Russian literature. Merezhkovskii's speech on Turgenev on the twenty-fifth anniversary of the writer's death in 1908 opened with these words:

> Turgenev, people say, is out of date. But forever? Two giant caryatids of Russian literature, Tolstoi and Dostoevskii, really have hidden Turgenev from us. But for how long? Are we not destined to return to him through them? In Russia, in the land of all kinds of revolutionary and religious maximalism, a country of self-immolation, of the wildest excesses, Turgenev, after Pushkin, is almost the sole *genius of measure* and therefore a genius of culture. For what is culture if not the *measuring*, the accumulation and preservation of values?[3]

[...]

It was measure—by which Turgenev understood the temperate, openend, equitable vision of life and not merely political or social compromise—that fell victim to the twentieth century. "In truth," Joseph Conrad wrote in his elegiac foreword to Edward Garnett's study of Turgenev in 1917, "it is not the convulsed terror-haunted Dostoevskii but the serene Turgenev who is under

---

2   Nikolai Berdiaev, *Mirosozertsanie Dostoevskogo* (Paris: YMCA-Press, 1968 [1921]), 235, 233, 234.

3   Dmitrii Merezhkovskii, "Turgenev," in *Polnoe sobranie sochinenii* (Moscow: Tip. I. D. Sytina, 1914), vol. 18, 58.

a curse."[4] He was right, but he might have added that serenity itself had come under a curse.

The Turgenev–Dostoevskii antinomy resolves itself finally into a cultural metaphor for the twentieth century. The profound differences between the art of the one and the other lie not so much in their conscious ideologies and philosophy as in their underlying vision of "nature," essential reality, being. Here, perhaps, one might posit a primary, deeply organic, and personal response to reality, a kind of *Urphilosophie* which determines the dynamics of a complex body of artistic thought and imagery, but not necessarily the final authorial point of view emerging from that dynamics. With Turgenev, we are certainly in the presence of an archetypal vision of the epic unity, wholeness, and organic character of nature and the vital life processes, one in which "beauty" (in the classical sense of "harmony," "clarity," and "serenity") is in the foreground; with Dostoevskii, a tragic vision of turbulence and fragmentation. One might say that the novel of Dostoevskii, which posits an ideal nonterrestrial unity and beatitude very classical in its formulation, is essentially an effort to contain and structure this turbulence, to find in man, or in man's relation to his universe, a structure of freedom and moral order. Turgenev's art, on the other hand, begins with a vision of a real order and beatitude in nature. The pathos of his art, however, emerges from a permanent contradiction between his aesthetic vision and his tragic sense of life, between the artist who is content to see and enjoy life in its wholeness and the subjective philosopher who is painfully aware of man's unfavored rank-and-file place in the ideal aesthetic order of nature.

The vision of unity and the vision of turbulence—the one centripetal, the other centrifugal—are not only points of departure for each artist: they translate into the very texture and forms of the artists' art, into their manner of representing reality, their style of writing, and finally into the impact of their art on the reader.

[...]

"Art is a plant," Turgenev once wrote.[5] The central images in this romantic organism metaphor are the root and the flower. In Turgenev's art, as in the plant, all energy flows into the visible and evocative form, and it is the flower, its flowering and fading, that is for Turgenev the fullest expression of the mission of art, the artist's preoccupation with beauty in form and form in beauty, and the pathos of human existence.

---

4 Joseph Conrad, foreword to Edward Garnett, *Turgenev* (London: Collins, 1927).
5 Letter to Ia. P. Polonskii, January 2, 1868. In I. S. Turgenev, *Polnoe sobranie sochinenii i pisem v dvadtsati vos'mi tomakh*, 28 vols. (Moscow-Leningrad: Izdatel'stvo Akademii nauk, 1960–68), *Pis'ma*, 7:26.

Turgenev, it is not surprising to learn, had difficulty with Tolstoi's psychological method, his "dialectics of the soul." He finds tedious, he writes in connection with *War and Peace*, "these quasi-subtle reflections and meditations and observations over his own feelings!"[6] Even more alien to him was Dostoevskii's psychological method. Dostoevskii's novel *The Adolescent* struck Turgenev as "chaos." "My God, what a sour smell, and hospital stench, and perfectly pointless mumbling and psychological nitpicking!!" he exclaims in a letter to the Russian writer M. E. Saltykov-Shchedrin at the publication of Dostoevskii's novel.[7] In spite of the uncongeniality of certain aspects of Tolstoi's artistic method, Turgenev remained a devoted admirer of the man whom, on his deathbed, he called the "great writer of the Russian land."[8] Tolstoi was ultimately great to Turgenev because of his "truth."[9] Turgenev's general antipathy to Dostoevskii and his art remained firm.

Many western European critics in the late nineteenth and early twentieth centuries were attracted to the very elements which were alien to Turgenev's artistic method. The art of Turgenev, by comparison with that of Tolstoi or Dostoevskii, seemed limited to many writers and readers. The Irish novelist and critic George Moore, though defending Turgenev's art, gave vivid expression in 1891 to the restive mood of the new generation of readers and critics that was discovering Tolstoi and Dostoevskii: "In reading [Turgenev] we are conscious of a thinness, of an irritating reserve. He has often seemed to us to have left much unsaid, to have, as it were, only drawn the skin from his subject. Magnificently well is the task performed; but we should like to have seen the carcass disemboweled and hung up."[10] In Dostoevskii Europe certainly found an artist who dealt with human psychology and stress in a more radical way than did Turgenev: it found an artist who met head-on the impending tragedy of violence and social disintegration in western civilization, a tragedy of which Moore's naturalistic "carcass disemboweled and hung up" seems in retrospect to give some fearful hint.

[. . .]

Not the flower but the root is the direct focus of Dostoevskii's "total realism." "They call me a psychologist," Dostoevskii observes in his notebook. "I am only a realist in the higher sense; that is, I depict all the depths of the

---

6 Letter to P. V. Annenskii, February 14, 1868; PSS: *Pis'ma*, 7:65.
7 Letter of November 25, 1875; PSS: *Pis'ma*, 11:164.
8 Letter to Lev Tolstoi, June 29, 1883; PSS: *Pis'ma*, 13/2:180.
9 Letter to I. P. Borisov, January 12, 1869, PSS: *Pis'ma*, 12:279.
10 George Moore, "Turgueneff," in *Impressions and Opinions* (London: David Nutt, 1891), 70–71.

human soul."[11] His realism, to borrow Turgenev's words, is loaded with a "wealth of veiled thoughts, secondary feelings and allusions"; it does not neglect surface, visible day-to-day reality, but it affirms, as in *Notes from the House of the Dead*, for example, that visible reality may be profoundly deceptive, at least as far as the everyday eye is concerned. One must penetrate through the "repulsive crust," through surface reality, Dostoevskii insisted, to arrive at the authentic core of human decency. To Turgenev's aesthetic of observation one may counterpose Dostoevskii's aesthetic of direct cognition. The artist must see, Dostoevskii believed, with the eyes of the soul. And he remained faithful to this image when he wrote elsewhere: "My critics understand only what goes on before their eyes, but because of nearsightedness they themselves are not only unable to look ahead, but cannot even understand how for another person the future results of present events can be crystal clear."[12] For Dostoevskii, art, vision is prophecy.

With respect to areas of psychological interest, scholars have noted that Dostoevskii and Turgenev often explore similar grounds. Turgenev's "Hamlet of Shchigrovo County" (1849), "The Diary of a Superfluous Man" (1849), *Rudin* (1855), and "A Correspondence" (1856) fully anticipate major psychological and philosophical emphases in Dostoevskii's *Notes from the Underground*. The Russian critic G. A. Bialyi has even suggested that the notion of a radical opposition in psychological style between Dostoevskii and Turgenev has been "greatly exaggerated." There is some basis for this assertion, but largely, perhaps, with reference to some of Turgenev's writing in the 1850s. But even in his comparison of some of these works with *Notes from the Underground* Bialyi underscores a crucial opposition. Thus the notion of "malice" in Turgenev's "Diary of a Superfluous Man" is manifested "within the limits of a psychological norm," whereas Dostoevskii consciously negates that norm, strives to violate it, intensifies the psychological situation to the "limits of the tragic, grotesque, fantasy, frenzy."[13]

Such hyperbole and straining of emotions were indeed uncharacteristic of Turgenev. The sense of a normative reality—aesthetically, a sense of measure—worked against this potential for hyperbole. For Dostoevskii, on

---

11 Dostoevskii, PSS 27:65.
12 Cited by V. V. Vinogradov in *Problema avtorstva i teoriia stilei* (Moscow: Khudozhestvennaia literatura, 1961), 535. See also Dostoevskii's remark in his notebook in the mid-1860s: "Realism is the mind of the crowd, of the majority, who do not see farther than their nose, but it is cunning and keen, quite adequate for the present moment" (PSS 20:182.)
13 G. A. Bialyi, "Dve shkoly psikhologicheskogo realizma (Turgenev i Dostoevskii)," in *Russkii realizm kontsa XIX veka* (Leningrad: Izd. Leningradskogo universiteta, 1973), 32, 36.

the other hand, essential reality is revealed not in the ordinary moment, but in a moment of crisis, of rupture, of moral, spiritual, psychological breakdown. Psychology in Dostoevskii, eruptive, is typically "from the underground"; in *Notes from the Underground* that is almost the only perspective.

[...]

In Dostoevskii's novelistic universe, the typical hero is very far from the "norm," or even a strong sense of the norm. He is far from that regulatory "nature" which provides Turgenev and the narrator of "A Journey to the Woodlands" with such a stable frame of reference, such a strong sense of inner order and equilibrium in the universe. Indeed, the whole quest of the Dostoevskii hero, consciously or unconsciously, is for the ethical and religious norm. "There's no order in me, no higher order," Dostoevskii's beloved Dmitrii Karamazov exclaims in anguish as he thunders across the stage of Russian life. The principle of order which reasserts itself in the epilogues to Pushkin's "Queen of Spades," Turgenev's *Fathers and Sons*, or Tolstoi's *War and Peace* (the ordinary routine of work, the affairs of the family, marriage, reproduction) is generally absent in Dostoevskii's novelistic universe. Such epilogues, it is true, have a distinct middle-class flavor, but for Turgenev, middle-class values appear to be precisely those of nature. *Harmony, measure, equilibrium* are key words in Turgenev's aesthetics of nature and in his vision of essential normative reality. This Turgenevian reality turns out to be full of cracks and fissures, contradictions and tragedy, for his heroes, yet like nature, it is self-restorative and hurls aside all those who like Bazarov in *Fathers and Sons* upset its equilibrium.

[...]

The notion of a higher order can also be found in Dostoevskii. If one concentrates attention, for example, on Father Zosima's vision in *The Brothers Karamazov* of ultimate reality in man and the universe, one might conclude that Dostoevskii conceives of nature and the cosmos in the aspect of world harmony, as a great ocean in a state of equilibrium wherein all flows and interacts. Certainly this vision is present and plays a structuring role in the Dostoevskii novel. It is the other dialectical pole of Dostoevskii's worldview—a primary vision of man and reality as turbulent, destructive, and contradictory—that is the real given and point of departure in Dostoevskii's novels. It is outside the monastery, outside Zosima's aesthetic and religious utopia, that one discovers the real material of Dostoevskii's "nature": the morally and aesthetically shapeless world of the Karamazovs [...]

"Reality strives toward fragmentation," remarks the narrator of *Notes from the House of the Dead* in an extraordinary phrase apropos the impossibility of reducing or simplifying reality into categories or typologies. What is striking, of course, is the use of the verb *strive*, the conception of reality as active, dynamic, centrifugal in movement. The necessity of mastering this explosive force of "reality"—not only in the realm of sensuality (as in Turgenev's world as well), but in crucial moral, aesthetic, and even psychic areas—is a central problem in Dostoevskii's universe. The art of Dostoevskii, many of its unique and innovative features, is itself an expression of this striving to master centrifugal reality, chaos, in himself, in man, in history.

Harmony, measure, equilibrium, health, and *beauty* are, of course, decisive words and concepts in Dostoevskii's worldview. But these values are not to be found in man or nature as organic attributes; it is not "nature," not any "law of nature" or any unalterable law of earthly life, that introduces these elements into man or society. These are attributes, in Dostoevskii's view, of divinity and faith, of a lofty spirituality in a quest for form and faith. This lofty spirituality enables man to transcend pure "nature" in himself. What health, equilibrium, and happiness there is on earth is a function of man's tension toward the ethical and religious ideal. "Man strives on earth for an ideal which is *contrary* to his nature," Dostoevskii wrote in his notebook in 1864. "When man does not fulfill the law of striving for the ideal, that is, does not sacrifice his 'I' through love for people or another being . . . he experiences suffering and has called this condition sin. And thus man continually must experience suffering, which is balanced by the divine joy in fulfillment of the Law, i.e., sacrifice. Precisely here earthly equilibrium is to be found. Otherwise the earth would be senseless."[14] The pawnbroker's frightening vision in "The Meek One" of "nature" and the "earth" as a stagnant, death-ridden wasteland is a direct projection of a life without love or sacrifice. Movement in Dostoevskii's universe is the illness and cure. Reality *strives* toward fragmentation, but man strives toward the ideal.

[. . .]

"But what is this life?" Turgenev asks rhetorically in an early letter to Pauline Viardot in 1849 apropos of the life of the universe, of the world of plants or insects in a drop of water:

> Oh, I do not know anything about it, but I do know that for the moment
> it is everything, it is in full flowering, in full swing; I do not know if all this

---

14 Dostoevskii, PSS, 20:175.

will last for a long time, but at least for the moment it exists, it makes my
blood flow in my veins without my doing anything about it, and it makes
the stars appear in the heavens like pimples on the skin, effortlessly and
without its seeming a great merit. This thing that is indifferent, imperious,
voracious, egoistic, encompassing, is life, nature, God; call it what you will
[...] All [this vitality in the world] is able to do nothing else but follow the
Law of its existence which is Life.[15]

Here is the heart of Turgenev, the objective artist whose love of life expresses
itself in a passion to reincarnate multiform reality. Yet side by side with this love
of life, as we have seen, is a melancholy, a gnawing consciousness of the tran-
sience of life, man, and happiness, which links him, perhaps, with his favorite
philosophers, Schopenhauer and Pascal, a kind of despair before the infinite.
"I can't bear the sky," Turgenev wrote to Pauline Viardot apropos the emotion
aroused in him by the sight of a green branch covered with young green leaves
etched against the blue sky. He is moved by the contrast between the little
branch with its fragile stirring of life and the eternal and immense emptiness of
the sky. "I can't bear the sky—but life, reality, its caprices, its accidentalities, its
patterns, its fleeting beauty . . . all this I adore."[16]

Turgenev's love of life, his sense for the objective, concrete universal in life,
dilutes his primordial dread of eternity. Indeed, his despair is never fully realized in the stern, tragic terms of Dostoevskii. Tragedy in Turgenev's universe is
not seldom modified, mitigated, almost neutralized by the author's pantheistic
sense of "life, nature, God." In this respect the concluding lines of *Fathers and
Sons* provide eloquent testimony. Bazarov is dead: Bazarov, that protagonist
who comes closest to giving really tragic embodiment to Turgenev's skepticism
and despair. Bazarov's parents come to visit his grave. Is it possible that their
tears and prayers are fruitless, that sacred love is impotent? asks the narrator.
He replies: "Oh no! However passionate, sinful, rebellious the heart that is concealed in the grave, the flowers, growing on it, peacefully look at us with their
innocent eyes: they speak to us not alone about eternal tranquility, about that
great tranquility of 'indifferent' nature; they speak also about eternal reconciliation and about endless life."

Turgenev's hosanna to life, his ultimate faith in it, despite all his melancholy,
his willingness in the end to accept the arbitration of nature, contrasts with

---

15 Letter of July 16–19, 1849; PSS: *Pis'ma*, 1:350–51.
16 Letter of May 1, 1848; PSS: *Pis'ma*, 1:297.

Dostoevskii's tragic questioning precisely of life, nature, God. As is well known, Dostoevskii parodied Turgenev's sketch "Enough," along with several other works of Turgenev, in *Demons*. Not the least irritant to Dostoevskii may have been Turgenev's concept of "radical contradiction" and (in "Enough" at least) his strongly esthetic and nonreligious resolution of the contradiction. For it is perhaps only in Dostoevskii's art that the radical contradiction may be said to be truly radical and unresolved, only in Dostoevskii that aesthetic and moral Don Quixotism acquires truly tragic character and serves to symbolize the human condition. The sense of "mud" and of "heaven," of disfiguration and opposing, perfect form; the despair over the evil in man, yet ecstatic faith in the transfiguring power of spiritual beauty—all this found supreme expression in Dostoevskii's art.

Beauty for Turgenev is tangible, real, however evanescent in life or nature. "The beautiful is the only thing that is immortal. [. . .] Nowhere does it shine more intensely than in the human personality." Few Russian writers equaled Turgenev in the perception of beauty and in the artistic crafting and modeling of the human physiognomy. For Dostoevskii, regardless of Ivan's delight in the "sticky little leaves," the highest beauty is not of this world. The beauty that in Turgenev's world conveys a poignant sense of vanished happiness, of man's incompleteness and yearning for some higher destiny, acquires philosophical and religious content in Dostoevskii's art. Beauty in the highest perception for Dostoevskii is linked with suffering and a sense of paradise lost. The motif of lost paradise is profoundly tragic not only because it expresses a deep yearning of man for an impossible return to innocence, but because it expresses his anguished quest for unity and balance. The classical harmonies, measure, and proportion, the beauty that Turgenev finds embodied in the living forms and processes of nature, in the play of character and human relations, Dostoevskii seeks finally in ecstatic aesthetic-religious experience. Turgenev, in his art and through his art, offers to man the epic vision of nature-divine; Dostoevskii holds out to man, tragic man, an aesthetic-spiritual transfiguration apocalyptic in character, inseparable from the Word of God.

The art of Dostoevskii, his vision of reality, challenges the very sense of unity and wholeness from which Turgenev's art emerges. When one imposes on this foundation the whole superstructure of social, psychological, and philosophical differences between these two writers, it is not difficult to understand Turgenev's deep-seated dislike of the art of Dostoevskii. Yet in turn, the art of Turgenev, quite apart from ideological differences, was part of the pathos of Dostoevskii's self-conception as an artist. Not without reason did Dostoevskii once refer to Turgenev as a "colossal artist," acknowledge in him (in *Crime and Punishment*) "the most artistic of all modern writers," and bracket him as pure artist with the writer he most revered in Russian literature—Aleksandr Pushkin.

The very values that are central in Dostoevskii's higher aesthetic—classical beauty, harmony, measure are to be found embodied not only in Turgenev's art, but in his personality. Dostoevskii's early admiration, as a young writer, of Turgenev is undoubtedly linked with a longing for these values. It is noteworthy that one of his earliest responses to Turgenev projects a largely aesthetic, one might even say Apollonian, image. Not long after his first meeting with Turgenev, Dostoevskii wrote his brother in 1845: "But, brother, what sort of person is he? I too have almost fallen in love with him. A poet, a man of talent, an aristocrat, handsome, wealthy, intelligent, educated, twenty-five years old—I do not know what nature has denied him. Finally: an inexhaustibly straightforward, splendid personality, shaped in the best school."[17]

[...]

Dostoevskii, the Parisian critic Elie Halperine-Kaminsky wrote prophetically in 1894, "will only be truly understood when the mounting tension of our century has reached its climax."[18] The tension of the century, real or fancied, contributed powerfully to the near eclipse of Turgenev, at least among some of the elite reading public. Tolstoi and Dostoevskii were making their presence felt on the European scene. "No one, or hardly anyone, thinks of reading [Turgenev] at the moment," wrote another Parisian critic in 1894.[19]

[...]

Such a view of Turgenev, of course, is entirely superficial. His art, with its aesthetic and ethical values of measure, moderation, and restraint, its accent on "middle culture," its acceptance of limitation, its open-ended view of human conflict, its profound understanding of human character, its realization of "seeing beautifully," and, last but not least, its tonic skepticism and principled war on rhetoric—all this is profoundly relevant to spirit, culture, and civilization.

---

17 Dostoevskii, PSS 20:175.
18 E. Halperine-Kaminsky, "La puissance des ténèbres sur la scène française," *La Nouvelle Revue*, February 1, 1888, 629.
19 T. de Wyzewa, "Revue russes," *Revue des deux mondes*, May 15, 1894, 458.

Part Two

Poetics

CHAPTER 3

Aesthetics

This chapter examines Dostoevskii's views on art and aesthetics, including his philosophy of art and ideas on beauty. As a student of German Romantic philosophy and literature in the 1840s, Dostoevskii was already developing his own philosophy of art before his exile to Siberia, yet aesthetic questions acquired a new significance for him following his return to St. Petersburg in 1859. During the years 1855–70, intense debates took place amongst the Russian intelligentsia over the questions of art's social responsibility and political commitment, its relationship to reality, the role of the ideal, and the possibilities of representing the contemporary moment in art. Though these debates can be traced back to the ideas of the radical critic, Vissarion Belinskii (1811–48), they took on a new urgency in the second half of the 1850s, when two opposing "camps" began to coalesce around the question of art's social mission. On one side was the utilitarian camp, which included the journal critics Nikolai Chernyshevskii (1828–89), Nikolai Dobroliubov (1836–61), and Dmitrii Pisarev (1840–68), who advocated art's social responsibility and political utility. On the other side were the aestheticians, defenders of the idea of art for art's sake, the journal critics Pavel Annenkov (1813–87), Aleksandr Druzhinin (1824–64), and Vasilii Botkin (1812–69). On his return from Siberian exile, Dostoevskii entered the fray, publishing a series of articles on art and society in the journal he founded with his brother Mikhail, *Time*.

"Mr. —bov and the Question of Art," which opens this chapter, is a response to Dobroliubov, who would often sign his articles "N. —bov." In this piece, Dostoevskii tries to find a middle ground between the utilitarian and aestheticist camps, acknowledging the value in both perspectives and yet rejecting the assumptions upon which their arguments are based. He agrees with the utilitarians that art should be useful, yet he redefines the nature of that usefulness, arguing that beauty is an essential human need.

Harmony is a central concept in Dostoevskii's aesthetics, one which unites the aesthetic and ethical realms. In "Mr. —bov" he advocates the distinctive harmony of a work of art, the classical unity of idea and form, and the value of harmony as an ideal for those marooned in the chaotic currents of contemporary life. Equally important in his aesthetics is the idea of disharmony. After *Notes from Underground* was published, critics seized upon the centrality of the underground as a concept in Dostoevskii's art and frequently referred to him as the "poet of the underground." Though it was intended as an insult, to draw attention to the squalor of the world portrayed in Dostoevskii's art, he reclaimed this label, arguing that the dissonant and discordant underground was a state of mind experienced by the majority. In the extract from the notebooks for *The Adolescent* included here, Dostoevskii expresses his pride in having presented, "for the first time, the real image of the *Russian majority*, and to have exposed, for the first time, its misshapen and tragic aspects." This sense of responsibility to represent the misshapen aspects of Russian society became increasingly important in his aesthetics in the 1870s.

As his novels gained more readers and received more critical attention, and as the concept of realism received a greater critical currency, Dostoevskii felt an increasing urge to defend his own particular conception of realism, which was often called idealism by his detractors, but which he preferred to call "realism in a higher sense." In the 1868 letter to Apollon Maikov, included here, written following criticism of the first serialized sections of *The Idiot* and its Christlike hero, Prince Myshkin, Dostoevskii defends the role of the ideal in realist art, arguing that idealism can express layers of experience which lie beyond the purview of conventional realism. This defense of the ideal remained central to Dostoevskii's aesthetics for the rest of his career. In the 1873 installment of *A Writer's Diary*, "Apropos of the Exhibition," also included here, a response to the Russian paintings at the Vienna International Exhibition, he is surprised to find idealism manifested in the normally tendentious Il'ia Repin's painting, *Barge Haulers on the Volga.* Unlike Nikolai Ge's *Christ*, which shows Jesus as a secular subject, real and unremarkable, Repin's painting conveys its author's higher purpose, representing the barge haulers in their distilled essence rather than in their everyday reality.

Central to Dostoevskii's art is the idea that beauty constitutes a riddle, as Dmitrii Karamazov puts it in the passage from *The Brothers Karamazov* included here. On the one hand, as Dostoevskii writes in the notebooks to *The Idiot*, "Beauty will save the world." On the other, evil can have the same kind of aesthetic appeal as beauty, even sometimes becoming confused with it. Dmitrii Karamazov sums up the two different competing aesthetic impulses he recognizes in himself as "the ideal of the Madonna" and "the ideal of Sodom." In another extract included here, which forms a commentary on the primary sources in the first half of the chapter, Robert Louis Jackson examines these two aesthetic impulses, one of which he defines as the longing for ideal form or *obraz*, the other of which is the attraction for its opposite, disfiguration or the deformation of ideal form, *bezobrazie*. He analyzes how, in the Dostoevskian universe, *bezobrazie* comes to fill the gap left when the act of striving towards the ideal disappears.

Dostoevskii's defense of the ideal in art led him to embrace another accusation leveled at him by his detractors: that his work veered into the realm of the fantastic. "Fantastic" frequently appears in Dostoevskii's works as part of a genre designation, and many scholars refer to his "fantastic realism." In the final extract in this chapter, Vladimir Zakharov analyzes Dostoevskii's use of the term "fantastic" to refer to his own work. He discusses the "fantastic pages" Dostoevskii included in the notebooks to *Demons,* pages that include utopian ideals and ideas that never made it into the final novel. For Zakharov, these pages constitute "Gospel Realism" which make explicit the Christian component of Dostoevskii's "realism in a higher sense." Zakharov, however, does not explain why these fantastic pages did not make it into the final novel. The balance between representing the misshapen aspects of contemporary reality and the utopian ideal is key to Dostoevskii's novelistic and aesthetic vision, and in his works we never find *obraz* without its opposite, *bezobrazie.*

Further Reading

Brunson, Molly. *Russian Realisms: Literature and Painting, 1840–1890*. DeKalb: Northern Illinois University Press, 2016.

Jackson, Robert Louis. *Dostoevsky's Quest for Form*. New Haven, CT: Yale University Press, 1966.

Jackson, Robert Louis. *The Art of Dostoevsky: Deliriums and Nocturnes*. Princeton, NJ: Princeton University Press, 1981.

Jones, Malcolm V. *Dostoyevsky after Bakhtin: Readings in Dostoyevsky's Fantastic Realism*. Cambridge: Cambridge University Press, 1990.

Moser, Charles. *Esthetics as Nightmare: Russian Literary Theory, 1855–1970*. Princeton, NJ: Princeton University Press, 1989.

Mr. —bov and the Question of Art (1861)*

Fedor Dostoevskii

In the January number of our journal, in concluding our introduction to "A Series of Articles on Russian Literature," we promised to talk about contemporary literary tendencies and questions.[1] One of the most important literary questions today we consider the question about art. This question divides many of our contemporary writers into two hostile camps. In this way forces become disconnected. We need not expatiate on the harm such a hostile difference of opinion entails. And the matter has already reached a point of open hostility [...]

Some declare and teach that art is an aim by itself and must find its justification in its inner content and that consequently there cannot be any question of the usefulness of art in the real meaning of the world. Creation is the fundamental principle of all art and it is an unbroken organic quality of human nature and has a right to exist and develop, if only for the reason that it is a necessary accessory of the human spirit. It is as legitimate in man as intellect and as all moral qualities of man, as legitimate, in fact, as two arms and two legs, as a stomach. It is inseparable from man and forms one whole with him. Intellect, of

---

* From "Mr. —bov and the Question of Art," *Dostoevsky's Occasional Writings*, trans. David Magarshack (New York: Random House, 1963), 89, 91–93, 95–98, 100–101, 124–27, 129–30. Printed with permission from the Magarshack family.

EDS: "Mr. —bov" is Nikolai Dobroliubov, the critic (1836–61), one of the leaders of the utilitarian camp. Dostoevskii is referring to a review written by Dobroluibov of a short story collection by Marko Vovchok, pseudonym of the Ukrainian female writer, Mariia Vilinskaia (1833–1907).

1 EDS: Dostoevskii's journal *Time*, where this article was first published, in 1861.

course, is useful and in the same sense man finds a pair of legs and arms useful. In the same sense art too is useful to man.

But as something integral, organic, creative art develops out of itself, it is not subject to anything and it demands full development. Above all, it demands absolute freedom in its development. For that reason any constraint, any sub-jection, any outside purpose, any exceptional aim put before it would be both illegitimate and unreasonable. If creative art were to be restricted or if man were forbidden to satisfy his creative and artistic needs by—shall we say?—by giving expression to certain sensations, if man were forbidden any creative occupations that certain natural phenomena would arouse in him, such a sun-rise, a storm at sea, etc., then all this would have been an absurd, ridiculous and illegitimate constraint of the human spirit in its development and activity.

This is what one party maintains, the party defending the freedom and the fullest independence of art.

"Of course that would have been an absurd constraint," reply the utili-tarians (the other party, which teaches that art must serve man by its direct, immediate, practical usefulness, which may even depend on circumstances), "of course such a constraint without any reasonable aim but simply at some-one's whim is a wicked and savage piece of stupidity. But you must surely agree (they could add) that for instance, if you found yourself in the midst of a battle and instead of assisting your comrades you, an artist at heart, suddenly felt that you must preserve a picture of the battle as a whole and so you so threw down your arms, took out a pencil: would you be doing right? No doubt you would be entitled to give yourself over to your inspirations, but would your artistic activity be reasonable at such a moment?

"In short," they conclude, "we do not reject your theory about the freedom of artistic development, but this freedom must at least be reasonable." [...]—

In short, the utilitarians demanded of art direct and immediate usefulness, which should take account of prevailing circumstances and be subject to them to such a degree that if, for instance, society were to be preoccupied at a given time with the solution of a certain problem, then art (according to the teachings of some utilitarians) should have no other aim that the solution of the same problem. If one were to regard this idea of usefulness not as a demand but only as a wish, it might in our view be even praiseworthy, though we are aware that such an idea is not quite right all the same. If, for instance, the entire society were preoccupied with the solution of some important internal problem, it would of course be agreeable to wish that all the forces of the society be directed toward the attainment of that aim and, therefore, that art too be inspired by the same idea and serve the general cause. Suppose that a certain society is on the brink of disaster; everyone possessing any intelligence, any feeling, any willpower, anyone conscious of his being a man, a citizen, is preoccupied with one single problem, one common cause. It is only poets and writers who need not have any intelligence, any feeling, any love for their country and sympathy with the general well-being of their people? But even if, as the poet contends, the service of the Muses cannot tolerate world-mindedness, it would not be a bad idea if poets, for instance, were not to seek refuge in the empyrean and look down from there on the rest of us mortals. For though a Greek anthology is an excellent thing, it is sometimes quite out of place and it would be much more agreeable to see in its place something more suitable to the business at hand and something more helpful to it. Besides, art can be of help to some cause by rendering assistance to it, for it comprises enormous means and great powers. We repeat: one can only wish it, one cannot demand it, if only because one demands mostly when one wishes to compel by force, and the first law of art is freedom of inspiration and creation. Everything that has been imposed from above, everything that has been obtained by force from time immemorial to our own day has never succeeded and, instead of being beneficial, has been only harmful. The defenders of "art for art's sake" are chiefly against the utilitarians because by prescribing certain aims for art, they destroy it, for they encroach on its freedom, and since they destroy art so easily, they cannot possibly value it and, therefore, cannot even understand what it could be useful for; they are first of all concerned about its usefulness. Therefore, say the defenders of art, if the utilitarians had any idea of the great usefulness of art to the whole of mankind, they would value it more and would not treat it with such disrespect. And indeed, they continue, even if one were to look at art from your point of view, that is to say, consider it only in the aspect of its usefulness, then it must be stated that the normal historical process of usefulness of art to mankind is still unknown. It is difficult to measure the whole mass of usefulness that has been and still is being brought to the whole of mankind by, for example, the *Iliad* or the *Apollo Belvedere*, things that are apparently quite unnecessary today. Suppose, for example, that a certain man when still in his youth, at a time when "all impressions of life are still new and fresh," had a look at the *Apollo Belvedere* and the god had imprinted himself in the young man's soul by his majestic and infinitely beautiful image. A seemingly unimportant fact: he stopped for a couple of minutes to admire the beautiful statue and went away. But this kind of admiration is quite unlike the admiration, for instance, of an elegant dress. "This marble is god," and spit at it as much as you like, you will not rob it of its divinity. Such an attempt to rob it has been made before, but nothing came out of it. And therefore the young man's impression may have been an ardent and nerve-racking one, an impression that sent a cold shiver down his spine; who knows, perhaps a kind of internal change takes place in man at the impact of such beauty, at such a nervous shock, a kind of movement of particles of galvanic current that in one moment transforms what has been before into something different, a piece of ordinary iron into a magnet. There are, of course, thousands of impressions in the world, but, surely, it is not for nothing that this sort of impression is a special one, the impression of a god. It is surely not for nothing that such impressions remain for the rest of one's life. And who knows? When twenty or thirty years later this young man came to the fore during some great social event in which he had taken a prominent part by acting in one way rather than another, who knows whether among the many reasons that made him act one way and not another there was, unconsciously, his impression of the *Apollo Belvedere* he had seen twenty years earlier? You laugh? Indeed, it does sound rather like the ravings of a lunatic. But, first of all, about these facts, in spite of their explicitness, you do not know anything positive yourself. Perhaps you will know about them in the future (we believe in science), but for the time being you do not know. Second, there are historic indications, certain historic facts, which seem to confirm our belief that our dreams are not altogether absurd. Who, for example, could have imagined that Corneille and Racine[2] would have exerted an influence on such unusual and decisive moments of the historic life of a whole people when at first it would have seemed unthinkable that such old dodderers as Corneille and Racine could have anything to do at such a period. It would seem however that souls do not die. If, therefore, one were to define the aims of art beforehand and determine what it ought to be useful for, one could make a terrible mistake and, instead of doing good, only do harm and, therefore, act against oneself, for utilitarians demand usefulness and not harmfulness. And since art demands full freedom first of all and freedom cannot exist without tranquility (any kind of disturbance is no longer freedom), it must function quietly and serenely, without haste, without being carried away by extraneous matters, having itself as its aim and believing that every activity will in time confer incontestable benefits upon humanity.

This is what the advocates of art for art's sake say to their opponents the utilitarians [...]

---

2   Pierre Corneille (1606–84) and Jean Racine (1639–99), French dramatists well known as the authors of tragedies.

Let us, incidentally, make one more observation. How does one recognize the high artistic quality of a work of art? By the fact that we see the fullest possible harmony between the artistic idea and the form in which it is embodied? Let us put it a little more clearly: the high artistic quality of, let us say, a novelist is his ability to express the idea of his novel in the characters and images of his novel so that after reading it the reader understands the writer's idea as well as the novelist understood it himself when creating his work. In simple words, then, it means that the artistic quality of a writer is his ability to write well. Therefore, those who claim that the artistic quality of a literary work is of no account admit that it is *permissible*, it is not far from saying quite simply that is *necessary* to write badly. In fact, they practically say that [...]

In one of your articles you say: "All right, let a literary work be artistic, but it must also be contemporary." And in another article: "If you want to exert any influence on me in a forceful way, if you want to make me love beauty, then be able to catch this general meaning in it, this breath of life, be able to point it out and explain it to me; only then will you achieve your aim." To put it in a nutshell: you do not reject artistic excellence, but you demand that the artist should talk about things that are important, should serve the general cause, should be true to contemporary reality, its needs and its ideals. An excellent wish. But such a wish which becomes a *demand* is, in our view, already a misunderstanding of the fundamental laws of art and its nature—freedom of inspiration. It means simply a refusal to recognize art as an organic whole. Therein lies the whole mistake in his confused question, which has resulted in misconceptions, disagreements and, what is worse, in extremes. You seem to think that by itself art has no standards, no laws of its own, that it can be ordered about just as you please, that inspiration is something everyone has in his pocket and can be fetched out on demand, that it serves this and that and follows the road you want it to follow. While we believe that art has an independent, inseparable, organic life of its own and hence also fundamental and unalterable laws for this life. Art is as much a necessity for man as eating and drinking. The need for beauty and creation embodying it is inseparable from man and without it man would perhaps have refused to live in the world. Man craves it, finds and accepts beauty *without any conditions* just because it is beauty and worships it with veneration without asking what it is useful for or what one can buy with it. And perhaps it is in this that the greatest secret of creative art lies, namely that the image of beauty created by art at once becomes something to be worshipped *without any conditions*. And why does it become an object of worship? Because the need for beauty is felt more strongly when men are at variance with reality, in a state of disharmony, in conflict, that is to say, when they are *most of all alive,* for men are most of all alive when they are searching for something and trying to obtain it; it is then that they are overcome by a most natural desire for everything that is harmonious and for tranquility, since in beauty there is both harmony and tranquility. When they find what they are looking for, life itself seems to slow down for a time, and we even know of examples of men who have attained the ideal of their desires and, not knowing what else to strive for, are completely satisfied, lapse into a kind of depression, even do their best to aggravate it, search for another ideal in life and, surfeited, no longer appreciate the things they had taken pleasure in; they even deviate from the straight path deliberately, stimulating in themselves all sorts of unhealthy, sharp, inharmonious and sometimes quite monstrous tastes, losing all sense of tact and esthetic flair for healthy beauty and instead demanding all sorts of exceptions. Beauty is therefore inherent in everything that is healthy, that is to say, everything that is most of all alive and is a necessity of the human organism. It is harmony; it holds the promise of tranquility; it is the embodiment of man's and mankind's ideals [...]

Beauty, it is true, is always useful; but we shall say nothing about it now (though we warn you beforehand that we might say something that is quite unheard of and shamelessly impudent, but do not be embarrassed, for all we say is mere surmise); what we are going to say is what if the *Iliad* is much more useful that the works of Marko Vovchok, and not only in the past but even today, when we are dealing with contemporary questions, more useful as a means for attaining certain aims, of dealing with these same questions, of solving the urgent problems of today? For even today the *Iliad* sends a thrill through a man's soul. For it is an epic so great and full of life, so high a moment of national life and, let us observe too, a life of so great a people, that in our time, a time full of aspirations, struggle, vacillations and faith (because our time is a time of faith), in short, because our time is a time of highly active life—that in our time too this eternal harmony which is embodied in the *Iliad* can most decidedly have an active influence on the soul [...]

Now let us turn to our chief and final reply to your just question of why the ideals of art do not always agree with the general and contemporary ideal, or, in other words, why art is not always true to reality.

Our reply to this question is ready.

We have already said that, in our opinion, the question of art is not properly formulated today, that it has gone to extremes and got hopelessly confused as a result of the mutual bitterness of either party of the dispute. No, the question has not been formulated properly and there is really no need to argue about it all, for:

Art has always been contemporary and real, it has never been different and, above all, it can never be different.

The Defense of the Ideal, Letter to Apollon Maikov, December 11, 1868*

Fedor Dostoevskii

The main thing I'm driving at is that I have on my mind two or even three publications, requiring an ox for the mechanical labor only, which would, by the way, undoubtedly bring in money. Sometimes I have even managed to do so. Now, though, I have on my mind an enormous novel, titled *Atheism* (just between us, for the love of God), but before I can start on it, I need to read almost an entire library of works by atheists, Catholics, and Orthodox Christians.[1]

It will be finished, even with full support, no sooner than two years from now. I have a character in mind: A Russian man from our society, *in advanced age*, not very educated, but not uneducated, without rank—*suddenly*, in mature age, he loses his faith in God. All of his life he did nothing but offer diligent service at work, he never did anything out of the ordinary, and until the age of 45 he never distinguished himself. (The answer to the riddle is psychological: deep feelings, a man, a Russian man.) His loss of faith in God affects him deeply. (The actual action and setting in the novel are grand.) He prowls among new generations, atheists, Slavs and Europeans, Russian fanatics and hermits, priests; he gets hooked quite firmly by one Jesuit, a Polish propagator; sinks

---

*   Translated from the Russian by Anton Nonin, redacted by the editors. This translation appears here under a Creative Commons BY-ND 4.0 license.

1   EDS: A plan for a novel which Dostoevskii never wrote, but elements of which entered his novels *Demons*, *The Adolescent*, and *The Brothers Karamazov*.

from there to the bottom with the *Khlysts*.[2] But in the end, he finds Christ and Russian land, the Russian Christ and the Russian God. (For the love of God, do not tell anyone.) But for me: to write this novel and then, let death come— I will have said all that I wanted.

Ah, my friend! I have completely different ideas about reality than our realists and critics. My idealism is realer than theirs. God! If I were to describe, meaningfully, everything that we, the Russians, have experienced in the past ten years, our spiritual development—would the realists not begin to yell that it's all fantasy? And all the while, this is the original, true realism! This is realism, only deeper. Theirs is shallow. Truly, is Liubim Tortsov not pitiable?[3] And he represents the peak of idealism that their realism offers. Deep realism, my foot! Their realism cannot explain one-hundredth of the real facts that actually happened. And we, without idealism, have even prophesied events that have come true facts. It has happened.

---

2   EDS: An underground ascetic Christian sect active in nineteenth century Russia, rumored to practise self-flagellation.

3   EDS: Character from the play by Aleksandr Nikolaevich Ostrovskii, *Poverty Is No Vice* (1853). Tortsov is a Russian national type, the "virtuous drunkard."

Apropos of the Exhibition (1873)*

Fedor Dostoevskii

I went in to see the exhibition.[1] Quite a number of paintings by our Russian artists are being sent off to the Vienna International exhibition. It's not the first time this has happened, and contemporary Russian artists are beginning to become known in Europe. But still the question arises: can they understand our artists there, and from what point of view will they judge them? [...]

I have a great fear when "tendency" takes hold of a young artist, especially at the beginning of his career; and what do you think causes me the most concern? Precisely that the purpose of this tendency will not be achieved. There is a certain dear critic whom I have been reading recently and whose name I don't wish to mention here. Will he believe that any work of art without a preconceived tendency, a work created exclusively out of the demands of art and even on an entirely noncontroversial subject which doesn't contain the least hint of anything "tendentious"—will this critic believe that such a work contributes far more *for his purposes* than all the "songs about the shirt," for instance (not Hood's, but those of our own writers),[2] even though superficially the work may appear to belong to the category called "satisfaction of idle

---

*   From Fyodor Dostoevsky, "Apropos of the Exhibition," *A Writer's Diary Volume I: 1873–1876*, trans. Kenneth Lantz (Evanston, IL: Northwestern University Press, 1993), 205, 210–16. Copyright © 1994 by Northwestern University Press. Published 1994. All rights reserved. The text is reproduced here with minor modifications: some footnotes have been removed.
1   Some hundred paintings and sculptures were exhibited in March 1873 at the Academy of Arts in St. Petersburg.
2   Thomas Hood (1799–1845), English poet. His "Song of the Shirt" (1843) is a poem of social protest against the exploitation of women's work.

curiosity"? If even scholars, apparently, have still not realized this, then what may sometimes happen in the hearts and minds of our young writers and artists? What a muddle of conceptions and preconceived notions they must have! To satisfy social demands, the young poet suppresses his own natural need to express himself in his own images, fearing that he will be censured for "idle curiosity"; he suppresses and obliterates the images that arise out of his own soul; he ignores them or leaves them undeveloped, while extracting from himself with painful tremors the images that satisfy common, official, liberal, and social opinion. What a terribly simple and naive mistake, what a serious mistake this is! One of the most serious mistakes is that the denunciation of vice (or what liberal opinion accepts as vice) and the arousal of feelings of hatred and vengeance is considered the only possible way to achieve the purpose! But even with such a narrow approach as this, a powerful talent could still wriggle free and not suffocate at the very beginning of his career; he need only keep in mind the golden rule that a word spoken may be silver, but one unspoken is gold. There are so many significant talents who promised so much but who were so badly corroded by "tendency" that it essentially put them into uniform [...]

No sooner had I read in the newspapers of Mr. Repin's barge-haulers than I got frightened.[3] Even the subject itself is terrible: we have accepted somehow that barge-haulers are the best means of representing the well-known social notion of the unpaid debt of the upper classes to the People. I came expecting to see these barge-haulers all lined up in uniforms with the usual labels stuck to their foreheads. And what happened? To my delight, all my fears turned out to be vain: they are barge-haulers, real bargehaulers and nothing more. Not a single one of them shouts from the painting to the viewer: "Look how unfortunate I am and how indebted you are to the People!" And in that alone we can credit the artist with a great service. They are marvelous, familiar figures: the two foremost haulers are almost laughing; at any rate they are certainly not crying, and aren't thinking at all about their social status. A little soldier is slyly trying to conceal the fact that he wants to fill his pipe. The little boy has put on a serious face; he is shouting, even arguing. He is a wonderful figure, almost the best in the picture and equal in conception to that of the very last hauler, a wretched, drooping little peasant who is trudging along on his own and whose face isn't even visible. One simply can't imagine that any notion of the politicoeconomic and social debts of the higher classes to the People could ever

---

3   Il'ia Efimovich Repin (1844–1930). His *Barge-haulers on the Volga* (1870–73) was the most discussed painting at the exhibition.

penetrate the poor, drooping head of this little peasant, oppressed by perpetual grief... and—and do you know, my dear critic, that the very humble innocence of the thought of this peasant achieves your purpose far more readily than you think?—precisely your tendentious, liberal purpose! More than one spectator will walk away with pain in his heart and with love (and with what love!) for this poor little peasant, or for this boy, or for this sly scoundrel, the soldier! Why, you can't help but love them, these defenseless creatures; you can't walk away without loving them. You can't help but think that you are indebted, truly indebted to the People. . . . You will be dreaming of this whole group of barge-haulers afterward; you will still recall them fifteen years later! And had they not been so natural, so innocent, and so simple, they would not have produced such an impression and would not have composed such a picture [. . .]

And so what else is the artist doing here if not trusting first his own idea (the ideal) more than the reality before him? The ideal is also reality after all, and just as legitimate as immediate reality. Many artists in Russia don't seem to realize that. Take Bronnikov's "Hymn of the Pythagoreans," for instance.[4] Some genre painter (even one of our most talented) might even be surprised at how a contemporary artist could pick such subjects. And yet subjects such as these (almost fantastic ones) are just as real and just as essential to art and to humans as is immediate reality.

What is genre, in essence? Genre is the art of portraying contemporary, immediate reality that the artist has himself felt personally and has seen with his own eyes, in contrast with historical reality, for instance, which cannot be seen with one's own eyes and which is portrayed not in its immediate but in its completed aspect. (Let me make a *nota bene* here: I said "seen with his own eyes." But Dickens never saw Pickwick with his own eyes; he perceived him only in a variety of forms of reality that he had observed; he created a character and presented him as the result of his observations. Thus this character is every bit as real as one who really exists, even though Dickens took only an ideal of reality.) But what happens here is a confusion of conceptions of reality. Historical reality in art, for instance, is naturally not that of immediate reality (genre) precisely because the former is completed and not current. Ask any psychologist you like and he will tell you that if you imagine some event of the past, especially of the distant past—one that is completed and historical (and to live without imagining the past is impossible)—then the even will *necessarily*

---

4 Fedor Andreevich Bronnikov (1827–1902). His painting *The Hymn of the Pythagoreans to the Rising Sun* (1869) was in the pseudoclassical academic style.

be imagined in its completed aspect, i.e., with the addition of all its subsequent developments that had not yet occurred at the historical moment in which the artist is trying to depict a person or event. And thus the essence of a historical event cannot even be imagined by an artist exactly as it probably happened in reality. And so the artist is overcome by a kind of superstitious fear of the fact that he will perhaps have to "idealize" despite himself, which to his mind means to lie. So, to avoid this imaginary error, he tries (and there were cases of this) to combine both realities—the historical and the immediate; from this unnatural combination arises the worst kind of untruth. In my view this pernicious error can be seen in certain of Mr. Ge's paintings.[5] For instance, he took his "Last Supper," which once created such a stir, and made a regular genre painting out of it. Look at it more carefully; this is an ordinary quarrel of some very ordinary people. There sits Christ—but is that Christ? It may be a very good young man, deeply hurt by his quarrel with Judas, who is standing there getting dressed to go off and denounce him, but this is not the Christ we know. His friends have crowded around the Teacher to comfort him; but we must ask the question: where are the eighteen centuries of Christianity that followed, and how are they connected with the event? How is it possible that from such an ordinary quarrel of such ordinary people gathered to have supper, such as Mr. Ge depicts, there could arise something so colossal?

Nothing at all is explained here; there is no historical truth here; there is not even any truth of genre here; everything here is false.

---

5   Nikolai Nikolaevich Ge (1831–94). His painting *Peter I interrogates the Tsarevich Aleksei Petrovich at Peterhof* (1871) was amongst those exhibited. His earlier *The Last Supper* (1863) was extremely controversial because of what many considered a mundane treatment of an event having profound religious significance.

Poet of the Underground (1875)*

Fedor Dostoevskii

March 22.[1]

For the preface.

Facts. They are passing by. They don't notice. There are no *citizens*, and nobody wants to make an effort and force himself to think and to notice things. I haven't been able to tear myself away, and all the shouts of our critics, ~~haven't dissuaded~~ who say that I am not depicting real life, haven't dissuaded me. Our society has no *foundations*, it hasn't worked out any rules <of life>, because there really hasn't been any life either. A colossal shock—and everything comes to a halt, falls down, and is negated as if it hadn't ever existed. And not just externally, as in the West, but internally, morally. Our most talented writers, who have been describing, in highly artistic form, the life of our upper middle class (from the vantage point of the family)—Tolstoi, Goncharov—thought that they were describing the life of the majority; in my opinion, what they were describing were the lives of some exceptions.[2] [Quite to the contrary, their life is the life of exceptions, while mine is the life of the general rule. Future generations will find that out, as they will be more objective, and the truth will be on my side. In this I believe.]

It has been said that I was describing real thunder, real rain, just as on stage. Where then? Could it be true that Raskol'nikov, Stepan Trofimovich

---

*   From The Notebooks for "A Raw Youth," trans. Victor Terras, ed. Edward Wasiolek (Chicago: University of Chicago Press, 1969), 424–26. Copyright © by the University of Chicago. All rights reserved. Published 1969. Elsewhere in this volume, we have used an alternative translation for this novel: The Adolescent.

1   EDS: 1875.

2   EDS: Lev Nikolaevich Tolstoi (1828–1910), whose *Anna Karenina* was being serialized in *The Russian Messenger* in 1875 in parallel with *The Adolescent*. Ivan Aleksandrovich Goncharov (1812–91), author of *Oblomov* (1859).

(the principal heroes of my novels) may give grounds for such an assertion? [Or Akul'ka's husband in *Notes from the House of the Dead*, for example? It was precisely this (civic) feeling that made me, for a moment, consider joining the Slavophiles, with the idea of resurrecting the dreams of my childhood (I had read Karamzin, <and was familiar with> the figures of Sergius, Tikhon).] And what about the underground and *Notes from Underground?* I am proud to have presented, for the first time, the real image of the *Russian majority*, and to have exposed, for the first time, its misshapen and tragic aspects. The tragic lies in one's awareness of being misshapen. As heroes, those beginning with Silvio and the Hero of our times down to Prince Bolkonskii and Levin stand for nothing but petty self-love, which is "not good," they were "brought up the wrong way," they have a chance to improve themselves, for excellent examples are available (Saks in *Polin'ka Saks*, also the German in *Oblomov*, Pierre Bezukhov, the tax farmer in *Dead Souls* and many others). But this is also because they are representative of nothing more than poets heroes of petty self-love. I have been the only one to bring out the tragedy of the underground, which consists of suffering, self-laceration, an awareness of a better <life> coupled with the impossibility of attaining it, and, most important of all, a strong conviction on the part of these unfortunate people that everybody else is like them and that it is, therefore, not worthwhile to improve oneself! What What can sustain those who do try to improve themselves? A reward, faith? Nobody is offering any reward, and in whom could one have faith? Another step from this position, and you have extreme depravity, crime (murder). A mystery.

They are saying that Olia has made it insufficiently clear why she is hanging herself.[3] However, I am not writing for fools.

Bolkonskii reforms as he sees Anatole's leg being cut off, and we've all been shedding tears over it, but a genuine underground man wouldn't have reformed.

"Underground, underground, *poet of the underground,*" our feuilletonists have been repeating over and over again, as if this were something derogatory to me. Silly fools, it is my glory, for that's where the truth lies. It is that very underground which made Gogol', in his solemn testament, speak of his [last] narrative which had risen from the bottom of his soul, *like a song*, and which actually would didn't even exist. Why, it is quite possible that, when he began to write his testament, he didn't even know that he would write this thing

---

3 EDS: Olia is a young provincial governess from *The Adolescent* who hangs herself mysteriously.

about his last narrative. Now, what is this power that makes even an honest and serious person lie and clown in this manner, and what's more, in his own testament? (This power is peculiarly Russian, in Europe people have more integrity, while our people are dreamers and scoundrels.)

The reason for the underground is the destruction of our belief in certain general rules. *"Nothing is sacred."*

Unfinished people (as a consequence of the Petrine reforms *in general*) like the *engineer* in *Demons.*

Dmitrii Karamazov on Beauty (1878)*

Fedor Dostoevskii

"Beauty is a terrible and awful thing! It is terrible because it has not been fathomed and never can be fathomed, for God sets us nothing but riddles. Here the boundaries meet and all contradictions exist side by side. I am not a cultivated man, brother, but I've thought a lot about this. It's terrible what mysteries there are! Too many riddles weigh men down on earth. We must solve them as we can, and try to keep a dry skin in the water. Beauty! I can't endure the thought that a man of lofty mind and heart begins with the ideal of the Madonna and ends with the ideal of Sodom. What's still more awful is that a man with the ideal of Sodom in his soul does not renounce the ideal of the Madonna, and his heart may be on fire with that ideal, genuinely on fire, just as in his days of youth and innocence. Yes, man is broad, too broad, indeed. I'd have him narrower. The devil only knows what to make of it! What to the mind is shameful is beauty and nothing else to the heart. Is there beauty in Sodom? Believe me, that for the immense mass of mankind beauty is found in Sodom. Did you know that secret? The awful thing is that beauty is mysterious as well as terrible. God and the devil are fighting there and the battlefield is the heart of man."

---

* From *The Brothers Karamazov*, trans. Constance Garnett (New York: The Modern Library, 1900), 127.

Two Kinds of Beauty (1966)*

Robert Louis Jackson

"Beauty will save the world—two kinds of beauty," Dostoevskii observes without further explanation in one of his notebooks to *The Idiot*.[1] This extremely condensed set of idea-signals points not only to the problem center of *The Idiot*, but to the complex dialectic of Dostoevskii's aesthetic thought. The first phrase—"Beauty will save the world"—is a model of syntactic precision and order; it promises direct, unimpeded action. But the second phrase is ominously disruptive; it shatters the integrity of the beauty-savior and bogs down the action in ambiguity and enigma. "Is it true, Prince, that you once said that 'beauty will save the world'?" Ippolit Terent'ev asks Myshkin in *The Idiot* and then mockingly adds: "What kind of beauty will save the world?" "The world will become the beauty of Christ," Dostoevskii answers in one of his notes to *Demons*.[2] But Myshkin gives no answer to Terent'ev; elsewhere in the novel he remarks: "It is difficult to judge beauty; I am still not ready. Beauty is an enigma." Dmitrii Karamazov also posits the enigma of beauty.

Where is Dostoevskii in this aesthetic confusion? Is he the one who believes in a single omnipotent beauty? Or does he acknowledge more than one kind of beauty? It is to be noted at the outset that when Dostoevskii, as critic or journalist, and speaking for himself, uses the word "beauty," it is invariably in the antique or neo-Platonist and Christian sense of ideal beauty.

---

* From Robert Louis Jackson, *Dostoevsky's Quest for Form* (New Haven, CT: Yale University Press, 1966), 40–44, 46–51, 56–60. Reprinted by permission of the author. The text is reproduced here with minor modifications: some footnotes have been removed.

1 P. N. Sakulin and N. F. Bel'chikov, eds., *Iz arkhiva Dostoevskogo, Idiot* (Moscow-Leningrad: Gos. izd-vo khudozhestvennoi literatury, 1931), 102.

2 F. M. Dostoevskii, *Zapisnye tetradi F. M. Dostoevskogo*, ed. E. N. Konshina (Moscow-Leningrad: Akademiia, 1935), 222.

It is this kind of beauty which will save the world; it is, to Dostoevskii, a beauty which finds an objective correlative in concrete form—form subject to definite formal aesthetic principles. Philosophically, Dostoevskii gives de jure recognition only to this classical beauty. At the same time, in his belles lettres, Dostoevskii quite consciously explores, or one might say poses the problem of, two kinds of beauty. Here he recognizes de facto a category of the beautiful, or of the experience of the beautiful, which is the very antithesis in both formal attributes and moral content to classical beauty; he recognizes, in short, a judgment of beauty of which the determining principle is wholly subjective. What is the relationship between these two areas or structures of aesthetic thought in Dostoevskii's thinking?

We cannot arrive at a proper understanding of Dostoevskii's aesthetic position without recognizing one paradoxical notion: *it is not beauty which is ambivalent, but man who experiences two kinds of beauty.* "But really to them (and indeed to many) this madness seems not a monstrosity but, on the contrary, *beauty*," Dostoevskii wrote N. N. Strakhov in 1871 apropos of the destructiveness of the Paris Commune. He continued: "And thus the aesthetic idea in the new humanity is beclouded. A moral foundation of society (taken from positivism) not only gives no results, but cannot even define itself, is confused in desires and in ideals."[3] Dostoevskii's position is clear. Man in his moral obloquy finds pleasure in ugliness, violence, bloodshed, and falsely calls it beauty. But the "aesthetic idea" alone (the idea of beauty which for Dostoevskii in the post-exile period, if not earlier as well, is always the religious idea), though beclouded in man's consciousness, is universal and absolute.

We must distinguish, then, between Dostoevskii's point of view and the point of view of his characters. This is not to deny that Dostoevskii enjoys a certain complicity with his heroes, even the most morally or ideologically questionable ones, but it is always within, and in relation to, a clearly defined structure of ideas and beliefs. It is especially important to distinguish this basic structure where Dostoevskii's aesthetic thought is concerned [. . .]

Dostoevskii's point of departure is the same as Plato's in *The Symposium*: the concept of love of beauty is necessarily love of something that is wanting to man, the concept of beauty as absolute. The conception of an absolute ideal beauty emerges from the postulation of man as incomplete, at variance with himself, and therefore ever seeking completion, unity, wholeness, and harmony. "Man strives on earth for an ideal which is *contrary* to his nature," Dostoevskii

---

3 *Pis'ma*, 2 (No. 387), 363.

observes in his notebook in the early 1860s.[4] At the core of Dostoevskii's aesthetic philosophy, then, is the tragic view of man's relation to himself and to reality as one of permanent discord, and the view of this discord as constituting a creative dialectic in human existence, the inner force of man's aesthetic strivings. Man's spirit is envisaged in a continual tension toward the ideal, the Absolute. "Peoples form and move," observes Shatov in *Demons*, "through the inexhaustible desire to come to an end . . . The spirit of life, as the Scriptures say, 'rivers of living water' . . . The aesthetic principle, as the philosophers say, the moral principle, with which they identify it. 'The seeking of God,' as I call it much more simply" (Pt. II, Ch. 7).

But when the ideal, or tension toward the ideal, vanishes from man's life, Dostoevskii notes, man loses his moral equilibrium. "Another ideal" replaces his higher ideal, and the striving for the abnormal replaces the vanished craving for the norm. Man in these moments excites in himself "alien tastes, unhealthy, sharp, inharmonic, sometimes monstrous ones, losing measure and aesthetic feeling for healthy beauty and demanding instead of it exceptions." Dostoevskii writes of such moral-aesthetic disintegration in his interpretation of the poetic improvisation, "Cleopatra e i suoi amanti," in Pushkin's story "Egyptian Nights."[5] All hope and faith have disappeared, Dostoevskii explains, from Cleopatra's decadent society; it is at the edge of an abyss.

> Life is choked because of the absence of a goal. There is nothing in the future; one must demand everything from the present; one must fill life with the immediate alone. Everything passes into the body, everything plunges into physical debauchery, and, in order to fill in for the higher spiritual impressions which are lacking, people excite their nerves, their body with everything that can possibly arouse sensations. The most monstrous aberrations, the most abnormal phenomena little by little become customary. Even the feeling of self-preservation disappears. Cleopatra is the representative of this society.[6]

---

4 Boris Vysheslavtsev, "Dostoevskii o liubvi i bessmertii (Novyi fragment)," *Sovremennye zapiski*, 50 (1932): 288–303 (297).

5 EDS: "Cleopatra and her lovers," improvised poem from Pushkin's "Egyptian Nights" which, in Dostoevskii's view, encapsulates the decadence of her society.

6 F. M. Dostoevskii, "Otvet russkomu vestniku," *Polnoe sobranie khudozhestvennykh proizvedenii*, 13 vols, ed. V. Tomashevskii and K. Khalabaev (Moscow, 1926-30), vol. 13: *Dnevnik pisatel'ia; stat'i*, 13, 216–17. Designated from now on as *Stat'i*.

Dostoevskii carefully avoids the use of the word "beauty" in his discussion of man's taste for "another ideal"; he does not explicitly state that man conceives and experiences this other ideal as beauty. Yet the idea of unhealthy beauty is suggested by the very notion of healthy beauty. What is involved here is the notion of a counter-ideal in the life of man, one that contrasts with the ideal of absolute beauty in that it is both temporal and accessible, fundamentally unhealthy, and full of the force of violence, disharmony, and unrest. There is no question of any good embodied in this other ideal. The phenomenon evoked here is aesthetically attractive evil—in its most basic form, sensuality. This is the "ideal of Sodom"—as opposed to the "ideal of the Madonna"—about which Dmitrii speaks in *The Brothers Karamazov*; it is the phenomenon of beauty in Sodom. These two ideals, taken in their dialectical relationship to one another in man, constitute the enigma that is beauty to Dmitrii Karamazov. On the aesthetic plane love of beauty in Sodom is posed in *The Brothers Karamazov* as the discordant element in man's inner being. But man does not renounce the ideal of absolute beauty—the ideal of the Madonna. It is precisely in the context of his inner discord, in struggle, as Dostoevskii noted, that the need for harmony, order, and form is felt.

The problem of beauty in Sodom—aesthetically, the problem of ugliness, disfiguration, deformation of the norm—is Dmitrii's point of departure in his dramatic peroration on the enigma of beauty in *The Brothers Karamazov*: here is man's condition, his dilemma, his struggle viewed in its earthly aspect. Dostoevskii's point of departure in his disquisition on beauty in "Mr. —bov and the Question of Art" is absolute beauty toward which man strives: here is man's struggle seen in the aspect of his highest destiny, of eternity. The concept of absolute beauty as the highest good and the eternal truth and the corresponding notion of an ideal form which symbolizes harmony and, therefore, beauty constitute the unalterable foundation of Dostoevskii's higher aesthetic [...]

Beauty to Dostoevskii is the beauty of what may be called ideal form—form that is the incarnation of harmony, measure, and repose. Dostoevskii's formal conception of beauty is the same as that found in Greek aesthetics. Beauty for him is figural, and it is in the plastic and representational arts of the antique and Renaissance periods that he seeks the form or "shape," the model, of his ideal beauty. Dostoevskii writes in 1861 of the "ideals of beauty created by the past,"[7] and in 1871, through Stepan Verkhovenskii (in *Demons*), of the "form of beauty already achieved." He calls attention to the "sublime beauty"

---

7 "G. —bov," *Stat'i*, 89.

of the Apollo of Belvedere;[8] he is infatuated with the beauty of the Venus of Milo and the Venus of Medici.[9] "The Exhibition in the Academy of Arts: 1860–1861"—attributed to Dostoevskii—expresses a preference for the Greek norm and ideal of beauty. The ancient Greeks greatly honored the human body; one reason for this is the Greek "reverence for the beautiful," a reverence which "we" share with the Greeks, "and, of course, nothing in the world is more beautiful than a beautiful body."[10]

But Dostoevskii finds no reverence for the beautiful body in the paintings on exhibit. He is disgusted with the manner in which women are depicted. Here there is no feeling for the ideal. "Where can one get a model so that one could draw a really beautiful body, the kind of model that would not leave a great deal to idealize?" There are no tolerable models, he complains; instead, "Feet are disfigured by shoes, the stomach spoiled like a potato, and by a foolish bind of the skirt, so that the poor artist even has to invent a woman." Dostoevskii is offended by one painting in which the goddess Bacchante is shown with an "excessively large breast," and by another painting—Manet's "Nymph with Satyr" ["La nymphe surprise"]—in which the body of the nymph has the "color of a five-day-old corpse." The latter painting, he suggests, had been exhibited with the intention of showing "to what limits of ugliness [bezobrazie] the imagination of the artist can go."[11]

Disfiguration, lack of proportion, deviation from the antique notion of the "beautiful body," is objectionable to Dostoevskii; he frankly insists on idealization in painting, as he does in his article "Apropos of the Exhibition" in 1873.[12] Disfigured bodies in no way evoke that religious reverence which is called forth by the "beautiful body." It is no accident that Dostoevskii, in "Mr. —bov and the Question of Art," assimilates the notion of the "image of beauty" to an idol (kumir), to a pagan statue of divinity, that he finds in the sculptured image of the goddess Diana an embodiment of ideal beauty. "Note that human nature unfailingly demands [something] to worship," Dostoevskii writes in his

---

8 Stat'i, 70.

9 "Obraztsy chistoserdechiia," Stat'i, 184; see also, "Otvet russkomu vestniku," Stat'i, 215.

10 "Vystavka v akademii khudozhestv za 1860–1861 god," Stat'i, 535. EDS: As Jackson points out, the authorship of "The Exhibition in the Academy of Arts: 1860–61," has never definitely been established, but since "the aesthetic positions it advances are identical with those advanced elsewhere by Dostoevskii, it seems clear that he is the author. See Jackson, Dostoevsky's Quest for Form, 231–32.

11 "Vystavka v akademii khudozhestv za 1860–1861 god," Stat'i, 535.

12 Cf. "Po povodu vystavki," Dnevnik pisatelia, Polnoe sobranie khudozhestvennykh proizvedenii, vol. 11, 77–79.

notebook.[13] In bowing before the image of beauty man gives expression to one of his deepest needs—the religious need to worship something.

Here it is important to note the centrality of *obraz* as an aesthetic as well as religious symbol in Dostoevskii's thinking on art. *Obraz* is the axis of beauty in the Russian language; it is "form," "shape," "image"; it is also the iconographic image, or icon—the visible symbol of the beauty of God. In a letter to Apollon Maikov in 1868, Dostoevskii admires the poet's poem, "At the Chapel" ("U chasovni"), at the center of which is an icon. He is troubled only by Maikov's tone: "You seem to *apologize* for the icon, *justify*," and Dostoevskii goes on to indicate in a few words his great regard (in the past as well as present) for the popular cult of the icon.[14] The icon, particularly the iconographic representation of the Madonna, appears in Dostoevskii's artistic universe as a religious-aesthetic symbol of great importance—a literal image of beauty toward which man turns in reverence and longing. "Her eyes were dimmed by a mute, tormenting anguish," Dostoevskii writes of the heroine Katerina in "The Landlady." "She slowly rose, took two steps forward, and with a piercing wail fell down before the image [of the Madonna]." Dostoevskii's whole conception of the role of beauty in the life of man is conveyed in his conception of Katerina: a woman torn between her voluntary enslavement to a corrupt passion and an anguished yearning for purity and unity. Man is created in the image and likeness of God, Dostoevskii repeats in his writings; his highest striving is to "imitate the perfection of that image." [. . .]

"The Greeks," Shatov remarks in *Demons*, "deified nature and bequeathed to the world their religion, that is, philosophy and art." The feelings aroused by beauty are basically religious to Dostoevskii. Man "bows" before beauty. The notion of an organic union of the religious and aesthetic elements, of beauty and prayer, in art is at the root of Dostoevskii's analysis, in "Mr. —bov and the Question of Art," of a poem by the lyric poet A. A. Fet, entitled "Diana":

> I saw between the trees over clear waters,
> In all the magnificence of splendid nakedness
> The rounded features of the virgin goddess.
> With colorless, oval eyes,
> The wide brow was upraised—
> Its undistracted glance all lapped in peace;

---

13 Konshina, ed., *Zapisnye tetradi*, 221.
14 *Pis'ma*, 2 (No. 318), 154.

And the stone virgin, sensitive, gave heed
To prayers of maidens suffering pangs of birth.
But the wind swept among the leaves—
A bright image of the goddess danced on the waters;
I waited—she will come forth with bow and arrows,
Flickering through the trees with a milky whiteness,
To glance at somnolent Rome, the eternal city of glory,
The Tiber of the yellow floods, the clustered colonnades,
The long broad avenues—But the still marble
Paled before me with its inaccessible beauty.

The statue of Diana—the structural and thematic center of the poem—is literally an image of beauty for the poet. The classical ideal of figural beauty is expressed in the poised motionlessness, rounded features, and lofty demeanor of the goddess; all this is focused against the background of the classical landscape of Rome. The poet's conception of this goddess as unattainable beauty, veiled in the mystery of birth, of dawn, echoes Plato's view of divine, harmonious beauty as "destiny or goddess of parturition who presides at birth, and therefore, when approaching beauty, the conceiving power is propitious."[15] The poet Fet has done what the painter Manet failed to do: he has started with an ideal model and he has sung a hymn to harmonious creation, to divine beauty.

"In this enthusiasm (Byronic as we call it) before the ideals of beauty created by the past and left us in eternal inheritance," Dostoevskii writes, "we pour out often the whole anguish for the present, and not from impotence before our own life, but, on the contrary, from a flaming thirst for life and from anguish for the ideal which we reach out toward in pain." Fet's poem "Diana," Dostoevskii feels, is an embodiment of this enthusiasm, "a passionate appeal, a prayer before the perfection of past beauty, and a hidden inner anguish for just such perfection which the soul seeks, but still must seek for a long time and for a long time must suffer birth pangs in order to find it."[16]

Dostoevskii's interpretation of the spiritual state of Fet's pagan goddess is of particular interest. The goddess has "already passed to the highest moment of life; she is already in eternity; for her time has stopped; this is the

---

15 See Plato's *Symposium*, in *The Works of Plato*, ed. Irwin Edman (New York: Modern Library, 1928), 373.
16 "G. —bov," *Stat'i*, 13, 89.

highest moment of life after which it ceases—Olympian tranquility draws near. The only thing that is endless is the future, eternally calling, eternally new, and there also is one's highest moment, which one must seek and eternally seek, and this eternal striving is called life."[17]

The aesthetic—and religious—character of Dostoevskii's mystical vision or anticipation of world harmony is very apparent in his interpretation of "Diana." Beauty in its visible expression in ideal form is immanent with a higher spiritual reality; the craving for beauty is a longing for a condition in which the formal aesthetic values of ideal form (*obraz*)—harmony, proportion, and repose—are realized on a spiritual plane. The craving for beauty is a craving for that highest moment of life which anticipates Olympian tranquility and eternality of time: it is a craving for transfiguration.

The most dramatic expression in Dostoevskii's writing of man's nostalgia before the infinite, his craving for beatitude, is to be found in Prince Myshkin's own description of the "highest moments" preceding his epileptic fits—moments filled with premonitions of universal harmony. Myshkin describes these highest moments as a kind of "beauty and prayer," "a higher tranquility full of clear and harmonious joy and hope, full of reason and of [knowledge of] the final cause." Here he experiences flashes of the "'highest mode of existence'... harmony, beauty of the highest order... a feeling... of completeness, measure, reconciliation, and ecstatic and prayerful fusion in the highest synthesis of life." "At that moment... I somehow or other began to understand the extraordinary saying that *there will be no more time*" (Pt. II, Ch. 5).

In Fet's poem the statue merely symbolizes to the observer the timeless beatitude toward which man strives; in *The Idiot*, however, subject and object merge: the observer (Myshkin) is assimilated, as it were, to the aesthetic object and experience itself. Here there is no Diana or Apollo of Belvedere or Venus of Milo: here for one moment there is only Myshkin in a state of transfiguration. What is striking about his moment of beauty and prayer is its plastic, almost kinesthetic character: this is an experience of classical form itself. For a moment Myshkin is transformed from the chaotic raw material of his dark spiritual reality into a work of art. And as with all transfiguration of reality in art, all creation of beauty, Myshkin's highest moment is one of profound moral purity and truth. In Myshkin's moment of beauty, truth, and revelation—and only in this moment—Dostoevskii approaches his ideal of depicting in Myshkin a "positively beautiful man," a perfect, sculptured embodiment of the good, the

---

17 Ibid., 90.

true, and the beautiful. The "chief beauty" of Pushkin's "positively beautiful Russian types," Dostoevskii wrote later in his *Diary of a Writer*, "is in their truth, an unquestioned and tangible truth, so that it is impossible to deny them; they stand as sculptured."[18] [...]

At the center of Dostoevskii's Christian aesthetic—as it becomes more explicit in his notebooks and belles lettres in the last decade of his life—is the image of Christ: here there are no teachings, Dostoevskii insists, only occasional words; "the main thing is the image of Christ from which comes all teaching... From Christ comes the thought that the chief acquisition and goal of mankind is the result of achieved morality."[19] "The moral ideal is in Christ."[20] Yet again, "not Christ's morality, not his teaching will save the world, but precisely faith that the Word became flesh. This faith is not alone intellectual recognition of his teaching, but direct attraction. One must believe precisely that this is the final ideal of man, the whole embodied Word, God embodied."[21] If one does not believe that "the ideal was in flesh, then the ideal is impossible and cannot be attained by mankind." Christ came so that mankind might know that the human spirit can be in heavenly glory "in fact and in flesh, and not only in the dream and in the ideal."[22] "Beauty will save the world," Dostoevskii observed in the notebooks to *The Idiot*. "The world will become the beauty of Christ," we read in the notebooks to *Demons*.[23]

The idea of the inseparability of the ideal (beauty) from its incarnation (Christ) is an aesthetic one for Dostoevskii. The ideal exists in the abstract only in its *need*, but it is embodied in the creative work, in the "image of beauty" before which man reverentially bows. The "utility" of a work (its moral element) is inseparable from the aesthetic element, from beauty incarnate, from form. It is not the abstract idea or ideal of a beautiful life that inspires the Ridiculous Man, but the vision of the *living image*, the ideal in flesh. Myshkin's premonition of a higher life is a concrete aesthetic experience, a self-incarnation.

The aesthetic and religious elements merge in the *obraz*. Artistic and religious vision are ultimately one vision, reveal the same absolute reality. "The Holy Spirit," Dostoevskii observes in his notebook to *Demons*, "is the direct understanding of beauty, the prophetic cognition of harmony and,

---

18 "Pushkin (ocherk)," *Dnevnik pisatelia*, 13, 385.
19 Konshina, ed., *Zapisnye tetradi*, 292.
20 Ibid., 207.
21 Ibid., 221.
22 Ibid., 155.
23 Ibid., 222.

therefore, a constant striving for it."[24] In turn, the artist, creating an image of beauty, gives intimations of the divine ideal lying beyond man's earthly existence. Art in the deepest sense is, like the Holy Spirit, prophetic, the incarnation of the Word itself, a premonitory symbol of the beauty of a transfigured humanity [...]

The moral-aesthetic spectrum of Dostoevskii begins with *obraz*—image, the form and embodiment of beauty—and ends with *bezobrazie*—literally that which is "without image," shapeless, disfigured, ugly. Man finds pleasure (he also calls it beauty) in *bezobrazie*, in the disfiguration of himself and others, in cruelty, violence, and, above all, sensuality—and "sensuality is always violence." Aesthetically, *bezobrazie* is the deformation of ideal form (*obraz'*). The humanization of man is the creating of an image, the creating of form (the verb *obrazit*). God created man in His own image. All violence against man is a dehumanization—a deformation, finally, of the divine image. Zosima recalls how, as a young man, in a moment of "monstrous rage" (*svirepyi i bezobraznyi*), he struck his servant in the face, and he remembers how he then reproached himself for his act of violence against another being created, like himself, "in the image and likeness of God." The brutalization of men is at the center of *Notes from the House of the Dead*; the narrator of this work writes of the sensualists (akin, he notes, to the Marquis de Sade and Marquise de Brinvilliers) who obtain an aesthetic delight in flogging others, in inflicting the last degree of humiliation "upon another being bearing in himself the image of God." Such a sensualist is Lt. Zherebiatnikov who "passionately loved the art of execution and loved it solely for the art. He enjoyed it and, like some jaded Roman patrician of the Roman Empire, running out of pleasures, invented for himself various refinements, various unnatural variations, so as in some way to stimulate and pleasurably titillate his soul lapped in its fat."

In his profound despair over the brutalization of men, Ivan, symbolically, is prepared to discard Dostoevskii's vital distinction between *obraz* and *bezobrazie* in the definition of man; commenting upon man's bestial and supremely "artistic" cruelty to his fellowman, Ivan declares: "I think if the devil does not exist and, therefore, man created him, he created him in his own image." Here the dual nature of man vanishes, and the spiritual countenance of man (*obraz*) is replaced by the mask of moral *bezobrazie*. Ivan in his near-atheism posits the idea that man is created in the image of the devil.

---

24 Ibid., 296.

The desecration of the iconographic image, the icon, or the religious painting quite understandably is symbolic in Dostoevskii's Christian universe of the deepest crime against man's humanity—murder. Petr Verkhovenskii's desecration of the icon in *Demons* parallels on the symbolic plane the murder of Stavrogin's saintly wife. Stepan Verkhovenskii, outraged at those who would place a pair of boots above Shakespeare or Raphael, wishes to speak out at the literary quadrille against the "stinking and debauched lackey who first will mount the ladder with a pair of scissors in his hands and slash the divine countenance of the great ideal" (a reference to the Sistine Madonna which he reveres). Rogozhin's sensual *bezobrazie* ends up by his slashing Myshkin's "image of pure beauty"—the Madonna-like Nastas'ia Filippovna— with a knife. Fedor Karamazov lasciviously blabbers (in "Over the Brandy") about his favorite topic—women—and concludes with a description of how he once spat on his wife's iconographic image of the Madonna. "Now look, you think it's a wonder working [icon]," Fyodor exclaims to his wife at that time, "but here and now I'm going to spit on it in your presence, and nothing will happen to me because of it." The theme of Fedor Karamazov—desecration—finds its most dramatic completion in this symbolic violation of the Madonna. He pays for his defiling of the ideal in life and image, for his hubris, with his death.

Moral-sensual *bezobrazie*, as we have noted, is for Dostoevskii the central area in which man disfigures both himself and his ideal. The Ridiculous Man's corruption (through sensuality) of paradise with its beautiful forms and images is on the same plane as Stavrogin's rape of a young girl. In both cases "cruel sensuality" consists precisely in a disfiguration of the moral ideal (here innocent beauty)—the ideality of *obraz*. Ugliness disfigures, ugliness kills. After reading Stavrogin's "confession," Tikhon remarks that he finds something ridiculous in the "essence" as well as the "form" of the confession. "Ugliness will kill it," he whispers to Stavrogin. "Ugliness! What kind of ugliness?" asks Stavrogin. "Of the crime," answers Tikhon.[25]

The disfiguration of another is simultaneously a self-disfiguration—a loss of image, form, humanity. The body of Dmitrii hunches up into a deformed position when he utters the terrible words: "Why is such a man alive?" (Dostoevskii significantly titles the tumultuous episode in which these words are spoken: "A Monstrous Scene"—"Bezobraznaia stsena.") "Insane cruelty had long ago

---

25   F. M. Dostoevskii, *Ispoved' Stavrogina* (Munich: Orchis Verlag, 1922), 40.

distorted this divine soul," Dostoevskii writes of Pushkin's Cleopatra, "and already frequently had degraded her to the likeness of a beast."[26]

The Underground Man's violation, both morally and physically, of the compassionate Liza, is in the deepest sense a despairing act of self-mutilation, a deliberate defacing of his own cherished ideal out of a feeling of its unattainability, a conscious laceration of his own nature, his own image. Man's being, then, is crucified by the opposite strivings of his divided nature: his corporeal self, with its destructive, carnal drives, and his spiritual self, with its higher strivings. The pleasure man finds in *bezobrazie*, in the ideal of Sodom, coexists in lacerating contact with his higher ideal; at the same time, the striving for that higher ideal is itself an effort to sublimate the forces of sensuality. (Fedor Karamazov indirectly gives expression to this idea when he calls Father Zosima a "sensualist.") The drama of Dmitrii Karamazov, of course, provides the most vivid example of this ceaseless interplay of opposites in man's nature as Dostoevskii conceives it.

---

26 "Otvet russkomu vestniku," *Stat'i*, 13, 217.

Dostoevskii's
Fantastic Pages (2006)*

Vladimir Zakharov

In his monograph *Dostoyevsky after Bakhtin: Readings in Dostoyevsky's Fantastic Realism*, Malcolm Jones correctly notes, "I am not sure that Dostoyevsky ever actually used the expression "fantastic realism" but his statements about his style fully justify its use as a shorthand term."[1] In fact, in spite of the continued existence of this delusion, Dostoevskii did not call his realism "fantastic." At the same time, the epithet attracts many scholars, and this is not a coincidence.

"Fantastic" is a favorite word of Dostoevskii's. In some cases, it has a single meaning; in others, its meanings are multiple. It has a single meaning as a concept (a *poetic category*, or "form of art," in Dostoevskii's expression). It has multiple meanings in its role as an *attribute* (its basic meanings are *fictitious, imaginary, invented, far-fetched; illusory, imagined, groundless; improbable, unlikely, unthinkable, inconceivable, implausible, unusual, uncommon*, and so on). These synonyms are appreciably inferior to the epithet *fantastic* in the richness of the "internal form" of the word: they are limited, clear, they hold no semantic mystery, they are not so attractive. In any case the word *fantastic* is an adjective, formed from the noun *fantasy*, and it defines its presence in phenomena belonging exclusively to the fantasy of man, but not to reality itself.

Dostoevskii had an original conception of the fantastic and his own rules for the fantastic in art. The fantastic is an essential property of art, a "form of art,"

* From Vladimir Zakharov, "Dostoevsky's Fantastic Pages," trans. Sarah Young, *Dostoevsky on the Threshold of Other Worlds: Essays in Honour of Malcolm V. Jones* (Ilkeston, UK: Bramcote Press, 2006), 239, 242–46, 248–49, 250–53. Reprinted with permission of the author and translator.

1   Malcolm V. Jones, *Dostoyevsky after Bakhtin* (Cambridge: Cambridge University Press, 1990), 1.

"boundless fantasy," a fantastic work is a "purely poetic (the most poetic) work." His rule is that "the fantastic must be so closely connected to the real that you almost have to believe in it." In the fantastic man has contact with other worlds, the essence becomes the phenomenon [...]

In the preparatory materials for the novel *Demons*, there is a body of notes which Dostoevskii isolated thematically and called the "Fantastic pages."[2] Anna Grigor'evna Dostoevskaia understood their exceptional significance: indeed, it was these very notes that she chose for publication in the eighth volume of the anniversary edition of the complete collected works of 1906.

The "Fantastic pages" express the innermost thoughts of Dostoevskii. In them all the fundamental themes which constitute the essence of Dostoevskii's work are concentrated: his characters have conversations about the meaning of life and history, the past and the future, God and Christ, faith and unbelief, Truth and Russia, they argue about words and interpret the Gospels. Many of these words, phrases and episodes do not appear in the novel, but remain in the working notebooks. Dostoevskii was conscious of their intimate nature. They are what Katkov would not permit to be discussed in *The Russian Messenger*, and what the author would not risk discussing in *Demons*.

In these scenes the characters often do not argue, but discuss problems, persuade each other, develop alien ideas as their own. Persuading others, they persuade themselves. These are distinctive dialogues by Dostoevskii, in which the final characters of the heroes are not yet elucidated, and their roles are not determined, but which ask the most pressing eternal questions: What is to be done? Is faith possible? Wherein lies happiness?

In one dialogue a character tells another, "There are a huge number of such conversations going on in Russia" (33).

The "Fantastic pages" embody a particular element of the novelistic life of the heroes. From one scene:

Sh[atov]: What must I do?
Pr[ince]: Repent, build yourself up, build up the Kingdom of Christ. [...]
[...]
Sh[atov]: So we have to take monastic vows if it is so?
Pr[ince]: What for? Proclaim Christ on Russian soil, and proclaim yourself. Great feats of heroism are needed. Is it necessary to perform great feats? It is necessary to be great in order to go against common sense. [...]

---

2   The text of the "Fantastic pages" is cited from the MS: RGB. f. 93.1.1.4, 27–40, 124–25, 127–29.

> The prince. A great feat is needed. Let Russian strength show what it can do. With a great feat you will conquer the world.
> Shatov became strangely pensive: you know this is all simply fantasy, he said, also books or—or religious lunacy. Can you attract everyone to great feats?
> Pr[ince]: Why everyone. Do you know how powerful one man can be? Only one has to appear and everyone will follow. We need self-accusation and great feats, this idea is necessary, otherwise we won't find Orthodoxy and there will be nothing. (27)

From Stavrogin's lips a sermon is issued:

> Strength is in the moral idea. The moral idea is in Christ. In the West Christ has been perverted and exhausted. The kingdom of the Antichrist. We have the Orthodox faith. This means that we are the bearers of the clear understanding of Christ and of the new idea for the resurrection of the world. Do you believe in the eternal presence of Christ in the world? And in order to declare the Orthodox faith a great feat is needed. (27)

However, Stavrogin is not a prophet. In the notebooks to the novel he is still prepared to perform a heroic deed, he says that which in the novel will be preached by Shatov, who in the notebooks pronounces his doubt—in the novel he has no such instability in his opinions.

The "Fantastic pages" communicate the typical condition of the soul of Dostoevskii's heroes, combining unbelief and the need for faith [...]

In the "Fantastic pages" the heroes speak out about morality and Christianity, religion and science—themes that are inescapable in their plenitude. The characters not infrequently formulate their opinions in paradoxes.

> The prince goes to Sh[atov]. (For the first time after the slap in the face). I've not come about that. I noticed one of your ideas: An atheist cannot love Russia and Russian life—and I was surprised at it.
> Pr[ince]: You don't have to. I know myself that an atheist can't love Russia. It's my idea. I've never come across it anywhere else. And suddenly you say the same thing. I'd like to know what are you looking at more, Orthodoxy or Lutheranism. (127)

Or:

"Moral foundations are given by revelation. Just destroy something in faith and the moral foundation of Christianity will all come crashing down, for everything is connected." (28)

In the "Fantastic pages" the prince expounds an original economic theory:

There they petition for credit, for the restoration of the Credit ruble. A terrible question. And in fact they will not understand that there is only one cure: in the firm idea of national origin. They'd even laugh if it were explained to them. (28)

It is as if he were speaking today:

The majority of our capital is gained by conjuring tricks. It's pretty often no wonder to hear that the heirs have joined the gentry, given up work and gone into the hussars or squandered everything. It means that everything is a conjuring trick, to the extent that there is no understanding of how capital is formed. And that there cannot be large capital where there is no small capital, an enormous majority of small capital, in its rightful natural proportion to the large. Large capital exists only because there is small capital. The whole of credit and the whole fall of the ruble depends only on the stability of small capital. Without it not even conjuring tricks will be able to repair or restore anything. (127–28)

Dostoevskii expresses similar ideas in the January issue of *Diary of a Writer* for 1881, in which he wrote about finances: about the devaluation of the ruble, the deficit, debts to foreign creditors, about the crisis in agriculture and trade, "nobody's buying anything," "factories are reducing production to the minimum," "they've all got their eyes greedily fixed on the treasury and public funds." Dostoevskii's advice is paradoxical. He could hardly be called an expert in macroeconomics: "restore the roots"—and everything will settle down; restore the spirit—and the ruble will climb, the budget deficit will disappear, trade and production will improve.

In raising critical problems Dostoevskii's heroes courageously discuss the Scriptures. The prince formulates his understanding of Christianity:

> They all (Renan, Ge) take Christ for an ordinary man and criticize his teaching as bankrupt for our time. But there is no teaching there, only fortuitous words, and the main thing is the image of Christ, from which all the teaching comes forth. On the other hand, look at the vanity and moral condition of these critics. Well, can they criticize Christ? From Christ came the idea that the main gain and aim of humanity is the result of the morality that is acquired. Just imagine that all these Christs—well, would they be possible in today's instability, bewilderment. pauperism? Whoever doesn't understand that doesn't understand anything about Christ or Christianity. (124)

Truth is not afraid of tests, contradictions, trials of the idea. From the unbelief and doubt of the heroes grows faith or the need for faith [...]

These are the same fantastic pages in which are manifested the essence of "realism in a higher sense," but in the author's voice. There is no fantasy in them, but there is a conflict: for the author the fantastic is real, utopia is attainable, the ideal is vitally important; in received opinion, the sermon is fantastic, striving towards the ideal, towards Christ's commandment.

Dostoevskii entered world literature with a new word about the world and about man. This word is dialogic. It always takes into consideration the "alien word" of another and is oriented towards the reader. It is deprived of the authority of "omniscience" and does not exhaust the complexity, completeness and depth of phenomena. The author consciously articulates to himself the reader's right to "guess and ... make mistakes." Who among contemporary and living writers needs this right? What writer today would trust his cherished word to an unauthoritative hero? In Dostoevskii this is the privilege not only of the authoritative and clever, but also of the lowly and stupid. In his works a stupid person is in principle impossible (precisely a "stupid person" (*glupets*); I do not use the word "fool" (*durak*): in Russian fairy tales the fool is sometimes cleverer than the wise man, and the Russian fool always has his wits about him). Shakespeare trusted the wise knowledge of the world to jokes, but their lofty intellectual reputation was sanctified by the popular tradition of the Middle Ages. In Dostoevskii a different ethical situation arose; in his works a liar can speak and tell the truth, a "fool" can utter a wise word, a scoundrel can yearn for a conscience, a cynic for the ideal, a sinner for sanctity. Man in Dostoevskii is complex and profound. Dostoevskii has no little people, everyone is boundless and significant, everyone has his own Face. With other writers the hero is frequently less than the author, whereas Dostoevskii was able to reveal the greatness of the simple man. In his artistic world, the Word creates the world, man, and connects him to God. In his soul "all contradictions live together," "God is fighting with the devil," "the ideal of the Madonna" and "the ideal of Sodom" come together, but the Faces of his heroes all shine, as in Rembrandt portraits, from the "darkness" with the light of conscience, which is the harmony of man not only with people, but above all with Christ.

Dostoevskii's hero is sometimes unknown to himself, unpredictable not only for the reader, but also for the author. He always has his cherished "suddenly," the unexpected "about face" in opinions and actions, the "rebirth of convictions," the transformation of the personality. Dostoevskii's artistic anthropology is based on the Christian conception of man [. . .]

The definition *fantastic* gives a form of realism to Dostoevskii. It is most fully revealed in Malcolm Jones's book, in which the scholar comes closest of all to a solution to "realism in a higher sense." There remains only to find an adequate synonymous substitution for the word *fantastic*. In my opinion, that which many people call "fantastic realism" is in fact *Christian realism*.

It was not Dostoevskii who discovered this aesthetic principle of poetry and prose. It is present in the Gospels and appears in the living details of life. In it is uncovered not only historical reality, but also the mystical meaning of the events that are occurring, which are accomplished as it were before the eyes of the reader. This Gospel realism presents events in their fortuitous manifestation and their divine destiny. It is not afraid to show doubt in the Messiah, it gives sinners the possibility to become Christ's apostles. It is sufficient to remember how the Evangelists told the story of the birth, service, passion and resurrection of the Savior. Their story contains such incidental and unexpected details which would be superfluous in a fictitious work, but in the Good News they are the historical testimony of eyewitnesses.

As an aesthetic principle, Christian realism appeared long before the discovery of realism in the arts. It is manifested in the New Testament conception of the world, man, and the dual (human and divine) nature of the Messiah. It is inevitable in hagiography, in which first the hero, then the author of the life followed the aesthetic canon of the Gospels. It is expressed in the highest artistic achievements of Christian painting—in the canvases of the titans of the Renaissance (and how can we not recall here the wondrous effect on Dostoevskii of Raphael's Madonna), in Rembrandt's pictures of stories from the Gospels, in the Russian painter Alexandr Ivanov's picture *The Coming of the Messiah*.

The "Christian idea" is presented by Dostoevskii as "the fundamental idea of art of the nineteenth century," and is revealed by him in the introduction to the translation of Victor Hugo's novel *Notre Dame de Paris*: "This is a Christian and to the highest degree a moral idea; its formula is the renewal of the dead man, who has been crushed unjustly by the yoke of circumstances, centuries of stagnation, and social prejudice. This idea is a justification of the insulted and of the pariahs of society who have been rejected by everyone."[3] Of course, the sources of this idea lie in Dostoevskii's early work, beginning with translation of *Eugénie Grandet*, but it was revealed in all its fullness in the writer's post-exile works, from *Notes from the House of the Dead* and *The Insulted and Injured* onwards.

This "Christian idea" sheds true light on the meaning of "realism in a higher sense." On this subject Dostoevskii wrote in his final notebook:

> With full realism to find the man in man. This is a Russian trait for the most part and in that sense I am of course of the people (for my direction flows from the depths of the Christian spirit of the people)—although the Russian people of today do not know this, those to come will. They call me a psychologist: this is not true; I am only a realist in a higher sense. That is, I depict all the depths of the human soul.[4]

These words have been quoted by many, by almost all critics. They have been used to explain the humanistic spirit of Dostoevskii's work: "to find the man in man." They have been seen as a prophecy, like that uttered at the Pushkin memorial: "although the Russian people of today do not know this, those to come will." They have been used to investigate the writer's psychological approach: "They call me a psychologist: this is not true, I am only a realist in a higher sense, that is, I depict all the depths of the human soul." The range of opinions is wide, right up to Bakhtin's categorical disagreement: Dostoevskii is not a psychologist.[5] Various questions remain unanswered: what is "full" realism? Why is "finding the man in man" a "Russian trait for the most part"? Surely the same spirit of seeking "the man in man" inspired Balzac and

---

3   *Vremia*, 9, 1862, 44–45.

4   RGALI, f. 121.1.17, 29. First published in F. M Dostoevskii, *Polnoe sobranie sochinenii*, t. 1: *Biografiia, pis'ma i zapisnye tetradi* (St. Petersburg: Suvorina, 1883), 73 (second pagination).

5   M. M. Bakhtin, *Problemy poetiki Dostoevskogo* (Moscow: Sovetskaia Rossiia, 1979), 71.

Hugo, about whom Dostoevskii wrote, proclaiming the "restoration of man" as the fundamental idea of all art of the nineteenth century? Why is this "a Russian trait for the most part and in that sense I am of course of the people (for my direction flows from the depths of the Christian spirit of the people)"? What does the expression "realism in a higher sense" mean? What are the "depths of the human soul"—and what does "all" mean here? Why does Dostoevskii's direction "flow from the depths of the Christian spirit of the people?"

Dostoevskii was the first of those who in their work expressed the idea of Christian realism. His "realism in a higher sense" is realism in which *God is alive, the presence of Christ is visible, and the revelation of the Word is manifested.* Dostoevskii gave a new understanding of art as service to Christ, the meaning of which he saw in its apostolic vocation (the propagation of the Holy Spirit).

The route of Russian literature in its highest achievements of the last centuries is the route of finding with Russian realism the Truth, which is manifested by Christ and "became the Word." Fantastic and Christian are two epithets, two sides of the same coin, two images of Dostoevskii's "realism in a higher sense": the obverse flickers with the enigmatic word "fantastic," on the reverse we have the revelatory expression of its essence: *Christian.*

CHAPTER 4

Characters

O ver the last century and a half, the protagonists of Dostoevskii's novels have made their way to the forefront of the Western literary imagination; Raskol'nikov, Prince Myshkin, Stavrogin, and Ivan Karamazov find themselves in the company of Odysseus, Hamlet, Don Quixote, Eugene Onegin, and Jean Valjean. It has been a daunting task to organize and select materials for a chapter devoted to Dostoevskii's characters. We chose a range of critical works focusing on particular characters that also demonstrate a range of different approaches to understanding those characters on both formal and thematic levels. Narrowing down the suggested works on the list of further reading also proved challenging, and this list should be viewed as a very modest beginning.

This chapter consists of pieces of contemporary literary criticism, which analyze individual protagonists of Dostoevskii's novels. Some of the pieces are chosen for their departure from the well-worn interpretations of Dostoevskii's characters. In the first of the character analyses, Carol Apollonio reads *Poor Folk*'s Makar Devushkin against the grain, as a predatory seducer taking literary inspiration from his sentimentalist predecessors in his dogged pursuit of his sweetheart Varen'ka, rather than as the meek civil servant escaping his desk job into literary daydreams.

One of the most significant paradigm shifts in Dostoevskii scholarship in the twentieth century was Mikhail Bakhtin's analysis of Dostoevskii's reinvention of the relationship between author and hero. Paradigmatic amongst Dostoevskii's heroes for Bakhtin was the underground man: aware of the fact that he can perceive himself only through the eyes of others, the underground man nonetheless fiercely maintains his right to have the "final word" about himself, even when it goes directly against his best interests. Bakhtin analyzes the underground man's discourse, finding it filled not only with "the word with a sidewards glance," that is, the anticipation of an interlocutor's response, but also "the word with a loophole," the right to take back anything he has already said the very next moment. In his reading of *Crime and Punishment*, Konstantine Klioutchkine reverses the usual critical reading of Raskol'nikov as shaped by his environment and focuses instead on how Raskol'nikov recycles the novel's world out of his reading matter, the journals and newspapers of his day. Sarah J. Young discusses the polarities of Nastas'ia's Filippovna's character and her complex role in *The Idiot*, where she is both central to the novel's plot and character dynamics, while at the same time sidelined, subdued, and silenced.

Two of Dostoevskii's most enigmatic protagonists are apparent opposites, Prince Myshkin of *The Idiot* and Stavrogin of *Demons*. Both aristocrats, both located at the very center of the structure of the novels they inhabit, both are also strangely absent from those novels. Proceeding from the commonly held view of Myshkin as a Christlike figure who is ultimately destroyed, Liza Knapp proposes that Dostoevskii meant us to perceive Myshkin through many layers; she adapts St. Paul's metaphor, arguing that we see him "through a dark glass, guessingly." In his analysis of Stavrogin, Joseph Frank shows how the evolving characterization of *Demons'* enigmatic antihero reveals the novel's developing design, its transformation from a "pamphlet-novel" to a "novel-tragedy." With the help of the notebooks to the novel, Frank shows how the initial model of generational conflict between the Verkhovenskiis, the original core of Dostoevskii's antinihilist novel, was gradually displaced by the emergence of a character known as the "Prince," who later evolved into Stavrogin.

The final three contributions to the chapter deal with the Karamazov family. Deborah A. Martinsen proceeds from the fact that Fedor Karamazov is characterized in the novel four separate times as an Aesop, examining him as a homegrown version of the legendary Greek storyteller. She analyzes his play with language and use of puns as verbal aggression designed to humiliate his interlocutors, but also to display his own shame and humiliation and to displace the novel's system of law and judgment. Harriet Murav reads *Brothers Karamazov* as a narrative icon, in which the stories of the brothers mirror the structure of the novel itself, and which contains katabasis, or the descent into hell, trial, and resurrection. Ivan plays a crucial role in this reading, becoming the source of the demonic history which counterbalances the sacred history figured in Zosima and in Alesha's final ascent at the end of the novel. Finally, Valentina Vetlovskaia shows how Dostoevskii characterizes Alesha within the terms of hagiography, creating parallels with the vita of a well-known saint, Aleksei the Man of God.

Further Reading

Apollonio, Carol. *Dostoevsky's Secrets: Reading against the Grain*. Evanston, IL: Northwestern University Press, 2009.

Cox, Gary. *Tyrant and Victim in Dostoevsky*. Ann Arbor, MI: Slavica, 1984.

Corrigan, Yuri. *Dostoevsky and the Riddle of the Self*. Evanston, IL: Northwestern University Press, 2017.

Dalton, Elizabeth. *Unconscious Structure in* The Idiot: *A Study in Literature and Psychoanalysis*. Princeton, NJ: Princeton University Press, 1979.

Martinsen, Deborah A. *Surprised by Shame: Dostoevsky's Liars and Narrative Exposure*. Columbus: Ohio State University Press, 2003.

Matzner-Gore, Greta. "Kicking Maksimov out of the Carriage: Minor Characters, Exclusion, and *The Brothers Karamazov*." *Slavic and East European Journal* 58, no. 3 ("Mini-Forum: Money and Minor Characters: Dostoevsky's *The Double* and *The Brothers Karamazov*") (Fall 2014): 419–36.

Naiman, Eric. "Kalganov." *Slavic and East European Journal* 58, no. 3 ("Mini-Forum: Money and Minor Characters: Dostoevsky's *The Double* and *The Brothers Karamazov*") (Fall 2014): 394–418.

Young, Sarah J. *Dostoevskii's* The Idiot *and the Ethical Foundations of Narrative. Reading, Narrating, Scripting*. London: Anthem Press, 2004.

Makar Devushkin (2009)*

Carol Apollonio

D ostoevskii enjoyed one of the most remarkable debuts in literary history when Russia's foremost literary critic, Vissarion Belinskii, welcomed the unknown writer's *Poor Folk* (*Bednye liudi,* 1846) as the long-awaited first Russian "social novel."[1] To this day, *Poor Folk* sustains reading as social criticism. Still, the most enduring feature of Dostoevskii's first novel is its "literariness." *Poor Folk* is saturated with influences from the Russian "natural school" and its western European predecessors, Pushkin's experiments with narrative fiction, the sentimental tradition in its native and foreign epistolary variants, and a more remote ancestor, the twelfth-century *Letters of Abelard and Heloise.*[2] Through a complex, layered parody of these earlier works, Dostoevskii's novel calls into question basic assumptions about the ethical and moral implications of reading and writing. Though highly derivative, *Poor Folk* is at the same time strikingly original. Already in this first published work the author sows the seeds of the unique tragic vision that will ripen in the late, great novels.

---

* Extracts from Carol Apollonio, *Dostoevsky's Secrets: Reading Against the Grain* (Evanston, IL: Northwestern University Press, 2009) 13–17, 23–26. Copyright © 2009 by Northwestern University Press. Published 2009. All rights reserved. The text is reproduced here with minor modifications: some footnotes have been removed.
1 See P. V. Annenkov, *The Extraordinary Decade,* trans. Irwin R. Titunik (Ann Arbor: University of Michigan Press, 1968), 150.
2 See V. V. Vinogradov's definitive study of the Russian literary background of *Poor Folk*: V. V. Vinogradov, "Shkola sentimentalnogo naturalizma (Roman Dostoevskogo 'Bednye liudi' na fone literaturnoi evoliutsii 40–kh godov)," in *Evoliutsiia russkogo naturalizma: Gogol' i Dostoevskii* (Leningrad: Akademiia, 1929), 291–389. Victor Terras's *The Young Dostoevsky* remains the most thorough English-language study of the broader literary traditions influencing the novel: see Victor Terras, *The Young Dostoevskii (1846–1849): A Critical Study* (The Hague and Paris: Mouton, 1969).

It is appropriate that literariness should be so central to the novel, for *Poor Folk* tells the story of Dostoevskii's own path to authorship. In a meticulous analysis, I. D. Iakubovich establishes a direct and convincing association between the dates and contents of the fictional letters in *Poor Folk* and specific events and experiences in the author's life. Iakubovich concludes that the novel is in part a disguised diary tracing the transformation of the young military engineer into a writer.[3] In this first novel, as in the later works, self-consciousness is bound up with an attraction to the printed word. While recognizing the autobiographical tensions, we should nevertheless avoid easy "indicative" readings. What the author creates is greater than what he is, "detached from the imperfect lie that produced it."[4]

Apophatic reading presumes a mismatch between words and truth. What characters say and write about themselves, on the one hand, and what they are and do, on the other, differ. Dostoevskii's message emerges from the tensions in this gap between word and world on the many levels of the text—the words of the two correspondents, their actions (stated and implied), the reactions of those around them, and the complex echoes of literary tradition. These discrepancies betray the author's own ambivalence as to the message and function of artistic literature.

Let us, then, consider Makar Devushkin. A middle-aged, low-level civil servant, a bachelor, Makar befriends Varvara Dobroselova (Varen'ka), a young lady with a tainted reputation. Although many of the best studies of *Poor Folk* have focused on Makar Devushkin, the depths and full implications of his character remain unexplored.[5] He is an extraordinarily complex figure, composed of ingredients from the sentimental lover of eighteenth-century epistolary fiction, the poor clerk of the Russian "natural school" (most notably, Gogol''s Akakii Akakievich from "The Overcoat" [1841]), the self-sacrificing and deeply caring father figure of Pushkin's "Stationmaster" from *Tales of Belkin* (1830), Balzac's *Le Père Goriot* (1835), and others. But Makar Devushkin also has a dark side that prefigures the most complex and sinister figures of Dostoevskii's later fiction [...]

Taking my cue from these new, skeptical lines of thought, I will explore the implications of a "dark" reading of Devushkin—focusing on him as

---

3 I. D. Iakubovich, "Dostoevskii v rabote nad romanom 'Bednye liudi,'" *Dostoevskii: Materialy i issledovaniia* 9 (1991): 50.

4 Thomas Nagel, "How to Be Free and Happy," review of *Bertrand Russell: The Ghost of Madness, 1921–1970*, by Ray Monk, *New Republic*, May 7, 2001: 31.

5 See Gary Rosenshield, "Varen'ka Dobroselova: An Experiment in the Desentimentalization of the Sentimental Heroine in Dostoevskii's *Poor Folk*," *Slavic Review* 45, no. 3 (Fall 1986): 525.

would-be seducer—in the context of Dostoevskii's artistic vision. Varen'ka is indeed besieged by both predatory males, as Andrew suggests, but Bykov and Devushkin represent fundamentally different, and mutually exclusive, values. The climax of the plot—Varen'ka's decision to marry Bykov—represents a renunciation of the dangers and temptations of literature personified in Devushkin. Dostoevskii conveys this message through a parody of sentimental novels, in the process endowing his heroine with a hidden power of her own. My analysis will radically readjust the hierarchies of moral virtue that have been accepted in nearly all critical readings of the novel [...]

Twice in his first letter Devushkin's figurative language betrays conflicting motives. The protector is a bird of prey, deflecting his desire for power into metaphoric expression: "I got up this morning all bright and bushy-tailed" (*iasnym sokolom*, "like a fine falcon"); "Why am I not a bird, a predatory bird?" (1:14). For socially minded critics, the metaphor of the bird of prey—taken from a poem by the Ukrainian poet M. P. Petrenko—represents Devushkin's incipient impulse toward rebellion against a repressive political system—a system that tolerates poverty. Yet at the same time it expresses a predatory urge against defenseless Varen'ka. Devushkin's letter to his "little dove" (*golubchik*) of August 4 reinforces this impression: "If I don't help you, it'll be the death of me, Varen'ka, my death, pure and simple, but if I do, then you will fly away from me, like a little bird from the nest that these owls, these predatory birds, are about to peck to pieces" (PSS 1:73). Devushkin expresses his desire to save Varen'ka, but the fact is, his love for her, bound up as it is in this correspondence, depends on her remaining in danger. Although Devushkin is powerless to act because he sublimates his impulses into literary expression, he represents both protective and predatory urges. The urge to protect is inseparable from the desire to ravish, and *both* are linked to the urge to rebel against the existing order.

As it establishes the premise for the correspondence between Varen'ka and Devushkin, this first letter introduces an erotic tension that will be sustained throughout the novel. The act of writing exposes guilty secrets— illicit sexual desire, thoughts of rebellion. The relevance of the concept of privacy—and the attendant need to guard secrets—in the rise of the Western novel, is well established in the critical tradition.[6] Much of Western literature after Rousseau's *Confessions* builds on the tension between the felt need to keep secrets and a contrasting desire to tell the truth. The novel, particularly the epistolary genre as

---

6 See Ian Watt, *The Rise of the Novel* (Berkeley and Los Angeles: University of California Press, 1957).

it develops in the eighteenth century, "invad[es] the private sphere by opening it up to the irrevocable publicity of writing."[7] Inevitably, literature will turn its attention to the secrets of sexual life, with the narrators serving as voyeurs [...]

The central hero of Dostoevskii's epistolary romance, though, is Makar Devushkin. When Makar's infatuation for Varen'ka is revealed, his gossiping neighbor, the writer Ratiaziaev, calls him "Lovelace," referring, in a shorthand comprehensible to every literate Russian of the time, to the ruthless seducer in another of Samuel Richardson's novels, the notorious *Clarissa* (1748–59). Here Richardson's sentimental heroine dies rather than live in dishonor. In Joseph Frank's interpretation of this reference, Dostoevskii juxtaposes his poor clerk to the English libertine in order to throw into relief "the moral preeminence of the humble clerk over the brilliant but selfish and destructive aristocrat."[8] My reading allows us to take the reference at face value. In other words, Devushkin is indeed a Lovelace [...]

Accepting the comparison to Lovelace encourages us to consider Devushkin from a more critical perspective than is usual. Look at his *actions*:

1. Influenced, perhaps, by an awareness of the seductive effects of sentimental literature on the morals of young girls, he gives Varen'ka books of dubious moral quality and copies out erotic passages for her to read. Having read Varen'ka's journal account documenting the powerful aphrodisiac effect of Pokrovskii's books, Devushkin cannot plead innocence from immoral intent (letter of June 26).

2. He wastes his money on frivolous gifts for her, causing her to feel guilty and indebted to him. Giving her candy, he tells her to eat it while she reads (romantic—and presumably erotic—novels), to suck it, rather than chew it, and to think of him as she does so (also letter of June 26).

3. When Varen'ka receives an offer of honest employment as a governess, he frantically persuades her not to accept it, in effect denying her an honorable means of extracting herself from her predicament. This, by the way, is doubly significant, given its parallel to young Pokrovskii's idiosyncratic refusal to take honest employment as a teacher—which dooms him to poverty and, we assume, death (letter of June 28).

---

7 Peter Brooks, *Body Work: Objects of Desire in Modern Narrative* (Cambridge, MA, and London: Harvard University Press, 1993), 32.

8 Joseph Frank, *Dostoevsky: The Seeds of Revolt, 1821–1849* (Princeton, NJ: Princeton University Press, 1976), 150.

4. Devushkin threatens to throw himself into the Neva if Varen'ka leaves him, and cruelly manipulates her most cherished memories by planting the image of his body in the coffin in her memory of Pokrovskii's funeral—anything to make her stay with him. Here again, the tenuous nature of Devushkin's clothing, with all the attendant implications of shame and guilty desire, is linked to his attempts to get closer to Varen'ka. To save her from having to accept the job offer, he will go out indecently dressed: "Go out into the world [*v liudi idti*]? Never! No, no, and no! And what can you be thinking, what has come over you? And to move out of the city too. No, little mother, I won't allow it, I'll muster all my forces against such an intention. I'll sell my old jacket and go out into the streets with just my shirt on, rather than let you want for anything" (PSS 1:56). Devushkin's way of referring to her proposed employment for which she must "go out into the world," literally to "go out among people," is enormously significant, given his isolation from the community of his fellow men (letters of June 28 and July 1).

5. He goes on a wild drunken binge, during which his attempts to confront one of Varen'ka's "suitors," an officer, draw attention to her plight and incriminate her further by implying that he himself has a romantic relationship with her (letter of July 27).

6. By carelessly allowing a draft of one of his letters to her to drop from his pocket and subsequently be read out loud at one of Ratiaziaev's gatherings, Devushkin reveals his secret passion to those around him. By betraying his secret, Devushkin compounds her dishonor (letter of August 11). She makes this clear herself: "You still don't know what I endure because of you! I can't even use the stairs without everyone looking at me, pointing their fingers, and saying such terrible things; yes, they say it right out loud, *She's taken up with a drunkard*" (PSS 1:80).

Devushkin's words are full of tender feeling, but his actions serve to prolong Varen'ka's misery and plunge her into ever greater danger. Thus, when Bykov proposes to her at the end, readers might very well rejoice at her good fortune, rather than condemn her for making a choice that to our romantic imagination seems based on cold calculation. By choosing to marry Bykov, she commits herself to a physical and sexual life *outside* literature. Her correspondence with Makar Devushkin cannot continue, since her choice necessitates a renunciation of the sentimental ideals that nourished their letters. She must leave this, and all books, behind. Although this is not the place to argue the feminist implications of the end of *Poor Folk*, Varen'ka's choice would seem to exemplify the Lacanian suggestion that "woman cannot enter the world of the symbolic, of language."[9] Tellingly, Varen'ka sees her decision as a submission to God's will: "God knows whether I will be happy; my destiny is in his holy, inscrutable power, but I have made my decision. What will be, will be, whatever God sends my way!" (PSS 1:101). For his part, Devushkin, representing intangible values and ideals, is left behind in a nonmaterial world, the world of writing and books. It is not surprising that readers, themselves seduced by the excitement and danger of a romantic plot, have refused to notice this stark truth.

This allegorical interpretation of *Poor Folk* leaves us with a curiously ambivalent attitude toward literary values. Makar Devushkin, professing tender, selfless concern for a girl in distress, turns out to be a dangerous predator who almost succeeds in ruining her—a direct descendant of Lovelace, whose interaction with Clarissa leads to her death. We are reminded again of the epigraph's warning about the dangers of writing. What seemed to be positive virtues in Devushkin—modesty and self-effacement—are exposed as the attempts of a predatory figure to conceal his true nature from his victim. The landlady's assertion, referring to Devushkin's relationship with Varen'ka, that "the devil has taken up with an infant" (PSS 1:70), no longer seems a mere figure of speech.

---

9 Joe Andrew, "The Seduction of the Daughter: Sexuality in the Early Dostoevsky and the Case of *Bednye liudi [Poor Folk]*," *Neo-Formalist Papers*, ed. Joe Andrew and Robert Reid (Amsterdam and Atlanta: Rodopi, 1998), 180.

Underground Man (1963)*

There is literally nothing we can say about the hero of "Notes from Underground" that he does not already know himself: his typicality for his time and social group, the sober psychological or even psychopathological delineation of his internal profile, the category of character to which his consciousness belongs, his comic as well as his tragic side, all possible moral definitions of his personality, and so on—all of this, in keeping with Dostoevskii's design, the hero knows perfectly well himself, and he stubbornly and agonizingly soaks up all these definitions from within. Any point of view from without is rendered powerless in advance and denied the finalizing word.

Because the dominant of representation in this literary work coincides maximally with the dominant of that which is represented, the formal task of the author can be very clearly expressed in the content. What Underground Man thinks about most of all is what others think or might think about him; he tries to keep one step ahead of every other consciousness, every other thought about him, every other point of view on him. At all the critical moments of his confession he tries to anticipate the possible definition or evaluation others might make of him, to guess the sense and tone of that evaluation, and tries painstakingly to formulate these possible words about himself by others, interrupting his own speech with the imagined rejoinders of others.

"Isn't that shameful, isn't that humiliating?" you will say, perhaps, shaking your heads contemptuously. "You long for life and try to settle the

---

* Extracts from Mikhail Bakhtin, *Problems of Dostoevsky's Poetics*, ed. and trans. Caryl Emerson (Minneapolis and London: University of Minnesota Press, 1984), 52–53, 227–34. Copyright © 1984 by the University of Minnesota. All rights reserved.

problems of life by a logical tangle ... You may be truthful in what you have said but you have no modesty; out of the pettiest vanity you bring your truth to public exposure, to the market place, to ignominy. You doubtlessly mean to say something, but hide your real meaning for fear, because you lack the resolution to say it, and only have a cowardly impudence. You boast of consciousness, but you are unsure of your ground, for though your mind works, yet your heart is corrupted by depravity, and you cannot have a full, genuine consciousness without a pure heart. And how tiresome you are, how you thrust yourself on people and grimace! Lies, lies, lies!"

Of course I myself have made up just now all the things you say. That, too, is from underground. *For forty years I have been listening to your words there through a crack under the floor. I have invented them myself. After all, there was nothing else I could invent.* It is no wonder that I have learned them by heart and that it has taken a literary form. [*SS* IV, 164–65; "Notes from Underground," Part One, XI]

The hero from the underground eavesdrops on every word someone else says about him, he looks at himself, as it were, in all the mirrors of other people's consciousnesses, he knows all the possible refractions of his image in those mirrors. And he also knows his own objective definition, neutral both to the other's consciousness and to his own self-consciousness, and he takes into account the point of view of a "third person." But he also knows that all these definitions, prejudiced as well as objective, rest in his hands and he cannot finalize them precisely because he himself perceives them; he can go beyond their limits and can thus make them inadequate. He knows that he has the final word, and he seeks at whatever cost to retain for himself this final word about himself, the word of his self-consciousness, in order to become in it that which he is not. His consciousness of self lives by its unfinalizability, by its unclosedness and its indeterminancy [...]

"Notes from Underground" is a confessional *Ich-Erzählung.*[1] Originally the work was entitled "A Confession."[2] And it is in fact an authentic confession. Of course, "confession" is understood here not in the personal sense. The author's intention is refracted here, as in any *Ich-Erzählung*; this is not a personal document but a work of art.

---

1   First-person narration.
2   "Notes from Underground" was originally announced by Dostoevskii under this title in *Time*.

In the confession of Underground Man what strikes us first of all is its extreme and acute dialogization: there is literally not a single monologically firm, undissociated word. From the very first sentence the hero's speech has already begun to cringe and break under the influence of the anticipated words of another, with whom the hero, from the very first step, enters into the most intense internal polemic. "I am a sick man . . . I am a spiteful man. I am an unpleasant man." Thus begins the confession. The ellipsis and the abrupt change of tone after it are significant. The hero began in a somewhat plaintive tone "I am a sick man," but was immediately enraged by that tone: it looked as if he were complaining and needed sympathy, as if he were seeking that sympathy in another person, as if he needed another person! And then there occurs an abrupt dialogic turnaround, one of those typical breaks in accent so characteristic of the whole style of the "Notes," as if the hero wants to say: You, perhaps, were led to believe from my first word that I am seeking your sympathy, so take this: I am a spiteful man. I am an unpleasant man!

Characteristic here is a gradual increase in negative tone (to spite the other) under the influence of the other's anticipated reaction. Such breaks in accent always lead to an accumulation of ever-intensifying abusive words or words that are, in any case, unflattering to the other person, as in this example:

> To live longer than forty years is bad manners; it is vulgar, immoral. Who does live beyond forty? Answer that, sincerely and honestly. I will tell you who: fools and worthless people do. I tell all old men that to their face, all those respectable old men, all those silver-haired and reverend old men! I tell the whole world that to its face. I have a right to say so, for I'll go on living to sixty myself. I'll live till seventy! Till eighty! Wait, let me catch my breath. [SS IV, 135; "Notes" Part One 1]

In the opening words of the confession, this internal polemic with the other is concealed. But the other's words are present invisibly, determining the style of speech from within. Midway into the first paragraph, however, the polemic has already broken out into the open: the anticipated response of the other takes root in the narration, although, to be sure, still in a weakened form. "No, I refuse to treat it out of spite. You probably will not understand that. Well, but *I* understand it." [. . .]

Thus the entire style of the "Notes" is subject to the most powerful and all-determining influence of other people's words, which either act on speech covertly from within as in the beginning of the work, or which, as the anticipated response of another person, take root in the very fabric of speech, as in those above-quoted ending passages. The work does not contain a single word gravitating exclusively toward itself and its referential object; that is, there is not a single monologic word. We shall see that this intense relationship to another's consciousness in the Underground Man is complicated by an equally intense relationship to his own self. But first we shall make a brief structural analysis of this act of anticipating another's response.

Such anticipation is marked by one peculiar structural trait: it tends toward a vicious circle. The tendency of these anticipations can be reduced to a necessity to retain for oneself the final word. This final word must express the hero's full independence from the views and words of the other person, his complete indifference to the other's opinion and the other's evaluation. What he fears most of all is that people might think he is repenting before someone, that he is asking someone's forgiveness, that he is reconciling himself to someone else's judgment or evaluation, that his self-affirmation is somehow in need of affirmation and recognition by another. And it is in this direction that he anticipates the other's response. But precisely in this act of anticipating the other's response and in responding to it he again demonstrates to the other (and to himself) his own dependence on this other. He *fears* that the other might think he *fears* that other's opinion. But through this fear he immediately demonstrates his own dependence on the other's consciousness, his own inability to be at peace with his own definition of self. With his refutation, he confirms precisely what he wishes to refute, and he knows it. Hence the inescapable circle in which the hero's self-consciousness and discourse are trapped: "Well, are you not imagining, gentlemen, that I am repenting for something now? . . . I am sure you are imagining that. However, I assure you it does not matter to me if you are . . ." [. . .]

As a result of Underground Man's attitude toward the other's consciousness and its discourse—extraordinary dependence upon it and at the same time extreme hostility toward it and nonacceptance of its judgments—his narration takes on one highly essential artistic characteristic. This is a deliberate clumsiness of style, albeit subject to a certain artistic logic. His discourse does not flaunt itself and cannot flaunt itself, for there is no one before whom it can flaunt. It does not, after all, gravitate naively toward itself and its referential object. It is addressed to another person and to the speaker himself (in his internal dialogue with himself). And in both of these directions it wants least of all to flaunt itself and be "artistic" in the usual sense of the word. In its attitude toward the other person it strives to be deliberately inelegant, to "spite" him and his tastes in all respects. But this discourse takes the same position even

in regard to the speaker himself, for one's attitude toward oneself is insepara-
bly interwoven with one's attitude toward another. Thus discourse is pointedly
cynical, calculatedly cynical, yet also anguished. It strives to play the holy fool,
for holy-foolishness is indeed a sort of form, a sort of aestheticism—but, as it
were, in reverse [. . .]

But the underground hero's word about himself is not only a word with a
sideward glance; it is also, as we have said, a word with a loophole. The influence
of the loophole on the style of his confession is so great that his style cannot
be understood without a consideration of its formal activity. The word with
a loophole has enormous significance in Dostoevskii's works in general, especially in the later works. And here we pass on to another aspect of the structure
of "Notes from Underground": the hero's attitude toward his own self, which
throughout the course of the entire work is interwoven and combined with his
dialogue with another.

What, then, is this loophole of consciousness and of the word?

A loophole is the retention for oneself of the possibility for altering the
ultimate, final meaning of one's own words. If a word retains such a loophole
this must inevitably be reflected in its structure. This potential other meaning,
that is, the loophole left open, accompanies the word like a shadow. Judged by
its meaning alone, the word with a loophole should be an ultimate word and
does present itself as such, but in fact it is only the penultimate word and places
after itself only a conditional, not a final, period.

For example, the confessional self-definition with a loophole (the most
widespread form in Dostoevskii) is, judging by its meaning, an ultimate word
about oneself, a final definition of oneself, but in fact it is forever taking into
account internally the responsive, contrary evaluation of oneself made by
another. The hero who repents and condemns himself actually wants only to
provoke praise and acceptance by another. Condemning himself, he wants and
demands that the other person dispute this self-definition, and he leaves himself a loophole in case the other person should suddenly in fact agree with him,
with his self-condemnation, and not make use of his privilege as the other.

Here is how the hero from the underground tells of his "literary" dreams:

> I, for instance, was triumphant over everyone; everyone, of course, lay in
> the dust and was *forced* to recognize my superiority *spontaneously*, and I
> forgave them all. I, a famous poet, and a courtier, fell in love; I inherited
> countless millions and immediately devoted them to humanity, and *at the
> same time I confessed before all the people my shameful deeds, which, of course,*

were not merely shameful, but contained an enormous amount of "the sublime and the beautiful," something in the Manfred style. Everyone would weep and kiss me (what idiots they would be if they did not), while I would go bare-foot and hungry preaching new ideas and fighting a victorious Austerlitz against the reactionaries. [*SS* IV, 181; "Notes," Part Two, ch. II]

Here he ironically relates dreams of heroic deeds with a loophole, dreams of confession with a loophole. He casts a parodic light on these dreams. But his very next words betray the fact that his repentant confession of his dreams has its own loophole, too, and that he himself is prepared to find in these dreams and in his very confessing of them something, if not in the Manfred style, then at least in the realm of "the sublime and the beautiful," if anyone should happen to agree with him that the dreams are indeed base and vulgar: "You will say that it is vulgar and base to drag all this into public after all the tears and raptures I have myself admitted. But why is it base? Can you imagine that I am ashamed of it all, and that it was stupider than anything in your life, gentlemen? And I can assure you that some of these fancies were by no means badly composed . . ."

And this passage, already cited by us above, is caught up in the vicious circle of self-consciousness with a sideward glance.

The loophole creates a special type of fictive ultimate word about oneself with an unclosed tone to it, obtrusively peering into the other's eyes and demanding from the other a sincere refutation. We shall see that the word with a loophole achieves especially sharp expression in Ippolit's confession, but it is to one degree or another inherent in all the confessional self-utterances of Dostoevskii's heroes. The loophole makes all the heroes' self-definitions unstable, the word in them has no hard and fast meaning, and at any moment, like a chameleon, it is ready to change its tone and its ultimate meaning.

Raskol'nikov (2002)*

Konstantine Klioutchkine

Critical literature on the novel commonly suggests that the setting of *Crime and Punishment* is crucial to Raskol'nikov's psychological makeup. It is important, however, to recognize the reverse dynamic: Raskol'nikov, whose operation is modeled on that of authors and narrators from the popular press, is responsible for the production of the novel's world. His influence on this world is generic rather than psychological. By way of Raskol'nikov as a quasi-author, popular writing endows the novel with generic organization. The character's authorial function is evident in an early draft of the novel where he narrates his own story. When Dostoevskii adjusted the narrative perspective, he made a note to himself: "The story is to come from the author, but he should not leave the character for a single minute."[1] The narrator's attachment to the character is crucial because the text advances along with Raskol'nikov's circuitous peregrinations. The nature of his wanderings finds reflection in a series of correspondences between a passage from the beginning of *Crime and Punishment* and the opening of the essay *The Lost but Affable Creature* (1862) by A. Levitov (a dropout from the St. Petersburg Medico-Surgical Academy).

Dostoevskii

The street bustling with people seemed frightfully hot and stuffy [. . .] with that special summer stench so familiar to Petersburgers . . . All this shook the already high-strung nerves of the young man [. . .] Drunks,

---

* Extracts from Konstantine Klioutchkine, "The Rise of *Crime and Punishment* from the Air of the Media," *Slavic Review* 61, no. 1 (Spring 2002): 101–6. Permission to reprint was granted by the American Association for the Advancement of Slavic Studies. The text is reproduced here with minor modifications: some footnotes have been removed.

1 PSS, 7:146.

constantly crossing his path, completed the picture ... Profound disgust
flashed on his sensitive features.

Levitov

You walk down a crowded street and see that its every point boils with life,
which, as every flaneur-observer knows, makes the provincials stop and
gape at the bustle ... All the time, odd people cross your path ...

People's speech and horses' trampling stun your ears so much that you
feel sick and angry.[2]

    In reproducing "familiar life," both narrators figure as experienced observ-
ers walking about the city and bringing their observations to experienced
readers. Their movement was associated with "flaneurism" common to feuilletonists, who wandered about the city and relayed what they saw and heard in
the street. In *Crime and Punishment*, Raskol'nikov walks, hears, speaks, and, as
it were, carries the observing and recording narrator on his back.

    Both opening passages depict the protagonist's shock at finding himself in
the street. This staging functions to charge Levitov's narrator and Dostoevskii's
character-narrator hybrid with generative energy: narratorial excitement powers
text production. This device was part of a strategy identified by Literary Medium
("Literaturnyi Medium," the pen name of a feuilletonist at *Peterburgskii listok*),
who wrote: "the litterateur artificially excites himself in order to suit the public
and make a buck by bringing to it his pseudo-literary product." Medium also
observed that writers who used such devices "shone at the beginning of their
careers but were headed for a sad conclusion at Sennaia Square."[3] The various
symbolic implications of this statement do not detract from its striking literal
accuracy. Raskol'nikov, of course, begins with an article for *Periodical Speech*[4]
and ends up at the Sennaia in more ways than one; Levitov's narrator heads for
a similar area in Moscow. So do scores of other fictional characters and narrators
in, as well as writers of, physiological sketches and feuilletons.

    These characters, narrators, and writers circulated in the press, verbalizing
trajectories through city streets, squares, markets, bars, clubs, and residential
hotels. By reiterating common descriptions of these locales, journalists and literati
navigated less the space of the city than the space of print. This dynamic is evident
in Raskol'nikov's peregrinations as he wanders in the space of the newspaper as

---

2 Ibid., 6:6. A. I. Levitov, *Izbrannye proizvedeniia* (Moscow: Khudozhestvennaia literatura
    1988), 84. Levitov used the title of Krestovskii's story verbatim.

3 "Zametki Literaturnogo Mediuma," *Peterburgskii listok*, 166 (1865).

4 Dostoevskii, PSS, 6:198.

much as in that of the city. His ear is constantly open to the noise of the street, but what he hears predictably comes from the press. At the beginning of the novel, a coachman, another street navigator, calls him a "German hat-maker," referring to his Zimmerman hat.[5] Zimmerman advertised his brand in newspapers, and the hat occasioned discussion by at least one narrator-character who was similar to Raskol'nikov.[6] In a pool and beer parlor, Raskol'nikov overhears a conversation about the implications of killing a useless person for money, which reminds him of conversations he has come across on many previous occasions—extending at least as far as Balzac's *Father Goriot*.[7] At the police department, he hears a story about a feuilletonist who has debauched a bordello: journalists' scandalous behavior was another common newspaper topic.[8] In each of these moments, Raskol'nikov operates, not as a character subject to the influences of the milieu, but as a product of the press, whose movement through the fictional topography of the city generates the text by actualizing what was in the media "air."

Raskol'nikov's function as a text producer in the novel accounts for a kind of self-referential world that was an extension of the media environment. This world is defined by the "hot and suffocating air" dominating the novel. The implications of the air theme, apparent to the reader of the time, were made explicit in the opening passage from a feuilleton:

> *Summer Heat and Literary Suffocation—Imaginary Theory—The Need for Fresh Air*
>
> Petersburg summers are always suffocating, but people condemned to the studious reading of books, newspapers, and journals are especially stifled . . . They are engulfed by an ocean of empty speech, banality, falsehood, and meaningless phrases.[9]

The "hot air" of *Crime and Punishment* is not just a realistic detail and is much more than the isolated symbol of "moral suffocation" commonly discussed in the press of the time. Rather, it is the environment that pervaded the novel as a result of Raskol'nikov's operation as a media man. The characters of

---

5 Dostoevskii, PSS, 6:7 (*nemetskii shliapnik*).
6 "When the rain falls not on a Zimmerman hat but on an oil-cloth cap, left over, so to speak, from the summer season." Levitov, "Krym," in *Izbrannye proizvedeniia*, 168.
7 Dostoevskii, PSS, 6:55. Honoré de Balzac, *Le Père Goriot* (Paris: Société d'éditions littéraires et artistiques, 1900), 168–69.
8 Ibid., 6:79.
9 "Smes': Nashi domashnie dela," *Vremia*, 4, pt. 2 (1861):13.

the novel are placed not only in the hot summer of 1865 but also in the stifling milieu of repetitive and nonreferential speech proliferating in the press. This milieu duplicates Svidrigailov's appeal "one needs air, air, air!" later reproduced in Raskol'nikov's conversations with Porfirii and Razumikhin.[10]

The meaning of Svidrigailov's appeal is explained in N. Akhsharumov's novel *Complicated Business, an Essay from the History of Russian Letters* (1864). Like Svidrigailov, Akhsharumov's main character arrives in Petersburg after several years of provincial life. Upon arrival, he explains: "I need fresh air [...] A verst before the city, I felt the smell of awful rot [...] Speaking figuratively, I mean the moral atmosphere of the capital, the openness and freedom of its varied life."[11] This ambiguous comment foreshadows the development of Akhsharumov's text by undermining the common expectation that Petersburg's intellectual atmosphere had to feel open and free. In partial parallel to Luzhin's trajectory, Akhsharumov's protagonist proceeds to meet with the "leading forces of society," marry an emancipated woman, and publish a journal *Delo* (two years before the appearance of the real journal *Delo* in 1866). After embarking on this project, he becomes embroiled in a journalistic scandal, his aspirations disintegrate, and he is forced to return to the provinces. Besides matching *Crime and Punishment* in a variety of ways, Akhsharumov's "essay from the history of Russian letters" offers a common lesson about the detrimental effects of the culture of the press.

Similar to many characters as well as writers of fiction, Raskol'nikov serves as a focal point for reenacting the predicament of a media-ridden contemporary. To an outside observer, the behavior of many younger men in the streets as well as in texts appeared as a frivolous wandering (*prazdnoshatanie*). In the new context of greater social mobility, many lacked an anchoring occupation. Physical wandering, predictably, extended to intellectual wandering (*shatanie umov*). The behavior of writers, although more intense, also seemed to lack coherence. One commentator observed: "All these feuilletonists hustle daily through the streets, read all kinds of newspapers [...] and still fail to notice anything that would excite the imagination." Writers' failure stemmed from readers' satiation: everything was already "familiar to the Petersburger." The impossibility of finding anything new was tantamount to the effacement of the writer's individuality. Losing his unique identity, he turned into a banal vehicle for circulating speech.

---

10 Dostoevskii, PSS, 6:336, 339, 352.
11 N. Akhsharumov, *Mudrenoe delo: Ocherk iz istorii russkoi slovesnosti* (St. Petersburg, 1895; originally in *Epokha*, 1864), 6.

As characters and narrators repeatedly registered an awareness of this condition and attempted to transcend it, they replicated the familiar pattern of the press collapsing on itself. "What am I?" wondered the wandering character of *The Lost but Affable Creature* by Krestovskii (a dropout from the University of St. Petersburg). In order to regain identity, the man of the press looked for new and meaningful words or attempted to transcend the bounds of speech altogether. "Find me a word that would have some meaning" pleaded a character in a story by Pomialovskii (finished penultimate in his seminary class). The protagonist in *The Arbuzov Building* by Voronov (a dropout from the University of Kazan') conceded the loss of individuality in a similar way: "Thinking of the banality and weakness of my character, I clearly realize what a petty fool I am, what a vile nonentity! We suffer precisely because we are constantly shouting and all for nothing! Because our hands dangle uselessly, because we struggle in a vicious circle and fear to cross the line."[12] Each of these statements contains recognizable correspondences to *Crime and Punishment*. Raskol'nikov, identified as an "author" and "littérateur,"[13] reproduces them when taking stock of his condition, as in these early thoughts: "Man's fate is in his hands. But he keeps bungling everything solely out of cowardice. He is most afraid of the new step. Yet, I do nothing because I babble too much. Or like this: I babble because I do nothing."[14] Entanglement in speech, fear of action, as well as the desire to cross the line and utter a new word are all recognizable afflictions of the media man. The tautological reversal at the end of his statement underscores Raskol'nikov's entrapment. Like many aspects of media man's existence, the reversibility of propositions received an early recognition in Balzac's novel *A Distinguished Provincial in Paris*, which was devoted to the press: "In literature every idea is reversible and no one can take it upon oneself to decide which is right and which is wrong."[15]

In Russian culture of the 1860s, the age-old quest for personal identity acquired a new dimension—belatedly in comparison with western Europe. The uncontrolled recycling of speech undermined public attempts to establish personal identity, and the commercial aspect of writing demeaned

---

12 "Chto ia, nu chto ia takoe?" V. V. Krestovskii, "Pogibshee, no miloe sozdanie," *Vremia* 1 (1861):202. N. G. Pomialovskii, *Molotov*, in *Izbrannoe* (Minsk: Nauka i tekhnika, 1980), 143. Voronov, *Arbuzovskaia krepost'*, 169.

13 Dostoevskii, PSS, 6:79, 264.

14 Ibid., 6:6.

15 Honoré de Balzac, "Un grand homme de province à Paris," in *La Comedie humaine* (Paris: Dumont, 1843), 8:306.

this formerly earnest pursuit. A certain austerity of words and fixity of definition, on which the search for identity depends, were undermined by the proliferation of the press.

The vicious circle of self-referential speech effaces Raskol'nikov's identity and accounts for the epistemological paralysis he attempts to overcome by answering the programmatic question what am I? In this context, "testing oneself" can be associated with the murderer's slogan "assez causé" from Balzac's *Father Goriot*.[16] Dostoevskii mentioned this slogan in an editorial note in *Vremia*, and Raskol'nikov reiterates it after reading the newspaper in a bar. Importantly, "assez causé" refers through Balzac's novel to the explosion of "causerie" in France of the 1830s, when the French press was undergoing an expansion similar to that of the Russian press in the 1860s. As long as Raskol'nikov remains in the sphere of speech, his identity will continue to dissolve in this duplicative and confusing environment. The act of murder, on the other hand, might afford him an opportunity to transcend the cycle of reproduction by committing an irreproducible act[17]—unlike a word, a life cannot be taken twice. Since the murder enters the novel from the press, however, it also lends itself to reproducibility. The function of the murder is not to give the protagonist a chance to develop an identity but to prefigure his own death ("I did not kill her—I killed myself"). The erasure of a character in Raskol'nikov's text prefigures his own disappearance as a speaking subject. Michael Holquist has observed that Raskol'nikov's "conversion dramatizes the condition of infancy (infari, infans, he who does not speak)." The conversion takes Raskol'nikov outside the media and into the stable sphere of myth, of the "wisdom tale with which the epilogue concludes."[18]

Raskol'nikov's crime, rather than opening a silent gap in the novel, fuels the production of its text. Following newspaper reports on double murders, the murder of the pawnbroker duplicates itself in the murder of Lizaveta, thus engendering at the event's inception the informational excess characteristic of the media. At the very start, the event contains no gaps, as the text identifies both perpetrator and victims and supplies all factual details. At issue, then,

---

16 Dostoevskii, PSS, 6:322: "Back then I had to find out and as fast as possible . . . I only wanted to test myself."

17 "I was so sick, so sick of all the talk. I wanted to forget and start again and stop blabbering," explains Raskol'nikov. Dostoevskii, PSS, 6:321.

18 Michael Holquist, *Dostoevsky and the Novel* (Princeton: Princeton University Press, 1977), 93–94.

is not the detective's questions who did it? or what happened? which aim at establishing the original fact, the basic premise whose discovery constitutes the teleology of the text. Rather, the question is of a journalistic kind: what kind of people among us could do this? This question sets up the development by way of induction, by finding new explanations and versions for the event and by conjuring up doubles of the perpetrator.

Myshkin (1998)*

Liza Knapp

In the wake of the death and destruction at the end of *The Idiot*, readers familiar with Dostoevskii's statements that he wanted, in Myshkin, to
portray a "positively beautiful" and Christlike man may well wonder whether
something has gone wrong with this novel. Critics have condemned Myshkin
(as an ineffectual hero), Dostoevskii (as an ineffectual novelist), and, for that
matter, Jesus himself (as an ineffectual savior or simply as a bad role model).[1]
And the fact that Dostoevskii expressed some dissatisfaction of his own with
the novel (without ever actually denying Myshkin) has only added grist to the
critical mill. Others have defended Myshkin, Dostoevskii, and Jesus. Still others
have come up with apologetic interpretations of the novel that rationalize the
novel's contradictions.

In order to understand the role played by Christ in the novel and
Dostoevskii's conception of that role, it is important to remember that
Dostoevskii envisioned this "positively beautiful man" to be *like* Christ, even
if in the privacy of his notebooks he at times seemed to equate Myshkin
with Christ (PSS 9:246, 249). *The Idiot* does not ask what would happen if
Jesus arrived in Saint Petersburg by train on November 27, 1867. Rather,
Dostoevskii set out to give us an imitation of Christ and to portray Christ by

* Extracts from Liza Knapp, "Myshkin Through a Murky Glass, Guessingly," *Dostoevskii's The
  Idiot: A Critical Companion*, ed. Liza Knapp (Evanston, IL: Northwestern University Press,
  1998), 191–98, 203–4. Copyright © 1998 by Northwestern University Press. Published
  1998. All rights reserved. The text is reproduced here with minor modifications: some footnotes have been removed.

1 Friedrich Nietzsche, according to Walter Kaufman, "conceived of Jesus in the image of
  Dostoevskii's *Idiot*." In his repudiation of Christ, *Der Antichrist* (The Antichrist) of 1895,
  Nietzsche elaborated on what he falsely (in my view) perceived as Dostoevskii's criticism of
  Jesus in *The Idiot*.

indirection. *The Idiot* thus formally imitates the New Testament; as Robin Feuer Miller has pointed out: "The figure of Christ and the style of the Gospels, which portray Him through parables and stories rather than through authorial explanations, provide Dostoevskii with models for characterization and narration."[2] Dostoevskii, in presenting a Christlike Myshkin, makes use of a process something like that practiced by Jesus when he spoke in parables, not defining the Kingdom of God but hinting at what it is like. The process is analogous to simile and metaphor as described by Aristotle: Dostoevskii challenges his reader to contemplate and intuit similarities between Myshkin and Christ so that the reader can, in the process, "learn" (for Aristotle argues that there is a "learning process" involved) something that was not previously known or obvious; it is often intended to be shocking.[3]

When it comes to the "fantastic," which Dostoevskii understood as matters bridging life and death, full knowledge and, for that matter, direct expression of partial knowledge are impossible, at least on earth. To use Paul's metaphor, we see "through a murky glass, guessingly" rather than "face to face."[4] And given the fact that *The Idiot* is a novel, with a Christ*like* hero, we are beholding Christ through many layers of murky glass [...]

In Myshkin, who arrives in Saint Petersburg in part I of the novel, may be seen reflections (of reflections) of Christ: he has traits that remind us of the early Christians who modeled their lives on Jesus', breaking with family and living at odds with the state. Myshkin has incorporated the attitudes that Paul tried to cajole the Philippians, Romans, and Corinthians into adopting. (Dostoevskii would later in his life declare Paul's Epistles to be an excellent source on faith: "There quite a bit is said specifically about faith and it cannot be said better" [30.1: 10, February 1878].) In the Myshkin who arrives in Saint Petersburg on November 27, 1867, Dostoevskii has presented what Paul had in mind when he said: "For I think that God has exhibited us apostles as last of all, like men sentenced to death. We are fools for Christ's sake, but you are wise in Christ. We are weak, but you are strong. You are held in honor, but we are in disrepute" (1 Cor. 4:9–10).[5] Myshkin, called a "holy fool" by Rogozhin on the train when they first meet, then greets the Epanchin household with stories of

---

2 Robin Feuer Miller, *Dostoevsky and "The Idiot." Author, Narrator, and Reader* (Cambridge, MA: Harvard University Press, 1981), 84.

3 Aristotle, "Rhetoric," in *On Poetry and Style,* trans. and introd. G. M. A. Grube (Indianapolis, IN: Bobbs-Merrill, 1958), 1410b–1413a.

4 A translation into English of the Russian I Cor. 13:12.

5 Roger Cox, *Between Earth and Heaven: Shakespeare, Dostoevsky and the Meaning of Christian Tragedy* (New York: Holt, Rinehart and Winston, 1969), 167.

executions, reminding his listeners that Jesus himself was sentenced to death and lived his life in the face of this agony and horror. Listening to Myshkin's stories, members of the Epanchin household, through a murky glass, guessingly, behold an imitation of Jesus [...]

Myshkin tells of having inspired through his own example the children of his Swiss village to love, during her last days, Marie, a young woman, seduced and abandoned, and suffering from consumption. An important component of Myshkin's story is that the love he imparted was subversive to the status quo of the village: initially, the parents of the children felt that Myshkin, Pied Piperlike, was leading their children astray. Especially disconcerting for the adults was that Myshkin did not judge Marie. Here Myshkin imitates Jesus in his refusal to judge a fallen woman. He loves in a seditious way that threatens authority and divides families. The tale of Marie—where Myshkin shows his Christlike love in action—is part dreamy Swiss miracle and part a warning of a socially subversive force that can create chaos.

On arriving at the Epanchins', Myshkin speaks man-to-man about questions of life and death with the Epanchins' servant, leaving the servant himself befuddled. (The servant wonders, Is the visitor "a poor little fool" without social ambition or is he a social climber with some scheme up his sleeve?) In humbling himself to the servant, Myshkin was imitating Jesus and thus following Paul's advice to the Philippians: "Do nothing from selfishness or conceit, but in humility count others better than yourselves. Let each of you look not only to his own interests, but also to the interests of others. Have this mind among yourselves, which you have in Christ Jesus, who, though he was in the form of God, did not count equality with God a thing to be grasped, but emptied himself, taking the form of a servant, being born in the likeness of men. And being found in human form he humbled himself and became obedient unto death, even death on a cross" (Phil. 2:3–8). But imitation of Christ can easily be misunderstood and misinterpreted, as the response of the Epanchins' servant reveals. Myshkin has so naturally taken "the form of a servant" that Nastas'ia Filippovna mistakes him for one when she first meets him at the Ivolgin apartment. This possible confusion and multiplicity is part of Dostoevskii's intention here [...]

Nastas'ia Filippovna and the Epanchin women, especially Aglaia, are drawn to Myshkin and to what he embodies. (Being distant cousins, the Epanchin women may see something of themselves reflected in Myshkin.) Nastas'ia Filippovna is prepared to allow Myshkin to decide her fate at her birthday party and sees him as someone who will liberate her from domination by another person: she will belong to no one and experience new independence. Aglaia, fed up with going to "their balls" and with everyone's attempts to marry her off, refuses to remain or become the dutiful daughter or wife she is expected to. And Myshkin seems to be her advocate in this rebellion. In citing her reasons for not wanting simply to be married off, she expresses her yearning to see a Gothic cathedral; at a certain point, her mother wonders whether she has not been infected by nihilism. But here Dostoevskii leaves the reader wondering whether her behavior is not also an attempt at imitation of the angels of God, residents of heaven who "neither marry nor are given in marriage" (Matt. 22:30). Here again Dostoevskii presents behavior that may be interpreted one way (Aglaia's behavior looks fishily like woman's emancipation), and yet, if one looks through a murky glass, guessingly, one sees glimmers of some otherworldly reality in these same actions.

When he is asked by the men he meets in the train whether he is a "great connoisseur of the female sex," Myshkin replies that because of his illness he has not known women. His response prompts Rogozhin to liken him to a God's fool, noting that God loves people like him. From the outset, Myshkin's virginal lack of erotic love seems part of his Christlike nature. His Christlike love is incompatible with marriage, as becomes apparent when Aglaia demands of Myshkin, "Why do you debase yourself?" and then in the next breath declares, "I wouldn't marry you for anything in the world" (PSS 8:283). At the very least, Aglaia presumes that an eligible suitor and successful husband should not behave humbly and meekly but rather should be more of a peacock. More than that, however, her hesitation also points to some deeper sense in which Myshkin is, in fact, not a fitting husband because marriage is predicated on certain selfish, un-Christlike qualities he seems to lack [...]

Dostoevskii's "fantastic" Myshkin, as he fondly called him later, through his epilepsy knew something of what it is like for there to be time no more, and also something of what it means to live like an angel of God. He rebels against isolating himself with one wife and having nothing left over for others. The "earthly balance," or compromise, Dostoevskii described to himself in his diary (and which Dostoevskii himself attempted in his life) eludes Myshkin, who, rather, attempts to have it both ways: he returns to Russia in search of family and sets himself up as a potential groom; yet, at the same time, he still wants to love others humbly, without isolating himself and without having "nothing left for everyone else."

For some of his critics, within the novel and without, Myshkin's whole problem, it would seem, is his inability to choose *either* Aglaia *or* Nastas'ia

Filippovna. Radomskii, speaking for the social order, criticizes Myshkin for acting as bridegroom almost simultaneously to two women. "You want to love them both, is that it?" says Radomskii. To which Myshkin replies, "O, yes, yes!" (8: 484). Once again, just as when he conversed with the servant, Myshkin's behavior can be interpreted in more than one way: either he's an ineffectual lover, unwilling or unable to make up his mind; or he's a modal bigamist, a selfish Don Juan, or worse. Or, looking guessingly through murky glass, perhaps one can see a reflection of Christ and of all the contradictions he represented. And indeed in Myshkin's leaving Aglaia and Nastas'ia Filippovna in the lurch, there is even some similarity to Jesus' treatment of Mary Magdalene, whom he allowed to wash and kiss his feet, to leave everything and follow him, only to abandon her a bit caddishly at the last moment, according to some apocryphal or blasphemous interpretations.

In *Adultery in the Novel*, Tony Tanner discusses the tension in novels of adultery between the Christlike forgiveness of the sinning woman, as described in John 8, and the scribe-like and Pharisee-like desire to stone her.[6] Tanner argues that the bourgeois novel of adultery depends largely on the tension that develops as the novel seeks to incorporate both responses to adultery: "a strictness that works to maintain the law, and a sympathy and understanding with the adulterous violator that works to undermine it" (14). And indeed, "it is arguable that it is just such a tension between law and sympathy that holds the great bourgeois novel together, and a severe imbalance in either direction must destroy the form" (14). If Tanner's assumptions about "the great bourgeois novel" are applied to *The Idiot*, then it just may be that the formal problems many critics have seen in *The Idiot* result from "severe imbalance" between sympathy and law.[7]

But perhaps it is an error to judge *The Idiot* by the standards of the bourgeois novel of adultery. *The Idiot* presents a main hero and, I would argue, an

---

6 "According to Old Testament Law, the adulterous man and woman are almost without exception to be excluded from society, canceled even to the point of execution. In the New Testament, Christ confronted with the woman taken in adultery makes the would-be lawgivers aware of her problematical reality, calling into question both the impersonal application of the law and the justification and rights of the would-be legislators. Effectively this implies the disintegration of society-as-constituted." Tony Tanner, *Adultery in the Novel: Contract and Transgression* (Baltimore: Johns Hopkins University Press, 1979), 14.

7 Although not a novel of adultery as such, *The Idiot* has many of the same concerns as the traditional novel adultery. Or perhaps the presence in the novel of Radomskii, Prince Shch., and even the narrator (as Robin Feuer Miller's work suggests) assures that the scribes and Pharisees are properly represented and that enough of Tanner's tension exists?

author, who both tip the scale toward compassion and a refusal to condemn, no matter what the destruction all this brings to traditional forms. This suggests that this novel is, indeed, different from the "great bourgeois" novels Tanner discusses. (According to Tanner, lack of the prescribed tension between sympathy and law results in a degeneration into sexuality or "linguicity,"[8]—but this does not quite fit Dostoevskii, although there may be elements of each.) Rather, in *The Idiot*, Dostoevskii sets forth a new type of novel, the novel of the *accidental* family, a family he himself in *Diary of a Writer* opposed to the *genetic* family, whose chronicler was Tolstoi.

The novel of the accidental family, as Dostoevskii understood it, had its own poetics, which Dostoevskii commented on, directly and indirectly, in his works.[9] In Dostoevskii's view, new artistic forms had to be created to represent disorder and decay. In order to arrive at these, however, the writer had to "guess and . . . make mistakes" (PSS 13:455).[10] In *The Idiot*, a novel with a Christlike hero, Dostoevskii works out these new forms, new forms that happen to bear some resemblance to the chronicle of Christ's life: the New Testament.

Much of the end of *The Idiot* is devoted to the narrator's throwing up his hands at the task of chronicling the last days of the action. Rather than go in search of the historical events or attempt to create a coherent narrative, the narrator chooses to give us several different reports, based on different accounts, and with various inconsistencies and contradictions.[11] Is this not a bit like the narratives of Jesus's life?

---

8 Tanner's term for an indulgence in words analogous to sexual indulgence.

9 Robert Louis Jackson has made this argument in his discussion of how Dostoevskii "undertook in his art to express the new social chaos," a prime manifestation of which was the "disintegrating family." This required a new form and a new type realism. See *Dostoevsky's Quest for Form: A Study of His Philosophy of Art* (New Haven: Yale University Press, 1966), 110–18.

10 Jackson, in reference to this quote, notes that "all art—we must remember—from one point of view for Dostoevskii is a guessing, a divining of the 'subsurface unexpressed future Word'" (Jackson, *Quest*, 116–17).

11 And, in the same vein, what occurs between part 1 and part 2 of the novel is left a mystery.

Nastas'ia Filippovna (2004)*

Sarah J. Young

One of the major problems facing the reader of *The Idiot* is the presentation of the character of Nastas'ia Filippovna. Her motivation and relationships with other characters remain largely obscure, owing to her absence from large sections of the narrative; she makes her entrance in the "real" time of the novel at the end of Chapter Nine of Part One, and in Parts Two and Three appears for just three brief scenes. In Part Four, we witness directly only her confrontation with Aglaia, as subsequent details of her marriage preparations and flight with Rogozhin are sketched in by the narrator after the event. In the novel as a whole Nastas'ia Filippovna makes only 131 speech acts—significantly fewer not only than Myshkin, Aglaia and Rogozhin, but also than Lizaveta Prokofievna, Lebedev, Ippolit and Gania.[1] [...]

As Nastas'ia Filippovna's absence is so central, and as her relationship with Myshkin is so essential to the direction of the narrative, we cannot begin to understand the hero's actions without first addressing hers. If the novel is "about" anything on the level of plot, it is surely the collision of the heroine's outraged suffering and the hero's compassion, and it is therefore necessary to examine both sides of the relationship. This chapter will therefore demonstrate how Nastas'ia Filippovna uses scripting strategies to place herself at the forefront of the other's consciousness and of the narrative even in her absence, the effect this has on others, and its implications for her motivation and self-image [...]

---

* Extracts from Sarah J. Young, *Dostoevskii's The Idiot and the Ethical Foundations of Narrative. Reading, Narrating, Scripting* (London: Anthem Press, 2004), 28–29, 35–36, 45–46, 53–54, 60–61, 67, 69. Permission to reprint granted by Wimbledon Publishing Company. The text is reproduced here with minor modifications: some footnotes have been removed.

1 See A. Ando, Y. Urai, and A. Renansky, *A Lemmatized Concordance to "The Idiot" of F M Dostoevskii* (Sapporo: Hokkaido University, 2003) vol. 4, 1911 (Appendix 3).

This tendency to objectify Nastas'ia Filippovna in both thought and deed is particularly evident in the reactions of the other characters to the photograph of herself she has given to Gania. In this object, as Dolezel notes, the heroine before her first appearance changes from being a verbal sign to a pictorial sign;[2] having already asserted her image through Rogozhin's story and established her place in the preoccupations of Gania, General Epanchin and Totskii, the photograph gives her an embodied presence to which the other protagonists respond in uninhibited fashion. While Myshkin's three examinations of the portrait are vital in establishing his view of her, the incidental gestures of the other characters are just as important as pointers to their attitudes towards her. Outside of Myshkin's hands, the portrait is generally connected to hostile reactions. Mrs. Epanchina, for instance, "with a haughty gesture threw the picture away from her on to the table" (VIII, 69), and it is treated with even less respect in the Ivolgin household; Varvara finds it on the floor, and Gania then "angrily took it from the table and threw it on to his writing desk, which stood at the far end of the room." (PSS 8:84) His violence towards Nastas'ia Filippovna is barely displaced,[3] and emphasizes the worthlessness of the heroine in the eyes of those who control or sanction control of her. However, the gift is also taken by all concerned as a sign of her assent to the proposed marriage and as such indicates both their propensity to misread her, and her own ability to confound expectations. The tension surrounding Nastas'ia Filippovna's determination to maintain her loophole is thus already present in her photograph, as the gift deliberately provokes incorrect, finalizing assumptions about the heroine and simultaneously provides an opportunity for these assumptions to be undermined, and the possibility of external finalization to be removed. In stark contrast to the treatment the portrait receives from others, Prince Myshkin treats it with reverence; it is notable that just before Mrs. Epanchina tosses the picture away casually, Myshkin kisses it (PSS 8:68). More importantly, he is the only character who actually pays attention to the image of Nastas'ia Filippovna [...]

The powerful melodramatic impulse in the novel, emanating particularly from the personality and actions of Nastas'ia Filippovna, and related to its Gothic elements, is thus both grounded in and complemented by an ethical system which both motivates her and informs the structure of the novel as a whole.

---

2 Lubomir Dolezel, "The Fictional World of Dostoevskij's *The Idiot*," *Russian Literature* 33 (1993): 239–48 (240).

3 Z. Malenko, and J. L. Gebhard, "The Artistic Use of Portraits in Dostoevskij's *Idiot*," *SEEJ* 5 (1961): 243–54 (245).

The opposition between Myshkin and Rogozhin is set up at the beginning of the novel by the narrator, but it becomes important to the novel precisely because it is evident to Nastas'ia Filippovna; it is her perception of herself and the world in extreme, polarized terms, which shapes the central plot-line. The heroine projects the divisions in her character onto the two men, to make them adopt supporting roles in the alternative scripts she is preparing. The rivalry between Rogozhin and Myshkin, the novel's most vital component, which is responsible for the fates of all three protagonists, is thus in large part a product of Nastas'ia Filippovna's imaginative perception, and the fact that the roles she offers both echo their natural desires with regard to her. In this we see the reciprocal nature of scripting; without the active participation of Myshkin and Rogozhin, Nastas'ia Filippovna has no effective script, and cannot assert her own self-image or influence the direction of the narrative. Both of her scripts depend on the perception of her by another being aligned with her own self-definition, and to this end she secures their attention and participation by presenting the sides of her character to which they will best respond.

The polarity inherent in Nastas'ia Filippovna's character and its reflection in the relationships of Myshkin and Rogozhin to the heroine (and to each other) are thus central to the novel. Burgin is therefore some way off the mark when she claims that Nastas'ia Filippovna rejects Myshkin's proposal of marriage because he arrives too late, after she has abandoned her dream of [4] salvation. In fact both extremes are present simultaneously, as her initially positive response to Myshkin's offer suggests. Recalling her dream of a good man who will tell her, "It's not your fault, Nastas'ia Filippovna, and I adore you!" she continues, "Dreaming like that can send you out of your mind [. . .] And then that man there would come, stay two months a year and disgrace, offend, inflame and corrupt, and then make his exit, and a thousand times I wanted to throw myself into the pond, but I was contemptible, I didn't have the courage." (PSS 8:144). Her direct reference to the reality of Totskii's abuse interrupting and destroying her dream also reminds her of her own guilt, and persuades her that she cannot accept or even believe in the prince's offer. Furthermore, the recollection of the suicidal ideation resulting from her abuse, immediately turns her thoughts back to Rogozhin as, having ignored him since Myshkin's proposal, she ends the above speech by announcing her final decision to leave with him; the guilt which led her to consider suicide in the past reasserts itself, and she takes the suicidal option again.

---

4   Diana Burgin, "The Reprieve of Nastas'ia: A Reading of a Dreamer's Authored Life," *Slavonic and East European Review* 29 (1985): 260.

Nastas'ia Filippovna's constant vacillations between the two men, and the conflicting desires for both punishment and forgiveness which they represent to her, inform the entire sub-structure of the novel. However, this factor also raises problems for both her character and her ability to determine the shape of the text, as her inability, or refusal, to choose one specific identity to form the basis of her scripting activity (the second stage of scripting), before breaking down others' views of her and making them dance to her own tune, creates a level of uncertainty verging on anarchy, which jeopardizes both the success of her own script and the coherence of the text as a whole. Nevertheless, in order to achieve her ultimate aim of avoiding finalization by others, it is essential for the heroine to keep different options alive; retaining the right to change her mind until the final moment is pointless unless she maintains alternative scripts. It is the presence of Myshkin which allows her to do this, and although she quickly hands back his script, she is, as we see throughout the novel, unwilling to surrender it definitively, as it gives her an additional dimension, enabling her to keep her options open. However, it is not merely the choice which is important; it is the heroine's use of these possible roles to play characters off against each other in order to create tension in the narrative and direct the course of events in her favor which classifies her interactivity as scripting. It is the interplay of the different components of her psychological make-up, the fatal, fallen and emancipated aspects,[5] which determine her self-image and the roles she allocates others [...]

After Nastas'ia Filippovna's disappearance, the fact that others incorporate her into their narrative presentations is a sign that they are still preoccupied with the heroine and her actions, and are trying to regain control of the narrative after her departure at the end of Part One left it in chaos and without a main plot to follow. Since the beginning of the novel, attention has concentrated on Nastas'ia Filippovna, at first indirectly, through her photograph and the characters' conversations and stories about her, then directly in her two appearances in Part One, which also set up the main plot of *The Idiot*, and then indirectly again after Myshkin's return from Moscow, when she is uppermost in the minds of both Myshkin and his two interlocutors, Lebedev and Rogozhin. When the action moves to Pavlovsk, there is a definite change of tone as the primary focus of attention moves away from Nastas'ia Filippovna. The other

---

5   Olga Matich, "*The Idiot*: A Feminist Reading," in *Dostoevski and the Human Condition After a Century*, eds. A. Ugrinsky, F. Lambasa, and V. K. Ozolins (New York: Greenwood, 1986): 53–60 (54).

protagonists try at this point to take advantage of her absence by re-imposing their common script for her, which has its origins in their shared assumptions about the moral code and social hierarchy, forcing their ideas of what she is and her lack of value as a human being on to the text and onto Myshkin's conscious- ness; Aglaia's reading of the Pushkin poem in particular is aimed at confronting the hero with the inadequacy and inappropriateness of the ideal he has chosen, in the hope that he will abandon the heroine and find a more suitable cause. However, in also voicing her strong approval of his quest, Aglaia provides the first hint that she has chosen Myshkin as a potential suitor not in spite of but precisely because of his connection with Nastas'ia Filippovna; in this way the heroine's influence over the actions and interactions of the other protago- nists begins to affect their relationships and, ultimately, the future direction of the plot.

The number of interpretations of Nastas'ia Filippovna in Part Two of the novel reminds the reader of her continued importance for the other char- acters. In spite of her absence, they recognize that she is still a central figure and that their relationships with her remain significant; Viktorovich notes the intense interest others have in Nastas'ia Filippovna, and more specifically in her relationship with Myshkin, which gives rise to the endless rumours and interpretations.[6] This contributes to the peculiar structuring of the novel, as the protagonists' attention, as well as the reader's, is constantly directed by the heroine away from the events depicted on the page.

However, it is when the heroine reappears in Part Two that her pivotal dynamic role in the structure of the narrative—as opposed to remaining the passive object and product of the interpretation and control of others—is grad- ually realized. Having abandoned Totskii's script for her in favor of "authoring her own life" at the end of Part One, and escaped the burden of being defined by others, Nastas'ia Filippovna not only has to create and assert her own script, but also has to make others redefine their scripts in line with her own. The strategy she adopts to try to achieve this is remarkable, and, for a long section of the novel, almost successful; whereas in Part One, her absence made it easier for the other characters to objectify and finalize her, now she uses her absence to avoid finalization by others. She not only controls them by drawing their attention back towards her, but also, by remaining enigmatically behind the scenes, creates a huge gap in the text, which forces the other characters into

---

6 V. A. Viktorovich, "Pushkinskii motiv v 'Idiote' F. M. Dostoevskogo," *Boldinskie chteniia* (Gorkii: Volgo-Viatskoe knizhnoe izdatel'stvo, 1980), 131.

interpretative mode, putting them under the influence of her script, and preventing them from reverting to their previous habit of finalizing the heroine [...]

The uncertainty and confusion surrounding Nastas'ia Filippovna's intentions continue throughout the novel. General Epanchin reports that Aglaia has spelled out Nastas'ia Filippovna's motives: "this deranged woman has taken it into her head to have me married off to Lev Nikolaevich no matter what, and that's why she's driving Evgenii Pavlych out of our house" (PSS 8:298). This confirms the suggestion previously made by Prince Shch., but cannot be corroborated. Aglaia may have more access to the thoughts of her rival than the other characters, as she has been receiving letters from her (a fact we have known since early in Part Two), but the same problems we have encountered since the first mention of Nastas'ia Filippovna by Rogozhin in Part One prevent us from accepting her interpretation without question: we do not know the heroine's intentions when she sent the letters, whether they represent an accurate reflection of her state of mind, or are merely a further example of her trying to manipulate another character. Her contradictory actions and divided impulses suggest that the letters are both sincere and part of a larger game. Thus, while Aglaia's explanation of Nastas'ia Filippovna's current behavior seems to fit the facts as we know them, we remain aware that owing to Nastas'ia Filippovna's strange behavior and deliberate withdrawal from the text, and the conflicting agendas of various characters, we are far from being in possession of the whole story. It is this absence of explanation and certainty which the protagonists feel—and resent—most forcefully. They suspect Nastas'ia Filippovna is trying to control events from the background, but do not know how or why, or what she might do next [...]

After the confrontation scene, Nastas'ia Filippovna effectively erases Aglaia from the remainder of the novel, proving both her enormous influence over the narrative, and the fact that she has, finally, made a decision about her identity, which allows her to return to the foreground and use her script to shape the denouement. This results in a significant change in the dynamics of the novel in the final chapters. Having wandered aimlessly through the central section, we are now rushed not only through the wedding preparations of Myshkin and Nastas'ia Filippovna, suggesting that their marriage is not the main issue for either character, but also through her departure with Rogozhin, and the murder scene is not shown at all. Moreover, much of what we are told about the climax of the novel reaches us second-hand and has its basis in rumor, as the narrator is unable to explain or control the action, leaving the reader with persistent doubts about its accuracy and little opportunity to define the

motivation behind these events. The elusiveness of the heroine, designed originally to prevent others finalizing her, reaches its peak in the finale of her script,
and the narrator is unable to find an adequate response.

The change of pace imposed by Nastas'ia Filippovna's decision, and the
rapidity with which the conclusion is reached after the long period in which the
action has failed to move forward, have a profound effect on the latter part of
the narrative. We can see this in the numerous loose ends which remain at the
end of the novel, leaving many of the minor characters in limbo. While Nastas'ia
Filippovna's actions have consistently initiated a series of explosions and rever-
berations, her death shatters the entire text, removing from the scene all the
major protagonists, leaving a void which the affairs of the minor characters,
who have by this stage demonstrated their inability to play leading roles, are
insufficient to fill. The suddenness of her demise catches the other characters
off guard, and their stories, which overlap with hers and Myshkin's, are cut off
by the narrator without resolution. Here we have ultimate proof that Nastas'ia
Filippovna's script succeeds, while many of those around her fail; the novel as
a whole is structured around her attempts to assert her script, in spite of the
narrator's design, to the extent that once she has chosen her denouement, it
cannot exist after her death [. . .]

By appointing another to fulfill her script, and mediating it through yet a
third person, Nastas'ia Filippovna also exposes the complicity of all others in
her life and death. Having lived according to the will of others for most of her
life, she continues her relationships with many of the same people through her
infrequent appearances in the central section of the novel, but shifts the balance of power so that she begins to exert control over them. By involving others
in her life to the very end, including agreeing to the meeting with Aglaia which
precipitates the denouement, she also involves them in her death, enabling her
to deflect part of the blame on to them. In choosing the manner of her death
as well as its perpetrator, Nastas'ia Filippovna simultaneously proves that she
has freed herself from the control of others, whilst implicating that control by
others in her death; Rogozhin kills her because it is the only way he can possess
(and therefore control) her.

Stavrogin (1969)*

Joseph Frank

O riginally, Dostoevskii's first grasp of his subject was purely satiric and caricatural; he had intended to concentrate on the comic confusion of the Liberal and Idealist generation of the 1840s confronted with the disastrous consequences of their own ideas in the Nihilists of the later 1860s. At this stage of his conception Dostoevskii referred to the novel as a "pamphlet," and said that he was resolved to sacrifice "art" to "tendentiousness." "Art" for Dostoevskii always meant the serious treatment of a basic moral conflict—a conflict which, whatever its point of departure in the contemporary socio-cultural situation, far transcended this context in the range of its human implications. In *Demons*, however, Dostoevskii did not set out to portray any such inner discord or dilemma from the inside; he thought he would limit himself only to castigating the beliefs and principles of the radicals (as well as the frivolity and stupidity of Russian "educated" society) with withering scorn. The narrative technique of the novel was thus conceived of very early in terms appropriate to this idea—as, that is, the report of a relatively detached observer, a provincial chronicler, setting down a series of unusual and grotesquely horrible events [. . .]

It is well known that, having already begun to write according to this original plan, Dostoevskii was confronted with a crisis when Stavrogin erupted into the manuscript as a major figure. Stavrogin was unquestionably a "tragic" character, and this meant that he would ordinarily have been treated internally and psychologically; but in this case Dostoevskii did not fundamentally change his

---

* Extracts from Joseph Frank, "The Masks of Stavrogin," *The Sewanee Review* 77, no. 4 (Autumn 1969): 660–62, 667–72, 676–79, 683–85, 690–91. First published in *The Sewanee Review* 77, no. 4 (Autumn 1969). Copyright 1969 by the University of the South. Reprinted with the permission of the editor.

narrative perspective. Stavrogin too is seen completely from the outside except in the confession-scene; and even here he "confesses" by means of a document which interposes itself between his consciousness in the scene and the reader. In other words, we are never inside Stavrogin, living with the life of his feelings, as we are inside the underground man, Raskol'nikov or Prince Myshkin. To be sure, neither Stavrogin nor his two main interlocutors, Shatov and Kirillov, are satirized or parodied; but while their obsessive quest for an absolute value has more inherent dignity than the posturings of Stepan Trofimovich, or the machinations of Peter Verkhovenskii and his "quintet," they are not presented in a radically different fashion. All the characters are seen from the outside, and their consciousnesses (as distinct from their emotive responses to particular situations) are rarely if ever dramatized directly at any length. Hence the book preserves a considerable degree of artistic unity, despite the marked differences in tone between the satirical and non-satirical sections [...]

Following the opening chapter devoted to Stepan Trofimovich, we are introduced next to Stavrogin; and this is the point at which, in my view, Dostoevskii's organization of his plot damages the effectiveness of his symbolic pattern. Nikolai Stavrogin, up to the age of sixteen, has been the pupil of Stepan Trofimovich, who was entrusted with his education. This makes a Liberal Idealist of the 1840s the spiritual progenitor of a Byronic type, a blood-brother of Eugene Onegin and Lermontov's Pechorin, associated in Russian culture with the 1820s and the 1830s. How can one account for this peculiar feature of the book?

With the aid of Dostoevskii's notebooks, it is not too difficult to reconstruct what occurred. Initially, the ideological center of the novel was to have been the relation between Stepan Trofimovich and his son, Peter. In this version, the plot contained a colorless character called the "Prince," a former pupil of Stepan Trofimovich's who had no particular socio-cultural function. The "Prince" then later emerged as Stavrogin, and replaced Stepan Trofimovich as the thematic center; it was the Byronic Stavrogin who, historically, had indeed been the original source of all the foreign ideologies that had infected the ailing body of Russia with madness. Trying, though, to preserve as much of his old manuscript as possible after Stavrogin appeared, Dostoevskii failed to alter the plot-pattern to fit his new thematic conception; and the result is an unfortunate confusion that obscures the real meaning of his symbolic chronology. Stavrogin's Byronism loses much of its historical point when he is turned into Stepan Trofimovich's disciple; and so does the nature of Stavrogin's relation to Kirillov and Shatov, which can be adequately understood only in historical-symbolic terms.

Dostoevskii accurately underlines the heritage of Romantic sensibility that linked the generations of Stepan Trofimovich and Stavrogin; but he anachronistically requires Stepan Trofimovich to bear the onus of having exercised a morbid and unhealthy influence on his youthful and impressionable charge. "More than once he awakened his ten-or-eleven year old friend at night, simply to pour out his wounded feelings and weep before him, or to tell him some family secret, without noticing that this was totally impermissible." The tutor communicated all the moral uncertainty and instability of his own character to his unfortunate pupil, without providing anything positive to counteract their unsettling effects; the result was to leave an aching emptiness at the center of Stavrogin's being. "Stepan Trofimovich succeeded in reaching the deepest chords in his pupil's heart, and had aroused in him a first vague sensation of that eternal, sacred longing which some elect souls, once having tasted and discovered it, will then never exchange for a cheap gratification. (There are some connoisseurs who prize this longing more than the most complete satisfaction of it, if such were possible)." This passage both defines Stavrogin as being emotionally engaged in the quest for an absolute of some kind, and also suggests the perversity springing from his lack of any positive goal. His quest is a spiritual experimentation totally preoccupied with itself, totally enclosed within the ego, and hence incapable of self-surrender to the absolute that it is presumably seeking [...]

The first physical description of Stavrogin given by the chronicler pinpoints his strange appearance of indefinable artificiality—an appearance that obviously derives from his symbolic function. "His hair was of a peculiarly intense black, his light-colored eyes were peculiarly light and calm, his complexion was peculiarly soft and white, the red in his cheeks was too bright and clear, his teeth were like pearls and his lips like coral—one would have thought the very acme of beauty, yet at the same time somehow repellent. It was said that his face suggested a mask . . ." Stavrogin's mask-like beauty reminds one of the vampires and ghouls of Gothic fictional mythology; like them he is a living corpse, whose unearthly beauty is the deceptive façade behind which festers the horror of evil and corruption. Several years later, however, when the chronicler observes him face-to-face again, a change has occurred. "Now—now, I don't know why he impressed me at once as absolutely, incontestably beautiful, so that no one could have said that his face was like a mask"; now he seemed to have "the light of some new idea in his eyes."

This "new idea" is clearly that of his decision to reject and transcend his past, to humiliate himself publicly and sincerely by acknowledging his marriage to Mar'ia Lebiadkin and confessing his violation of Matriosha. By seeking forgiveness and absolution, he hopes to save himself from the madness that he feels to be his impending fate. On the purely moral-personal level, Stavrogin's rôle as a character is defined by his despairing struggle to triumph over the egoism of his self-will and to attain a state of genuine humility. The first overt manifestation of this "new idea" is the self-control that he exhibits under the provocation of Shatov's blow; but in the same scene he lies about his relation to the crippled Mar'ia, which he wishes to reveal only under the conditions of his own choosing. And this is the first evidence for Tikhon's later judgment that Stavrogin's egoism, far from having been conquered by his new resolution, has taken on its subtlest form of all as a carefully staged martyrdom of contempt [. . .]

The action in the first four chapters of Part II, which concentrate on Stavrogin as he makes a round of visits to Kirillov, Shatov, and the Lebiadkins, indirectly illuminates both his historical-symbolic significance and the tragedy of his yearning for an unattainable absolution and humility. The first two figures represent an aspect of himself that he has discarded, but which has now become transformed into one or another ideological "devil" permanently obsessing his spiritual disciples. In the case of Kirillov, this "devil" is the temptation to self-deification logically deriving from the atheistic humanism of Feuerbach [. . .]

Stavrogin has thus here again inspired a mutilated version of the Truth, which falls short of its ultimate grounding in true religious faith—even though he knows abstractly that such faith is the only answer to the chaos of his unlimited freedom. Shatov diagnoses the malady afflicting them both in a key speech which helps to place them in Dostoevskii's perspective:

> "You're an atheist [Shatov tells Stavrogin] because you're a nobleman's son, the last nobleman's son. You've lost the distinction between good and evil because you've ceased to know your people. A new generation is coming, straight from the heart of the people, and you will know nothing of it, neither you nor the Verkhovenskiis, father or son, nor I, because I am also a nobleman's son, I, the son of your serf-lackey Pashka . . ."

On the symbolic level of the book, this can only mean that all the ideologies deriving from Stavrogin (and here one feels very acutely that Stepan Trofimovich should be among them!) are equally tainted by the original sin of their birth among a Western educated "aristocracy" totally divorced from the people; all are doomed to be swept away by an authentically Russian culture of the future springing from the people's faith [. . .]

It is not necessary to decide here between the various allegorical and theological interpretations that have been offered of Mar'ia; but she can scarcely be, as some critics have maintained, the positive heroine of the book. Certainly, in some sense, she represents Dostoevskii's vision of the primitive religious sensibility of the Russian people, particularly in her feeling for the theurgic union between the Russian soil and "the Mother of God." But the debasement and pathos of her condition recall Dostoevskii's statement, in an article, that while the *raskolniki* demonstrated the unconquerable desire of the Russian people not to submit to alien ways of life, they themselves sometimes went to "hideous" and "misshapen" extremes as a reaction. In this context, Mar'ia's poignant longing for a "Prince" who would not be ashamed to acknowledge her as his own takes on a good deal of historical-symbolic force; and her false and unnatural *mariage blanc* with Stavrogin, which has never been consummated, surely indicates that no true union is possible between the Christian Russian people and even the very finest flower of godless Russian Europeanism.

Symbolically, again, it is entirely appropriate that Mar'ia should finally unmask Stavrogin and label him unequivocally as the "impostor." Whatever confusions might have existed in the past, her demented second sight has now pierced through to his ultimate incapacity for true selflessness. "As soon as I saw your mean face when I fell and you picked me up—it was as if a worm had crawled into my heart," she says; "it's not *he*, I thought to myself, not *he*! My falcon would never have been ashamed of me in front of a young society lady!" Stavrogin starts with rage and terror when she prophetically alludes to his "knife," i.e., his lurking desire to have her murdered (on which Peter Verkhovenskii hopes to capitalize). And at the same time that she reads his inmost soul, she also speaks for the Russian people in assigning him his true historical-symbolic dimension. He is not the "Prince," not the genuine Lord and Ruler of Russia, but only Grishka Otrep'ev, "cursed in seven cathedrals," the impious and sacrilegious "impostor" and "false pretender" to the throne of God's Anointed Tsar [. . .]

Dostoevskii had planned to place Stavrogin's confession to the true God (in the person of His servitor Tikhon) following Verkhovenskii's "confession" to the false God Stavrogin. This would have dramatized all the horror and abomination of the "idol" that Peter Verkhovenskii was worshiping. After a sleepless night spent in warding off his hallucinations, Stavrogin was to have gone to Tikhon; and here the secret of his past, which has been repeatedly hinted at, was finally to have been revealed. Like Onegin and Pechorin, Stavrogin is a victim of the famous *mal du siècle*, the all-engulfing *ennui* that haunts the literature of the first half of the nineteenth century and whose cause is invariably the disappearance of religious faith. Baudelaire, its greatest poet, called ennui the deadliest of the vices:

> *Quoiqu'il ne pousse ni grands gestes ni grands cris,*
> *Il ferait volontiers de la terre un débris*
> *Et dans un bâillement avalerait le monde* [...]

Ennui is one of the symptoms of that "romantic agony" whose dossier has been so industriously compiled by Mario Praz, and, as he has shown, its usual result is one or another form of moral perversion. Dostoevskii has depicted it as such previously in Prince Valkovskii (*The Insulted and Injured*), Svidrigailov (*Crime and Punishment*), and in the sudden appearance of Cleopatra in *Notes from Underground* sticking golden pins into her slave-girls for amusement. With Stavrogin, it has led to the abominable violation of little Matriosha and his unspeakably vile observation of her death-throes.

All this is the result of Stavrogin's attempt to pass beyond the limits of good and evil, to put into practice, with the maniacal determination of Dostoevskii's negative heroes, the conviction that good and evil simply do not exist. "I have neither the feeling nor the knowledge of good and evil," Stavrogin tells himself just after the little girl's death, formulating the rationale by which he has tried to live, "and not only have I lost the sense of good and evil, but good and evil really do not exist (and this pleased me) and are but a prejudice; I can be free of all prejudices, but at the very moment when I achieve that freedom I shall perish." These were, as Stavrogin says, "old familiar thoughts" that he was at last putting clearly to himself for the first time; these were the convictions that had been responsible for all his behavior in the past. Like Raskol'nikov's crime, Stavrogin's revolting and despicable escapades had been a great moral philosophical experiment; and this is why Dostoevskii had taken such pains from the very start to dissociate his conduct from any kind of banal and self-indulgent debauchery.

Stavrogin's desire to transcend the human, to pass entirely beyond the bounds of good and evil, nonetheless runs aground on the hidden reef of conscience. No matter what Stavrogin may *think* he believes, he cannot entirely suppress his *feeling* for the difference between good and evil; and this irrepressible instinct erupts from his subconscious—almost always the guardian of morality for Dostoevskii—in his famous dream of "The Golden Age" inspired by Claude Lorrain's painting *Acis and Galatea*. The vision of a primeval Earthly Paradise of happiness and innocence fills his heart with overflowing joy. "I woke and opened my eyes, for the first time in my life literally wet with tears . . . A feeling of happiness, hitherto unknown to me, pierced my heart till it ached." But then a tiny red spider, associated in Stavrogin's subconscious with Matresha's death, replaces this dream-reverie of bliss, and he sees in his mind's eye the little girl standing on the threshold of his room and threatening him with her little fist. "Pity for her stabbed me," he writes, "a maddening pity, and I would have given my body to be torn to pieces if that would have erased what had happened." Stavrogin finds this vision of his own evil unbearable, but he continues to evoke it voluntarily and unendingly all the same; it is this unsupportable need to expiate his crime—a need that nothing he knows of or believes in can help him to absolve—that is gradually driving him mad.

Stavrogin's confession thus makes clear the source of his inner torments; but these torments have never been strong enough totally to triumph over his supreme egoism and self-will. Even his confession, as Tikhon rightly senses, is only another and extreme form of the "moral sensuality" that has marked all his previous attempts at self-mastery. "This document," Tikhon says of his confession, "is born of a heart wounded unto death . . . But it is as though you were already hating and despising in advance all those who will read what you have written, and challenging them to an encounter." Tikhon knows that Stavrogin by himself can never achieve the true humility of genuine repentance; his need for suffering and martyrdom can thus only lead to more and more terrible and disastrous provocations. This is why he urges Stavrogin to submit his will *completely* to the secret control of a saintly *starets*, and thus discipline himself by a total surrender to another as the first step along the path to the acceptance of Christ and the hope of forgiveness. But Stavrogin, irritably breaking an ivory crucifix that he has been fingering during the conversation, rejects this final admonition and goes to his self-destruction [. . .]

Stavrogin's suicide, which terminates the action, had been foreseen by Dostoevskii from his very first grasp of the character; but if he had been able to include the confession-chapter, it is likely that Stavrogin would have been given a greater place in the last third of the text. Some of Dostoevskii's notes show Stavrogin instrumental in solving the murder of Shatov, assembling the town for a special service of repentance, making a speech denouncing the horrors of atheistic destruction, and only *then* unexpectedly committing suicide.

There is no way of knowing, of course, whether Dostoevskii would have used these ideas in his final redaction; but they would have been far more consistent with Stravrogin's importance in the first two-thirds of the book. In the present version, the reader knows neither that Stavrogin has made a superhuman endeavor to transcend the boundaries of good and evil, nor that his conscience has driven him to the point of madness; thus his act loses much of its symbolic meaning as a self-condemnation of all the ideologies that he had spawned.

Fedor Karamazov (2003)*

Deborah A. Martinsen

While General Ivolgin and Stepan Verkhovenskii die after shocks to their identity, Captain Lebiadkin and Fedor Karamazov are murdered in part because they expose, or threaten to expose, others' shame. Like Lebiadkin, Fedor Karamazov responds to social shame by verbal aggression. When humiliated, or potentially humiliated, he humiliates.[1] By doing so publicly, he not only provokes a desire for revenge within his victim but also arouses audience anxiety. By doing so with stories, Fedor Karamazov earns the epithet "Aesop," which situates him at the center of metaliterary play in *The Brothers Karamazov*. Though commentators usually focus on Ivan's and Alesha's literary activities, their provocative progenitor regales those assembled in Zosima's cell with four stories that signal the novel's metaliterary dimension. Like Aesop's stories, Fedor Karamazov's contain hidden messages. And like Aesop's, they provoke hostile audience response.

Dostoevskii reveals authorial intent to associate Fedor Karamazov with Aesop by having three characters refer to him as "Aesop" four times within a hundred pages of the novel's beginning and once at its end. Miusov calls him "Aesop" once in Book Two, Chapter 8 (PSS 14: 78;84); Dmitrii Karamazov once and Ivan Karamazov twice in Book 3, Chapter 9 (PSS 14:129, 132;140, 143);

---

* Extracts from Deborah A. Martinsen, *Surprised by Shame: Dostoevsky's Liars and Narrative Exposure* (Columbus: The Ohio State University Press, 2003), 175–83. Permission to reprint granted by The Ohio State University Press. The text is reproduced here with minor modifications: some footnotes have been removed.

1 As Andrew Morrison points out, "Humiliation specifically reflects the social, interpersonal manifestation of shame, or internalized representation of the 'humiliator' [...] Humiliation is that manifestation of shame which is the product of *action* perpetrated against the self by someone else." Andrew Morrison, *Shame: The Underside of Narcissism* (London: Routledge, 1989), 15.

Dmitrii once again in Book Twelve, Chapter 2 (PSS 15:99; 666). Dostoevskii further underscores the epithet's metaliterary function by joining Miusov's first and Dmitrii's last references to Fedor as "Aesop" with references to him as "that Pierrot." Aesop and Pierrot share humble social origins and ambiguous identities as well as scatological, gastronomical, and clown-like associations. Both are identified with arbitrary violence and comic wit. Both are subverters of hierarchy as well as performers. And both link Fedor Pavlovich to the European literary tradition. Though Fedor Pavlovich is referred to as "Pierrot" only twice, he is repeatedly referred to as, and even professes himself to be, a "buffoon" (*shut*), keeping his identity as a performer alive to Dostoevskii's readers [. . .]

Like the legendary Aesop, Fedor Karamazov's career moves from private to public spheres. As Annabel Patterson points out in her study *Fables of Power*, most collections of Aesop's fables from the Middle Ages through the eighteenth century begin with the legendary life of Aesop.[2] Though the *Life* itself consists of a series of anecdotes, many of them scatological, Patterson points out that together they form a complex fable that was often amply illustrated. In the legendary *Life*, Aesop (or Aethiops) was an ugly,[3] black slave who acquired the gift of eloquence after he hosted two priests of Diana. He was then sold to the philosopher Xanthus, whom he entertained with his wit and one-upmanship. Weary of his role as servile prankster, he achieved manumission by successfully interpreting portents. Aesop then attained international fame as a counselor, which proved his undoing, for the good citizens of Delphi, either jealous of their own reputation as readers of oracles (Patterson) or angry because Aesop reminded them of their slave origins (Daly), had him framed for sacrilegious theft and threw him over the cliff at Delphi. Patterson points out that though there were fables before and after Aesop, he became associated with animal fables employed as ruses by the underprivileged for survival in a hostile world and was thus seen as a symbolic figure of challenge from below. Furthermore, she associates him with sexual and political violence and locates him at the crossroads of gross body and ironic wit, slavery and liberty, self-destructive ambition and an ideal of emancipation. The account of Aesop in the nineteenth-century Russian encyclopedia published by Brockhaus-Efron

---

2 Patterson also points out that the lives were revised at various junctures, depending on the author's political agenda. Thus, for instance, La Fontaine omitted all the scatological incidents in his version of Aesop's life. Annabel Patterson, *Fables of Power: Aesopian Writing and Political History* (Durham, NC: Duke University Press, 1991).

3 Iconographically, Aesop was often contrasted to Apollo, as two antipodal images of ugliness and beauty, formlessness and form.

also characterizes the father of the animal fable as a person who, though constantly humiliated by his owners as well as his fellow slaves, was able to revenge himself successfully.[4] The name "Aesop" thus evokes the image of a man who rose from servitude to independence by using his god-given wit, a legendary figure associated with physicality, sacrilege, and theft, both generating fiction and generated by it, the site of revenged humiliation and opposites clashing. What better epithet for Fedor Pavlovich Karamazov? [. . .]

When readers first meet him, Fedor Karamazov has lived and prospered by his verbal wit, the Aesopian quality he has used to raise himself in the world. He sang for his supper, as it were, during his days as a sponger. He managed to convince his first wife, an intelligent young woman with a romantic imagination, "if only briefly," that he "was one of the boldest and most sarcastic spirits of that transitional epoch" (PSS 14:8;8). From this marriage he gained enough capital to make his future fortune. Like the Aesop in Swift's "The Battle of the Books," Fedor Karamazov breaks the silence in Zosima's cell by apologizing for his son Dmitrii's tardiness. He introduces himself with a well-worn cliché attributed to Louis XVIII, thereby identifying himself as an imitator of social decorum: "I myself am always very punctual, to the minute, remembering that punctuality is the courtesy of kings." An upholder of social decorum, Miusov responds to his shame at witnessing Fedor's gaucherie by acrimoniously retorting that Fedor Pavlovich is not a king. Thus, early in the novel, Dostoevskii sets up a scenario of shame and exposure that draws readers into the action. To the intense embarrassment of the homodiegetic audience, including his son Alesha, Fedor Pavlovich parries by proclaiming himself a buffoon:

> "That's quite true, I'm not a king. And just imagine, Petr Aleksandrovich, I even knew it myself, by God! You see, I'm always saying something out of place! Your reverence," he exclaimed with a sort of instant pathos, "you see before you a buffoon! Verily, a buffoon! Thus I introduce myself! It's an old habit, alas! And if I lie inappropriately sometimes [*nekstati inogda vru*], I do it even on purpose, on purpose to be pleasant and make people laugh. One ought to be pleasant, isn't that so?" (PSS 14:38; 40)

Fedor Pavlovich here pays lip service to the *Diary* writer's observation that most liars sacrifice themselves to their audiences, thereby hoping to provide

---

4 *Entsiklopedicheskii slovar'* (St. Petersburg: Izd. Brokgauz-Efron, 1898), vol. 27, 187.

pleasure. In Dostoevskii's article, however, audience pleasure encourages social harmony, whereas Fedor Pavlovich voices the cliché about punctuality to criticize his son. He thereby demonstrates that he is not an altruistic, but an aggressive liar. His shameless exhibitionist display also discomfits the homodiegetic audience, whose members serve as models for the narrative audience, including Alesha, a model for Dostoevskii's authorial audience. Guided by the audience in the text, Dostoevskii's readers experience the same anxiety at witnessing a flagrant violation of social norms as the character audience.

This small scenario dramatizes an instance of inappropriate wit, thus preparing both literally and thematically for the two anecdotes that immediately follow. Fedor Pavlovich's blasphemous use of the interjection "by God" (*ei-bogu*) in a monastery underlines his conscious toying with social and religious taboos. He presents himself as a self-conscious buffoon, a playactor and entertainer, a Pierrot. But he goes even further. Fedor Pavlovich recounts two anecdotes about how wit can backfire. These anecdotes wittily explain the aforementioned exchange with Miusov by anticipating their own effect; they also link him to Aesop, whose wit frequently angered his audience.

By wittily exposing himself, Fedor Karamazov aggressively shares his shame with his audience:

> I came to a little town seven years ago, I had a little business there, and went around with some of their merchants. So we called on the police commissioner, the *ispravnik*, because we wanted to see him about something and invite him to have dinner with us. Out comes the *ispravnik*, a tall man, fat, blond, and gloomy—the most dangerous type in such cases—it's the liver, the liver. I spoke directly with him, you know, with the familiarity of a man of the world: "Mr. Ispravnik," I said to him, "be, so to speak, our Napravnik!" "What do you mean, your Napravnik?" I can see from the first split second that it's not coming off, that he's standing there seriously, but I keep on: "I wanted," I say, "to make a joke, for our general amusement. Mr. Napravnik is our famous Russian Kappelmeister, as it were [. . .]" I explained it all and compared it quite reasonably, didn't I? "I beg your pardon," he says, "I am an *ispravnik*, and I will not allow my title to be used for the construction of puns." He turned around and was about to walk away. I started after him, call out: "Yes, yes, you are an *ispravnik*, not Napravnik." "No," he says, "have it your way. I am Napravnik." And just imagine, our deal fell through! And that's how I am, it's always like that with me. I am forever damaging myself with my own courtesy! (PSS 14:38; 40–1)

Fedor Karamazov's pun, as he himself realizes, might have worked with a different audience. The word *ispravnik*, which designates a police commissioner, literally means "corrector." By contrast, *napravnik*, which literally means "director," is a fabricated word that is also the last name of the Russian composer who first directed the Mariinskii Theater, the imperial opera and ballet theater in Petersburg. Fedor Pavlovich appeals to the police commissioner not to criticize or correct, the police commissioner's literal job, but to direct Fedor Pavlovich's business enterprise. Fedor Pavlovich thus puns on the police commissioner's identity as well as his title. He asks him to be a "director," rather than a "corrector," to harmonize people rather than to isolate them. While Fedor Karamazov puns with a very concrete commercial goal in mind, Fedor Dostoevskii situates this pun in a novel that thematizes social and spiritual harmony. Fedor Dostoevskii's pun also plays with the shared root *prav*, which denotes "justice" and "truth," other thematic issues in the novel.

Fedor Karamazov's pun demonstrates his deliberately aggressive wit. He tells this anecdote about misfired wit after Miusov rudely refuted his cliché about punctuality. By telling a story about the police commissioner's humorless response to his pun, Fedor Pavlovich exposes Miusov's. At the same time he looks to his son's spiritual director, the Elder Zosima. Like the police commissioner, the Elder Zosima upholds order, in his case, spiritual order. Unlike the police commissioner, who "corrects" his charges, Zosima "directs" his spiritual flock. Fedor Pavlovich thus tells his anecdote about literal and figurative understanding to a divided audience—which either literally or figuratively understands him. Unlike most Dostoevskian liars, Fedor Karamazov is acutely aware of his audience. Dostoevskii thus uses him to inscribe his Aesopian poetics into the scene's mimetic action. In reading this scene, Dostoevskii's readers may follow the different examples of Fedor Pavlovich's homodiegetic audience. Like the police commissioner and Miusov, we may respond to his pun with shame and punish him. Or, like Zosima, we may listen to the shame behind it and respond with compassion [...]

Fedor Karamazov's second anecdote also involves word play. In it, for the sake of a pun, he slanders a woman whose husband then beats him. Though I reserve discussion of this anecdote for Chapter 11, it, like Fedor Pavlovich's first anecdote, has an internal audience and is about audience response. Both anecdotes thus self-consciously anticipate Fedor Pavlovich's homodiegetic audience's responses, for they are about business or social interchanges spoiled by Fedor's love of wordplay. The dynamic of backfired wit, in turn, links Fedor Karamazov to Aesop. First of all, like Aesop, Fedor Pavlovich constantly provokes others into beating him—including his own son Dmitrii. Next, like Aesop, Fedor Pavlovich is partly responsible for his own violent death: Aesop reminds the citizens of Delphi of their origins as the progeny of slaves. Likewise, Fedor Pavlovich's names for Smerdiakov remind his illegitimate son of his shameful origins.[5] Again, like Aesop, Fedor Pavlovich is betrayed by the child he takes under his roof. In an Aesopian twist, in a novel about divine and human justice, the self-proclaimed "son of lies" is killed by the son of a liar.

Finally, by establishing the Aesop/Fedor Karamazov connection, Fedor Dostoevskii draws readers' attention to the covert message of Fedor's stories—for *The Brothers Karamazov* is a novel about justice and judgment. Fedor Karamazov, who worries about the Last Judgment, tells stories about being judged and punished [. . .]

Fedor Karamazov and his creator pose a further problem for their audiences. Both note that positive audience response causes pleasure. Furthermore, as Fedor Karamazov's anecdotes show, negative audience response causes pain. His second anecdote underlines the fact that a disapproving audience can even beat a storyteller—as happened so frequently in Aesop's case. So why does a storyteller who knows that storytelling can provide pleasure tell stories that deliberately provoke displeasure? While I do not believe I can explain fully, I think that the shame dynamics encoded in the Aesop/Pushkin connection provide a partial explanation.

When Fedor Karamazov responds to Miusov's initial rejection by aiming his anecdotes at him, he acts like Aesop, engaging in wit and one-upmanship with a social superior. In winning the battle of wits, Aesop frequently incurred physical punishment from his master. Thus the cycle of shame and triumph would resume and continue until Aesop wins his freedom. Once free, he not only becomes his master's social equal, but also gains universal recognition as his master's intellectual superior. Fedor Pavlovich starts from an analogous position. Though he is Miusov's class equal and a relative by marriage, he is not Miusov's social equal. Miusov is ashamed of their relation by marriage. Fedor Pavlovich resents and reacts to his shame. Miusov exposes and shames Fedor Pavlovich, reminding him of his social inferiority. Fedor Pavlovich, in turn, exposes and shames Miusov. Their rivalry thus keeps shame alive for both of them. As mentioned earlier, there are three major defenses against shame: denial, flight, and fight. The first two are more conventional and socially

---

5   Readers might want to remember that Dostoevskii believed that his father was murdered by his own serfs.

acceptable. The decorum-conscious Miusov engages in the first, denial. Fedor Pavlovich, on the other hand, chooses aggression, which is both unconventional and unacceptable. He shares his shame, thus equalizing the relationship. Fedor Dostoevskii uses this Aesopian struggle mimetically to illustrate sociopolitical and economic inequalities in a modernizing country, thematically to raise questions of justice, and synthetically to spotlight issues of audience response.

The epithet "Aesop" functions mimetically as well as metaliterarily in Dostoevskii's novel. Aesop is smart enough to know that he should not provoke the Delphians, yet he does. Fedor Karamazov is smart enough to know that the police commissioner would resent the pun on his name, that the important official would resent the pun on his wife's honor, that the humorless Miusov would expose and shame him. But the pleasure of wordplay, a pleasure that links Fedor Karamazov with Dostoevskii's Lebedev and Lebiadkin, impels Dostoevskii's exhibitionist liars to display themselves whatever the cost. In this, Dostoevskii's liars differ from their creator.

In literary history there are two Aesops: the Aesop of legend and the writer of fables. The name "Aesop" thus evokes the story of a slave who lives and dies by his wit. It also suggests apparently simple stories with hidden depths, thus signaling a time-honored practice favored by writers constricted by censorship. Aesopian subterfuge became a commonplace in the Russian literary tradition, where writers and readers alike conspired to inscribe forbidden materials and messages in and extract them from texts that passed through the scrutiny of government censors.[6] In attributing the epithet "Aesop" to Fedor Karamazov, Dostoevskii deliberately evokes Aesop's legendary life story as well as his poetics. As I have shown, Fedor Karamazov's life story resembles that of the legendary Aesop. But Fedor Karamazov as an Aesopian storyteller is a cover for Fedor Dostoevskii, who uses his comic namesake to plumb dangerous thematic depths. On the surface, *The Brothers Karamazov* is the story of parricide. Beneath the surface, it is the story of regicide and deicide, topics forbidden by Russian censors. Though Dostoevskii counted on his Russian audience's Aesopian reading practices, the epithet "Aesop" clues us to look for depths in Fedor's stories that we might otherwise overlook.

---

6 Laura Kristan Wilhelm, "The Aesopic Legacy in Russian Literature," unpublished article.

Ivan Karamazov and Smerdiakov (1992)*

Harriet Murav

The Brothers Karamazov will be examined as a narrative icon, in which the stories of the brothers and the structure of the novel mirror each other. The icon consists of three parts: katabasis, or descent into hell; trial; and resurrection, or ascent. This tripartite structure corresponds to the traditional structure of the icon, in which the uppermost part represents heaven, the middle section, earth, and the lowermost, hell.[1] In the novel, as we will see, hell takes up the largest space. The possibility of ascent is suggested only at the novel's end by the holy-foolish Alesha [...]

The theme of katabasis is introduced in the most well-known section of the novel, Ivan's "Legend of the Grand Inquisitor." Ivan prefaces his "poem" by describing various literary and dramatic works, popular in both Europe and Russia, in which angels, the Virgin Mary, the saints, and even God make their appearance. Ivan gives as an example "The Tour of the Virgin in Hell," which, he says, is a translation from the Greek. Ivan compares the force and daring of the "Tour" to Dante's *Inferno*. The Virgin visits hell and, led by the archangel Michael, sees the sinners and their various torments. She comes to a fiery lake and sees "those whom God has forgotten" (PSS 14:225, *BK* 2.5.5). Greatly moved, she pleads with God on their behalf. God is at first reluctant. He shows her the hands and feet of his son, pierced through by nails, and asks,

* Extracts from Harriet Murav, *Holy Foolishness: Dostoevsky's Novels and the Poetics of Cultural Critique* (Palo Alto, CA: Stanford University Press, 1992) 135, 139–41, 144–48. Copyright © 1992 by the Board of Trustees of the Leland Stanford Jr. University. All rights reserved. Used by permission of the publisher, Stanford University Press, sup.org.

1 V. I. Uspenskii, *Ocherki po istorii ikonopisaniia* (St. Petersburg: Sinod. tip., 1899), 20.

"How can I forgive his tormentors?" Mary persists and, with the help of all the saints, angels, and martyrs, wins a yearly respite for all the sinners, which lasts from Good Friday to Trinity day.

As Ivan suggests, "The Tour of the Virgin in Hell" represents an important aspect of popular apocrypha.[2] Like the *Inferno*, to which Ivan compares them, the various "Tours" present a fully articulated topography of human sinfulness. The fiery river or lake is but one of the torments. Others include a tree of iron, from which sinners are hung, a chamber of iron, circles of fire, a vile fog, and "insatiable worms" (Pypin, "Drevniaia russkaia literatura," 351). The sins include not bowing to icons, laughing in church, fornication, crooked judgment, and, in some of the later versions, the shaving of beards and the use of tobacco. The loose format provides the opportunity for an ongoing cultural critique. The overall texture of "The Tour of the Virgin in Hell" can be described as pictorial, encyclopedic, topical, and cosmological—qualities that are also characteristic of Dostoevskii's novel.

Ivan's use of the "Tour" in conversation with his brother suggests one of the ways that we can understand Alesha's role not only in this scene but in the novel as a whole. Ivan's theological rebellion is based in part on conclusions he has drawn from the sufferings of children. Before he quotes from the "Tour," Ivan describes to Alesha a whole catalogue of atrocities committed against children. The episodes he describes are not hypothetical cases but actual events, culled from the newspapers of the day. Ivan's catalogue, in other words, has the same sort of topicality that we saw in the "Tour." Alesha experiences the full force of Ivan's journalism: he cries out, "Why are you tormenting me?" Ivan's description of the children's suffering and Alesha's response suggest that the scene can be understood as a verbal tour of hell, with Ivan as the guide and Alesha as the tourist.

The miniature verbal tour of hell provides a key to the overall structure of the novel to this point as Alesha's katabasis. He descends from the monastery to the secular world (in Book 2), where he ceaselessly moves between sites of "laceration" (*nadryv*) and despair. At Katerina Ivanovna's, in

---

2　For more on the "Tour," see Martha Himmelfarb, *Tours of Hell: An Apocalyptic Form in Jewish and Christian Literature* (Minneapolis: Fortress Press, 1985). In the 1860s, N. Tikhonravov, I. Sreznevskii, and F. I. Buslaev all published studies of Russian apocrypha. In 1857, the "thick journal" *Notes of the Fatherland* (*Otechestvennye zapiski*) published A. Pypin's article, "Legends about the Tour of the Virgin in Hell," which contained a detailed description of various "Tours." See Pypin, "Drevniaia russkaia literatura: I: Starinnye apokrify. II: Skazanie o khozhdenii bogoroditsy po mukam," *Otechestvennye zapiski* 115, no. 2 (1857): 335–60.

Snegirov's hut, and especially at his father's house, which Fedor Pavlovich calls his *skvernia* ("foul place"), Alesha plays the role of a tourist in hell, similar to that of Mary in the apocryphal "Tour of Hell." [...]

Thus far, I have traced in Dmitrii's subplot a katabasis narrative in which descent into hell has, if not a happy, then at least a hopeful ending. Another aspect of katabasis in *The Brothers* can be found in what Robert Belknap has described as Alesha's vicarious journey through the philosophical hell in which Ivan resides. The rubric of a philosophical hell applies to the series of interrelated models—of human history, of the relationship between fathers and children, of God and his creatures, even of the author and his hero—implicit in Ivan's "Rebellion," his "Legend of the Grand Inquisitor," and his discussions with the devil, all of which challenge the promise of renewal in the theological models that I have just discussed. The novel, as a whole, offers alternatives to Ivan's models in a number of ways, one of the most important being Alesha himself, whose role as a holy fool has complexities we have yet to explore. But to search for a concrete response, to seek to match up a "pro" for every "contra," would be misguided. To look for a solution to Ivan's dilemma in the terms that he proposes means never to escape from it. If we want to escape from his dilemma, we cannot read *The Brothers Karamazov* in terms of "pro and contra." We have to come up with another way of reading the novel. Dostoevskii does not leave us completely to our own devices, however. The novel teaches us how it ought to be read.

In order to see how this process works, we must first understand Ivan's "rebellion." In a letter written in 1879 to his editor at *The Russian Messenger*, N. A. Liubimov, Dostoevskii characterized Ivan's position as follows: "My hero chooses a theme I consider irrefutable: the senselessness of children's suffering, and develops from it the absurdity of all historical reality" (PSS 30.I:63). Dostoevskii's emphasis on history is crucially important. What Ivan sees as the ordering of the world makes no sense to him. As Ivan puts it to Alesha, he knows, with his earthly Euclidean mind, that "one thing follows another, directly and simply," and that "everything flows and reaches equilibrium." The kind of story that Ivan would tell about history, his chronotope, is one that would link events into linear chains of cause-and-effect relationships.[3] [...]

---

3 In his *Diary of a Writer* for October 1876, Dostoevskii had given this mode of thinking precise formulation. In an article entitled "Two Suicides," he attributed Liza Gertsen's suicide to the despair that he believed necessarily arises from the positivist thinking in which she was raised: the kind of thinking that organizes the relations anlong phenomena in a straightforward linearity of cause and effect (PSS 23:145). Dostoevskii called this model of causality *priamolineinost'*.

Ivan's dilemma is not exhausted by the opposition between science and theology. If the matter ended there, if Ivan were a pure scientist, his lot would be easier to bear. What torments him, however, is that his model of history effectively silences the suffering of the children. There is no answering cry in any other part of the universe; instead, "everything flows and reaches equilibrium." Ivan also has a sense of justice: he demands retribution for the suffering of the children, not in infinity but in the here and now. Because his model of history is inadequate, he turns to God, calling God to account in his own terms. Another way to put it is to say that Ivan tries to limit all possible relationships between the infinite and the finite to purely finite terms. And in the resulting equation, God comes up short. Ivan argues that if everyone must suffer in order to buy eternal harmony, why must children suffer as well? Why have they been reduced to material for the future harmony? We cannot afford that sort of harmony, Ivan concludes, and he therefore rejects God's world; he "returns his ticket."

Ivan's model is not, strictly speaking, a scientific one, for he believes in the infinite value of the innocent child. We can restate his position as follows. Everything seems to flow, effect seems to follow cause, but, in reality, there is no order because of the un-righted wrong of the suffering of children. There has been a terrible skewing of the balance sheets, which masquerades as order. The world rests not on a divinely ordered harmony but on "absurdities." God's creation is nothing other than "demonic chaos" (PSS 14:209, BK 2.5.4).

The polarity that we earlier defined between scientific and sacred history needs to be restated in a somewhat different form as the polarity between sacred and demonic history. The first envisions the possibility of salvation; the second sees it as impossible. In this schema, the scientific model of history can be subsumed under the demonic.

Just as the devil is a false imitation of God, demonic history is a bad imitation of sacred history. In the beginning of the chapter, we drew upon the theology of the icon to describe the central concept of sacred history, namely, replication that includes change. The demonic version amounts to replication without change, sheer repetition. Ivan's devil articulates such a philosophy, for example, when he says that the present earth may have come into existence, been destroyed and reborn an infinite number of times, the whole process repeated in exactly the same way each time, "down to the last detail" (PSS 15:79, BK 4.11.9). Nothing new could ever enter the cycle; everything is already given and already known. There can be no surprises; as the devil himself concludes, "It is horribly boring." To anticipate, the model implicit in Zosima's thinking suggests, in contrast to both the predictability of the scientific model of causality and the demonic principle of eternal return, that human history is open-ended. In the notebooks to the novel, Zosima says that the directions taken by history cannot be known in advance (*gde znat' vse khody istorii*) (PSS 15:253).

The principle of eternal return is no mere philosophical abstraction, isolated from the novel's dramatic and psychological structure. Demonic repetition can also be found in the relationship between Ivan and his father. Smerdiakov says that, of all the brothers, Ivan is the one who most closely resembles his father, "with one and the same soul" (PSS 15:68, *BK* 4.11.8). The notebooks to the novel suggest more than a resemblance. Ivan remarks to Alesha that Liza pleases him, and adds, "I'm afraid that I'm turning into Fedor Pavlovich" (PSS 15:324). The son repeats his father, reiterating in individual, psychological terms what the devil has articulated as a principle of history: that we are utterly bound by the past. The inescapability of the past, the father's hold over his son, is also suggested by the fact that Smerdiakov's first name and patronymic, Pavel Fedorovich, are the reverse of those of his father, Fedor Pavlovich.

Smerdiakov, like Fedor Pavlovich is associated with the devil and with that which is unclean. Smerdiakov's name means something like "Stinker." The words *smert'*, ("death"), *osmerdit'*, ("to befoul"), *smerdiashchii* ("stinking"), and the name Smerdiakov are all related. Smerdiakov, who *smerdit* ("stinks"), carries the sign of death (*smert'*,). In his childhood he used to hang cats and then perform funeral rites over them; as an adult, he commits murder and then suicide. Smerdiakov's excessive fastidiousness, his squeamishness about his food, for example, and his fondness for pomade and perfume indicate an impurity from which he cannot escape.[4] It is part of his birth, as Grigorii, the old servant, tells him: "You come from the bathhouse mildew" (PSS 14:II4, *BK* l.3.6). Smerdiakov blasphemes: he laughs because God created light on the first day but did not create the sun, moon and sars until the fourth day. Grigorii slaps him, and "it just so happened" that a week later, Smerdiakov showed the first signs of epilepsy, a disease preeminently associated with demonic possession.

---

4 For more on Smerdiakov and impurity, see Gary Saul Morson, "Verbal Pollution in *The Brothers Karamazov*," *Poetics and Theory of Literature* 3 (1978): 223–33. Morson's analysis rests on the concepts of purity and danger developed by Mary Douglas. Smerdiakov's roles as cook, gatekeeper, and intermediary reveal his position "betwixt and between"; he is powerful and dangerous because he is the "anomaly to all classifications."

Alesha Karamazov (1977)*

Valentina Vetlovskaia

"The main narrative is the second," explains the narrator of *The Brothers Karamazov* in his introductory remarks, "—it is the action of my hero in our day, at the very present time. The first novel takes place thirteen years ago, and it is hardly even a novel, but only a period in my hero's early youth. I cannot do without this first novel, because much in the second would be unintelligible without it."[1]

Clearly Dostoevskii conceived of his work in the form of two novels, of which the second (not known to us) is the main one. It follows that without this second novel much in the first cannot be entirely comprehensible. It is essential, therefore, that we seek out and consider elements which might provide some clue to the overall structure of the two novels [. . .]

The introductory remarks provide some indication of the sense of the whole. The opening phrase of the introduction speaks of a biography: "In beginning the biography of my hero, Aleksei Fedorovich Karamazov," etc. The narrator continues: "I have two novels and only one biography." What is important here, first, is that the narrator-author conceives of the whole as a biography, and, second, that Aleksei Fedorovich Karamazov is the center of this biography. The preeminence of precisely this hero is emphasized throughout the entire story, in spite of the fact that the first novel is called *The Brothers Karamazov.*

---

*   Extracts from Valentina Vetlovskaya, "Alyosha and the Hagiographic Hero," trans. Nancy Pollak and Susanne Fusso, in *Dostoevsky: New Perspectives*, ed. Robert Louis Jackson (New York: Prentice Hall, 1984), 206–13, 219–20, 222, 224–26. The text reproduced here has been updated by the original translators and, additionally, some footnotes have been removed.

1   *The Brothers Karamazov*, trans. by Constance Garnett (New York: Modern Library, 1950), xviii. All subsequent references are to this edition. (Translator's note.)

The first line of the novel, closely related to the introduction, reads as follows: "Aleksei Fedorovich Karamazov was the third son of [. . .] a landowner [. . .] in our district." The main hero is singled out. Further, the introductory story of Alesha appears in a special chapter entitled, "The Third Son, Alesha." By contrast, the more laconic and dry accounts of Dmitrii and Ivan appear in chapters that seem to diminish rather than accentuate the importance of these heroes: "He Gets Rid of his Eldest Son," "The Second Marriage and the Second Family" (here Fedor Pavlovich is in the foreground).

We may recall at this point that the word used for "biography," *zhiz-neopisanie,* signifies *"vita."* The narrator of The Brothers Karamazov emerges— not obtrusively, but clearly enough—as the narrator of a *vita,* with his "main": hero, Alesha, as hero-saint.[2] [. . .]

Like the typical hero of a hagiographic narrative, even in early youth Alesha feels the urge to depart from the vain world, because earthly passions are alien to him.

The complex relations between the ideal hero of the *vita* and the surrounding world make this hero strange to ordinary people and ordinary perception. This is the way Alesha is presented to the reader. The narrator speaks right away of a strangeness, a certain eccentricity in him, but at the same time explains that these qualities do not, nevertheless, signify isolation: "[. . .] on the contrary, it happens sometimes that such a person [the eccentric—V. V.], I dare say, carries within himself the very heart of the universal, and the rest of the men of his epoch have for some reason been temporarily torn from it . . ." As a result Alesha is both set off against other people (this is typical for the hero of a *vita*), and closely linked to them, because it is impossible to go far from the "heart," impossible to entirely break off from it. Such a twist is unusual for a *vita* [. . .] Alesha's "wild fanatical modesty and chastity" also belongs to the obligatory attributes of the hero of the *vita*—another feature that makes him strange from an ordinary point of view and that, for example, makes "all his schoolfellows from the bottom class to the top want to mock at him" and to look upon him "with compassion" (I, 1, iv).

---

2 A. L. Volynskii, in connection with the portrait characterization of Alesha in the novel, noted the latter circumstance: "His [Alesha's—V. V.] quiet gaze, the longish oval of his face, the animation of expression—all this created the impression of a painted icon from the Tsarist school from the seventeenth century—an image in which there is nothing provocative, nothing sharply individual." A. L. Volynskii, *Tsarstvo Karamazovykh* (St. Petersburg: Tip. M. M. Stasiulevicha, 1901), 148–49.

In general, the motifs that are enumerated here exhaust the preliminary characterization of Alesha. They are all marked and coordinated with the usual representation of the hero of the *vita*, who, even in childhood, exhibits the uncommon characteristics of the future great ascetic and saint [...]

With the exception of the element of self-admiration (which is in no way connected with Alesha), everything in the characterization of "contemplative" love corresponds to the feeling with which Alesha enters on the "monastic road." The hero is not yet ready for an "active" love, for the "harsh and dreadful," for "labor and fortitude." Therefore his choice, despite the fact that it is natural for this essentially saintly hero, has as yet the most hasty and preliminary character. It perhaps serves as a premonitory allusion to the future, but it is not very important in the present, for the hero begins directly from that with which he should have ended.

As a result the image of the main hero of the "biography" is presented as mobile, capable of further change, and lacking that schematic straightforwardness and fixity of form which burdens the typical hero of a *vita*. Let us stress that this changeability and mobility is indicated not so much in spite of the hagiographic canon, as within its boundaries, thanks to the ambiguity, created by the narration, of certain motifs originating in that canon [...]

The above-cited motifs (on the one hand, the hero's uncommonness even in early youth, his decision to go into a monastery; on the other, his lack of inner preparation for this exploit, his dispatch into the world for such preparation) signify that in this case we are dealing with the organic combination in one character of the two usual types of hagiographic hero. The first type is the hero who senses, almost from infancy, his lofty calling, and subsequently follows it without swerving (like Theodosius of Pechersk or Sergius of Radonezh). The second type is the hero who turns to God and gives himself up to the same asceticism after many trials, mistakes and errors (Ephraim Sirin). Alesha's dispatch from the monastery does confront him with this set of trials, for in relation to the hero of the *vita*, the world can only appear in its tempting aspect.

After the presentation of the main hero, a motif arises that links his name with that of Aleksei the Man of God. This motif is at first heard obliquely. The hero of the *vita*, widely known in its time, is only recalled to the reader's mind. The occasion for this reminder is the eider's conversation with one of the devout women, who is wasting away with grief over her dead boy. To the eider's question as to what her son was called, the mother answers:

"Aleksei, Father."
"A sweet name. After Aleksei, the Man of God?"

"Of God, Father, of God, Aleksei the Man of God!"
"What a saint he was! I will remember him, mother . . ." (I, 2, iii)

Since the name of the main hero has already been mentioned and he himself has been presented to the reader in a hagiographic halo, the reminder of Aleksei the Man of God brings to mind certain details of the "biography" that support the idea of Alesha's closeness to the hagiographic hero mentioned here.

Aleksei the Man of God was born in Rome; his parents were rich and distinguished Romans: "Under the emperors Arcadius and Honorius, at the end of the fourth century, there lived in Rome a distinguished man by the name of Euphimian, and his wife Aglaida . . ."[3]

In the version of the life found in the *Lives of the Saints* by Dimitrius of Rostov, we read: "There was in ancient Rome a pious man by the name of Euphimian, at the time of the pious emperors Arcadius and Honorius, great among the nobles and exceedingly wealthy . . ." In the *Prologue* version of the life of Aleksei the Man of God we read: "He was from ancient Rome, the son of Euphimian the patrician, his mother was Aglaida. . . ."[4]

Clearly it is not by chance that it is precisely in the chapter, "The Third Son, Alyosha," that the portrait of Fyodor Pavlovich is given, which ends with the words: "He was fond indeed of making fun of his own face, though, I believe, he was well-satisfied with it. He used particularly to point to his nose, which was not very large, but very delicate and conspicuously aquiline. "A regular Roman nose," he used to say, "with my goiter I've quite the countenance of an ancient Roman patrician of the decadent period." (I, 1, iv). To be sure, the evident resemblance between Fyodor Pavlovich and the father of the ancient hero of the *vita*, who was by habit quite pious, is confined to this casual remark. [. . .]

The basic features of the *vita* of Aleksei the Man of God and of the sacred poem about him are Aleksei's departure from home to perform the exploits customary for the hero of a *vita*, and his life in his parents' home upon his

---

3   *Izbrannye zhitiia sviatykh, kratko izlozhennye po rukovodstvu Chet'ikh Minei*, 2nd ed., revised and supplemented (Moscow, 1860), March 17. This edition was in Dostoevskii's library. See L. Grossman, *Biblioteka Dostoevskogo* (Odessa : A. A. Ivasenko, 1919), 154. Especially interested in the *vita* of Aleksei the Man of God, Dostoevskii undoubtedly did not limit himself to the short exposition of it in this edition. *The Lives of the Saints* by Dimitrius of Rostov and the *Prologue*, quite authoritative and accessible in their time, were well known to him.

4   Both the *vita* in the edition of Dimitrius of Rostov and the *Prologue* redaction are cited according to the texts included by V. P. Adrianova-Peretts in the appendix to her *Zhitie Alekseia, cheloveka bozhiia, v drevnei russkoi literature i narodnoi slovesnosti* (Petrograd: Ia. Bashmakov, 1917), 501, 512.

return.[5] It is precisely from the time when the saint, unrecognized, lodges in his parents' home, that a grave temptation begins: the saint is faced not with a rejection of the world in order to save himself and, perhaps, others, but with a sojourn in the world for those same goals.

In accordance with the spirit and meaning of the *vita* and the poem about Saint Aleksei, Alesha Karamazov's rapprochement with the world and his relations at first turns out to be a trial for him. The narrative is constructed so that after the scene in the monastery, which serves as the starting point of the action, Alesha is sent on errands by first one, then another character; he listens to others' stories, usually filled with perturbation and grief, that cast doubt on the affirmation of God's endless love, charity, and beneficence. The tempting character of these encounters, commissions, and confessions is conveyed through various motifs [...]

Fulfilling others' requests, listening to others (above all his brother Ivan), Alesha gives way to temptation. The "darkness" of the world does not remain alien to this hero's heart, and not only because he is too young, but also because Alesha, as he himself explains more than once, is a Karamazov. Notwithstanding his strangeness, Alesha is the same sort of man as everyone else (in contrast to the *vita* and the poem, in the novel this motif is carried out quite definitely). The very deep affinity of the "angel" Alesha for the other "sinners" presumes, for the young and inexperienced hero, the possibility of committing the same errors as the others. "Yes, yes, it is he, it is Pater Seraphicus, he will save me—from him and forever!" (II, 5, v)—races helplessly through Alesha's mind when he hurries to the monastery after the conversation with Ivan [...]

If Alesha had loved the elder more "correctly," that is, not with an exceptional love but in the same way that he loved others, he would not have found grounds in the righteous man's "shame" for the condemnation of "God's world." Everything in this world is connected. And just as there are

---

5   In contrast to the *vita*, the poem sometimes emphasizes Aleksei's desire, in his departure from home, to serve not only his own salvation but that of his relatives:

... I went to an alien land,

to pray for papa's sins,

to work for mama's sins! (Var. of Kireevskii)

See also Bessonov, var. Nos. 29, 30. An echo of this motif (which is omitted by T. I. Filippov's variant) appears in *Brothers Karamazov*, in Fedor Pavlovich's reply to his son's request to allow him to go back to the monastery: "After all I'll miss you, Alesha ... However, here's a good opportunity: pray for us sinners; sitting here, we've sinned too much. I've been thinking all the time about this: who's ever going to pray for me? Is there such a person in the world?" (I, 1, iv).

none who are completely righteous, so there are none who are completely sinful. For this reason the scene of Alesha and Grushen'ka, coming after the scene of the young hero's bitter suffering, harmoniously complements the story about the righteous man's "shame." Here the sinful woman unexpectedly reveals a degree of love, reverence for sanctity, and compassion for her dispirited brother that, considering her "incorrect" view of things, would not be supposed of her. Thanks to this, Grushen'ka is able to encourage Alesha: the loftiness of her soul, made manifest "at that moment," is the essential link in the chain of phenomena that, according to the author's conception, makes their entire relationship not frightfully incongruous but comforting and harmonious.

Alesha's dream ("Cana of Galilee") naturally concludes these scenes. The boundlessness of God's love for all people and the joy of those who are united by this love are manifested here to the young ascetic as if before his very eyes. The link of everyone with each other, salutary and joyful when God is among people (a circumstance which must be construed in a broad sense), staggers Alesha's soul with ecstasy. The idea of the primordial beauty and purity of "God's world," and of the responsibility of all people for the fact that they make this beautiful world vicious, is what the author tries to emphasize in "Cana of Galilee." It is just this idea that Alesha suddenly grasps, "for the rest of his life and forever and ever": "What was he weeping over? Oh! in his rapture he was weeping even over those stars, which were shining to him from the abyss of space . . . He longed to forgive everyone and for everything, and to beg forgiveness. Oh, not for himself, but for all men, for all and for everything. 'And others are praying for me too,' echoed again in his soul [. . .] He had fallen on the earth a weak boy, but he rose up a resolute champion, and he knew and felt it suddenly at the very moment of his ecstasy" (III, 7, iv).

Thus the young ascetic's passionate and exceptional love for his spiritual father yields, at this important moment, to a just as passionate love for the world and for all people without exception [. . .]

True, it is possible that the moment of Alesha's ecstasy before "God's world" is only an anticipation. It is possible that subsequently Alesha will turn from the "correct road" once more. All this is possible. But if Alesha does turn from this road, then it would certainly be in order for him to enter onto it later, once and for all. It is precisely this outcome that the logic of the artistic narrative demands.

A person who joyfully takes into his soul the entire world ("both the whole, and every grain of sand") without exception, accepting all people in spite of their "stinking sin," loving it all with an equally deep love, in other words, a person who comprehends the beauty and blessing of God's creation and along with it the beauty and blessing of the creator, is, of course, a "man of God." The world and God are harmoniously reconciled in the soul of this hero.

So Alesha emerges (or must emerge) from the grave trial to which the "divine" elder sends him. And thus Dostoevskii interprets the central figure and the central confrontation of the *vita* of Aleksei the Man of God against a new background. In the continuation of the novel about Alesha this interpretation would, it is likely, appear more clearly, but even now it is sufficiently obvious.

CHAPTER 5

The Novel

Dostoevskii is best known as a novelist, though he also wrote short fiction and journalism, and his novels are often regarded as milestones in the development of the novel form. Throughout the twentieth century, his novels played a central role in the growing field of novel theory as either paradigmatic or pathbreaking examples of the genre. Two of the pioneers of the field, Mikhail Bakhtin and Georg Lukács, began by writing critical works on Dostoevskii's novels, which transformed into theories of the novel, Bakhtin's *Problems in Dostoevskii's Art* (1929) (and its later edition, *Problems of Dostoevskii's Poetics,* 1963) and Lukács's *Theory of the Novel* (1914–15). The main part of this chapter is made up of secondary sources, which consider Dostoevskii's novels from different perspectives within the broad realm of novel theory. However, Dostoevskii himself also gave a lot of consideration to the novel as a genre, particularly in the mid-1870s when he was working on his most experimental late novel, *The Adolescent.*

The Adolescent, published in 1875, Dostoevskii's messiest novel, is about the problem of how to write about the contemporary moment. Dostoevskii even considered giving it the title *Disorder.* The first part of this chapter shows how *The Adolescent* showcases some of the dilemmas facing the novelist of the 1870s. It consists of an extract from the notebooks to *The Adolescent,* as well as the fictional letter included in the novel's epilogue. This letter responds to some of the criticisms leveled at the novel's first serialized installments and provides Dostoevskii's answer to those criticisms. In the extract from the notebooks to the novel that opens this chapter, he declares that, "disintegration is the principal visible idea of the novel." Taken together, these two pieces show Dostoevskii's attempt to think about what a novel of disorder and disintegration might look like. In the chapter's third extract, Kate Holland shows how Dostoevskii conceives of *The Adolescent* as a response to Tolstoi's *Childhood* trilogy, how he reconceives the noble family novel for a new historical moment.

The rest of the chapter provides a survey of theoretical and critical works dealing with Dostoevskii's responses to different realms of the novel and the novelistic. An important strand of novel theory focuses on Dostoevskii's revolutionary approach to narration in the novel. In an extract taken from probably the most influential work on Dostoevskii and the novel, *Problems of Dostoevskii's Poetics*, Bakhtin argues that Dostoevskii's greatest contribution to the genre is in the new relationship of author to hero. Where traditional novelists depict a hero with a fixed and concrete place in the world, Dostoevskii shows him as an ever-changing consciousness. His novels hinge on how the hero sees himself and how he interacts with the world. Every aspect of novelistic reality is now mediated by the hero's self-consciousness, as even author and narrator are brought into the hero's field of vision. To show the uniqueness of Dostoevskii's treatment of the self-conscious hero, Bakhtin analyzes the way in which Tolstoi, as author, always has a surplus of vision, is always in full control of his hero. We do not have to subscribe to Bakhtin's reductionist view of Tolstoi to appreciate his insight into Dostoevskii's poetics. Narration is also the subject of the extract from Robin Feuer Miller's analysis of *The Idiot*. Miller examines the shifting narrative voice in the novel, showing how Dostoevskii uses themes and techniques taken from Gothic novelists to convey the horror mixed with the beautiful, which constitutes the sublime, an important mode in this account of the fall of a Christlike hero.

Dostoevskii's representation of time in the novel has also been the subject of much scholarly attention. In a section from his book on the poetics of Russian literature, Dmitrii Likhachev examines how Dostoevskii "emancipates" time, just as he liberates the novelistic hero in Bakhtin's account. Time seems to flow on its own in Dostoevskii's novels, and everything happens suddenly. Events are recorded in their full chaos and immediacy by a narrator-chronicler who has no time to organize or analyze it. It is organized instead by an author-narrator who stands above the narrator-chronicler. Likhachev shows how Dostoevskii transposes the medieval form of the voice of the narrator-chronicler, with its collective consciousness of time, to a new historical moment, when it serves to self-consciously represent the time of chaotic modernity. Gary Saul Morson also examines Dostoevskii's treatment of time in the novel, arguing that he uses a technique called "sideshadowing," which shows that each moment leads to multiple possible scenarios in order to demonstrate the openendedness of time. He shows how, in *Demons*, rumors and narrative prevarications help to create a sense of open time which counteracts the linear time of the revolutionaries and their utopian models.

In final extract of the chapter, Robert Belknap examines Dostoevskii's plotting in *Crime and Punishment*. While the architectonics and intricate plotting of Tolstoi's novels have occasioned many scholarly debates, Dostoevskii's plots have too often been sidelined or dismissed as imitations of the contrived plot devices of lowbrow literature or genre fiction. Belknap shows how parallelism and situation rhyme among the plots helps to locate the center of the action as taking place within the mind of Raskol'nikov. By means of a set of oppositions that reverberate throughout the novel, Dostoevskii never permits his reader to leave the capacious mind of Raskol'nikov, which seems to stretch to encompass the novel's own limits.

Further Reading

Bakhtin, Mikhail. *Problems of Dostoevsky's Poetics*. Minneapolis: University of Minnesota Press, 1984.

Holland, Kate. *The Novel in the Age of Disintegration: Dostoevsky and Genre in the 1870s*. Evanston, IL: Northwestern University Press, 2013.

Holquist, Michael. *Dostoevsky and the Novel*. Princeton, NJ: Princeton University Press, 1977.

Ivanov, Vyacheslav. *Freedom and the Tragic Life: A Study in Dostoevsky*. New York: Noonday Press, 1959.

Miller, Robin Feuer. *Dostoevsky and The Idiot: Author, Narrator and Reader*. Cambridge, MA: Harvard University Press, 1981.

Morson, Gary Saul. *Narrative and Freedom: The Shadows of Time*. New Haven, CT: Yale University Press, 1994.

A Novel of Disintegration from the Notebooks for *The Adolescent* (1874)*

*M*ost important. The idea of disintegration is present everywhere, for everything is falling apart, and there are no remaining ties not only in the Russian family, but even simply between people in general. Even children are apart.

[*Disintegration is the principal visible idea of the novel.*]

"The tower of Babel," he says. "Here we are, for example, a Russian family. We speak different languages and cannot understand each other. Society is chemically disintegrating."

[. . .]

Title of the novel: "Disorder."

The whole idea of the novel is to demonstrate that we have now general disorder, disorder everywhere and wherever you go, in society, in business, in guiding ideas (of which, [for that very reason,] there aren't any), in \<our\> convictions (which, [for the same reason,] we don't have), in the disintegration of the family unit. "If there are any passionate convictions, they are all destructive (socialism). There aren't any moral ideas; suddenly not a single one is left, and above all," He the Youth says, "one has the impression that there never were any."

---

* From Fyodor Dostoyevsky, *The Notebooks for "A Raw Youth,"* trans. Victor Terras, ed. Edward Wasiolek (Chicago: University of Chicago Press, 1969), 37–38, 120. Copyright © by the University of Chicago. All rights reserved. Published 1969. Elsewhere in this volume, we have used an alternative translation for this novel: *The Adolescent.*

An Exceptional Family from *The Adolescent* (1875)*

Fedor Dostoevskii

"If I had been a Russian novelist and had talent I should certainly have chosen my heroes from the old nobility, because only in that type of cultivated Russian is it possible to find at least that outward semblance of fine order and aesthetic beauty so necessary in a novel to produce an artistic effect on the reader. I am not joking when I say this, although I am not a nobleman myself, as you are indeed aware. Pushkin selected the subject for his future novels from the 'Traditions of the Russian Family,' and believe me that everything beautiful we have had so far is to be found therein. Everything that has been brought to some sort of perfection, anyway. I don't say this because I am accepting unconditionally the truth and justness of that beauty; but at least there were completely worked out forms of honor and duty which have never existed anywhere in Russia except in the nobility, even in the most rudimentary shape. I speak as a calm man seeking calm.

"Whether that honor was a good thing, and whether that duty was a true one—is a secondary question. What to my mind is of most consequence is the finality of the forms and the existence of some sort of order, not prescribed from above, but developed from within. Good heavens, what matters most of all for us is to have any sort of order of our own! All hopes for the future, and, so to say, restfulness of outlook lie in our having something at last built up, instead of this everlasting destruction, instead of chips flying in all directions, rubbish and disorder which has led to nothing for two hundred years.

From *A Raw Youth, trans.* Constance Garnett (Melbourne, London, Toronto: William Heinemann Ltd., 1916), 557–60.

"Don't accuse me of Slavophilism; I only say this from misanthropy, for my heart is heavy! Something is happening to us today and in the recent past, the very opposite of what I have imagined above. It is not that the worthless attach themselves to the highest stratum of society, but, on the contrary, with light-hearted haste, fragments are torn from what is fine and noble and thrown into one mass with the lawless and the envious. And there have been many instances of fathers and head of what have been cultured families, laughing at what their children perhaps would have liked to believe in. What is more they eagerly display to their children their spiteful pleasure at the sudden license to be dishonest which they have all at once deduced, wholesale, from something. I am not speaking of the true progressives, dear Arkadii Makarovich, but, only of that rabble, so numerous it seems, of whom it has been said '*grattez le Russe et vous verrez le Tatare*,'[1] and believe me there are by no means so many true liberals, true and noble friends of humanity among us, as we have imagined.

"But all this is theorizing; let us come back to our supposed novelist. The position of our novelist in this case would be perfectly definite; he could not write in any other form but the historical, for there is no fine type in our day, and if there were remnants of it left they would not, according to the prevalent ideas of the day, have retained their beauty. Oh! and in historical form it is possible to depict a multitude of extremely attractive and consolatory details! It is possible so to fascinate the reader indeed that he will take the historical picture for the possible and the actual. Such a work, if executed with great talent, would belong not so much to Russian literature as to Russian history.

"It would be a picture artistically worked out of the Russian ideal, having a real existence so long as it was not guessed that was an ideal. The grandson of those heroes who have been depicted in a picture of a Russian family of the upper middle cultivated class during three generations, side by side with and in connection with Russian history—that descendant of his forefathers would not be depicted in his modern type except in a somewhat misanthropic solitary and distinctly melancholy aspect. He is even bound to appear a somewhat strange figure, so that there the reader might from the first glance recognize him as one retreating from the field of action, and might be convinced there was no field of action left for him. A little further and even that misanthrope, that grandson of heroes, will disappear entirely; new characters will appear, unknown to us as yet, and a new ideal; but what sort of characters? If they are without beauty,

---

1 EDS: "Scratch a Russian and you will find a Tatar."

then the Russian novel is impossible in the future. But alas! will the novel be the only thing impossible?

"I will not pursue this further, but will hasten back to your manuscript. Consider, for instance, both the families of M. Versilov (for this once I will venture to be quite open). I won't enlarge on Andrei Petrovich himself; but he is anyway of a good old family. He is a nobleman of ancient lineage, and at the same time a Parisian communard. He is a true poet and loves Russia, yet denies her absolutely. He is without any sort of religion, but yet almost ready to die for something indefinite, to which he cannot give a name, but in which he fervently believes, like a number of Russian adherents of European civilization of the Petersburg period of Russian history. But enough of him. As for his legitimate family, I won't discuss his son, and indeed, he is not worth of the honor. All who have eyes know what upstarts like that come into Russia, and what they bring others to as well. Then his daughter, Anna Andreevna— she is surely a girl of strong character? A figure on the scale of the Mother Abbess Mitrofaniia, not that I mean to predict anything criminal—which would be unjust on my part.

"If you can assure me Arkadii Makarovich, that that family is an exceptional phenomenon it will rejoice my heart. But would it not be on the contrary a truer conclusion, that a multitude of unquestionably aristocratic Russian families are with irresistible force passing in masses into exceptional families and mingling with them in the general lawlessness and chaos. A typical example of such an exceptional family is sketched by you in your manuscript. Yes, Arkadii Makarovich, you are *a member of an exceptional family*, in contrary distinction to the aristocratic types who have had such a very different childhood and adolescence from yours.

"I must say I should not like to be a novelist whose hero comes from an exceptional family!

"To describe him is an ungrateful task and can have no beauty of form. Moreover these types are in any case transitory, and so a novel about them cannot have artistic finish. One might make serious mistakes, exaggerations, misjudgments. In any case, one would have to guess too much. But what is the writer to do who doesn't want to confine himself to the historical form, and is possessed by a longing for the present? To guess . . . and to make mistakes.

"But such an autobiography as yours might serve as material for a future work of art, for a future picture of a lawless already passed. Oh, when the angry strife of the day has passed, and the future has come, then a future artist will discover beautiful forms for depicting past lawlessness and chaos.

Then such autobiographies as yours—so long as they are sincere—will be of use and provide material in spite of their chaotic and fortuitous character [...] they will preserve at any rate some faithful traits by which one may guess what may have lain hidden in the heart of some raw youth of that troubled time—a knowledge not altogether valueless since from raw youths are made up the generations."

Remaking the Noble Family Novel (2013)*

Kate Holland

I argue here that in his attempt to answer the conflicting demands of fragmented reality and formal clarity, Dostoevskii directly challenges the traditional forms of the Russian novel, particularly a subgenre I call the "noble
family novel," which he saw encapsulated in the works of Tolstoi, Turgenev,
and to a lesser extent Goncharov. This challenge brings together the voices
of Dostoevskii and his protagonist, each of whom has a different endgame
in mind. As well as revealing the central creative dilemma of *The Adolescent*,
Nikolai Semenovich's commentary reveals the parallel existence of two literary projects: Arkadii's "notes," of which he is a reader, and Dostoevskii's novel,
within which he is a character. Located within the novel's frame, Nikolai
Semenovich's commentary highlights the complex narrative structure of *The
Adolescent*. One fictional character's commentary on another's creative choices
draws attention to the fictionality of both, thus foregrounding the figure of the
implied author. The problem of the relationship between Arkadii's "notes" and
the larger novel itself moves into focus. Nikolai Semenovich's comments on
Arkadii's decision to focus on the formlessness of his own accidental family
point the reader toward his creator's choice of hero and in so doing reveal the
divergences between *The Adolescent*'s two literary projects. Arkadii is merely
writing his autobiography; he has not chosen himself as an accidental hero.

---

* From Kate Holland, *The Novel in the Age of Disintegration: Dostoevsky and Genre in the 1870s*
(Evanston, IL: Northwestern University Press, 2013), 103–4, 115–19, 122–23. Copyright
© 2013 by Northwestern University Press. Published in 2013. All rights reserved.

It is Dostoevskii who has embraced the formlessness of this novelistic subject as an alternative to the "finished forms" of the traditional Russian novel, as his "new word" in novelistic representation. As Nikolai Semenovich explores Arkadii's narrative motivation, providing a critical reading far beyond what the notes seem to merit, we are asked to consider Dostoevskii's own creative impulses, the wisdom and daring of his choice of a hero, yet such consideration flouts the text's hermeneutic order, for how can a fictional character comment on the text he himself inhabits? As Nikolai Semenovich meditates on the differences between Arkadii's "notes" and the Russian noble family novel, he reveals the creative potential in the "notes" and argues for their status as the provisional model for a literary project of the future. Speaking through his character, Dostoevskii questions *The Adolescent*'s success as a project, its relationship with traditional Russian novelistic models, and its status as a blueprint for a novel for the present and the future. Arkadii's autobiography is revealed to be far more than the story of an adolescent's botched involvement in a series of family plots that he does not completely understand; it emerges as a radical novelistic experiment.

Representing the process of Arkadii's formation as a narrator allows Dostoevskii to dramatize his own attempts to find a novelistic form to express the social disintegration of the 1870s, to include within the novel an account of his own authorial motivations. While Arkadii examines earlier novelistic models as the means by which he can come to know his father's narrative legacy and his own narrative inheritance, Dostoevskii uses them to inscribe into *The Adolescent* the history of the Russian novel as a genre. He thus explores his own place in the history of the Russian novel as he revisits his own past as a novelist and explores its significance for his current project. Arkadii's examination of earlier novels thus allows Dostoevskii to explore the origins and allegiances of the Russian novel, as well as its thematic and formal preoccupations.

Narrating his protagonist's development as an author allows Dostoevskii to lay bare his own novelistic process; the text turns out to be not only an attempt to represent the moment of social transition in all its fragmentation, but also a novelistic meditation on whether and how such representation can be possible within the form of the novel. With their double framing, Arkadii's "notes" serve as both an example of fragmented novelistic discourse and an account of the *process* of representing fragmentation. As subject of one text and object of the other, Arkadii is both agent and victim of disintegration. At once the embodiment of the disintegrating family and its chronicler, Arkadii both symbolizes and narrates social breakdown. This multilayered narrative structure creates the dynamic effect of a work in progress, not merely a narrative *of* transition, but a narrative *in* transition [...]

If *The Adolescent* begins by invoking the originary moment of the Russian novelistic tradition, it soon moves on to engaging the works of Dostoevskii's immediate contemporaries, Tolstoi, Turgenev, and Goncharov. At the turn of the 1870s Dostoevskii had pushed back against the novel as practiced by Tolstoi and Turgenev, first in his correspondence with Strakhov over *War and Peace* and then in *Demons*, his allegory of the alienation of Russian Westernism. *The Adolescent* invokes the genre with which the trio of Tolstoi, Turgenev, and Goncharov are associated throughout Dostoevskii's letters, notebooks, and journalism from the late 1860s onward: the noble family novel. This novelistic model helps to differentiate between the narrative perspectives of Arkadii and the implied author and takes on the central role in the drama of genre that plays itself out formally and symbolically in *The Adolescent*.

The publication circumstances of *The Adolescent* cemented a sense of competition with Tolstoi that significantly shaped both the evolution of the novel itself and Dostoevskii's perception of his own novelistic vision. *The Adolescent* was originally supposed to have been published in *The Russian Messenger*, but Katkov had taken Tolstoi's new family novel, *Anna Karenina*, instead, and the two novels began to be published simultaneously in January 1875. Dostoevskii began to read *Anna Karenina* immediately, and he soon became aware that the reading public was comparing his new novel unfavorably with Tolstoi's (PSS 29/2:11). Vladimir Solov'ev describes how, at the beginning of 1875, he visited Dostoevskii while the latter was working on *The Adolescent*. Dostoevskii asked him if he thought he envied Tolstoi and proceeded to demonstrate that envy.[1] During the summer of 1875 in Bad Ems, as he struggled with the third part of *The Adolescent*, Tolstoi was clearly on his mind, and there are repeated references to him in the letters and in the notes for the novel (PSS 16:360, 390, 424; 29/2:40, 49).[2]

In a famous passage in the notebooks, written on March 22, 1875, Dostoevskii responds to criticisms following the publication of the novel's first installment in *Fatherland Notes* (PSS 16:329–30). Accused of crude naturalism by a number of critics in the periodical press, Dostoevskii defends his own representation of a society without foundations, his own underground men and

---

1 V. V. Grigorenko et al., *F. M. Dostoevskii v vospominaniakh sovremennikov* (Moscow: Izdatel'stvo khudozhestvennoi literatury, 1964).

2 Dostoevskii's later high praise of *Anna Karenina* in the 1877 *Diary*, his criticism of part 8 notwithstanding, once *The Adolescent* was behind him, suggests that he was well aware of the evolution that had taken place in Tolstoi's style in that novel: PSS 25:198–202.

"unfinished people."[3] He compares his own poetics of fragmentation to the creative vision of "our most talented writers, who have been describing, in highly artistic form, the life of our upper middle class (from the vantage point of the family)—Tolstoi, Goncharov—[who] thought that they were describing the life of the majority; in my opinion what they were describing were the lives of some exceptions" (PSS 16:329). In the 1871 letter to Strakhov, he had complained that what he called the "landowner's literature [*pomeshchich'ia literatura*]" practiced by such luminaries as Tolstoi and Turgenev had nothing left to say, yet the new word that would replace it did not yet exist (PSS 29/1:216).[4] At work on his own experimental novel, Dostoevskii insists that Tolstoi, Turgenev, and Goncharov rely on an outmoded concept of the novelistic subject, limiting their novelistic focus to the noble estate and the traditional family, both of which are being washed away by the advancing tide of history. He revels in the intended insult "poet of the underground," arguing that underground characters such as Arkadii have more verisimilitude and psychological accuracy than the heroes of *War and Peace*: "Bolkonskii reforms as he sees Anatole's leg being cut off, and we've all been shedding tears over it, but a genuine underground man would never have reformed" (PSS 16:330).

It is Tolstoi's bildungsroman, *Childhood. Boyhood. Youth* (1851–57), rather than his *War and Peace*, that frames *The Adolescent*. The trilogy is invoked by Nikolai Semenovich in his letter, and its memory permeates Dostoevskii's own bildungsroman. The old man writes, "Yes Arkadii Makarovich, you are a member of an accidental family, as opposed to our still-recent hereditary types, who had a childhood and a boyhood [*detstvo i otrochestvo*] so different from yours" (PSS 13:455). This apparently casual invocation of Tolstoi's trilogy in the novel's closing paragraphs reveals its most richly contradictory and meaningful intertextual relationship, a relationship that plays a crucial role in the process of narrative *Bildung* underlying *The Adolescent* [...]

As A. L. Bem points out, in the notebooks for *The Adolescent* Dostoevskii seems to refer to all of Tolstoi's major novels without differentiation, as if to some unitary Tolstoian text that remains consistent over the decades, and he

---

3 The populist critic A. M. Skabichevskii found the first installment of *The Adolescent* excessively naturalistic. See his article "Mysli po povodu tekushchei literatury: Nechto o romanakh g. F. M. Dostoevskogo voobshe. 'Podrostok,' roman g. F. M. Dostoevskogo, chast' pervaia," *Birzhevye Vedomosti* 35 (February 6, 1875). For commentary, see Dostoevskii, PSS 17:349–50, 421.

4 This letter is included in Chapter 2 of this volume.

consistently refers to Tolstoi as "the historian of the Russian nobility."[5] This sense of Tolstoi can be contrasted with Dostoevskii's sense of himself as the biographer of a hero whose social class as yet has no historian, and his growing realization throughout 1875 that his readers have failed to understand his creative mission. While continually measuring himself against Tolstoi, Dostoevskii at times expresses nostalgia for the literary and social certainties the latter seems to represent. By focusing his criticism and nostalgia on Tolstoi's trilogy rather than on *Anna Karenina*, Dostoevskii underlines his own position as chronicler of the accidental family as radically new. At the same time, however, he demonstrates the ambivalence of a novelist who feels intellectually obliged to represent the processes of social change, but who has a palpable sense of anxiety about the future artistic legacy of *The Adolescent*. The complexity of his attitude toward Tolstoi's novels is explicitly represented in *The Adolescent's* epilogue, but the combination of criticism of the trilogy as having outlived its time and a simultaneous nostalgia for its certainties permeate the novel. The precision, clarity, and completeness of the image of the family in Tolstoi's trilogy represent the antithesis of the accidental family Dostoevskii represents in *The Adolescent*. Yet the representation of the disintegration of the family unit could only be possible if the memory of an integrated family unit was present in the novel. *The Adolescent* can only be understood in relation to *Childhood*.

In *The Adolescent*, Dostoevskii engages with Tolstoi's trilogy in many different ways. He borrows elements of the narrative structure of *Childhood*, and through these structural echoes he both underlines the contrasting qualities of his own novelistic vision, the "accidental" nature of the family that forms his novelistic subject, and reveals its generic history, its relationship to the noble family novel, which plays such a dominant role in the history of the Russian novel. Yet with the exception of the mention of the trilogy in Nikolai Semenovich's letter, outside the frame of the "notes," Dostoevskii does not embed any direct intertextual references to Tolstoi's works in the final text. This is in marked contrast to the direct invocation of the works of the Natural School discussed previously. And whereas Arkadii introduces the genre models of the prose works of the Natural School as prototypes for Versilov's character, there is no evidence to suggest that Arkadii evokes Tolstoi in *The Adolescent*,

---

5 A. L. Bem, "Khudozhestvennaia polemika s Tolstym: K ponimaniu 'Podrostka,'" in *O Dostoevskom: Sbornik statei pod redaktsiei A. L. Bema*, 3 vols. (Prague: Petropolis, 1936), vol. 3, 192–214.

as Perlina points out.[6] Instead, it is Nikolai Semenovich, in the epilogue, who most directly invokes Tolstoi's trilogy as an intertext. The trilogy functions as an alternative model in Dostoevskii's novel, rather than in Arkadii's autobiography, operating within the perspective of the implied author rather than the author. Rather than referring directly to the trilogy, Dostoevskii chooses several of the work's essential structural and thematic features and models them within *The Adolescent* in a radically different hermeneutic context, at a radically different historical and literary moment. Articulating these features, Dostoevskii brings to mind not Tolstoi's work itself, but a memory of it, or, rather, the genre memory of the novel of the Russian noble family, the generic tradition within which Nikolai Semenovich (and Dostoevskii) places Tolstoi's trilogy. This memory is preserved in the structural fragments of Tolstoi's trilogy still present in Dostoevskii's novel and serves as a double-voiced reminder of the tradition out of which *The Adolescent* emerges and against which it sets itself.

Dostoevskii invokes the memory of Tolstoi's trilogy through the very title of his novel, which points toward another age of man just beyond the three stages Tolstoi describes, an age that had formed part of Tolstoi's original conception.[7] (Dostoevskii's twenty-year-old adolescent is a couple of years older than Tolstoi's youth when the trilogy ends.) But Dostoevskii's title also suggests a reclassification and depoeticization of the states of Tolstoi's trilogy. Dostoevskii's adolescence both supplements and supplants Tolstoi's ages of man. It also shifts the focus from a state or a stage, an age of man, *Childhood*, to a concrete character, the adolescent, whose identity hovers indeterminately between that of an individual and that of a type. Dostoevskii also borrows from the opening of *Childhood* the temporal marker of the exact date without the year. In *Childhood* the date without a year, August 12, the day of Irten'ev's first memory of childhood, introduces a model of cyclical time outside of history, which includes the sequence of the seasons but excludes any possibility of social or historical development. This model of cyclical time, as Bakhtin notes, characterizes the chronotope of the idyll, the remnants of which can be found in the noble family novel.[8] It is accompanied by a model of spatial unity that in

---

6 Nina Perlina, "Rethinking Adolescence," *Celebrating Creativity. Essays in Honour of Jostein Börtnes,* ed. Knut Andreas Grimstad and Ingunn Lunde (Bergen: University of Bergen Press, 1997), 216–26.

7 On Tolstoi's original conception, see Boris Eikhenbaum, *Molodoi Tolstoi: Vospominaniia, pis'ma, dnevniki,* ed. A. G. Ostrovskii (Moskva: Agraf, 1999).

8 M. M. Bakhtin, "Formy vremeni i khronotopa v romane," in *Voprosy literatury i estetiki* (Moscow: Khudozhestvennaia literatura, 1975), 234–407; and "Forms of Time and

the case of *Childhood* centers on the estate which has been inhabited by generations of Irtenievs, and on the manor house, where each room is occupied by the shades of Nikolai's ancestors [...]

Perhaps the most significant reconfiguration of Tolstoi's trilogy in *The Adolescent* is the narrative displacement enacted through the choice of Arkadii as narrator. Although Arkadii occupies Irten'ev's structural position within the work, it is his father, not the adolescent, who shares Irten'ev's symbolic genealogy. Versilov carries the ancient noble pedigree that Irten'ev shares with Tolstoi himself, and is around the same age as Irten'ev the narrator. Versilov's idealized love for Sophia seems to resemble Irten'ev's love for his distant mother more than Arkadii's confused and awkward fondness for his. Even Versilov's romanticized vision of the peasant Makar evokes Irten'ev's confused wonderment at the peasants who occupy the fringes of his family estate. It is Versilov who shares Irten'ev's idealized memories of a childhood on a country estate, memories that consist of the smiling faces of the servant women and the beloved nanny who raised him in lieu of his absent parents (PSS 13:86). Dostoevskii twice parodies those nostalgic memories: first by Versilov's own identification of this childhood recollection as the source of his disgust for women working and his abiding love of idleness, and second by Arkadii's subsequent account of his own neglected childhood as an angry rejoinder to Versilov's reminiscences (PSS 13:91–100). This double parody exemplifies the way *The Adolescent* reframes the trilogy's structural elements. Dostoevskii is simultaneously revealing the illusory and dangerous elements of Tolstoi's vision of the gentry childhood, overcoming them and moving on from them, as demonstrated in the shift from the old hero and symbolic descendant of Irten'ev, Versilov, to the new, hybridic hero, Arkadii. That symbolic shift from the old aristocratic protagonist to the new socially cross-bred hero occurs during the novel's creative evolution, as the father gives way to the son, but is also narratively present in the novel itself, as Arkadii's attempt to take on his father's narrative mantle is gradually replaced by the perception that he can forge a new narrative path independent of past literary models.

Arkadii's access to the future is blocked by Versilov and the need to understand his own past. He longs to put together the confused fragments

---

Chronotope in the Novel," in *The Dialogic Imagination: Four Essays by M. M. Bakhtin*, ed. Michael Holquist, trans. Michael Holquist and Caryl Emerson (Austin: University of Texas Press, 1981), 224–36.

of his own history and understand his own present by accessing the "whole" of his father (PSS 13:111). His nostalgia for his father's narrative certainties mirrors Dostoevskii's own inability to reject traditional novelistic family values entirely. The fact that critics almost universally seem to prefer Versilov to Arkadii may indicate Dostoevskii's own inability to relinquish his own nostalgia for the Tolstoian family novel, a nostalgia that we see represented in Nikolai Semenovich's commentary.[9] But Versilov's novelistic identity is itself fractured; the multiplying dualities within his character form the shards of his psychological and narrative disintegration, which finally materializes in his breaking of the icon, his attempted suicide, and his attempted murder of Akhmakova. As a character, Versilov contains within himself the generic residue of the Russian novel of the noble family, from the shade of the idealistic pedagogue of *Polinka Saks*, through the echoes of the childhood rural paradise of *Childhood*, to his Turgenevian exile in Europe. But these episodes in the novel's history are preserved within him only as the fragments of genre memory, their generic contexts forgotten in the new and dislocated novelistic world Versilov inhabits. The reader of *The Adolescent* can no more reassemble the noble family novel from the generic fragments that remain in Dostoevskii's novel of the accidental family than Arkadii can return his father to wholeness. Versilov ultimately disintegrates along with the family he has fathered and the noble family novel he evokes. Arkadii is left on the threshold of a new stage in his life, and we as readers are left to contemplate the possibilities of the future artistic work whose vague outlines Nikolai Semenovich sees in Arkadii's notes. In the novel's closing chapters, Dostoevskii projects Versilov's collapse onto a larger national historical screen, inscribing into it a narrative of national and social division. Versilov's disintegration becomes a figure for the social fragmentation of Russia after the Petrine reforms, a symbolic manifestation of the historical culpability of his social estate in this process of fragmentation. Arkadii's narratological education is revealed as the figure for Russia's own troubled transition to modernity.

---

9 Joseph Frank writes, "Versilov is far and away the most interesting character in the book, and after Part I Dostoevskii is unable to prevent him from taking center stage": Joseph Frank, *Dostoevsky: The Mantle of the Prophet, 1871–1881* (Princeton: Princeton University Press, 2003), 176.

A New Kind of Hero (1963)*

Mikhail Bakhtin

The hero interests Dostoevskii not as some manifestation of reality that possesses fixed and specific socially typical or individually characteristic traits, nor as a specific profile assembled out of unambiguous and objective features which, taken together, answer the question "Who is he?" No, the hero interests Dostoevskii as a *particular point of view on the world and on oneself*, as the position enabling a person to interpret and evaluate his own self and his surrounding reality. What is important to Dostoevskii is not how his hero appears in the world but first and foremost how the world appears to his hero, and how the hero appears to himself.

This is a very important and fundamental feature of the way a fictional character is perceived. The hero as a point of view, as an opinion on the world and on himself, requires utterly special methods of discovery and artistic characterization. And this is so because what must be discovered and characterized here is not the specific existence of the hero, not his fixed image, but the *sum total of his consciousness and self-consciousness*, ultimately *the hero's final word on himself and on his world*.

Consequently those elements out of which the hero's image is composed are not features of reality—features of the hero himself or of his everyday surroundings—but rather the *significance* of these features for the *hero himself*, for his self-consciousness. All the stable and objective qualities of a hero— his social position, the degree to which he is sociologically or characterologically typical, his habitus, his spiritual profile and even his very physical

---

* Extracts from Mikhail Bakhtin, *Problems of Dostoevsky's Poetics*, trans. Caryl Emerson (Minneapolis: University of Minnesota Press, 1984), 47–54, 67–73. Copyright © 1984 by the University of Minnesota. All rights reserved.

appearance—that is, everything that usually serves an author in creating a fixed and stable image of the hero, "who he is," becomes in Dostoevskii the object of the hero's own introspection, the subject of his self-consciousness; and the subject of the author's visualization and representation turns out to be in fact a *function* of this self-consciousness. At a time when the self-consciousness of a character was usually seen merely as an element of his reality, as merely one of the features of his integrated image, here, on the contrary, all of reality becomes an element of the character's self-consciousness. The author retains for himself, that is, for his exclusive field of vision, not a single essential definition, not a single trait, not the smallest feature of the hero: he enters it all into the field of vision of the hero himself, he casts it all into the crucible of the hero's own self-consciousness. In the author's field of vision, as an object of his visualization and representation, there remains only pure self-consciousness in its totality.

Even in the earliest "Gogolian period" of his literary career, Dostoevskii is already depicting not the "poor government clerk" but the *self-consciousness* of the poor clerk (Devushkin, Goliadkin, even Prokharchin). That which was presented in Gogol's field of vision as an aggregate of objective features, coalescing in a firm socio-characterological profile of the hero, is introduced by Dostoevskii into the field of vision of the hero himself and there becomes the object of his agonizing self-awareness; even the very physical appearance of the "poor clerk," described by Gogol', Dostoevskii forces his hero to contemplate in the mirror.[1] And thanks to this fact all the concrete features of the hero, while remaining fundamentally unchanged in content, are transferred from one plane of representation to another, and thus acquire a completely different artistic significance: they can no longer finalize and close off a character, can no longer construct an integral image of him or provide an artistic answer to the question, "Who is he?" We see not who he is, but *how* he is conscious of himself; our act of artistic visualization occurs not before the reality of the hero, but

---

1   Devushkin, on his way to the General, sees himself in a mirror: "I was so flustered that my lips were trembling, my legs were trembling. And I had reason to be, my dear girl! To begin with, I was ashamed; I glanced into the looking-glass on the right hand and what I saw there was enough to send one out of one's mind [. . .] I remembered what I had seen in the looking-glass: I flew to catch the button!" (Fedor Dostoevskii, *Sobranie sochinenii*, 10 vols., Moscow: Gosizdat, 1956–58, designated hereafter as *SS*, 1:186; *Poor Folk*, Letter of September 9) Devushkin sees in the mirror exactly what Gogol', when he described the coat and appearance of Akakii Akakievich, had depicted, but Devushkin sees what Akakii Akakievich himself could not see or become aware of; the constant agonizing reflection of the heroes on their external appearance is the function, for them, of the mirror; for Goliadkin, it is his double.

before a pure function of his awareness of that reality. In this way the Gogolian hero becomes Dostoevskii's hero.[2]

One might offer the following, and somewhat simplified, formula for the revolution that the young Dostoevskii brought about in Gogol''s world: he transferred the author and the narrator, with all their accumulated points of view and with the descriptions, characterizations, and definitions of the hero provided by them, into the field of vision of the hero himself, thus transforming the finalized and integral reality of the hero into the material of the hero's own selfconsciousness. Not without reason does Dostoevskii force Makar Devushkin to read Gogol''s "Overcoat" and to take it as a story about himself, as "slander" against himself; this is how Dostoevskii literally introduces the author into the hero's field of vision.

Dostoevskii carried out, as it were, a small-scale Copernican revolution when he took what had been a firm and finalizing authorial definition and turned it into an aspect of the hero's self-definition. The content of Gogol''s world, the world of "The Overcoat," "The Nose," "Nevskii Prospect," and "Notes of a Madman," remained quite unchanged in Dostoevskii's earliest works, *Poor Folk* and *The Double*. But in Dostoevskii the distribution of this identical material among the structural elements of the work is completely different. What the author used to do is now done by the hero, who illuminates himself from all possible points of view; the author no longer illuminates the hero's reality but the hero's self-consciousness, as a reality of the second order. The dominant governing the entire act of artistic visualization and construction had been shifted, and the whole world took on a new look—although in essence almost no new non-Gogolian material had been introduced by Dostoevskii.[3]

---

2 Dostoevskii often gives external portraits of his heroes, directly from the author, or from the narrator, or through other characters. But in Dostoevskii these external portraits do not perform the function of finalizing the hero; they do not create a fixed and predetermining image. The functions of one or another of a character's traits do not, of course, depend solely upon the elementary artistic methods used to reveal this trait (self-characterization by the hero, or directly from the author, or by some indirect route, etc.).

3 "Prokharchin" also remained within the boundaries of this same Gogolian material, and also the piece "The Shaved-off Sideburns" [Sbritye bakenbardy], which Dostoevskii destroyed. But here Dostoevskii began to sense that his new principle applied to the same Gogolian material was already becoming a repetition, and that it was imperative to tackle material essentially new in content. In 1846 he wrote to his brother: "I'm not writing 'The Shaved-off Sideburns' either. I threw everything out. Because all of it is nothing but a repeat of the old things I finished saying long ago. Now brighter, more original and alive thoughts are begging me to put them down on paper. As soon as I had finished writing 'Shaved-off Sideburns' this all came to me spontaneously. In my position, monotony is ruin." [Letter to Mikhail

Not only the reality of the hero himself, but even the external world and the everyday life surrounding him are drawn into the process of self-awareness, are transferred from the author's to the hero's field of vision. They no longer lie in a single plane with the hero, alongside him and external to him in the unified world of the author—and for this reason they cannot serve as causal or genetic factors determining the hero, they cannot fulfill in the work any explanatory function. Alongside and on the same plane with the self-consciousness of the hero, which has absorbed into itself the entire world of objects, there can be only another consciousness; alongside its field of vision, another field of vision; alongside its point of view on the world, another point of view on the world. *To the all-devouring consciousness of the hero the author can juxtapose only a single objective world—a world of other consciousnesses with rights equal to those of the hero* [...]

Self-consciousness, as the artistic dominant governing the construction of a character, cannot lie alongside other features of his image; it absorbs these other features into itself as its own material and deprives them of any power to define and finalize the hero.

Self-consciousness can be made the dominant in the representation of any person. But not all persons are equally favorable material for such a representation. The Gogolian clerk in this respect offered too narrow a potential. Dostoevskii sought a hero who would be occupied primarily with the task of becoming conscious, the sort of hero whose life would be concentrated on the pure function of gaining consciousness of himself and the world. And at this point in his work there begin to appear the "dreamer" and the "underground man." Both "dreamer-ness" and "underground-ness" are socio-characterological features of people, but here they also answer to Dostoevskii's artistic dominant. The consciousness of a dreamer or an underground man—who are not personified, and cannot be personified—is most favorable soil for Dostoevskii's creative purposes, for it allows him to fuse the artistic dominant of the representation with the real-life and characterological dominant of the represented person.

> Oh, if I had done nothing simply out of laziness! Heavens, how I would
> have respected myself then. I would have respected myself because
> I would at least have been capable of being lazy; there would at least have

Dostoevskii, end of October 1846; *Pis'ma*, 1, 100.] Then he began work on *Netochka Nezvanova* and "The Landlady"; that is, he sought to apply his new principle to another area of the same Gogolian world ("The Portrait," and somewhat in "The Terrible Vengeance").

been in me one positive quality, as it were, in which I could have believed myself. Question: Who is he? Answer: A loafer. After all, it would have been pleasant to hear that about oneself! It would mean that I was positively defined, it would mean that there was something to be said about me. "Loafer"—why, after all, it is a calling and an appointment, it is a career, gentlemen. [SS IV, 147; "Notes from Underground," Part One, VI]

The Underground Man not only dissolves in himself all possible fixed features of his person, making them all the object of his own introspection, but in fact he no longer has any such traits at all, no fixed definitions, there is nothing to say about him, he figures not as a person taken from life but rather as the subject of consciousness and dream. And for the author as well he is not a carrier of traits and qualities that could have been neutral toward his self-consciousness and could have finalized him; no, what the author visualizes is precisely the hero's self-consciousness and the inescapable open-endedness, the vicious circle of that self-consciousness. Thus the real-life characterological definition of the Underground Man and the artistic dominant of his image are fused into one [...]

There is literally nothing we can say about the hero of "Notes from Underground" that he does not already know himself: his typicality for his time and social group, the sober psychological or even psychopathological delineation of his internal profile, the category of character to which his consciousness belongs, his comic as well as his tragic side, all possible moral definitions of his personality, and so on—all of this, in keeping with Dostoevskii's design, the hero knows perfectly well himself, and he stubbornly and agonizingly soaks up all these definitions from within. Any point of view from without is rendered powerless in advance and denied the finalizing word [...]

The hero from the underground eavesdrops on every word someone else says about him, he looks at himself, as it were, in all the mirrors of other people's consciousnesses, he knows all the possible refractions of his image in those mirrors. And he also knows his own objective definition, neutral both to the other's consciousness and to his own self-consciousness, and he takes into account the point of view of a "third person." But he also knows that all these definitions, prejudiced as well as objective, rest in his hands and he cannot finalize them precisely because he himself perceives them; he can go beyond their limits and can thus make them inadequate. He knows that he has the final word, and he seeks at whatever cost to retain for himself this final word about himself, the word of his self-consciousness, in order to become in it that which he is not.

His consciousness of self lives by its unfinalizability, by its unclosedness and its indeterminancy.

And this is not merely a character trait of the Underground Man's self-consciousness, it is also the dominant governing the author's construction of his image. The author does indeed leave the final word to his hero. And precisely that final word—or, more accurately, the tendency toward it—is necessary to the author's design. The author constructs the hero not out of words foreign to the hero, not out of neutral definitions; he constructs not a character, nor a type, nor a temperament, in fact he constructs no objectified image of the hero at all, but rather the hero's *discourse* about himself and his world [...]

Here it is again appropriate to emphasize the positive and active quality of the new authorial position in a polyphonic novel. It would be absurd to think that the author's consciousness is nowhere expressed in Dostoevskii's novels. The consciousness of the creator of a polyphonic novel is constantly and everywhere present in the novel, and is active in it to the highest degree. But the function of this consciousness and the forms of its activity are different than in the monologic novel: the author's consciousness does not transform others' consciousnesses (that is, the consciousnesses of the characters) into objects, and does not give them secondhand and finalizing definitions. Alongside and in front of itself it senses others' equally valid consciousnesses, just as infinite and open-ended as itself. It reflects and recreates not a world of objects, but precisely these other consciousnesses with their worlds, recreates them in their authentic *unfinalizability* (which is, after all, their essence).

The consciousnesses of other people cannot be perceived, analyzed, defined as objects or as things—one can only relate to them dialogically. To think about them means to talk with them; otherwise they immediately turn to us their objectivized side: they fall silent, close up, and congeal into finished, objectivized images. An enormous and intense dialogic activity is demanded of the author of a polyphonic novel: as soon as this activity slackens, the characters begin to congeal, they become mere things, and monologically formed chunks of life appear in the novel. Such chunks, which fall out of the polyphonic design, can be found in all of Dostoevskii's novels, but they do not of course determine the nature of the whole [...]

The new position of the author in the polyphonic novel can be made clearer if we juxtapose it concretely with a distinctly expressed monologic position in a specific work.

We shall therefore analyze briefly, from the vantage point most relevant to us, Leo Tolstoi's short story "Three Deaths" (1858). This work, not large in size but nevertheless tri-leveled, is very characteristic of Tolstoi's monologic manner.

Three deaths are portrayed in the story—the deaths of a rich noblewoman, a coachman, and a tree. But in this work Tolstoi presents death as a stage of life, as a stage illuminating that life, as the optimal point for understanding and evaluating that life in its entirety. Thus one could say that this story in fact portrays three lives totally finalized in their meaning and in their value. And in Tolstoi's story all three lives, and the levels defined by them, are *internally self-enclosed and do not know one another*. There is no more than a purely external pragmatic connection between them, necessary for the compositional and thematic unity of the story: the coachman Serega, transporting the ailing noblewoman, removes the boots from a coachman who is dying in a roadside station (the dying man no longer has any need for boots) and then, after the death of the coachman, cuts down a tree in the forest to make a cross for the man's grave. In this way three lives and three deaths come to be externally connected.

But an internal connection, *a connection between consciousnesses*, is not present here. The dying noblewoman knows nothing of the life and death of the coachman or the tree, they do not enter into her field of vision or her consciousness. And neither the noblewoman nor the tree enter the consciousness of the dying coachman. The lives and deaths of all three characters, together with their worlds, lie side by side in a unified objective world and are even externally contiguous, but they know nothing of one another and are not reflected in one another. They are self-enclosed and deaf; they do not hear and do not answer one another. There are not and cannot be any dialogic relationships among them. They neither argue nor agree.

But all three personages, with their self-enclosed worlds, are united, juxtaposed and made meaningful to one another in the *author's* unified field of vision and consciousness that encompasses them. He, the author, knows everything about them, he juxtaposes, contrasts, and evaluates all three lives and all three deaths. All three lives and deaths illuminate one another, but only for the author, who is located *outside* them and takes advantage of his *external position* to give them a definitive meaning, to finalize them. The all-encompassing field of vision of the author enjoys an enormous and fundamental "surplus" in comparison with the fields of vision of the characters. The noblewoman sees and understands only her own little world, her own life and her own death; she does not even suspect the possibility of the sort of life and death experienced by the coachman or the tree. Therefore she cannot herself understand and evaluate the *lie* of her own life and death; she does not have the dialogizing background for it. And the coachman is not able to understand and evaluate the wisdom and truth of his life and death. All this is revealed only in the author's field of vision, with its "surplus." The tree, of course, is by its very nature incapable of understanding the wisdom and beauty of its death—the author does that for it.

Thus the total finalizing meaning of the life and death of each character is revealed only in the author's field of vision, and thanks solely to the advantageous "surplus" which that field enjoys over every character, that is, thanks to that which the character cannot himself see or understand. This is the finalizing, monologic function of the author's "surplus" field of vision.

As we have seen, there are no dialogic relationships between characters and their worlds. But the author does not relate to them dialogically either. A dialogic position with regard to his characters is quite foreign to Tolstoi. He does not extend his own point of view on a character to the character's own consciousness (and in principle he could not); likewise the character is not able to respond to the author's point of view. In a monologic work the ultimate and finalizing authorial evaluation of a character is, by its very nature, a *second-hand evaluation*, one that does not presuppose or take into account any potential *response* to this evaluation on the part of the character himself. The hero is not given the last word. He cannot break out of the fixed framework of the author's second-hand evaluation finalizing him. The author's attitude encounters no internal dialogic resistance on the part of the character.

The words and consciousness of the author, Leo Tolstoi, are nowhere addressed to the hero, do not question him, and expect no response from him. The author neither argues with his hero nor agrees with him. He speaks not with him, but about him. The final word belongs to the author, and that word—based on something the hero does not see and does not understand, on something located outside the hero's consciousness—can never encounter the hero's words on a single dialogic plane.

That external world in which the characters of the story live and die is the *author's world*, an objective world vis-à-vis the consciousnesses of the characters. Everything within it is seen and portrayed in the author's all-encompassing and omniscient field of vision. Even the noblewoman's world—her apartment, its furnishings, the people close to her and their experiences, the doctors, and so forth—is portrayed from the author's point of view, and not as the noblewoman herself sees and experiences that world (although while reading the story we are also fully aware of her *subjective* perception of that world). And the world of the coachman (the hut, the stove, the cook, etc.) and of the tree (nature, the forest)—all these things are, as is the noblewoman's world, parts of one and the same objective world, seen and portrayed from *one and the same authorial position*. The author's field of vision nowhere intersects or collides dialogically with the characters' fields of vision or attitudes, nowhere does the word of the author encounter resistance from the hero's potential word, a word that might illuminate the same object differently, in its own way—that is, from the vantage point of its own *truth*. The author's point of view cannot encounter the hero's point of view on one plane, on one level. The point of view of the hero (in those places where the author lets it be seen) always remains an object of the author's point of view.

Thus, despite the multiple levels in Tolstoi's story, it contains neither polyphony nor (in our sense) counterpoint. It contains only *one cognitive subject*, all else being merely objects of its cognition. Here a dialogic relationship of the author to his heroes is impossible, and thus there is no *"great dialogue"* in which characters and author might participate with equal rights; there are only the objectivized dialogues of characters, compositionally expressed within the author's field of vision.

In the above story Tolstoi's monologic position comes to the fore very distinctly and with *great external visibility*. That is the reason we chose this story. In Tolstoi's novels and in his longer stories, the issue is, of course, considerably more complex.

In the novels, the major characters and their worlds are not selfenclosed and deaf to one another; they intersect and are interwoven in a multitude of ways. The characters do know about each other, they exchange their individual "truths," they argue or agree, they carry on dialogues with one another (including dialogues on ultimate questions of worldview). Such characters as Andrei Bolkonskii, Pierre Bezukhov, Levin, and Nekhliudov have their own well-developed fields of vision, sometimes *almost* coinciding with the author's (that is, the author sometimes sees the world as if through their eyes), their voices sometimes *almost* merge with the author's voice. But not a single one ends up on the same plane with the author's word and the author's truth, and with none of them does the author enter into dialogic relations. All of them, with their fields of vision, with their quests and their controversies, are inscribed into the *monolithically monologic whole* of the novel that finalizes them all and that is never, in Tolstoi, the kind of "great dialogue" that we find in Dostoevskii. All the clamps and finalizing moments of this monologic whole lie in the zone of authorial "surplus," a zone that is fundamentally inaccessible to the consciousnesses of the characters.

Let us return to Dostoevskii. How would "Three Deaths" look if (and let us permit ourselves for a moment this strange assumption) Dostoevskii had written them, that is, if they had been structured in a polyphonic manner?

First of all, Dostoevskii would have forced these three planes to be reflected in one another, he would have bound them together with dialogic relationships. He would have introduced the life and death of the coachman and the tree into the field of vision and consciousness of the noblewoman, and the noblewoman's life into the field of vision and consciousness of the coachman. He would have forced his characters to see and know all those essential things that he himself—the author—sees and knows. He would not have retained for himself any *essential* authorial "surplus" (essential, that is, from the point of view of the desired truth). He would have arranged a face-to-face confrontation between the truth of the noblewoman and the truth of the coachman, and he would have forced them to come into dialogic contact (although not necessarily in direct compositionally expressed dialogues, of course), and he would himself have assumed, in relation to them, a dialogic position with equal rights. The entire work would have been constructed by him as a great dialogue, but one where the author acts as organizer and participant in the dialogue without retaining for himself the final word; that is, he would have reflected in his work in the dialogic nature of human life and human thought itself. And in the words of the story not only the pure *intonations of the author* would be heard, but also the intonations of the noblewoman and the coachman; that is, words would be double-voiced, in each word an argument (a microdialogue) would ring out, and there could be heard echoes of the great dialogue.

Of course Dostoevskii would never have depicted three *deaths*: in his world, where self-consciousness is the dominant of a person's image and where the interaction of full and autonomous consciousnesses is the fundamental event, death cannot function as something that finalizes and elucidates life. Death in the Tolstoian interpretation of it is totally absent from Dostoevskii's world.[4] Dostoevskii would have not depicted the deaths of his heroes, but the *crises* and *turning points* in their lives; that is, he would have depicted their lives *on the threshold*. And his heroes would have remained internally *unfinalized* (for self-consciousness cannot be finalized from within). Such would have been a polyphonic treatment of the story [...]

---

4 Characteristic for Dostoevskii's world are murders (portrayed from within the murderer's field of vision), suicides, and insanity. Normal deaths are rare in his work, and he usually notes them only in passing. [See the eloquent expansion of this idea in Bakhtin's notes for the 1963 edition, "Toward a Reworking of the Dostoevsky Book," Appendix II of *Problems of Dostoevsky's Poetics*.]

"Chronicle Time" in Dostoevskii (1979)*

Dmitrii Likhachev

There are writers for whom the problem of time is not of special importance, and who are therefore satisfied with traditional forms of artistic time. For Dostoevskii, on the other hand, artistic time was one of the most essential aspects of artistic representation. He constantly sought new forms for representing processes, action, duration, the change from one point of view in time to another. The problem of the eternal, the extra-temporal, was for him connected with the problem of time. This problem entered the very essence of his worldview. The temporal was for him a form of realization of the eternal. Through time he guessed at the eternal, discovered this eternal and extra-temporal [. . .]

All Dostoevskii's principal novels are written "in short segments." An extremely small time lies between the time of action and the note about this action. Dostoevskii's imaginary author follows "on the heels" of events, almost catches up with them, hurries to record them, as if not yet having had time to interpret them enough, not knowing how and in what way they will finish, amazed at their suddenness, their sharp twists, their "scandalousness," constantly noting their incompleteness. In the course of his narrative the author or "chronicler" in whose name the narrative is conducted changes his

---

* Extracts from Dmitry Likhachev, *The Poetics of Early Russian Literature,* trans. Christopher Arden-Close (Lanham, MD: Lexington Books, 2014), 295–99, 301–5. *Poetics of Early Russian Literature* edited by Christopher M. Arden-Close Copyright © 2014. Used by permission of Rowman & Littlefield Publishing Group. All rights reserved. The text is reproduced here with minor modifications: some footnotes have been removed.

evaluation of events, is intensely expectant about what will happen, confused and uncertain about whether he has communicated the very essence of what happens exactly, anxious about the future, in ignorance but with presentiments and premonitions about this future. Moreover, the author, or the narrator created by him, as though distrusts the correctness of his own interpretation of events, and therefore evaluates them from the point of view of different characters, introduces continual self-corrections.

This following closely after the time of the action creates dramatic intensity. But this intensity is one of the secondary phenomena. It is not the main thing in this "short segment." But first we shall examine how this "short segment" is realized.

Poor Folk is a novel in letters. This form was not new in Dostoevskii's time, it was even fairly old-fashioned: it had already been a favorite in sentimentalism.[1] But I would like to draw attention to this point. The correspondents write to each other every day, sometimes up to twice a day. This allows them to write not of events of the distant past, but of what has just happened, and even of what is happening at the very moment of writing the letter. The letters of each turn into a monologue, an "inner monologue," as we would now say. Both characters are as if in a state of uninterrupted conversation—a conversation accompanying the action and which is this very action. This correspondence is unreal, since it is impossible to imagine a situation in which such a protracted correspondence would be possible. It is also impossible to imagine such high literary culture in characters in the social position they occupied. Thus the letters of each are not only a correspondence between characters, but also the pronouncements of the author, Dostoevskii himself, through the mouths of his characters.

Should one not see a retreat from realism and artistic quality in the blending of author and authorial character (mainly Devushkin)? No. What is represented in *Poor Folk* is a conversation between two spirits, and spirits can speak not with their temporal language, but can overcome all barriers of confused everyday articulation, lack of education, lack of instruction. The characters speak more than they could speak in life. Their conversation has a feeling of being above life, above everyday things. This is a conversation between their beings, their essences.

And all the same, *byt*, life, their official position, their lack of means for existence, the disgusting states of their apartments—all this has weighed down on both. All this stifles both. And all this is needed to show their extratemporal,

---

1   See Iurii Tynianov, *Arkhaisty i novatory* (Leningrad: Priboi, 1929), 21–24.

eternal existence. For their genuine union in the otherworldly and eternal, it is necessary to show that they are different in age, that they cannot unite, that they are deeply unhappy. It is the same with time. The temporal is necessary to show the eternal in the characters, their otherworldly essences. Both characters in some way overcome *byt*, become above it. The author overcomes time, representing time as pursuing him, and himself as pursued by time, suffocating, not making any progress, "unhappy" in this sense, stifled by worries, his lack of success in writing, his search for words, his division in himself, and by the image of a narrator-correspondent created by him, and also in the later novels of a chronicler, storyteller, interrupting the author and taking words away from him, as though "struggling" with him.

Dostoevskii "emancipates" time, as he emancipates the heroes of his novels, as he even emancipates the narrators. He attempts to leave them to act alone, as though independent of the author. Just as exactly, he wants to grant the flow of time freedom from his own notions of time. This is why events so often happen "suddenly" in Dostoevskii, "somehow suddenly," "at this moment"—suddenly not only for the characters, but as if for himself also. Time flows quickly, and the author has no time to keep up with it. In this very way, time becomes independent of the author, it moves "inexorably"; events flow as if without any connection. The connection is only later recognized by the author. The narrator-chronicler seems not to understand the significance of what is happening. Events are recorded first, interpreted later. "Chaotic" notes are to give an impression of the chaos of life. In this lies the meaning of the image of the chronicler in Dostoevskii's novels. The imaginary author in Dostoevskii's novels (in *The Adolescent*, for example) stands, like a chronicler also, "too low" to understand the significance of events. In this way much is left to be guessed at by the reader. It is as though the reader understands more than the imaginary narrator-chronicler wants to convey explicitly and consciously to the reader. The causal-effective connection between events in Dostoevskii's novels appears insufficiently clear for their imagined author. Thus this causal-effective connection is revealed not simultaneously with events, but *afterwards*. Much is interpreted by the narrator as if later. The narrator (the imaginary author) sometimes runs ahead, but this running ahead is not isolated from the position of an author who is telling about the past, about what has happened. Thus if the narrator also recounts the meaning of what is happening, it is as if from the future, when all has become clear.

The flowing and unsteady quality of the surrounding world is emphasized by this chronicle style of exposition. The adolescent in Dostoevskii's novel of the same name attempts to "note the history of his first steps in the field of life" in the most artless, "chronicle" way. Through the lips of the raw youth, Dostoevskii proclaims his protest against literature and literariness. The adolescent writes that he will expound events "avoiding with all my might everything extraneous, and mainly literary beauty" (SS 8:5).[2] Thus there are a multitude of declarations like this in the novel: "I do this so that it will be more comprehensible to the reader, and since I cannot foresee where l could *stick* this list in the later course of the story" (SS 8:85). Thus the composition of the story consists in *sticking* something somewhere. This is a sharp degradation of the image of a writer's work. Dostoevskii emphasizes this "casualness" of composition, noting different cases of "running ahead": "But again, anticipating the course of events, I find it necessary to explain this to the reader, although it may be a little premature, for so many chance events have been added here to the logical course of this story, that without explaining them in advance they will be impossible to make out" (SS 8:551); "so that this does not turn into a muddle, before describing the catastrophe I will explain the whole real truth and for the last time will run ahead" (SS 8:606); "I will run ahead with two or three words!" (SS 8:539). The adolescent sometimes conducts his story as though immediately after the event, on the run, and sometimes writes after that. This position of the author of the notes, which changes all the time, is externally illogical, unnatural, but should not be regarded as "artistic oversight." [...]

Dostoevskii forces the reader to cover the whole course of interpreting events with him, forces him to live it through and interpret it with him. Hence the reservations in the text, the hesitations in evaluation. It seems as if Dostoevskii is not sure of the correctness of his own interpretation of events. Hence the continual self-corrections, and hence the attempt to note the events down immediately. This tracking of time, of which we have already spoken, creates a dramaturgical intensity and sharpens the feeling of unfamiliarity, the feeling of unexpectedness.

It is important to note that the "chronicler" of the novel *The Adolescent* is a young, immature person. He sees the world without understanding it to a sufficient extent. The reader perceives events through the psychology of this adolescent, and is gripped by his all-enveloping "idea." This is not the naivety of an old chronicler who has partially renounced life, who has already become indifferent to it (the image of Pimen), but the naivety of an ardent youth, who wishes to

---

2 F. M. Dostoevskii, *Podrostok, Sobranie sochinenii v 10-ti t.* (Moscow: Gosizdat 1957). Subsequently indicated in the text as *SS* with volume number.

assert himself in life whatever happens, who has fallen into its whirlpool, is lively (this liveliness makes it possible for him to be a witness of events, to act quickly, in the "tempo" of the whole narrative). This is a perception of the world from an emphasized "hesitant" point of view, showing the relativity of all that is happening. Sometimes the adolescent cannot make sense of the world, and then, like a chronicler, he will attempt to write down only facts: "I will not describe my confused feelings . . . I will continue only with facts . . . facts, facts! I remember how these very facts stifled me then and would not let me make sense of anything, so that towards the end of that day I was totally confused" (*SS* 8:539).

Facts in themselves are meaningless; they are deprived of real truth. This is vanity. Meaning is somewhere beyond the boundaries of facts, in the depths, in their essence. This is a mirage. An adolescent like this is needed to describe facts. It is impossible to invest a definite meaning in them as such, one has to be a "factographer," a "chronicler." But the adolescent cannot sustain this— he interprets facts, interprets them patently wrongly, since he is an adolescent, slow-witted, and also gripped by an "idea," for which the reader cannot have sympathy, since it comes from his aggrieved nature, full of hate for the surrounding society. In this sense the adolescent's interpretations cannot be accepted by the reader, cannot be taken seriously. But at the same time, there is much intelligence in his reflections, he also expresses wise truths in his own way against his will, gives deep interpretations, but the latter are as if fortuitous: the reader himself has to separate the wise from the stupid, "puppyish." Objectivity of artistic generalizations is created in this way. It is as if the reader himself makes generalizations, imperceptibly prompted towards this by Dostoevskii.

In the novel, which attempts to communicate facts (this is announced from the lips of the adolescent), there are an extraordinary number of discussions and judgments. They burst into the novel's fabric in their own way, involuntarily.

At the end, in critical remarks made by the adolescent's former tutor, Nikolai Semenovich, it is said of the adolescent's notes that they could "give material" for the characterization of a "troubled time," "in spite of all their chaotic and casual character" (*SS* 8:625). We would say that the notes give a characterization of their time just *thanks* to their chaotic and casual character. The essence of things appears through just this chaotic and casual character. Here is a pledge of the objectivity of the picture created, not juggled by the author, but recorded in a chronicle style by a chronicler [. . .]

Dostoevskii emphasizes the narrowness of the chronicler's information. The chronicler does not know everything, or finds out about it later. He constantly declares: "as it has turned out now," "as it turned out later," "he remembered," "by all the signs, he was hiding," "even now I do not know exactly who he is," etc. Sometimes the chronicler simply declines to give information: "Of course, no one has a right to demand from me as a storyteller too exact details concerning one point: there is a secret here, there is a woman" (*SS* 7:490). Dostoevskii emphasizes that his chronicler grasps only the external aspect of phenomena [...]

Dostoevskii's nearest predecessors and contemporaries represented time from one point of view, moreover a motionless one. It was as if the narrator (the author himself, or the "image of the narrator") sat down in front of the viewer in an imaginary comfortable chair (slightly lordly, let us allow, in Turgenev's case) and began his narration, knowing its beginning and end. The author seemed to suggest that the reader should listen to a narrative in which the author himself occupied a firm and unmoving position as a witness to what had happened, narrating that which had already occurred, that which already had its ending. "Novels in letters" (of which I have already spoken) and diary entries were slightly different from this. The positions of Dostoevskii's narrators are completely different. The narrator runs through the town, finds out about what has happened, spies, sometimes even hiding behind curtains (as in *The Adolescent*), writes and describes "on the move." There is something journalistic in his work. It is not for nothing that Dostoevskii liked journalistic activity so much. His *A Writer's Diary* is also a pursuit of contemporaneity in a "short segment." But this is not enough. In general, one point of view does not suit Dostoevskii, even if it is moving, dynamic, freely moving from place to place after what has just occurred. He needs at least two points of view—that of the author and that of the narrator—so as to describe the action and characters from all sides, so as to create a certain "stereoscopic quality" of representation. The author looks on what is happening from a certain height, he is further removed in time from the narrator. He can judge events and people from the point of view of their "eternal" significance. The chronicler is all in a bustle. He looks and follows events without any distance from them. As a result of such double representation, each person and each action is shown in Dostoevskii, as in a Renaissance painting, from several sides or from the side from which it can be most clearly viewed. This is why in the end Dostoevskii so often has resort to the image of the chronicler, "a chronicler of contemporaneity" (Dostoevskii's own expression). For in the chronicle there is no single point of view, nor a single narrator. Thus both significant and insignificant events turn up in the chronicle. This creates an effect of the vanity and fragility of human existence. An effect which, as we shall see, is not without interest for Dostoevskii.

The difference between Dostoevskii's narrators and the chronicle narrators, however, is the fact that the chronicle was "really" written by many chroniclers. Compilers composed each chronicle from many other chronicles, combining the different points of view of actually different chroniclers. In Dostoevskii this is a conscious method. And this method of his was created earlier than European painting decided to return to a pre-Renaissance "examination" of objects from several sides simultaneously [...]

In the literature about Dostoevskii it has been pointed out more than once it is impossible to identify his characters' views with the views of Dostoevskii himself. And this is true. However, it is also impossible not to notice the fact that no other author has expounded his views so often through the mouths of his characters. And in this respect we are again obliged to emphasize that there are no "pure" heroes in Dostoevskii, as there is no "pure" author.

Thanks to such authorial incursion into the speeches, actions, and judgments of his characters, the very figures of the author and his narrator appear far from distinct. And a distinction between them is also not needed. They are not "in focus," insofar as they are moving all the time. The representations are impressionistically washed away by their movement. This is an artistic method. What are important are actions, events, characters, not narrators. Sometimes the reader does not even immediately recognize who are. The reader finds out the name and patronymic of the "chronicler" in *Demons* (Anton Lavrentevich) as though by chance, and can easily forget it is not important. The narrators of Dostoevskii's novels are often conventional and one has to a certain extent to forget about them. This is almost the same as in Japanese dolls' theater, where actors in black move the dolls on the stage under the viewers' gaze, but the viewers *do not have to* notice them, and do not recognize them. The dolls play. The dolls can sometimes represent more than the living actors. One should not take those who move the dolls for characters. The author and narrators in Dostoevskii are servants of the proscenium, who help the reader to see all that is happening from the best positions in each situation. This is why they are in such a bustle.

Dostoevskii is in pursuit of time, but not of "time past," which has once been, has passed, and is now remembered, as M. Proust was later to do, but of the present, of what is happening. Like a chronicler, he wants to record the fleeting, in order to secure it and bring out the eternal in it. What Dostoevskii writes about is the past which has still not cooled down, has not ceased being the present. This is a chronicle—a "quick chronicle," and its chronicler is very similar to a reporter, which is why he is so agile, unlike Pimen, and young, unlike Pimen. But all the same there is a connection with Pimen. Dostoevskii ascribes equal significance, also like a chronicler, to the significant and insignificant, combines in his exposition the essential and the minor. This allows him to see in trifles signs of eternity, premonitions of the future, and the as yet unborn future itself [...]

The "quick chronicle" of Dostoevskii's novels is a contemporary form literature. It is by no means an attempt to archaicize the narrative, to resurrect forgotten forms of artistic time mechanically. It is sometimes a shorthand report. The character of the shorthand report influenced Dostoevskii's style, mingling with chronicle compositional methods. Compare, for example, the remarks in brackets with which Dostoevskii accompanies the speeches at the meeting of the revolutionaries in *Demons*: "(Laughter was heard)," "(Laughter again)" (*SS* 7:421), "(General movement and approval)," "(Again movement, several guttural noises)," "(Exclamations: "Yes, yes! General support)" (*SS* 7:567), etc. Here even the clumsiness of stenographic language communicated: "movement"! Shorthand is the contemporary form of the chronicle, of the documentary entry. Not fortuitously, the chronicler-annalist emphasizes the protocol exactness of the speeches communicated by him: "will quote this jerky and inconsistent speech word for word" (*SS* 7:492).[3]

Dostoevskii is in constant pursuit of events because authenticity is necessary for him as a chronicler. Only a month or so passes, and truth disappears. Ivan Karamazov's trial shows this. It is impossible to establish the truthfulness of the past. And about the distant past only legends exist.

But all the same Dostoevskii was drawn to the narrative manner of the past, and consequently also to the fantastic time of medieval genres, when it was necessary to expound a pure idea. It is not by chance that Ivan Karamazov reproaches Alesha that "contemporary realism has spoilt him" and he "cannot accommodate anything fantastic." "The Legend of the Grand Inquisitor" is conventionally transferred to the sixteenth century, when, in Ivan's words, "it was the custom in works to bring celestial forces to earth" (*SS* 9:909). It is typical that Father Zosima's notes are an attempt to resurrect old forms of narrative. It is not by chance that Father Parfenii's notes served as a model for their style.[4]

---

3 On the stenography of Dostoevskii's works see B. N. Kapeliush and Ts. M. Poshemanskaia, "Stenograficheskie zapisi A. G. Dostoevskoi," in *Literaturnyi arkhiv, Materialy po istorii literatury i obshchestvennogo dvizheniia*, vol. 6, (Moscow-Leningrad: Izdatel'stvo Akademii nauk SSSR, 1961). However, the influence of stenography on Dostoevskii's works has not been studied.

4 *Skazanie o stranstvii i puteshestvii po Rossii, Moldavii, Turtsii i Sviatoi zemle postrizhenika sviatye gory Afonskia inoka Parfeniia*, 2nd ed. (Moscow, 1856).

Written in the nineteenth century, these notes nonetheless followed the traditions of early Russian literature—the traditions of the genre of pilgrimage to the holy land, which represented a curious form of mixing different languages and styles, demonstrating the vitality of old methods of depicting the vanity of everything temporal and the significance of the extra-temporal. And all the same, Dostoevskii had resort to these early Russian methods only in interspersions foreign to his basic stylistic manner.

Basically, Dostoevskii tried to find signs of reliable and "eternal" truth in the "vanity of vanities" of accumulations of facts close to the contemporary world. As a guide in this search Dostoevskii chose an imaginary "chronicler"—an annalist, a clumsy writer, who, by sometimes not distinguishing the significant from the insignificant, and running across the essential by chance, gave him the most objective evidence.

We shall now note the most important difference between the chroniclers and Dostoevskii in relation to time. Chronicle time in the former was a natural expression of their relation to history, to the contemporary world, to the world of events. This was an epic, collective consciousness of time, which was formed in the genre as such. In Dostoevskii, chronicle time is an artistic method for representing the world, he recreates it artificially, as an artist, *represents* this very chronicle time, creating the image of the chronicler and annalist. Chronicle time for the chroniclers is the nature of their vision of the world. Chronicle time in Dostoevskii is a landscape painted by a great artist. Moreover, Dostoevskii does not attempt to recreate the chronicler's artistic time—he only makes use of the achievements of this ancient method of expounding events from the standpoint of eternity. He reworks his method artistically, transforms it, and makes it amazingly mobile.

The Narrator of
The Idiot (1981)*

Robin Feuer Miller

B ecause Dostoevskii considered form to be inseparable from idea, the
search for the proper narrative mode mattered almost as much to him as
finding the idea itself: "for various forms of art there exist series of poetic ideas
which correspond to them, so that one idea can never be expressed in another
form that doesn't correspond to it" (*Pis'ma*, III, 20). The form of *The Idiot*
subsumes within it several simultaneously coexisting modes of narration: the
voice of a sympathetic and omniscient narrator; a voice—ironically detached
from the action—which passes along the current local rumors, a comic voice
of limited intelligence which relates a kind of novel of ill manners; and a
Gothic voice which employs techniques of arbitrary disclosure and heightened
terror. At times the narrative style becomes completely dramatic.[1] A reader of

---

* From Robin Feuer Miller, *Dostoevsky and The Idiot: Author, Narrator and Reader* (Cambridge, MA: Harvard University Press, 1981), 90–92, 107–10, 115–17. Copyright © 1981 by the President and Fellows of Harvard College.

1 Mixing of modes is not peculiar to Dostoevskii; it prevails in the works of most great novelists. In disagreeing with Percy Lubbock's emphasis on the *point of view* in a novel, E. M. Forster finds that for him this question resolves itself into "the power of the writer to bounce the reader into accepting what he says—a power which Mr. Lubbock admits and admires, but locates at the edge of the problem instead of at the centre. I should put it at the centre." See his *Aspects of the Novel*, (New York: Harcourt, Brace and World, 1927), 78–79. His example is *Bleak House*: "Logically, *Bleak House* is all to pieces, but Dickens bounces us, so that we do not mind the shiftings of the viewpoint" (ibid., 79). The lack of a single consistent point of view enriches rather than diminishes the novel; the multiplicity of narrative modes in a work serves to make a novel more real. "Indeed this power to expand and contract perception (of which the shifting view-point is a symptom), this right to intermittent knowledge:—I find it one of the great advantages of the novel-form, and it has a parallel in our perception of life. We are stupider at some times than others; we can enter into people's minds occasionally but not

The Idiot rapidly becomes accustomed to the variety of narrative tones that emerge in the first two parts of the novel.

They are all different voices of a single narrator, who ventures at times to introduce his own opinions and interpretation of events, and must not be confused with the voice of the author, or in Booth's terminology, the voice of the implied author. We know that in his fiction Dostoevskii always sought to conceal his own voice as a matter of policy. The entire novel, except for the purely dramatic scenes, is written through the voices of the narrator.

Narration generally implies communication of the details of a story. Those who judge this novel to be a failure tend to do so on the grounds that the reader has lost touch with the author and that the narrative medium—in this case the narrator's voices—has muddied rather than clarified the channels of communication between the novelist and the reader. In short, the author has failed to express his idea in a convincing way.[2] In Parts I and II of *The Idiot*, however, the narrator does establish a definite modal pattern; the reader is invited to expect the use of a particular voice to describe a particular character or group of characters. After identifying the main voices of the narrator and the patterns that allow the reader's prediction of their occurrence, one can begin to assess the balance of these voices in the novel and their possible effect on the reader.[3] Does he become too bewildered, or, conversely, is he burdened with a too heavy-handed narrative irony?

---

always, because our own minds get tired; and this intermittence lends in the long run variety and colour to the experiences we receive" (ibid., 81). Dostoevskii takes this method of shifting viewpoint to its extreme limits, so that the reader is often rudely jolted rather than bounced.

2   The reactions of the reader I know best, myself, did not correspond to the enriching, interlacing layers of response that repeated readings of great novels usually produce, but were, instead, opposite, mutually exclusive reactions. At a first reading I felt Dostoevskii had failed in his creation of Myshkin as a "positively beautiful man." I located this failure in the fact that vestiges of the vengeful Idiot of the notebook remained in the novel. A second reading convinced me of Myshkin's authentic goodness. A comparison of Robert Lord's with Joseph Frank's readings of the novel yields the same extreme variance but for both, it is precisely the experience of being a reader of *The Idiot* that becomes the most crucial aspect of this novel. See Robert Lord, "An Epileptic Mode of Being," in his *Dostoevsky: Essays and Perspectives* (Berkeley: University of California Press, 1970), 81–102, and Joseph Frank, "A Reading of *The Idiot*," *Southern Review* 5 (April 1969): 303–32.

3   Leo Spitzer has characterized criticism as a "to and fro voyage from certain outward details to the inner center and back again to other series of details." See his *Linguistics and Literary History: Essays in Stylistics* (Princeton: Princeton University Press, 1948), 19–20. Criticism can claim for itself no scientific methodology; to understand the whole you must seek a detail or a part which will illuminate the whole. But the critic's happy choice of a productive part to examine presupposes some understanding of the whole, and Spitzer aptly quotes

The novel opens with a straightforward, factual account by a narrator-observer. The narrator's sense that he is telling a story predominates from the outset; he tries to restrict himself to a tempered, measured disclosure of the identities of the two young men on the railroad car, yet he cannot resist, in the second paragraph, forewarning the reader that this is a remarkable meeting. "Since dawn, in one of the third-class cars, facing each other by the window, sat two passengers—both young people, both with practically no luggage, both unfashionably dressed, both with rather remarkable physiognomies, and both wishing, finally, to enter into conversation with the other. If they had both known about one another, why they were especially remarkable at that moment, then of course they would have marveled that chance had so strangely seated them opposite one another in a third class car of the Petersburg-Warsaw train" (PSS 8:5; 25). The reader immediately connects the two passengers with each other; they are linked by the narrator's insistent repetition of "both." The narrator has also managed to assert twice that they are each remarkable and that their presence on the third-class coach is somehow odd. These compartments are usually crowded with "ordinary people"; his is to be a story of extraordinary men [. . .]

Thus by the end of Part I a definite pattern of narration has emerged; the reader has become acquainted with the narrator's voices and has acquired grounds for expecting when a particular voice will appear. The narrator will describe Totskii and the general in an ironic mode, relying heavily upon public opinions and rumors. He will use a similar voice for the rest of the Epanchin family, but there, in addition, he has an eye for the details of domestic life and manners. Though entering the prince's mind rarely, when he does so, the narrator bewilders the reader; he refrains from an ironic, distanced presentation of the hero. All this seems fitting and proper, and the reader's trust in the narrator's judgment, taste, and tact has been established. The narrator's slight lapses of logic and taste have caused no serious offence. At the same time the reader knows the narrator is manipulating him and sometimes withholding information. However, the dramatic scenes counterbalance the effect of the narrator's mystifications. The narrator has successfully maintained the reader's bewilderment and curiosity about the plot and the characters, yet he has

---

Pascal's God, "Tu ne me chercherais pas si tu ne m'avais pas déjà trouvé" (ibid., 24). My own study of the narrative manner in *The Idiot* and its effect upon the reader has assumed the qualities of a "to and fro voyage" and should not be construed as an effort occurring under the banner of any particular critical ideology.

also endowed the reader with a sense of his own acuity by sharing ironies and witticisms with him.

In Part II these narrative patterns become even more pronounced. Here the narrator also reveals a new voice, a mode reminiscent of the Gothic novel. Although it was Leonid Grossman who first pointed out Dostoevskii's debt to the Gothic novel, he and others have rather stressed Dostoevskii's artistic debt to writers such as Sue, Soulié, Hugo, Dumas, George Sand, Poe, Hoffman, Balzac, Scott, and Dickens.[4] But these writers themselves drew on the tradition of the Gothic novel as it developed in the works of Horace Walpole, Ann Radcliffe, Matthew Lewis, and Charles Maturin, and so did Dostoevskii; the themes and techniques explored by the Gothic novelists find a direct echo in his work.[5] But Dostoevskii raises the themes and techniques of the Gothic novelists to new heights, for he forges a metaphysical system out of a language which, in the hands of lesser novelists, remains merely a style, an effective fictional point of view. The language of the Gothic novel and its themes offered Dostoevskii a powerful rhetoric for describing modern man's predicament.

As a child and young reader Dostoevskii himself delighted in the "tales of terror." In 1863, on the first page of his *Winter Notes on Summer Impressions*, Dostoevskii recalled his early love for the fiction of Ann Radcliffe, "when, during the long winter evenings, before I could read, I would listen, agape and rooted to the spot with delight and terror, as my parents read, at bedtime, the novels of Radcliffe; I would then rave deliriously about them in my sleep" (PSS 5:46).[6] Dostoevskii had expressed his earliest response to the Gothic novel in terms of the sublime—a mixture of terror and delight. Nevertheless, Dostoevskii's explicit references to Radcliffe in his fiction are slight and always ironic. (PSS 3:134; 15:158). But even though Dostoevskii had no real use for

---

4 Leonid Grossman, "Kompozitsiia v romane Dostoevskogo," in *Sobranie sochinenii*, vol. 2, 9–59; Bakhtin, "Characteristics of Genre and Plot Composition in Dostoevskii's Works," in his *Problems of Dostoevsky's Poetics*, 83–150; Konstantin Mochulsky, *Dostoevsky: His Life and Work*, trans. Michael Minihan (Princeton: Princeton University Press, 1967); Donald Fanger, *Dostoevsky and Romantic Realism: A Study of Dostoevsky in Relation to Balzac, Dickens, and Gogol* (Chicago: University of Chicago Press, 1965).

5 See Robin Feuer Miller, "Dostoevsky and the Tale of Terror," in *The Russian Novel*, ed. John G. Garrard (New Haven: Yale University Press, 1983), 103–25.

6 See also Dostoevskii's letter of 1861 to Iakov Polanskii (*Pis'ma*, 1: 302). Moreover, as a student in engineering school, Dostoevskii had read to his friends from the works of Maturin (See Leonid Grossman, *Sobranie sochinenii*, 2:73). See also Vsevolod Setchkarev, "Ch. R. Maturins Roman 'Melmoth, the Wanderer' und Dostojevskij," *Zeitschrift für slavische Philologie* 30 (1951): 99–106.

debauched monks, mysterious castles, and the rest of the paraphernalia of the Gothic novel, he learned much from the "fantastic romanticism" of this genre. By linking some of Dostoevskii's techniques and themes directly back to this older genre of the Gothic novel rather than to the intervening traditions of the roman-feuilleton, the historical romance, and the novels of romantic realism, we can gain a more thorough understanding of Dostoevskii's narrative technique.

In "A Philosophical Enquiry into the Origin of Our Ideas of the Sublime and Beautiful" (1757) Edmund Burke wrote, "Whatever is fitted in any sort to excite the ideas of pain and danger, that is to say, whatever is in any sort terrible, or is conversant about terrible objects, or operates in a manner analogous to terror, is a source of the sublime." Burke rigorously separated the beautiful from the sublime. One fills us with pleasure, the other with delight; the beautiful induces "in us a sense of affection and tenderness," but the sublime "is productive of the strongest emotion which the mind is capable of feeling."[7]

The Gothic novelists of the late eighteenth and early nineteenth century, though profoundly influenced by Burke's understanding of the terrible as a necessary part of the sublime, were not interested in reproducing Burke's entire aesthetic system: they did not attempt to separate the beautiful from the sublime.[8] Instead, they described a world in which the beautiful and the sublime were tightly entangled. "The discovery of Horror as a source of delight reacted in men's actual conception of Beauty itself: the Horrid, from being a category of the Beautiful became eventually one of its essential elements, and the 'beautifully horrid' passed by insensible degrees into the 'horribly

---

7 Edmund Burke, *A Philosophical Enquiry into the Origin of Our Ideas of the Sublime and Beautiful*, ed. James T. Boulton (Notre Dame: University of Notre Dame Press, 1958), 39, 51, 39. Burke was not the first to associate the sublime with greatness of dimension or to analyze the psychological effects of experiencing the sublime. He was, however, the first to attempt a "physiological explanation" of the sublime and the first to convert the link between sublimity and terror into a system. See Boulton, "Introductory Essay," i–vi, in Burke, *A Philosophical Enquiry*.

8 The impact of Burke's essay was almost immediate—the phrase "the sublime and the beautiful" quickly entered everyday speech (ibid., xcvi–xcvii, xcii), and "it became commonplace among both writers and readers to consider the emotions of terror and awe as sources of 'the Sublime'—a ready conduit to ideas of Divinity, Omnipotence, and all Final Things." See Joel Porte, "In the Hands of an Angry God: Religious Terror in Gothic Fiction," in *The Gothic Imagination: Essays in Dark Romanticism*, ed. G. R. Thompson (Pullman, Wash.: Washington State University Press, 1974), 43. In Dostoevskii's *Notes from Underground* the underground man does battle with countless writers, thinkers, and catch-all phrases— among them "the sublime and the beautiful." Although this phrase has often been linked to Schiller as well, the editors of the ongoing Soviet edition of Dostoevskii's works have turned back to Burke and Kant (PSS 5 [1973], 102; 383).

beautiful."[9] In his fiction Dostoevskii partakes of the "new sensibility" inherent in this Gothic tradition: his themes, plots, and characters all embody the heady mixture of the awful and the beautiful.

As one might expect, in the Gothic novel descriptions of beauty and horror often coalesce in the same image: "By the side of three putrid half-corrupted bodies lay the sleeping beauty [. . .] She seemed to smile at the images of death around her."[10]

Or "so he lay [. . .] in a kind of corpse-like beauty [. . .] A St. Bartholomew flayed, with his skin hanging about him in a graceful drapery—a St. Laurence, broiled on a gridiron, and exhibiting his finely formed anatomy on its bars [. . .] even these were inferior to the form half-veiled half-disclosed by the moonlight as it lay."[11] The final description of Nastas'ia Filippovna at the end of *The Idiot* invokes, though to a lesser degree, the same responses from the reader. The sight of Nastas'ia's white foot protruding from the cover, the buzzing fly, and the moonlight emphasize both her deadness and her loveliness; they merge into one image. As Dostoevskii may have learned from the Gothic novelists, the death of a beautiful woman offered a powerful way of holding the reader's attention: the "death of a beautiful woman is, unquestionably," as Poe observed, "the most poetic topic in the world."[12] [. . .]

Part II had opened with the narrator's familiar ironic, detached voice, a voice that repeatedly reminded the reader that he was reading a story. Predictably, the narrative centered around the Epanchin family. The second chapter of Part II begins in a tone of straightforwardly descriptive narration: the subject—again predictably—is the prince. He has arrived on the Petersburg scene once again, this time from the opposite direction—from the heart of Russia. Suddenly a new narrative mode, the

---

9 Mario Praz, "Introductory Essay," in *Three Gothic Novels: The Castle of Otranto, Vathek, Frankenstein,* ed. Peter Fairclough (Harmondsworth, UK: Penguin Books, 1968), 10. Burke himself had briefly suggested that the qualities of the sublime and the beautiful could be "sometimes found united" both in nature and in art, despite the fact that one is "founded on pain, the other on pleasure." Edmund Burke, *A Philosophical Enquiry,* 124.

10 Matthew G. Lewis, *The Monk* (New York: Grove Press, 1952), 363–364.

11 Charles Robert Maturin, *Melmoth the Wanderer: A Tale* (Lincoln: University of Nebraska Press, 1961), 322.

12 Edgar Allan Poe, *Philosophy of Composition,* quoted by Mario Praz in his *The Romantic Agony,* trans. Angus Davidson, 2nd ed. (New York: Oxford University Press, 1970), 27. Throughout the chapter "The Beauty of the Medusa" (23–53) Praz gives other examples of the mingling of Beauty and Horror, and he later cites Mitia's famous speech in *The Brothers Karamazov* that begins, "Beauty is a terrible and awful thing!" (ibid., 350). He does not link this passage directly back to the Gothic novel, however, but forward to the language of Baudelaire.

Gothic voice, wafts in and then quickly subsides for several chapters. "No one met him at the station; but as he left the carriage suddenly it seemed to the prince that he felt a strange, burning glance from a pair of eyes in the crowd, which had gathered to meet the train. He looked around more attentively, but he already could not make out anything more. Of course, it had only seemed that way; but an unpleasant impression remained. And even without that the prince was melancholy and pensive and seemed worried about something" (PSS 8:158; 210). The narrative ingredients are reassuringly familiar to the reader, who finds that the narrator has entered Myshkin without really explaining his thoughts and observes that the prince, as before, is susceptible to "impressions." But a new, slightly fantastic element has crept into the narrator's tone. He does not undercut Myshkin's sense of premonition and foreboding, nor does he relieve us with an explanation of what Myshkin is really sensing. This tone (almost a melodic prefiguring of a fragment to be later expanded) quickly dissipates, however, and the narrator reverts to his former voices.

The most extended passage in the Gothic mode that offers no moments of comic realism occurs in Chapter 5 of Part II. The narrative resembles the stereotyped half of the Gothic tradition, for the whole chapter, save the last two paragraphs, is like the tale of terror in its heightened mood and in the extreme use of the technique of arbitrary disclosure by the narrator. Fears merely intimated provoke a greater effect than ones that are fully described. Here Myshkin, having left Rogozhin's house, wanders in a state of feverish reverie through St. Petersburg. "Solitude soon became unbearable to him; a new impulse seized his heart feverishly, and for a moment the darkness, in which his soul was languishing, was lit up by a bright light. He took a ticket for Pavlovsk [...] but, now something was pursuing him, and it was something real, and not a fantasy, as, perhaps, he was inclined to think [...] Some time later [...] it was as if he suddenly remembered something, as if he had seized hold of something very strange, something that had already troubled him a long time [...] Then he would forget it [...] then suddenly again he would look around" (PSS 8:186–87; 243–44). He finds the shop window with the sixty-kopek article in the window (Rogozhin's knife—not named here) and remembers the sensation of Rogozhin's eyes being fixed upon him.

In what is now a familiar pattern, he tries to force this thought out of his mind; he thinks of the moment before an epileptic fit. "He thought of this, sitting on a bench, under a tree, in the Summer Garden [...] It was stifling, as if the weather were presaging thunderstorms . . . There was a certain appeal for him in his present contemplative state [...] he wanted at all costs to forget something, something real and pressing, but from his first glance around him he again immediately recognized his gloomy thought, the thought, from which he so wanted to escape [. . .] he gazed at the sky [. . .] Perhaps his epileptic condition was becoming more and more acute. The thunderstorm [. . .] was really advancing, although slowly. Distant thunder had begun already. It had become very stifling" (PSS 8:189; 246–47). Having called at Nastas'ia Filippovna's in vain, he continues his reverie under the spell of Rogozhin's eyes: "A strange and terrible demon had finally attached itself to him and would no longer let him go. This demon had whispered to him in the Summer Garden" (PSS 8:193; 251). At last, he sees Rogozhin on the other side of the street standing before him like an accuser and a judge. It appears that Rogozhin had hardly bothered to conceal himself. That simple disclosure of reality by the narrator, after having been for so long in Myshkin's mind, produces a more nightmarish effect than did the hero's shadowy inklings and forebodings. As Myshkin enters the gate of the hotel the storm finally breaks and he again catches sight of Rogozhin: "'Now everything will be decided!' he thought to himself with a strange conviction . . . Those two eyes, *those very ones*, suddenly met his stare" (PSS 8:194–95; 253–54).

A typical narrator in a Gothic novel seeks to interest the reader by any means whatsoever, whether by making things look mysterious or by describing events in ghastly detail. In this chapter the narrator seeks to create an air of overbearing, all-encompassing mystery in order to heighten Myshkin's premonitions while clouding his rational faculties. The language is deliberately mysterious. The narrator has stretched his usual mode of describing Myshkin to its extreme. Previously he used the word "something" to describe Myshkin's imprecise thoughts; now he adds an aura of external mystery to his use of indefinite nouns. "Something" pursues Myshkin; a "demon" has attached itself to him. Myshkin's forebodings, in Gothic fashion, inexorably come to pass, for the scene climaxes with Rogozhin's attempted murder and with Myshkin's epileptic fit. The narrator vacillates between fantasy and reality, although, like Ann Radcliffe's narrator, at the end he offers a rational explanation for events. The reader finds himself in a world far removed from the easy ironies of the Epanchin household.

Sideshadowing in Dostoevskii's Novels (1994)*

Gary Saul Morson

*F*oreshadowing robs a present moment of its presentness. As we have seen, foreshadowing lifts the veil on a future that has already been determined and inscribed. Somehow, a specific later event is already given at the time of an earlier event. Thus the sense of many possible futures, which we experience at every present moment, is revealed as an illusion. What *will* be *must* be; events are heading in a single direction; time is entirely linear or, as the underground man says, "logarithmic," because the future is either known for certain or calculable (at least in principle) with mathematical certainty.

Wisdom in such a world consists in the appreciation of inevitability. As readers or viewers of a story with foreshadowing, we recognize a character's struggle for alternatives as doomed and deluded. If the real world is governed by the same kind of temporality, then we would do well never to forget the singularity of the future. Whether or not we hear the voice of Tiresias, the time in which we live is oracular.

As we have seen, those who have believed time to be genuinely open have sought to invent ways of telling a story that elude foreshadowing and closure. They have sought to restore presentness to the present. To do so, Dostoevskii and Tolstoi made effective use of a device that may be viewed as the antithesis of foreshadowing: sideshadowing.

Whereas foreshadowing works by revealing apparent alternatives to be mere illusions, sideshadowing conveys the sense that actual events might just

---

* From Gary Saul Morson, *Narrative and Freedom: The Shadows of Time* (New Haven, CT: Yale University Press, 1994), 117–18, 120–22, 126–28. Copyright © 1994 by Yale University. All rights reserved.

as well not have happened. In an open universe, the illusion is inevitability itself. Alternatives always abound, and, more often than not, what exists need not have existed. *Something else* was possible, and sideshadowing is used to create a sense of that "something else." Instead of casting a foreshadow from the future, it casts a shadow "from the side," that is, from the other possibilities. Along with an event, we see its alternatives; with each present, another possible present. Sideshadows conjure the ghostly presence of might-have-beens or might-bes. While we see what did happen, we also see the image of what else could have happened. In this way, the hypothetical shows through the actual and so achieves its own shadowy kind of existence in the text.

In sideshadowing, two or more alternative presents, the actual and the possible, are made simultaneously visible. This is a simultaneity not in time but of times: we do not see contradictory actualities, but one possibility that was actualized and, at the same moment, another that could have been but was not. In this way, time itself acquires a double and often many doubles. A haze of possibilities surrounds each actuality.

When sideshadowing is used, it seems that distinct temporalities are continually competing for each moment of actuality. Like a king challenged by a pretender with an equal claim to rule, the actual loses some temporal legitimacy. It can no longer be regarded as inevitable, as so firmly ensconced that it does not even make sense to consider alternatives. Or to adapt one of Bakhtin's favorite metaphors, a present moment subjected to sideshadowing ceases to be Ptolemaic, the unchallenged center of things. It moves instead into a Copernican universe: as there are many planets, so there are many potential presents for each one actualized [. . .]

Let us consider some examples from a master of sideshadowing, Dostoevskii. Used extensively in his fiction, the device nevertheless dominates some novels more than others. It is essential to the temporality of *Demons*, in which it serves as a counterpoint to the utopianism of the revolutionaries. The linear time of their theories is silently opposed by the novel's open time, as their drive toward completion vies with the work's temporality of continuing and open-ended sequence. Operating both in major events and in the most minor scenes, sideshadowing endows the novel with a sense of the unexpected and the mysterious. Other possibilities threaten to erupt at any moment and cast their shadow over everything that actually happens.

More often than not, Dostoevskii's chronicler (a resident of the town) tells us what might have happened or what could have happened. Moreover, the "actions" he does describe are frequently checked impulses, which might or might not indicate a possibility contemplated but not actualized. Such actualities are themselves aborted possibilities, and they evoke the middle realm of things that could have happened. Remembered by the character who "performs" them, and perceived by witnesses, these possibilities acquire a substantiality of their own. *Demons* is thick with events that might have happened.

At about midpoint of the novel, several characters, in order to relieve their boredom, take a trip to the mad "prophet" Semen Iakovlevich. Having completed a lengthy description of the journey and of the visit itself, the chronicler unexpectedly announces that none of these events is important. "At this point, however, there took place, I am told, an extremely enigmatic incident, and I must own, it was chiefly on account of it that I have described this expedition so minutely," he announces.[1] Here, as elsewhere, the chronicler has evidently given us "too many facts," including all sorts of apparently "irrelevant" details about the expedition. We recognize their presence as characteristic of Dostoevskian narration. Too many facts, presented with no clear explanation and an air of mystery, lead us to construct or intimate many possible stories. What is irrelevant to one account, after all, may be central to another, and the reader, like many characters in the novel, seeks to reconstruct many stories from each one.

Stories also multiply if the facts may not be facts at all or if other "facts" lie behind the ostensible ones, with ever-receding layers of possibility and orders of suspicion. Although the chronicler has himself witnessed a great deal, has collected firsthand accounts, and has apparently spoken with almost everyone about almost everything, he seems, for all his research, to be unable to decide on a single version of events. Instead, he typically reports a range of rumors, doubts his own best sources, and obsessively offers alternative possibilities. "Some say," "others affirm," "it is absurd to suppose," "the papers were surely mistaken to say," "now everyone at the club believed with the utmost certainty," "it is maintained in all seriousness"—these and countless similar expressions give each of his accounts an aura of endless alternatives and an air of unresolvable enigma. That is surely true of the "extremely enigmatic" incident—if incident it was—at Semen Iakovlevich's.

---

1 EDS: Morson makes reference to the following edition: Fyodor Dostoevsky, *The Possessed*, trans. Constance Garnett (New York: Modern Library, 1963), 341. Subsequent references to this title appear in the text as "P."

It appears that as everyone was leaving, Stavrogin and Liza Nikolaevna, whose relations everyone regarded as profoundly mysterious, jostled against each other in the doorway. Or, at least, "I am told" they did, says the chronicler:

> I fancied they both stood still for an instant, and looked, as it were, strangely at one another, but I may not have seen rightly in the crowd. It is asserted, on the contrary, and quite seriously, that Liza, glancing at Nikolai Vsevolodovich [Stavrogin], quickly raised her hand to the level of his face, and would certainly have struck him if he had not drawn back in time. Perhaps she was displeased with the expression of his face, or the way he smiled, particularly just after such an episode with Mavriky Nikolaevich. I must admit I saw nothing myself, but all the others declared they had, though they certainly could not all have seen it in such a crush, though perhaps some may have. But I did not believe it at the time. I remember, however, that Nikolai Vsevolodovich was rather pale all the way home. (P, 341)

Readers will identify this rhetoric as quintessentially Dostoevskian. "Though . . . though . . . however"; "I fancied," "perhaps," "it is asserted quite seriously": with qualification piled on qualification, tentative judgments no sooner made than withdrawn and perhaps ambiguously reasserted, the narrator claims not be sure what he himself has witnessed. Reports of others are (probably) even more unreliable and apparently contradictory, though not necessary groundless. Frivolous people with a taste for scandal seriously say things that differ from what the narrator himself has seen, although, of course, he may have witnessed such a vague event and does not trust his own eyes "in such a crush." He concludes by saying he did not believe in the reported event—does he accept it now?—and then giving evidence that it might just be true anyway. Moreover, the action in question was checked before it happened, and so one has in any case to distinguish between as unrealized possibility and nothing at all.

Something may or may not have happened, and if it did, it may have been one thing or another. Liza and Stavrogin may have simply stared strangely at each other, or "on the contrary," she may have intended to slap him. If that was her purpose, it may have had various motivations, including, presumably, others not mentioned here at all.

What we are given here is not one but many possible stories. The real point is that whatever did happen, any of these incidents could have happened.

What is important is the field of possibilities, not the one actualized. By depriving any version of undeniable actuality, Dostoevskii reveals the field itself. The sideshadows crowd out the actual event. Indeed, nothing may have happened, in which case the sideshadows themselves are all there is [...]

Demons never settles on a single set of events or interpretation but invites us to contemplate this range of political possibilities.

At first the head of the police responds to the assembled workers, and then when he arrives, the governor takes over. In each case, the chronicler again reports not what did happen but the countless things said to have happened. As for the police chief, "it was not true that he galloped to the spot with three horses at full speed, and began hitting out right and left before he alighted from his carriage," although it is true that he had behaved with even less restraint on other occasions (P, 444). "There is a still more absurd story that soldiers were brought up with bayonets, and that a telegram was sent for artillery and Cossacks; those are legends which are not believed now even by those who invented them. It's an absurd story, too" that people were drenched by water from the fire brigade (P, 444). In the chronicler's opinion, this last account, which was repeated in the Moscow and Petersburg papers, evidently derived from the fact that the police chief shouted that "he wouldn't let one of them come dry out of the water" (P, 444). If the chronicler is right, then language itself seems to generate stories, as rumor progresses by an energy of its own. Whatever did happen, any of these events might well have happened.

Still more confusing was the behavior of the governor, who was later declared mad. Once someone is known to be mad, of course, it is possible to believe he did almost anything. "From the facts I have learned and those I have conjectured," the chronicler characteristically begins his account, "it's an absolute fabrication that everyone was flogged; at most two or three were" (P, 452). "It's a nonsensical story, too, that a poor but respectable lady was caught as she passed by and promptly thrashed," even though this story, as well, was reprinted in the Moscow and Petersburg papers and even though the chronicler himself not only believed in the story but also contributed to a subscription for the poor lady, who, it turned out later, did not even exist (P, 452). In short, it is virtually impossible to tell what did or did not happen, and no version makes sense of everything. Whatever possibility was actualized this time, a different one could easily take place on a similar occasion. The chronicler's uncertainty in ascertaining facts becomes the author's way of evoking the field of possibilities present in chaotic or politically charged situations.

Twice *Possessed*

Demons interweaves two plots, the story of Petr Stepanovich's conspiracy and the story of Stavrogin's search for meaning. Petr Stepanovich manufactures secrets, and Stavrogin conceals mysteries behind the "mask" of his face. In each story, an immense number of contradictory possibilities emerge. Sometimes it eventually becomes clear what happened, but only after a long interval of uncertainty in which the reader has become accustomed to contemplating fields rather than points. Other mysteries are never resolved, and contradictory explanations remain possible. For example, we never learn who killed Fed'ka. Liputin is struck by the fact that shortly after an angry Petr Stepanovich predicts Fed'ka's death, the escaped convict is indeed found murdered, and the reader no doubt shares Liputin's suspicions. And yet it is apparently determined that someone with no connection to Petr Stepanovich committed the crime. Or was that determination itself simply the result of deceit? Liputin never learns, and neither do we.[2]

Such multiplicity unreduced to singularity pertains not only to occasional incidents but also to the novel's central events. Several people suggest that Petr Stepanovich may in fact be a police agent, either an infiltrator or a provocateur. Of course, such suspicions are bound to arise in any case. Nevertheless, they cannot be easily dismissed. How else did Petr Stepanovich manage to return from his exile abroad, move about freely, and even obtain recommendations from influential officials in Petersburg? At the end of the novel, he receives secret information from Petersburg that allows him to avoid arrest, and, unlike his associates, he escapes. The other revolutionaries suspect him, and even Stavrogin puts the question directly:

> "And listen, Verkhovenskii [Petr Stepanovich], you are not one of the higher police, are you?"
> "Anyone who has a question like that in his mind doesn't utter it."
> "I understand, but we are by ourselves."
> "No, so far I am not one of the higher police." (P, 394)

"So far" [*pokamest*]—this is a denial that almost cancels itself. Does it mean that Petr Stepanovich is trying to prove himself so as to join the higher police? He may be working for the authorities even if not for the "higher" police.

---

2 As Susanne Fusso suggested to me, the intimations that Dar'ia is pregnant are neither confirmed nor dispelled.

Is he perhaps lying altogether, as any police agent would? And what if he is both a genuine revolutionary and a police spy at the same time, a sort of double agent, Working ultimately—for whom? Possibilities multiply. If Dostoevskii had not meant to suggest them, there would have been no need to insist so frequently and so explicitly that Petr Stepanovich may be the opposite of what he seems.[3]

As it is usually read, *Demons* depends on Petr Stepanovich being, like his real-life model Nechaev, a genuine revolutionary. If he is an agent of the secret police, then the whole significance of the events changes. *Demons* then becomes a different novel, a sort of sideshadow of itself.

To be sure, the most likely interpretation is that Petr Stepanovich is not a police agent but cultivates the rumor that he is in order to increase his power with the authorities, just as he probably invents his connections with the Internationale to magnify his power with the revolutionaries. And yet Dostoevskii allows these rumors to go unrefuted, draws attention to them, and leaves mysteries easily explained by them to go unresolved. As particular incidents in the novel seem haunted by shadows of contradictory alternatives, so does the novel as a whole.

---

3 At the end of "A Meeting," the lame man observes that even though Petr Stepanovich has asked whether others would inform, he "hasn't answered the question either; he has only asked it. The remark produced a striking effect" (P, 419).

The Plot of *Crime and Punishment* (2016)*

Robert L. Belknap

The plot that emerges in *Crime and Punishment* reflects much of Dostoevskii's background in the history of literature as well as his own evolution as a novelist. Part I of the novel can be isolated for a moment and studied as a novella called *Crime* whose much longer sequel would be called *Punishment*. This book begins with a rich depiction of the hero's alienation from the educational, economic, social, and moral worlds; it ends with him committing a murder. The second and third chapters contain two long embedded narratives: Marmeladov's monologue in the tavern and the letter from Raskol'nikov's mother describing Dunia's trials as a governess for the Svidrigailovs and her engagement to Luzhin. These accounts contain much of the background of the novel, but in the construction of the causal system, Dostoevskii has given Raskol'nikov no part in the events Marmeladov relates and little influence on the events in his mother's letter except for his absence and his need for money, about which his mother's account is silent. Except when Raskol'nikov is involved, these two sets of events and characters continue to have little effect on one another, although Dostoevskii foregrounds Dunia's courtesy to Sonia Marmeladova and uses Svidrigailov's fortune to provide for the Marmeladov children. Luzhin persecutes Sonia partly for political, partly for prurient, purposes, but primarily to offend and discredit Raskol'nikov. But this lack of causal interconnection forces Dostoevskii to emphasize two other kinds

* From Robert L. Belknap, *Plots* (New York: Columbia University Press, 2016), 101–7. Copyright © 2016 Columbia University Press. Reprinted with permission of the publisher.

of relationship between the Marmeladov fabula and the Svidrigailov-Dunia fabula. One is spatial: Svidrigailov lives adjacent to Sonia, and Luzhin lives among the other Marmeladovs.

Far more important are the parallels between the Marmeladov and the Dunia plots. Dunia's plan to sacrifice her happiness to support her brother's career is one of his strongest motives for the murder, and in one of the most puzzling passages in the novel, Raskol'nikov tells Sonia that he had planned to confess the crime to her even before he had met her. To remind his readership of this organizing principle, parallelism, Dostoevskii begins the next chapter, the fourth in the novel, with a five-page interior monologue that is primarily Raskol'nikov's literary criticism of his mother's letter, partly of its diction, use of the word "apparently," etc., but also of its plot, particularly the motivations of Luzhin, Dunia, and his mother. This third monologue in the novel ends with a comparison of the other two, an eloquently bitter linking of Sonia and Dunia: "Oh, dear and unjust hearts! . . . Sonechka, Sonechka Marmeladova, the eternal Sonechka, as long as the World lasts! . . . Do you know, Dunechka, that Sonechka's destiny is in no way more vile than a destiny with Mr. Luzhin?" (pt. 1, chap. 4). Dostoevskii is using Raskol'nikov to instruct his readers in how to read the relationship among the incidents in *Crime and Punishment*. Causation is important, and certainly time and space are, but as Raskol'nikov forces us to see at this point, the Dunia plot is related to the Sonia plot centrally by analogy. Calculated marriages have been compared to prostitution by characters in Dickens, Hugo, George Sand, and other favorites of Dostoevskii's, but the nagging attention to the parallel constitutes one of the central elements of the Sonia plot. Of the five ways incidents can be related in a novel like *Crime and Punishment*, parallelism has probably received the most admiring attention. For Shakespeare, we have studied how parallelism leads to abstraction, or rather how it makes abstraction concrete by enabling readers to see and feel the common features for themselves. In *Crime and Punishment*, the multitude of parallelisms carries much of the ideological argument that drove Dostoevskii to write this particular novel at this time. Chapter 4 continues with Raskol'nikov meeting a disheveled teenager staggering down the boulevard. Raskol'nikov reflects that her destiny is also prostitution and death before she is twenty, and he calls the hovering lecher "Svidrigailov," creating a cluster of three helpless women sacrificed to the lust of moneyed selfishness. By calling our attention to this "situation rhyme," Dostoevskii makes us see the consistency in Raskol'nikov's responses to the three women. With Sonia's family, his first impulse is generous; he places money on the windowsill as he leaves, then in a fit of *esprit de l'escalier*, repents cynically on the staircase: "They have Sonia" (pt. 1, chap. 2). With Dunia, his first reaction to the Luzhin engagement is spirited. He wants to prevent the marriage, but then angrily asks himself what right he has to forbid it, which leads him to thoughts about murdering the pawnbroker. With the drunken teenager, he gives a policeman money to help her home, then calls to the puzzled policeman to forget the whole idea, telling himself that statistics prove that a certain percentage of women have to be ruined every year. By the end of the fourth chapter, therefore, Dostoevskii has trained his readers to expect parallel events producing parallel responses, and specifically to expect Raskol'nikov to alternate between impulsive generosity and cynical afterthought. By the fifth chapter, the character of this alternation becomes clearer because it is laid out in Raskol'nikov's interior monologue: "After *that*," he cried, springing from the bench, "but is *that* really going to happen? Can it be that it will happen?" (Pt. 1, chap.5).

Earlier, the italicized words had been part of an authorial strategy to inspire *curiosité*, the reader's drive to figure out what is going on, but by now it is clear to the reader that "*that*" refers to the murder; the italicized words are a part of Raskol'nikov's system for tabooing explicit enunciation of the principal matter on his mind. By the end of the fifth chapter, Dostoevskii has laid out the chief algorithm for creating or interpreting *Crime and Punishment*—the alternation in Raskol'nikov's mind between two fully established bodies of imagery and ideology:

dream (*son*) vs. daydream (*mechta*)
unconsciousness vs. consciousness
impulse vs. afterthought
generosity vs. economics
religion vs. mathematics
nature vs. science
humanity vs. statistics
intuition vs. reason
freedom vs. burden (*bremia*)
air vs. enslavement
revulsion vs. murder

After the murder, more elements enter the picture, notably the opposition between confession and suicide and between resurrection and death, but by the end of the fifth chapter, the plan for the novel is in place, and it is daringly simple.

The plot of *Crime and Punishment* has its main action within the mind of Raskol'nikov. He is on stage almost all the time, usually as a central actor, but sometimes, as in Chapters 2 and 3, as the audience for the account of another character. When he is not on stage, one of his two surrogates, Razumikhin or Svidrigailov, usually occupies our attention. In this sense, Dostoevskii has abandoned the plot of the letter novel, in which two or more narrators can see the same event. We know that Dostoevskii first planned to narrate the novel in the first person, through Raskol'nikov's eyes and voice. But first-person narration never worked as well for Dostoevskii in full-length novels as it did in his greatest shorter works, probably for technical reasons: the need for eavesdropping, letters, or outside reports to inform a narrator cut off from authorial omniscience. But the obsessive, sometimes oppressive involvement in Raskol'nikov's life survived the shift to third-person narration. Critics often call Raskol'nikov unpredictable and the novel tormentingly disorienting, just as they call Moscow's Cathedral of the Blessed Basil wild and violent. But the power of that cathedral rests in part on the rigid formality of its floor plan, and the power of *Crime and Punishment* rests in part on the clarity of the central split, or *raskol,* in Raskol'nikov's mind and its enactment in alternating states of mind, often separated by the word *vdrug,* "suddenly!"

Once he has trained us to expect this algorithm, Dostoevskii sets to work to implicate us in the crime. He ends Chapter 4 by setting up a parallel for Raskol'nikov, embedding a brief portrait of Razumikhin, another ex-student, but one who is companionable, practical, cheerful, and simple-hearted, as opposed to Raskol'nikov, who is a loner, unable or unwilling to help himself, grim, haughty, and excessively intellectual. In exactly the same position, they are heading in opposite directions. Next, Dostoevskii introduces the first great scene in the novel, again an embedded one—a dream. In this dream, we see another moment in Raskol'nikov's background, his childhood when his father was alive, seeing it again with Raskol'nikov as spectator at two levels, adult spectator to the dream and child spectator to the beating of the horse within the dream. This double layering involves us with Raskol'nikov, whose impulses at both ages coincide with our own, and the vividness of the dream—its play on personal power, personal possession of a living female creature, savage glee in that possession and in the destructive use of it—all link this passage with the passages about Luzhin, Svidrigailov, and the lecher passing the ruined teen-ager on the boulevard. Our experience of Raskol'nikov's experience retains its obsessive integrity.

The aftermath of this dream near the end of Chapter 5 repeats the paired bodies of imagery and ideology that we have already assimilated but may not have noticed as organized polar oppositions until now:

> He wants to catch his breath, cry out, and wakes up . . . all in a sweat, his hair drenched with sweat, gasping, and sat up in horror. "Thank God, it's just a dream," he said [. . .] taking a deep breath [. . .] "Isn't this a fever starting up in me, such a hideous dream." [. . .]
>
> "Oh, God, [. . .] Can it be, can it really be that I will take an axe and start beating her head, and smash her skull—will slip on sticky, warm blood, smash a lock, steal and tremble, hide, all bloodied—with an axe— Lord, can it be? [. . .] "No, I won't endure it, I won't. Suppose, suppose there's not even any doubt at all in all these calculations, suppose that all that's been decided this month were clear as day, fair as arithmetic. Lord! I still would not decide to do it." [. . .] He suddenly breathed more easily. He felt that he already had cast off this fearsome burden that had been crushing him so long, and his heart suddenly grew light and was at peace. "Lord, show me my way, and I renounce this damned—daydream of mine."
>
> Crossing the bridge, he gazed quietly and peaceably at the Neva, at the brilliant setting of a bright red sun [. . .] It was as if a boil on his heart that had been swelling all month had suddenly burst. Freedom! Freedom! He was free now from these hexes, these enchantments, these obsessions. (pt. I, chap. 5)

This passage is so powerful that most readers probably form a new expectation at this point to replace the alternation they have been trained to expect. The fate of that new expectation is the subject of a later chapter, but here we will turn to the end of part I, after Raskol'nikov has done exactly what he envisioned with such revulsion in the passage just quoted. Raskol'nikov— whose actions, passions, and experiences we have shared without interruption (waking, sleeping, listening, and committing murder)—has unhooked the door and listened at the stairhead, waiting patiently to escape. He hears voices in the distance, then silence, then the noisy painters quitting work, and then someone's footsteps approaching, heavily, evenly, unhurriedly. He freezes, as in a nightmare when one dreams pursuers are catching up, closing in, want- ing to kill, and it's as if one has taken root there and can't move one's hands. He finally slips back to the pawnbroker's room, rehooks the door, and hides, not breathing. As Raskol'nikov stands in the room with the two bleeding corpses, holding his breath as he listens at the door, inches from his potential discoverers, who may leave or summon the police, we readers hold our breath, exert our will upon him not to give up and confess, and then suddenly realize that we are accessories after the fact, trying to help this merciless, calculating hatchet-murderer to escape.

This complicity in the crime alternates with the reader's horror and revulsion at it, just as Raskol'nikov alternates between a drive towards murder and escape and a drive toward freedom from the murderous impulse and—after the murder—towards confession. Dostoevskii's siuzhet manipulates his readers into the fabula of the novel by almost never letting them outside the mind of Raskol'nikov. We have mentioned that this intensity of narrative concentration on a single figure implicates the readers in his predicament much as readers willed the escape of picaresque scamps in earlier novels. *Crime and Punishment* has a beginning, a middle, and an end, but it retains the algorithmic integrity of Gogol' and his masters. In *Crime and Punishment*, the shaping rule is not accretive and perverse as in *Dead Souls*, but is rather the terrifying alternation between the crime and the punishment, the rational calculation that the destruction of a bloodsucking insect was an action worthy of a great man and the direct, emotional realization that this was the murder of a helpless fellow human being. Dostoevskii uses his narrative tools to draw the reader inside this vacillation.

By constructing a siuzhet that makes us live with his protagonist so intimately for ninety pages, Dostoevskii has implicated us in a crime that is vicious, greedy, cold, and despicable. This is the manipulative novel at its strongest. It tells us what is happening, shows us what is happening, but more than that, it makes us experience what is happening. From the end of part I, the reader, like Raskol'nikov, will alternate between a strong drive towards his escape and a drive toward his confession. The siuzhet programs the reader's experience to track the hero's experience in the fabula.

CHAPTER 6

From Journalism to Fiction

An avid reader of news, Dostoevskii frequently drew inspiration from the press for his fiction. He was also a journalist himself, publishing feuilletons, editorials, and opinion pieces over the course of his career. In 1847 he wrote four feuilletons—short sketches which appeared in *Petersburg News*. Returning from Siberia, in the 1860s, he began writing fiction but also founded two journals: first *Time*, which was suppressed after a few years, then *Epoch*, which went bankrupt. Finally, between 1873 and 1881 Dostoevskii published *A Writer's Diary*, a journal that built on his success as a novelist and gave him an outlet to discuss the events of the day. In the *Diary* Dostoevskii challenged the distinction between journalism and imaginative literature, as well as that between author and reader in order to engage more deeply with his audience. The result is an unparalleled creation that blends journalism and literary fiction into a new artistic form. This chapter is organized to give readers a sense of different ways Dostoevskii's fiction and journalism are linked, and how they can be read together for more insight into both.

The chapter begins with the feuilletons; an excerpt from one of Dostoevskii's own feuilletons appears, in which the author meditates on what "news" is, while the two subsequent pieces from Joseph Frank's biography give insight into how Dostoevskii's Petersburg emerged in these journalistic sketches and his fiction. The second piece includes the "Vision on the Neva" sequence from "A Weak Heart" (1848), which builds on the personal experience aspect of the feuilleton to create a dramatic climax in the story. These early pieces describing urban experience show the influence of Gogol', and can be compared to Dostoevskii's works set in a dreamy St. Petersburg like "White Nights" and *The Double*. In them, however, we also see the Petersburg of Raskol'nikov, who spends so much time walking the streets and interacting with the city's residents. Dostoevskii republished the "Vision on the Neva" in the first issue of *Time* in 1861, and there called it an autobiographical episode, part of a series of "Petersburg Dreams and Verse."

The years in Siberia had put Dostoevskii in direct and regular contact with murderers, thieves, and other criminals, and prompted his fascination with the criminal mind. His return to European Russia coincided with the advent of Alexander II's Great Reforms, among them the introduction of jury trials in 1864. Dostoevskii avidly followed the trials reported in the press. Reproduced here are documents related to Dostoevskii's engagement with the trial of Ol'ga Umetskaia in the autumn of 1867 and Dostoevskii's novel *The Idiot* (1869). In the working notebooks for *The Idiot*, Umetskaia appears and readers can see how Dostoevskii tested different scenarios for the character. In the finished novel, parts of Umetskaia's story remain in the backstory of tempestuous femme fatale Nastas'ia Filippovna. Katherine Bowers's essay gives insight into how this process—from trial to journalism to notebooks to fiction—occurred.

As we move into the 1870s, we include two excerpts from *A Writer's Diary*: "Two Suicides" and "The Meek One," published in October and November 1876, respectively. "Two Suicides" is a journalistic piece, while "The Meek One" is a work of fiction. Both, however, deal with the same subject, and it is interesting to see how Dostoevskii treats the material differently in the two genres. Through these pieces we get a sense of Dostoevskii's voice as a journalist, and how it differs from his voice as an author of fiction. Kate Holland's analysis of the section provides context and several ways of reading the two passages together. Just as Dostoevskii used his novels as "laboratories" for his ideas, so the *Writer's Diary* was an experimental place where fiction and nonfiction comingled productively. Igor' Volgin considers the *Diary*'s place in world literature, and within Dostoevskii's oeuvre, admiring its artistry while critically addressing its contradictions.

The section concludes with an uncut issue of *A Writer's Diary*, from April 1877. The issue includes the story "Dream of a Ridiculous Man," often published and read as a standalone, as well as a wide range of journalistic pieces. Opinion pieces about Russia entering into war with the Ottoman Empire comprise the first chapter of the issue. Dostoevskii's support of war and, specifically, killing in "Does Shed Blood Save Us?" may surprise readers more familiar with the messages of compassion and universal brotherhood that appear in *Brothers Karamazov* (1880) and other works. As we will see in other chapters of the present volume—"Dostoevskii's Others" and "Russia"—Dostoevskii's beliefs readily contradicted each other. Chapter 2 of the issue includes just three pieces: "Dream of a Ridiculous Man," an account of a woman who defenestrated her stepchild, and a note to readers. "Dream of a Ridiculous Man," too, is an exercise in contradictions, as Gary Saul Morson describes in "Meta-utopia" (included in Chapter 7 of the present volume). The story's final scene gives rise to a utopian hope, but this is then juxtaposed with a report of child cruelty, reminiscent of the cases that appear in Ivan's discussion with Alesha in *Brothers Karamazov*.

Further Reading

Catteau, Jacques. *Dostoevsky and the Process of Literary Creation*. Cambridge: Cambridge University Press, 1989, particularly Part 2.

Dianina, Katia."The Feuilleton: An Everyday Guide to Public Culture in the Age of the Great Reforms." *Slavic and East European Journal* 47, no. 2 (2003): 186–208.

Fusso, Susanne. *Editing Turgenev, Dostoevsky, and Tolstoy: Mikhail Katkov and the Great Russian Novel*. DeKalb: Northern Illinois University Press, 2017.

Holland, Kate. "The Fictional Filter: "Krotkaia" and *The Diary of a Writer*." *Dostoevsky Studies* n.s. 4 (2000): 95–116.

Martinsen, Deborah, ed. *Literary Journals in Imperial Russia*. Cambridge: Cambridge University Press, 1997.

Moser, Charles. "Dostoevsky and the Aesthetics of Journalism." *Dostoevsky Studies* vol. 3 (1982): 28–41.

Vassena, Raffaella. *Reawakening National Identity: Dostoevsky's "Diary of a Writer" and Its Impact on Russian Society*. Bern: Peter Lang, 2007.

Feuilleton, April 22, 1847*

Fedor Dostoevskii

Only a short while ago I could not imagine a Petersburg citizen except in a dressing gown and nightcap sitting in a shut-up room with his doctor's strict orders to take something in a tablespoon every two hours. I don't expect that all of them were ill. Some were forbidden to be ill by their duties. Others were saved by their strong constitutions. But at last the sun is shining and this is undoubtedly the greatest piece of news everyone has been waiting for. The convalescent is at a loss what to do: he takes off his nightcap hesitatingly, gets dressed thoughtfully and at last makes up his mind to go out for a walk, armed to the teeth, of course, that is to say, in a sweater, a fur coat and galoshes. He is pleasantly surprised by the warmth of the air, the kind of festive look of the crowds and the deafening roar of the carriages on a roadway no longer covered with snow and slush. On Nevskii Avenue, at last, the convalescent swallows a mouthful of new dust. His heart begins to throb and something in the nature of a smile twists his lips, till then skeptically and questioningly closed. The first Petersburg dust after the deluge of slush and something very moist in the air is, of course, in no way inferior to the delight of the ancient smoke of native hearths, and the convalescent, whose look of skepticism has vanished from his face, makes up his mind to enjoy the spring at long last. Generally speaking, there is something good-natured and ingenious about the Petersburg citizen who makes up his mind to enjoy the spring at long last. On meeting a friend, he even forgets the usual question, "What's the news?" and changes it to a more interesting one: "How do you like this splendid weather?" And, as is well known, after the weather, especially if it is filthy, the most offensive question

* From *Dostoevsky's Occasional Writing*, ed. and trans. David Magarshack (New York: Random House, 1963), 10–11. Printed with permission from the Magarshack family.

to ask anyone in Petersburg is, "What's the news?" I have often observed that when two Petersburg friends meet in the street and, after greeting each other, ask with one accord, "What's the news?" there is a piercing feeling of desolation in the sound of their voices, whatever the intonation they started their conversation with. Indeed, this Petersburg question conceals a feeling of utter hopelessness. What is so unforgivable, however, is that very often the man asking this question, a Petersburger born and bred, is completely indifferent to the answer, for he knows that it is merely an empty phrase to which he will get no reply, that there is no news, that he has put this question at least a thousand times [...]

The Petersburg Feuilletons (1979)*

Joseph Frank

Dostoevskii's chronic indebtedness not only forced him to write more rapidly than he would have liked, and to hurry the completion of work that should have matured; it also impelled him to keep a sharp eye on the literary marketplace, and to snap up any assignments that could bring a little extra cash [. . .] Earlier, in the spring of [1847], he had picked up a more important assignment from the *St. Petersburg Gazette*. The writer who regularly supplied the feuilletons for this newspaper died unexpectedly; and the editor hastily filled the gap by appealing to some of the young St. Petersburg literati to furnish him with copy. Aleksei Pleshcheev wrote one for the issue of April 13, and it was perhaps through him that Dostoevskii learned of this journalistic opportunity. The next four feuilletons, signed F. D., were written by Dostoevskii himself [. . .]

All the up-and-coming young talents of the Natural School—Grigorovich, Panaev, Turgenev, Goncharov, Sollogub, Pleshcheev—also wrote feuilletons, and Dostoevskii was simply joining a general literary trend [. . .] Balzac's *Illusions perdues*, published in 1843, had glorified the feuilleton as a form created to capture all the glitter, excitement, and variety of Parisian social-cultural life. Eagerly on the alert for the latest literary novelties, the younger Russian writers immediately adopted it as a vehicle for their own self-expression.

The invention of the feuilleton in France had been stimulated by a new, popular mass-circulation press which served as a medium of publicity and

---

* From Joseph Frank, *Dostoevsky: The Seeds of Revolt, 1821–1849* (Princeton, NJ: Princeton University Press, 1979), 133–35. The text has been excerpted. Republished with permission of Princeton University Press, from *Dostoevsky: The Seeds of Revolt, 1821–1849*, Joseph Frank, © 1979.

could influence the success or failure of books, plays, operas, and public spectacles of all kinds. Originally, the feuilleton had been simply a column of information about all such cultural novelties; but it quickly developed into the form of the modern book or theater review. Lucien de Rubempré's famous column was a scintillating account of a new play in which a young actress, his future mistress, was making her first important appearance. The feuilleton, however, in branching out to describe urban types and social life, also gave birth to the physiological sketch [. . .]

It is difficult to distinguish the feuilleton from the physiological sketch in any clear-cut fashion. One can say that the former is less marked by the ambition to portray the life of a particular social environment, and allows more freedom for the writer to roam wherever his fancy pleases and to display his personality [. . .] The writer of feuilletons ordinarily used this privilege to indulge in lyrical effusions and pseudo-personal "confessions"; and these created an atmosphere of intimacy between writer and reader that became a stylistic convention. Indeed, as we learn from Belinskii, the persona of the feuilletonist was always understood to be highly conventional and stylized. The writer of a feuilleton, he says, is "a chatterer, apparently good-natured and sincere, but in truth often malicious and evil-tongued, someone who knows everything, sees everything, keeps quiet about a good deal but definitely manages to express everything, stings with epigrams and insinuations, and amuses with a lively and clever word as well as a childish joke."[1]

These words fit the personality assumed by the young Dostoevskii to the life. At first sight, his feuilletons may seem little more than unpretentious familiar essays, leaping from topic to topic solely according to the whimsical moods of the narrator. Depictions of Petersburg life and landscape, sketches of various social types, reflections and reminiscences, the stereotyped purveyance of the latest cultural tidings—all the standard ingredients are there, thrown together haphazardly to distract the casual reader. But the moment one reads a little less casually, it is evident that the feuilletons mean much more than they appear to say. With all their reticences and sly evasions, they do "definitely manage to express everything" (or at least a good deal) of what was preoccupying Dostoevskii—and many others like him—in the spring of 1847.

---

1 Cited in V. S. Nechaeva, *V. G. Belinskii*, 4 vols. (Leningrad: Nauka, 1949–1967), 4:298.

Dostoevskii's "Vision on the Neva" (1979)*

Joseph Frank

O ne other document can also help to clarify the process of Dostoevskii's artistic maturation. This is a feuilleton that he wrote in 1861 when, turning back to look at his early work in the 1840s, he felt called upon to defend it. With some slight changes, the feuilleton reproduces the famous "vision of the Neva" that Dostoevskii first used in his short story *A Weak Heart* (1848) [...]

In general, the feuilleton provides a sketch of Dostoevskii's literary evolution from the days of his early Romanticism up to his discovery of the theme of his first novel. Writing in the first person, he places himself on the same social level and in the same surroundings as the characters of his book. This transposition is of course fictitious, but the account given of his cultural and literary formation is quite accurate. Educated, like his entire generation, on the historical novel and Romantic tragedy, he tells us that his imagination as a youth had been filled with the fantasies inspired by such reading. "[...] What did I not live through with all my heart and soul in my impassioned and golden dreams—exactly as if from opium?"[1]

This state of mind continued to persist even when (here is where the fiction begins) the narrator becomes a lowly government clerk in St. Petersburg and, like all the others, lodges in a poverty-stricken garret.

---

* From Joseph Frank, *Dostoevsky: The Seeds of Revolt, 1821–1849* (Princeton, NJ: Princeton University Press, 1979), 133–35. The text has been excerpted. Republished with permission of Princeton University Press, from *Dostoevsky: The Seeds of Revolt, 1821–1849*, Joseph Frank, © 1979.

1 F. M. Dostoevskii, *Polnoe sobranie khudozhestvennykh proizvedenii*, ed. B. Tomashevskii and K. Khalabaev, 13 vols. (Leningrad: Gos. izd-vo, 1926–1930), vol. 13, 157. EDS: Hereafter PSKhP vol.: page.

His neighbor, another poor clerk, has a family of five daughters; and a shy flirtation develops with the eldest of the brood. They read Scott and Schiller together, and, though her name is Nadia, he calls her Amalia (after the heroine of *The Robbers*). But he pays no attention to her virginal blushes and her confusion in his presence because "I preferred to read *Kabale und Liebe* or the stories of Hoffmann" (PSKhP 13:158). One day she suddenly announces that she is going to marry still another clerk—a much older man—who has just obtained a new post; and she kisses the narrator on the brow, at parting, with a strange and twisted smile.

It is probably after this event (the time-sequence is not too clear) that the narrator experiences his "vision." This is how he describes it:

> I remember once on a wintry January evening I was hurrying home from the Vyborg side. I was still very young then. When I reached the Neva, I stopped for a minute and threw a piercing glance along the river into the smoky, frostily dim distance, which had suddenly turned crimson with the last purple of a sunset that was dying out on the hazy horizon. Night lay over the city, and the whole immense plain of the Neva, swollen with frozen snow, under the last gleam of the sun, was strewn with infinite myriads of sparks of spindly hoar-frost. There was a twenty-degree frost. . . . Frozen steam poured from tired horses, from running people. The taut air quivered at the slightest sound, and columns of smoke like giants rose from all the roofs on both embankments and rushed upward through the cold sky, twining and untwining on the way, so that it seemed new buildings were rising above the old ones, a new city was forming in the air. . . . It seemed, finally, that this whole world with all its inhabitants, strong and weak, with all their domiciles, the shelters of the poor or gilded mansions, resembled at this twilight hour a fantastic, magic vision, a dream which would in its turn vanish immediately and rise up as steam toward the dark-blue sky. Some strange thought suddenly stirred in me. I shuddered, and my heart was as if flooded with a hot rush of blood that boiled up suddenly from the surge of a powerful but hitherto unknown sensation. I seemed to have understood something in that minute which had till then only been stirring in me, but was still uninterpreted; it was as if my eyes had been opened to something new, to a completely new world, unfamiliar to me and known only by certain obscure rumors, by certain mysterious signs. I suppose that my existence began from just that minute . . . (ibid.).

No further attempt is made to explain the meaning of this "vision"; but it effects a radical transformation in the whole relation of the narrator to reality. Earlier, he had either paid no attention to his surroundings, or had immediately reshaped them into the consecrated images of his Romantic fantasy-world [. . .] Now the narrator suddenly begins to look around, and to see "some strange figures, entirely prosaic, not at all Don Carloses or Posas, just titular councilors, and yet, at the same time, fantastic titular councilors" (ibid.). Behind all these suddenly strange and fascinating figures, there was someone "who made faces before me, concealed behind all that fantastic crowd, and pulled some kind of strings or springs and all these puppets moved and laughed and everybody laughed!" (ibid.). But then the narrator catches a glimpse of another story that was no laughing matter at all—"some titular heart, honorable and pure, moral and devoted to the authorities, and together with him some young girl, humiliated and sorrowing, and all their story tore deeply at my heart" (PSKhP 13:158–59). This story, of course, is the one that Dostoevskii tells in *Poor Folk*.

There has been a great deal of rather overheated speculation about this feuilleton, and an unfortunate tendency to take it as literal autobiography. "Up until this moment," writes Konstantin Mochul'skii, "Dostoevskii had lived in a world of romantic dreams [. . .] He was blind to reality, and everything that was mysterious, fantastic, and out-of-theordinary would lure him into its captivating sphere," etc.[2] Even a cursory glance at Dostoevskii's letters in the early 1840s, however, is enough to show that he was very far from having been "blind to reality" (whatever that means) before his "vision."

---

2 Konstantin Mochulsky, *Dostoevsky*, trans. Michael Minihan (Princeton NJ: Princeton University Press, 1967), 27.

Excerpts from the Notebooks for *The Idiot* (1867)*

Fedor Dostoevskii

THE FIRST PLAN

The main family also includes an adopted child, the stepdaughter of the mother's sister—the wrathful Mignon, a Cleopatra. [Ol'ga Umetskaia.] And finally there is the *Idiot*. He was dubbed an idiot by his mother, who hates him. He supports the whole family, but in their opinion he does nothing for them. He is an epileptic and has nervous seizures. He has never finished his university studies. He lives with the family. He is in love with the fiancé's cousin— secretly. She detests him and treats him worse than an idiot or a footman. (*On the street as he is accompanying her, he kisses her.*) Seeing that he is in love with her, she teases him, for lack of anything better to do, and sets him beside himself. She is twenty-four. *After one of these occasions* he rapes Mignon. *He sets fire to the house.* On her command he burns his finger. *The Idiot's* passions are violent, he has a burning need of love, a boundless pride, and out of pride he means to dominate himself, conquer himself. He takes delight in humiliation. Those who do not know him make fun of him; those who do know him begin to fear him [. . .]

Mignon is terribly downtrodden and terribly timid, but inwardly she is dreadfully spiteful, insolent, and vindictive; she hates the handsome youth's fiancée. Mignon's history is altogether like that of Ol'ga Umetskaia [. . .]

---

* Extracts from Fyodor Dostoyevsky, *The Notebooks for* The Idiot, trans. Katharine Strelsky, ed. Edward Wasiolek (Chicago: University of Chicago Press, 1967), 31–34, 42, 97, 103. Copyright © by the University of Chicago. All rights reserved. Published 1967.

His attention shifted to Mignon, and they told him her biography, *in her presence*, saying that she was the daughter of a landowner, that no one had troubled to see that she was fed, that she had tried to hang herself and had been cut down. The beauty (the heroine) then arrived. The uncle turned his attention to the Idiot, for they were already hastening to explain about him. He listened absently. (His handwriting. The clerk had already told him <about the Idiot>.) "I'll have to deal with him; I have a whip. How can he be an idiot? No one knows this for a fact." The handsome youth's fiancée. Everyone jeered at the Idiot. He went away.

Mignon is in love with the handsome youth and hates his fiancée. And she hates the heroine, because the latter hovers round the handsome youth; but since she is extravagantly beautiful, Mignon kisses her hands and feet when left alone with her (and because of that intensifies her hatred). She even kisses her feet for the special purpose of hating her the more. "Therefore I will hate her all the more fiercely." Mignon is envious and proud. One could chop her into mincemeat, but she would not ask forgiveness; yet she trembles like a coward (out of nerves). She could hang herself, but if no one gave her a crust she would never beg. Her desires are naïve, to revenge herself on everyone, to swim in gold. She makes common cause with the Idiot. Her friendship for him is passionate to the point of enslavement, though they are on terms of equality. Mignon worships him. Once when the handsome youth was already engaged, *he made an attempt* on her while in his cups, and Mignon nearly killed him in a fury of pride, taking it as an insult, despite the fact that she was in love with him; but when the Idiot violated her, she gave in to him (without love) and never even referred to it again. Once done, neither gave it another thought.

Now and then the Idiot and she would meet and talk, she with her naïve daydreams, he gloomy and incommunicative. Mignon tells him all her dreams. She daydreams incessantly [. . .]

The main point. *Nota bene.*

From the outset he frightened her *to such a terrible degree* that she would suddenly be seized with an urge to run away from him and hide; but also she would have a sudden urge to play with fire or leap off a tower: the voluptuousness in a sinking of the heart. She would exasperate him to frenzy, then dart out of reach, as it were, keeping her distance, gazing avidly at him yet dreading to approach him. *The lines of her character are emerging.* She is extraordinarily proud, she rides roughshod over all the conventions, and *therefore* the worst extravagances of the Idiot neither shock nor outrage her (once he almost killed her, another time he broke her hands). But once such moments are over, she flees in aversion. These moments arise partly out of her terribly abnormal and incongruous position in the family. In general, she is unquestionably of an original, frivolous, capricious, *provocative* and poetic nature, superior to her environment. She understands, for example, that one can set the house on fire.

THE FIFTH PLAN

On leaving for Switzerland and on returning from there, the Idiot ordered the Umetskiis under threat of his wrecking everything (N.B. "I won't support her any longer or give you any subsidy") not to dare inform the uncle but to keep matters hushed up. On his return they moved [. . .] His wife and Umetskaia went to live with an old lady related to them.

Umetskaia is a *iurodivaia*,[1] an avenging angel. The wife was finding out
...... [. . .]

He had always *hated* her, but at times he gave up and shut himself away, alone. He raped Umetskaia. It appeared that Umetskaia had always loved him and had been sacrificing herself completely *to him and his wife.*

His brutal defilement of her was both an overwhelming happiness to her and death itself.

She became obsessed with the idea of universal brotherhood [. . .]

Umetskaia reads the *New Testament.* In her demented state, she sermonizes. She disconcerts the uncle. (*Umetskaia's naïveté is boundless.—This is the chief trait in her character.*) About heads being cut off, about fingernails being torn out, in the beginning she had set a fire—.

---

1 EDS: A holy fool.

Nastas'ia Filippovna's History from *The Idiot* (1869)*

Fedor Dostoevskii

T his complicated and troublesome "factor" had, as Totskii himself expressed it, come on to the scene a long time—some eighteen years— before.

Afanasii Ivanovich had one of his finest estates in a central province of Russia. His nearest neighbor was the owner of a small and poverty-stricken property, and was a man remarkable for his continual and almost incredible ill luck. He was a retired officer of good family—better, in fact, than Totskii's own—by name Filipp Aleksandrovich Barashkov. Burdened with debts and mortgages, he managed after working fearfully hard, almost like a peasant, to get his land into a more or less satisfactory condition. At the smallest success he was extraordinarily elated. Radiant with hope, he went for a few days to the little district town to see and, if possible, come to an agreement with one of his chief creditors. He had been two days in the town when the elder of his little village rode in with his beard burnt off and his cheek scarred, and informed him that the place had been burnt down the day before, just at midday, and "that his lady had graciously been burnt, but his children were unhurt." This surprise was too much even for Barashkov, accustomed as he was to the buffetings of fortune. He went out of his mind and died in delirium a month later. The ruined property with its beggared peasants was sold to pay his debts. Afanasii Ivanovich Totskii

---

*   From *The Idiot*, trans. Constance Garnett (New York: Macmillan, 1913), 36–39.

in the generosity of his heart undertook to bring up and educate Barashkov's children, two little girls of six and seven. They were brought up with the children of Totskii's steward, a retired government clerk with a large family, and, moreover, a German. The younger child died of whooping cough, and little Nastas'ia was left alone. Totskii lived abroad and soon completely forgot her existence. Five years later it occurred to him on his way elsewhere to look in on his estate, and he noticed in the family of his German steward a charming child, a girl about twelve, playful, sweet, clever and promising to become extremely beautiful. On that subject Afanasii Ivanovich was an unerring connoisseur. He only spent a few days on his estate, but he made arrangements for a great change in the girl's education. A respectable and cultivated elderly Swiss governess, experienced in the higher education of girls and competent to teach various subjects besides French, was engaged for her. She was installed in Totskii's country house, and little Nastas'ia began to receive an education on the broadest lines. Just four years later this education was over; the governess left, and a lady who lived near another estate of Totskii's in another remote province came, by his instructions, and took Nastas'ia away. On this estate there was also a small recently built wooden house. It was very elegantly furnished, and the place was appropriately called "The Pleasaunce." The lady brought Nastas'ia straight to this little house, and as she was a childless widow, living only three-quarters of a mile away, she installed herself in the house with her. An old housekeeper and an experienced young maid were there to wait on Nastas'ia. In the house she found musical instruments, a choice library for a young girl, pictures, engravings, pencils, paints and brushes, a thoroughbred lap-dog, and within a fortnight Afanasii Ivanovich himself made his appearance . . . Since then he had been particularly fond of that remote property in the steppes and had spent two or three months there every summer. So passed a fairly long time—four years, calmly and happily in tasteful and elegant surroundings.

It happened once at the beginning of winter, four months after one of Totskii's summer visits, which had on that occasion lasted only a fortnight, a rumor was circulated, or rather reached Nastas'ia Filippovna, that Afanasii Ivanovich was going to be married in Petersburg to a beautiful heiress of good family—that he was, in fact, making a wealthy and brilliant match. The rumor turned out to be not quite correct in some details. The supposed marriage was only a project, still very vague; but it was a turning point in Nastas'ia Filippovna's life. She displayed great determination and quite unexpected strength of will. Without wasting time on reflection, she left her little house in the country and suddenly made her appearance in Petersburg, entirely alone, going straight to

Totskii. He was amazed, and, as soon as he began to speak to her, he found almost from the first word that he had completely to abandon the language, the intonations, the logic, the subjects of the agreeable and refined conversations that had been so successful hitherto—everything, everything! He saw sitting before him an entirely different woman, not in the least like the girl he had left only that July.

This new woman turned out, in the first place, to know and understand a great deal—so much that one could not but marvel where she had got such knowledge and how she could have arrived at such definite ideas. (Surely not from her young girl's library!) What was more, she understood many things in their legal aspect and had a positive knowledge, if not of the world, at least of how some things are done in the world; moreover, she had not the same character as before. There was nothing of the timidity, the schoolgirlish uncertainty, sometimes fascinating in its original simplicity and playfulness, sometimes melancholy and dreamy, astonished, mistrustful, tearful and uneasy.

Yes, it was a new and surprising creature who laughed in his face and stung him with venomous sarcasm, openly declaring that she had never had any feeling in her heart for him except contempt—contempt and loathing which had come upon her immediately after her first surprise. This new woman announced that it was a matter of absolute indifference to her if he married at once any one he chose, but she had come to prevent his making that marriage, and would not allow it from spite, simply because she chose not to, and that therefore so it must be— "if only that I may have a good laugh at you, for I too want to laugh now."

Ol'ga Umetskaia and
The Idiot (2017)*

Katherine Bowers

In September 1867 Dostoevskii began to plan the novel that would eventually become *The Idiot* (1869). Before the final version was published he drafted a number of different plans in three different notebooks as he worked on finding the precise configuration of characters, setting, and plot that would enable him to convey the idea he wanted to articulate.[1] Dostoevskii did not finalize his outline for *The Idiot* until he had begun the final version of the novel, and even after Part I was published (serially), he continued to adjust his overall plan.

The news was a significant influence on him while he was working on the novel. As Jacques Catteau notes, "Dostoevskii could not live without the Press, especially abroad, where he needed to keep in touch with his native country [. . .] he found true 'happiness' in reading the Russian Press from cover to cover."[2] Dostoevskii often referred to newspaper stories in his correspondence, and his wife, Anna Grigor'evna, regularly mentions the couple's discussion of the daily news in her diaries. Recent news items also informed the writer's working notebooks, among them, the story of Ol'ga Umetskaia.

In late September 1867 fifteen-year old Umetskaia was on trial for arson in the town of Kashira, near Moscow; in response to her parents' abuse (beatings and starvation), she had set fire to the family estate four times, and at least twice attempted suicide. The press reported on the sensationalistic details that emerged in the course of the trial, painting a picture of monstrous parents

---

* This piece was written for the present volume.

1 For a discussion of this process in *The Idiot*, see Robin Feuer Miller, *Dostoevsky and* The Idiot: *Author, Narrator, Reader* (Cambridge, MA: Harvard University Press, 1981), 46–89.

2 Jacques Catteau, *Dostoyevsky and the Process of Literary Creation*, trans. Audrey Littlewood (Cambridge: Cambridge University Press, 1989), 180.

who tormented and abused their children. Dostoevskii was able to follow the trial from Geneva in the Russian newspapers: the issues of *Moscow* (Moskva), dated 23 and 24 September (nos. 136 and 137), and *The Voice* (Golos), dated 26, 27, and 28 September (nos. 266–68).[3]

Umetskaia did not deny the arson charge, but was acquitted by the jury, who sympathized with her story and judged her crime to be a result of the abuse she had suffered. This outcome does not seem extraordinary today, but in 1867 jury trials were a relatively recent development in Russia; they had been introduced in the Judicial Reform of 1864, only three years earlier. Widely reported in the press, trials were a source of fascination for the late nineteenth-century Russian public, and critique of them came to inform many of Dostoevskii's later works, from the prose experiments in *A Writer's Diary* to the famous courtroom scenes in *The Brothers Karamazov*.[4] In the case of *The Idiot*, the integration of the Umetskii trial details into the text provides insight into Dostoevskii's writing process.

Before he read Ol'ga Umetskaia's story, Dostoevskii had begun to plan a novel centered on the Russian family. One of the character types he had included in the first plan is "Mignon," taken from Goethe's *Wilhelm Meister's Apprenticeship* (1795–96). Goethe's Mignon is a mysterious heroine, kidnapped as a child, forced to work for a nefarious circus master, rescued from an abusive environment, and characterized by a romantic longing for freedom and love. While Dostoevskii's Mignon also longs for love and freedom, she resents her situation and hates her abusive foster family. At some point, the writer connected Mignon and Ol'ga Umetskaia. In the margins of the first plan, Dostoevskii jotted "Ol'ga Umetskaia" next to the sentence, "The main family also includes an adopted child, the stepdaughter of the mother's sister—the wrathful Mignon, a Cleopatra."[5] Later he wrote directly into the plan:

> Mignon is terribly downtrodden and terribly timid, but inwardly she is dreadfully spiteful, insolent, and vindictive; she hates the handsome youth's fiancée. Mignon's history is altogether like that of Ol'ga Umetskaia.[6]

---

3 These are the Russian old-style calendar dates of the issues; Dostoevskii would have read them in early to mid October. See Catteau, 180. By the 1860s Moscow and St. Petersburg newspapers reached Western Europe in only a few days thanks to the rail network.

4 On true crime and the press during this period, see Louise McReynolds, *Murder Most Russian: True Crime and Punishment in Late Imperial Russia* (Ithaca, NY: Cornell University Press, 2013). On Dostoevskii's use of the jury trial in his fiction, see Gary Rosenshield, *Western Law, Russian Justice: Dostoevsky, the Jury Trial, and the Law* (Madison: University of Wisconsin Press, 2005).

5 Fyodor Dostoyevsky, *The Notebooks for* The Idiot, trans. Katharine Strelsky, ed. Edward Wasiolek (Chicago: University of Chicago Press, 1967), 31.

6 *The Notebooks for* The Idiot, 32.

As the notebooks progress, Dostoevskii begins to refer to the character simply as "Umetskaia." Troubled by the Umetskii case, Dostoevskii incorporated its details into his working model for the novel, embellishing or changing them as he built his narrative. In various plans, Umetskaia becomes a rape victim, a victim of incest, or both. The Idiot character is her abuser in some, but her accomplice in others. In every case, however, the Umetskaia character loves the Idiot character and shows him compassion, even for his cruellest acts. She struggles with indecision; she is vengeful, but seeks redemption. Her mental anguish becomes madness in some versions. In several she becomes a Holy Fool. In others she marries.

While Dostoevskii describes the Idiot character—the future Myshkin—in the notebooks as an "enigma" or a "Sphinx," the Umetskaia character is the real mystery. She does not appear in the novel, but she appears in every plan. The notebooks do not provide an account of the character's backstory, motivations for committing violence, or eventual fate, although some aspects linked to Umetskaia appear in *The Idiot*. This correspondence is most readily visible in Nastas'ia Filippovna's gothic-inspired history, in which she is violently orphaned by a fire, isolated through misfortune, and exploited by an unscrupulous guardian. Like some versions of the Umetskaia character, Nastas'ia Filippovna is seduced by her guardian, then abandoned. Like Umetskaia, she feels violently angry, and her irrational and self-destructive tendencies stem from her humiliation, yet she remains blameless. This dual nature emerges in the description of her portrait in the novel:

> The face, extraordinary in its beauty and in something else, astonished him even more now. There was something like immeasurable pride and contempt, almost hatred, in that face, and at the same time something trusting, something wonderfully simple-hearted; these two contrasting elements aroused a feeling almost of compassion at the sight of these features. Her dazzling beauty was positively unbearable, the beauty of a pale face, almost sunken cheeks and glowing eyes; a strange beauty![7]

In Nastas'ia Filippovna's fiery gaze we see Ol'ga Umetskaia grown up as Dostoevskii might hope she would: a survivor of abuse, a product of suffering, but a woman with her soul intact, still capable of trust and love.

---

7 Fyodor Dostoevsky, *The Idiot*, trans. Constance Garnett and revised by Anna Brailovsky (New York: Modern Library, 2003), 85.

In addition to Ol'ga Umetskaia's story, Dostoevskii incorporated other newspaper items into *The Idiot*, many of them accounts of murders. Perhaps most striking for the final novel's conception is the way Dostoevskii incorporates the details of the notorious Mazurin murder. V. F. Mazurin, a merchant, killed a jeweller in his home. He then concealed the corpse in an oilcloth and surrounded it with Zhdanov fluid, a disinfectant and deodorizing compound that is also mentioned in *The Idiot*. Nastas'ia Filippovna has clearly read about the crime when she mentions her dream of a corpse under the floorboards of Rogozhin's house surrounded by jars of Zhdanov fluid, and Rogozhin mimics these details in the murder that concludes the novel. Furthermore, as V. S. Dorovatovskaia-Liubimova observes, the beginning of the novel's events in late November 1867 would have occurred just as Mazurin's trial was reported in the press, so Nastas'ia Filippovna would have read about the crime perhaps even on the day she meets Rogozhin and Myshkin, associating them with Mazurin in her mind (a point not lost on contemporaneous readers, Dorovatovskaia-Liubimova argues).[8]

In another news item, a man murdered an acquaintance in order to steal his silver watch; in the investigation, it emerged that the murderer had prayed for forgiveness as he was slitting his victim's throat. Myshkin recounts the incident as an example of the paradoxical nature of the Russian people, who are deeply religious but simultaneously have the potential for extreme violence.[9] Of this last crime, Myshkin later observes, "I know a genuine case of murder over a watch—it's in the newspapers now. Let some author invent that— pundits of the national way of life and critics would have cried out at once that it was improbable; but when you read it in the newspapers as a fact, you feel that it is just through such facts that you learn Russian reality."[10] Indeed, for Dostoevskii, incorporating these sensationalistic news items, printed in the press and pored over by the masses, enabled him to achieve realism "in a higher sense" by allowing him to turn the glass on Russia and reflect the best and worst facets of society.

---

8   V. S. Dorovatovskaia-Liubimova, "*Idiot* Dostoevskogo i ugolovnaia khronika ego vremeni," *Pechat' i revoliutsiia* 3 (1928): 31–53.

9   This passage appears in Chapter 10 of the present volume.

10   Dostoevskii, *The Idiot*, 538.

Two Suicides from
A Writer's Diary (1876)*

Fedor Dostoevskii

About a month ago all the Petersburg newspapers carried several short lines in fine print concerning a suicide in the city. A poor young girl, a seamstress, threw herself out of a fourth-floor window "because she was absolutely unable to find enough work to make a living." These accounts added that she leapt and fell to the ground *holding an icon in her hands*. This icon in the hands is a strange and unprecedented feature in suicides! This, now, is a meek and a humble suicide. Here, apparently, there was no grumbling or reproach: it was simply a matter of being unable to live any longer—"God did not wish it"—and so she died having said her prayers. There are some things which, no matter how simple they seem on the surface, one still goes on thinking about for a long time; they recur in one's dreams, and it even seems as if one is somehow to blame for them. This meek soul who destroyed herself torments one's mind despite oneself. It was this latter death that reminded me of the suicide of the emigré's daughter I had heard about last summer.[1] But how different these two creatures are—just as if they had come from two different planets! And how different the two deaths are! And which, I ask, of these two souls bore more torment on this earth—if such an idle question is proper and permissible?

---

* From Fyodor Dostoevsky, *A Writer's Diary Volume 1: 1873–1876*, trans. and ed. Kenneth Lantz (Evanston, IL: Northwestern University Press, 1994), 653. Copyright © 1994 by Northwestern University Press. All rights reserved.

1 The girl was Elizaveta Aleksandrovna Gertsen, daughter of Aleksandr Gertsen [. . .] who committed suicide in Florence at the age of seventeen. The suicide note Dostoevskii quotes here is an abbreviated paraphrase of the original. The original also does not contain the phrase "Ce n'est pas chic!" [It isn't *chic*.] This, apparently, was a comment made by Konstantin Pobedonostsev, who wrote to Dostoevskii about the suicide, and which the latter assumed to be part of Miss Gertsen's note.

From "The Meek One: A Fantastic Story" (1876)*

Fedor Dostoevskii

Luker'ia says [. . .] that after I left the house, and only some twenty minutes before I came back, she suddenly went to the mistress in our room to ask something—I don't remember what—and noticed that her icon (that same icon of the Virgin Mary) had been removed from the icon case and was standing before her on the table; the mistress, it seemed, had just been praying before it.

"What is it, ma'am?"

"It's nothing, Luker'ia, you may go . . . Wait, Luker'ia."

"She came up to Luker'ia and kissed her.

"Are you happy, ma'am?" Luker'ia asked.

"Yes, Luker'ia."

"The master should have come to ask your forgiveness a long time ago, ma'am. Thanks be to God you've made it up."

"That's fine, Luker'ia," she said. "You may go now."

And she smiled, but oddly somehow. It was such an odd smile that ten minutes later Luker'ia came in again to have a look at her: "She was standing by the wall, right near the window, her arm against the wall and her head against her arm, just standing there, thinking. And she was so deep in thought that she didn't even notice me standing there watching her from the other room. I could see that she had a kind of smile on her face, standing there, thinking and

---

smiling. I looked at her, turned and went out on tiptoe, wondering about her. But suddenly I heard the window open. Right away I went in to tell her that it was still cool outside and she might catch a cold if she wasn't careful. And I saw that she'd climbed up on the windowsill and was standing upright in the open window, her back to me, holding the icon. My heart just sank inside me, and I shouted 'Ma'am, ma'am!' She heard me and made a move as if to turn toward me, but didn't. She took a step, pressed the icon to her bosom, and leapt out the window!"

I remember only that when I came through the gate she was still warm. The worst thing was that they were all staring at me. They shouted at first, and then suddenly they all fell silent and made way before me, and . . . and she was lying there with the icon. I have a vague memory of coming up to her, silently, and looking for a long time. They all surrounded me and were saying something to me. Luker'ia was there, but I didn't see her. She tells me she spoke to me. I only remember some fellow shouting to me "there wasn't but a cupful of blood came out of her mouth, you could hold it in your hand!" And he showed me the blood there on the paving stone. I think I touched the blood and smeared the end of my finger with it; I recall looking at my finger while he kept on: "You could hold it in your hand!"

"What do you mean, in your hand?" I yelled at the top of my voice (so people say) and raised my arms to attack him . . .

A Case Study:
October, November,
December 1876 (2013)*

Kate Holland

The October and November 1876 issues of *A Writer's Diary* most clearly exemplify Dostoevskii's novelistic preoccupations. Focusing on the actual suicides of two women, Gertsen's illegitimate daughter Liza and a young seamstress who threw herself out of a Petersburg window holding an icon, the Diarist explores an ongoing theme: the phenomenon of ideological suicide ("Two Suicides"). Young *raznochintsy*,[1] torn between sense of self and enslavement to the grand narratives of historical determinism, are driven to take their own lives. For Dostoevskii, they are casualties of Russia's transition to modernity. In the May 1876 entry, "One Unconnected Idea," he had written about the death of Pisareva, a young radical who had killed herself, leaving a suicide note full of ressentiment. Despite their very different psychological contexts, the deaths of Liza and the seamstress both lead him to continue his May meditations. Quintessentially modern heroines, Pisareva and Liza suffer

---

* From Kate Holland, *The Novel in the Age of Disintegration: Dostoevsky and the Problem of Genre in the 1870s* (Evanston, IL: Northwestern University Press, 2013), 154–60. Copyright © 2013 by Northwestern University Press. All rights reserved. The text has been excerpted and some notes have been excised.

1   EDS: *Raznochintsy* literally means "those of various ranks"; by the mid-nineteenth century it referred to those in Russia's urban centers who, though not of noble extraction, had some education and were upwardly mobile. They became increasingly numerous and important as Russia's system of *sosloviia*, or estates, began to break down. Many of the liberal and radical intellectuals in Russia came from the *raznochintsy*.

from the same atrophied consciousness as the underground man.[2] Seeking in death the freedom they had failed to find in life, they sacrifice the self that is so dear to them on the altar of brute causality. In their double-voiced suicide notes, they attempt to assign themselves meaning by audaciously asserting the emptiness of their deaths. Like the novelistic subject, they are at once unique individuals, the psychological and metaphysical circumstances that led to their suicides irreducible to any common mean, and types, universal signifiers of a psychic disintegration that is all-embracing [. . .]

The Diarist explores the phenomenon of the suicide note, seeing in it the ultimate example of the collapse of narrative, and connecting it to his task of exploring the narrative implications of *obosoblenie*.[3] The suicide note finalizes its author, fixes her identity forever at the moment before death. Only by bringing Pisareva and Liza Gertsen back to life in narrative can one defer the terrible finality of their suicide notes. The Diarist seeks the meaning behind these women's deaths by exploring the final moments of their lives, examining the circumstances that led up to their fatal decisions. In so doing, he defies determinism, showing through the multiplicity of possible narrative threads that it could have been otherwise, that the brute causality they perceive to be leading their every move is in fact an illusion. Thus, within the *Diary*, the suicides are resurrected as novelistic heroines [. . .]

In the fictional work "The Meek One: A Fantastic Story," which takes up the *Diary*'s entire November issue, Dostoevskii provides the most complete representation of the kind of narrative breakdown about which he writes so often in the *Diary*. The story is structured in the same way as the *Diary*'s other sections; it is divided into two parts, each of which is subdivided into four or five sections. It thus blends seamlessly into the structure of the *Diary* and invites comparisons with the work's other issues. The story begins with a foreword explaining that the work's subtitle, "A Fantastic Story," refers to its form, a chaotic transcription of the fractured internal thoughts of its pawnbroker protagonist. The author of the foreword, presumably the Diarist,

---

2   On the suicides in the *Diary*, see Irina Paperno, *Suicide as a Cultural Institution in Dostoevsky's Russia* (Ithaca, NY: Cornell University Press, 1997), 162–84.

3   EDS: "*Obosoblenie*" means the practice of isolating, or segregating. It is one of the underlying themes of *A Writer's Diary*, where it takes on a broader meaning, suggesting a process of social dislocation, whereby there are no longer any common ideas, values, forms, institutions, even languages; therefore communication between people becomes increasingly difficult. It is translated by Kenneth Lantz in *A Writer's Diary* as "dissociation" and is the subject of a March 1876 entry.

heads off any possible criticism of the form as unrealistic by declaring it to be fantastic. By inviting comparisons with Victor Hugo's *The Last Day of a Man Condemned*, which he calls "among the most real and most truthful of his writings," the Diarist implies that this fantastic story reveals something true about contemporary Russian society and thus shares some of the *Diary*'s broader preoccupations. Indeed, the foreword suggests that the story can be seen as another kind of diary, albeit one that deals with private, rather than public, impressions. Inspired by the suicide of the seamstress he had discussed in "Two Suicides," Dostoevskii writes the fictional narrative of the events leading up to her death [. . .]

The work draws its dynamism from the contradiction between the organized, ordered certainty of the pawnbroker's narrative, and the horrific incomprehensibility of the act of suicide itself. His narrative attempts to "rewrite" the story of what should have happened. It attempts both to assuage his guilt and to find comfort in the security of form [. . .] However, there are chinks in the ordered certainty of the pawnbroker's narrative that reveal the turmoil underneath. These chinks become more frequent as the narrative progresses. The ellipses, which hint at doubt and the failure to articulate some deeper repressed feeling, are accompanied by admissions of misunderstanding and a gradual creeping awareness that his is not the only perspective. Doubts about his point of view are compounded by more and more questions, self-laceration, and an increased awareness of his imagined reader. His anguished reproaches are increasingly directed at himself as the "shroud fell." In the second part of the text the dialogue between the narrative certainty and uncertainty becomes more intense still. His narrative speeds up and becomes more confused as the pawnbroker nears his conclusion. He stops his self-flattery; his tone becomes more frantic, his narrative more punctured by frenzied adjectives. He changes from his own voice to the indirect speech of Luker'ia the maid, to her direct speech, in a desperate attempt to formulate a narrative capable of expressing the inexpressible, of explaining the inexplicable, of comprehending the incomprehensible [. . .]

Finally all narrative certainty is gone. His narrative is his last defense against the appalling reality of his wife's death and the evidence of his own culpability, but finally even that breaks down into incoherence [. . .] leaving him with the prospect of either silence, which dominated his relationship with his wife, or the incessant repetition of the word *bred* (delirium). His narrative account has become disembodied, devoid of signifier and signified, bereft of addressee, existing only to fill the vacuum left by her body. Just as the laws on which the pawnbroker has based his worldview collapse, so does his narrative itself [. . .]

In the astonishing virtuosity of its portrayal of narrative breakdown, "The Meek One" lies at the heart of the *Diary*'s vision. It is both profoundly typical and atypical of the larger work within which it is embedded: typical in its embodiment of a central theme of the *Diary*, the problem of how narrative responds to death, particularly death by suicide, atypical in the success of its execution, in the way Dostoevskii creates a narrative that is both open and closed, subject and object, representing and represented. It is a "fantastic story" based on a real incident, a story that conveys through its fantastic form both the delusions of the pawnbroker's fantasy and the reality of the seamstress's religious belief even at the moment of suicide. This belief could strike the reader as fantastic, but Dostoevskii is at pains to show that it is real [. . .]

In the December 1876 *Diary*, underlining his ownership of the Diarist's voice, Dostoevskii is determined to have the last word on the story. Annihilating the space between his own voice and that of his narrator, he attempts to rein in the open-endedness of his novelistic explorations of suicide and doubt in the October and November issues. It should be noted that the second half of the October issue constitutes a journalistic commentary on the war in the Balkans, followed by a historical narrative that seeks to explain the Russian Idea and a prophetic interpretation of the Russian volunteer movement. It reads as a profoundly jarring sequel to the narratives of suicide in the first half and exemplifies the problems of combining novelistic and journalistic narratives within a single issue. In December, the Diarist continues in the same doctrinaire journalistic voice he had employed in the second half of the October issue. Launching into an analysis of "The Sentence," he takes on the voice of the prophet-pedagogue, explaining how the whole work is intended to illustrate the impossibility of living without the idea of immortality. By means of authoritative discourse that assigns a single meaning to the story, he reduces not only "The Sentence" but the entire October issue to a dogmatic sermon. Having teased out the idiosyncratic and individual identities of the suicides, he fixes them as uncompromisingly as their own suicide notes had done [. . .]

As he looked for new ways to embody in literary form the changing social landscape of mid-1870s Russia, Dostoevskii turned from the novelistic form back to journalism. Journalism offered new ways of looking at the world, the possibility of greater engagement with the present, dialogue with his readers, and liberation from the novel's formal constraints. *A Writer's Diary* was perhaps his boldest generic experiment, an encyclopaedic work that sought to model the heterogeneous narratives of the post reform era within its very structure. A journal born of a struggle with novelistic form, it shares many of the novel's formal devices: a tension between particular and universal perspectives, a dynamic hierarchy of narrative voices, and an ability to embody social transition within narrative. Yet combining different genres with their often contradictory structures and worldviews carries the inherent risk of narrative breakdown.

A *Writer's Diary* as a Historical Phenomenon (2004)*

Igor' Volgin

A nd so, real facts come into collision with the historical literary tradition that unconditionally associated *The Diary* with strictly conservative publications, and regarded its ideology as wholly reactionary and defensive. We ought to raise a question about the specificity of *The Diary's* artistic and ideological nature, and in that context, about its special situation within the context of Russian periodical publications of the second half of nineteenth century.

Up until now, the ideology of *The Diary* has been characterized exclusively outside of its "material medium" (i.e., *The Diary* itself) and only in evaluative terms. Meanwhile, an opportunity arises to address the question: how, and in which specific historical form, did this ideology reach the reader? And, consequently, how did the audience receive *The Diary*?

A Writer's Diary is a unique occurrence in the history of Russian and world journalism. Its quality was characterized by two interrelated factors: the individual characteristics of Dostoevskii's artistic personality on the one hand, and particularities of the specific historic situation on the other. The inception of *The Diary* and its institutionalization as a monojournal appeared as the culmination of a lengthy process of literary evolution. Dostoevskii's artistic genius

* From Igor' Volgin, *Vozvrashchenie bileta. Paradoksy natsional'nogo samosoznaniia* (Moscow: Grant", 2004), 143–45. The text has been translated by Anton Nonin, with the permission of the author, and is published here under a Creative Commons BY-ND 4.0 license.

and the presence of specific social efforts were required in order for the results of this process to emerge at this historical moment, and in this particular historical form.

At the same time, the amalgamation of all of the basic functions of the journal (authorial, editorial, and publishing) does not, in our opinion, determine the typology of *The Diary* or its genre. This aspect is merely formal and, in fact, unoriginal, while *The Diary* possesses qualities of artistic and historical uniqueness.

Unable to express himself as a novelist in *The Diary*, Dostoevskii, nevertheless, managed to infuse it with novelistic thought. This allowed *The Diary* to partly solve issues inherent in the novels. If, until now, the influence of journalistic genres on Dostoevskii's writing has been noted (his greatest novels can be considered serial novels), then, we believe, it is appropriate to pose a question about the opposite influence, i.e. the pervasion of the novel into the feuilleton.

Seeing it from this perspective, *The Diary* appears as an unparalleled artistic experiment.

And it was also a public experiment. *The Diary* was an attempt to push off from literature (which, in practice, only created the opposite: more complex forms of literature), and to speak directly to the audience "over the barriers." Aiming to destroy the familiar model "author – reader," The Diary took the first step towards achieving its ultimate goal: a selfless, seamless form of communication.

Therefore, the very mode of existence of *The Diary* is deeply ideological.

This being said, *The Diary* retains its cohesiveness only as long as it remains within the frame of its own artistic conception. As soon as *The Diary* steps over these lines (and, wishing to become a "theory, loses its inherent higher meaning"), it discovers its own vulnerability.

The Diary reaches its "higher" objective only when it rejects its "practical" objective, the one that it supposedly was created for it by virtue of its journalistic conception. Therefore, we can say that *The Diary's* aim (its "purpose") contradicts its own artistic status (its "greater purpose").

The Diary turns out to be "greater" than itself because the identity of its author is "greater" than the ideological means at his disposal.

But in this case, a question arises: can Dostoevskii's ideology be seen as a worldview in the narrow sense of the word? That is, as something that can be painlessly removed from his identity, and observed autonomously—as independent, strictly rational, whole. Would this worldview remain the same if one removed its core —the identity of Dostoevskii?

Or would this be the same as trying to separate the music from a song?

If one were to take certain ideological moments in *A Writer's Diary* out of context, they would become their opposite. The "aims" of *The Diary*, isolated from its own artistic environment, are not its aims anymore.

It is not some "parenthetical" ideological constructions, but Dostoevskii's identity, which fills the lacunae of his "worldview," and allows him to retain the wholeness of his artistic world.

We hope that, when we speak about the wholeness of Dostoevskii's world, we will not be suspected of trying to claim that his creative output is without contradictions. Quite the opposite: it is an understanding of its wholeness that allows us to acknowledge Dostoevskii's contradictions—not as a random and chaotic assortment of paradoxes, but as a *system*, as a *cohesive ideological paradox*, with a consistent pattern.

His identity, binding, as intended, Dostoevskii's entire *universum*, imbues it with such intensity that separate ideologemes, as if sucked into a magnetic field, are able to change their own nature. In this "fantastical" world, ideological space bends under a superpowerful artistic dominance. Ideology does not exist here in a "pure" sense—as an independent and final entity. In order to be realized it must receive a certain artistic permission.

But in this case, the ideology is bound up, first of all, with the identity of the artist, not with an ideologue's guise.

Dostoevskii's wordview, attempting to realize itself as such, is in fact his *artistic sense of the world* and can only adequately manifest itself through that sense.

As for the "regular reader," he, as we discovered, felt this from the beginning; it makes no difference that he did so purely intuitively.

A Writer's Diary, April 1877 issue*

Fedor Dostoevskii

CHAPTER 1

1. War. We Are Stronger Than the Others.

"It's war! War has been declared!" Such were the shouts we heard two weeks ago.[1] "Is it to be war?" asked others when they heard. "It's true, it's been declared!" was the reply. "It may have been declared, but will it happen?" the others kept asking . . .

And, truly, questions such as these were asked; perhaps they are being asked even now. And it's not only the drawn-out diplomatic dawdling that has made people so skeptical; it's something else, an instinct. Everyone senses that something decisive has begun, that there is somehow going to be a resolution of an issue from the past—a long, drawn-out issue from the past—and that a step is being taken toward something quite new, toward something that means a sharp break with the past, that will renew and resurrect the things of the past for a new life and . . . that it

---

* From Fyodor Dostoevsky, *A Writer's Diary Volume 2: 1877–1881*, trans. and ed. Kenneth Lantz (Evanston, IL: Northwestern University Press, 1994), 929–64. Copyright © 1994 by Northwestern University Press. All rights reserved.

1 Alexander II declared war on Turkey on April 12, 1877. The immediate cause of the war was Turkey's refusal to implement the reforms for its Christian population that had been set forth by the Constantinople Conference of 1876, as well as Turkish atrocities committed against Bulgarian civilians in response to a Bulgarian uprising in May 1876. Pan-Slavist sentiments, Russian rivalry with Austro-Hungary in the Balkans, and Russia's desire for free and safe egress from the Black Sea were other causes.

is Russia who is taking this step! This is just the thing that makes our "wise" people so skeptical. There is an instinctive premonition, yet the skepticism continues: "Russia! But how can she? How does she dare? Is she ready? Is she ready inwardly and morally, never mind materially? That's Europe over there, and Europe is no small matter! While Russia . . . well, what is Russia? And to take such a step?"

But the People believe that they are ready for a great, new, and regenerating step. It is the People themselves who rose to go to war, with the tsar at their head. When the word of the tsar rang out, the People rushed into the churches, and this happened all over the Russian land.[2] When they read the tsar's manifesto the People crossed themselves and everyone *congratulated* each other on the war. We have seen this with our own eyes and heard it, and all this is happening even here in Petersburg. And once more the same activities have begun and the same facts come to light as last year: peasants in rural districts are donating money, as their means allow, and sending carts; and suddenly these thousands of people exclaim as one, "Donations and carts are little enough; we will all go off to fight!" Here in Petersburg we see people giving money for wounded and sick soldiers; they give sums of several thousand and ask that they be listed *anonymously*. There is a host of such facts; there will be tens of thousands of similar ones, and no one will be surprised at them. They signify only that the entire People have risen up for the truth, for a sacred cause, that the entire People have risen up to go to war and are on their way. Oh, the wise men will deny these facts as well, as they did last year's; the wise men still laugh at the People, as they did even recently, although they have plainly lowered their voices. Why do they laugh? From where do they draw so much faith in themselves? They continue to laugh precisely because they still see themselves as a power, that very power without which nothing can be achieved. And meanwhile, their power is drawing to its end. They are approaching a dreadful collapse, and when the pieces start to fall on their heads they, too, will begin talking in a different language, but everyone will see that they are only mumbling someone else's views and echoing someone else's voice; and everyone will turn away from them and invest their hopes in the tsar and his People.

We also need this war for ourselves; we rise up not only for our "brother Slavs" who have been suffering[3] at the hands of the Turks but for our own

---

2 Dostoevskii's wife notes that when he learned of the declaration of war, he went directly to Kazan Cathedral and spent half an hour in fervent prayer. A. G. Dostoevskaia, *Vospominaniia* (Moscow: Khudozhestvennaia literatura, 1971), 315–16.

3 EDS: Here Dostoevskii refers to the massacre of Bulgarians by the Ottoman Turkish army in 1875.

salvation as well: war will clear the air we breathe and in which we have been suffocating, helplessly decaying within our narrow spiritual horizons. The wise men shout that we are perishing and suffocating from our own internal disorganization and that therefore we should seek not war but, rather, a prolonged peace so that we may be transformed from beasts and blockheads into real people and learn about order, honesty, and honor: "And then go off and help your brother Slavs," they conclude, singing in close harmony. In such a case, it would be interesting to know how they conceive the process by which they would become better. And how could they acquire any honor for themselves through a clearly dishonorable act? It would be interesting, finally, to know how and with what they would justify their refusal to share the feeling we find everywhere among the People. Yes, evidently it's right that the truth is purchased only at the cost of martyrdom.

Millions of people are moving and suffering and passing away without a trace, as if destined never to comprehend the truth. They live by the ideas of others; they seek the readymade word and example and latch onto causes suggested by others. They shout that the authorities are on their side, that Europe is on their side. They jeer at those who do not agree with them, at all who despise flunkyism of thought and who believe in their own and their People's independence. And, indeed, these masses of shouting people are destined to serve only as a passive means for a scant few individuals among them to draw a little closer to the truth, or at least to get some slight premonition of it. It is these same individuals who later lead all the others, who take control of the movement, who give birth to an idea and leave it as a legacy to the teeming masses of people. We have already had such individuals among us. Some of us—even many of us—already understand them. But the wise men still continue to laugh and believe that they are a great power. "They'll have a little spree, and then they'll come home"—that's what they are now saying about our forces that have crossed the border; they even say it aloud. "There won't be a war—what war? How can we go to war? It's just a military review and some maneuvers, at the cost of some hundreds of millions, so as to bolster our honor." That is the private view of the matter. But is it really only a private war?

Indeed, if we should be beaten, or if, after beating the enemy, we still were pressured by circumstances to come to terms cheaply—oh, then, of course, the wise men would be triumphant. And what dreadful jeering and racket and cynicism we'd have for years to come; what a bacchanalia of self-contempt, face slapping, and jeering at ourselves there would be again—and it would not be a summons to resurrection and strength but specifically to celebrate their own lack of honor, personality, and strength. And a new nihilism would begin, absolutely the same as the old one, with a rejection of the Russian People and their independent view. And the main thing is that is would acquire such force and become so strong that it would certainly begin, even openly, to ride roughshod over Russia's most sacred values. And young people would again spit upon their homes and families and flee from their elders, mindlessly repeating the endless platitudes and boring old words about the grandeur of Europe and our duty to be as lacking in personality as possible. And the main thing is—the same old song, the same old words, and nothing new for a long time! No, we need the war and the victory. With war and victory will come a new word, and a living life will begin, not merely the mind-numbing twaddle we used to hear— what do I mean, we used to hear? That we hear to this day, gentlemen!

But we must be ready for everything; and indeed, if we, assume even the worst, even the impossibly worst outcome for the war that has now begun, then, although we may endure much of that disgusting old misery that has sickened us all to death, the colossus will still not be shaken and, sooner or later, will take all its due. This is not merely a hope; it is a complete certainty, and in this impossibility of shaking the colossus lies our entire strength over Europe, where now virtually everyone fears that their old edifice will be shaken and the ceilings will crash down upon them. This colossus is our People. And the beginning of the current *People's* war, and all the recent circumstances that preceded it, have merely made it patently obvious to everyone who knows how to look that the People truly are one, that we are fresh, and that our People's strength has not been touched to any real extent by the decay that has spoiled our wise men. And what a service these wise men have rendered us in our dealings with Europe! Only recently they were still shouting to the whole world that we were poor and insignificant; with a jeer they assured everyone that there was no spirit whatsoever among our People because there were no *People* whatsoever, since our People and their spirit were mere products of the fantasies of homegrown Moscow dreamers; that eighty million Russian peasants were nothing more than millions of inert, drunken taxation units; that there was no unity between tsar and People; that this was only some copybook maxim; that, on the contrary, everything had been shaken and corroded by nihilism; that our soldiers would throw down their arms and run like sheep; that we had neither cartridges nor provisions; and finally, that we ourselves could see that we had been merely talking to keep our spirits up and had gone too far, and now were only looking anxiously for any pretext to retreat without the ultimate disgrace of having our face slapped—something that "even we would be unable to endure"—and were praying for Europe to invent such a pretext for us.

This is the sworn testimony of our wise men and, indeed, one can scarcely get angry at them; this is their view and their understanding, their utterly sincere view and understanding. And truly, yes, we are poor; yes, we are pitiful in many respects; yes, there really is so much wrong with us that the wise man, and particularly if he is one of our wise men, cannot "betray" himself and cannot help but exclaim, "Russia is *kaputt* and we needn't feel sorry about it!" And so it is these heartfelt ideas of our wise men that have flown around Europe, particularly through the channel of European correspondents who flocked here on the eve of the war to study us at first hand, to examine us from their European viewpoints and to measure our strength by their European yardstick. And it goes without saying that they have been listening only to our "most wise and sensible" people. All of them have overlooked the strength of the People, the spirit of the People, and the news has flown around Europe that Russia is perishing, that Russia is nothing—she was nothing, she is nothing now, and she will be brought to nothing. The hearts of our age-old enemies and Russophobes, whom we have annoyed in Europe for two centuries now, started to quiver; the hearts of many thousands of European Yids, along with the hearts of millions of "Christians" who practice the Yiddish trade along with them, also began to quiver; Beaconsfield's heart[4] quivered: he had been told that Russia would endure everything, right to the most disgraceful and final slap in the face, but would not go to war—such, he was told, was the strength of her "peaceable nature." But God saved us, having sent blindness upon them all; they have put far too much faith in the ruination and the insignificance of Russia and have overlooked the very most important thing. They have overlooked the entire Russian People as a living force and have overlooked a colossal fact: the union of the tsar with his People! It's *only this* they have overlooked! Besides, they simply could not comprehend and believe that our tsar truly is peaceable and truly does regret the blood that will be shed: they thought that all this was merely "politics." And even now they see nothing: they shout that suddenly, after the tsar's manifesto, "patriotism" has reared its head among us. But is this patriotism? This is where our main strength lies: that they do not understand Russia at all, that they understand nothing in Russia! They do not know that nothing in the world can conquer us, that we may, perhaps, lose battles but will still remain unconquerable precisely because of the unity of our People's spirit and by our People's consciousness; that we are not France, which is entirely in

---

4 EDS: "Beaconsfield" refers to British Prime Minister Benjamin Disraeli, who had been created Earl of Beaconsfield in 1876.

Paris; that we are not Europe, which completely depends on the stock markets of its bourgeoisie and on the "placidity" of its proletariats, a placidity purchased by the last resorts of their governments there—and this only for an hour. They do not understand and do not know that if such is our *will*, we will not be conquered by all the Yids of Europe taken together, nor by the millions of their gold, nor by the millions of their armies; that if such is our will, we cannot be compelled to do that which we do not wish to do, and that there is no power on earth that could compel us. The only problem is that people not only in Europe but in Russia as well will laugh at these words, and that not only our wise and sensible people but even genuine Russian people of our educated class will laugh as well—such is our lack of understanding of ourselves and our age-old strength, which, thank God, has not yet been broken. These good people do not understand that in Russia, in our vast, unique, utterly un-European land, even military tactics (so common a thing as that!) can be quite unlike European ones, that the bases of European tactics—money and the scientific organization of six-hundred-thousand-man invading armies—may stumble in our land and fall against what for them is a new and unknown power, whose bases lie in the nature of the endless Russian land and in the nature of the all-uniting Russian spirit. But never mind that, *for the time being*, so many good people among us still do not know this (they do not know and are hesitant). Yet our tsars do know it, and our People sense it. Alexander I knew about this unique power of ours when he said that he would let his beard grow and go off into the forest with his People, but would not lay down his sword and submit to the will of Napoleon.[5] And, of course, should the whole of Europe come up against such a force, it would all be shattered, because they have neither the money nor the unified organization to conduct such a war. When all our Russians realize that we are that strong, then we shall have reached a point where we shall no longer have to wage war; then people will believe in us and will *discover* us for the first time, as Europe once discovered America. But for that to happen we must discover ourselves before they do, and our intelligentsia must understand that it can no longer remain isolated and estranged from its People ...

2. War Is Not Always a Scourge; Sometimes It Is Salvation.

But our wise men have seized upon yet another aspect of the matter: they preach benevolence and humaneness, they grieve over the blood to be shed

---

5 Alexander I is quoted as saying this in N. V. Putiata, "Obozrenie zhizni i tsarstvovaniia imperatora Aleksandra I," in *Deviatnadtsatyi vek* (Moscow: P. Vartenev, 1871), vol. 1, 456–57.

and over the fact that we will become even more bestial and defiled in a war and thereby move even further away from our goal of domestic well being, from the true path, from science. Yes, war, of course, is a misfortune, but there is also much that is wrong in these arguments; and the main thing is that we have had enough of this bourgeois moralizing! The feat of sacrificing our blood for all that we consider sacred is, of course, more moral than this entire bourgeois catechism. The nation's surge of spirit for the sake of a noble idea—that is an impulse toward progress and not bestialization. Of course, we may be mistaken in what we regard as a noble idea; but if the thing we consider our holy of holies is shameful and flawed, then we will not escape punishment from Nature herself: that which is shameful and flawed bears death within it and sooner or later will exact its own punishment. For instance, a war fought to acquire wealth, for the demands of the insatiable stock market, may arise from the same law of development of national personality common to all nations, yet there is a limit to this development that must not be crossed and beyond which every acquisition and every development means excess; it bears a disease within it, a disease that ends in death. So it is that England, should she take the side of Turkey in this current conflict in the East, having utterly ignored the groans of tormented humanity for the sake of her commercial interests, would surely be raising her sword against herself, a sword that, sooner or later, will fall on her own head. On the other hand, what is more sacred and pure than the feat of a war such as Russia is presently undertaking? People will say: "But though Russia, too, may truly be setting out only to liberate the oppressed peoples there and to restore their independence, in so doing she will acquire future allies in these same peoples and, accordingly, acquire power; and so it is all just another example of this same law of development of national personality toward which England is also striving. And since the colossal scope of this proposed 'panslavism' may truly frighten Europe, then the same law of self-preservation certainly entitles Europe to stop us; on the same basis, however, we are entitled to go ahead, paying no heed to her fears and guided in our movement only by political foresight and prudence. Thus there is nothing here either sacred or shameful; there is only the age-old life instinct of peoples to which all of the earth's insufficiently and improperly developed tribes respond without differentiation. Nevertheless, as consciousness, science, and humaneness accumulate, sooner or later the age-old and bestial instinct of improperly developed nations must weaken and inspire, rather, a desire for peace, international unity, and humane development in all peoples. Accordingly, one must still preach peace, not blood."

Holy words! But in the present instance they somehow do not apply to Russia, or, to put it even better—Russia, at the present historical moment of Europe, is a kind of exception, and this is really so. In fact, if Russia, who has so selflessly and justly now taken up arms for the salvation and renewal of the oppressed tribes, should later increase her power through them, then in such a case she is still a most exceptional example that Europe, who measures by her own yardstick, simply cannot anticipate. If Russia is strengthened, even excessively, through her alliance with the tribes she has liberated, she will not fall upon Europe with a sword, will not seize and take away anything from her, as Europe certainly would do should she find the opportunity to unite herself once more against Russia, and as all the nations of Europe have been doing all their lives, the moment they found the opportunity to increase their strength at the expense of their neighbor. (And this has been going on from the most savage, primordial times of Europe right up to the modern and so recent Franco-Prussian War. And what became of all their civilization then? The most educated and enlightened of all nations attacked another nation, just as educated and enlightened and, taking advantage of the opportunity, tore the life out of it like a wild beast, drank its blood, squeezed the juices out of it in the form of billions in reparations, and cut off its whole side in the form of two of its best provinces! Yes, in truth, can Europe be blamed if, after that, she cannot understand Russia's mission? How can they, proud, educated, and strong, understand and admit, even in their wildest fantasies, that Russia is predestined and created, perhaps, for their salvation as well and that only she, perhaps, will at last pronounce this word of salvation?) Oh, yes, yes, of course, not only will we seize nothing from them and take nothing away, but the fact that we will be vastly strengthened (through an alliance of love and brotherhood, not through seizure and violence) will at last allow us not to bare our sword but, rather, in the calm assurance of our strength, to give an example of sincere peace, international unity, and selflessness. We shall be the first to declare to the world that it is not by suppressing the national personalities of other tribes that we strive to achieve our own well-being; on the contrary, we see that well-being only in the freest and most independent development of all other nations and in fraternal unity with them, each one enhancing the other, grafting their organic features onto ourselves and giving them our branches to graft onto themselves, communing with them in soul and in spirit, learning from them and teaching them; and so it will be until such time as humanity, having achieved universal unity through the communion of nations of the world, will, as a great and magnificent tree, cast its shade over the happy earth. Oh, let today's "universal men" and those full of contempt for their own People laugh at these "fantastic" words, but we cannot be blamed if we believe these things, that is, if we go hand in hand with our People who believe precisely these things. Ask the People; ask the soldier; why do they rise up, why do they go to war, what do they expect from the war that has just begun? They will tell you, as one man, that they are going to serve Christ and to liberate their oppressed brethren, and not a single one of them is thinking about seizing territory. Indeed, it is precisely here, in this present war, that we shall demonstrate our whole idea about Russia's future mission in Europe and demonstrate it precisely by the fact that when we do liberate the Slavic lands, we shall not acquire a single inch of them for ourselves (as Austria now has visions of doing); we shall, rather, watch to see that they live in mutual harmony and shall defend their freedom and independence, from the whole of Europe if need be. And if such is the case, then our idea is sacred, and our war is not at all "the age-old and bestial instinct of improperly developed nations," but is precisely the first step toward attaining that eternal peace in which we are fortunate enough to believe, toward attaining international unity *in truth*, and a humane state of well-being *in truth*! And so, one need not always preach only peace, and it is not in peace alone, despite everything, that salvation is to be found; sometimes it is also in war.

3. Does Shed Blood Save Us?

"But the bloodshed; we are talking of bloodshed, after all," the wise men kept repeating, and truly, all these official phrases about bloodshed are often nothing more than a collection of most insignificant, high-sounding words spoken with a definite purpose in mind. Stock-exchange operators, for instance, are extremely fond of talking about humaneness. And many of those who now talk of humaneness are nothing more than traders in it. And yet, even more blood might be shed without a war. Believe me, in some instances, if not in almost all instances (except in those of civil wars), war is the process *precisely* through which international peace is achieved with the least amount of bloodshed, the least amount of misery, the least expenditure of effort, and in which at least some approximation of normal relationships between nations are worked out. Of course, it's a sad thing, but what can be done if such is the case? It's better, after all, to draw the sword than to suffer endlessly. And in what way is the current peace among civilized nations better than war? On the contrary, it is not war but peace, a prolonged peace, that bestializes and hardens people. A prolonged peace always gives rise to cruelty, cowardice, and coarse, bloated egoism and, above all, to intellectual stagnation. During a prolonged peace only the hangman and the exploiters of peoples grow fat. We hear again and again that peace generates wealth, but this is true only for a tenth of people, and this ten percent, having become infected with the diseases of wealth, pass on the infection to the remaining ninety percent, although they do not pass on the wealth. The former become infected with vice and cynicism. An excessive accumulation of wealth in the hands of a few generates coarseness of feeling in the possessors of that wealth. The sense of refinement is transformed into a thirst for frivolous luxuries and abnormality. There is a terrible spread of voluptuousness. Voluptuousness generates cruelty and cowardice. The bloated and coarse soul of the voluptuary is more cruel than any other—even one with many flaws. A voluptuary who faints at the sight of blood from a cut finger will not pardon some poor wretch and will have him sent to prison for a tiny debt. Cruelty, in turn, generates an intensified and most cowardly anxiety over one's own safety. This cowardly anxiety over one's security is always ultimately transformed, during a prolonged peace, into a kind of panic fear for oneself, and that spreads through all levels of society; it generates a terrible greed for the acquisition and accumulation of money. Faith in human solidarity, in human brotherhood and in the help of society, is lost; the slogan Every Man for Himself is loudly proclaimed; the poor man sees all too clearly what the wealthy man is and what sort of brother he is to him, and so each one isolates himself and dissociates himself. Egoism kills noble feelings. It is only art that still supports the higher life in society and awakens the souls that have fallen into slumber during periods of prolonged peace. And that is why people have conjured up the notion that art can flourish only in a time of prolonged peace, yet there is an immense error here: art, I mean genuine art, develops during a prolonged peace precisely because it is at odds with the heavy and immoral slumber of souls; in such periods the creations of art always invoke an ideal, generate protest and indignation, rouse society, and often cause suffering for those who long to awaken and climb out of the stinking pit. Ultimately, the result is that a prolonged, bourgeois peace almost always generates an urge for war; this is its miserable consequence, and it is not a war for a grand and just purpose, worthy of a great nation, but for some wretched bourgeois interests, for new markets needed by the exploiters, for acquiring new slaves essential to those who own the sacks of gold—in short, for reasons that are not justified even by the need for self-preservation but, rather, for reasons that testify to the frivolous, pathological state of the national organism. These interests, and the wars that are undertaken to support them, corrupt and even utterly destroy nations, whereas a war for some noble purpose, for the liberation of the oppressed, for the sake of a selfless and sacred idea—such a war can only clear the air befouled by accumulated miasmas, cure the soul, drive out shameful cowardice and laziness, declare and set forth a firm goal, provide and clarify an idea that this or that nation is summoned to put into effect. Such a war strengthens every soul with the awareness of self-sacrifice, and the spirit of the entire nation with the awareness of the mutual solidarity and unity of all the members that constitute it. And the most important thing is the awareness of a duty fulfilled and of a good deed accomplished:

"We have not entirely fallen and become corrupt; there remains something human even in us!" And just look at how these proponents of peaceableness and humaneness began their preaching so recently: they began directly with the most inhuman cruelty. They themselves did not want to help the martyrs who were calling out to us, and they restrained others from doing so. These people, evidently so humane and so sensitive, cold-bloodedly and mockingly denied our need to sacrifice ourselves and accomplish a great spiritual deed. They sought to push Russia onto the lowest and most unworthy path for a great nation; and beyond that, there was their contempt for the People who saw the Slavic martyrs as their brothers and, consequently, their haughty alienation from the will of the People, above which they placed their own false "European" enlightenment. Their favorite slogan was Physician, Heal Thyself. "You go off to heal and to save others, but you haven't even built schools of your own"—such was the evidence they provided. "Well, and what of it? that's why we are going—to heal ourselves. Schools are an important thing, of course; but schools need a spirit and a direction—and that's why we're going now: to gather up some spirit and to acquire a proper direction. And we will acquire these things, particularly if God sends us a victory. We shall return with the awareness of the selfless deed we have accomplished, with the awareness that we have gloriously served humanity with our blood, with the awareness of our renewed strength and energy—and all of this in place of our so recent shameful infirmity of purpose, in place of the deathly stagnation of our mindlessly borrowed Europeanism. And the most important thing is that we shall commune with the People and unite ourselves more firmly with them—for in them and in them alone shall we find the cure for our two-hundred-year-old ailment, for our twohundred-year-old unproductive impotence."

Indeed, one can say generally that if society is unhealthy and infected, then even such a fine thing as a prolonged peace can, instead of benefiting society, be harmful to it. One can even apply this to all of Europe generally. It is not without reason that no generation has passed in the history of Europe, as far as we can remember it, without a war. And so, evidently, even war is essential for something; it is healing; it relieves humanity. This is shocking if one thinks in abstract terms, but in practice it turns out that way, it seems, and precisely because in an infected organism even such a fine thing as peace is transformed into something harmful. But still, the only useful war is one undertaken for a grand idea, for a higher and noble principle and not for material interests, not for greedy seizure of territory, not for contemptuous violence. Wars of that sort have only led nations along wrong paths and have always destroyed them. If not we, then our children, will see how England ends. Now, for everyone in the world, "the time is at hand."[6] And about time, too.

4. The Opinion of the "Most Serene" Tsar on the Eastern Question

I have been given an excerpt from a book published in Kiev last year: *The Moscow State under Tsar Alexis and Patriarch Nikon, from the Records of Archdeacon Pavel of Aleppo,* by Ivan Obolenskii, Kiev, 1876, 90–91. This is a page from someone else's work, but it is so characteristic and so interesting at our present moment, and the work itself probably so little known to the general public, that I decided to include these few lines in the *Diary.* The passage reveals the opinion on the Eastern Question[7] of Tsar Alexis—also a "most serene" tsar—and his lament that he was unable to be a tsar-liberator.[8]

> It was said that Easter in the year 1656 the sovereign, exchanging Easter greetings with some Greek merchants who were visiting Moscow, asked them, "Is it your wish and expectation that I liberate and ransom you from captivity?" And when they replied: "How could it be otherwise? How could be not wish it?"—he added, "So therefore, when you return to your lands, ask all the monks and bishops to pray to God and to hold services

---

6 Matthew 26:18: "And he said, Go into the city to such a man, and say unto him, The Master saith, My time is at hand; I will keep the Passover at thy house with my disciples."

7 EDS: The "Eastern Question" asks what Europe should do with an unstable and slowly decaying Ottoman Empire.

8 Tsar Alexis [Aleksei] reigned from 1645–1676. His reign was not as serene as Dostoevskii suggests here but was marked by frequent popular uprisings and the Great Schism in the Orthodox church. Alexis was the first Russian tsar to begin adopting, though in small measure, elements of Western culture. He earned the sobriquet "most serene" (*tishaishii*) because of his pleasant disposition, warmth, and humility.

for me so that through their prayers I may be given strength to cut off the head of their enemy." And having shed many tears over this, he then addressed the nobles, saying: "My heart is filled with grief over the enslavement of these poor people who suffer in the clutches of the enemies of our faith; God will call me to account on judgment day *if, having the power to liberate them, I neglect my duty.* I do not know how long government affairs will continue in such a lamentable state, but since the time of my father and his predecessors we have been visited unceasingly by patriarchs, bishops, monks, and ordinary poor people bearing complaints of their conqueror's oppression, and not one of them has come save because he was burdened with most bitter sorrow and was fleeing from the cruelty of his masters. *And I dread the question the Creator will put to me on that day: and I have resolved in my mind, should it please God, to use all my armies and my treasury, and shed my blood to the last drop, yet will I strive to liberate them."* To all this the nobles replied, *"O Lord, grant thy heart's desire."*

CHAPTER 2

The Dream of a Ridiculous Man: A Fantastic Story

1

I'm a ridiculous man. Now they call me a madman. It would have been a promotion if I hadn't remained just as ridiculous in their eyes as before. But now it doesn't bother me; now they're all dear to me, and even when they laugh at me—even then there are things that make them especially dear. I'd laugh along with them—not at myself, but loving them—if I didn't feel so sad when I look at them. I feel sad, because they don't know the truth, while I know the truth. Ah, what a hard thing it is to be the only one who knows the truth! But they won't understand that. No, they won't understand.

But in times past I used to worry a good deal because I seemed a ridiculous man. Not seemed: I was. I was always a ridiculous man, and I've known it, I suppose, ever since I was born. Perhaps I knew it already at the age of seven. Then I went to school, and then to university, and what do you think? The more I studied, the more I came to realize that I was a ridiculous man. So as far as I was concerned, the more deeply I became involved in my university studies, the more its ultimate purpose seemed only to prove and make clear to me that

I was a ridiculous man. My life followed the same pattern as my studies. With every year the same awareness—that I looked like a ridiculous man in every respect—grew and strengthened within me. Everyone always laughed at me. But not one of them knew or suspected that if there was one person on earth who knew better than anyone that I was a ridiculous man, then that person was I myself; and this was just the thing that was most painful to me—that they didn't know it. But that was my own fault: I was always so proud that I could never have admitted this to anyone. This pride grew inside me over the years, and if there had ever come a time when I permitted myself to admit to someone that I was a ridiculous man, then I think that at once, that very same evening, I would have blown my head off with a revolver. Oh, the pains I suffered in my adolescence, thinking that I might give in and suddenly somehow confess to my comrades. But as I grew to manhood, for some reason I became calmer, even though with every year I became more and more aware of my awful quality. I say "for some reason" because even now I can't explain why. Perhaps it was because in my soul there kept growing a terrible ache caused by one thing that was infinitely beyond anything in my own self—namely, the conviction that everywhere on earth *nothing mattered*. I had sensed this long before, but the complete conviction somehow suddenly struck me in the last year. I suddenly sensed that, as far as I was concerned, *it wouldn't matter* whether the world existed or whether there were nothing anywhere. I began to sense and feel with all my being that *nothing existed around me*. At first I kept thinking that a good many things used to exist in the past; then I concluded that even in the past there had not been anything, but that for some reason it had only seemed as if there had been something. Little by little I became convinced that there would never be anything in the future either. At that point I suddenly stopped being angry at people and almost ceased to notice them. It's true that this showed itself even in the most trivial things: for instance, I'd be bumping into people as I was walking along the street. And this wasn't because I was deep in thought: what did I have to think about? At that point I'd stopped thinking altogether; it didn't matter to me. It would have been very well if I'd answered my questions; oh, but I hadn't answered a single one, and yet how many of them were there! But I began to feel *that nothing mattered*, and all the questions vanished.

And so, just after that, I discovered the truth. I discovered the truth last November, on the third of November to be precise, and I can recall every moment of my life since then. It happened on a gloomy evening, the gloomiest evening there could ever be. Some time after ten o'clock I was going back home, and I recall thinking specifically that there could be no gloomier time than this. Even in a physical sense. Rain had been pouring down all day, and it was the coldest and gloomiest rain, even a sort of menacing rain, I recall, with an open hostility toward people; and then, suddenly, towards eleven o'clock it stopped and a horrible dampness set in—damper and colder than when the rain was falling, and a kind of vapor rose from everything, from every stone on the pavement and from every side street, if you peered down to its farthest recesses. I suddenly imagined that if they were to shut off the gas everywhere it would be more cheerful, but one's heart was heavier with the lights on, because they illuminated everything. I had scarcely had any dinner that day and had spent the whole evening visiting an engineer, who had two of his friends there as well. I never opened my mouth the whole time and, I imagine, must have got on their nerves. They were discussing some controversial topic and suddenly even grew excited. But I could see that it really didn't matter to them and that they were excited just for form's sake. And suddenly I told them so: "Gentlemen," I said, "this really doesn't matter to you, does it?" They didn't take offense, and they all laughed at me. That was because I said what I did with no reproach and simply because it didn't matter to me. They saw very well that it didn't matter to me and were amused.

When the thought about the gaslight occurred to me out on the street, I looked up at the sky. The sky was awfully dark, but you could clearly make out some tattered clouds and bottomless black depths among them. Suddenly I noticed a tiny star in one of these depths and began looking at it intently. That was because this tiny star had given me an idea: I resolved that night to kill myself. I had made such a firm resolution even two months before, and despite my poverty I had bought a beautiful revolver and had loaded it that same day. Two months had passed, and it was still lying in my drawer; but so little did it matter to me that I wanted, at last, to catch a moment when it might matter, even just a little—for what reason, I don't know. And so it was that every night for these two months I came home thinking I would shoot myself. I kept waiting for the right moment. And now this tiny star had given me the idea, and I resolved that it would *definitely* happen on this very night. Why the tiny star gave me that idea I don't know.

And so, just as I was looking up at the sky, this little girl suddenly seized me by the elbow. The street was already deserted and there was scarcely a soul about. Off in the distance a cabbie was dozing in his droshky. The girl was about eight, wearing a kerchief and only a wretched little dress, and was soaked to the skin; but I particularly noticed her tattered boots, and remember them even now. The boots struck me particularly. She suddenly began tugging at my elbow and calling me. She wasn't weeping, but kept jerkily crying out some words that she couldn't pronounce clearly because she was all atremble from the cold. She was terrified of something and kept crying out desperately, "Mamma! Mamma!" I considered turning to face her, but said not a word and went on my way; but she ran after me and plucked at my sleeve, and I could hear in her voice the note that in very frightened children means despair. I know that sound. Although she didn't say so in words, I understood that her mother lay dying somewhere, or something had happened to them there and she had run out to call someone or find something to help her mother. But I didn't follow her and, on the contrary, suddenly got the notion to drive her away. First I told her that she should find a policeman. But she suddenly folded her tiny hands and, sobbing and choking, kept running alongside me and would not leave. At that point I stamped my foot and shouted at her. She only cried out, "Sir, oh sir! . . ." But suddenly she left me and rushed across the street: some passerby had appeared there, and she rushed over to him.

I went up to my fifth floor. I rent a place in a rooming house. My room is wretched and small, with a semicircular garret window. I have an oilcloth sofa, a table with some books on it, two chairs and a comfortable armchair, a very ancient thing but a "Voltaire one,"[9] for all that. I sat down, lit a candle, and fell to thinking. In the room next door, behind the partition, the row was still going on. They'd been at it for three days now. A retired captain lived there, and he had visitors—six or more good-for-nothings who were drinking vodka and playing faro with some old cards. Last night there had been a brawl, and I know that two of them spent a long time tearing at each other's hair. The landlady wanted to complain, but she's awfully afraid of the captain. The only other lodgers in our place are a short, skinny lady—an army officer's wife from out of town—with three small children who have already fallen ill since coming to live here. She and the children are deathly afraid of the captain and spend their nights trembling and crossing themselves; the smallest child was so afraid he had a fit of some kind. I know for certain that this captain sometimes stops passersby on Nevskii Prospect and begs money from them. They won't take him into the civil service, yet the strange thing is (and this is why I'm telling you this), the whole month the captain has been living here he hasn't caused me the least bit of annoyance. From the very beginning, of course, I shied away from any acquaintance with him, and in fact he was bored with me from our first meeting; but no matter how much shouting went on behind the partition and

---

9 A low-seated, high-backed armchair.

no matter how many of them there were, it didn't matter to me. I sit up all night long and, truly, I don't hear them—that's how well I'm able to ignore them. I never get to sleep until dawn, you see, and it's been that way for a year now. I sit by the table in my armchair all night long and do nothing. Books I read only during the day. I sit, not thinking about anything in particular, just like that; vague thoughts wander through my mind, and I let them flow as they please. A whole candle burns up during the night. I sat down quietly by the table, took out the revolver and put it down in front of me. I recall asking myself as I put it down, "Is this how it is to be?" And I answered myself absolutely affirmatively, "Yes, it is." That's to say, I'll shoot myself. I knew that I would certainly shoot myself that night, but how much longer I would go on sitting by the table—that I didn't know. And of course I would have shot myself had it not been for that little girl.

2

You see, even though it didn't matter to me, I could still feel pain, for instance. If someone were to strike me, I would feel pain. It was just the same way in a moral sense: if something very sad were to happen, I would feel pity, just as before, when things in life still did matter to me. I had felt pity earlier that evening: I would certainly have helped out a child. So why didn't I help the little girl? It was because of a thought that came to me then: when she was tugging at my sleeve and calling me a question suddenly arose in my mind, and I wasn't able to answer it. It was an idle question, but it made me angry. I got angry because if I had already decided that I would kill myself that same night, then nothing on earth ought to matter to me, now more than ever. Why was it, then, that I suddenly felt that I was not indifferent to everything and pitied the little girl? I recall that I felt a great deal of pity for her, to the point even of a strange pain, even an improbable pain, given my situation. Truly, I don't know how better to convey that fleeting sensation I had then, but the sensation continued at home as well, when I had taken my seat by the table, and I was very irritated, as I hadn't been for a long time. One train of thought followed another. It seemed clear that if I were a human being and not yet a nonentity—and until such time as I became a nonentity—was living, and accordingly could suffer, get angry, and feel shame for my actions. Granted. But if I were going to kill myself in two hours, say, then what should I care about this girl and about shame and about anything on earth? I was going to be transformed into a nonentity, an absolute nonentity. Could it be that the awareness of the fact that shortly I would *absolutely* cease to exist and that, accordingly, nothing else would exist—could that not have had the least influence either on the feeling of pity for the little girl or on the feeling of shame after the vile thing I had done? After all, that was the reason I had stamped my foot and shouted in a savage voice at the unfortunate child—that I could think "not only do I feel no pity but I can permit myself to commit some inhuman, vile deed because in two hours everything will be extinguished." Can you believe that this was why I shouted? Now I'm almost convinced of it. It seemed clear that from this point life and the world were dependent on me, as it were. I can even say that now the world had been created for mc alone, as it were: I'll shoot myself and the world will exist no longer, at least as far as I'm concerned. To say nothing of the possibility that, perhaps, nothing really would exist for anyone else after me and that as soon as my consciousness was extinguished, the whole world would be extinguished with it, like a mirage, like a product of my own consciousness alone; and it would be done away with because this entire world and all these people were, perhaps, nothing more than myself. I recall that as I sat there thinking this out, I gave all these new questions that were crowding into my mind one after the other an entirely different twist and conceived something quite new. For example, I suddenly had the following strange notion: suppose I had formerly lived on the moon or on Mars and had committed there the most disgraceful and dishonorable act one can imagine for which I had been defamed and dishonored to an extent one can imagine only in some dream or nightmare; and, if I had later found myself on earth, still with the awareness of what I had done on the other planet, and knew, as well, that I would never ever return there, then would I, as I looked from the earth to the moon, feel as if *it didn't matter*? Would I have felt shame for my act or not? These were idle, unnecessary questions, since the revolver was lying on the table before me, and I knew with all my being that it would certainly happen; yet they excited me and worked me into a frenzy. It seemed I could not die now without having first resolved something. In short, that little girl saved me because the questions led me to put off shooting myself. Meanwhile, everything began to quiet down in the captain's room: they finished their card game and were settling down to sleep, still grumbling and lazily abusing one another. And at this point I suddenly dropped off to sleep in my chair by the table, something that had never happened to me before. I didn't notice falling asleep at all. Dreams, as we know, are extraordinarily strange things: you'll have one that has an awful clarity, with all its details presented with lapidary precision, while in another you don't even notice how you swoop through time and space. Dreams, I think, are governed not by reason but desire, not by the head but the heart; and yet what crafty tricks my reason sometimes plays on me in dreams! Furthermore, some quite incomprehensible things happen to my reason in sleep. My brother, for instance, died five years ago. I sometimes dream of him: he takes part in my affairs; we are deeply involved with one another, yet throughout the dream I know and remember full well that my brother is dead and buried. How is it that I'm not amazed at the fact that even though he's dead, he's still right here beside me, concerning himself with my affairs? Why does my reason accept all this so completely? But enough. I'll get back to my dream. Yes, this is the dream I had then, my dream of the third of November. They tease me about it now, saying that it was only a dream, after all. But surely it doesn't matter whether it was a dream or not since this dream revealed the Truth to me. If once you've recognized the truth and have seen it, then you surely know that it is the truth and that there is not and cannot be any other, whether you are asleep or awake. Well, it was a dream—let it be so; yet I was going to put an end to this life which you make so much of, but my dream—oh, my dream revealed to me a new life, renewed, intense, and majestic!

Listen.

3

I said that I drifted off to sleep without noticing it and even went on mulling over those same matters, as it were. Suddenly I dreamed that I took up the revolver and, still sitting in my chair, was aiming it right at my heart—at my heart and not my head; earlier I had decided that I would definitely shoot myself in the head, in the right temple, to be specific. With the revolver pointed at my chest I hesitated for a second or two, and suddenly my candle, the table, and the wall before me began to move and sway. Quickly I fired.

In dreams you sometimes fall from a great height or are being stabbed or beaten, but you never feel any pain unless you somehow bump yourself against the bedpost; then you feel pain and almost always wake up. So it was in my dream: I felt no pain, but it seemed that after my shot everything within me was shaken, and suddenly everything went blank and there was an awful blackness all around me. I seemed to be blind and mute and was lying on my back, stretched out full-length on something hard, seeing nothing, and unable to make the least movement. All around me people were walking and shouting; the captain rumbled and the landlady screeched—and suddenly there was another quiet interval, and now I was being carried in a closed coffin.

And I could feel the coffin swaying and was thinking about that; and suddenly for the first time I was struck by the thought that I was dead, quite dead, and knew it without a doubt; I could not see and could not move, yet I could feel and think. But I quickly become resigned to that and, as usual in a dream, accepted the facts with no argument.

And so they were burying me. Everyone went away, and I was alone, completely alone. I made no move. Formerly, whenever I used to imagine what it would be like to be buried, the only sensation I would associate with the grave was cold and damp. And so it was now: I felt very cold, especially the tips of my toes; but I felt nothing more than that.

I lay there and, strangely enough, expected nothing, accepting without demur that a dead man had nothing to expect. But it was damp. I don't know how much time passed—an hour or a few days or many days. But suddenly a drop of water that had seeped through the lid of the coffin fell on my left eye, which was closed; a minute later there was another one, and a third minute later; and so it continued, a drop every minute. Deep indignation suddenly welled up in my heart, and suddenly I felt a physical pain there: "That's my wound," I thought, "it's the shot, there's a bullet there. . ." and the drops kept falling every minute, directly on my closed eyelid. And suddenly I called out—not with my voice, for I could not move, but with my whole being—to the One who governed all that was happening to me: "Whoever Thou may be, but if Thou art and if there does exist anything more rational than what is now coming to pass, then grant that it happen here as well. But if Thou art taking vengeance upon me for my unwise suicide, through the ugliness and absurdity of life after death, then know that no torment that might ever befall me could compare with the contempt that I shall always feel in silence, though it be through millions of years of martyrdom! . . ."

I cried out and fell silent. A profound silence continued for almost a whole minute, and one more drop of water even fell; but I knew, I knew and believed infinitely and unshakably that now everything must certainly change. And then suddenly my grave opened wide. I mean to say, I don't know whether all the earth had actually been dug away, but I was taken up by some dark and unfamiliar creature and we found ourselves in open space. I suddenly recovered my sight: it was the depths of night, and never ever had there been such darkness! We were flying through space, and the earth was already far behind us. I did not ask anything of the one who bore me; I waited, proud. I assured myself that I was not afraid and was dizzy with delight at the thought that I was not afraid. I don't recall how long we flew and can't even imagine it: everything happened as it always does in dreams, when one leaps through space and time and over the laws of existence, stopping only where one's heart longs to stop. I recall that I suddenly caught sight of one tiny star in the darkness. "Is that Sirius?" I asked, suddenly unable to hold back, for I had decided not to ask about anything. "No," answered the creature who bore me, "it is that same star you saw among the clouds when you were coming home." I knew that the face of the creature was in the likeness of a human. But, strangely enough, I did not like that creature and even felt a deep aversion toward it. I had been expecting complete nonexistence, and with that in mind had shot myself in the heart. And now I was in the hands of a creature which was not human, of course, but which *was*, which existed. "And so there is a life beyond the grave!" I thought, with the bizarre frivolity of dreams, but the real essence of my heart remained unchanged: "And if I must *be* once more," I thought, "and live again by someone else's intractable will, then I will not be vanquished and humiliated!"

"You know that I am afraid of you, and therefore you despise me," I said suddenly to my companion, unable to resist a humiliating question that held an admission and sensing the humiliation in my heart like a pinprick. He did not answer my question, but I suddenly sensed that I was not despised and that I was not being laughed at, that I was even being pitied, and that our journey had a goal, unknown and mysterious and concerning only me. Fear welled up in my heart. Something was passing from my silent companion to me, mutely but agonizingly, and it seemed to pierce to the core of my being. We were rushing through dark and unknown regions of space. I had long lost sight of the constellations familiar to me. I knew that there are such stars in the vastness of the heavens whose rays reach the earth only after thousands and millions of years. Perhaps we were already flying through these spaces. I was expecting something, in a terrible agony that gripped my heart. And suddenly I was shaken by a familiar and most nostalgic feeling: I suddenly caught sight of our sun! I knew that it could not be our sun that had given birth to *our* earth and that we were an infinite distance from our sun, but somehow I realized, with all my being, that this was just the same kind of sun as our own, its duplicate and twin. A sweet, welcoming feeling roused an ecstasy in my soul: the old, familiar power of the light, the same light that had given me life, made my heart respond and restored it, and I sensed life, the former life, for the first time since my burial.

"But if this is the sun, if this is exactly the same sun as ours," I cried, "then where is the earth?" And my companion pointed to a little star that glittered in the darkness with an emerald light. We were rushing directly toward it.

"And are such duplicates really possible in the universe? Is there really such a law of nature? . . . And if that is the earth over there, then is it really the same kind of earth as our own . . . just the same—unhappy, wretched, yet dear and eternally beloved, one that engenders as painful a love in its most ungrateful children as does our own?" I cried, trembling with irresistible, rapturous love for that once native earth I had abandoned. The image of the wretched little girl whom I had offended flitted before me.

"You shall see it all," answered my companion, and there was a kind of sorrow in his words.

But we were quickly drawing near the planet. I could see it seeming to grow in size; I could already make out the ocean, the outlines of Europe; and suddenly a strange feeling of some tremendous and sacred journey began to burn in my heart: "How can there be such a duplication, and why? I love—I can love only the earth I have left behind, which I have spattered with my blood when I, ungrateful wretch, extinguished my life with a bullet in my heart. But never, never did I cease to love that earth, and even on the night I parted with it I loved it, perhaps, more agonizingly than ever. Does suffering exist on this new earth? On our earth we can truly love only with suffering and only through suffering! We know not how to love in any other way, and know no other love. I want to suffer in order to love. This very instant I want, I long, to kiss and to water with my tears the one and only earth I have abandoned, and I do not want and do not accept life on any other! . . ."

But my companion had already left me. Suddenly, without really knowing how it happened, I was standing on this other earth in the sunny brightness of a day as lovely as paradise. I think I was on one of those islands that on our earth form part of the Greek archipelago, or somewhere on the mainland coast adjacent to that archipelago. Oh, it was all just the same as it is on our earth, but everything seemed to have a festive glow, as if some glorious and holy triumph had at last been achieved. The friendly emerald-green sea lapped quietly against the shore and kissed it with a love that was unmistakable, visible, almost conscious. Tall, beautiful trees stood in full splendor, and their countless little leaves—I'm convinced of it—welcomed me with their gentle, calming rustle and seemed to be whispering words of love. The meadow was ablaze with bright, fragrant flowers. Flocks of little birds wheeled through the air and landed unafraid on my shoulders and hands, beating joyfully at me with their dear little fluttering wings. And at last I met and came to know the people of this happy land. They came to me themselves, gathered around me, and kissed me. Children of the sun, children of their sun—and oh, how beautiful they were! Never on our earth have I seen such beauty in people. Perhaps only in our children of tenderest age could you find a distant, though pale reflection of this beauty. The eyes of these happy people shone with a clear light. Their faces radiated wisdom and a consciousness that had attained serenity, but their faces were happy: the voices and words of these people rang with childlike joy. Oh, at once, the moment I looked at these faces, I understood everything, everything! This was an earth that had not been defiled by sin; on it lived people who had not sinned, who lived in just such a paradise in which our fallen ancestors had once lived, according to the traditions of all of humanity, the only difference being that the entire earth here was one and the same paradise. These people, laughing joyously, crowded around and caressed me; they took me to their dwellings, and each one of them was anxious to comfort me. Oh, they did not question me about anything but seemed to know everything already and wanted quickly to banish suffering from my face.

4

Now, I'll say it once more: what would it matter if it had been only a dream! Still, the feeling of the love of these innocent and beautiful people has remained ever within me, and I feel that their love comes pouring down on me even now. I saw them myself, came to know them, and became convinced; I loved them and I suffered for them afterward. Oh, even then I realized at once that there were many things about them I would never understand; for instance, I, a modern Russian progressive and wretched inhabitant of Petersburg, found it inexplicable that they, who knew so much, had none of our science. But I soon realized that their knowledge was supplied and nourished by insights different from those on our earth and that their aspirations were also quite different. They had no desires and were content; they did not strive for knowledge of life as we strive to comprehend it, because their lives were complete. But their knowledge was more profound and more elevated than our science; for our science seeks to explain what life is and itself strives to comprehend it so as to teach others how to live, while they knew how to live even without science; I realized that, but could not understand their knowledge. They showed me their trees, and I could not understand the intensity of love with which they regarded these trees: it was just as though they were speaking to creatures like themselves. And, you know, I may not be wrong in saying that they spoke with them! Yes, they had found their language, and I am convinced that the trees understood them. They regarded the whole of nature in the same way—the animals, which lived peaceably with them and did not attack them, conquered by their love. they showed me the stars and told me something about them that I was unable to grasp, but I am convinced that they were able somehow to make contact with these heavenly stars, not only through thought but in some living way. Oh, these people did not strive to make me understand them, they loved me without that; and yet I knew that they would never understand me either, and therefore I scarcely ever spoke to them of our earth. I merely kissed the earth on which they lived, in their presence, and adored them wordlessly; and they saw this and let me adore them, unashamed that I was doing it because they themselves deeply loved me. They felt no pain for me when I, in tears, would kiss their feet, for in their hearts they joyously knew the strength of love with which they would return my feeling. At times I would ask myself in amazement how they managed never to offend a person like me and never to make me feel any jealousy or envy. Many times I asked myself how I, a braggart and liar, could refrain from speaking of the things I knew, things of which they, naturally, hadn't the least conception. How could I not want to astonish them with my knowledge, even if only out of love for them? They were as full of life and joy as children. They wandered through their magnificent groves and forests; they sang their beautiful songs; they ate but lightly, of the fruits of their trees, the honey of their forests, and the milk of their devoted animals. Acquiring food and clothing cost them little and easy toil. They loved and begot children, but never did I see in them the outbursts of cruel sensuality that befall almost everyone on our earth—each and every one—and serve as the single source of almost all the sins of our human race. They rejoiced in their newborn children as new participants in their bliss. There were no quarrels and jealousy among them, and they did not even understand what these things meant. Their children were the children of all because they all were part of one family. They had scarcely illnesses, although there was death; but their old people died peacefully, as if sinking into slumber, surrounded by people who had come to bid them farewell, blessing them, smiling at them, and departing life accompanied by the radiant smiles of others. I saw no grief or tears on these occasions, only a love that seemed to multiply to the point of rapture, but a rapture that was calm, contemplative, and complete. There was reason to think that they were able to keep in touch with their dead even after death and that the earthly union among them was not broken by death. They could scarcely understand me when I asked them about eternal life, but apparently they were so utterly convinced of it that it was not even a question for them. They had no temples, but they did have a kind of essential, living, and continuous union with the

Totality of the universe; they had no religion; instead they had a certain knowledge that when their earthly joy had fulfilled itself to its limits there would ensue—both for the living and for the dead—an even broader contact with the Totality of the universe. They awaited this moment joyfully but unhurriedly, not with painful longing but as if their hearts held a presentiment of it that they communicated to one another. Before going to sleep in the evenings they loved to sing in harmonious and melodious chorus. In these songs they expressed all the feelings the passing day had brought them; they sang praise to the day and bade it farewell. They sang praises to nature, the earth, the sea, the forests. They loved to compose songs to one another and heaped praises on each other like children; these were the simplest of songs, but they came from the heart and moved the heart. And not only their songs but, it seemed, their whole lives were devoted only to admiring one another. It was a kind of complete, all-encompassing devotion to one another. Yet some of their songs were solemn and ecstatic, and I could scarcely understand them at all. While understanding the words, I could never comprehend their full meaning. That remained inaccessible to my mind, as it were, yet my heart seemed more and more to grasp instinctively its essence. I often told them that I had had a presentiment of all this long ago, that all this joy and glory had affected me while still on our earth by evoking a longing that at times reached unbearable sorrow; that the dreams of my heart and the fancies of my mind had given me a presentiment of all of them and their glory; that on our earth I often could not look upon the setting sun without tears . . . That my hatred for the people of our earth was always touched with anguish: why could I not hate them without loving them? why could I not help but forgive them? And in my love for them there was anguish: why could I not love them without hating them? They listened, and I saw that they could not comprehend what I was telling them; but I did not regret telling them of this: I knew that they understood the full force of my anguish over those I had left behind. And, indeed, when they looked at me with their tender gaze so filled with love, when I sensed that in their presence my heart as well was becoming as innocent and as honest as theirs, then I was not sorry I could not understand them. The sensation of the fullness of life almost took my breath away, and I could only worship them in silence.

Oh, how everyone laughs in my face and tells me that it's impossible to dream all of these details I'm telling you here; they say that in my dream I saw or felt only some sensation that my own heart engendered in a fit of delirium, while I invented all the details after I woke up. And when I admitted that, perhaps, this is really how it was—Lord, how they laughed in my face and what entertainment I provided them! Oh, yes, of course, I was overcome only by the sensation of that dream, and it alone survived in my wounded and bleeding heart; yet the actual images and forms of my dream—I mean those things I actually saw during the very time of my dreaming—were so filled with harmony, were so filled with charm and beauty, and were so filled with truth, that when I awakened I was naturally unable to embody them in our feeble words, so they were bound to become blurred in my mind; and so I may very well have been unconsciously forced to invent some of the details afterward and, of course, I distorted them, especially in my passionate longing to express them in some way or other as quickly as possible. And yet; how can I not believe that all this happened? That it happened, perhaps, a thousand times better, more brightly and joyously than I am telling it? Let it be a dream, but all of this had to have happened. You know, I'll tell you a secret: this whole thing, perhaps, wasn't a dream at all! For at this point something happened, something so awfully true that it could not have been the product of a dream. Let's suppose that my heart did give birth to my dream; but could my heart alone have been able to give birth to that awful truth that befell me then? How could I alone have invented it? How could it have been a product of my heart's fancy? As if my petty heart and my frivolous, trivial mind could have risen to such a revelation of the truth! Oh, judge for yourselves: I've kept this from you until now, but now I shall tell you this truth as well. The fact is that I . . . I corrupted them all!

5

Yes, yes, it ended in my corrupting them all! How it could have happened I don't know, I don't remember clearly. The dream encompassed thousands of years and left me merely with a sense of the whole. I know only that the cause of their fall into sin was I. Like some filthy trichina, like some atom of the plague that infects entire countries, so I infected that whole happy earth which had been sinless until my coming. They learned to lie, they came to love falsehood and to know the beauty of the lie. Oh, it may well have begun innocently, with a joke, with a bit of flirtation or amorous play, or it may really have been from an atom, but this atom of falsehood penetrated their hearts and pleased them. And then it was not long before sensuality was born; sensuality gave birth to jealousy, jealousy to cruelty . . . Oh, I don't know, I can't remember, but soon—very soon—the first blood was shed: they were astonished and horrified and began to separate from one another and lose their unity. Alliances were formed, but now they were against one another. Recriminations and reproaches began. They came to know shame and elevated shame as a virtue. The concept of honor was born, and its banner was raised in each of the alliances. They began to abuse the animals, and the animals fled from them into the forests and became their enemies. There began a struggle for separation, for dissociation, for individuality, for "mine" and "thine." They began to speak in different languages. They tasted of sorrow and came to love it; they longed for suffering and said that Truth was attained only through suffering. At that point science made its appearance among them. When they had become wicked, they began to speak of brotherhood and humaneness and understood the meaning of these ideas. When they had become criminal, they invented justice and prescribed entire codes of law in order to maintain it; and to enforce these codes they set up a guillotine. They could scarcely remember what they had lost, and did not even want to believe that they had once been innocent and happy. They even laughed at the thought that they had once been happy and called it an idle fancy. They could not even imagine it in specific forms and images, yet the strange and marvelous thing was that though they had lost all faith in their former happiness and called it a fairy tale, they wanted so much to be innocent and happy again that, like children, they succumbed to the desires of their hearts and deified those desires, built temples and began to worship this idea of theirs, these "desires" of theirs, even while believing fully that these desires would never be fulfilled or achieved; still, they worshiped them in tears and bowed down to them. And yet, had it become possible for them to return to the innocent and happy state that they had lost, and should someone have suddenly shown it to them again and asked whether they wanted to return to it, they would certainly have refused. They told me: "We may be deceitful, wicked, and unjust; we *know* this and we lament it and torment ourselves over it; we inflict more punishment and torture on ourselves, perhaps, than will that merciful Judge who will weigh our sins and whose name we know not. But we have science, and with its help we shall again find the truth, but now we shall accept it consciously. Knowledge is higher than feelings, consciousness of life is higher than life. Science will give us true wisdom, wisdom will reveal the laws, and a knowledge of the laws of happiness is higher than happiness." That is what they said, and after saying it each one began to love himself more than he loved the others; and, indeed, they could not do otherwise. Each one became so jealous of his own individuality that he tried with all his might only to humiliate and belittle the individuality of others; and therein he saw the very purpose of his life. Slavery appeared, even voluntary slavery: the weak eagerly submitted to the strong merely so that the strong could help them crush those who were still weaker than they. Righteous men appeared, and they came to these people in tears and spoke to them of their arrogance, of their loss of measure and harmony, of their loss of shame. But the righteous men were mocked or stoned. Sacred blood was spilled on the porches of the temples. Then there appeared people who began trying to find some manner in which all might be united once again so that each, without ceasing to love himself more than everyone else, might at the same time not interfere with anyone else, so that they all might live in a harmonious society. Entire wars were waged for the sake of this idea. At the same time, all the warring parties believed that science, true wisdom, and a sense of self-preservation would at last compel humanity to unite in a harmonious and rational society; and so in the meantime, to speed the matter, the "wise" attempted as quickly as possible to annihilate all the "unwise" who did not understand their idea, so that the latter should not stand in the way of its triumph. But the sense of self-preservation began quickly to weaken; proud men and sensualists appeared who flatly demanded, "All or nothing." To achieve everything, they wanted they resorted to crime and, if that failed, to suicide. Religions appeared with a cult of nonexistence and self-destruction for the sake of eternal peace in nothingness. At last, these people tired of their senseless labor and suffering appeared on their faces; and they proclaimed that suffering was beauty, for in suffering alone was there thought. Their songs were hymns to suffering. I walked among them wringing my hands, and I wept over them, yet I loved them even more, perhaps, than I had before, when suffering had not yet been written on their faces, when they were innocent and so beautiful. I came to love the earth they had defiled even more than when it had been a paradise, solely because grief had made its appearance on it. Alas, I have always loved grief and sorrow, but only for myself, only for myself, while I wept over them in pity. I stretched out my arms to them, accusing, cursing, and despising myself in despair. I told them that I had done all this, I alone, and that it was I who had brought them corruption, contamination, and falsehood! I implored them to crucify me; I taught them how to make a cross. I could not, I did not have the strength to kill myself, but I wanted to suffer at their hands; I longed for suffering, I longed for my blood to be spilled to the last drop in these sufferings. But they only laughed at me and at last began to consider me a holy fool. They tried to defend me, saying that they had taken only that which they themselves desired and that everything that now was happening could not have been otherwise. At last they declared that I was becoming a danger to them and that they would put me into a madhouse if I did not keep silent. Then sorrow entered my soul with such force that my heart contracted and I felt that I would die, and then . . . well, and then I woke up.

It was already morning; I mean, it wasn't daylight, but it was about six o'clock. I awoke in my same armchair, my candle had already burned itself out; everyone in the captain's room was asleep, and all around there was a silence that is rare in our house. I at once jumped to my feet in extreme amazement; nothing like this had ever happened to me before, even so far as the little details were concerned: I had never fallen asleep this way in my armchair, for instance. Then suddenly, while I was standing there coming to my senses, I caught sight of my revolver lying in front of me, loaded and ready—but in an instant I pushed it away! Oh, now I wanted life, and more life! I raised my arms and called out to eternal Truth; or rather, I did not call out but wept; rapture, infinite rapture elevated my entire being. Yes, life and—preaching! I decided on preaching at that very moment and, of course, to go on preaching for my whole life! I am going off to preach; I want to preach, but what? The Truth, for I have beheld it, beheld it with my own eyes, beheld all its glory!

And since then I have been preaching! What's more, I love all those who laugh at me, love them more than all the others. Why that is so I do not know and cannot explain, but so be it. People say that even now I'm confused, and that if I'm so confused now, what will happen in the future? It's absolutely true: I am confused, and perhaps in the future it will be even worse. And of course I shall get confused a few times before I find out how to preach—I mean to say, which words to use, and which deeds, because this is a very difficult thing to do. Why, even now I see it all as clear as day, but listen: who doesn't get confused? And yet we're all moving toward the same thing, at least we're all striving toward one and the same thing, from the wise man to the meanest bandit, only we're traveling by different roads. It's an old truth, but here's what's new: even I can't be all that confused, you know. Because I've seen the truth, I've seen it and know that people can be beautiful and happy without losing their capacity to live on the earth. I don't want to believe, and can't believe, that evil is man's normal state. And yet they all just laugh about that belief of mine. But how can I not believe it: I have seen the truth—it was not some invention of the mind; I saw it, I truly saw it, and its *living image* has filled my soul forever. I saw it in such consummate wholeness that I cannot believe it could not exist among people. And so, how will I get confused? I'll stray from the path, of course, and do so more than once, and I may even speak with someone else's words, although not for long: the living image of what I saw will always be with me and will always correct and guide me. Oh, I am of good cheer and full of strength, and I am on my way, though the trip may take a thousand years. Do you know, at first I even wanted to hide the fact that I had corrupted them all, but that was a mistake—my first mistake already! But truth whispered to me that I was lying and preserved and guided me. But how we are to build paradise I do not know, because I do not have the words to express it. I lost the words after my dream. At least all the main words, the most essential ones. But never mind: I shall go off and shall keep talking tirelessly, for I have indeed seen it with my own eyes even though I do not know how to tell of what I saw. But this is just what the scoffers do not understand: "He had a dream," they say. "It's just ravings and hallucinations." Well! How wise is that? And they're so proud of themselves! A dream? What's a dream? Is our very life not a dream? I'll say even more: suppose this never comes to pass, suppose paradise never is realized (that much I do understand, after all)—well, I shall still go on preaching. And yet it could happen so easily: in a single day, in a single hour—everything could be established at once! The main thing is that you must love others as you love yourself; that's the main thing, and that's everything, and absolutely nothing more than that is needed: you'll at once find a way to build paradise. And yet this is only an old truth that has been read and repeated a billion times, but it has still not managed to take root! "Consciousness of life is higher than life, knowledge of the laws of happiness is higher than happiness"—that's what we need to fight against! And I shall. If only we all want it, everything will be arranged at once.

And I've found that little girl . . . And I shall go on! Yes, I shall go on!

The Defendant Kornilova Is Freed

On April 22 of this year the defendant Kornilova was tried a second time in the local circuit court by new judges and jurors.[10] The former verdict, pronounced last year, was quashed by the Senate on the grounds that the medical evidence produced was insufficient. Most of my readers, perhaps, remember this case well. A young stepmother (who at the time had still not reached the legal age of maturity), pregnant, angry at her husband who kept citing the example of his first wife to reproach her, and after a bitter quarrel with him, threw her six-year-old stepdaughter (her husband's daughter by his former wife) from a fourth-floor window, nearly forty feet above the ground; a near-miracle occurred: the girl was not dashed to pieces, she sustained no fractures or other injuries, and quickly regained consciousness; she is now alive and well. The young woman's bestial act took place within the context of her other

---

10 Dostoevskii discusses Kornilova's case in October 1876, 1.1, December 1876, 1.1, and again in December 1877, 1.1–1.6.

actions, so senseless and mysterious that one could not help but wonder whether was she acting in her right mind. Was she not, at least, in a state of temporary derangement caused by her pregnancy? When she woke up in the morning, after her husband had gone off to work, she let the child sleep; then she dressed the little girl and gave her some coffee. Then she opened the window and threw the girl out of it. Without even bothering to look down to see what had happened to the child, she closed the window, got dressed, and set off for the police station. There she stated what had happened and answered questions rudely and strangely. When she was told, several hours later, that the child had survived, she displayed neither joy nor chagrin and remarked, quite indifferently and cold-bloodedly, as if deep in thought, "She's got the lives of a cat." For nearly a month and a half thereafter, in the two prisons where she happened to be confined, she continued to be sullen, rude, and uncommunicative. And suddenly all these traits disappeared at once: through all the four months that remained until her delivery, and through all her trial and after it, the wardress of the women's section of the prison could not say enough in her praise: her disposition became stable, calm, kind, and serene. However, I have described all this before. In short, the former verdict was quashed, and then on April 22 a new verdict was rendered by which Kornilova was acquitted.

I was in the courtroom and took away many impressions. It is a pity, though, that I'm quite unable to pass them on to you and am literally compelled to limit myself merely to a very few words. Besides, I am discussing this case only because I wrote a good deal about it earlier and so I feel that it is not superfluous to inform the readers about its outcome. The trial went on twice as long as the former one. The composition of the jury was particularly noteworthy. A new witness was called—the wardress of the women's section of the prison. Her testimony about Kornilova's character weighed heavily in the defendant's favor. The testimony of Kornilova's husband was also quite remarkable: he spoke with extraordinary frankness and hid nothing—neither the quarrels nor the things he had done to abuse her; he spoke from the heart—directly and openly. He is still only a peasant, though it's true he's dressed in European style, reads books, and has a monthly salary of thirty rubles. Then came the assortment of expert witnesses, which was also remarkable. Six people were called, all of them well-known luminaries of medical science; five of them gave testimony: three of them declared unequivocally that the pathological condition peculiar to a pregnant woman *certainly could* have had an influence on the crime that had been committed in this instance. Only Dr. Florinskii was not in agreement with this opinion, but fortunately he is not a psychiatrist and his opinion was not given any particular weight.[11] The last to testify was our well-known psychiatrist, Diukov.[12] He spoke for almost an hour, answering questions from the prosecutor and the presiding judge. It's hard to imagine a more subtle understanding of the human soul and its pathological states. The wealth and variety of his extraordinarily interesting observations, culled over many years, was also striking. As for me, I listened to parts of the testimony of this expert with real admiration. The opinion of this expert witness was entirely in favor of the defendant; he stated *positively* and *conclusively* that, in his opinion, when the defendant had committed the crime she was in pathological mental state. The result was that the prosecutor himself, despite his formidable speech, withdrew the charge of premeditation, i.e., the most serious aspect of the indictment. Lustig, the defense attorney, also very skillfully countered several accusations; one of the most damaging ones—the stepmother's alleged long-standing hatred for her stepdaughter—he discredited entirely by clearly showing it was no more than backstairs gossip.[13] Then, after a lengthy speech by the presiding judge, the jury retired and in less than a quarter-hour brought back an acquittal, which produced near delight among the large crowd of spectators. Many crossed themselves, some congratulated each other and shook hands. The husband of the acquitted took her home that same evening, after ten o'clock; the happy woman entered her own home again after nearly a year's absence, with the impression of the enormous lesson she had learned, a lesson that would last for her whole life, and an impression of the clear intervention of the hand of God in this case—beginning with the miraculous sparing of the child, to take but one example.

To My Readers

I crave the forbearance of my readers. Last year, because of my summer trip to Ems to be treated for an illness, I was compelled to publish the July and August issues of my *Diary* as a single issue, on August 31, but of course with double the number of pages. This year, because of the increasingly serious nature of my illness, I am compelled to publish the May and June issues

---

11 Vasilii Markovich Florinskii (1833–99), physician; in the late 1870s and 1880s, professor of obstetrics and gynecology at Kazan University; author of a number of books on obstetrics.

12 Petr Andreevich Diukov (1834–99), psychiatrist and author of many articles on mental illness.

13 Vil'gel'm Iosifovich Lustig (1843–1915), prominent St. Petersburg lawyer.

together, under one cover, at the end of June or the very first part of July.[14] Then the July and August issues will be published again in August, as they were last year. Beginning in September, the *Diary* will again be published regularly on the last day of each month.

Leaving Petersburg on the advice of doctors, I wish to say that although the editorial office in Petersburg will be closed until September, all out-of-town subscribers and readers, as well as those living in the city, can, if need be, still contact the editorial office by mail, exactly as they did before. These letters will be promptly forwarded by the manager of the office, and each complaint, misunderstanding, etc., will, as in the past, be seen to as quickly as possible. All letters addressed to me will be promptly forwarded in the same manner. Quite specific arrangements for this have been made by the editor. Subscriptions will be maintained as before: new subscribers will be promptly taken care of.

I trust that those who read and subscribe to my *Writer's Diary* will excuse me. Given such unforeseen circumstances as the complication of an illness, it was difficult to anticipate all this. I know, on the basis of valid facts that until now the vast majority of my readers have treated me in a most benevolent manner. I venture to anticipate their kindness on this occasion as well.

---

14 During the early spring of 1877 Dostoevskii had a renewed series of attacks of epilepsy and was advised by doctors to spend the summer in quieter surroundings in the country. He also suffered from bronchial problems, which were growing increasingly severe. He and his family spent the summer in Kursk Province, southwest of Moscow, at the country estate of his brother-in-law, I. G. Snitkin.

Part Three

Themes

CHAPTER 7

Captivity, Free Will, and Utopia

A major idea that informs Dostoevskii's works from *Poor Folk* to *Brothers Karamazov* is individual freedom. He explores aspects of this idea through the connected themes of captivity, utopia, and free will. This chapter provides a sample of texts that engage with these themes as they develop across Dostoevskii's works, beginning with his imprisonment in Siberia and ending with universal brotherhood, the cornerstone of the writer's late philosophy. Utopia—the notion of an ideally constructed society—runs throughout Dostoevskii's works, and studying it reveals an intriguing dissonance: in *Notes from Underground* (1864) Dostoevskii rejects utopia as put forward by Chernyshevskii in *What Is to Be Done?* (1863), yet *Brothers Karamazov* (1880) ends on a triumphant utopian note with Alesha's joyful "Speech at the Stone."

One of the reasons for Dostoevskii's shift from supporting socialist utopian ideas in the 1840s and so ardently arguing against them in the 1860s was his decade of penal servitude and military service in the 1850s. During this time, Dostoevskii experienced significant deprivation and suffering, interacted with criminals, and learned to prize freedom in a more authentic way than in his earlier writings, which had been heavily influenced by romanticism and German idealist philosophy. James P. Scanlan's essay provides historical and biographical context for Dostoevskii's imprisonment, while the letter to Mikhail Dostoevskii reproduced here gives a first-hand account of the writer's experiences. In *Notes from the House of the Dead* (1862), Dostoevskii ruminates on freedom and human nature. In Siberia he also experienced a religious awakening, and in 1859 he returned to European Russia convicted in his faith.

After his return, Dostoevskii's fiction took on a more philosophical quality as he grappled with concepts like fate, free will, and human nature. In his response to the St. Petersburg Censorship Committee, as recounted by Joseph Frank, the link between captivity and free will is delineated in terms of a utopian paradise, which Dostoevskii compares to a prison. Extending this view, *Notes from Underground* sharply critiques *What Is to Be Done?*—which advocates a socialist paradise, a Crystal Palace where everyone is equal and everything is shared by all in equal parts. As Dostoevskii argues, such theories are naïve as they fail to take into account the complexity of the individual; as Underground Man observes, twice two equals four is rational, but sometimes twice two equals five is pleasant too.

Dostoevskii champions free will, the freedom to choose one's path, and views Chernyshevskian utopia as an ideal that reduces individual freedom. Utopia in Chernyshevskii's formulation is predicated on the idea that the individual will always choose what is in the group's best interest because it is also in his or her own best interest; *Notes from Underground*, on the other hand, presents a character who constantly acts against his own best interests, and demonstrates that this idea is fantasy. The freedom to act against one's own best interest if one wishes is an intrinsic part of free will, one of the key elements that gives us our humanity. Dostoevskii builds on this idea in *Crime and Punishment* (1866); Robert Louis Jackson's discussion of "Philosophical *Pro et Contra*" in the novel lends insight into the link between fate and free will, and how they can determine human action. In Jackson's analysis, determinism binds Raskol'nikov to his murderous path, entrapping him. Jackson concludes with a link to Christian love, which, as one outcome of *Crime and Punishment*, lays a cornerstone for the development of universal brotherhood.

Universal brotherhood—each person loving others as he loves himself—is biblically inspired, but in Dostoevskii's view, the concept presents a solution to Russia's (and the world's) problems of inequality, cruelty, deprivation, and suffering. Dostoevskii begins to articulate the idea in a piece called "Masha is lying on the table. Will I ever see Masha again?" Written on the occasion of his first wife's death as he was sitting vigil with her corpse, in this meditation on life, death, love, and sacrifice, Dostoevskii questions the New Testament mandate to love others as oneself because, as he writes, this is impossible. This work reveals Dostoevskii's strong faith, but also his questioning, which then gives rigor to his later novelistic experiments in philosophy.

Dostoevskii develops the concept of universal brotherhood across his later fiction—first with Sonia's strong faith in *Crime and Punishment*, then in Myshkin's compassion in *The Idiot*, through the utopian vision in "Dream of a Ridiculous Man" (in Chapter 6 of the present volume), and finally in Zosima's conviction and Alesha's foundational "Speech at the Stone" in *Brothers Karamazov*. Gary Saul Morson discusses the difficulty of reading "The Dream of a Ridiculous Man" as an affirmational utopia in his work on meta-utopia; in his discussion of *The Idiot* we also see this problem.

In *Brothers Karamazov*, the idea has its synthesis. Acts of compassion and kindness, and their transformative affect on others, demonstrate readily the potential for goodness that exists within each individual. As each person is transformed, as Father Zosima relates, paradise is possible on earth, that is, through individual kindnesses, the utopian universal brotherhood can be born. The key to success, in Dostoevskii's view, is that universal brotherhood accepts the unpredictability of human nature and free will, and, indeed, is built out of them. Robert Louis Jackson's analysis of the chorus in Alesha's "Speech at the Stone" ends this chapter on a joyful note.

Further Reading

Girard, René. *Resurrection from the Underground: Feodor Dostoevsky*. East Lansing: Michigan State University Press, 2012.

Kelly, Aileen. "Irony and Utopia in Herzen and Dostoevsky: *From the Other Shore* and *Diary of a Writer.*" *Russian Review* 50, no. 4 (October 1991): 397–416.

Morson, Gary Saul. *The Boundaries of Genre: Dostoevsky's* Diary of a Writer *and the Traditions of Literary Utopia*. Austin, TX: University of Texas Press, 1981.

Scanlan, James P. *Dostoevsky the Thinker*. Ithaca, NY: Cornell University Press, 2002.

Thompson, Diane Oenning. The Brothers Karamazov *and the Poetics of Memory*. Cambridge: Cambridge University Press, 2009.

Dostoevskii's Prison Years (2013)*

James P. Scanlan

*N*otes from the House of the Dead by Fedor Dostoevskii is appropriately classified as a novel, but its extraordinary appeal to readers both in Russia and abroad stems in part from the fact that the story it tells is as much auto-biography as fiction. The book might be called a thinly fictionalized memoir, chronicling a transformative period in the great Russian writer's life—the four years (1850–54) he spent as a political prisoner in a military labor camp in Siberia [. . .]

Even in prison, where writing materials were hard to come by, he had managed with the aid of a sympathetic doctor in the prison hospital to pro-cure and hide notebooks in which he jotted down his thoughts and obser-vations. In exile after 1854, he had more opportunity to write but at first was denied permission to publish. In 1856 permission was granted, and he proceeded to write and publish the stories "A Little Hero," "Uncle's Dream," and "The Village of Stepanchikovo and Its Inhabitants" while still in Siberian exile. In 1860, settled in St. Petersburg, he published the introduction and first chapter of Notes from the House of the Dead. Further installments fol-lowed through 1861 and the first half of 1862, with one chapter delayed by censorship until January 1863.

---

* From James P. Scanlan, "Dostoevsky's Prison Years," in Fyodor Dostoevsky, Notes from the House of the Dead, trans. Boris Jakim (Grand Rapids, MI: Wm. B. Eerdmans Publishing Company, 2013), vii–xii. Fyodor Dostoevsky, Notes from the House of the Dead © 2013. Wm. B. Eerdmans Publishing Company, Grand Rapids, MI. Reprinted by permission of the publisher; all rights reserved. The text has been excerpted with permission from the publisher.

Concerns about censorship no doubt played a role in Dostoevskii's decision to cast the memoir in the form of a novel rather than a firsthand, autobiographical account, but his public was not misled. Aside from fictionalizing his identity—he gives the name "Aleksandr Petrovich Gorianchikov" to the book's narrator and protagonist—and disguising the names of many of his fellow prisoners, he makes little effort to conceal the fact that the book, which was published under his own name, recounts his own experiences. Gorianchikov, like himself, is a former convict of noble birth and education and thus is separated by a huge social gulf from the largely peasant and illiterate mass of convicts, who in prison openly display their hatred of their former masters. Dates given in the text for some of Gorianchikov's experiences match the corresponding dates in Dostoevskii's biography. Perhaps most significant for the course of Dostoevskii's narrative is that Gorianchikov exhibits a distinctively Dostoevskian fascination with what he and his fellow convicts think and feel, and what makes them behave in the ways they do. One notable difference between the two is that Gorianchikov is said at the outset to be in prison not for political reasons but for murdering his wife. The careful reader, however, will note that in later chapters Dostoevskii appears to ignore this first characterization and treats Gorianchikov as if he were a political prisoner like himself.

The clear correspondence between the actual Dostoevskii and his literary stand-in allows us to consider *Notes from the House of the Dead* on two levels—as fiction and as nonfiction. More than a novel, it is also a historical document, a detailed account of the experiences of a victim of one of the most appalling practices of pre-1900 tsarist rule in Russia—the large-scale, forcible exile of criminals and other undesirables from European Russia to Siberia, the vast expanse of northern Asia that stretches across eight time zones from the Ural Mountains in the west to the Bering Strait in the east. Dostoevskii's gripping story is in fact one of the few detailed, firsthand accounts to come down to us of the workings of the Russian exile system in imperial Russia in the mid-nineteenth century, and the only one produced by a perceptive, gifted writer.

Having effectively conquered the Siberian lands by the middle of the seventeenth century, the Russian government began systematic efforts to colonize and Russify the sparsely populated region. A major objective was to provide manpower to exploit the rich natural resources found there—furs, salt, lead, silver, gold. Voluntary emigration from European Russia was encouraged, and many took part—not only fortune hunters but asylum seekers such as serfs, fugitive criminals, and members of dissident religious communities. But more than voluntary relocation was needed in order to bring enough workers to the more remote and inhospitable destinations such as the mines of eastern Siberia, where the climate was punishing and the labor arduous. Accordingly, already in the eighteenth century and still more actively in the nineteenth, the tsarist government employed forced emigration, which took two forms.

One form was the banishment, to designated locations in Siberia where labor was needed, of individuals who had committed no crime warranting a prison sentence but were deemed in some way socially troublesome or unworthy. Living as supposedly free citizens in their Siberian communities, these reluctant colonists had, of course, little choice but to accept whatever employment was available to them in the mines or other enterprises with which their communities were associated. Involuntary exile of this sort grew exponentially in the nineteenth century with the expansion of the practice of administrative exile (as opposed to judicial exile, which required a verdict of a court of law). Administrative exile allowed local authorities to consign individuals to exile virtually at will: a serf master could banish a trouble-making serf; a peasant community could rid itself of an unwanted member. Russian government statistics show that in the year 1885, for example, a total of 3,751 peasants were consigned to exile "on account of their generally bad character" by the village communes to which they belonged.[1]

The second type of involuntary exile—the type Dostoevskii experienced and describes in Notes from the House of the Dead—is the notorious Russian system of *katorga*, or penal servitude in exile. *Katorga* was reserved for legally convicted criminals and was spent in prisons or penal colonies typically connected with mining or other enterprises requiring hard labor; some, such as Dostoevskii's prison, were operated by the military and known for particularly harsh discipline. Crimes of every sort were represented in the prison population, from the most foul and violent to the purely political, with sentences supposedly appropriate to the seriousness of the crime. All the prisoners wore heavy leg-irons, day and night, and had half of their heads shorn for quick identification. Branding on the forehead or cheeks was sometimes employed (though not for the political prisoners) to indicate the type of crime committed.

Most of the prisoners were peasants or former soldiers of peasant origin, though the gentry was represented as well, particularly among the political prisoners. A few inmates, as Gorianchikov describes in Chapter Five of Part One, were not criminals at all: they were individuals sentenced to exile only, not to *katorga*, but who ended up in *katorga* nonetheless because each of them naively

---

1 George Kennan, *Siberia and the Exile System*, 2 vols. (New York: Century, 1891), vol. 1, 458.

(or drunkenly) accepted an attractive bribe from a scheming criminal to trade identities with him. Exact figures for the total number of victims of the *katorga* system through the nineteenth century are not available, but some estimates place the number at over one million persons.

The value of *Notes from the House of the Dead* as a historical record of the workings of the *katorga* system in the mid-nineteenth century is unparalleled with regard to such features of the prisoners' lives as their daily routines, their wretched diet, their unbelievably cramped and squalid quarters, their floggings and other cruel punishments, and their social interactions and diversions. At the same time, the limitations of the book as a historical record must also be acknowledged, for in many respects Dostoevskii's experiences in *katorga* were different from those of most of its victims.

In large part these differences stemmed from his status as a member of the Russian gentry—indeed, in his case the hereditary nobility. Gorianchikov comments at length on the resentment felt by the common criminals against their former masters for the privileges the latter enjoyed in the past and even in *katorga*, where they were spared some of its discomforts and deprivations. Ordinarily the gentry prisoners had access to funds with which they could buy additional food and pay willing fellow prisoners for what amounted to valet services, such as doing laundry, cooking, and preparing tea. Some also benefited from having relatives or friends in high places who could intercede on their behalf with prison authorities.

Surpassing all other advantages, however, was the fact that gentry prisoners such as Dostoevskii, like the Decembrists of the earlier nineteenth century before him, were typically assigned to prisons not in remote eastern Siberia but in western Siberia, and were provided with relatively comfortable transportation to their less-distant destinations. Dostoevskii's prison was in Omsk, on the border separating Siberia from Kazakhstan—east of the Ural Mountains, to be sure, but still many time zones short of the far east. His trip from St. Petersburg took eighteen days, traveling day and night. Already shackled in his leg-irons and accompanied by a guard, he was conveyed in an open sledge through January snow and ice, with only post stops for food and fresh horses [. . .]

Dostoevskii's detailed description of their life in prison came to the Russian public as a sensational expose of conditions that previously had been the subject of rumor only. Dostoevskii had worried that the authorities might not appreciate his revelation of the atrocities to which the inmates of the tsar's prisons were subjected, but to his surprise the censors were more interested in deterring crime than in concealing the inhumanity of the prisons. One censor even wondered whether life in *katorga* as Dostoevskii described it was sufficiently frightening to potential evildoers; some, the official suggested, might find it "alluring."[2]

The book was an instant bestseller in its original Russian, and as early as 1863 it was translated into German. Many other translations followed later, beginning with English in 1881, after Dostoevskii's great novels had drawn international attention to him. Together with the American reporter and explorer George Kennan's exhaustive and searing study *The Siberian Exile System* (first published serially in 1888–1889 and soon translated into all the major European languages, including Russian), *Notes from the House of the Dead* was one of the two publications most responsible for turning Russian and world public opinion against what Kennan called "one of the darkest blots upon the civilization of the nineteenth century."[3] In 1900, the tsarist government resolved to end the exile system and began dismantling it.

---

2   PSS 4:276.
3   Kennan, *Siberia and the Exile System*, vol. 2, 471.

Prison Life
Letter to Mikhail Dostoevskii,
February 22, 1854*

Fedor Dostoevskii

I had made acquaintance with convicts in Tobol'sk; at Omsk I settled myself down to live four years in common, with them. They are rough, angry, embittered men. Their hatred for the nobility is boundless; they regard all of us who belong to it with hostility and enmity. They would have devoured us if they only could. Judge then for yourself in what danger we stood, having to cohabit with these people for some years, eat with them, sleep by them, and with no possibility of complaining of the affronts which were constantly put upon us.

"You nobles have iron beaks; you have torn us to pieces. When you were masters, you injured the people, and now, when it's evil days with you, you want to be our brothers."

This theme was developed during four years. A hundred and fifty foes never wearied of persecuting us—it was their joy, their diversion, their pastime; our sole shield was our indifference and our moral superiority, which they were forced to recognize and respect; they were also impressed by our never yielding to their will. They were forever conscious that we stood above them. They had not the least idea of what our offence had been. We kept our own counsel about that, and so we could never come to understand one another; we had to let the whole of the vindictiveness, the whole of the hatred, that they cherish against the nobility, flow over us. We had a very bad time there. A military prison is

---

* From *Letters of Fyodor Michailovitch Dostoyevsky to His Family and Friends*, trans. Ethel Colburn Mayne (New York: The Macmillan Company, 1917), 59–62.

much worse than the ordinary ones. I spent the whole four years behind dungeon walls, and only left the prison when I was taken on "hard labor." The labor was hard, though not always; sometimes in bad weather, in rain, or in winter during the unendurable frosts, my strength would forsake me. Once l had to spend four hours at a piece of extra work, and in such frost that the quicksilver froze; it was perhaps forty degrees below zero. One of my feet was frostbitten. We all lived together in one barrack-room. Imagine an old, crazy wooden building that should long ago have been broken up as useless. In the summer it is unbearably hot, in the winter unbearably cold. All the boards are rotten. On the ground filth lies an inch thick; every instant one is in danger of slipping and coming down. The small windows are so frozen over that even by day one can hardly read. The ice on the panes is three inches thick. The ceilings drip; there are drafts everywhere. We are packed like herrings in a barrel. The stove is heated with six logs of wood, but the room is so cold that the ice never once thaws; the atmosphere is unbearable—and so through all the winter long. In the same room, the prisoners wash their linen, and thus make the place so wet that one scarcely dares to move. From twilight till morning we are forbidden to leave the barrack-room; the doors are barricaded; in the anteroom a great wooden trough for the calls of nature is placed; this makes one almost unable to breathe. All the prisoners stink like pigs; they say that they can't help it, for they must live, and are but men. We slept upon bare boards; each man was allowed one pillow only. We covered ourselves with short sheepskins, and our feet were outside the covering all the time. It was thus that we froze night after night. Fleas, lice, and other vermin by the bushel. In the winter we got thin sheepskins to wear, which didn't keep us warm at all, and boots with short legs; thus equipped, we had to go out in the frost.

To eat we got bread and cabbage soup: the soup should, by the regulations, have contained a quarter pound of meat per head; but they put in sausage meat, and so I never came across a piece of genuine flesh. On feast-days we got porridge, but with scarcely any butter. On fast-days—cabbage and nothing else. My stomach went utterly to pieces, and I suffered tortures from indigestion.

From all this you call see for yourself that one couldn't live there at all without money; if I had none, I should most assuredly have perished; no one could endure such a life. But every convict does some sort of work and sells it, thus earning every single one of them, a few pence. I often drank tea and bought myself a piece of meat; it was my salvation. It was quite impossible to do without smoking, for otherwise the stench would have choked one. All these things were done behind the backs of the officials.

I was often in hospital. My nerves were so shattered that I had some epileptic fits—however, that was not very often. I have rheumatism in my legs now, too. But except for that, I feel right well. Add to all these discomforts, the fact that it was almost impossible to get one's self a book, and that when I did get one, I had to read it on the sly; that all around me was incessant malignity, turbulence, and quarreling; then perpetual espionage, and the impossibility of ever being alone for even an instant— and so without variation for four long years: you'll believe me when I tell you that I was not happy.

The Prison from *Notes from the House of the Dead* (1862)*

Our prison stood at the edge of the fortress grounds, close to the fortress wall. One would sometimes, through a chink in the fence, take a peep into God's world to try and see something; but one could see only a strip of the sky and the high earthen wall overgrown with coarse weeds, and on the wall sentinels pacing up and down day and night. And then one would think that there are long years before one, and that one will go on coming to peep through the chink in the same way, and will see the same wall the same sentinels and the same little strip of sky, not the sky that stood over the prison, but a free, far away sky. Imagine a large courtyard, two hundred paces long and a hundred and fifty wide, in the form of an irregular hexagon, all shut in by a paling, that is, a fence of high posts stuck deeply into the earth, touching one another, strengthened by cross-way planks and pointed at the top; this was the outer fence of the prison. On one side of the fence there is a strong gate, always closed, always, day and night, guarded by sentinels; it is opened on occasion to let us out to work. Outside that gate is the world of light and freedom, where men live like the rest of mankind. But those living on this side of the fence picture that world as some unattainable fairyland. Here there is a world apart, unlike everything else, with laws of its own, its own dress, its own manners and customs, and here is the house of the living dead—life as nowhere else and a people apart. It is this corner apart that I am going to describe.

---

* From *The House of the Dead*, trans. Constance Garnett (New York: Macmillan, 1915), 5–6.

The Eagle from
Notes from the House of the Dead (1862)*

Fedor Dostoevskii

W̶e had for some time in the prison an eagle, one of the small eagles of the steppes. Someone brought him into the prison, wounded and exhausted. All the prisoners crowded round him; he could not fly; his right wing hung down on the ground, one leg was dislocated. I remember how fiercely he glared at us, looking about him at the inquisitive crowd, and opened his crooked beak, prepared to sell his life dearly. When they had looked at him long enough and were beginning to disperse, he hopped limping on one leg and fluttering his uninjured wing to the furthest end of the prison yard, where he took refuge in a corner right under the fence. He remained with us for three months, and all that time would not come out of his corner. At first the convicts often went to look at him and used to set the dog at him. Sharik would fly at him furiously, but was evidently afraid to get too near. This greatly diverted the convicts. "Savage creature! He'll never give in!" they used to say. Later Sharik began cruelly ill-treating him. He got over his fear, and when they set him on the eagle he learnt to catch him by his injured wing. The eagle vigorously defended himself with his beak, and, huddled in his corner, he looked fiercely and proudly like a wounded king at the inquisitive crowd who came to stare at him.

At last every one was tired of him; every one forgot him, abandoned him, yet every day there were pieces of fresh meat and a broken pot of water near

---

* From *The House of the Dead*, trans. Constance Garnett (New York: Macmillan, 1915), 5–6.

him. So some one was looking after him. At first he would not eat, and ate nothing for several days; at last he began taking food, but he would never take it from anyone's hand or in the presence of people. It happened that I watched him more than once. Seeing no one and thinking that he was alone he sometimes ventured to come a little way out of his corner and limped a distance of twelve paces along the fence, then he went back and then went out again as though he were taking exercise. Seeing me he hastened back to his corner, limping and hopping, and throwing back his head, opening his beak, with his feathers ruffled, at once prepared for battle. None of my caresses could soften him; he pecked and struggled, would not take meat from me, and all the time I was near him he used to stare intently in my face with his savage piercing eyes. Fierce and solitary he awaited death, mistrustful and hostile to all. At last the convicts seemed to remember him, and though no one had mentioned him, or done anything for him for two months, everyone seemed suddenly to feel sympathy for him. They said that they must take the eagle out. "Let him die if he must, but not in prison," they said.

"To be sure, he is a free, fierce bird, you can't get him used to prison," others agreed.

"He's not like us, it seems," added some one.

"That's a silly thing to say. He's a bird and we are men, aren't we?"

"The eagle is the king of the forest, brothers," began Skuratov but this time they did not listen to him.

One day after dinner when the drum had just sounded for us to go to work, they took the eagle, holding his beak, for he began fighting savagely, and carried him out of the prison. We got to the rampart. The twelve men of the party were eagerly curious to see where the eagle would go. Strange to say, they all seemed pleased as though they, too, had won a share of freedom.

"See, the cur, one does something for his good, and he keeps biting one," said the convict who was carrying him, looking at the fierce bird almost with affection.

"Let him go, Mikitka!"

"[. . .] Give him freedom, freedom full and free!"

He threw the eagle from the rampart into the plain. It was a cold gloomy day in late autumn, the wind was whistling over the bare plain and rustling in the yellow, withered, tussocky grass of the steppes. The eagle went off in a straight line, fluttering his injured wing, as though in haste to get away from us anywhere. With curiosity the convicts watched his head flitting through the grass.

"Look at him!" said one dreamily. "He doesn't look round!" added another. "He hasn't looked round once, lads, he just runs off!"

"Did you expect him to come back to say thank you?" observed a third.

"Ah to be sure it's freedom. It's freedom he sniffs."

"You can't see him now, mates . . ."

"What are you standing for? March!" shouted the guards, and we all trudged on to work in silence . . .

Dostoevskii Responds to the Censorship Committee (1986)*

Joseph Frank

The first chapter cleared the censorship without any trouble. The second, however, did run into a snag—but not at all of the kind that Dostoevskii had anticipated. It was not, as he had feared, that his account of prison conditions might be considered too harsh; rather, he was accused of painting them in such rosy colors that some enticing details might positively prove an *incitement* to crime. "Individuals who are not morally developed," declared the worried president of the St. Petersburg Censorship Committee, "and whom only the rigor of punishment restrain from crime ... might conclude from the humanity of the actions of the government that serious crimes are punished by the law only in a feeble fashion."[1] Such an outlandish opinion may appear to be merely another of those countless idiocies that often turn the history of tsarist censorship into a black comedy; but a brief look at Dostoevskii's pages will show that, in this instance, there was some justification for the response. Early in the second chapter, for example, we come across the following passage: "My first impression on entering the prison was most revolting, and yet

---

* From Joseph Frank, *Dostoevsky: The Stir of Liberation, 1860–1865* (Princeton, NJ: Princeton University Press, 1986), 29–31. The text has been excerpted and some notes have been removed. Republished with permission of Princeton University Press, from *Dostoevsky: The Stir of Liberation, 1860–1865*, Joseph Frank © 1986.

1 F. M. Dostoevskii, *Stat'i i materialy*, ed. A. S. Dolinin, 2 vols. (Moscow-Leningrad: Mysl', 1922–1925), vol. 1, 361.

strange to say it seemed to me that life in prison was much easier than on the journey I had fancied it would be. Though the prisoners wore fetters, they walked freely about the prison, swore, sang songs, did work on their own account, smoked, even drank vodka (though very few of them), and at night some of them played cards. The labor, for instance, seemed to me by no means so hard, so *penal*, and only long afterwards I realized that the hardness, the penal character of the work lay not so much in its being difficult and uninterrupted as in its being *compulsory*, obligatory, enforced. The peasant in freedom works, I dare say, incomparably harder [. . .]"[2] Dostoevskii also remarks that "the food too seemed to me fairly sufficient," and adds that "our bread was particularly nice, and was celebrated throughout the town."[3]

Such words hardly portray prison life as very forbidding; and the Censorship Committee was not entirely misguided in believing that to a Russian peasant, living under the heel of his landowner and on the edge of destitution, it might even sound very attractive. Of course the possibility of Dostoevskii's pages ever reaching such a reader (even assuming he was literate) was extremely remote—as Dostoevskii hastened to point out in a letter to the president of the committee, Baron Medem. *The Russian World*, he explained, even though a weekly, "was a journal intended primarily for the more or less educated classes and not for the masses [. . .]" (The Baron had expressed the opinion that Dostoevskii's prison opus might be more suitable for a less easily accessible monthly.) Dostoevskii, though, did not content himself only with such general reassurances; he decided to write a supplement that could be inserted into the chapter to allay any further doubts: "If the reason for the refusal to allow my article to be printed was the fear that it could serve to create, among the people, a distorted impression of prison life, so now the article [with the supplement] has the goal of creating the impression that, regardless of any alleviations in the fate of the convicts made by the government—the prison camp [*katorga*] does not cease to be a moral torture, which automatically and inescapably punishes crime.[4]

As it turned out, the misgivings of the St. Petersburg Censorship Committee were not shared by the Central Censorship Authority, and Dostoevskii's chapter was approved two months later in its original form. Nothing further was said about the proposed supplement, which was

---

2 PSS 4:19–20.

3 Ibid., 4:22.

4 *Pis'ma* 1: 299–300; September 20, 1860.

dutifully deposited in the capacious files of the censorship administration and remained there undisturbed for over sixty years until unearthed by A. S. Dolinin in 1922. Dostoevskii never used it in subsequent editions of his book for reasons that can only be surmised. The fragment may have been too intrusive an authorial statement, too much of a break in the tonal impersonality that he wished to maintain; but this only makes it all the more valuable as a clue to what had now become one of Dostoevskii's major themes—a theme that would soon occupy a crucially central place in his creations of the early 1860s.

The supplement begins by squarely confronting the objections raised by the censorship and assimilating them into the text. "In a word," Dostoevskii writes, "a total, terrible, genuine torment reigned in the camp without ceasing. And yet (this is exactly what I wish to say) to a superficial observer, or some fine gentleman, at first sight the life of a convict may sometimes seem agreeable. 'But my God!'—he says—'just look at them: there are some (who doesn't know it?) who have never eaten white bread, and who didn't even know that such delicious bread existed in the world. And now, look at what kind of bread he is fed—he, a worthless rascal, a robber! Look at him: how he looks around, how he walks! Yes, he doesn't give a rap for anybody even though he is in shackles! How do you like that!—he's smoking a pipe; and what's that? Cards!!! Bah, a drunk! So he can drink hard liquor in prison camp?! Some punishment!!!' This is what, at first sight, someone coming from the outside will say, perhaps a well-intentioned and kind person . . ."[5]

After dramatizing such a possible reaction, Dostoevskii suddenly confronts this shocked outside observer with a question. Why, if life in the prison camp is so apparently agreeable, are the convicts ready to exchange it at any moment for one of hardship and suffering, for a hazardous and grueling existence as fugitives on the run in the forests and steppes of the Siberian wilderness? The answer is given in a passage that, more powerfully than anything Dostoevskii has written so far, expresses the essence of what he had learned in the house of the dead about the human spirit:

> What is bread? They [the convicts] eat bread to live, but they have no life! The genuine, the real, the most important is lacking, and the convict knows that he will never have it; or he will have it, if you like, but when? . . . It's as if the promise is made only as a joke . . .

---

5 PSS 4:250.

Try an experiment and build a palace. Fit it out with marble, pictures, gold, birds of paradise, hanging gardens, all sorts of things . . . And step inside. Well, it may be that you would never wish to leave. Perhaps, in actual fact, you would never leave. Everything is there! "Let well enough alone!" But suddenly—a trifle! Your castle is surrounded by walls, and you are told: "Everything is yours! Enjoy yourself! Only, don't take a step outside!" And believe me, in that instant you will wish to quit your paradise and step over the wall. Even more! All this luxury, all this plenitude will only sharpen your suffering. You will even feel insulted as a result of all this luxury . . . Yes, only one thing is missing: a bit of liberty! a bit of liberty and a bit of freedom.[6]

This remarkable passage reveals, in the first place, an increasingly important trait of Dostoevskii's literary imagination: his tendency to invent an extreme situation, an end-of-the-line set of circumstances, in which he places a character in order to bring out the appropriate moral-psychological reaction that he wishes to exemplify. Clearly, too, we are here at the core of what, just a few years later, will become the underground man's hysterical defense of the irrepressible and indestructible need of the human spirit to maintain the sense of its own freedom—his preference for suffering, if need be, rather than for a life of plenitude in a Socialist Utopia in which such freedom would be eliminated as a matter of principle. Shortly after leaving prison camp, Dostoevskii had compared his years there to living in a world of "compulsory communism";[7] and such words indicate how spontaneously he had identified prison-camp conditions with those that might result if some of the Utopian social worlds dreamed of by the radicals were ever realized in practice. In addition, as if by design, the very latest mutation of Russian radical thought had taken a form which irrefutably confirmed Dostoevskii's instinctive association between the intolerable lack of personal freedom in the prison-camp world and the "scientific" ideas of the Russian Socialists.

---

6 Ibid.
7 *Pis'ma*, 1: 299–300; September 20, 1860.

Vera Pavlovna's Fourth Dream from *What Is to Be Done?* (1863)*

Nikolai Chernyshevskii

And Vera Pavlovna dreams a dream [...]
The cornfield shines with golden hues. The meadow is decked with flowers; hundreds, thousands of blossoms are waving on the copse encircling the meadow, and the forest which rises behind the copse grows green, and whispers and gleams with flowers [...] Little birds are flying from twig to twig, and thousands of voices come forth from the branches with the fragrance; and beyond [...] are other cornfields shining in gold, other meadows decked with flowers, other copses thick with blossoms, stretching away to the distant mountains [...] gleaming in the sun, and on their summits, here and there, bright, silvery, golden, purple, translucent clouds, changing and casting on the horizon their brilliant blue shadows; the sun mounts on high; it rejoices, and nature rejoices [...] a song of joy and tenderness pours forth; of love and goodness from the heart: "Oh, earth! Oh, sun! Oh, happiness! Oh, joy! Oh, love! Oh, love so golden-beautiful, like morning clouds on yonder heights!["] [...]

At the foot of the mountain, at the edge of the forest, amid the blooming copse, surrounded by lofty trees, a palace is built [...]

An edifice; an enormous, enormous edifice, such as can be seen only in the largest capitals—or, no, at the present time there is none such in the world.

---

* Extracts from Nickolay Gavrilovich Chernyshevsky, *A Vital Question: or, What Is to Be Done?*, trans. Nathan Haskell Dole and S. S. Skidelsky (New York: Crowell and Co., 1886).

It stands amid fields of grain, meadows, gardens, and groves. The fields of grain—this is our grain —they are not such as we have now, but rich, rich, abundant, abundant. Is it wheat? Who ever saw such heads? Who ever saw such grain? Only in forcing-houses is it possible to make such heads of wheat, such royal grain! The meadows are our meadows; but such flowers as these are now found only in flower gardens. Orchards are full of lemon-trees, oranges, peaches, and apricots. How can they grow in the open air? [. . .] But this edifice! what is it? What style of architecture? There is nothing like it now; no, but there is one that points toward it,—the palace which stands on Sydenham Hill,[1] built of cast-iron and glass—cast-iron and glass, and that is all. No, not all; that is only the integument of an edifice,—the outside walls. [Inside this palace] is a real house, a tremendous house! This integument of cast-iron and glass only covers it as by a sheath [. . .] How simple is the architecture of the inward house! [. . .]

But how rich everything is! Everywhere is aluminum [. . .] and all the spaces between the windows are adorned by large mirrors. And what carpets on the floors! Here in this parlor half of the floor is bare, and so you can see that it is made of aluminum [. . .] Here children are playing, and together with them their elders; and here in this other hall the floor is also bare, for the dancers. And everywhere are tropical trees and flowers; the whole house is a large winter garden."

But who lives in this house, which is more magnificent than palaces? "Here live many, very many. Come, we will see." [. . .]

The groups, which are working in the fields, are almost all singing. What work are they doing? *Ah*, it is harvest time. They are getting in the grain. How quick the work goes on! But how can it help going on quickly, and how can they help singing? Almost all the work is done by machines, which are reaping and binding the sheaves, and carrying them away. The men have scarcely more to do than look on, drive and manage the machines, and how well everything is arranged for them! It is a hot day, but they of course dont mind it. Over that part of the field where they are working is stretched a huge awning; as the work advances, this also moves. What a fine shadow they have manufactured! How can they help working quickly and gaily? How can they help singing? In such a way I too would become a harvest hand [. . .]

"Are these really our people? Is this really our country? I heard their song; they speak Russian."

---

1 EDS: Here Chernyshevskii refers to the Crystal Palace, the centerpiece of the Great Exhibition held in London in 1851. The structure was moved from Hyde Park to Sydenham in 1854.

"Yes, you see not far from here is a river —it is the Oka; these people belong to us; for when I am with you I am a Russian!" [...]

"Remember your shop, your sewing union. Did you have great means? Did you have more than others? [...] And yet your seamstresses have tenfold more conveniences, twenty-fold more happiness in life, and they experience a hundred-fold less unpleasantness than others with such small means as you had. You yourself have proved that even in your time people can live very comfortably. It is only necessary to be reasonable, to make a good start, to know how to use your moans to the best advantage [...] Now go and see a little more carefully how these people are living some time after they began to understand what you understood long ago [...]"

They enter a house; again the same sort of enormous, magnificent parlors. A party is in progress, full of gaiety and joy. It is three hours since sunset; it is the very tide of joy. How bright the parlor is lighted! With what? no candelabra are to be seen anywhere, nor gas-jets. *Ah*! it is from here—in the rotunda of the hall is a great pane through which the light falls; of course it must be such—just like sunlight, white, bright, and soft; this is the electric light. There are a thousand people in the hall, but there is room enough for thrice as many [...]

This evening is an everyday, ordinary evening; they dance and enjoy themselves every evening in this way. But did I ever see such energetic joy? And how can their joy help having an energy unknown to ours? They work well in the morning. Whoever has not worked enough does not give his nervous system the zest, and so cannot feel the fullness of the enjoyment. And even now the happiness of the common people, if by chance they succeed in living happy, is more intense, keen, and fresh than ours; but the chances for our common people to be happy are very poor. But here the means of happiness are richer than for us; and the happiness of our common people is disturbed by the remembrance of the inconveniences and deprivations, misfortunes and sufferings in the past, and by the anticipation of similar things to come. Their happiness is a transitory forgetfulness of want and woe. But can want and woe be absolutely forgotten? Do not the sands of the desert spread? Do not the miasmas of the swamp bring contagion upon the small plan of the good land, which may have good air between the desert and the swamp?

But here there are no remembrances, no dangers of want and woe; there are only remembrances of free labor with full satisfaction, of abundance, of good, and of enjoyment. Here the expectations of the time to come are the same. What a comparison! And again, the nerves only of our working people are strong, and therefore they are able to endure a great deal of enjoyment; but they are coarse, obtuse; but here the nerves are strong as those of our laborers, and developed, susceptible, just as with us. The preparation for enjoyment, a healthy, keen thirst for it, such as none of our day have, such as is given only by perfect and physical labor, are combined in people here with all the delicacy of sense such as we have. They have all our mental culture together with the physical development of our strong working people. It is comprehensible that their enjoyment, their pleasure, their passions are more lively, keener, wider, and sweeter than with us. Happy people! [...]

"[...] You shall see that every happiness here is suited to every one's special faculty. All live here in the way that it is best for each to live; there is a full volition, a free volition for every one here.

"What you have been shown here will not soon reach its full development as you have just seen it. A good many generations will pass before your presentiment of it will be realized [...] you know the future. It is bright, it is beautiful. Tell everybody. Here is what is to be! The future is bright and beautiful. Love it! Seek to reach it! Work for it! Bring it nearer to men! Transfer from it into the present whatever yon may be able to transfer. Your life will be bright, beautiful, rich with happiness and enjoyment, in proportion as you are able to transfer into it the things of the future. Strive to reach it! Work for it! Bring it nearer to man. Transfer from it into the present all that you are able to transfer."

The Prison of Utopia (1986)*

Joseph Frank

For the Dostoevskii who had just written *House of the Dead* and *Winter Notes*, Chernyshevskii's novel, with its touchingly naive faith in Utilitarian reason, could hardly have been felt except as a direct challenge. And the challenge was all the more provoking because, in the famous fourth dream of Vera Pavlovna, one of Dostoevskii's own key symbols is used with a significance directly opposed to his interpretation. In this climactic passage, Chernyshevskii brushes in a tableau of the evolution of humanity in the pseudo-epical style used by French Social Romantics like Ballanche and Lamennais at the beginning of the century—an evolution that culminates in the advent of the Socialist Utopia. Not surprisingly, this Utopia turns out to resemble the life that Fourier had imagined for his ideal phalanstery; and it would certainly have brought back for Dostoevskii memories of his days in the Petrashevskii circle, where Fourier's ideas had been passionately revered and debated in an atmosphere of candid exaltation. Even then, however, the details of the Fourierist blueprint for the future had seemed to him rather ridiculous, and he had agreed with his friend Valerian Maikov that the phalanstery hardly left any leeway for the freedom of the individual.[1] Fourteen years later—and what years for Dostoevskii and Russia!—the resurgence of such fantasies could only have appeared to him as the height of absurdity. Once again he was confronted with this dream image of a future in which man had completely conquered nature, and established a way

---

* From Joseph Frank, "The Prison of Utopia," in *Dostoevsky: The Stir of Liberation, 1860–1865* (Princeton, NJ: Princeton University Press, 1986), 288–89. Some notes have been excised. Republished with permission of Princeton University Press, from *Dostoevsky: The Stir of Liberation, 1860–1865*, Joseph Frank © 1986.

1 Joseph Frank, *Dostoevsky: The Seeds of Revolt, 1821–1849* (Princeton: Princeton University Press, 1976), 252–56.

of life allowing all desires to be freely and completely satisfied. No gap exists in this world between every appetite and its satisfaction; all conflict, all unhappiness, all inner striving and spiritual agitation have totally vanished. This is the literal end of history, whose attainment marks the final stasis of mankind in an unending round of pleasure and gratification. For Dostoevskii, the ideal of such a world immediately called up images of Greco-Roman decadence and the inevitable growth of the most perverse passions in an effort to escape from the sheer boredom of total satiation.

To make matters worse, Chernyshevskii had selected as an icon of this glorious world of fulfillment the Crystal Palace of the London World's Fair— precisely the same edifice that Dostoevskii had seen as the monstrous incarnation of modem materialism, the contemporary version of the flesh goddess Baal. But, to Chernyshevskii's bedazzled eyes, this structure represented the first hint of what would become the gleaming visual embodiment of the Socialist Utopia of the future, the manifest goal of all human aspirations [...]

The "palace that stands on Sydenham Hill," as everyone knew, was the Crystal Palace, which Chernyshevskii had probably visited on his secret trip to London to consult with Herzen, and which, in any event, he had written about sight unseen in 1854. In Chernyshevskii's pages, then, Dostoevskii once again encountered all the old Utopian dreams of the 1840s with which he was so familiar, now allied with the new faith in Utilitarian reason that ran so squarely counter to the sense of human life he had so painfully acquired.

The Crystal Palace from
Notes from Underground
(1864)*

Fedor Dostoevskii

But these are all golden dreams. Oh, tell me, who was it first announced, who was it first proclaimed, that man only does nasty things because he does not know his own interests; and that if he were enlightened, if his eyes were opened to his real normal interests, man would at once cease to do nasty things, would at once become good and noble because, being enlightened and understanding his real advantage, he would see his own advantage in the good and nothing else, and we all know that not one man can, consciously, act against his own interests, consequently, so to say, through necessity, he would begin doing good? Oh, the babe! Oh, the pure, innocent child! Why, in the first place, when in all these thousands of years has there been a time when man has acted only from his own interest? What is to be done with the millions of facts that bear witness that men, CONSCIOUSLY, that is fully understanding their real interests, have left them in the background and have rushed headlong on another path, to meet peril and danger, compelled to this course by nobody and by nothing, but, as it were, simply disliking the beaten track, and have obstinately, willfully, struck out another difficult, absurd way, seeking it almost in the darkness. So, I suppose, this obstinacy and perversity were pleasanter to them than any advantage . . . Advantage! What is advantage? And will you take it upon yourself to define with perfect accuracy in what the advantage of

---

* From *Notes from Underground*, in *White Nights and Other* Stories, trans. Constance Garnett (London: Macmillan, 1918), 64–68.

man consists? And what if it so happens that a man's advantage, SOMETIMES, not only may, but even must, consist in his desiring in certain cases what is harmful to himself and not advantageous. And if so, if there can be such a case, the whole principle falls into dust. What do you think—are there such cases? You laugh; laugh away, gentlemen, but only answer me: have man's advantages been reckoned up with perfect certainty? Are there not some that not only have not been included but cannot possibly be included under any classification? You see, you gentlemen have, to the best of my knowledge, taken your whole register of human advantages from the averages of statistical figures and polit-ico-economical formulas. Your advantages are prosperity, wealth, freedom, peace—and so on, and so on. So that the man who should, for instance, go openly and knowingly in opposition to all that list would to your thinking, and indeed mine, too, of course, be an obscurantist or an absolute madman: would not he? But, you know, this is what is surprising: why does it so happen that all these statisticians, sages and lovers of humanity, when they reckon up human advantages invariably leave out one? [. . .]

I want to compromise myself personally, and therefore I boldly declare that all these fine systems, all these theories for explaining to mankind their real normal interests, in order that inevitably striving to pursue these interests they may at once become good and noble—are, in my opinion, so far, mere logical exercises! Yes, logical exercises. Why, to maintain this theory of the regeneration of mankind by means of the pursuit of his own advantage is to my mind almost the same thing . . . as to affirm, for instance, following Buckle,[1] that through civ-ilization mankind becomes softer, and consequently less bloodthirsty and less fitted for warfare. Logically it does seem to follow from his arguments. But man has such a predilection for systems and abstract deductions that he is ready to distort the truth intentionally, he is ready to deny the evidence of his senses only to justify his logic [. . .]

And what is it that civilization softens in us? The only gain of civilization for mankind is the greater capacity for variety of sensations—and absolutely nothing more. And through the development of this many-sidedness man may come to finding enjoyment in bloodshed. In fact, this has already hap-pened to him. Have you noticed that it is the most civilized gentlemen who have been the subtlest slaughterers [. . .] civilization has made mankind if not

---

1 EDS: Here Dostoevskii refers to Henry Thomas Buckle's unfinished *The History of Civilization in England* (London: Longmans Green, 1857–61). Buckle is sometimes called the "father of scientific history."

more bloodthirsty, at least more vilely, more loathsomely bloodthirsty. In old days he saw justice in bloodshed and with his conscience at peace exterminated those he thought proper. Now we do think bloodshed abominable and yet we engage in this abomination, and with more energy than ever. Which is worse? Decide that for yourselves. They say that Cleopatra (excuse an instance from Roman history) was fond of sticking gold pins into her slave-girls' breasts and derived gratification from their screams and writhings. You will say that that was in the comparatively barbarous times; that these are barbarous times too, because also, comparatively speaking, pins are stuck in even now; that though man has now learned to see more clearly than in barbarous ages, he is still far from having learnt to act as reason and science would dictate. But yet you are fully convinced that he will be sure to learn when he gets rid of certain old bad habits, and when common sense and science have completely re-educated human nature and turned it in a normal direction. You are confident that then man will cease from INTENTIONAL error and will, so to say, be compelled not to want to set his will against his normal interests. That is not all; then, you say, science itself will teach man (though to my mind it's a superfluous luxury) that he never has really had any caprice or will of his own, and that he himself is something of the nature of a piano-key or the stop of an organ, and that there are, besides, things called the laws of nature; so that everything he does is not done by his willing it, but is done of itself, by the laws of nature. Consequently we have only to discover these laws of nature, and man will no longer have to answer for his actions and life will become exceedingly easy for him. All human actions will then, of course, be tabulated according to these laws, mathematically, like tables of logarithms up to 108,000, and entered in an index; or, better still, there would be published certain edifying works of the nature of encyclopedic lexicons, in which everything will be so clearly calculated and explained that there will be no more incidents or adventures in the world [. . .]

Then—this is all what you say—new economic relations will be established, all ready-made and worked out with mathematical exactitude, so that every possible question will vanish in the twinkling of an eye, simply because every possible answer to it will be provided. Then the "Crystal Palace" will be built. Then . . . In fact, those will be halcyon days. Of course there is no guaranteeing (this is my comment) that it will not be, for instance, frightfully dull then (for what will one have to do when everything will be calculated and tabulated), but on the other hand everything will be extraordinarily rational.

Twice Two from
Notes from Underground
(1864)*

Fedor Dostoevskii

G entlemen, I am tormented by questions; answer them for me. You, for instance, want to cure men of their old habits and reform their will in accordance with science and good sense. But how do you know, not only that it is possible, but also that it is desirable, to reform man in that way? And what leads you to the conclusion that man's inclinations need reforming? In short, how do you know that such a reformation will be a benefit to man? And to go to the root of the matter, why are you so positively convinced that not to act against his real normal interests guaranteed by the conclusions of reason and arithmetic is certainly always advantageous for man and must always be a law for mankind? So far, you know, this is only your supposition. It may be the law of logic, but not the law of humanity [. . .] Man likes to make roads and to create, that is a fact beyond dispute. But why has he such a passionate love for destruction and chaos also? Tell me that! [. . .] [M]an is a frivolous and incongruous creature, and perhaps, like a chess player, loves the process of the game, not the end of it. And who knows (there is no saying with certainty), perhaps the only goal on earth to which mankind is striving lies in this incessant process of attaining, in other words, in life itself, and not in the thing to be attained, which must always be expressed as a formula, as positive as twice two makes four, and such positiveness is not life, gentlemen, but is the beginning

---

* From *Notes from Underground*, in *White Nights and Other* Stories, trans. Constance Garnett (London: Macmillan, 1918), 74–76.

of death. Anyway, man has always been afraid of this mathematical certainty, and I am afraid of it now. Granted that man does nothing but seek that mathematical certainty, he traverses oceans, sacrifices his life in the quest, but to succeed, really to find it, he dreads, I assure you. He feels that when he has found it there will be nothing for him to look for. When workmen have finished their work they do at least receive their pay, they go to the tavern, then they are taken to the police station—and there is occupation for a week. But where can man go? Anyway, one can observe a certain awkwardness about him when he has attained such objects. He loves the process of attaining, but does not quite like to have attained, and that, of course, is very absurd. In fact, man is a comical creature; there seems to be a kind of jest in it all. But yet mathematical certainty is, after all, something insufferable. Twice two makes four seems to me simply a piece of insolence. Twice two makes four is a pert coxcomb who stands with arms akimbo barring your path and spitting. I admit that twice two makes four is an excellent thing, but if we are to give everything its due, twice two makes five is sometimes a very charming thing too [. . .]

And why are you so firmly, so triumphantly, convinced that only the normal and the positive—in other words, only what is conducive to welfare—is for the advantage of man? Is not reason in error as regards advantage? Does not man, perhaps, love something besides well-being? Perhaps he is just as fond of suffering? Perhaps suffering is just as great a benefit to him as well being? Man is sometimes extraordinarily, passionately, in love with suffering, and that is a fact. There is no need to appeal to universal history to prove that; only ask yourself, if you are a man and have lived at all. As far as my personal opinion is concerned, to care only for well being seems to me positively ill-bred. Whether it's good or bad, it is sometimes very pleasant, too, to smash things.

Philosophical
Pro et Contra in Part I of
Crime and Punishment (1981)*

Robert Louis Jackson

"Freedom, freedom!" is Raskol'nikov's predominant sensation after his nightmare. "He was free now from those spells, that sorcery, that enchantment, that delusion." The nightmare is catharsis, purgation, momentary relief. It is only a dream, yet it brings him face to face with himself. "Lord! is it really possible, really possible that I will actually take an ax, will hit her on the head, split open her skull . . . slip in the sticky warm blood?" he wonders. "Good Lord, is it really possible?" The day before, he recalls, he had recoiled from the idea of crime in sick horror. Now he remarks inwardly, and significantly: "Granted that everything decided upon this month is as clear as day, true as arithmetic. Lord! Yet I really know all the same I shall never come to a decision!" Indeed, Raskol'nikov will never decide to commit the crime. He will never consciously, actively, and with his whole moral being choose to kill—or, the reverse, choose not to kill. His "moral resolution of the question" will never go deeper than "casuistry." And yet he will kill! He will lose his freedom (which in any case, after his nightmare, is deceptive) and be pulled into crime and murder—so it will seem to him—by some "unnatural power." [. . .]

Raskol'nikov's deeply passive relationship to his crime often has been noted. Yet this passivity is not a purely psychological phenomenon. It is,

* Extracts from Robert Louis Jackson, "Philosophical *Pro et Contra* in Part I of Dostoevsky's *Crime and Punishment*," in *The Art of Dostoevsky: Deliriums and Nocturnes* (Princeton, NJ: Princeton University Press, 1981), 202–7. Reprinted with the author's permission. Some notes have been excised.

Dostoevskii clearly indicates, closely linked with Raskol'nikov's worldview, an area of very intense activity for him. As Raskol'nikov realizes later on, and as his own thinking and choice of language suggest, he is dominated at the time of the crime by a belief in fate, a general superstitious concern for all sorts of chthonic forces, perhaps even a taste for the occult (elements that, in Svidrigailov, have already surfaced in the form of ghosts). Dostoevskii alludes to Raskol'nikov's problem directly in his notes to the novel. "That was an evil spirit: How otherwise could I have overcome all those difficulties?" Raskol'nikov observes at one point. And a few lines later these significant lines: "I should have done that. (*There is no free will. Fatalism*)." And, finally, these crucial thoughts: "Now why has my life ended? Grumble: But God does not exist and so forth."[1] Dostoevskii's own belief emerges even in these few notes: a loss of faith in God, or in the meaningfulness of God's universe, must end with the individual abandoning himself to a notion of fate.

Raskol'nikov shares his proclivity toward fatalism with a number of Dostoevskii's heroes—for example, the Underground Man, the hero of "A Gentle Creature," and Aleksei Ivanovich in *The Gambler*. The similarities between Raskol'nikov's and the gambler's problems are striking. Both men are dominated by a sterile, rationalistic outlook; both place themselves in a position of challenging fate; both lose their moral awareness in the essential act of challenge (murder, gambling); both seek through their acts to attain to an absolute freedom from the so-called laws of nature that are binding on ordinary men; both, in the end, conceive of themselves as victims of fate. Such types continually are seeking their cues or directives outside of themselves. Quite symptomatic, in this connection, is Raskol'nikov' s prayerful remark after his dream: "O Lord!" he prayed, "show me my path, and I will renounce this cursed dream of mine!"

The fateful circumstance that strikes Raskol'nikov "almost to the point of superstition" and that seems a "predestination of his fate" is his chance meeting with Lizaveta, a meeting that, in Raskol'nikov's view, sets into motion the machinery of fate. Raskol'nikov returns home after that meeting "like a man condemned to death. He had not reasoned anything out, he was quite incapable of reasoning; but suddenly he felt with all his being that he no longer had any freedom to reason or any will, and that everything suddenly had been decided once and for all." Similarly, he responds to a conversation he overhears in a restaurant—by "coincidence" two men give expression to "precisely the

---

1 PSS 7:81.

same thoughts" that had been cropping up in his own mind—as constituting "some kind of prefiguration, a sign":

> This last day which had begun so unexpectedly and had decided every-thing at once, had affected him in an almost completely mechanical way, as though somebody had taken him by the hand and were drawing him after him, irresistibly, blindly, with unnatural force, without objection on his part; as though a piece of his clothing had got caught in the wheel of a machine and had begun to draw him into it. (part 1, chpt. 6)

Dostoevskii is not projecting an "accident" theory of personal history; but neither does he deny the role of chance. Chance is the eternal given. Without it there would be no freedom. Raskol'nikov's encounter with Lizaveta was accidental (though not pure accident), and it was by chance that he over-heard the conversation in which he recognized his own thoughts (although, as Dostoevskii wrote in his letter to M. N. Katkov on the novel, the ideas that infect Raskol'nikov "are floating about in the air").[2] But these chance elements only set into motion a course of action that was seeking to be born, albeit with-out the full sanction of moral self.

What is crucial in Raskol'nikov's situation is not so much the factor of chance as *his disposition to be guided by chance,* his readiness, as it were, to gamble, to seek out and acknowledge in chance his so-called fate. What is crucial to his action is the general state of consciousness that he brings to the moment of crit-ical accident; and consciousness here is not only his nervous, overwrought state but the way he conceives of his relationship to the world [...]

Raskol'nikov seizes upon the various chance incidents that precede the murder as the action of fate, but he does not recognize that fate here has all the iron logic of his own, inner fatality. His passivity—that state of drift in which he evades the necessity of choice and abandons all moral responsibility—is motivated, then, not only by his deep and unresolved moral conflicts but by a muddled rationalistic, fatalistic outlook that itself denies freedom of choice or moral responsibility, an outlook that in the end posits an incoherent universe. This outlook is not something that Raskol'nikov merely picked up in reading or table talk. The sense of a blind, meaningless universe, of a loveless world dominated by an evil spirit—and this is conveyed in part one—emerges from Raskol'nikov's confrontation with the concrete social reality of Russian life, with the tragedy of its lower depths: its hopeless poverty, its degradation, its

---

2 *Pis'ma* 1:418.

desolation. It is this confrontation with the human condition that violates the purity of Raskol'nikov's ideal, that ruptures his faith in moral law and human nature that bends him toward a tragic view of man and toward the view of a universe ruled by blind fate. It is this confrontation, in which compassion and contempt for man form an intimate dialectic, that nourishes the related structures of his ideas or ideology: his altruistic utilitarian ethics and his Napoleonic self-exaltation and contempt for the "herd." It is this confrontation that underlies his murder of the old pawnbroker.

Consciousness, of course, is not passive here. Raskol'nikov, half-deranged in the isolation and darkness of his incomprehensible universe (the model of which is his little coffinlike room), actively reaches out into "history," into his loveless universe, to rationalize his own responses to reality and his own psychological needs. He is an intellectual. His ideas, moreover, acquire a dynamic of their own, raise him to new levels of abstraction and fantasy, and provide him, finally, with a theoretical framework and justification for crime. Yet whatever the independence of these ideas, as we find them in his article or circulating freely in taverns and restaurants, they acquire their vitality only insofar as they mediate the confrontation between individual consciousness and social reality, only insofar as they give expression to Raskol'nikov's intimate social and psychological experience and his deepest, organic responses to the world about him.

In one of his notebooks [. . .] Dostoevskii prided himself as being the first writer to focus on

> the tragedy of the underground, consisting of suffering, self-punishment, the consciousness of something better and the impossibility of achieving that something, and, chiefly, consisting in the clear conviction of these unhappy people that all are alike and hence it is not even worth trying to improve. Consolation, faith? There is consolation from no one, faith in no one. But another step from here and one finds depravity, crime (murder). Mystery.[3]

The profoundly responsive Raskol'nikov, we might say, voluntarily takes on himself this tragedy of the underground. He experiences it internally, morally, in all its aspects and agonizing contradictions. His final step should have been love—a step toward humanity. Instead, experiencing the tragedy of life too deeply, and drawing from that tragedy the most extreme social and philosophical conclusions, Raskol'nikov (a victim of his own solitude, ratiocination, and casuistry) takes a step away from humanity into crime, murder, mystery.

---

3 PSS 16:329.

Meta-utopia (1981)*

Gary Saul Morson

L ike its generic relatives, the *Diary* invites interpretation as a "dialogue of
the mind with itself," an "adventure of the soul among Utopian inquiries."
It regards those inquiries, and the reader is expected to regard them, "with almost
every possible degree of approbation and shade of assent; from the frontiers of
serious and entire belief, through gradations of descending plausibility [...] and
to which some wild paradoxes are appended." In it, as in More's *Utopia*, utopianism predominates, but that predominance is precarious; and "serious and entire
belief" is ever threatened by an uncertain shadow of irony. In part, that shadow
is cast by the *Diary*'s playful, metaliterary passages, passages which, for reasons
discussed above, have no place in unambiguous utopias and which therefore suggest the possibility of parody. The antitheses of metaliterary play and dogmatic
assertion produce meta-utopian ambivalence—that is, not a synthesis, but an
intensified dialectic of utopian "pro" and anti-utopian "contra." That dialectic
is, in turn, the reflection of Dostoevskii's deepest ambivalence toward what he
regarded as the most fundamental moral, religious, and political issues.

Dostoevskii's complex attitude toward his own utopianism recalls Prince
Myshkin's attitude toward the ecstatic visions of universal harmony that he experiences during his epileptic fits. Just before the fit, Myshkin explains to himself,

> His mind and his heart were flooded with extraordinary light; all his uneas-
> iness, all his doubts, all his anxieties were relieved at once [...] But these

---

*   From Gary Saul Morson, *The Boundaries of Genre: Dostoevsky's* Diary of a Writer *and the
Tradition of Literary Utopia* (Austin, TX: University of Texas Press, 1981), 177–82. From
The Boundaries of Genre: Dostoevsky's Diary of a Writer and the Tradition of Literary
Utopia by Gary Saul Morson, Copyright © 1981. By permission of the University of Texas
Press. The text has been excerpted and some notes have been excised.

moments, these flashes were only the prelude of that final second (it was never more than a second) with which the fit itself began [...] Thinking of that moment later, when he was all right again, he often said to himself that all these gleams and flashes of the highest self-awareness and self-consciousness, and therefore also of the "highest form of existence," were nothing but disease, the interruption of the normal condition; and if so, it was not at all the highest form of being, but on the contrary must be reckoned the lowest. And yet, all the same, he came at last to an extremely paradoxical conclusion. "What if it is a disease?" he decided at last. "What does it matter that it is an abnormal intensity, if the result, if the minute of sensation, remembered and analyzed afterwards in health, turns out to be the acme of harmony and beauty, and gives a feeling, unknown and undivined till then, of completeness, of proportion, of reconciliation, and of ecstatic devotional merging with the highest synthesis of life?"[1]

In the *Diary*, the ridiculous man also asks what it matters that his vision may have been an impossible dream, if that dream "announced to me a different life, renewed, grand, and full of power!" (ch. 2). In part, the identification of such visions as "the interruption of the normal condition" reflects the fact that they are necessarily experienced alone—*idio*syncratically—and can scarcely be communicated. The ridiculous man's recognition that he "lost the words" to describe the "live image" (ch. 5) possessing his soul is comparable to the Idiot's regret that his visions are ultimately beyond language and therefore beyond sharing. Reflecting on the words he has used to describe them to himself, he continues (214),

These vague expressions seemed to him very comprehensible, though too weak. That it really was "beauty and worship," that it really was "the highest synthesis of life" he could not doubt, and could not admit the possibility of doubt. It was not as though he saw abnormal and unreal visions of some sort at that moment, as from hashish, opium, or wine, destroying the reason and distorting the soul [...] These moments were only an extraordinary quickening of self-consciousness—if the condition was to be expressed in one word—and at the same time of self-awareness in the

---

1 Fyodor Dostoevsky, *The Idiot*, trans. Constance Garnett (New York: Random, Modern Library Giant, 1935), 213–14. All references to *The Idiot* in the excerpt refer to this translation and edition.

highest degree of immediacy. Since at that second, that is, at the very last conscious moment before the fit, he had time to say to himself clearly and consciously, "Yes, for this moment one might give one's whole life!" then without doubt that moment was really worth the whole of life. He did not insist on the dialectical part of his argument, however. Stupefaction, spiritual darkness, idiocy stood before him conspicuously as the consequence of these "higher moments"; seriously, of course, he could not have disputed it. There was undoubtedly a mistake in his conclusion—that is, in his estimate of that minute, but the reality of the sensation somewhat perplexed him. What, indeed, was he to make of that reality?

The direct sensation of existence which is nevertheless a disease, the height which is also the abyss, the threat of idiocy which reveals the highest wisdom—all these contradictions, already implicit in its ambivalent title, are developed and intensified in this extraordinary novel. The Idiot himself is a direct literary descendant of the wise fool so often and so ambiguously praised in Renaissance literature, especially of the fool to whom he is so often compared, Don Quixote. When Aglaia compares him to this and other quixotic figures, the prince, wondering at her frequent shifts from "genuine and noble feeling" to "unmistakable [. . .] mockery" (239), cannot decide "whether she was in earnest or laughing" (236).

Don Quixote is also a central figure in the self-consciously quixotic *Diary*, where he plays a complex—multiple and inconsistent—role. In some articles, for example, in "The Metternichs and the Don Quixotes" (February, 77, I, 4), the type exemplified by Cervantes' hero turns out not to be ridiculous, but only to be called such by scoffers who are themselves, like their counterparts in most utopias, ridiculous. These scoffers, maintains Dostoevskii, who in his pre-Siberian days was himself given the mocking epithet "Knight of the Mournful Countenance,"[2] fail to understand that in the Last Days the most practical policies are the most idealistic, while the most Machiavellian strategies are the most likely to fail. "Believe me," he concludes, "Don Quixote also knows an advantage and is able to calculate." But in other articles (e.g., "A Lie Is Saved by a Lie," September, 77, II, 1), Don Quixote is alluded to as truly foolish, both because he takes fiction for nonfiction and because, like the dreamers of Dostoevskii's early stories, he will not recognize or acknowledge unpoetic fact.

---

2   For an account of this incident, see Joseph Frank, *Dostoevsky: The Seeds of Revolt, 1821–1849* (Princeton, NJ: Princeton University Press, 1976), 168.

These contradictions are similar to those of the diarist himself. At times, he portrays himself as the only one to understand apocalyptic politics, and, therefore, as the greatest realist. At other times, however, he portrays himself as a somewhat ludicrous and harmless flâneur, imagining an impossible golden age when pompous generals and their wives have become "cleverer than Voltaire, more sensitive than Rousseau, incomparably more seductive than Alcibiades, Don Juan, the Lucreces, the Juliets, and the Beatrices! [...] And can it be, can it really be, that the golden age exists only on porcelain cups?" ("The Golden Age in the Pocket," January, 76, I, 4) [...]

The diarist seems to react with a similar mixture of irony and agreement in his assessments of the *Diary*'s other quixotic figures, especially the "paradoxicalist" and a second paradoxicalist, the "witty bureaucrat." These wise and foolish figures speak in exemplary rhetorical paradoxes, praising the unpraisable and advising the unadvisable. Their contradictions seem to epitomize those of the *Diary* itself, and to point to its generic roots. When the paradoxicalist praises war, for instance, it is hard to tell whether to take the article as a satire on European conflicts and their apologists, or—in view of the fact that Dostoevskii himself advances quite similar arguments in "War Is Not Always a Scourge, Sometimes It Is Salvation" and other apparently un-ironic articles— as quite the opposite, that is, as a call to arms. Is the paradoxicalist's encomium to hypocritical politeness as the closest approximation to the golden age to be taken as an oblique endorsement of Dostoevskii's plans for a genuine utopia— plans to which the paradoxicalist is eventually converted—or, on the contrary, as a wry satire on "a man whom absolutely no one knows" but a type whom everyone knows: "he is a *dreamer*" (April, 76, II, 2). Or is he perhaps not an impractical dreamer, but only called such (as the diarist implies at the end of one article) by those who do not wish to consider his arguments? When he is at last converted to the diarist's political program, in what light, or shadow, is that program placed?

And is the ridiculous man really ridiculous or only called ridiculous? We may observe that the interpretive history of this story repeats that of More's *Utopia* (and parallels that of Dostoevskii's Grand Inquisitor legend). Whereas most readers have taken the "Dream" as an unambiguous utopia, and the narrator's conversion as his genuine salvation, a number have interpreted the story in the opposite way. "The Golden Age, like every other important concept in Dostoevskii's world, is a dialectical concept: it can be sacrament or blasphemy, the vision of regeneration in Christ or the vision of degeneration in the imitation of Christ," Edward Wasiolek has observed. "*The Dream of a Ridiculous*

Man is *blasphemy,* and yet it has been taken universally by Dostoevskii's interpreters as *sacrament.*"[3] This school of interpretation usually argues that the story's narrator converts not from solipsistic atheism to the true faith, but rather from nihilistic egoism to monomaniacal egoism. The solipsist, it is contended, is recognizable in his religious rebirth, especially in his conviction that he alone knows the Truth: he is, in short, another one of *The Possessed.*

Each proponent of this reading discovers in the ridiculous man's sermons what I called earlier an "irony of origins. "That is, his beliefs are discredited as the product of his personality and biography and therefore, if not necessarily false, at least compromised in their advocacy. According to Wasiolek,

> The dream of the Ridiculous Man is *his dream,* and it is as good as his motives, and his motives are self-interested. Dostoevskii has presented in his story what he has presented so often: he has placed some cherished truth in the mouth and being of a self-interested person [. . .] Dostoevskii criticism will always go wrong when it separates Dostoevskii's ideas from those characters who carry the ideas [. . .] What we must not forget is that the dream is the Ridiculous Man's dream. Psychology has taught us that we are all the actors in our dreams [. . .] He corrupts the truth by making it his [. . .][4]

By contrast, those who take the story as an unambiguous utopia implicitly or explicitly rule out psychological readings as inappropriate. They compare the story not to psychological novels or stories, but rather to the lives of the saints (such as the embedded Life of Zosima in *Karamazov*) or to religious narratives of conversion (sometimes citing the conversion of Markel in Karamazov or of Raskol'nikov in the epilogue to *Crime and Punishment*). In the story of Markel, it may be recalled, the doctor regards the dying man's conversion as evidence that "he is going insane because of the disease" (344-pt. 2, bk. 6, ch. 1). But this crude psychology, like that of other "psychologists" in *Karamazov,* seems to be an example of self-serving narrow-mindedness, a complacent refusal to accept the possibility of a Truth reached not by personal need, motive, or experience, but by grace: a Truth, that is, which is inexplicable solely in terms of biography.

There are, in other words, works in which one will go wrong to "separate [. . .] ideas from those characters who carry the ideas" and those in which one

---

3   Edward Wasiolek, *Dostoevsky: The Major Fiction* (Cambridge, Mass.: M.I.T. Press, 1964), 145.

4   Wasiolek, *Dostoevsky: The Major Fiction,* 145–47.

will go wrong if one does not so separate them. In novels or novelistic short stories one must understand ideas as someone's ideas; in utopias, saints' lives, certain philosophical parables (such as Voltaire's), or medieval dream-visions, one must not. *The question, in short, is one of genre*; and unless that question is addressed, arguments are bound to be circular or at cross purposes. One cannot *show* the story to be anti-utopian by means of psychology, because it is precisely this method of interpretation which is in question. Conversely, one cannot demonstrate it to be an unambiguous utopia (or an account of a genuine conversion) by identifying the hero's views with the author's, because the appropriateness of such an identification is what needs to be proved. One can only show that *if* one takes the story to be of this kind, *then* certain readings are implausible. But *whether* to take it one way would seem to be a question about which sophisticated readers may and do disagree. "The Dream," in other words, is what we have been calling here a boundary work—that is, one which has come to be interpreted according to contradictory generic conventions.

No one, to my knowledge, has tried to resolve these contradictions by reading the story in the context of the *Diary*—that is, by taking it not as a self-sufficient but as an embedded work. But even this contextual interpretation ultimately fails to resolve them. When I first tried to read "The Dream" in this way, the story seemed to be an unambiguous utopia. Appearing in the same issue of the *Diary* in which Dostoevskii proclaims that the Eastern War is the "exception" to history, that "War Is Not Always a Scourge, Sometimes It Is Salvation," and that Russia has taken "the first step toward the achievement of that eternal peace in which we are fortunate to believe—toward the achievement in truth of international unity and in truth of philanthropic prosperity!" (April, 77, I, 2)—appearing in this context, the story seemed to be a fictional exemplification of those beliefs. But as I read further, and re-read earlier passages of the *Diary*, I discovered ambiguity. The story's immediate context was undoubtedly utopian, I reasoned, but it also seemed to allude to more distant sections that are not. Is the ridiculous man, perhaps, another paradoxicalist? Are we expected to think of the diarist's warnings against "false Christs" and his psychological studies of those who, convinced that they alone know the way to brotherhood, are themselves the most extreme example of unbrotherly "Dissociation" (March, 76, I, 3)? Does his dream, we may ask, resemble the saving visions of "The Peasant Marei" (February, 76, I, 3) and "Vlas" (1873) or, on the contrary, the insane one of "Bobok"? And does the narrative's subtitle, "A Fantastic Story," indicate that it is not a psychological story, or is it rather designed to recall the Diary's earlier study of monomaniacal egoism with the same subtitle, "The Meek One"?

The *Diary*, in short, is itself an ambiguous context, and the story appears to be not only a boundary work—that is, one that has been interpreted according to contradictory generic conventions—but also a threshold work, that is, one designed to resonate between opposing genres and interpretations. Or to put it differently, *the "Dream" is a meta-utopia embedded in a metautopia*, an epitome of the larger work's genre *and* of its ambivalence. If one chooses to take it this way, the passage that will be foregrounded is the one immediately before the ending in which the ridiculous man, admitting his vision to be impossible, still refuses to surrender it. "I'll go further," he writes, "let this never be realized, and let paradise never come (this much I already understand!)—well, all the same, I will go on preaching it." Those who read *Utopia* as a meta-utopia may recall the concluding lines of book 2, in which "More"—or is it More?—observes that "I cannot agree with all that he [Hythloday] said. But I readily admit that there are many features in the Utopian commonwealth which it is easier for me to wish for in our countries than to have any hope of seeing realized."[5] When the "Dream" is read in this ambiguous way, its import seems closest neither to *The Demons* nor to the epilogue of *Crime and Punishment*, but to *The Idiot*; and its title—like that of *The Idiot*—seems to invite the contradictory readings it has in fact received.

---

5   St. Thomas More, *Utopia*, in *The Complete Works of St. Thomas More*, vol. 4 (New Haven, CT: Yale University Press, 1965), 245–47.

A Note on His Wife's Death (1864)*

Fedor Dostoevskii

April 16, 1864. Masha is lying on the table. Will I ever meet Masha again?

To love others as thyself, as per Christ's commandment, is impossible. The law of individuality on Earth constrains; the *I* obstructs. Only Christ was able to do this, but Christ was the eternal, everlasting ideal towards which man strives, and must strive, according to the law of nature. Meanwhile, it has become clear as day that since the appearance of Christ as *the ideal man in the flesh*, the highest and ultimate development of the individual (the final development, at the very final moment of reaching that goal) must be the realization by man that he must find, realize, and with all his nature understand that the highest goal of his individuality, the full development of his *I*, is to in a sense destroy that *I*, to give it away completely to each and every one, wholeheartedly and selflessly. And that is the greatest happiness. Thus, the law of *I* fuses with the law of humanism, and in this fusion, both the *I* and every one (which appear to be total opposites) are mutually destroyed—while simultaneously reaching the height of individual development on their own.

And that is Christ's paradise. The entire history of humanity, and of every individual, is the history of development, struggle, and endeavour towards that goal. But if that is humanity's final goal (upon achieving it, humanity, despite its failings, will no longer need to develop—that is, to reach, to struggle, to see the light, to eternally strive for the ideal—therefore, will no longer need to live),

---

*   This translation was done by Anton Nonin and is published here under a Creative Commons BY-ND 4.0 license. The original appeared in Dostoevskii's notebooks.

consequently, man, upon achieving the ideal, will cease his earthly existence. And so man is an earthly creature that is developing, i.e. not completed yet, and only transitional.

But it seems to me that reaching that lofty goal is completely senseless if, upon reaching it, everything fades and disappears—that is to say, if man will live no longer upon reaching the goal. Therefore, there is a future life in paradise.

What kind of life is it, where will it take place, on which planet, in which center, is it the final center, i.e. in the bosom of universal synthesis, i.e. God? We do not know. We only know one trait of the nature of future creatures, which we doubtfully call "man" (we have no idea what kind of creatures we will be). This trait has been foretold and foreshadowed by Christ—the highest and ultimate ideal of human development—who appeared before us in the flesh, according to the law of our history.

The trait is this:

"They neither marry nor are they given in marriage; they live like God's angels." This is profoundly significant.

1. Neither *marry*, nor *are given in marriage*—because there is no need. There is no longer any need to develop, to achieve that goal, by means of the changing generations, and:

2. Marriage, and the act of giving away the woman in marriage, is the greatest rejection of humanism, the complete isolation of the couple from *everyone* else (very little is left for everyone else). While to have a family, is to conform with the law of nature, it is still an abnormal, egotistical endeavor compared with the fullest meaning of the condition of a man. Family is man's most sacred thing on earth, because by means of this law of nature, the main goal is achieved (that is, the making of new generations). But at the same time, man, as per the law of nature, for the sake of achieving his ideal goal, must constantly reject the ideal. (Duality)

NB. The antichrists are wrong, when they deny Christianity with the following refutation:

1. "If Christianity is true, then why does it not reign on Earth? Why do men still suffer and why are they not brothers to each other?"

It is clear why: because this state is the ideal of the future, the final life of man. On Earth, man is in a transitional state. It will happen, but it will happen when the man is reborn according to the laws of nature as a new being that does not marry, and is not given away in marriage.

2. Christ himself preached his teachings only as an ideal. He himself prophesied struggle and development of man (the parable about the sword) until the end of the world, because it is the law of nature, because life on earth goes on changing, but there—life is a complete synthesis, eternal pleasure and fulfillment, in which, as a result, "time will no longer exist."

NB2. Atheists who deny God and the future life are terribly inclined to imagine all of this in a human form, thus their sin. God's nature is the complete opposite of man's nature. Man, according to the great findings of science, moves from multiplicity to Synthesis, from facts to their generalization and comprehension. God's nature, on the other hand, is different. It is a complete synthesis of all existence, which examines itself in multiplicity, in Analysis.

But if man is not man—what will be his nature?

It is impossible to understand this on earth. But the law of nature can be anticipated by all of humanity, and each private individual, in direct emanations (Proudhon,[6] the origin of God).

This is a fusion of the complete *I*, that is to say of the knowledge and synthesis with *everything*. "Love everything, like thyself." To do so is impossible on earth because to do so would contradict the law of the development of the individual and the achievement of the final goal, to which the man is bound. Therefore, this law is not ideal, as the antichrists say, but of our ideal.

NB. And so, everything depends on this question: is Christ accepted as the final expression of ideal on earth, that is on Christian faith. If you believe in Christ, then you believe that you will live forever.

Is there, in this case, a future life for any *I*? They say that man self-destructs and dies *entirely*.

We already know that he doesn't die entirely because, by physically giving birth to a son, a man passes on part of his individuality, and leaves his memory to people. (NB. *The desire for eternal memory*[7] expressed in funerals is significant), that is he passes a part of his previously living individuality on to the future development of humanity. We clearly see that the memory of the great

---

6   EDS: Pierre-Joseph Proudhon (1809–65) was an anarchist philosopher (the first to call himself an "anarchist") and founder of mutualist philosophy

7   EDS: "Eternal memory" (in Russian *vechnaia pamiat'*) is part of the Byzantine Rite (the liturgy of the Eastern Orthodox Church) said at the end of a funeral service. "Memory" in the liturgical statement refers to remembrance by God, not by the living, and is said as a prayer that the soul has entered heaven and enjoys eternal life. Dostoevskii here gives the phrase an additional layer of meaning in his interpretation of "memory."

developers of mankind lives on within people (as well as within evildoers), and for man, the greatest happiness is to be like the developers. Therefore, part of these individuals is found in the flesh and spirit of other people. Christ entered humanity entirely, and man strives to transform himself into the *I* of Christ as in his own ideal. Having achieved this ideal, he will clearly see that everyone who strived to reach the same goal on earth is part of his final nature —that is, the nature of Christ. (The synthetic nature of Christ is amazing. After all, synthesis is the nature of God, and Christ is the reflection of God on earth.) It is difficult to imagine how every *I* will be resurrected —into the general Synthesis. But the living, not having died before the achievement of the ideal, and having been reflected in the final ideal, must come alive into final, synthetic, eternal life. We will live without stopping to fuse with everything, without marrying or being given away in marriage, and in various ways (in my father's house are many mansions). Everything will feel and know itself forever. But how it will happen, what form it will take, in what nature—it is difficult for man to fully imagine.

And so, man on earth strives for an ideal that is the *complete opposite* of his nature. When man has not fulfilled the law of striving towards his ideal—that is, he has not sacrificed his *I through love* to people and other beings (Masha and I), he feels suffering and calls this condition sin. And so, man must endlessly feel suffering, which is counterbalanced by the heavenly joy of fulfilling the law—that is, by sacrifice. Herein lies earthly balance. Otherwise, earth would be senseless.

The teaching of the materialists is universal stagnation and mechanism of matter, thus death. The teaching of true philosophy is the destruction of stagnation; it is a thought, it is the center and Synthesis of the universe and its outer form—matter—that is, it is God. Life is eternal.

The Speech at the Stone from *Brothers Karamazov* (1880)*

Fedor Dostoevskii

"Let us make a compact here, at Iliusha's stone, that we will never forget Iliusha and one another. And whatever happens to us later in life, if we don't meet for twenty years afterwards, let us always remember how we buried the poor boy at whom we once threw stones, do you remember, by the bridge? and afterwards we all grew so fond of him. He was a fine boy, a kind-hearted, brave boy, he felt for his father's honor and resented the cruel insult to him and stood up for him. And so in the first place, we will remember him, boys, all our lives. And even if we are occupied with most important things, if we attain to honor or fall into great misfortune—still let us remember how good it was once here, when we were all together, united by a good and kind feeling which made us, for the time we were loving that poor boy, better perhaps than we are. My little doves—let me call you so, for you are very like them, those pretty blue birds, at this minute as I look at your good dear faces. My dear children, perhaps you won't understand what I am saying to you, because I often speak very unintelligibly, but you'll remember it all the same and will agree with my words some time. You must know that there is nothing higher and stronger and more wholesome and good for life in the future than some good memory, especially a memory of childhood, of home. People talk to you a great deal about your education, but some good, sacred memory, preserved from childhood, is perhaps the best education. If a man carries many such memories with him into life, he is safe to the end of his days, and if one has only one good memory left in one's heart, even that may sometime be the means of saving us. Perhaps we may even

---

* Extract from *The Brothers Karamazov*, trans. Constance Garnett (New York: The Lowell Press, 1912), 876–77.

grow wicked later on, may be unable to refrain from a bad action, may laugh at men's tears and at those people who say as Kolia did just now, 'I want to suffer for all men,' and may even jeer spitefully at such people. But however bad we may become—which God forbid—yet, when we recall how we buried Iliusha, how we loved him in his last days, and how we have been talking like friends all together, at this stone, the cruelest and most mocking of us—if we do become so—will not dare to laugh inwardly at having been kind and good at this moment! What's more, perhaps, that one memory may keep him from great evil and he will "reflect and say, 'Yes, I was good and brave and honest then!' Let him laugh to himself, that's no matter, a man often laughs at what's good and kind. That's only from thoughtlessness. But I assure you, boys, that as he laughs he will say at once in his heart, 'No, I do wrong to laugh, for that's not a thing to laugh at.'"

"That will be so, I understand you, Karamazov!" cried Kolia, with flashing eyes.

The boys were excited and they, too, wanted to say something, but they restrained themselves, looking with intentness and emotion at the speaker.

"I say this in case we become bad," Alesha went on, "but there's no reason why we should become bad, is there, boys? Let us be, first and above all, kind, then honest and then let us never forget each other! I say that again. I give you my word for my part that I'll never forget one of you. Every face looking at me now I shall remember even for thirty years. Just now Kolia said to Kartashov that we did not care to know whether he exists or not. But I cannot forget that Kartashov exists and and that he is not blushing now as he did when he discovered the founders of Troy, but is looking at me with his jolly, kind, dear little eyes. Boys, my dear boys, let us all be generous and brave like Iliusha, clever, brave and generous like Kolia (though he will be ever so much cleverer when he is grown up), and let us all be as modest, as clever and sweet as Kartashov. But why am I talking about those two? You are all dear to me, boys, from this day forth, I have a place in my heart for you all, and I beg you to keep a place in your hearts for me! Well, and who has united us in this kind, good feeling, which we shall remember and intend to remember all our lives? Who, if not Iliusha, the good boy, the dear boy, precious to us forever! Let us never forget him. May his memory live for ever in our hearts from this time forth!"

"Yes, yes, forever, forever!" the boys cried in their ringing voices, with softened faces.

"Let us remember his face and his clothes and his poor little boots, his coffin and his unhappy, sinful father, and how boldly he stood up for him alone against the whole school."

"We will remember, we will remember," cried the boys. "He was brave, he was good!"

"Ah, how I loved him!" exclaimed Kolia.

"Ah, children, ah, dear friends, don't be afraid of life! How good life is when one does something good and just!"

"Yes, yes," the boys repeated enthusiastically.

"Karamazov, we love you!" a voice, probably Kartashov's, cried impulsively.

"We love you, we love you!" they all caught it up. There were tears in the eyes of many of them.

"Hurrah for Karamazov!" Kolia shouted ecstatically.

"And may the dead boy's memory live forever!" Alesha added again with feeling.

"Forever!" the boys chimed in again.

"Karamazov," cried Kolia, "can it be true what's taught us in religion, that we shall all rise again from the dead and shall live and see each other again, all, Iliusha too?"

"Certainly we shall all rise again, certainly we shall see each other and shall tell each other with joy and gladness all that has happened!" Alesha answered, half laughing, half enthusiastic.

"Ah, how splendid it will be!" broke from Kolia.

"Well, now we will finish talking and go to his funeral dinner. Don't be put out at our eating pancakes—it's a very old custom and there's something nice in that!" laughed Alesha. "Well, let us go! And now we go hand in hand."

"And always so, all our lives hand in hand! Hurrah for Karamazov!" Kolia cried once more rapturously, and once more the boys took up his exclamation: "Hurrah for Karamazov!"

Ode to Joy (2004)*

Robert Louis Jackson

To return to the beginning of Alesha's speech: he and the boys come upon the stone as they are walking along the path. Alesha's reactions to seeing the stone, like Smurov's, are spontaneous: the "whole picture" of Snegirev and Iliusha arises in his memory. "Something shook, as it were, in his soul." He looks at the boys and "suddenly" speaks to them. "Suddenly," here, is not the theatrical "suddenly" that preludes Ivan's speech: "Ivan was silent for a moment, his face suddenly became very sad." Alesha's impulse to speak is devoid of artificial gesture or melodrama. Alesha's "suddenly" is prompted by a fresh memory, a recollection arising from his own feeling and experience [. . .]

The speech that follows this moment of silence is not something Alesha has been preparing for, as in the case of Ivan. The boys gather naturally around the stone, around the memory of Iliusha. Alesha's speech, his effort to unite the boys in solemn recollection, emerges organically out of that moment of silence, reverence, and respect for the child.

Both Ivan's and Alesha's speeches have at their center a "picture" of a suffering child. Ivan's child, one of his "little pictures," is drawn from a newspaper account of a landowner who baits his dogs with a child in front of the mother. Ivan holds this little picture, figuratively speaking, before Alesha's eyes, as he, Ivan, rejects the idea of the suffering child as a basis for "solidarity in sin."[1]

---

*   Extract from Robert Louis Jackson, "Alyosha's Speech at the Stone: 'The Whole Picture,'" in *A New Word on* The Brothers Karamazov (Evanston, IL: Northwestern University Press, 2004), 240–43, 246–48. Copyright © 2004 by Northwestern University Press. All rights reserved. The text has been excerpted and some notes have been removed.
1   Fyodor Dostoevsky, *The Brothers Karamazov,* trans. Richard Pevear and Larissa Volokhonsky (San Francisco: North Point Press, 1990), 244. Hereafter BK.

Alesha speaks concretely about a real person, a child, whom he has known. His "whole picture" comes directly from life, from direct contact with Iliusha; it includes the boys who had played a fatal role in Iliusha's life. Alesha's compassion is direct, comprehensible. Iliusha's suffering and sacrifice are presented as grounds for the moral and spiritual unity of the boys. In contrast to Ivan's parody of the notion of "solidarity in sin," Alesha advances the idea of the suffering child as a basis for *solidarity in love*.

Dostoevskii's accent on the "whole picture" is an important one; this is not just a picture focused on a horrendous moment of cruelty and injustice or on the victim or perpetrator alone, but one focused on the entire tragedy, one encompassing the actions and behavior of a whole community of people. Most important, however, the whole picture encompasses not only evil but also the potential for good and the momentary expression of good in human nature. Here is the whole picture. Not without reason does Dmitrii, indirectly culpable in Iliusha's tragedy and directly culpable in the tragedy of his father, Fedor Pavlovich Karamazov, say early in the novel, in reference to his ethical conflicts: "God knows my heart, he sees all my despair. He sees the whole picture" (121). That is what Dostoevskii ultimately insists upon: the *whole picture* [. . .]

Alesha's whole picture, his opening recollection of Snegirev's recollection of Iliusha at the stone, leads directly into the main, or outer, theme of his speech: the importance of remembering, the importance of the purified and purifying image of recollection as a way of maintaining or reconstituting, when necessary, moral and spiritual health.

"Russian children," Dostoevskii wrote in the January 1876 issue of his *Writer's Diary*, "are brought up to behold repulsive pictures such as a peasant whipping a helpless, overburdened horse across the eyes" (PSS 22:26). To counteract these terrible impressions, to root them out and plant new ones, Dostoevskii recommends "a series of pure, holy, beautiful pictures [that] would have a strong impact upon souls thirsting for beautiful impressions" (PSS 22:24). Scarcely noticed by the reader of Raskol'nikov's monstrous dream of a peasant beating his horse is his recollection in the prelude to the dream of his earliest and positive childhood memories, pictures that include the family church with its green cupola and its ancient icons. Dostoevskii's inclusion of this detail was not an accident: the possibility of Raskol'nikov's redemption, in Dostoevskii's view, is rooted partly in the existence of such early pure memories, recollections that lie at the base of his consciousness.

The real meaning, or inner core of Alesha's speech, of course, is embodied not so much in words, as in the embodied gospel Word. Like Christ's speech at the Last Supper, "Whither I go, ye cannot come; so now I say to you" (John 13:33), Alesha's talk opens on a note of separation: "Gentlemen, we shall be parting soon." But it is a separation like that facing Christ and his disciples, which will be overcome, ultimately, through memory. "But these things have I told you"—here the utterance of Christ—"that when the time shall come, ye may remember that I told you of them [. . .] Remember the word that I said unto you" (John: 16:4; 15:20 AV).

Alesha's separation from the boys will be overcome, first of all, in a merging, a coming together, a joining of voices—such merging as we see at the end of Alesha's speech and at the end of the novel. That joining of voices is heralded at the outset of Alesha's speech by the Russian verb *soglasimsia*—"let us agree"—a verb that consists of the preposition "with" and of a root that is found in the Russian *golos*, or "voice." "And so we shall part, gentlemen. Let us agree here, by Iliusha's stone, that we will never forget—first, Iliushechka, and second, one another." The expression "one another" or "each other" in Russian, *drug o druge*, consists of two words, each meaning "friend," each word separated by a preposition, thus accenting, in Alesha's context, the idea of remembering friends.

The first appeal of Alesha is for *so-glas*, a joining of voices: one may go one's separate way in life, but one can and must, first of all, before taking leave of one another, voluntarily agree, concur, coordinate voices, sing in unison, live in spiritual reconciliation, in a condition of free concord involving everybody. One can and must agree—the act is a free one—*not* to forget Iliusha and "each other."

The act of remembering, of calling upon each other to remember—reiterated throughout Alesha's speech by a variety of Russian words signifying remembering—is itself an act of consecration, of bringing together, of re-creating a moment of spiritual unity and harmony: "All the same, let us never forget how good we once felt here, all together, united (*vsem soobshcha, soedinennymi*) by such good and kind feelings as made us too, for the time that we loved the poor boy, perhaps better than we actually are" (BK 774).

The moment of spiritual unity and harmony Alesha refers to is that moment when everyone reveals himself or herself as he or she is at heart. The potential for good, Dostoevskii believed, lies in each of us [. . .]

The harmonious family on earth, in the final chorus of *Brothers Karamazov*, is a premonition of the harmonious family in heaven. Ivan, as we know, indignantly refuses to take part in that chorus or concert, that moment when the universe will be shaken, when all in heaven and under the earth will merge in one voice of praise, when all that lives and has lived will exclaim: "Just art Thou, O Lord, for thy ways are revealed" (BK 244). Ivan refuses to participate in this glorious moment out of respect for the unexpiated tears of children and out of a general feeling of indignation. Yet we might also surmise that Ivan, the archetypal soloist, refuses to sing in the chorus just because it is a chorus. Alesha, as his interaction with the boys attests, is not a soloist. He interacts emotionally and spiritually with his audience through a dialogue of words and glances. His voice, at the end, merges with the chorus of the boys' voices [...]

Kolia and the boys, and along with them, Alesha, are carried forward on a wave of extraordinary jubilation, indeed, exalted ethical-religious emotion. The presence of the eighteenth-century German poet, dramatist, and thinker Friedrich von Schiller—specifically, his "Ode to Joy" (An die Freude, 1785)—is unmistakable in this final episode. Schiller, that youthful love of Dostoevskii; Schiller, the champion of brotherhood and of the loftiest ideals of humanity; Schiller, who Dostoevskii said belonged more to Russia than to Europe; Schiller, whom the divided Dmitri Karamazov invokes in his moments of ecstasy and despair; Schiller, whose poem "Resignation" forms a subtext to Ivan's rebellion; Schiller, of whom it has been said that he missed his vocation as a religious preacher—this same Schiller asserts his magic power at the end of *Brothers Karamazov*, as he does in other parts of the novel.

There is an overexcited, euphoric, precisely exclamatory quality to the final choral scene, one that goes far beyond the lofty but spiritually contained affirmations of those silent iconographic representations of medieval Russian spirituality, "O Tebe raduetsia" ("All Creation Rejoiceth in Thee"). Here at the end of *Brothers Karamazov* is a scene that borders on the kind of romantic Schilleresque *Brüderschaft*, or sentimental brotherliness, that Dostoevskii, at other moments in his earlier works, knew how to parody mercilessly in heroes who had lost contact with Russian reality. Yet this was clearly not that kind of a moment for Dostoevskii. In this period, Dostoevskii himself, as we know, fondly recollected the beneficent power that Schiller (for example, in his play "The Robbers") had exercised on him in his youth (PSS 30/1:212).

The final choral moment in the novel is a complex one: it joins an authentic note of spiritual-religious fervor with a romantic exuberance—precisely the kind of synthesis that lies at the basis of Schiller's "Ode to Joy" and Beethoven's

Ninth Symphony—two works that merge in the final swelling chorus of the last movement of the Ninth:

> Joy, O beauteous spark divine,
> Daughter of Elysium,
> Fire-drunk we enter now,
> Heavenly one, your sacred shrine.
> Your magic power joins again
> What fashion sternly did divide;
> All mankind shall be as brothers
> Where your gentle wings abide.
> Take now this embrace, you millions!
> This kiss—for the whole world wide!
> Brothers—above the starry heavens
> There must a loving Father dwell.

These and other verses from "Ode to Joy," constituting almost a religious hymn, a spiritual dithyramb, celebrate the theme of friendship, familial harmony, good will on earth, and the existence of a loving Father. "Joy" itself, a kind of universal law, is the enabling element that brings people together. In Schiller's ode there is no "I," only "we." The stanzas themselves, divided into two parts (a speaker and chorus), joyfully interact with one another. The utopian spirit and themes of Schiller's poem, memorialized in the chorale movement of Beethoven's Ninth, find expression, too, in the chorus of voices that concludes *Brothers Karamazov*. And Beethoven's own verses, introducing Schiller's "Ode to Joy"—"O friends, not these sounds! / Rather let us intone more pleasant ones, and more full of joy!"—seem the unspoken words of Dostoevskii as we are lifted, at the end of *Brothers Karamazov*, on a great wave of joyful enthusiasm, faith in friendship, and universal love.

CHAPTER 8

Dostoevskii's Others

"Others" is, admittedly, a chapter heading that rather clumsily brings together various distinct marginalized groups in nineteenth-century Russia: religious minorities, such as Jews and Muslims; national minorities, such as Tatars and Poles; and women, who remained unequal in the patriarchal culture and society of the Russian Empire. While we are aware that treating these groups together in a single chapter could potentially reinforce, rather than challenge, their marginalization, we believe that there is, nonetheless, a value in treating them alongside one another. Together, the representation of these groups helps show how Dostoevskii—like other writers—constructed his notion of Russianness in opposition to the real or imagined features of its "Others." Moreover, these identity categories intersect with each other in fascinating and often problematic ways. For example, Dostoevskii brings together nationality, gender and religion when he expresses the notion that Russian women have preserved some inner core of Christian goodness that their male counterparts have lost. Gender, sexuality, ethnicity and religion all coalesce in Dostoevskii's affectionate—if arguably patronizing and Orientalizing—portrait of the feminized Muslim prisoner Alei in *Notes from the House of the Dead*.

Notes from the House of the Dead provides a good starting point for this chapter because of the multinational and religious diversity of its characters. Dostoevskii's fictionalization of his own experiences in a Siberian prison camp describes encounters with Jewish, Polish and Tatar prisoners. Two portraits are included in this book: the aforementioned Alei, "pure as a chaste girl," and the much less flattering portrait of the Jew Isai Fomich, that "most comical mixture of naiveté, stupidity, craft, impudence, good-nature, timidity, boastfulness and insolence." More troubling, however, is Dostoevskii's 1877 essay "The Jewish Question" that appeared in *A Writer's Diary*. Here, he responds to allegations of antisemitism, countering that he believes in equal rights for Jews. However, in an astonishing set of intellectual gymnastics, he then puts the blame on the victims, suggesting that the Jews themselves are the real oppressors of the Russian people and it is they who need to repent of their actions.

Such antisemitism has proved alarming to Dostoevskii critics, particularly after the horrors of the Holocaust and the Second World War. The extent to which it is possible to divorce Dostoevskii's antisemitism—mostly, but not exclusively—found in his journalism from the ideal of universal love set forth in his fiction remains a challenging question. Susan McReynolds speaks for many when she wonders "How could the author of *The Brothers Karamazov* also be the source of the slurs against the Jews contained in *A Writer's Diary*?" (3). Her reading of Alei and Isai Fomich, and their role in the construction of Russian identity, is reproduced here.

Many of Dostoevskii's most memorable characters are women: one thinks of the abused protagonist of *Netochka Nezvanova*, the self-sacrificing Sonia Marmeladova in *Crime and Punishment*, or the fiery Nastas'ia Filippovna in *The Idiot*. Some feminist critics, such as Barbara Heldt, have objected to the way in which Dostoevskii relies on idealized women to save or redeem troubled male protagonists. However, *A Writer's Diary* testified to the complexity of its author's views about women. In an obituary for George Sand, the French writer famed for her depiction of emancipated women, Dostoevskii speaks highly of her and her heroines. In "Again about Women," he speaks passionately about the ambition of young women and the need for women's education. However, as his wife Anna Grigor'evna points out in her memoirs, Dostoevskii was suspicious of a certain kind of masculinized woman who had renounced all traces of femininity, whom he found among the intelligentsia of the 1860s. Yet when it came to depicting such women in fiction, as he did with Aglaia Ivanovna in *The Idiot*, his portrayal of them was often more sympathetic and multifaceted than his wife's account suggests.

Gender and sexuality have been some of the most productive subfields in literary studies in recent years, but it is possible to reproduce only a couple of examples from the secondary literature here. Nina Pelikan Straus's reading of *Crime and Punishment* not only offers a feminist interpretation of the novel's representation of women that posits Dunia, rather than Sonia, as the novel's heroine, but also suggests that Dostoevskii explodes myths of masculinity. For Straus, Dostoevskii's novel contains "scenes in which no authentic male heroism exists without a man's willing entry into dialogic relations and identifications with women, substantiating certain feminist hopes for the future of both sexes." By contrast, Carol Apollonio's "The Mothers Karamazov" offers an unsettling interpretation of women's roles in *Brothers Karamazov*. Defying conventional readings that see Fedor Pavlovich as the absolute embodiment of evil, Apollonio instead suggests that his first wife, Adelaida Ivanovna, may be the ultimate source of the "demon" that enters the family. The contrast between Straus's approach and Apollonio's shows the diversity of possible readings of women in Dostoevskii's fiction and, perhaps, the novels' unfinalizability. As feminist theory continues to develop, and new modes of inquiry such as gender studies, masculinity studies, and queer theory gain traction, we can look forward to these methodologies generating new insights about Dostoevskii and his work.

Further Reading

Briggs, Katherine Jane. *How Dostoevsky Portrays Women in His Novels: A Feminist Analysis.* Lewiston, NY: The Edwin Mellen Press, 2009.

Fusso, Susanne Grace. *Discovering Sexuality in Dostoevsky.* Evanston, IL: Northwestern University Press, 2006.

Goldstein, David I. *Dostoevsky and the Jews.* Austin: University of Texas Press, 1981.

Heldt, Barbara. *Terrible Perfection: Women and Russian Literature.* Bloomington: Indiana University Press, 1987.

Hoisington, Sona Stephan, ed. *A Plot of Her Own: The Female Protagonist in Russian Literature.* Evanston, IL: Northwestern University Press, 1995. See especially Harriet Murav's essay, "Reading Women in Dostoevsky," 44–57 and Gary Rosenshield's "Afterword: The Problems of Gender Criticism; or, What Is to Be Done about Dostoevsky?", 114–28.

McReynolds, Susan. *Redemption and the Merchant God: Dostoevsky's Economy of Salvation.* Evanston, IL: Northwestern University Press, 2008.

Morson, Gary Saul. "Dostoevsky's Anti-Semitism and the Critics: A Review Article." *Slavic and East European Journal* 27 (1983): 302–17.

Perlina, Nina. "Dostoevsky and His Polish Fellow Prisoners from the House of the Dead." In *Polish Encounters, Russian Identity*, ed. David L. Ransel and Bożena Shallcross, 100–109. Bloomington: Indiana University Press, 2005.

Straus, Nina Pelikan. *Dostoevsky and the Woman Question: Rereadings at the End of a Century.* New York: St. Martin's Press, 1994.

Portrait of Alei in *Notes from the House of the Dead* (1862)*

Fedor Dostoevskii

The Dagestan Tatars were three in number and they were all brothers. Two of them were middle-aged men, but the third, Alei, was not more than two-and-twenty and looked even younger. His place on the bed was next to me. His handsome, open, intelligent, and at the same time good-naturedly simple face won my heart from the first minute. I was so thankful that fate had sent me him as a neighbor rather than any other. His whole soul was apparent in his handsome, one might even say beautiful, face. His smile was so confiding, so childishly trustful, his big black eyes were soft, caressing, that I always found a particular pleasure in looking at him, even a consolation in my misery and depression. I am not exaggerating. When he was in his native place one of his elder brothers—he had five of them, two of the others had been sent to some sort of penal factory—ordered him to take his sabre, to get on his horse and to go with them on some sort of expedition. The respect due to an elder brother is so great among the mountaineers that the boy did not dare ask, did not even dream of asking, where they were going, and the others did not think it necessary to inform him. They were going out on a pillaging expedition, to waylay and rob a rich Armenian merchant on the road. And so indeed they did: they killed the escort, murdered the Armenian and carried off his goods. But the affair was discovered; all the six were caught, tried, convicted, punished, and sent to penal servitude in Siberia. The only mercy shown by the court to Alei was that he received a shorter sentence: he had been sent to Siberia for

---

* Excerpted from *The House of The Dead*, trans. Constance Garnett (London: Heinemann, 1915), 58–59.

four years. His brothers were very fond of him, and their affection was more like a father's than a brother's. He was their comfort in exile, and sullen and gloomy as they usually were, they always smiled when they looked at him, and when they spoke to him (though they spoke to him very little, as though they still thought of him as a boy with whom it was useless to talk of serious things) their surly faces relaxed, and I guessed that they spoke to him of something humorous, almost childish; at least they always looked at one another and smiled good-humoredly after listening to his answer. He hardly dared to address them, so deep was his respect for them. It was hard to imagine how this boy was able during his prison life to preserve such a gentle heart, to develop such strict honesty, such warm feelings and charming manners, and to escape growing coarse and depraved. But his was a strong and steadfast nature in spite of all its apparent softness. As time went on I got to know him well. He was pure as a chaste girl, and any ugly, cynical, dirty, unjust or violent action in the prison brought a glow of indignation into his beautiful eyes, making them still more beautiful. But he avoided all strife and wrangling, though he was not one of those men who allow themselves to be insulted with impunity and knew how to stand up for himself. But he never had quarrels with anyone, everyone liked him and was friendly to him. At first he was simply courteous to me. By degrees I began talking to him; in a few months he had learned to speak Russian very well, which his brothers never succeeded in doing all the time they were in Siberia. He seemed to me a boy of marked intelligence and peculiar modesty and delicacy, who had in fact reflected a good deal. I may as well say at once that I consider Alei far from being an ordinary person, and I look back upon my meeting with him as one of the happiest meetings in my life. There are natures so innately good, so richly endowed by God that the very idea of their ever deteriorating seems impossible. One is always at ease about them. I am at ease about Alei to this day. Where is he now?

Portrait of Isai Fomich in *Notes from the House of the Dead* (1862)*

Fedor Dostoevskii

One day, in the leisure hour towards evening, a rumor suddenly spread through the prison that a Jew had been brought, and was being shaved in the guardroom and that he would come in directly. There was not a single Jew in the prison at the time. The convicts waited with impatience and surrounded him at once when he came in at the gate. The sergeant led him to the civilian room and showed him his place on the common bed. Isai Fomich carried in his arms a sack containing his own belongings together with the regulation articles, which had been given to him. He laid down the sack, climbed on to the bed and sat down tucking his feet under him, not daring to raise his eyes. There were sounds of laughter and prison jokes alluding to his Jewish origin. Suddenly a young convict made his way through the crowd carrying in his hand his very old, dirty, tattered summer trousers, together with the regulation leg-wrappers. He sat down beside Isai Fomich and slapped him on the shoulder.

"I say, my dear friend, I've been looking out for you these last six years. Look here, how much will you give?"

And he spread the rags out before him.

Isai Fomich, who had been too timid to utter a word and so cowed at his first entrance that he had not dared to raise his eyes in the crowd of mocking,

---

* Excerpted from *The House of The Dead*, trans. Constance Garnett (London: Heinemann, 1915), 108–11.

disfigured and terrible faces which hemmed him in, was cheered at once at the sight of the preferred pledge, and began briskly turning over the rags. He even held them up to the light. Everyone waited to hear what he would say.

"Well, you won't give me a silver ruble, I suppose? It's worth it, you know," said the would-be borrower winking at Isai Fomich.

"A silver ruble, no, but seven kopecks maybe."

And those were the first words uttered by Isai Fomich in prison. Everyone roared with laughter.

"Seven! Well, give me seven then; it's a bit of luck for you. Mind you take care of the pledge; it's as much as your life's worth if you lose it."

"With three kopecks interest makes ten," the Jew went on jerkily in a shaking voice, putting his hand in his pocket for the money and looking timidly at the convicts. He was fearfully scared, and at the same time he wanted to do business.

"Three kopecks a year interest, I suppose?"

"No, not a year, a month."

"You are a tight customer, Jew! What's your name?"

"Isai Fomich."

"Well, Isai Fomich, you'll get on finely here! Goodbye!"

Isai Fomich examined the pledge once more, folded it up carefully and put it in his sack in the midst of the still laughing convicts.

Everyone really seemed to like him and no one was rude to him, though almost all owed him money. He was himself as free from malice as a hen, and, seeing the general goodwill with which he was regarded, he even swaggered a little, but with such simple-hearted absurdity that he was forgiven at once. Luchka, who had known many Jews in his day, often teased him and not out of ill-feeling, but simply for diversion, just as one teases dogs, parrots, or any sort of trained animal. Isai Fomich saw that clearly, was not in the least offended and answered him back adroitly.

"Hey, Jew, I'll give you a dressing!"

"You give me one blow and I'll give you ten," Isai Fomich would respond gallantly.

"You damned scab."

"I don't care if I am."

"You itching Jew."

"I don't care if I am. I may itch, but I am rich; I've money."

"You sold Christ."

"I don't care if I did."

"That's right, Isai Fomich, bravo! Don't touch him, he's the only one we've got," the convicts would shout, laughing.

"Aie, Jew, you'll get the whip, you'll be sent to Siberia."

"Why, I am in Siberia now."

"Well, you'll go further."

"And is the Lord God there, too?"

"Well, I suppose he is."

"Well, I don't mind then. If the Lord God is there and there's money, I shall be alright everywhere."

"Bravo, Isai Fomich, you are a fine chap, no mistake!" the convicts shouted round him, and, though Isai Fomich saw they were laughing at him, he was not cast down.

The general approval afforded him unmistakable pleasure and he began caroling a shrill little chant "la-la-la-la-la" all over the prison, an absurd and ridiculous tune without words, the only tune he hummed all the years he was in prison. Afterwards, when he got to know me better, he protested on oath to me that that was the very song and the very tune that the six hundred thousand Jews, big and little, had sung as they crossed the Red Sea, and that it is ordained for every Jew to sing that song at the moment of triumph and victory over his enemies.

The Jewish Question (1877)*

Fedor Dostoevskii

O h, don't think that I'm really planning to raise "the Jewish question"! I wrote the title as a joke. Raising a question of such magnitude as the position of the Jew in Russia, and the position of Russia, who numbers three million Jews among her sons, is too much for me. This question is beyond my limits. But I still can have some opinion of my own, and it turns out that some Jews have suddenly begun to take and interest in my opinion. I have been getting letters from them for some time now; they reproach me severely and bitterly for "attacking" them and for "hating the Yids," hating them not for their flaws, "not as an exploiter," but specifically as a race, supposedly because "Judas betrayed Christ." Such things are written by "educated" Jews, i.e., by those who (I have noted this, but I am in no way making a generalization—this I wish to point out in advance) always seem to try to let you know that they, with their education, have long ceased to share the "prejudices" of their nation; that they no longer carry out their religious rites as do other petty Jews; that they consider this beneath the level of their enlightenment; that, moreover, they do not even believe in God. I note, apropos of this and in parentheses, that all these gentlemen from the "higher Jews" who defend their nation in this way find it too great a sin to ignore their forty-centuries-old Jehovah and to renounce him. And it is a sin, not only because of feelings of nationality, by any means; there are also other reasons of very great importance. It's an odd thing, indeed: a Jew without God is somehow unthinkable; one can't even imagine a Jew without God. But this is one of those immense topics, and we will drop it for the moment. What surprises me most is how and why I could be placed among the haters of the Jews as a people, as a nation. Even these gentlemen themselves permit me, to some extent, to condemn the Jew for some of his flaws and for being an exploiter, but—but this is only in words: when it comes to deeds, it is difficult to find anything more irritable and punctilious than an educated Jew and more ready than he to take offense—as a Jew. But once again: when and how did I declare my hatred for the Jews as a people? Since there was never any such hatred in my heart—and those Jews who are acquainted with me and who have had dealings with me know this—I, from the very outset and before saying anything else, reject this accusation once and for all so as not to make special mention of it later. Might they not be accusing me of "hatred" because I sometimes call the Jew a "Yid"?[1] But in the first place, I never thought this was so offensive, and in the second place, as far as I can recall, I always used the word "Yid" to denote a well-known idea: "Yid, Yid-ism, the Kingdom of the Yids," etc. These designated a well-known concept, a tendency, a characteristic of the age. One can argue with that idea, one can disagree with it, but one should not take offense at a word [...]

Hatred, and hatred caused by prejudice—that is the accusation the Jews make against the native population. But since we've begun on the topic of prejudices, then what do you think: does the Jew harbor fewer prejudices toward the Russian than the Russian toward the Jew? Doesn't he have a few more of them? I just gave you some examples of how the Russian common person regards the Jew; but I have before me letters from Jews, not common people but educated Jews, and how much hatred these letters express toward the "native population"! What's most important is that they don't notice the hatred contained in what they write.

You see, in order to exist on the earth for forty centuries, i.e., for almost the entire historical period of humanity, and to exist in such a close and indissoluble unity; in order to lose so many times their territory, their political independence, their laws, almost even their religion—to lose these things and each time to unite once more, to be reborn once more *in their old idea*, even though in another form, and to create themselves, their laws, and almost their religion once more—no, a people of such vitality, a people so unusually strong and energetic, a people so unprecedented in the world cannot exist without *status in statu*, something they have maintained always and everywhere during their

---

1   EDS: Dostoevskii here distinguishes between the word *evrei*, translated here as "Jew," and *zhid*, translated here as "Yid." By the 1860s, *evrei* had become the standard word for Jew, whereas *zhid* was marked as pejorative and offensive.

most awful, thousand-year-long Diaspora and persecution.[2] When I speak of *status in statu* I am certainly not making any accusation. But still, what is the meaning of the *status in statu*; what is its centuries-old, unchanging idea, and where does the essence of this idea lie?

To expound this would take a long time and, indeed, would be impossible in a short little article; it would also be impossible because, despite the forty centuries that have elapsed, *all the times and the seasons* have not yet arrived, and the final word of humanity about this great tribe still remains to be said. But without entering into the essence and the depth of this subject, one can outline at least some of the characteristics of this *status in statu*, even if only superficially. These characteristics are: alienation and estrangement on the level of religious dogma; no intermingling; a belief that there exists but one national individuality in the world—the Jew, and though there may be some others, one still has to think of them as nonexistent, as it were. "Go forth from the other nations, form thine own entity and know that henceforth thou art *the only one before God*; destroy the others or enslave them or exploit them. Have faith in thy victory over the whole world; have faith that all will submit to thee. Shun everyone resolutely, and have no communication with any in thy daily life. And even when thou art deprived of thy land, thy political individuality, even when thou art scattered over the face of the earth and among all the other peoples—pay no heed; have faith in all these things that have been promised unto thee; believe, once and for all, that all this will come to pass; and meanwhile thou must live, shun, cling together, exploit and—wait, wait . . ." That is the essential idea of this *status in statu*; and then, of course, there are the internal and, perhaps, mysterious laws that preserve this idea [. . .]

But what am I talking about, and why? Or am I, too, an enemy of the Jews? Can it be true, as one Jewish girl who is—of this I have no doubt—most honorable and educated (that's quite evident from her letter and from the sincere, ardent feeling expressed in it)—can it be true that I, too, am (in her words) an enemy of this "unfortunate" race which I "seem to attach so cruelly at every opportune moment"? "Your scorn for the race of Yids which 'thinks of nothing but itself,' etc., etc., is obvious." No, I will speak up against this "obviousness" and deny even the fact itself. On the contrary, I say and write specifically that "everything required by humaneness and justice, everything required by compassion and Christian law—all this must be done for the Jews." I wrote

---

2   EDS: Lantz here uses the Latin term *status in statu* to translate Dostoevskii's *gosudarstvo v gosudarstve*, literally "a state within a state."

these words above, but now I will add that, despite all the considerations I have already set forth, in the end I still stand for the full extension of rights to the Jews in formal legislation and, if such is possible, also for the fullest equality of rights with the native population (N.B.: although in some instances, perhaps, they already now have more rights or, to put it better, more *possibility to exercise them*, than the native population itself). Of course, a fanciful picture like the following occurs to me: what if, for some reason, out rural commune, which defends our poor, native peasant from so many evils, should collapse? What if the Jews should descend like a horde upon that liberated peasant who has so little experience, who is so little able to restrain himself from temptation and who, until now, has been watched over by the entire commune? Why, that would be the end of him at once: all his possessions, all his strength would tomorrow pass into the hands of the Jew, and an era would begin that could not be compared with serfdom, or even with the Tatar yoke.

But despite all the "fanciful pictures" and despite everything that I wrote above, I still stand for complete and conclusive equality of rights—because this is Christ's law, because this is a Christian principle. But if that is so, then why on earth did I fill so many pages with writing, and what point did I want to make if I *contradicted myself* in such a fashion? Precisely this: that I am not contradicting myself and that from the standpoint of the Russians—the native population—I can see no obstacles to broadening Jewish rights; yet I do contend that there are many more of these obstacles on the Jewish side than on the Russian, and that if this thing so wholeheartedly desired has still not come to pass, then the Russian is much, much less to blame for it than the Jew himself. What I indicated about the common Jew—who did not want to associate and eat with the Russians, while they not only did not get angry at him and reply in kind but, rather, immediately understood the situation and forgave him, saying, "That's because of his religion"—in just the same way as in this common Jew we often see the same boundless and arrogant anti-Russian prejudice in the educated one as well. Oh, they shout that they love the Russian People; one of them even wrote to me along those lines, saying that he was grieved that the Russian People were without a religion and understood nothing of their own Christianity. This is too strongly said for a Jew and only gives rise to the question as to whether this highly educated Jew himself understands anything about Christianity. But self-importance and arrogance are traits of the Jewish character that are very painful for us Russians. Which of us, the Russian or the Jew, is less able to understand the other? I avow that I would rather vindicate the Russian: the Russian, at least, has no (absolutely no) religious hatred for the Jew. And who had more of the other prejudices, and on which side are they? Now we hear the Jews shouting that they have been oppressed and persecuted for so many years, that they are oppressed and persecuted even now, and that the Russian must at least take this into account when he makes judgements on the Jewish character. Very well, we do take that into account and can prove it: among educated classes of the Russian people voices have been raised in favor of the Jews on more than one occasion. Now what about the Jews: have they ever, and do they now, when they complain and make accusations against the Russians, take into account the many centuries of oppression and persecution the Russian People themselves have endured? Can one really claim that the Russian People have endured fewer misfortunes and evils "in their history" than the Jews, in any place you care to mention? And can one really claim that it was not the Jew who, so very often, joined with the oppressors of the Russians, who indentured the Russian People and became their oppressor himself? All this happened, after all; such things went on; this is history, historical fact, but we've never heard anywhere that the Jewish people have repented for it, yet they still accuse the Russian People of having little love for them.

But still: "Let it come to pass! Let it come to pass!" May there be complete and spiritual union of the tribes and no disparity in their rights! And to this end I first implore my opponents and Jewish correspondents to be, on the contrary, a bit more indulgent and fair to us Russians. If their arrogance, if the perennial "resentful affliction" of the Jews toward the tribe of Russians is only a prejudice, a "historical tumor," *and is not buried among some far deeper mysteries of their law and their makeup*, then may all this disappear as quickly as possible and may we all join together in a single spirit, in complete brotherhood, for mutual help and for the great cause of service to our land, our state, and our fatherland! May the mutual accusations be softened; may the perennial intensification of things, vanish away. But one can vouch for the Russian People: oh, they will accept the Jew in complete brotherhood, despite the difference in religion, and with complete respect for the historical fact of this difference; nevertheless, for brotherhood, for complete brotherhood, *brotherhood is needed on both sides*. Let the Jew himself show the Russian even a little brotherly feeling so as to encourage him. I know that among the Jewish people even now one can find enough individuals who seek and long for the misunderstanding to be dispelled; these are humane people as well, and I will not be the one to ignore the fact and hide the truth. It is specifically in order that these useful and humane people should not grow despondent and lose courage, that their prejudices might be weakened in some small measure and that they might thus find it easier to begin to act—it is for these reasons I would like to see the complete broadening of the rights of the Jewish race, as far as is possible, at least, precisely in so far as the Jewish people themselves demonstrate their capacity to accept and to use these rights without damaging the interests of the native population. It might even be possible to make some concessions in advance, to take still more steps forward on the Russian side . . . The only question remains: will the new, good people among the Jews manage to do this, and to what extent are they themselves capable of serving the new and beautiful cause of *genuine* brotherly unity with people who are alien to them by religion and blood?

Christians, Muslims, and Jews in *Notes from the House of the Dead* (2008)*

Susan McReynolds

M̲ost surprising in light of the anachronistic expectations readers bring to *Notes from the House of the Dead* is the way this text portrays Christian Russians, Muslims, and Jews. The most uplifting episodes of the book, which come closest to moments of brotherly reconciliation across cultural divides, involve the narrator and Muslim inmates. The community that does emerge in *Notes* is not one that encompasses the Russian elite and common people as envisioned in *Time*, but a new brotherhood that unites Gorianchikov, his beloved Alei, and Alei's brothers, in common appreciation of Jesus's message.[1]

The Russian Christian prisoners are morally inferior to the Muslims. Among the Russians, Gorianchikov writes, "Backbiting and scandal-mongering went on ceaselessly," and "gossip, intrigue, cattiness, envy, squabbles, malice were always to the fore" (*MHD*, 14).[2] The prison is a place of inexpressible cynicism and shameless laughter, relieved only by the moral goodness of the Dagestanian Tatars. Gorianchikov's description of the Tatars has the

---

*   From Susan McReynolds, *Redemption and the Merchant God: Dostoevsky's Economy of Salvation and Antisemitism* (Evanston, IL: Northwestern University Press, 2008), 109–16. Copyright © 2008 by Northwestern University Press. All rights reserved.

1   EDS: *Time* (Russian *Vremia*) is the journal launched by Dostoevskii and his brother Mikhail in 1861. The journal aimed to bridge the growing divide between Westernizers and Slavophiles, and between the elites and the ordinary people.

2   EDS: In this excerpt, *MHD* refers to *Notes from the House of the Dead*. The edition used by McReynolds is: Fyodor Dostoevsky, *Memoirs from the House of the Dead*, ed. Ronald Hingley, trans. Jessie Coulson (Oxford: Oxford University Press, 1992).

same curious blending of feminine and masculine qualities and almost erotic attraction that characterize the later description of Marei. *Notes* offers some of the first examples of iconic, transformative beauty Dostoevskii creates, and they are Muslim tribesmen.

Nurra is "built like a Hercules, very fair, with light blue eyes like a Finnish woman's"; he "produced a most comforting, a most pleasing impression on me from the very first," Gorianchikov confides.

> The other prisoners all liked him. He was always cheerful and friendly towards everybody, did his work without repining and was good-natured and placid, although he often showed his dislike of the filth and squalor of prison life and was roused to fury by every instance of theft, drunkenness, swindling and general knavery, and vice [...] He himself never stole anything or did one wrong thing all the time he was in prison. (*MHD*, 71)

During Gorianchikov's first half hour in prison and over the next days, he recalls, Nurra "wanted to show me that he was friendly, and to cheer me up and assure me of his help. Good, simple Nurra!"; "it was impossible to miss his kind, sympathetic face among all the sullen, spiteful, jeering faces of the other prisoners" (*MHD*, 72).

Gorianchikov confesses an attraction to Alei's beauty as well. He is "as chaste as a pure young girl," and "his handsome, candid, intelligent and at the same time naively good-natured face attracted my heart to him at first sight" (*MHD*, 72). Gorianchikov is grateful that he sleeps next to Alei. "I was very glad that fate had sent me him, and not somebody else, as a neighbor" in the barrack, he writes. Alei's iconic beauty improves those who look at him. "His whole soul was reflected in his handsome—one might almost say beautiful—face. His smile was so trustful, so childishly artless, his big black eyes were so melting and tender, that I always felt particular satisfaction, even a lightening of my grief and longing, when I looked at him" (*MHD*, 72). Alei's face has a similar effect on his older brothers, who "always smiled when they looked at him"; when they talked with him, "their grim faces relaxed" (*MHD*, 73). "I think of Alei as no ordinary being and I remember my meeting with him as one of the most valuable in my life," Gorianchikov asserts (*MHD*, 73–74).

Among the depraved Russian prisoners, Alei "kept himself so strictly honest, so sincere, and so attractive, and never became hardened or corrupted. His personality, moreover, was strong and direct in spite of all his seeming gentleness" (*MHD*, 74).

Any evil, cynical, filthy, or unjust instance of violent conduct lit the fires of indignation in his fine eyes, making them even more beautiful. But he avoided disputes and strife, although he was not one of those who allow themselves to be insulted with impunity and was able to stand up for himself. But he had no quarrel with anybody; everybody liked him and was kind to him. (*MHD*, 74)

A brotherly community encompassing Gorianchikov and Alei's brothers arises around appreciation of Alei's beauty and the message of the Gospels. Gorianchikov gives Alei lessons in the Russian language and reading the New Testament, which the young Muslim "learned with zeal and enthusiasm."

Once we read through together the Sermon on the Mount. I noticed that he seemed to pronounce some parts of it with special feeling. I asked him whether he had liked what he read. He looked up quickly and his cheeks were flushed.

"Oh, yes!" he answered. "Yes, Jesus is a holy prophet. Jesus spoke the word of God. How wonderful!" (*MHD*, 76)

Seeing this special friendship between their younger brother and the Russian prisoner, Alei's brothers reach out to Gorianchikov. Alei and his brothers take pleasure in doing things for Gorianchikov. "It was plain that it gave him great pleasure to make things even a little easier and pleasanter for me," he writes of Alei. "In this endeavor there was not the slightest abasement or search for personal advantage, but only the warmth of his friendship for me, which he made no attempt to hide" (*MHD*, 75). A community based in spiritual love, not national, biological, or sectarian ties, emerges. Alei, Gorianchikov reflects, "loved me perhaps as much as he loved his brothers," who "vied with each other in helping me" (*MHD*, 77, 76). When Alei leaves prison, he kisses Gorianchikov and weeps, saying he has done more for him than his own father or mother would and telling him, "You have made me a man" (*MHD*, 77).

"Nurra is a lion," the prisoners say, but the Jewish prisoner Bumshtein is a plucked chicken.[3] Gorianchikov recalls "his little figure: fiftyish, puny,

---

3 The portrait of Bumshtein is perhaps the earliest representation of a Jew in Dostoevskii's writings. The real-life prototype, Isai Bumstehl, was a jeweler imprisoned for murder, whipped and branded. The records say that he was a convert to Greek Orthodoxy. David Goldstein notes that Gorianchikov uses the word "Jew" (*evrei*) rather than the term "Yid" (*zhid*), which occurs frequently in Dostoevskii's later writings. David I. Goldstein, *Dostoevsky and*

wrinkled, with horrible brands on his cheeks and forehead, with a skinny, feeble, white body like a plucked chicken's" (*MHD*, 136). The physically beautiful Muslims stand out as beacons of moral rectitude among the degenerate Russians, but the ugly Jew is the butt of the prison's laughter. "Lord, how comical, how laughable, that man was!" Gorianchikov exclaims. All the prisoners liked the Jew, "although absolutely all of them, without exception, laughed at him" (*MHD*, 78). "Isaiah Fomich evidently served as an entertainment and a perpetual diversion for them" (*MHD*, 137). The prisoners tease him "exactly as one amuses oneself with a dog, a parrot, a trained animal, or something of that kind" (*MHD*, 139). Everyone laughed at him, Gorianchikov recalls, "and even now I cannot remember him without laughing" (*MHD*, 78).

Beneath his comic/grotesque characterization, however, the truth is that this branded Jew actually embodies the spiritual disfigurement of the Russians. Bumshtein concentrates in himself all the moral flaws of the superficially Christian prisoners: formalism, vanity, and lack of true values and conscience. The shallowness of their Christianity is exposed through their association with the Jew.

The moral flaws tragically disfiguring the Russians are comic/grotesque in the Jew. Bumshtein is "cunning and yet distinctly stupid," Gorianchikov observes, "impudent and insolent, and at the same time terribly cowardly" (*MHD*, 78). "There was in him a most comical mingling of naivete, stupidity, sharpness, impudence, artlessness, timidity, boastfulness, and effrontery," Gorianchikov explains (*MHD*, 137). "Generally speaking," he says of the Russians, they have "a certain peculiar personal dignity," observing that "the whole tribe [. . .] was sullen, envious, terribly conceited, boastful, touchy, and preoccupied in the highest degree with forms" (*MHD*, 13, 12). Bumshtein is "innocently vain and conceited"; the Russian prisoners are "in the highest degree vain and frivolous" (*MHD*, 140, 184).

Bumshtein and the Russians have no moral conscience; prison holds no shame for them. Bumshtein "was always in excellent spirits. Prison life was easy for him"; he is a jeweler and busy with orders from town; he's the moneylender and pawnbroker (*MHD*, 78). "The expression of his face revealed unwavering, unshakeable self-satisfaction and even beatific happiness. He felt apparently not the slightest regret at having fallen into prison" (*MHD*, 136). He is wrinkled and branded; he is accused of murder; yet he nurses absurd hopes

---

the Jews (Austin: University of Texas Press, 1981), 15. There is some question as to whether the record stating Bumstehl's conversion is correct (169).

that are repulsive in him—about fifty years old, he plans on absolutely getting married when he's released, an intention that Gorianchikov relays with
repugnance.

The Russians, including Gorianchikov, "did not like to talk, and
evidently tried not to think, of the past" (*MHD*, 11). The prisoner on the bed
next to him in the hospital is in for counterfeiting; he is "far from stupid, an
extremely cheeky and confident young man, morbidly vain and quite seriously convinced that he was the most honest and upright person in the world,
and even that he was completely innocent of all wrongdoing" (*MHD*, 202).
Many of them "are even glad to have reached the prison at last (a new life is
sometimes so great an attraction!) and are consequently disposed to settle
down in peace and quiet" (*MHD*, 62). The situation is the same on both
sides of the class line. The nobleman Aristov entered prison "without the
least distress or even repugnance, suffered no moral disturbance and feared
nothing in it" (*MHD*, 90). They act "as if the status of convict, or condemned
man, constituted some kind of rank, and that an honorable one. Not a sign of
shame or remorse!" (*MHD*, 13).

Nurra, Alei, and his brothers live the Sermon on the Mount even though
they are not Christian; Christ's message continues to elude the Russian prisoners, on the other hand, because they are mired in a kind of formalism they share
with the Jew. Bumshtein and the Russians live by empty words, formalism,
and the law instead of living conscience. "Preoccupied in the highest degree
with forms," the prisoners frequently repeated "proverbs and sayings" such as
"'You wouldn't heed your father and mother, now be ruled by the drum,' [. . .]
but never seriously. They were only words. There was hardly one of the prisoners who in his heart acknowledged his own lawlessness" (*MHD*, 13). Akim
Akimovich, who "had even settled himself in prison as though he were preparing to spend the rest of his life there," produced in Gorianchikov "immeasurable dejection" (*MHD*, 323). "I would be hungry sometimes for a living word
of some kind," but instead Akim Akimovich would patter on "in a sedate, even
tone, like water falling drop by drop" (*MHD*, 324).

Bumshtein practices his Sabbath "with forced and pedantic solemnity";
everything he does is "prescribed by his ritual" (*MHD*, 140). The old believers
have "fanatical literal belief in their religious books" (*MHD*, 79). "They were
highly developed people, shrewd peasants, believing pedantically and uncrit-
ically in the literal truth of their old books, and very powerful dialecticians
in their own way; a haughty, arrogant, crafty, and highly intolerant people"
(*MHD*, 44). Akim Akimovich "was not particularly pious, because morality

had apparently swallowed up all his human talents and particular qualities, all his passions and desires, both good and evil" (*MHD*, 157). "Generally speaking, he did not like to have to do much thinking. He never troubled his head, apparently, about the meaning of any act, but he fulfilled a principle, once it had been shown to him, with religious accuracy" (*MHD*, 158).

Akim Akimovich's preparations for Christmas, like Isaiah Fomich's for his Sabbath, emphasize form and ritual to the exclusion of living spirit. "Blindly devoted to ritual, he regarded even his Christmas suckling pig, which he had stuffed with kasha, and roasted [...] with a kind of anticipatory esteem, as though it were not an ordinary piglet, which might be bought and roasted at any time, but a special, Christmas one" (*MHD*, 158). "I am sure that if he had ever once failed to eat pork on that day he would have felt a certain pang of conscience all his life for the obligation unfulfilled" (*MHD*, 158). Sarcastically describing Akim Akimovich's attention to the details of the new clothes he has saved for Christmas, Gorianchikov writes, "Pious respect for a button, for a shoulder knot, a loop had been ineffably imprinted in his mind from his childhood as an incontestable obligation, and in his heart as the highest degree of beauty attainable by an honest man" (*MHD*, 159). He executed his obligations "with calm, methodical seemliness of conduct, just as much as was required for the performance of his obligations and the ceremonies laid down once and for all" (*MHD*, 158).

Gorianchikov critically describes how Bumshtein delights in fulfilling the "ingenious provision of the Law" in his religious observances and observes Russians misusing the concept of the law (*MHD*, 141). Overseeing a flogging, Lieutenant Zherebiatnikov takes recourse to the law as a substitute for individual moral conscience.

> "My dear friend," says he, "what am I to do with you? The law punishes you, not I."
>
> "Your honor, everything depends on you. Be merciful!"
>
> "Do you not think I am sorry for you? Do you think it will be a pleasure for me to watch you being beaten? After all, I too, am a man! [...] I am quite well aware that I must, in all humanity, look with compassion and even indulgence on you, sinner though you are [...] But this is a matter for the law, not for me!" (*MHD*, 227–28)

Russia has too many people who believe that "the relentless application of the letter of the law" is foremost in human affairs, Gorianchikov maintains (*MHD*, 176).

"These advocates of the application of the law definitely do not under-stand, and are incapable of understanding, that the mere literal fulfillment of the law, without reason or comprehension of its spirit, leads straight to disor-der and has never led to anything else," Gorianchikov objects (*MHD*, 176). The prisoners, he critically observes, dispute "as an exercise in style." The formal qualities of argument eclipse content and critical thinking among them. "Not infrequently they got carried away and began to dispute with passion-ate heat and frenzy," he recounts, only to part company as though nothing had happened. "The man who could argue down or shout down his opponent was highly esteemed and all but applauded like an actor," Gorianchikov notes with disapproval (*MHD*, 31). Isaiah Fomich's arguing skills are highly regarded in the prison.

The Christmas theatricals do effect a temporary transformation in the prisoners. It is what happens in the audience—the spectacle enacted among the viewers—that has some regenerative power. "For me," Gorianchikov explains, "the greatest interest lay in the audience" (*MHD*, 189). "Alei's charming face shone with such beautiful child-like joy that I confess it made me immensely happy to look at him," Gorianchikov recalls (*MHD*, 188). Alei has a similar effect on other usually glum prisoners as well. Their joy momentarily trans-forms them into a brotherly community, with each man seeking to communi-cate his impressions to the others. They nudge one another, look around; one "would turn in an ecstasy of appreciation to the crowd, embrace them with a rapid glance as though exhorting them to laugh" (*MHD*, 189). After such expe-riences, "they all went to sleep, not as on any other night, but almost with a quiet spirit" as if "their moral nature was changed, even if only for a few min-utes" (*MHD*, 198).

Several factors serve to render the theater's promise as a vehicle of moral redemption problematic, however. Gorianchikov's reflections on the tempo-rary transformation accomplished in the prisoners are interrupted by the real-ity of how the "ugly dream" of their lives continues on as before (*MHD*, 198). Most important, however, is the contrast between the audience's joy and what is actually portrayed on stage.

"Kedril the Glutton," one of the pieces performed, is a strange, one-act fragment lacking a beginning and ending; like the prisoners' lives, it seems abortively disconnected. "There is not the slightest reason or logic in the whole thing" Gorianchikov observes (*MHD*, 191). Set in a provincial Russian inn, "something like Don Juan," it tells of a master and servant being dragged off to hell. The servant Kedril is in one sense a victim—his fate is tied to that of his master, who has sold his soul to the devil. But Kedril is not simply a victim; his own gluttony and moral immaturity, rather than oppression by a master, doom him. This fragment enacts the contrast between the moral irresponsibility of the people and the (alleged) acceptance of accountability in the elite. The master accepts the consequences of his crime—he displays volition and understanding of his sin and its repercussions—whereas Kedril is taken against his will because he lacks the strength to resist.

As they are shown to their room, the innkeeper warns the gentleman and his servant Kedril, "a great glutton," that it is haunted (*MHD*, 191). The gentleman replies that he knows of the devils and orders Kedril to prepare supper; Kedril, "a coward and a glutton" (these qualities are emphasized several times), "turns pale and trembles like a leaf" (*MHD*, 191). Kedril has several opportunities for escape, but base emotions outweigh his desire to save himself. "He would run away, but he is very afraid of his master. Besides, he is very hungry. He is lustful, stupid, cunning in his own way, and cowardly" (*MHD*, 191). When the master explains to him that he once long ago sold his soul to the powers of darkness and that tonight they will come for him "in accordance with the bargain he made," Kedril "begins to grow terrified. His master, however, has not lost heart and bids him prepare supper" (*MHD*, 192). Kedril consumes almost an entire chicken while the gentleman paces; the master, "gloomily preoccupied and noticing nothing," pays no attention to the fact that only one chicken leg remains for him, a fact that sets the audience laughing (*MHD*, 193).

Kedril and his master react differently to the appearance of the devils. "The gentleman turns sufficiently boldly to the devils and cries that he is ready for them to take him" (*MHD*, 193). Kedril, on the other hand, is torn between his fear of eternal damnation and his more powerful physical desires. Turning "timid as a hare," he hides under the table, "not forgetting, in spite of all his fright, to seize the bottle as he goes" (*MHD*, 193). He ignores his master's cry of "Kedril, save me!" and enjoys his meal after the devils have taken the gentleman away. Instead of escaping and saving himself, he stays to eat and drink. The devils pounce on him just as he pours himself a glass of wine; "he is too faint-hearted to dare turn around. Neither is he able to defend himself; in his hands are the bottle and glass, which he cannot find the strength to put down" (*MHD*, 194). He is dragged off to hell with a "comical expression of lily-livered terror," while "still holding the bottle" (*MHD*, 194).

Like Petrov and many of the other prisoners, Kedril seems to know nothing higher than his immediate, physical inclinations. This figure—joyfully acclaimed by the prison audience as one of their own—exemplifies the complex contributions even the victims make to their hopeless condition in the dead house. One of the most distressing obstacles to resurrection portrayed in *Notes from the House of the Dead* is surely this: that it is not even clear who the victims in need of saving are because the very category of victim seems to break down; and that when salvation is offered, the supposed victim himself seems incapable of accepting it.

From "A Few Words about George Sand" (1876)[*]

Fedor Dostoevskii

Very quickly, right from the beginning of the thirties, we learned of this immense movement of European literatures. The names of the many newly fledged orators, historians, publicists, and professors became known. We even knew, though incompletely and superficially, the direction in which this movement was heading. And this movement manifested itself with particular passion in art—in the novel and above all in George Sand. It is true that Senkovskii and Bulgarin had warned the public about George Sand even before her novels appeared in Russian. They tried to frighten Russian ladies, in particular, by telling them that she wore trousers; they tried to frighten people by saying she was depraved; they wanted to ridicule her.[1] Senkovskii, who himself had been planning to translate George Sand in his magazine *Library for Reading* began calling her Mrs. Egor Sand in print and, it seems, was truly pleased with his witticism.[2] [. . .] People who met her in Europe then said that she was propounding a new status for women and foreseeing the "rights of the free wife" (this is what Senkovskii said about her). But that was not quite correct, because she was by no means preaching only about women and never invented any

---

[*]   From Fyodor Dostoevsky, *A Writer's Diary Volume 1: 1873–1876*, trans. and ed. Kenneth Lantz (Evanston, IL: Northwestern University Press, 1994), 508–11; 513. Copyright © 1994 by Northwestern University Press. All rights reserved.

[1]   Osip Ivanovich Senkovskii (1800–58), journalist, critic and humorist. His reviews of contemporary writers display cynicism and contempt. Faddei Venediktovich Bulgarin (1789–1859), Russian writer, journalist, and publisher of *Severnaia pchela* [The Northern Bee], a conservative newspaper. Bulgarin was notorious for his denunciations of writers to the secret police of Nicholas I.

[2]   Egor is the Russian form of George.

notion of a "free wife." George Sand belonged to the whole movement and was not merely sermonizing on women's rights. It is true that as a woman she naturally preferred portraying heroines to heroes; and of course women all over the world should put on mourning in her memory, because one of the most elevated and beautiful of their representatives has died. She was, besides, a woman of almost unprecedented intelligence and talent—a name that has gone down in history, a name that is destined not to be forgotten and not to disappear from European humanity.

As far as her heroines are concerned, I repeat that from my very first reading at the age of sixteen I was amazed by the strangeness of the contradiction between what was written and said about her and what I myself could see in fact. In actual fact, many, or at least some, of her heroines represented a type of such sublime moral purity as could not be imagined without a most thorough moral scrutiny within the poet's own soul; without the acceptance of one's full responsibility; without an understanding and a recognition of the most sublime beauty and mercy, patience, and justice. It is true that along with mercy, patience, and the recognition of one's obligations there was also an extraordinary pride in this scrutiny and in protest, but this pride was precious because it stemmed from that higher truth without which humanity could never maintain its high moral ideals. This pride is not a feeling of hostility *quand même*, based on the fact that I am supposedly better than you and you are worse than I; it is only a sense of the most chaste impossibility of compromise with falsity and vice, although, I repeat, this feeling excludes neither universal forgiveness nor mercy. Moreover, along with the pride came an enormous responsibility, voluntarily assumed. These heroines of hers sought to make sacrifices and do noble deeds. Several of the girls in her early works particularly appealed to me; these were the ones depicted, for example, in what were called at the time her Venetian tales (including *L'Uscoque* and *Aldini*).[3] These were of the type that culminated in her novel *Jeanne*, a brilliant work which presents a serene and, perhaps, a final solution to the historical question of Joan of Arc.[4] In a contemporary peasant girl she suddenly resurrects before us the image of the historical Joan of Arc and graphically makes a case for the actual possibility of this majestic and marvelous historical phenomenon, a task quite characteristic of George Sand, for no one but she among contemporary poets, perhaps, bore within her

---

3   *La Derniere Aldini* (1837–38), novel. Dostoevskii translated the novel into Russian in 1844, only to learn that a Russian translation already existed.

4   *Jeanne* (1844), novel.

soul such a pure ideal of an innocent girl, an ideal that derives its power from its innocence.

[...]

George Sand was not a thinker, but she had the gift of most clearly intuiting (if I may be permitted such a fancy word) a happier future awaiting humanity. All her life she believed strongly and magnanimously in the realization of those ideals precisely because she had the capacity to raise up the ideal in her own soul. The preservation of this faith to the end is usually the lot of all elevated souls, all true lovers of humanity. George Sand died a *déiste*, firmly believing in God and her own immortal life, but it is not enough to say only that of her: beyond that she was, perhaps, the most Christian of all her contemporaries, the French writers, although she did not formally (as a Catholic) confess Christ. Of course, as a Frenchwoman George Sand, like her compatriots, was unable to confess consciously the idea that "in all Creation there is no name other than His by which one may be saved"—the principal idea of Orthodoxy.[5] Still, despite this apparent and formal contradiction, George Sand was, I repeat, perhaps one of the most thoroughgoing confessors of Christ even while unaware of being so.

---

5   Paraphrase of Acts 4:12: "Neither is there salvation in any other; for there is no other name in heaven given among men, whereby we must be saved."

From
"About Women Again"
(1876)*

Fedor Dostoevskii

I was about to conclude my *Diary* and was already checking the proofs when a young girl unexpectedly called on me.[1] I had met her in the winter after I had begun publishing my *Diary*. She wants to take a rather difficult examination and is energetically preparing for it; she'll pass it, of course. She's from a wealthy family and doesn't lack means, but is very concerned about her education. She would come to ask my advice on what to read and what to pay particular attention to. She has been visiting me about once a month, staying no more than ten minutes; she would speak only of her own affairs, but briefly, modestly, almost shyly, showing remarkable trust in me. Yet I could also see she had a very resolute nature, and it seems I was not mistaken. This time she came to me and said directly: "People are needed to tend the sick in Serbia.[2] I have decided to postpone my examination for the time being so I can go look after the wounded. What do you think?"

---

* From Fyodor Dostoevsky, *A Writer's Diary Volume 1: 1873–1876*, trans. and ed. Kenneth Lantz (Evanston, IL: Northwestern University Press, 1994), 532–34. Copyright © 1994 by Northwestern University Press. All rights reserved.

1 The girl was Sof'ia Efimovna Lur'e (1858–189?), identified by Anna Dostoevskaia as the daughter of a wealthy banker from Minsk (Leonid Grossman, *Seminarii po Dostoevskomu* [Moscow-Petrograd: Gos. izd-vo, 1922], 65). Dostoevskii publishes a portion of a letter from her in *A Writer's Diary*, March 1877, 3.1. She in fact conceded to the wishes of her family and did not go to Serbia.

2 EDS: Serbia declared its independence in 1876, leading to the Serbo-Ottoman War (1876–78); Russia supported the Serbs and the conflict developed into the Russo-Turkish War (1877–78).

And she looked at me almost timidly, yet her look told me clearly that she had already made her decision and that it was an absolutely firm one. She wanted some parting words of approval from me, however. I cannot convey all the details of our conversation lest I might in some small way violate her anonymity; I am passing on only its general content.

I suddenly felt very sorry for her—she is so young. It would have been quite pointless to frighten her with the difficulties, the war, the typhus in the field hospitals; this would mean only pouring oil on the flames. Here was a pure case of longing for sacrifice, for some noble feat, for some good deed; most significant and most precious was her total lack of conceit and self-infatuation; she wanted only to "look after the wounded" and to be of help.

"But do you know anything about treating wounded soldiers?"

"No, but I've been collecting information and have been to the Committee. Those who enlist are given two weeks to prepare, and of course I'll manage."

And she will, of course; here the word is equal to the deed.

"Listen," I told her, "I don't want to frighten you or dissuade you, but consider my words well and try to weigh them in your conscience. You have grown up in surroundings quite different from those you'll encounter there; you've seen only good society and have met people only in that calm state of mind where they remain within the bounds of etiquette. But the same people at war, in crowded conditions, in hardship and labor, may change utterly. Suppose you spend a whole night tending the sick; you've worn yourself out and are so exhausted that you can barely stand, when a doctor—a very good man at heart, perhaps, but tired and overstrained after just amputating a number of arms and legs—turns to you in irritation and says: 'All you do is make a mess of things; you can't do anything! If you've taken on this job, then do it properly!' and so on. Won't you find that hard to bear? Yet you certainly have to expect that sort of thing, and what I'm suggesting is only a tiny part of what's ahead of you. Real life often surprises us. And finally, are you certain that, even with all your resolve, you'll be able to cope with looking after the wounded? Might you not faint at the sight of some death, some wound or operation? This happens despite one's will, unconsciously . . ."

"If I'm told that I'm doing things wrong and not working properly, then I'll certainly understand that this doctor is himself irritable and tired; it's enough to know in my own heart that I'm not to blame and have done everything properly."

"But you're still so young; how can you be certain what you'll do?"

"What makes you think I'm young? I'm already eighteen; I'm not so young at all . . ."

In short, it was impossible to dissuade her: she was ready to go off the very next day, in any case, regretting only that I did not approve of what she was doing.

"Well, God be with you," I said. "Go on; but come back just as soon as the thing is finished."

"Of course. I have to take my examination. But you'll never believe how happy you've made me."

She went away radiant and, of course, she will be there in a week.

At the beginning of this *Diary*, in the article about George Sand, I wrote a few words about the young female characters I had found particularly appealing in the stories of her earliest period. Well, this girl was just like one of them. She had just the same sort of direct, honest, but inexperienced young feminine character, along with that proud chastity which is unafraid and which cannot be stained even by contact with vice. This girl felt the need for sacrifice, for undertaking a task that seemed to be asked of her specifically; she had the conviction that she must first begin herself, with no excuses, to do all those fine things that we expect and demand from others. This is a conviction which is genuine and moral to the highest degree, but which, alas, is most often characteristic only of youthful purity and innocence. But the main thing, I repeat, is that here there is only a cause and not the slightest element of vanity, conceit, or infatuation with one's own heroism, something that we very often see among today's young people, even among mere adolescents.

After she had left I could not help but think once more about the need for higher education for women in Russia, a need that is most urgent at this moment in particular, in view of the serious pressure among today's women to be active, to be educated, and to participate in the common cause. I think that the fathers and mothers of these daughters ought themselves to insist on it for their own sake, if they love their children. In fact, it is only higher learning that is serious, attractive, and powerful enough to settle what is almost an agitation that has begun among our women. Only science can provide answers to their questions, strengthen their intellects, and take their heterogeneous thoughts under its wing, as it were. As far as this girl was concerned, though I had pity for her youth (and even though I was unable to stop her in any case), I rather think that this journey might even be of some value to her in a sense: this is not the world of books or abstract convictions after all; it is an immense experience that awaits her, an experience that perhaps God Himself, in His immeasurable goodness, fated for her in order to save her. Here a lesson in the living life is being prepared for her; before her stands the possibility of expanding her ideas and her views; she will have something to remember all her life, something precious and beautiful in which she participated, something that will compel her to value life and not weary of it before she has lived, as did the unfortunate suicide Pisareva of whom I spoke in my last, May, Diary.

The Woman Question in *Crime and Punishment* (1994)*

Nina Pelikan Straus

While feminist approaches to Dostoevskii's other novels may be promising, the murder-of-women and salvation plot of *Crime and Punishment* offers the most concentrated exposure of the relation between a young man's experience of violence toward women and the construction of his masculine identity. Other Dostoevskian narratives offer the construction (or destruction) of the hero's character in relation to women, yet none explores so relentlessly the identity confusions such relations generate. In *Crime and Punishment* Dostoevskii dramatizes men's experience in response to "the feminine" and points to the possibility of Raskol'nikov's becoming a representative "life poised on the threshold"[1] of reinvented forms of the "masculine." In this chapter, I indicate how stereotypes about gender have structured previous readings of the heroic in the novel, and how it is precisely these stereotypes that are challenged by Dostoevskii's polyphonic language.

Feminist approaches to the novel may meet with resistance because of Dostoevskii's overt repudiation of a socialism concerned with woman's oppression and his Slavophile nationalism. The recasting of Sonia in his notebooks to embody the philosophy of the soil (*pochvennichestvo*), expressed in her demand that Raskol'nikov bow down and kiss the Russian earth, seems evidence of Dostoevskii's conservatism. Yet Bakhtin's description of Dostoevskii's

* From Nina Pelikan Straus, *Dostoevsky and the Woman Question: Rereadings at the End of a Century* (New York: Palgrave Macmillan, 1994), 19, 21–22, 24–27, 30–36. Reprinted with permission of the publisher.
1 Mikhail Bakhtin, *Problems of Dostoevsky's Poetics*, trans. Caryl Emerson (Minneapolis: University of Minnesota Press, 1984), 63.

multivoiced discourse invites feminist speculation, particularly in terms of Bakhtin's emphasis on the idea of the *other*. In his notes, Bakhtin offers an image that might serve as the germ of a feminist hermeneutics: "Just as the body is initially formed in the womb of the mother (in her body), so human consciousness awakens surrounded by the consciousness of others."[2] [. . .]

For feminists, "the feminine" may be socially constructed, but for Raskol'nikov its polarity to "the masculine" is initially experienced as essentialist. Raskol'nikov is obsessed with guilt about his landlady and her daughter, and with responsibility for his mother and sister whose female dependencies "stifl[e] and cram[p]" him (*CP*, 57).[3] He is immersed in the dream of the beaten nag and in revolting visions of the female pawnbroker whom he perceives, in contrast to himself, as "vermin." Female images (nag, pawnbroker, landlady, sister, mother) are sources of uncontrollable misery that he longs to transcend through the "fascinating audacity" of a violent, manly act. This act, associated with the fantasy of man's unlimited freedom and the "uttering [of] a new word" (*CP*, 20), receives its charge from the contrasting idea of woman's bondage to an old world: from Dunia's potential bondage to Luzhin in marriage, from his mother's bondage to himself as her "guardian angel" (*CP*, 213), and from Sonia's bondage to prostitution. Raskol'nikov's encounters with women continually test whether "everything is in a man's own hands" (*CP*, 20), whether he can conceive of his identity as (metaphysically) bound or unlimited, as (socially) victimized or heroic, as (dialogically) related to women or severed from them in sublime masculinist autonomy. He links women with ideas of cowardice, limitation, and victimization, and masculinity with power, money, courage, and the capacity to create victims. The pawnbroker and Lizaveta are Raskol'nikov's victims; his mother and sister are Luzhin's and Svidrigailov's; and "Mother Russia" is Napoleon's. He murders the pawnbroker as the cab driver of his dream murders the nag, as Napoleon murders "vermin," and as Svidrigailov may have murdered his wife. Patterned so that Raskol'nikov's gendered associations are gradually contradicted, the novel moves toward pandemonium, the "terrible uproar" of the funeral scene in which women scream, Luzhin is unmasked (*CP*, 404), and Dunia resists and defeats Svidrigailov. Only through the experience of gender roles reversed or conflated can Raskol'nikov glimpse the transformed image of manhood Dostoevskii seeks for him.

---

2   Tzvetan Todorov, *Mikhail Bakhtin: The Dialogical Principle*, trans. Wlad Godzich (Minneapolis: University of Minnesota Press, 1984), 96.

3   EDS: In this excerpt, *CP* refers to Fyodor Dostoevsky, *Crime and Punishment*, trans. David McDuff (London: Penguin Books, 1991).

Dostoevskii's diffusion of sex-stereotyped images is nevertheless at odd with Raskol'nikov's initial gender essentialism. The novel begins with Raskol'nikov's dream of a (male) cart driver beating a (female) nag and continues with Raskol'nikov hacking the female pawnbroker to death, but the image of men beating women is finally inverted. Duplicated images of beating, several of them reversing the gender relations of the others, show how Raskol'nikov discovers that what he beats *beats him*. An early image of Katerina pulling her husband "by the hair" (*CP*, 32) is followed by the image of Raskol'nikov hitting the "crown" of the female pawnbroker's head with a hatchet (*CP*, 96). Raskol'nikov then dreams of "hitting the old woman on the head with all his strength, but at every blow of the hatchet... [she] simply rocked with laughter" (*CP*, 194). His fall into a "fathomless chasm" and into a simultaneously "higher" realm where his dialectic "vanishes" (*CP*, 132–133) is also dramatized by Marmeladov's being crushed to death by a horse, implying the retaliation of the beaten mare in Raskol'nikov's dream upon her male persecutor (*CP*, 195). The idea of "the feminine" in *Crime and Punishment* is the symbolic hatchet that breaks open men's heads by destroying the distinctions between "low" and "high," "docile" and "powerful," victim and master, the coward and the hero. The hierarchy of Raskol'nikov's sexist imagery decomposes as he discovers that he is "a louse . . . nastier than the louse [he] killed" (*CP*, 292) and that his Napoleon fantasy is a "frightful muddle" (*CP*, 470). By exploring the ways in which the masculine-feminine polarities reflected in Raskol'nikov's consciousness are undermined, *Crime and Punishment* appears as a text in which Dostoevskii discovers the politics of gender, and in which Raskol'nikov's crime and punishment are engendered by them [...]

What is missing from Raskol'nikov's discourse and experience is present in the resonating relations between the two men, Dunia, and other women: in their "hidden polemic, polemically colored confession, hidden dialogue,"[4] which defines "man" as he who violates women, which defines masculinity at femininity's expense, and which defines a new kind of woman as a resisting heroine or martyr (*CP*, 487). This hidden polemic about men and women is not disclosed by Raskol'nikov's murdering of the pawnbroker. Instead, that crime serves as an opening for Raskol'nikov to come in contact with Svidrigailov, who in turn comes in contact with Dunia which enables both men to admit their to each other their "insect" suffering and hopelessness (*CP*, 305) [...]

---

4   Bakhtin, *Problems*, 203.

Dostoevskii's convergence of the crime and sex-crime categories in the novel's second half forces the woman question and the Napoleonic question (whether Raskol'nikov is a "man" or a "vermin") to mirror each other. Svidrigailov's words about Dunia ("I assure you this look of your sister's haunted me in my dreams" [*CP*, 489]), suggesting obsession with female sexuality, are dialogically related to Raskol'nikov's words about the beaten mare in his dreams. The nonsexual words that inform Raskol'nikov's dream reveal the contexts of Russian women's lives. In axing the pawnbroker, the symbolic master Raskol'nikov will "whip the little grey-brown mare." Taking things into "a man's own hands," he is compelled not to "spare her"; she must be "showered with blows"; she must drown in blood because she is a man's "property" (*CP*, 74–76). Or, in a dreamlike reversal of meanings, he must kill her because she has taken his property (as Alena takes Raskol'nikov's property in pawn), or because he is not, psychologically, his own property. All these words reveal the contexts to which the novel's women are subjugated in varying degrees and the pattern through which Raskol'nikov becomes more and more identified with women and their contexts. Katerina carries the load of her family upon her sickly, tortured back, crying out on her deathbed that "they've beaten the mare to death" (*CP*, 448); Sonia can be bought or sold as sexual property; Svidrigailov beats his wife until she dies; Dunia's virgin blood will flow if she cannot convert the master or persuade him to spare her.

Dunia's relations with men, like Sonia's, disclose the masculinist desire (as dramatized by Luzhin and Svidrigailov) to purchase woman as a thing to violate her morally or physically as the instantiation of man's superior power. Raskol'nikov's resistance to Sonia, as well as his hatred of the female pawnbroker, demonstrates a terror of the sex-violence complex he associates with men and fears in himself, an association verified by Svidrigailov's attempted rape of Dunia. The question of what men do to, for, or with women drives Raskol'nikov toward others beside Sonia, thus enlarging the dialogue between masculinist identity and crimes against women. His emotional turmoil unravels in relation to Sonia or what Peace calls "the 'Elizaveta' in [Raskol'nikov's] make-up";[5] through conversations with Porfirii that trivialize his Napoleonism; but also in terms of the "Dunia" who evolves within him and through the "Svidrigailov" he confronts.

---

5 Richard Peace, *Dostoyevsky: An Examination of His Major Novels* (Cambridge: Cambridge University Press, 1971), 54.

The pattern that relates Raskol'nikov's Napoleon ideology to both his and Svidrigailov's crimes involves images of violence done to women, even though Raskol'nikov's conversations with Porfirii suppress the connection. The novel is saturated with writings about crime (Raskol'nikov's article), arguments about crimes redeemed by penitence (with Sonia), conversations about criminal motivation (with Porfirii), and disclosures of the pleasures of sex-crimes (with Svidrigailov). Yet nowhere does Dostoevskii employ words that describe connections between Raskol'nikov's notion that there are "two categories" of human being—the "inferior" and the "talent[ed]" capable of both crime and of saying a "new word" (*CP*, 279)—and his responses to two categories of the human: the male and the female. These connections are made because Raskol'nikov's consciousness is increasingly penetrated by other peoples' words. Women's words in particular tell him a different story than he has told himself. Through Sonia's and Porfirii's words, Raskol'nikov begins to understand the connections between his Napoleonic theory and the murder that he, a possibly *talented* young man, has perpetrated against a distinctly *inferior* and nearly *wordless* old woman. As the novel progresses, Raskol'nikov's words become more and more a part of "agitated, verbal surface" of a work in which "everything is on the borderline . . . everything is prepared . . . to pass over into its opposite."[6] The crossing over or mutual identification between Raskol'nikov and Svidrigailov becomes increasingly close. Although Raskol'nikov commits crimes "on principle" and Svidrigailov is compelled by sensuality, each man's experience with women mirrors the genderized structure of an action imagined as necessary for male transcendence in the Napoleon fantasy.

The two worst crimes, murder and attempted rape, are positioned at opposite ends of the novel; bookends that symbolize the two "supreme effort[s]" of a perverted masculinist script (*CP*, 279). While Raskol'nikov's article, "On Crime," articulates the supreme fantasy, the novel reveals that fantasy's consequence, which is violence toward "vermin" (who turn out to be female). What the novel articulates as a rethinking of male roles, Raskol'nikov's article perverts; yet each reveals that male criminality is never disassociated from fantasies about women and sex. If "it takes a strong soul to endure [Dostoevskii's] works,"[7] this is because the novel and its "intellectual" discussions are haunted by images of battered, violated, and murdered women. Raskol'nikov's vision

---

6   Bakhtin, *Problems*, 167.
7   Jacques Catteau, *Dostoevsky and the Process of Literary Creation*, trans. Audrey Littlewood (New York: Cambridge University Press, 1989), 455

of the "masses" as "cows" (*CP*, 279) points to "Napoleon" as a bull or phallic signifier. Only a "Napoleon" is capable of violating "Mother Russia." Thus Raskol'nikov's question to himself suggests the nature of Dostoevskii's "borderline" feminist inquisition: "Why did I say 'Women!'?" (*CP*, 268).

Raskol'nikov's Napoleonism, like his relation to women, is in Bakhtin's terms a "*live* event," a masculinist "idea-prototype" whose "resonance" must be played out and exposed.[8] Overtly expressed in Raskol'nikov's writings and his conversations with Porfirii, the little-Napoleon actions of other male characters in the novel express this idea-prototype in nearly parodic form. Initially experienced through Raskol'nikov's murder of the female pawnbroker, whose life "amounts to no more than the life of a louse" (*CP*, 84–85), the idea is later played out through Luzhin's and Svidrigailov's relations with Sonia and Dunia. Treated as inferiors, each female figure enters Raskol'nikov's "thoroughly dialogized interior monologue [. . .] a dialogue of ultimate questions and ultimate life decisions."[9] These ultimate decisions are related to problems involving women's bodies, women's social-economic role, and the religious and mythic symbolisms that entrap both sexes. Sonia, Dunia, her mother, Katerina, Lizaveta, and the pawnbroker each represent a familiar feminine situation. All of them indicate how "woman" is a dominant fetish of Raskol'nikov's culture, constituted by her lack of phallic, social, and political power.[10]

Sonia's woman problem is that she lacks money and must sell her body to men. Dunia's deprivation and sacrificial impulse for her brother's sake tempts her to sell herself in marriage to Luzhin. If Alena brokers jewelry, Sonia and Dunia broker youth and sexuality. The pawnbroker's suspiciousness, the way she jumps back "in panic" when a man "advance[s] straight on" (*CP*, 94), dramatizes the elderly female's experiences of male brutality even before her encounter with Raskol'nikov. Lizaveta is not just any docile woman, but one who "always seemed to be pregnant" and who "acquiesces in everything," including sex, as the officers who describe her with "keen relish" indicate to Raskol'nikov (*CP*, 83–84). Along with Katerina, Alena, and Sonia, she represents the socially

---

8 Bakhtin, *Problems*, 88–92. The italics are Bakhtin's.

9 Ibid., 74.

10 I use the word *lack* in the sense of Lacan's interpretation of Freud's notion of the female as "castrated," stressing a linguistic rather than physical meaning. Raskol'nikov's Napoleonism can be understood as a symptom of phallocentric narcissism in the sense that "the human social order [. . .] refracted through the individual human subject is patrocentric," reflecting not biological but "cultural-symbolic language conditions." Juliet Mitchell, Intro. to Jacques Lacan, *Feminine Sexuality: Jacques Lacan and the École Freudienne* (New York and London: W. W. Norton, 1985), 23.

degraded female whom Raskol'nikov must extinguish within himself in his attempt to establish a sense of male superiority. Like Svidrigailov, Raskol'nikov must initially mock, penetrate, or hack at a woman to assert a masculine identity otherwise indistinguishable from its status as "vermin."

Dostoevskii represents Raskol'nikov as magnetized toward two symbolically gendered extremities, each of which is psychologically imprisoning. Whereas the Napoleon idea embodies masculine fantasies of freedom and modernity, reacting to cruelty by embodying it, the idea of Sonia embodies docility and Christianity, reacting to cruelty by bearing it. In acting out both these roles, Raskol'nikov reveals the socially constructed sexual polarities within himself, experiencing fully the Russian "feminine." Not only the novel's women but its central male figures are represented as oppressed by patriarchal hierarchies and by myths about masculine freedom. Svidrigailov's question, "Am I a monster or am I myself the victim?" (*CP*, 297), is also Raskol'nikov's. The consequence of the "self's capacity to exercise its freedom without limit" is a suffering that Raskol'nikov shares with men who make women suffer [...]

Running between the physically undeveloped Sonia and the androgynous Porfirii, both of whose bodily attributes signify gender confusions, Raskol'nikov is led toward the undermining of his masculine role. Victimized by Porfirii's inquisition, Raskol'nikov's sickness appears as a defense against the cruelties of a legal system that treats men without power like women and perpetuates misogyny by allowing men to symbolically retaliate against that system by beating women. Raskol'nikov's transformation thus has multiple sources, reinforced by Porfirii's appearance in the novel as a peculiar feminine-masculine compound. "The expression of [Porfirii's] eyes was strangely out of keeping with his whole figure, which reminded one somehow of the figure of an old peasant woman" (*CP*, 267). Raskol'nikov is provoked to partial confession through Porfirii's maternal image and through his strangely castrating discourse: "he'll fly straight into my mouth, and I'll swallow him!" (*CP*, 355). Attempting to liberate him from the world of dead men's voices, Porfirii insists that Raskol'nikov's crime bears "no resemblance whatever to any previous case" (*CP*, 354). Yet the reader may remember that "exactly the same ideas" about murdering the pawnbroker "just beginning to stir in [Raskol'nikov's] own mind" were articulated by ordinary young officers in a Petersburg restaurant a short while before Raskol'nikov committed the crime (*CP*, 84–85). Porfirii's discourse exists alongside other words and images that overlap to form a pattern revealed to the reader: the notion of Raskol'nikov's crime as a disease (*CP*, 90), the resonance between Raskol'nikov's Napoleon theory and other misogynist worldviews shared by men of his generation. Because Porfirii has not heard the young officers' words about murdering the old woman, because he has no knowledge of Svidrigailov's sexual violence toward young women, his solutions for Raskol'nikov, like Sonia's, remain partial. Porfirii intuits Raskol'nikov's suicidal impulses, but he is not privy to the female-imaged crisis that Raskol'nikov's confession to Sonia suggests:

> Was it the old hag I killed? No, I killed myself, and not the old hag. I did away with myself at one blow and for good. (*CP*, 433)

Related to his growing identification with women, Raskol'nikov's suicidal impulses foreshadow the motive behind Svidrigailov's suicide. Raskol'nikov's self-knowledge emerges partially from his ambiguous struggles with Sonia's Christianity and partially through Porfirii's mockery of his Napoleonism. But knowledge also comes to him by way of Dunia's resistance to Svidrigailov and Raskol'nikov's identification with them both. A series of events connected with women leads to the confession of his crime. Svidrigailov confesses his "disgusting stories" of lust and violence to Raskol'nikov (*CP*, 494); he attempts the rape of Dunia and she shoots at him (*CP*, 507). In what appears as a non sequitur in the police station, Raskol'nikov listens to the assistant superintendent discuss "short-haired young females" who "have a most immoderate desire for enlightenment," and the issue of "what more do [women] want" (*CP*, 540–541). This textual glancing at feminist questions and Dunia is followed by the announcement that Svidrigailov has shot himself, and by Sonia's appearance at the police station. Only then does Raskol'nikov admit "It was I who killed the old woman" (*CP*, 541–542). Although Dostoevskii has sought to keep Raskol'nikov's crime clean of sexual implications, he is finally unable to forestall the convergence of sex with violence, of Raskol'nikov's "disease" with Svidrigailov's, and of feminist with religious and ethical issues.

The Dunia-Svidrigailov chapter therefore occupies a peculiar position in the novel because it is explicitly about sexual relations and the masculine problematic. Melodramatic as the Lazarus scene between Raskol'nikov and Sonia, it is that scene's reversal, with the man rather than the woman humiliated by the struggle. Dostoevskii's intention to transform man through woman's religious faith is complicated in the second scene by the intrusion of a psychology of a new woman and a transformed man whose life framework is power and sexuality rather than religion and theory. Although Dunia's experience with Svidrigailov is not mentioned in the police station where her brother makes his

confession, the assistant-superintendent's words about "short-haired" (emancipated) women and "educated" men (*CP*, 540–1) forge dialogic connections
between the Svidrigailov-Dunia scene and the scene of Raskol'nikov's confession in the police station with Sonia present. While Raskol'nikov's fantasy is to
reform the world of heroes through his Napoleon theory (which Sonia resists),
Dunia's "passion for reform" moves in a feminist direction toward advocacy for
other women (*CP*, 489) to which Svidrigailov submits. This glance in a feminist
direction through Dunia on Dostoevskii's part is not a fully developed or integrated part of the novel's surface. In fact, the image of Dunia and Svidrigailov
interrupts that surface somewhat the way the central clue to a dream's meaning appears extraneous to the dream's manifest content. It shifts the notion of
transformation away from religious conversion to what looks like the feminist
conversion of a male chauvinist.

Dunia, much less fully realized as a character than Svidrigailov, remains
part of what Bakhtin calls the novel's "hidden interior," perhaps its most hidden
part, justifying the impression that the novel's "narrative practices and psychology [are] violently at odds with [its] ideological intentions."[11] It is the
religiously pure and simple Sonia, and not the complex Dunia, who must
appear to be the source of Raskol'nikov's conversion, even if the novel's imagery, its self-interception, and its hidden dialogue suggest the contrary. Slipping
from Dostoevskii's anti-feminist/socialist stance, Dostoevskii's "encounter"
with Dunia, once set in verbal motion, forms new aspects and new functions
of the word for the novel and for the reader. It is only through Dunia's effect
on Svidrigailov that Raskol'nikov's confession and self-transformation can be
achieved. Only through the connections between religious and feminist ideologies of conversion that "the woman question" can be contextualized. Dunia's
visit to Svidrigailov's rooms explores the question that Dostoevskii has treated
satirically through Lebeziatnikov—whether "in the future men and women can
have access to each other's rooms" (*CP*, 384)—a question that must henceforth be taken seriously.

Dunia's capacity for a violent act against Svidrigailov undermines the
gendered contraries at the heart of Raskol'nikov's fantasy of male freedom
and female bondage. Locked in Svidrigailov's room, threatened with the fact
that "rape is very difficult to prove," Dunia shoots at her violator with his own

---

11 Michael André Bernstein, "'These Children that Come at You with Knives': Ressentiment,
Mass Culture, and the Saturnalia," *Critical Inquiry* 17 (1991): 365.

gun, first grazing his hair with the bullet. In the following passage the narrator describes Svidrigailov's state of mind:

> Now she would kill him—at only two feet away! Suddenly she threw away the gun. A heavy weight seemed to have lifted suddenly from his heart, but possibly it was not only the weight of the fear of death [. . .] It was a release from another more forlorn and somber feeling which he himself could scarcely have defined in all its strength. (*CP*, 506–8)

Dunia's response to Svidrigailov combines (stereotypically male) self-defense with (stereotypically female) compassion for the other, dramatizing a cross-gendered role that Raskol'nikov can "grasp" only "to a certain extent" (*CP*, 540) and that Svidrigailov can "scarcely define." Release from Svidrigailov's masculinist monologue turns upon Dunia's final refusal to use the man's own methods against him, leading to his being "seized by the other's discourse, which has made its home in it."[12] Dunia's image and voice invade Svidrigailov just as the images of beaten mare, axed pawnbroker, and prostituted Sonia invade Raskol'nikov's narcissistic solitude. Her interception in the genderized nightmare destroys stereotypes as it exposes the masculinist disease and "something in common" (*CP*, 302) from which Svidrigailov and Raskol'nikov suffer.

Woman readers may be particularly sensitive to the implications of Dostoevskii's connection of Raskol'nikov with Svidrigailov. In *Crime and Punishment* the rapist is the murderer's double, and each symbolizes the degenerate form to which the secular Westernized "metaphysic" of free male individuality and genderized oppositions have driven him. Dostoevskii's critique of "man's" freedom suggests the woman-violating form to which socially constructed masculinity is sometimes addicted. The novel makes clear that just as the peasant Mikolka beats the mare because she is his "property" (*CP*, 77), just as Napoleon is the conqueror of territories, so Svidrigailov imagines himself the "conqueror of women's hearts" (*CP*, 488), and Raskol'nikov temporarily imagines he can become "one man out of a thousand" by killing a greedy old woman. Svidrigailov's question to Dunia, "So you don't love me?" (*CP*, 508) co-exists with Raskol'nikov's question, "Why did I say 'Women!'?" and with the assistant superintendent's question, "What more do [women] want?" For both Raskol'nikov and Svidrigailov, disease has its origins in male fantasies that

---

12 Bakhtin, *Problems*, 219.

construct women as barriers men must penetrate to achieve masculinity—fantasies symbolized in the novel's last section by Svidrigailov's dream.

The dream that Bakhtin characterizes as *Menippea* marks the alpha and omega of masculine images of women as it assimilates the temptress to the victim, the Orthodox Madonna to Magdalene, the girl to the woman, and both to the whore who is man's desire and debasement. As Svidrigailov lifts the covers from the sleeping girl-child, Dostoevskii uncovers the fantastic core of his female image repertoire:

> But how strange! The color of the little girl's cheeks seemed brighter . . . her eyelids were opening slowly, as though a pair of sly, sharp little eyes were winking at him not at all in a childish way, and as though the little girl was only pretending to be asleep.

Svidrigailov's dream suggests "the universal genre of ultimate questions"[13] involving masculine relations to power and female sexuality. The dream asks whether women are human, whether women mean what they say; whether women desire rape:

> Yes, yes, that was so: her lips parted in a smile; the corners of her mouth twitched [. . .] She was laughing! [. . .] There was something shameless and provocative in that no longer childish face. It was lust, it was the face of a whore, the shameless face of a French whore [. . .] But at that moment he woke up. (*CP*, 520–21)

Replicating fragments of Raskol'nikov's experience, the dream echoes the "winking" of the "peasant woman" Porfirii and the laughing of the pawnbroker in his dream, as well as her "sharp, sly" eyes. The child's face mirrors the childish face of Sonia, the fact that Sonia is a "whore," and that whores like Napoleon are "French." Like Sonia, Dunia is tempted to sell herself to men such as Luzhin, but in Svidrigailov's dream, men also prostitute themselves to degraded identity and dreams that drive them to despair and suicide, Dostoevskii's religious intentions for Raskol'nikov do not disguise what his society has projected upon women.

Learning that Svidrigailov has shot himself, Raskol'nikov "felt as if some heavy weight had descended on him and pinned him to the ground" (*CP*, 541).

---

13 Ibid., p. 146.

His feeling inverts Svidrigailov's sense that "a heavy weight seemed to have lifted suddenly from his heart." The weight of sexual crisis, no longer sublimated into abstract questions of freedom or power, shifts to Raskol'nikov. He is weighed down by Dunia's and Sonia's meanings, by the "key" that Svidrigailov has literally thrown to his sister and, by symbolic implication, to him (*CP*, 509). If he does not fully incorporate Sonia's Christianity, he nevertheless falls into a new world that Sonia and Dunia occupy. In this world where women affect men intensely, the dialectic between masculinity and femininity, hero and vermin, oppressor and oppressed, begins to close. For Raskol'nikov, "Life had taken the place of dialectics, and something quite different had to work itself out in his mind" (*CP*, 580).

This difference discloses Dostoevskii's new version of a masculinity that will escape violence but resist impotence. Raskol'nikov attempts but ultimately fails to live out the most heroic version of male courage available to him (Napoleonism), yet Dostoevskii represents his failure as a triumph. Each defeat of an unwanted sexual advance on the part of other men in the novel can also be read as Dostoevskii's undermining of a false conception of masculinity that must be extinguished in Raskol'nikov. Against these masculinist fantasies, Dostoevskii empowers Sonia with a hardly believable compassion and Dunia with a virtue, understanding, and strength that can be read as Dostoevskii's alternative to the virtues of feminine passivity. As matured variants of the raped girl-child figure that haunted Dostoevskii all his lie, Dunia and Sonia perform a partial revenge against their male violators. If for Dostoevskii child rape ending in murder was the worst crime, then the resistance to rape by a young woman, leading to the self-conscious transformation of the rapist, would constitute a transformed male consciousness. More importantly it would acknowledge female power in an alternate form to Sonia's. If Svidrigailov is Raskol'nikov's double, Svidrigailov's conversion from pathological sexuality to a momentary dialogic relation with Dunia is the feminist parallel to Raskol'nikov's religious conversion through Sonia [...]

Originating in Raskol'nikov's experience with women, Dostoevskii's challenge to himself ends *Crime and Punishment*: "He would have to pay a great price for it [...] he would have to pay for it by a great act of heroism in the future" (*CP*, 559). This heroic act is Dostoevskii's creation of male figures, particularly Prince Myshkin and Alesha Karamazov, who incorporate socially constructed "feminine" traits and are intensely sensitive to the problem of man's violence against women. In *The Brothers Karamazov*, Alesha is haunted and motivated by his mother's miserable life. He faints when his father describes how he tortured Alesha's mother, "the shrieker" (Bk. 3, ch. 8), repeating Raskol'nikov's fainting scene with his mother and sister but with a new development in consciousness. Neither Myshkin nor Alesha can be imagined without their most important predecessor, Raskol'nikov. *Crime and Punishment* presents scenes in which no authentic male heroism exists without a man's willing entry into dialogic relations and identifications with women, substantiating certain feminist hopes for the future of both sexes.

The Mothers
Karamazov (2009)*

Carol Apollonio

In *The Brothers Karamazov* Dostoevskii offers one of the great paternal portraits in world literature. Fedor Pavlovich Karamazov dominates the novel: he is the great elemental force at its center, the mystery of the seed in the Gospel of John, the "evil urge" without which no life is possible. This last novel is so obviously an exploration of the question of fatherhood that the reader may be excused for forgetting that the Karamazov brothers had mothers—two, and possibly even three, of them. Adelaida Ivanovna, Sof'ia Ivanovna, and Lizaveta Smerdiashchaia are long dead by the time the novel's action begins; they occupy the narrator's sustained attention only in cursory introductory material, and although reminders of them surface now and then through the course of the novel, our attention is generally focused elsewhere.[1] Nevertheless, the

---

* From Carol Apollonio, *Dostoevsky's Secrets: Reading against the Grain* (Evanston, IL: Northwestern University Press, 2009), 144; 148–58. Copyright © 2009 by Northwestern University Press. All rights reserved.

1 Some excellent recent studies have directed attention to the mothers. In "Mothers and Sons in *The Brothers Karamazov*: Our Ladies of Skotoprigonevsk," in *A New Word on "The Brothers Karamazov,"* ed. Robert Louis Jackson (Evanston, IL: Northwestern University Press, 2004), 31– 52, Liza Knapp explores the significance of the Marian motif and the hysterical affliction of Ivan and Alesha's mother. Susan Amert explores the Ophelia motif in the Adelaida Ivanovna story, in "The Reader's Responsibility in *The Brothers Karamazov*: Ophelia, Chermashnia, and the Palpable Obscure," in *Freedom and Responsibility in Russian Literature,* ed. Elizabeth Cheresh Allen and Gary Saul Morson (Evanston, IL: Northwestern University Press, 1995), 105–18. See also Straus, *Dostoevsky and the Woman Question;* and Harriet Murav, "Reading Women in Dostoevsky," in *A Plot of Her Own: The Female Protagonist in Russian Literature,* ed. Sona Stephan Hoisington (Evanston, IL: Northwestern University Press, 1995). All of these studies represent a wealth of new work devoted to the role of women in Dostoevskii's writings.

central catastrophe of the novel builds upon the tensions they left behind. The chain of events leading to the murder of Fedor Pavlovich Karamazov began some thirty years before when he eloped with the headstrong Miusov girl [. . .]

Adelaida marries Fedor Pavlovich, and then realizes that she feels only contempt for him. The strong word *prezirat'* (to feel scorn or contempt) associates her with such troubled and scornful characters as Ivan Karamazov, Katerina Ivanovna, Lisa Khokhlakova, and Rakitin, whose love of money renders them unable to experience grace and pure love. The telltale conjunctive *takim obrazom* ("in this way" or "thus") suggests that the "consequences of the marriage," the couple's "disorderly life," and "constant scenes" are due to *Adelaida's* scorn for her husband rather than his behavior or character itself. It is she who beats him, not the reverse; and she commits the worst crime a mother can commit when she leaves not just her husband, but her child as well. Although—like Ivan Karamazov rebelling against God because he has abandoned his children—we concentrate our blame on the father, the cycle of misery and sin begins with the mother's action. There is no indication that Fedor Pavlovich was unfaithful to his wife during their marriage; he began drinking and carousing with other women (that "harem") *after* his wife abandoned him. In the distinctive moral system of Dostoevskii's novel, Adelaida Ivanovna bears a significant share of the blame for her husband's unruly behavior, which, according to the logic of the narrative, would not have taken place if she had stayed home where she belonged. A very charitable reader may choose to view Fedor Pavlovich's preparations to travel to St. Petersburg in search of his runaway wife ("What for? Of course he himself did not even know"; PSS 14:9) as an attempt *to save her*. Significantly, Adelaida Ivanovna chooses a seminary student for her lover. In Dostoevskii's world (both in the novels and in the cultural context of mid-nineteenth-century Russia), this well-established type, the proto-nihilist *raznochinets*, represents the abandonment of Christian faith and a commitment to radicalism, feminism, and atheism. Adelaida's move from a provincial town in the heart of Mother Russia to "the most complete emancipation" (*v samuiu polnuiu emansipatsiiu*; PSS 14:9—note the foreign word) in St. Petersburg is also symbolically significant, representing a dangerous openness to the evils of Westernization. These choices turn Adelaida Ivanovna away from the life principle embodied in her husband and lead inexorably to her *death*.

Clearly Adelaida Ivanovna has abrogated her moral responsibilities. But how can Fedor Pavlovich's behavior with his wife's money be justified? He essentially stole her dowry, which "was as good as gone forever." The narrator's report that her behavior was considered more noble and dignified than her husband's guides this conventional interpretation. Still, under what conditions does a husband's use of his wife's dowry constitute wrongdoing? Fedor Pavlovich invested the money and built a fortune from it; a faithful wife who shares her property with her husband could only stand to benefit from such prudent financial management. Only in retrospect, and only from a point of view *sympathetic* to Adelaida, could his behavior be condemned. Furthermore, if she hadn't left him, the money would have belonged to them both and their son. This is not a trivial issue, for Dmitrii's misery originates in the enigmatic remnants of her dowry, and of course in his mother's abandonment of him and his father.

The events depicted in *The Brothers Karamazov* demonstrate the powerful, morally weighted forces inherent in family relationships and passed down through the generations. Adelaida Ivanovna's selfish behavior, which can be blamed for the sufferings of her abandoned husband and son, is consistent with her own brand of "family values." Her death involves her cousin Petr Aleksandrovich Miusov in the Karamazovs' affairs. Petr Aleksandrovich represents one of the most reprehensible types in Dostoevskii's palette: the outwardly cultured, charitable, and righteous but inwardly selfish, grasping, and corrupt nobleman. Miusov's continuing legal battles with the monastery over property boundaries surely symbolize a deeper struggle between Western secular values and an elemental Russian Christianity. Upon Adelaida's death, Miusov becomes joint guardian of the motherless boy. Having attended to his own financial interests, however, he too abandons Mitia to a distant relative. This *dvoiurodnaia tetka* (aunt once removed) establishes a faint but deadly association between Miusov and Ivan's devil, who, the narrator informs us, resembles those bachelor spongers (*prizhival'shichiki*) of noble birth "who might even have children, but their children are brought up somewhere far away, by some *aunt* or other [*u kakikh-nibud' tetok*], whom a gentleman practically never mentions in decent society, as though somehow ashamed of such a relationship" (PSS 15:71). It seems possible to argue that the Miusovs serve as a conduit for the devil through the matrilineal line—in the form of a woman's lust, greed, and selfishness, and the money that comes with her—into the inner sanctum of the Karamazov family.

[…]

Counterintuitive as it may seem, Adelaida Ivanovna's marriage to Fedor Pavlovich may be viewed symbolically, from her point of view, as a life-affirming step. The similarity of her precipitous marriage to a provincial Russian girl's suicidal imitation of Ophelia paradoxically reinforces this interpretation—in spite of the narrator's attempts to characterize the elopement as impulsive and self-destructive.[2] For the juxtaposition of elopement and suicide is a relation of contrast, not similarity. Adelaida Ivanovna's marriage to Fedor Pavlovich in the symbolic structure of the novel serves as an alternative to death. Indeed, it leads to the creation of new life (the birth of her son Dmitrii). Only when she abandons him and her husband does she die.[3]

Fedor Pavlovich's second marriage contrasts sharply to his first. Sof'ia Ivanovna, Ivan's and Alesha's mother, is presented to the reader as a naive, gentle child bride victimized by her husband's lechery and raucous behavior. But her marriage too saves her life. Life in the house of her benefactress had reportedly been so miserable that "it would have been better for her to throw herself into the river than remain with her" (PSS 14:13). This turn of phrase recalls the Ophelia motif of her predecessor Adeleida Ivanovna (whose twenty-five-thousand-ruble cash dowry, by the way, "disappeared as if into the water"; PSS 14:9). Furthermore, Sof'ia had not metaphorically, but in fact, attempted suicide. Here again, marriage to Fedor Pavlovich serves as an *alternative to death*. A woman's entrance into Fedor Pavlovich's house exposes her to the raw power of his sexual energy (yeast for the dough) and offers the potential for creation of new life—the babies Ivan and Alesha.

Based on the narrator's account, readers generally credit Sof'ia Ivanovna for Alesha's gentle spirituality. Her son's memories of her serve as "bright points in the darkness" (PSS 14:18). One scene remains particularly vivid in Alesha's mind:

> He remembered one quiet summer evening, an open window, the slant-
> ing rays of the setting sun (he remembered those slanting rays most of
> all), the icon in the corner of the room with the lamp burning in front of
> it, and in front of the icon, on her knees, sobbing as if in hysterics, with
> shrieks and exclamations, his mother, snatching him up in her arms, grip-
> ping onto him so tightly it hurt, and praying to the Mother of God for him,
> stretching him away from her embrace with both hands toward the icon

---

2 Amert, "The Reader's Responsibility," 107–9.

3 This perspective will clash with approaches that identify the woman as the silenced victim in Dostoevskii's work. Readers interested in learning "whether Dostoevskii's narratives in general, or indeed, narrative in general, require a (female) victim" should turn to Harriet Murav's provocative "Reading Women in Dostoevsky" (46). Asking this question in reference to *The Brothers Karamazov* leads to a negative answer: here the narrator's victim (of slander) is Fedor Pavlovich.

as though turning him over to the protection of the Mother of God, [. . .] and suddenly his nurse rushes into the room and tears him away from her in terror. What a picture! At that moment Alesha recalled the face of his mother as well: he said that it was frenzied, but beautiful, at least as far as he could recall. (PSS 14:18)

The son's gentleness and reverence for his mother's memory—along with those potent "slanting rays" that have made such an impression on critics through the years—have led to interpretations of this vision as a source of spirituality and grace:

Persisting memories from childhood, spots of light amid darkness, a still summer evening, an open window, the slanting rays of the setting sun, a holy icon, a lighted lamp, a parent's tears, a picture created through memory—each of these elements somehow, according to Dostoevskii's private mythology, contributes intimately and directly to an ever-shifting yet unified design that reflects the epiphanic moments of grace that can occur unexpectedly in human life.[4]

Robert Belknap associates this passage with the sunlit scenes of joyful religious experience Zosima remembers from his own childhood in the novel's "cluster of associations centering upon divine grace."[5] It is possible, though, that the positive aspects of Zosima's related vision have tended to overshadow the darker side of Alesha's memory, for the scene contains disturbing, dissonant elements as well. Sof'ia Ivanovna's shrieks and sobs differ qualitatively from the cathartic weeping of Zosima's theology—the bereaved peasant mother's tears that will eventually lead to quiet joy, the redemptive tears that flow around little Iliusha Snegirev's bedside, and Alesha's own rapturous tears after the Cana of Galilee revelation.

[. . .]

The narrator identifies her as a *klikusha*, a "shrieker." In Russian folk culture, "shrieking" (*klikushestvo*) was a mental illness resembling hysteria that afflicted peasant women and was often perceived as a form of demonic possession. Ivan Pryzhov, a contemporary of Dostoevskii's who studied Russian

---

4   Robin Feuer Miller, *"The Brothers Karamazov": Worlds of the Novel* (Toronto: Maxwell Macmillan Canada, 1992), 21.

5   Robert Belknap, *The Structure of "The Brothers Karamazov"* (Evanston, IL: Northwestern University Press, 1989), 39–42.

folk belief, describes the *klikusha* as a diminished descendant of the prescient maiden (*veshchaia deva*) of old Russia, in whom the Holy Spirit took residence and granted the gift of prophecy. With time, however, and with the worsening of the material conditions of peasant life, the status of these women "descends lower and lower" until by the seventeenth century the deva has become a baba and the holy spirit has mutated into "unclean spirits," demonic forces that provoke shrieking and hysterics in their human hosts.[6] *Klikushestvo* was widespread in Russia, even in Dostoevskii's time. It was "primarily a woman's condition characterized by howling, cursing, and falling to the ground during the liturgy, in the midst of church processions, or in the presence of icons, incense, and other religious objects."[7] *Klikushestvo* clearly signaled the presence of the devil in its victims, although they were treated with sympathy among the peasantry.[8] The servant Grigorii's tenderness toward Sof'ia Ivanovna in *The Brothers Karamazov* may be taken as a case in point.[9] In her discussion of Russian witchcraft, including the related phenomenon of *klikushestvo*, Christine Worobec documents a "feminization of witchcraft and sorcery" in Russia in the second half of the nineteenth century that "reflected a growing identification of women and their sexuality, if unrestrained, as potentially dangerous to the patriarchal world."[10] The shrieking affliction came on at sexually sensitive times; for example, women would be "seduced by demons who appeared before them in the shape of their dead or absent husbands."[11] "The devil's nocturnal visit to women, particularly on their wedding night, is a common folk motif."[12] One sufferer "dated the beginning of her demon

---

6 Ivan Pryzhov, *26 Moskovskikh prorokov, iurodivykh, dur i durakov i drugie trudy po russkoi istorii i etnografii* (St. Petersburg: Ezro, 1996), 82–83. Dostoevskii's brief discussion of *klikushestvo* in the "Peasant Women Who Believe" chapter of *The Brothers Karamazov* draws on Pryzhov's study. See PSS 14:44 and the editors' notes in 15:531–32. See also Knapp, "Mothers and Sons," 36–39.

7 Linda J. Ivanits, *Russian Folk Belief* (Armonk, NY: M. E. Sharpe), 106.

8 Ibid., 106–8.

9 Vladimir Golstein's recent discovery and disclosure of demonic aspects in Grigorii's character are highly relevant here. See his "Accidental Families and Surrogate Fathers: Richard, Grigorii, and Smerdiakov," in *A New Word on "The Brothers Karamazov,"* ed. Robert Louis Jackson (Evanston, IL: Northwestern University Press, 2004), 90–106.

10 Christine Worobec, "Witchcraft Beliefs and Practices in Prerevolutionary Russian and Ukrainian Villages," *Russian Review* 54 (April 1995): 168. See also her book *Women, Witches, and Demons in Imperial Russia* (DeKalb: Northern Illinois University Press, 2001), which offers an in-depth exploration of Russian *klikushi*.

11 Ibid., 174.

12 Christopher Putney, *Russian Devils and Diabolic Conditionality in Nikolai Gogol's "Evenings on a Farm near Dikanka"* (New York: Peter Lang, 1999), 70, note 18.

possession to her wedding day."[13] In one "epidemic" of demon possession, "a majority of the possessed women lived in households without their husbands," but all of them had been married.[14] Shrieking episodes came on in the presence of sacramental objects. This form of demonic possession clearly relates to both Russian spirituality and female sexuality. The fact that Sof'ia Ivanovna suffers from this affliction complicates the traditional interpretations of the "slanting rays" scene in *The Brothers Karamazov*; this is not a simple case of innocent suffering and supplication.

In a recent essay on "maternal grief" in *The Brothers Karamazov*, Liza Knapp explores the boundaries between the Russian phenomenon of *klikushestvo* and Western psychological, literary, and religious models. She identifies antecedents of Sof'ia Ivanovna's story in Victor Hugo's tale of the grieving mother and lost child in *Notre Dame de Paris*, and in the image of Our Lady (Mother of God) in its Western as well as Eastern manifestations. Knapp contrasts the specifically Russian phenomenon of "shrieking" with "Freudian and Platonic" forms of hysteria. Hysteria in these Western variants was assumed to afflict women with "restless wombs," that is, those who were not sexually active and were barren. Dostoevskii's peasant women, in contrast, are overworked wives and mothers, and their ailment reflects the rigors and travails of their lives rather than a deficit of sex. Knapp examines Sof'ia Ivanovna as a literary manifestation of this type and shows her derivation from the numerous real-life examples recounted by the author in his *A Writer's Diary* of "women who retaliated violently" against abuse by men.[15] Tellingly, in the Hugo novel, the church (Our Lady, the Cathedral of Notre Dame) is unable to save the mother's child.

These meticulous readings reveal previously undiscovered layers of complexity in Dostoevskii's treatment of the theme of *klikushestvo* in his characterization of Alesha's mother. Still, the violence, pain, and terror of Alesha's memory of his mother are disturbing, and the question of demonic possession, which Pryzhov identifies as a key element in the affliction, cannot be ignored. The critics sidestep the issue, although Knapp suggests that Ivan's fanatical obsession with the suffering of children may reflect the legacy of the shrieking demon. Some details of the scene simply do not make sense. If the icon truly offers "solace and salvation," it doesn't seem to be working in this case. If the mother is grieving for her son, it is not because any harm has come to him, for

---

13 Worobec, "Witchcraft Beliefs and Practices in Prerevolutionary Russian and Ukranian Villages," 179.

14 Ibid., 185.

15 Knapp, "Mothers and Sons," 40.

he is right there in her arms where he belongs. Here the reader would do well to recall Zosima's conversation with the peasant women, in which he tells one of them that it is a great sin to grieve for a person who *is still alive* (PSS 14:47): little Alesha Karamazov, of course, is very much alive. Furthermore, nothing terrifies a small child more than his mother's fear. In Alesha's memory the child appears to be in *physical danger*. Why is the mother thrusting him *away from herself*? A very plausible answer is that *she* is the source of the danger. After all, there is no one else in the room until the nurse rushes in, terrified for the child's safety, and rescues him, forcibly wresting him from his mother's arms. What if the nurse hadn't come in at that moment? The evidence suggests not a vision of spiritual grace and comfort, but *a traumatic memory*. Sof'ia's identity as a *klikusha* suggests that in this twinned image of mother and child there is a demon at work.

Thus, the human mother stands in sharp contrast to the iconic Mother of God in Alesha's vision. The two opposing elements here are not simply "one serenely divine, merciful and elevated, the other mortal, innocently suffering and supplicating." In fact, the child Alesha finds himself suspended between the divine and the demonic, where, to borrow a phrase from his half-brother Dmitrii, "the devil is fighting against God here, and the field of battle is human hearts" (PSS 14:100). This perspective may help explain the enigmatic hints throughout the novel that Alesha is, or will be, a sinner like his brothers.

The image of his mother is associated subliminally in Alesha's mind with fear, religious frenzy, and sexuality. "Over cognac," Fedor Pavlovich starts telling his sons stories about their mother, including an incident that occurred when another man (who was attracted to her) slapped Fedor Pavlovich. Sof'ia Ivanovna insisted that her husband rise to the challenge and duel the man. In this way she associated love (or sex) with violence. Fedor Pavlovich's account reminds the reader of Zosima's story about his epiphany, which began with a similar refusal to fight a duel.

Instructing his sons in seduction techniques, Fedor Pavlovich launches into a salacious description of his marital relations with their mother. The details of Fedor Pavlovich's reminiscences make clear the link between sexuality and *klikushestvo*:

> Listen, Alesha, I always used to surprise your late mother, only it turned
> out to be a different sort of thing. I'd never show her any tenderness, and
> then suddenly, when the moment was right—I'd suddenly go to pieces,
> I'd crawl on my knees and kiss her feet, and would always, always bring

her to the point—I can recall it clearly now, as then—where she'd let out this special little giggle, nervous, bubbly, resonant but not loud. Only she could laugh that way. I know that that was always the beginning of an attack of her illness, that the next day she would begin shrieking like a *klikusha*, and that this little laugh of hers did not signify any ecstasy, or rather, though it was false, still, it was ecstasy. That's what it means to find your own special touch in everything. (PSS 14:126)

Alesha's hysterical fit in response to his father's tale of his threat to spit on his wife's icon echoes the symptoms of Sof'ia Ivanovna's *klikushestvo* and reveals the dark side of his maternal legacy. This crude medical reality underlies a wealth of symbolic associations. What exactly in his father's tale triggers Alesha's violent reaction? Is it purely a sensitive and pious young man's reaction to blasphemy? The sorrow of a son for his mother? Or the association between sexuality and his mother's religious fervor? Fedor Pavlovich's method of bringing his wife back to her senses—sprinkling water on her from his mouth—models a sexual act and reminds us of the scenes of the heroine's seduction that we examined in *Poor Folk* and *White Nights*. Depending on the reader's perspective, it becomes either an act of blasphemy (spitting on an icon) or the ultimate human expression of love. The tension between these two extremes—united as they are in a single act—triggers Alesha's "fall to the floor." [...]

In *The Brothers Karamazov*, Alesha's sin is passivity. His violation of the elder's command to "be with your brothers" (PSS 14:72), no less than Ivan's subconscious wish for his father's death, leads to the parricide. After all, violating the wishes of an elder, as the narrator took great care to tell us, is the worst possible sin. Alesha's plan to retreat from engagement in the world and devote himself to a monastic life relates to that traumatic memory of his mother. Indeed, it was his quest to locate her grave that brought him onto the stage of the novel: "When he arrived in our town, and his father began questioning him as to 'Why did you come here without completing your studies?' he gave no direct answer, but was, as they say, unusually pensive. Soon it became clear that he was seeking his mother's grave. [...] And rather soon after his discovery of his mother's grave, Alesha suddenly announced to him that he wanted to enter the monastery" (PSS 14:21–22). The monastic path, says the narrator, struck Alesha as the ideal escape for his "soul striving out of the darkness of earthly malice to the light" (PSS 14:25). This cumbersome language verbally recapitulates the visual gesture of the shrieking mother scene: the frantic soul of the youth seeks a calm, spiritual home in the icon. The discordant elements suggest that Alesha's entrance into the monastery is as much a flight from human engagement as a positive spiritual journey.

[...]

When Alesha visits his mother's grave, Fedor Pavlovich oddly chooses to give money to the monastery for requiems not in her name, but in the name of his *first* wife, Dmitrii's mother. We might solve this mystery by considering Adelaida Ivanovna to be the original source of Sof'ia's demonic infection. Fedor Pavlovich is the ostensibly guilty party. He is identified as the abuser, and Sof'ia Ivanovna's ailment is attributed to him by proximity: the shrieking started soon after their marriage. Still, none of the cited sources on *klikushestvo* suggest that the husband might serve as the source of the demon. Yet Sof'ia Ivanovna's affliction would make sense if Fedor Pavlovich were to be seen as a carrier of the disease. In this scenario, the demon enters with his first marriage, stays with him after Adelaida abandons him, and infects his second wife, Sof'ia. It plagues the lives of all three Karamazov sons, causing Dmitrii's struggles with his mother's money, Alesha's passivity, and Ivan's internal divisions.

CHAPTER 9

Russia

This chapter, which consists mainly of Dostoevskii's own writings, examines his views on Russia's past, present and future, on the country's relations with the West, and on the Russian people, or *narod*. While Dostoevskii's writings on Russia often reveal a darker and more unpalatable side to the writer than can be found even in his novels and serve as a window onto a nationalism that makes modern readers in the West uneasy, they are also central to understanding the historical and social circumstances that underlie his fiction. Towards the end of his life, Dostoevskii's views on Russia developed into a utopian religious nationalist vision which saw Orthodox Russia as representing an alternative future for a Europe divided by ideological and class conflict, yet these views developed gradually during the 1860s and 1870s in response to the changing social and political situation of Russia under the reforming tsar, Alexander II.

To understand Dostoevskii's evolving views on Russia, we must begin with the eighteenth-century reforms of Peter the Great and his attempt to "open a window to the west" through the founding of St. Petersburg as the new imperial capital and the import of Western European cultural and political models. Dostoevskii, along with many of the Russian intelligentsia of the middle of the nineteenth century, blamed the Petrine reforms for having created a rift within Russian society, between the nobility, who adopted the new Western models, and the *narod*, who rejected them, continuing to live as they had always done. An earlier generation of intelligentsia in the 1840s had themselves exacerbated these divisions, spawning the divide between the Westernizers, who saw Russia's future as lying with the West, and the Slavophiles, who believed the nation should follow its own distinct path. The Emancipation of the Serfs in 1861 offered an unprecedented possibility for the reconciliation of nobility and *narod* and for the reunification of Russian society, yet the promise of reconciliation seemed to fall away in the 1860s and 1870s as social and political divisions intensified. The hope of a regenerated Russian society continued to motivate Dostoevskii's thinking until his death and comes to a head in his "Pushkin speech," the last of the extracts presented here.

During his exile in a Siberian prison camp, Dostoevskii was thrown together with prisoners of all social backgrounds and thus had more personal experience of Russia's complicated national and social mix than any other writer of his generation. He later wrote about his experiences in fictional form in *Notes from the House of the Dead*, and the first passage provided here is taken from that work. Here the fictional narrator, Gorianchikov, describes his gradual acculturation to prison camp life. The vast gulf that separates the educated prisoners from the peasants becomes complicated by the contradictions within the peasant convicts as the complexity and diversity of the Russian national character grows into a central theme in the work.

Dostoevskii reframed his experiences with his fellow convicts in his account of the regenerative power of a childhood memory during his conversion experience in Siberia in his 1877 *A Writer's Diary* entry, "The Peasant Marei," also reproduced here. Remembering a childhood encounter with a peasant who saved him from an imaginary wolf, the political prisoner is able to look at the peasant convicts in a new light, investing them with Marei's humanity and tenderness. Marei becomes the symbol of the potentiality of the Russian peasant, which the Polish political prisoners are unable to see in their brutalized fellow inmates.

In the years immediately following his return from Siberian exile, Dostoevskii, together with his brother Mikhail Dostoevskii (1820–64), and the literary critics Apollon Grigor'ev (1822–64) and Nikolai Strakhov (1828–96), published a monthly journal, *Time*, which elaborated a set of beliefs they called *pochvennost'*, sometimes translated as "native soil conservatism." *Pochvennost'* called for a search for national values in the life and ideas of the Russian *narod*. The 1860 *Time* manifesto, included here, probably written by Fedor Dostoevskii, declares that the Emancipation has ended the separation of nobility and *narod* that began as a result of the Petrine reforms, lessons have been learned from Peter's westernization, and Russians should not reject their national values and unquestioningly follow a Western European path. The task ahead, argues the manifesto, is to take ideas from both the nobility and the *narod* and create new social forms which will reflect Russia's position in the "great family of nations." Here we find the first invocation of the "Russian idea" which will become the core of the later prophetic nationalism Dostoevskii espouses in *A Writer's Diary*. Also included here is the *Time* article "Two Camps of Theoreticians," ("Going Beyond Theory") which discusses the Petrine reforms and their meaning for Slavophiles and Westernizers, and tries to carve out a middle ground for native soil conservatism. These two extracts from *Time* are accompanied by Sarah Hudspith's commentary, which contextualizes them within the ideological context of the time and shows how Dostoevskii's idea of Russianness is related to those of his Slavophile antecedents.

By the 1870s, Dostoevskii's sense of the possibilities of national regeneration had acquired more than a hint of messianism as he began to develop the view that "the Orthodox idea" was Russia's main contribution to world culture. A passage included here from the notebooks to *Demons* presents Russia as offering Europe moral and spiritual resurrection in the shape of the Orthodox religion. These ideas are attributed to the character of the Prince, later to become Stavrogin, but Dostoevskii voices some of the same ideas in the nationalist passages of his monojournal, *A Writer's Diary* (1876–77, 1880, 1881).

The final piece in this chapter is Dostoevskii's famous "Pushkin Speech," given at the festivities for the unveiling of a statue to Pushkin in Moscow in 1880 and published in a special issue of *A Writer's Diary*. Along with several other famous writers of the day, including Ivan Turgenev, Dostoevskii was invited to give a speech on Pushkin and his influence; the speech came to have a profound effect on its audience and became an event in Russian cultural history. Dostoevskii presents Pushkin as an ideal, the pinnacle of Russian cultural achievement and a writer capable of articulating both the alienation of Russia's educated classes and the moral and spiritual values of the Russian people. He sees Pushkin as advocate for the Russian people's unique contribution to world culture. In the final phase of his career, Dostoevskii argues, Pushkin became a truly national poet, who embodied the Russian people's responsiveness to the entire world and brotherly love for all humanity, which gave them the redemptive potential to save Europe from atomistic individualism. Yet Dostoevskii's desire to see Pushkin as a creative synthesizer reveals more about his own art than it does about Pushkin's. Dostoevskii pulls back from his account of Pushkin's complexity and depicts Pushkin as prophet of his own messianic world view.

Further Reading

Dowler, Wayne. *Dostoevsky, Grigor'ev and Native Soil Conservatism*. Toronto: University of Toronto Press, 1982.

Hudspith, Sarah. *Dostoevsky and the Idea of Russianness*. London: Routledge-Curzon, 2004.

Ivanits, Linda. *Dostoevsky and the Russian People*. Cambridge: Cambridge University Press, 2008.

Kabat, Geoffrey C. *Ideology and Imagination: The Image of Society in Dostoevsky*. New York: Columbia University Press, 1978.

Levitt, Marcus C. *Russian Literary Politics and the Pushkin Celebration of 1880*. Ithaca, NY: Cornell University Press, 1989.

Ruttenberg, Nancy. *Dostoevsky's Democracy*. Princeton, NJ: Princeton University Press, 2010.

Ward, Bruce K. *Dostoyevsky's Critique of the West*. Waterloo, ON: Wilfred Laurier University Press, 1986.

Fellow Convicts from
Notes from the House of the Dead (1862)*

I have already said that I did at last become accustomed to my position in
prison. But this came to pass painfully and with difficulty and far too gradually. It took me almost a year, in fact, to reach this stage, and that was the hard-
est year of my life. And that is why the whole of it is imprinted on my memory
forever. I believe I remember every successive hour of that year. I said, also,
that other convicts too could not get used to that life. I remember how in that
first year I often wondered to myself what they were feeling, could they be
contented? And I was much occupied with these questions. I have mentioned
already that all the convicts lived in prison not as though they were at home
there, but as though they were at a hotel, on a journey, at some temporary
halt. Even men sentenced for their whole life were restless or miserable and
no doubt every one of them was dreaming of something almost impossible.
This everlasting uneasiness, which showed itself unmistakably, though not in
words, this strange impatient and intense hope, which sometimes found involuntary utterance, at times so wild as to be almost like delirium, and what was
most striking of all, often persisted in men of apparently the greatest common
sense—gave a special aspect and character to the place, so much so that it constituted perhaps its most typical characteristic. It made one feel, almost from
the first moment, that there was nothing like this outside the prison walls.

---

* From *The House of the Dead*, trans. Constance Garnett (New York: Macmillan, 1915),
238–41.

Here all were dreamers, and this was apparent at once. What gave poignancy to this feeling was the fact that this dreaminess gave the greater number of the prisoners a gloomy and sullen, almost abnormal expression. The vast majority were taciturn and morose to the point of vindictiveness, they did not like displaying their hopes. Candor, simplicity were looked on with contempt. The more fantastical his hopes, and the more conscious the dreamer himself was of their fantastical character, the more obstinately and shyly he concealed them in his heart, but he could not renounce them. Who knows, some perhaps were inwardly ashamed of them. There is so much sober-mindedness and grasp of reality in the Russian character, and with it such inner mockery of self. Perhaps it was this continual hidden self-dissatisfaction which made these men so impatient with one another in the daily affairs of life, so irritable and sneering with one another, and if, for instance, some one of them rather simpler and more impatient than the rest were to make himself conspicuous by uttering aloud what was in the secret mind of all, and were to launch out into dreams and hopes, the others roughly put him down at once, suppressed him and ridiculed him; but I fancy that the harshest of his assailants were just those who perhaps outstripped him in their own hopes and dreams. Candid and simple people were as I have said already looked upon generally as the vulgarest fools, and they were treated with contempt. Every man was so ill-humored and vain that he despised anyone good-natured and free from vanity. All but these naive and simple chatterers, all the taciturn, that is, may be sharply divided into the ill-natured and the good-natured, the sullen and the serene. There were far more of the ill-natured and the sullen, and those of them who were naturally talkative were infallibly uneasy backbiters and slanderers. They meddled in everyone's affairs, though of their own hearts, their own private affairs, they showed not one glimpse. That was not the thing, not correct. The good-natured—a very small group—were quiet, hid their imaginings in their hearts, and were of course more prone than the ill-natured to put faith and hope in them. Yet I fancy that there was another group of prisoners who had lost all hope. Such was the old dissenter from the Starodubovskii settlements; there were very few of these. The old man was externally calm (I have described him already), but from certain symptoms I judge that his inner misery was terrible. But he had his means of escape, his salvation—prayer, and the idea of martyrdom.

The convict whom I have described already, who used to read the Bible, and who went out of his mind, and threw a brick at the major, was probably one of the desperate class too, one of those who have lost their last hope, and as life impossible without hope he found a means of escape in a voluntary and almost artificial martyrdom. He declared that he attacked the major without malice, simply to "accept suffering." And who knows what psychological process was taking place in his heart then! Without some goal and some effort to reach it no man can live. When he has lost all hope, all object in life, man often becomes a monster in his misery. The one object of the prisoners was freedom and to get out of prison.

But here I have been trying to classify all the prison, and that is hardly possible. Real life is infinite in its variety in comparison with even the cleverest abstract generalization, and it does not admit of sharp and sweeping distinctions. The tendency of real life is always towards greater and greater differentiation. We, too, had a life of our own of a sort, and it was not a mere official existence but a real inner life of our own.

But as I have mentioned already I did not, and indeed could not, penetrate to the inner depths of this life at the beginning of my time in prison, and so all its external incidents were a source of an unutterable misery to me then. I sometimes was simply beginning to hate those men who were sufferers like myself. I even envied them for being, anyway, among their equals, their comrades, understanding one another; though in reality they were all as sick and weary as I was of this companionship enforced by stick and lash, of this compulsory association, and everyone was secretly looking towards something far away from all the rest. I repeat again, there were legitimate grounds for the envy which came upon me in moments of ill-humor. Those who declare that it is no harder for a gentle man, an educated man and all the rest of it, in our prisons and in Siberia, than it is for any peasant, are really quite wrong. I know have heard of theories on the subject of late, have read of them. There is something true and humane at the back of this idea—all are men, all are human beings. But the idea is too abstract. It overlooks too many practical aspects of the question, which cannot be grasped except by experience. I don't say this on the grounds that the gentleman, the man of education may be supposed to be more refined and delicate in his feelings, that he is more developed. There is no standard by which to measure the soul and its development. Even education itself is no test. I am ready to be the first to testify that, in the midst of these utterly uneducated and downtrodden sufferers, I came across instances of the greatest spiritual refinement. Sometimes one would know a man for years in prison and despise him and think that he was not a human being but a brute. And suddenly a moment will come by chance when his soul will suddenly reveal itself in an involuntary outburst, and you see in it such wealth, such feeling, such heart, such a vivid understanding of its own suffering, and of the suffering of others that your eyes are open and for the first moment you can't believe what you have seen and heard yourself. The contrary happens too; education is sometimes found side by side with such barbarity, such cynicism, that it revolts you, and in spite of the utmost good nature and all previous theories on the subject, you can find no justification or apology.

After the Emancipation (1860)*

Fedor Dostoevskii

Time: September 1860

Before proceeding to explain why we consider it necessary to publish a new literary periodical, we must say a few words about what we understand the nature of our time to be and, particularly, the nature of the present moment of our social life. This will also serve to elucidate the spirit and the tendency of our journal.

We live in a highly remarkable and critical epoch. As proof of our view we need not emphasize those new ideas and needs of Russian society, which have been proclaimed with such unanimity during recent years by the thinking section of Russian society. Nor shall we deal with the great peasant problem, the solution of which has begun in our own time. All these are only the signs and the facts of that prodigious change which is about to take place peacefully and with the consent of our entire nation, though when we consider its tremendous importance, we cannot help feeling that it is equivalent to the most outstanding events in our history and even to the great reforms of Peter the Great. This change consists chiefly of the total union between the educated section of our population with its national element and the participation of the whole of our great Russian people in all the events of our current life—the people who recoiled from the Petrine reform one hundred and seventy years ago and who

---

* Announcement for the publication of *Time*, September 1860. From "Four Manifestoes," *Dostoevsky's Occasional Writings*, trans. David Magarshack (New York: Random House, 1963), 229–35. Permission to reprint granted by the Magarshack family.

have since been separated from the educated section, which carried on its own special and independent life.

We have mentioned signs and facts. No doubt the most important of these is the question of the amelioration of the conditions of life of our peasantry. Now millions and not only thousands of Russians will enter into Russian life, introduce their fresh, pristine forces into it and utter its new word. It is not the hostility of the classes, of the conquerors and the vanquished, as everywhere else in Europe, that must lie at the foundation of the development of the future elements of our life. We are not Europe and we must have neither conquerors nor vanquished.

The reform of Peter the Great has cost us too much as it is: it separated us from the common people. The common people repudiated it from the very start. The forms of life that were left to them by the reform were not in accordance with their spirit or their aspirations; they did not fit the common people; they were not opportune. The common people regarded them as alien, as due to the great tsar's wish to follow the example of foreigners. The very fact of the moral dissociation of the common people with the upper classes, with their leaders and guides, shows how much we had to pay for that new life of ours. But having repudiated the reform, the common people did not lose heart. They proclaimed their independence again and again, proclaimed it by extraordinary, convulsive efforts because they were alone and they found things difficult. They walked in darkness, but they went on their separate ways regardless. They thought deeply about themselves and their position and tried to create their own views on life, their own philosophy, broke up into all sorts of mysterious, ugly sects, looked for new solutions of their problems, for new forms. It was impossible to recoil more from the old shores; it was impossible to burn one's boats in a braver fashion that it was done by our common people on entering upon the new ways they had been looking for with such torment. And yet they where calling the common people the custodians of old pre-Petrine forms, of the stupid dogmas of the old believers.

Of course the ideas of the common people, left without leaders and thrown back upon their own resources, were sometimes quite monstrous and their attempts at new forms of life hideous. But they had all arisen from one common cause, one spirit, unshakable faith in oneself, untried strength. After the reform there was only one case of unity between ourselves, the educated classes, and the common people—the campaign of 1812—and we saw how splendidly the common people behaved in that crisis. The trouble is that they do not know us, that they do not understand us.

But now the separation has come to an end. The Petrine reform, which continued up to our own times, at last reached the outermost limit of its influence. We cannot go any further; besides, it is impossible to go further, for there is no road; it has been completely traversed. All those who followed Peter got to know Europe, adopted the European mode of life, but did not become Europeans. Time was when we reproached ourselves for being unable to become Europeans. Now we think differently. Now we know that we cannot become Europeans, that we are incapable of squeezing ourselves into one of the European forms of life, forms Europe has produced out of its own national sources, which are alien and contrary to ours, just as we could not wear somebody else's clothes which did not fit us. We have at last come to the conclusion that we too are a separate, highly subjective nationality, and that our task is to create a new form, our own native form, taken out of our soil, out of our national spirit and our national resources. But we returned unvanquished to our native soil. We do not renounce our past: we realize its wisdom, too. We realize that the reform has widened our horizon, that through it we have come to understand our future importance in the great family of nations.

We know that now we cannot erect a Chinese wall as a protection against the rest of the world. We foresee, and we foresee with a sense of veneration, that the character of our future activity must be to the highest degree universal, that the Russian idea will perhaps be the synthesis of all those ideas that Europe is developing with such stubbornness and with such courage within its separate nationalities; that perhaps everything that is hostile in those ideas will find reconciliation and further development in the Russian nationality. Surely it is not for nothing that we spoke all languages, understood all civilizations, sympathised with the interests of every European nation, realized the reason and wisdom of phenomena that are quite alien to us. Surely it is not for nothing that we have manifested a power of self-criticism that has astonished all foreigners. They reproached us for it, they called us impersonal, people without a native land, without noticing that the ability to renounce one's native soil for a time is by itself already a sign of the greatest ability to examine oneself as soberly and impartially as possible; on the other hand, the ability to assume a reconciliatory attitude toward the things that divide the foreigner is the highest and the most noble gift of nature which is bestowed only on a few nationalities. The foreigners still do not have the slightest idea of our infinite powers [. . .] But now, it seems, we too are entering a new life.

And it is before we enter this new life that a reconciliation has become necessary between the followers of the Petrine reform and our common people's fundamental ideas. We are not referring here to Slavophiles and the Westerners. Our time is completely indifferent to their dissensions. We are referring to the reconciliation of civilization with the basic ideas of common people. We feel that both sections must at last understand each other, must clear up all the innumerable misunderstandings that have arisen between them and then advance together in concord and harmony along the new glorious wide road. Union at all costs, regardless of any sacrifices and as soon as possible—this is our motto, our advanced idea.

But where is this point of contact with the common people? How is one to take the first step toward unity? That is the question, that is the worry that must be shared by everyone who holds the Russian name dear, by everyone who loves the common people and holds dear their happiness. For their happiness is our happiness. It goes without saying that the first step toward obtaining an agreement is literacy and education. The common people will never understand as if they are not prepared for it first. There is no other way and we know that by saying this we are not saying anything new. But while the educated class has still to take the first step, it has to make use of its position and do its utmost to do so. The spread of education in an intensified form and as soon as possible is the chief task of our time, the first step to any activity.

We have only expressed the main and foremost idea of our journal and given a hint as to its character and the spirit of its future activity. But there was another reason that impelled us to found a new, independent literary periodical. We have noticed for some time that during recent years a kind of peculiar, acquiescent dependence on literary authorities has developed in our literature. We do not, of course, accuse our journals of selfishness and venality. No one in our country sells his convictions for money, as it is the case in European journals, where writers change their odious service and their masters because others pay them more. But one can sell one's convictions not only for money. One can sell oneself, for example, out of innate servility or fear to be thought a fool because one does not agree with the literary authorities. Mediocrity sometimes quite unselfishly trembles before opinions of literary luminaries, especially if those opinions are expressed boldly, insolently and impertinently. Quite often it is just this insolence and impertinence that provide the literary luminary with his great, though only temporary, influence on the masses. Mediocrity, for its part, in spite of its apparent arrogance, is almost always pusillanimous and submits readily. Pusillanimity begets literary servitude and there must not be any servitude in literature. The craving for literary power, literary superiority, literary prestige will induce even a distinguished old writer sometimes to undertake an activity so unexpected and strange that it willy-nilly arouses astonishment, lead his contemporaries into temptation and be sure to be passed on to posterity as some scandalous story about Russian literature of the mid-nineteenth century. And such things are occurring more and more often and such people enjoy an influence that lasts a long time, while the journals say nothing about them and indeed do not dare touch them. There are still in our literature a few fixed ideas and opinions that exist in the form of immutable truths solely because the leading literary men had declared them to be so a long time ago. Criticism gets more and more vulgar and petty. In some journals, certain writers are completely ignored for fear of saying something they would not like. They engage in literary polemics for the sake of getting the better of their opponents and not for the sake of truth. Cheap skepticism, harmful by its influence on the majority of readers, successfully conceals mediocrity and is used in order to attract subscribers. The stern word of true and profound conviction is heard more and more seldom. Finally, the desire for making money, which is now so rife in literature, turns certain periodicals into essentially commercial enterprises, while literature, and the benefits it confers, is being pushed back into the background and sometimes no one bothers about it at all.

We have therefore decided to found a journal that is completely independent of literary authorities—notwithstanding our respects for them—with the aim of a bold and full exposure of all the literary quirks of our time. We undertake this exposure out of a most profound feeling of respect for Russian literature. Our journal will have no literary antipathies or predilections. We shall be quite ready to acknowledge our own mistakes and blunders, to acknowledge them in print, and we do not think we are ridiculous in being proud of that (though in anticipation). We shall not eschew polemics, either. We shall not be afraid to "tease" the literary geese occasionally; the gaggle of geese is sometimes very useful: it forecasts the weather, though it doesn't always save the Capitol. We shall pay particular attention to the section dealing with criticism. Not merely every remarkable book, but also every remarkable literary work published in other journals, will be analyzed without fail in our periodical. Criticism must not be allowed to go by default merely because books are now beginning to be serialized in journals and not published separately as before. Leaving personalities aside, ignoring everything mediocre, provided it is not harmful, *Time* will follow every movement in literature, however insignificant, drawing attention to both positive and negative facts and exposing with evasiveness mediocrity, every kind of evil intent, sham enthusiasm, misplaced pride and literary aristo-cratism—wherever they may appear. Everyday facts, current opinions, estab-lished principles, which have grown into clichés from too frequent use, strange and disappointing aphorisms, are as subject to criticism as a newly published book or magazine article. Our journal regards as its unalterable rule to declare frankly what it thinks of every honest literary work. A famous name makes it necessary for our judgement to be stricter and our journal will never descend to the now generally accepted trick of showering a famous writer with compli-ments so as to earn the right to make one unflattering remark about him. Praise is always chaste; flattery alone smells of the servant's hall.

Going Beyond Theory (1862)*

Fedor Dostoevskii

Now is the time when we need an honest, direct, and, most importantly, truthful discourse about our common people [*narod*]. The common people have entered the stage, called to participate in public life by the legislation of February 19th. But what is it, this unknown country of which we heard something, which we have apparently approached closely; what is this new element of Russian life? In short, what is *Russian local government* [*zemstvo*]? Historically we have known only that it is one of the fundamental principles of our life—then it was pushed into the background due to various circumstances; then, for a long time, it apparently faded out, and only occasionally announced itself, often in the form of terrible protests against bitter reality . . . The question of the people has now become a question about life . . . Perhaps the future of Russian progress depends on the kind of decision we will make. And that is because the question about the Russian people has changed into the following question: do we currently have, in the *zemstvo*, an element that is distinct from the service class? Is there any life still remaining in the *zemstvo*? Can the *zemstvo* still renew the vitality of our modest society?

A vital question like this one will never be solved theoretically. It had already arisen among us long ago, although not as prominently, when our society came to the realization of its distinction from other European peoples. But the love of theory prevented theoreticians from looking at the facts directly,

---

* From "Two Camps of Theoreticians (Apropos of *Day* and a Bit More)," published in *Time* in 1862, translated by Anton Nonin from the original Russian, which can be found in PSS 20:5–10, 12–13, 22. Nonin's translation appears here under a Creative Commons BY–ND 4.0 license.

from understanding them properly. A theory is good but only under certain conditions. If a theory wants to explain life, then it has to comply with life's strict rules. Otherwise, theory will start encroaching on life, ignoring facts—it will, as they say, bend reality to itself. Westerners, having developed a theory of Western European life as universal, and having then encountered the completely different Russian life, judged that life. Slavophiles, having accepted the old Moscow ideal as the norm, *also immediately* judged everything about Russian life that did not fit in their narrow margins. Of course, this could not be otherwise be any other way. Once set, a false basis leads to false conclusions: theory likes consistency. Once set, a narrow, one-sided basis, following the same theoretical consistency, will necessarily lead to the denial of those aspects of life that contradict the assumed principle.

But perhaps that's the merit of theoreticians—that they are, in some cases, too consistent, and are not afraid of the conclusions they may reach . . . One camp of theoreticians currently denies the existence of the Russian *zemstvo* and refuses to acknowledge it as a beginning that must build on—it simply denies the existence of the nationality in principle. We will not analyze closely the view held by this camp, because to do so would take up a lot of space and time— and above all because this theory is too narrow and superficial, as well as old. Schiller's Marquis of Posa already dreamed of cosmopolitanism. Regarding the subject that interests us now, the theory does not bear criticism; therefore, we will limit ourselves to a few words only.

"Our ideal," says one camp of the theoreticians, "is characterized by universal qualities. We need a human who would be the same no matter where he is—in Germany, or in England, or in France—and who would embody a general type of humanity that developed in the West. Everything universal that he acquired—he would boldly give it to all other people, bringing universal elements into any environment, no matter its qualities? What's the point in talking about the soil, with which one is supposed to cope, when applying principles worked out by other peoples?" Therefore, out of all humanity, out of all peoples, the theoreticians want to make something totally impersonal, which would be the same in any country of the world, under any climactic or historical conditions . . . The task here, evidently, is broad, and the objective is grand. It is too bad that the issue is not the broadness of the task, and the grandness of the objective. We would really appreciate it if someone from this ilk of theoreticians could solve the following questions: is that true that humanity will gain a good deal if every nation appeared as a worn-out penny; and what good would this bring? Let one of these theoreticians show us that universal ideal which every personality has to develop. Humanity has yet to develop such an ideal because education is, in fact, found only in 1/20 of humankind. And if the universal ideal that they do have has been developed *solely* by the West, can it be called so perfect that all other nations must abandon all attempts to bring something from themselves into the development of the perfect human ideal, content with merely passively absorbing an ideal based on Western books? No. Humanity will begin to live a fulfilling life only when every nation progresses based on its own principles, and bringing into the collective life the particular aspects that it has developed. Perhaps only then can we dream about a wholesome universal ideal. Sometimes it occurs to us that each person, developing under specific circumstances, peculiar to the country in which he lives, inevitably creates his own worldview, his own patterns of thought, his own customs, his own organization of communal life . . . And it seems that, if it is physically impossible to force a nation to reject everything that it has amassed and developed for the good of the supposed universal ideal, one acquired only in other countries, then inevitably we must pay attention to the national character if we wish this people any development [. . .]

Because the theoreticians deny the very existence of nationality, they do not understand what it means to "bond with the people." They cannot understand that *zemstvo* is the most necessary element in our Russian life; they do not understand what is required in order to bond with the people. "Either we have to approach the people," says *The Contemporary*, "or the people should approach us?" "The people should approach us, or even better, we should bring the people to us, because universal ideals live within us. We are the representatives of progress and civilization in Russia. Because the people are stupid, they haven't developed anything yet. The people's lives are meaningless, dumb." But it occurs to us that perhaps the people will never approach us, unless we come down from our Olympian heights and, instead of offering words, give the people a real helping hand. Because the people do not feel that they need us: *they will remain strong without us* . . . They won't wither, like we do without a foundation under our feet, without masses of people behind us. The people are strong by themselves. It is we, the so-called educated society that are weak and lifeless [. . .]

But there is yet another phalanx of theoreticians who, for the sake of consistency, reject much: we mean the Moscow Slavophiles, who now publish the newspaper *Day*. In its time, Slavophilism did a great deal for the study of the everyday life of our people . . . The Slavophiles showed many sides of Russian life, they identified the meaning of *zemstvo* in our history, and showed its immediate expression—community life. Even today Slavophilism serves our literature. *Day* has been in publication only since February 15 of last year, but even during this short period it has managed to attract the attention of our reading community. And we must admit that the public's attention to *Day* is worthwhile. It possesses a strength that unwittingly attracts the reader to its side. You cannot but sympathize with *Day's* intensive search for truth, with that deep (albeit sometimes unjust) indignation at lies and falsehood. In its acrimonious commentary on the current state of affairs, one hears a certain aspiration for fresh air, a desire to destroy those barriers that prevent Russian life from progressing freely and independently [. . .]

We understand that this voice can be sincere; but it's evident that this is the voice of a fanatic [. . .] *Day* refuses to descend from its pre-Petrine heights, it views contemporary Russian life with contempt, gazing through its Moscow lorgnette it finds nothing with which it can sympathize . . .

Two months ago we asked *Day*: Do you really think that during the century-and-a-half of quasi-European life we haven't developed anything good and have only corrupted our core, faded, and lost all our potential? Do you really think that Pushkin, Lermontov, Turgenev, Ostrovskii, Gogol'—the pride of our literature, all these names that gave us the right to participate in Pan-European life, everything that enlightened Russian life and shines within in—all this amounts to zero?

Do you really think that the urgent striving of the literature of recent years towards progress, civilization, the passionate desire to improve Russian life as much as possible, the attention to social issues (to the extent allowed by external circumstances), do you really think that the very deep disappointment with contemporary life, all this, is nothing but lies, and falsehoods? [. . .]

Indeed, there were plenty of lies and falsity in pre-Petrine Russia, especially during the Muscovite period . . . These were lies in social relationships, in which hypocrisy, pretend humility, servility, and so on dominated. Falsity in religiosity, underneath which hid, if not crude unbelief, then at the very least apathy and hypocrisy. Falsity in family relations, in which women were degraded to the level of animals, considered a thing and not a person . . . In pre-Petrine, Muscovite Russia, there was too much of Oriental, eastern laziness, pretence, and lies. This quietism, the sad monotony of pre-Petrine Russia, points to a certain inner weakness. If life in Moscow was so good, then please explain what made the people reject the Muscovite way of life and turn to the other side? In short, what caused our Russian schism? It turns out that you cannot fuse Moscow with the people, it's impossible to recognize the

Muscovite, pre-Petrine life as a truthful, and ideal expression of a people's life. *Day* says the pre-Petrine Russia had flaws but not falsity . . . The expression is too ambiguous . . . Then what is falsity after all this? Was it not falsity that caused the flaws, the lack of which one cannot complain about in pre-Petrine Russia? According to this Muscovite ideal, the Slavophiles wish to rebuild Russia . . . For them, all our development, which may not amount to much, but was development nonetheless, that we had since the times of Peter—all that amounts to nothing . . . They scold Peter for, in Aksakov's words, stirring up the porridge too thick, while their porridge is not too thin either. One can see in them the same pre-Petrine unceremonious attitude towards life . . . The theory of Slavophilism is just as merciless, just as hasty as any other . . . No, a lot of water has flowed since the time of Peter, that water has reached far and wide, and it is physically impossible to turn back its tide or destroy it completely [. . .]

There is no doubt that Peter's reforms tore one segment of the people from the other, leading segment. The reform was conducted from top to bottom and not from bottom to top. It never had time to reach the lowest population. And total success wasn't possible anyway, considering the methods used by Peter. The reformation could not encompass the entire people: it is very difficult to rebuild a people. For that, the iron will of one man is not enough. The development of a people lasts for centuries; and the destruction of everything it has obtained can only be the work of centuries as well . . . And therein lies Peter's mistake—the fact that he wanted to change the ways, customs, and opinions of the Russian people during his lifetime. The despotism of his reformation methods incited only reactions from the masses; they strove all the more to preserve themselves from the Germans, the more the latter infringed upon the people's own nationality. On the other hand, it would be a serious mistake to claim that Peter's reforms brought into our Russian life mainly universal Western elements. At first, only the most frightening decadence was established in our land—German bureaucracy, officialdom. Not feeling any benefits from the reformation, not seeing any practical relief under the new order, the people felt only terrible oppression. With a heavy heart the people bore the desecration of what they had long been used to view for ages as sacred. That is why the people remained as they were before the reform; if the reform had any influence on the people, it was far from beneficial. Speaking thus, we do not dare deny all the universal meanings of Peter's reform . . . According to Pushkin's wonderful expression, it opened a window to Europe, it *showed* us the West, from which there is much to learn.

But therein lies the problem—the reforms remained nothing but the window from which select members of the public looked at the West and saw what they should not have seen, learned what they should not have learned … That is why Peter's reform had the character of betrayal of our people, of our national spirit. There are certain times in the life of a people when a particular need to breathe fresh air is felt, a particular kind of discontent with the present, a need for something new. Undoubtedly, in the times leading up to Peter, the people already felt the scragginess of life, protested against reality, and attempted to step outside for fresh air … At the very least, this is how we understand the historical fact of our schism. Such a historical event as Peter grew in Russian soil naturally without any miracles. Undoubtedly it was brought up by the times … The makings of the storm of reformation were already felt in the Russian air; and the fiery public desire to give our historical life a new direction was merely concentrated in Peter … But the nature of any transitional period is such that during them, a strong desire is felt to leave the past order, but how to leave and where to go—that is poorly perceived and understood … Therein lay Peter's problem—the fact that he understood Russia's desire for renewal according to his ideas, and conducted change according to himself as well—in a despotic manner he implanted into life that which it did not need [. . .]

Will all our negation end in nothing but destruction? Will nothing be built where half-ruined buildings once stood, and will this place remain an empty scene of conflagration? Have we suffocated so much, become so frozen, that no hope remains for our revival? But if life is frozen in us, then it doubtless still remains untouched in the people's soil … That is our sacred belief.

We admit that there are many shortcomings in the people, but we will never agree with the camp of theoreticians that claims that the people are hopelessly stupid, and haven't done anything with their lives in a thousand years. We don't agree, because such superfluous rigor is never in order … If friends have such an opinion about the people, then what remains for their enemies?

Dostoevskii and the Slavophiles (2003)*

Sarah Hudspith

Time was launched in 1861 and very soon attracted a respectable number of subscribers, thus demonstrating that there was a demand for a moderate journal with a fresh argument. The editors made much of the selling point that the reading public was bored with the old squabbles between the Slavophiles and the Westernizers, and they advertised their publication as showing the way to reconciling the two factions, as well as healing the rift between intelligentsia and *narod*. The timing of the publication was also to their advantage, as it came in the same year as the long-awaited and much-discussed Emancipation of the Serfs. Optimism was therefore high, and the "peasant question" was on everyone's minds.

Time began by situating itself in the debate over the significance of the reforms of Peter the Great. The position the editors took was conciliatory, emphasizing the inappropriate nature of the reforms for the common people, but also acknowledging the necessity of those reforms. The Call for Subscriptions published ahead of the journal in 1860 described how the form of Peter's reforms was against the soul and the strivings of the people, and thus they chose to make their own way in the dark (PSS 18:36). By contrast, for the educated classes the reforms did not turn them into Europeans, but showed Russia its potential and revealed to it the need to find its own national principle to contribute to humanity (PSS 18:36–7). In this announcement, confirmed by Strakhov as authored by Dostoevskii,[1] the *pochvenniki* even took the unique

---

* From Sarah Hudspith, *Dostoevsky and the Idea of Russianness: A New Perspective on Unity and Brotherhood* (London: Routledge, 2003), 41–46. Copyright © 2003 Routledge, reproduced by permission of Taylor & Francis Books UK.

step of arguing that although the time for the division between the gentry and the people was now past and a new era must begin, this division had been both necessary and a sign of Russia's unique character: "the capacity to uproot oneself from the soil for a time, in order to scrutinize oneself all the more soberly and impartially, is already in itself a sign of the greatest special quality" (PSS 18:37).

This bold statement stands out against Dostoevskii's later proclamations on the subject of Peter's reforms as being strikingly positive, for in the years to come, although he never went so far as to suggest that there were no benefits to the gentry from the reforms, Dostoevskii did not again assert that the resulting split through Russian society had any worthwhile outcomes. The possibility of pandering to the censor may be dismissed, for Dostoevskii was more likely by nature to err on the side of outspokenness than obsequiousness. It seems more probable that he too was buoyed up by the mood of hope and optimism preceding the Emancipation edict, and that as this mood gradually ebbed in the subsequent years, so did Dostoevskii's generous attitude towards Peter's reforms.

Despite its claim to be a journal of reconciliation, *Time* devoted many pages to criticizing the arguments of the Slavophiles and Westernizers, and its first year of publication saw more censure of the former than the latter. This bias was in part due to the fact that Dostoevskii, who had the largest share of the input into the journal, had not read the works of the early Slavophiles and based his opinion on the content of the contemporary Slavophile journal *Day*. In addition, Dowler suggests that Mikhail Dostoevskii had more sympathies with the liberal journals and that his influence counterbalanced the more conservative leanings of Grigor'ev and Strakhov in editorial decisions.[2] However, I disagree with V. S. Nechaeva, whose argument that Dostoevskii unambiguously sided with the Westernizers[3] rather oversimplifies the complex nature of his tendency, as my analysis will show. In the eleventh issue of *Time* Dostoevskii published an article entirely devoted to attacking the tendency of *Day*. Entitled "The latest literary occurrences," the article denounces Slavophilism for being moribund, blinkered and negative. Dostoevskii begins by expressing agreement with the recently deceased Konstantin Aksakov on the worth of the peasant

---

1   As cited by the editors of PSS 18, 229.
2   Wayne Dowler, *Dostoevsky, Grigor'ev and Native Soil Conservatism* (Toronto: University of Toronto Press, 1982), 73.
3   V. S. Nechaeva, *Zhurnal M. M. i F. M. Dostoevskikh "Vremia," 1861–1863* (Moscow: Nauka, 1972), 271.

obshchina,[4] conceding that his understanding of it as set down in one of his last, unfinished articles, was better than that of any Westernizer (PSS 19:59).[5] But this acknowledgement of common ground is overshadowed by the list of faults he finds with the Slavophiles. He writes:

> The Westernizers have not wanted to shut their eyes and ears, fakir-like, against certain phenomena they do not understand; they have not wanted to leave these matters without settlement and *at all costs* take a hostile attitude towards them, as the Slavophiles have done [...] Slavophilism to this day rests on its vague and ill-defined ideal, which consists, *in essence,* of certain successful studies of our ancient way of life. (PSS 19:60)

He is particularly frustrated with the attitude of the same Konstantin Aksakov towards Russian literature, which the latter saw as being false, over-Europeanized and hostile to its own native principles. As a writer, Dostoevskii could not help but feel indignant at this accusation. He justifies his profession with the argument that literature is motivated by a spirit of ruthless self-criticism, standing as much against extreme Westernism as do the Slavophiles themselves (PSS 19:60), and that the European influence in Russian literature has been given a national perspective (PSS 19:62).

"The latest literary occurrences" provides us with (as it were) a snapshot of Dostoevskii's interaction with Slavophilism: he was becoming aware of correspondences between his ideas and those aspects of the movement that have been enumerated in the preceding chapter, but at that time the points on which he took issue with the Slavophiles outnumbered these correspondences, thanks to his as yet limited acquaintance with their works. Frank further elaborates on the issue with the comment that, like many of his contemporaries, Dostoevskii had absorbed certain ideas fundamental to Slavophilism as self-evident truths; for example, both Gertsen and Chernyshevskii accepted the notion, first put forward by the Slavophiles, that the principle behind the peasant commune was morally superior to Western individualism.[6]

---

4 EDS: The peasant commune, a form of local self-governance, which the Slavophiles placed at the center of their belief system.

5 It is uncertain to which article Dostoevskii is referring, although the editors of the Academy edition make various suggestions in PSS 19: 259–60.

6 Joseph Frank, *The Stir of Liberation, 1860–1865* (Princeton: Princeton University Press, 1988), 104.

In its first year of publication, *Time* gained the reputation for being a relatively progressive publication. The reasons for this included, as we have seen, Dostoevskii's open frustration with what he viewed as the narrow-mindedness of *Day*, and the brothers' moderation of the more pro-Slavophile tendencies of Strakhov and Grigor'ev. It is also true, as Frank remarks, that public opinion at that time was mostly hostile to the Slavophile movement, and this may explain the brothers' caution in their initial editorial policy.[7] Offord concurs, noting that Dostoevskii may have felt obliged to tread carefully with the younger generation when referring to the "authorities of *The Contemporary*" so as not to alienate his readers. He points out that there was "a measure of genuine respect" for the likes of Chernyshevskii and Dobroliubov in the early years of *Time*.[8] However, during the course of 1862, certain articles indicated that the editors were experiencing a growing sympathy with Slavophile principles, although a measure of criticism was still directed towards the contemporary representatives of that camp. The most important of these articles is "Two camps of theoreticians." It is a remarkable piece, in that, perhaps more clearly than any other *Time* article authored by Dostoevskii, it tackles head on the issue of the deficiencies of the main ideological movements within the Russian intelligentsia, and attempts to offer something of an alternative. It also shows how Dostoevskii was beginning to formulate the idea-feelings inspired by *katorga*[9] into a set of beliefs, although it should be noted that at this time these beliefs were still in development and were yet to have the input of many key events of the writer's life. Written in the wake of the 1861 Emancipation of the Serfs, "Two camps of theoreticians" stands in contrast to Dostoevskii's pre-Siberian journalism with regard to his attitude towards the Russian people. In this article he indicates right from the outset that because of the Emancipation edict alone, there is a need to consider the part the *narod* has played and will play in the life of Russia. In addition to this, he brings to bear on the matter his knowledge gained in Siberia of the relations between the educated classes and the common people, in order to expose the weaknesses in the arguments of the Slavophiles and the Westernizers. He begins by stating that the question of the people is directly linked to the future of

---

7 Ibid., 53.
8 Derek Offord, "Dostoevskii and Chernyshevskii," *Slavonic and East European Review* 57, no. 4 (1979): 509–30 (512).
9 EDS: Siberian prison colony.

Russia, and shows that the connection is organic by speaking of the people and the vitality of society in the same phrase:

> The question of the *narod* is today a question of life [. . .]: do we today have a *zemstvo* that stands as an element distinct from the conscript classes, does it today have any kind of life, can it renew our society that is so lacking in vitality? (PSS 20:5)

Dostoevskii concedes in "Two camps of theoreticians" that both Westernizers and Slavophiles recognize the existence of a gulf between the educated classes and the *narod*, which must be bridged. Outlining the arguments of each camp, he examines their different attitudes to healing the rift and highlights the inadequacies therein. He portrays the Westernizers as seeking to raise the common people to their level, seeing the people as the needy party and the intelligentsia as a repository of progress and enlightenment. But in Dostoevskii's view, the situation is the reverse: it is the educated classes who are in need, whereas the people have their own reserves of strength. He refers to the common belief—one that he himself once held—that the *narod* is stupid and so steeped in routine as to function virtually like machines, citing Uspenskii and Pisemskii, two writers for the progressive journal *The Contemporary*, as propagating this view, and calls it slander. He sees this belief as expressing in a contemporary form the old antagonism felt by the boyar aristocracy for the *zemstvo* (PSS 20:8). Here the reader can feel the resonance of Dostoevskii's Siberian experience in his assertion that the people will not appreciate any attempt by the gentry to make magnanimous gestures to them, as he writes, "The *narod* will not approach us, unless we lose our air of Olympian grandeur [. . .] For the *narod* does not recognize need in us: *it will remain strong even when we are gone*" (PSS 20:8).

On the other hand, Dostoevskii praises the Slavophiles for having raised awareness of the positive attributes of peasant society and for having recognized the value of the *obshchina*. *Day*, he writes, has a deep and honest thirst for the truth, supports the free and independent development of Russian life and upholds Russian interests on issues that are as flesh and blood to society, so much that he finds that *Day* plays an invaluable part in literary debate (PSS 20:9). High praise indeed from Dostoevskii, especially when compared to his comments from just the year before. But he still finds points of disagreement with the Slavophiles, criticizing the arguments that stem from such noble motives. In their zeal to emphasize the worth of the traditional peasant way of life, he asserts, they are unjust towards the educated classes and write off all aspects of post-Petrine civilization as false. In order to refute their claims, Dostoevskii points to the flowering of Russian literature from Pushkin onwards and its ability to absorb the best of European learning as well as to turn a critical eye on the flaws in Russian society (PSS 20:10).

True to *Time*'s claim to hold the middle ground, Dostoevskii acknowledges that a part of the truth is to be found in each camp. In a passage that sets out the position of the *pochvenniki* on the reforms of Peter the Great, he argues that those reforms were a genuine response to the increasing need felt by all Russians for intellectual development and spiritual renewal. He pays homage to the pre-Petrine period idealized by the Slavophiles for its emphasis on spiritual life, but cautions that renewal cannot come from dreams of nostalgia. By contrast, according to Dostoevskii, the reforms sprang from Peter's correct apprehension of his native people's needs, and so were truly Russian in nature and quite necessary. However, Peter's despotic will caused him to try to reconstruct the whole of society in his lifetime. In opening a window on the West, says Dostoevskii, the reforms allowed Russians to take from Europe not only beneficial education but also ideas and structures not appropriate to Russia. The *narod*, seeing no advantage to them in the reforms, turned their back on them, thus proving that in their implementation they were anti-Russian, as Dostoevskii explains:

> Therefore one can say that Peter's reforms were a national [*narodnyi*] phenomenon insofar as they epitomized the striving of the *narod* for renewal and more space in life—but only in that respect were they national . . . To put it more precisely, only the *idea* of the reforms was national. But the reforms as a fact were antinational to the greatest degree . . . Firstly, he betrayed the national spirit by the despotic methods of his reforms, having treated the transformation not as a matter for the whole people, but as a fact of his own arbitrary rule [. . .] The *narod* renounced its well-meaning reformers [. . .] because such a method of transformation was quite contrary to its spirit. (PSS 20:15)

Thus Dostoevskii shows that the price paid for the benefits of Peter's reforms was an ever-increasing rift between the educated classes and the people, a rift that had become so large that the intelligentsia did not know how to bridge it, as typified by the squabbling of the Westernizers and the Slavophiles. Dostoevskii's solution is based on the deep appreciation for the peasant classes that he learned in Siberia. He underlines the native principle of voluntary unity in the peasant commune, the innate wisdom shown by the people in their response to the Emancipation edict, and their ability to recognize and judge their own faults. These, he writes, are proof that the *narod* has something to offer and is capable of growth (PSS 20:21). Also interesting is Dostoevskii's contention that the *raskol*[10] demonstrates the Russian people's ability to create their own indigenous cultural forms in preference to accepting changes imposed by the authorities (PSS 20:20–21). Here he shows that his fervent faith in Christ does not preclude him from departing from official Church teaching; on the contrary, this comment, in my interpretation, indicates that Dostoevskii preferred to look to the people as the true authority on Orthodoxy and that he sympathized with Grigor'ev's concept of "humble Orthodoxy" as outlined above.

As a contrast with his portrayal of the people, Dostoevskii depicts the gentry as running out of fresh energy because, thanks to their separation from their native soil, their range of activity is too limited to take Russia far. He lays the blame on the upper stratum of society for the poor regard the peasantry has of it; it is because of the gentry's former lack of concern with the peasantry and because of its dubious moral standing that the people do not understand them (PSS 20:17). Therefore, Dostoevskii proposes three necessary courses of action. First, literacy must be disseminated among the common people as a means to their moral and spiritual self-improvement. Second, the system of estate borders, which prevents the free movement of the peasantry, must be abolished. Third, the gentry must also be prepared to undergo moral reform and learn to respect the peasant in a manner that transcends abstract theories (PSS 20:20). He concludes:

> Have we really suffocated and stagnated so much that there is no hope of our revival? But if life has stagnated in us, then it most certainly exists in the as yet untouched soil of the people [...] this is our sacred conviction. (PSS 20:22)

In Dostoevskii's summation of the problem facing Russian society, of the pitfalls in the arguments of the Slavophile and Westernizer movements, and in his proffered solutions, it is possible to discern several points that indicate his

---

10 EDS: Split in the Russian Church following Patriarch Nikon's church reforms in 1653, which resulted in a group leaving the Orthodox Church. This group subsequently became known as the Old Believers.

increasing awareness of common ground with the Slavophiles and his growing admiration for them. Of particular interest for the purposes of this study are the role he accords to the *narod* in renewing Russia and the peasant commune, for these matters are central to Slavophilism. In his esteem for the people he sides with the Slavophiles, and implies as much by his parting criticism of the Westernizers in "Two camps of theoreticians": "We concede that the *narod* has many faults, but we will never agree with one camp of theoreticians that the *narod* is inescapably stupid and has done nothing for the thousand years of its life" (PSS 20:22). He also shows a partial agreement with the Slavophiles on the question of the disruptive and anti-Russian implementation of Peter the Great's reforms, although he puts more emphasis on their benefits than can be found in the works of Khomiakov or Kireevskii.

The Coming Apocalypse from The Notebooks for *Demons* (1870)*

Fedor Dostoevskii

*T**he Prince's ideas.* A new idea. This isn't Anglo-Saxon law, nor is it Democracy or the formal equality of the French (Romance) world. This is natural brotherhood. The tsar is at the head. Slave and yet free (St. Paul).[1] The Russian people will never rise against their tsar (which some tsars failed to realize, fearing an uprising). But they will come to realize it. The tsar is for his people an incarnation of their soul, of their spirit. Uprisings could only occur as long as there existed a division of society into estates: the Moscow of December 14 (the people were always set against it). All this has come to an end with the emancipation of the peasants. Russia is not a republic, it is not Jacobinism, or communism. (Foreigners, as well as our Russian foreigners, will never understand this!) Russia is no more and no less than the embodiment of Orthodoxy (a slave, and yet free), and those Russians who have betrayed Christianity. In Russia, there live peasants. The Apocalypse. The millennium. The Roman Whore (for their Christ has accepted the earthly kingdom rejected in the desert). We have reached the last stage of our submission to Europe, to civilization, to the curse of Peter's reform. Intellectual irresponsibility—(socialism, communism, baseness)—but we shall eventually grasp this not only with our vigorous vitality (as we did finally grasp) [. . .] i.e., immediately and alive,

---

*   From Fyodor Dostoyevsky, *The Notebooks for* The Possessed, trans. Victor Terras, ed. Edward Wasiolek (Chicago: University of Chicago Press, 1968) 225–26. Copyright © by the University of Chicago. All rights reserved.

1   A free quotation from I Corinthians 7:22.

but also with out intellect; we shall smash those European fetters which have been clinging to us for so long, and they will break like cobwebs; and we shall all realize, finally, that the world, the terrestrial globe, the Earth has never *seen such* a gigantic idea as the one which is now taking shape here, in the East, and moving to take up place of the European masses <*sic*> to regenerate the world. Europe will flow into our waters as a living stream, and the part of it which is dead and doomed to die will serve as ethnographic material for us. We are bringing the world the only thing we can give it, which is, however, the only thing it needs: Orthodoxy, the true and glorious, eternal creed of Christ and a full moral regeneration in his name. We are bringing the world the first paradise of the millennium. —And from amongst us, there will appear Elias (ENOCH AND ELIAS) and Enoch, who will give battle to the Antichrist, i.e., the spirit of the West which will become incarnate in the West. Hurray to the future.

Peasant Marei (1876)*

Fedor Dostoevskii

B ut reading all these *professions de foi* is a bore, I think, and so I'll tell you a story;[1] actually, it's not even a story, but only a reminiscence of something that happened long ago and that, for some reason, I would very much like to recount here and now as a conclusion to our treatise on the People. At the time I was only nine years old [. . .] But no, I'd best begin with the time I was twenty-nine.

It was the second day of Easter Week. The air was warm, the sky was blue, the sun was high, warm, and bright, but there was only gloom in my heart. I was wandering behind the prison barracks, examining and counting off the pales in the sturdy prison stockade, but I had lost even the desire to count, although such was my habit. It was the second day of "marking the holiday" within the prison compound; the prisoners were not taken out to work; many were drunk; there were shouts of abuse, and quarrels were constantly breaking out in all corners. Disgraceful, hideous songs; card games in little nooks under the bunks; a few convicts, already beaten half to death by sentence of their comrades for their particular rowdiness, lay on bunks covered in sheepskin coats until such time as they might come to their senses; knives had already been drawn a few times—all this, in two days of holiday, had worn me out to the point of illness. Indeed, I never could endure the drunken carousals of peasants without being disgusted, and here, in this place, particularly. During these days even the prison staff did not look in; they made no searches, nor did they check for alcohol, for they realized that once a year they had to allow even these outcasts

---

* From Fyodor Dostoevsky, *A Writer's Diary Volume 1: 1873–1876*, trans. and ed. Kenneth Lantz (Evanston, IL: Northwestern University Press, 1994), 351–55. Copyright © 1994 by Northwestern University Press. Published 1994. All rights reserved.
1   According to the memoirs of Dostoevskii's younger brother, Andrei, Marei was an actual personage.

to have a spree; otherwise it might be even worse. At last, anger welled up in my heart. I ran across the Pole M—cki, a political prisoner;[2] he gave me a gloomy look, his eyes glittering and his lips trembling: "Je hais ces brigands!" he muttered, gritting his teeth, and passed me by. I returned to the barrack despite the fact that a quarter hour before I had fled it half-demented when six healthy peasants had thrown themselves, as one man, on the drunken Tartar Gazin[3] and had begun beating him to make him settle down; they beat him senselessly with such blows as might have killed a camel; but they knew that it was not easy to kill this Hercules and so they didn't hold back. And now when I returned to the barracks I noticed Gazin lying senseless on a bunk in the corner showing scarcely any signs of life; he was lying under a sheepskin coat, and everyone passed him by in silence: although they firmly hoped he would revive the next morning, still, "with a beating like that, God forbid, you could finish a man off." I made my way to my bunk opposite a window with an iron grating and lay down on my back, my hands behind my head, and closed my eyes. I liked to lie like that: a sleeping man was left alone, while at the same time one could daydream and think. But dreams did not come to me; my heart beat restlessly, and M—cki's words kept echoing in my ears: "Je hais ces brigands!" [I hate these brigands!] However, why describe my feelings? Even now at night I sometimes dream of that time, and none of my dreams are more agonizing. Perhaps you will also notice that until today I have scarcely ever spoken in print of my prison life; I wrote *Notes from the House of the Dead* fifteen years ago using an invented narrator, a criminal who supposedly had murdered his wife. (I might add, by the way, that many people supposed and are even now quite firmly convinced that I was sent to hard labor for the murder of my wife.)

Little by little I lost myself in reverie and imperceptibly sank into memories of the past. All through my four years in prison I continually thought of all my past days, and I think I relived the whole of my former life in my memories. These memories arose in my mind of themselves; rarely did I summon them up consciously. They would begin from a certain point, some little thing that was often barely perceptible, and then bit by bit they would grow into a finished picture, some strong and complete impression. I would analyze these impressions, adding new touches to things experienced long ago; and the main thing was that I would refine them, continually refine them, and in this

---

2   The Polish revolutionary Aleksandr Mirecki was an exile in Omsk while Dostoevskii was serving his term of hard labor there. The conversation he describes probably took place in April 1851. He also figures in Dostoevskii's *Notes from the House of the Dead*.

3   Gazin likewise appears in Notes from the House of the Dead.

consisted my entire entertainment. This time, for some reason, I suddenly recalled a moment of no apparent significance from my early childhood when I was only nine years old, a moment that I thought I had completely forgotten; but at that time I was particularly fond of memories of my very early childhood. I recalled one August at our home in the country: the day was clear and dry, but a bit chilly and windy; summer was on the wane, and soon I would have to go back to Moscow to spend the whole winter in boredom over my French lessons; and I was so sorry to have to leave the country. I passed by the granaries, made my way down into the gully, and climbed up into the Dell—that was what we called a thick patch of bushes that stretched from the far side of the gully to a grove of trees. And so I make my way deeper into the bushes and can hear that some thirty paces away a solitary peasant is plowing in the clearing. I know he's plowing up the steep side of a hill and his horse finds it heavy going; from time to time I hear his shout, "Gee-up!" I know almost all our peasants, but don't recognize the one who's plowing; and what difference does it make, anyway, since I'm quite absorbed in my own business. I also have an occupation: I'm breaking off a switch of walnut to lash frogs; walnut switches are so lovely and quite without flaws, so much better than birch ones. I'm also busy with bugs and beetles, collecting them; some are very pretty; I love the small, nimble, red-and-yellow lizards with the little black spots as well, but I'm afraid of snakes. I come across snakes far less often than lizards, however. There aren't many mushrooms here; you have to go into the birch wood for mushrooms, and that's what I have in mind. I liked nothing better than the forest with its mushrooms and wild berries, its insects, and its birds, hedgehogs, and squirrels, and with its damp aroma of rotting leaves that I loved so. And even now, as I write this, I can catch the fragrance from our stand of birches in the country: these impressions stay with you all your life. Suddenly, amid the deep silence, I clearly and distinctly heard a shout: "There's a wolf!" I screamed, and, beside myself with terror, crying at the top of my voice, I ran out into the field, straight at the plowing peasant.

It was our peasant Marei. I don't know if there is such a name, but everyone called him Marei. He was a man of about fifty, heavyset, rather tall, with heavy streaks of gray in his bushy, dark-brown beard. I knew him but had scarcely ever had occasion to speak to him before. He even stopped his little filly when he heard my cry, and when I rushed up to him and seized his plow with one hand and his sleeve with the other, he saw how terrified I was.

"It's a wolf!" I cried, completely out of breath.

Instinctively he jerked his head to look around, for an instant almost believing me.

"Where's the wolf?"

"I heard a shout . . . Someone just shouted, 'Wolf'" . . . I babbled.

"What do you mean, lad? There's no wolf; you're just hearing things," he said, reassuring me. But I was all a-tremble and clung to his coat even more tightly; I suppose I was very pale as well. He looked at me with an uneasy smile, evidently concerned and alarmed for me.

"Why you took a real fright, you did!" he said wagging his head. "Never mind, now, my dear. What a fine lad you are!"

He stretched out his hand and suddenly stroked my cheek.

"Never mind, now, there's nothing to be afraid of. Christ be with you. Cross yourself, lad." But I couldn't cross myself; the corners of my mouth were trembling, and I think this particularly struck him. He quietly stretched out a thick, earth-soiled finger with a black nail and gently touched it to my trembling lips.

"Now, now," he smiled at me with a broad almost maternal smile. "Lord, what a dreadful fuss. Dear, dear, dear!"

At last I realized that there was no wolf and that I must have imagined hearing the cry of "Wolf." Still, it had been such a clear and distinct shout; two or three times before, however, I had imagined such cries (not only about wolves), and I was aware of that. (Later, when childhood passed, these hallucinations did as well.)

"Well, I'll be off now," I said, making it seem like a question and looking at him shyly.

"Off with you, then, and I'll keep an eye on you as you go. Can't let the wolf get you!" he added, still giving me a maternal smile. "Well, Christ be with you, off you go." He made the sign of the cross over me, and crossed himself. I set off, looking over my shoulder almost every ten steps. Marei continued to stand with his little filly, looking after me and nodding every time I looked around. I confess I felt a little ashamed at taking such a fright. But I went on, still with a good deal of fear of the wolf, until I had gone up the slope of the gully to the first threshing barn and here the fear vanished entirely, and suddenly our dog Volchok came dashing out to meet me. With Volchok I felt totally reassured, and I turned toward Marei for the last time; I could no longer make out his face clearly, but I felt that he was still smiling kindly at me and nodding. I waved to him, and he returned my wave and urged on his little filly.

"Gee-up," came his distant shout once more, and his little filly once more started drawing the wooden plow.

This memory came to me all at once—I don't know why—but with amazing clarity of detail. Suddenly I roused myself and sat on the bunk; I recall that a quiet smile of reminiscence still played on my face. I kept on recollecting for yet another minute.

I remembered that when I had come home from Marei I told no one about my "adventure." And what kind of adventure was it anyway? I forgot about Marei very quickly as well. On the rare occasions when I met him later, I never struck up a conversation with him, either about the wolf or anything else, and now, suddenly, twenty years later, in Siberia, I remembered that encounter so vividly, right down to the last detail. That means it had settled unnoticed in my heart, all by itself with no will of mine, and had suddenly come back to me at a time when it was needed; I recalled the tender, maternal smile of a poor serf, the way he crossed me and shook his head: "Well you did take a fright now, didn't you, lad!" And I especially remember his thick finger, soiled with dirt, that he touched quietly and with shy tenderness to my trembling lips. Of course, anyone would try to reassure a child, but here in this solitary encounter something quite different had happened, and had I been his very own son he could not have looked at me with a glance that radiated more pure love, and who had prompted him to do that? He was our own serf, and I was his master's little boy; no one would learn of his kindness to me and reward him for it. Was he, maybe, especially fond of small children? There are such people. Our encounter was solitary, in an open field, and only God, perhaps, looking down saw what deep and enlightened human feeling and what delicate, almost feminine tenderness could fill the heart of a coarse, bestially ignorant Russian serf who at the time did not expect or even dream of his freedom. Now tell me, is this not what Konstantin Aksakov had in mind when he spoke of the advanced level of development of our Russian People?

And so when I climbed down from my bunk and looked around, I remember I suddenly felt I could regard these unfortunates in an entirely different way and that suddenly, through some sort of miracle, the former hatred and anger in my heart had vanished. I went off, peering intently into the faces of those I met. This disgraced peasant, with shaven head and brands on his cheek, drunk and roaring out his hoarse, drunken song—why he might also be that very same Marei; I cannot peer into his heart, after all. That same evening, I met M—cki once again. The unfortunate man! He had no recollections of any Mareis and no other view of these people but "Je hais ces brigands!" No, the Poles had to bear more than we did in those days.

Pushkin Speech (1880)*

Fedor Dostoevskii

Pushkin (A Sketch)
Delivered on June 8 at a Meeting of the Society of Lovers of Russian Literature
  "Pushkin is an extraordinary and, perhaps, unique manifestation of the Russian spirit," said Gogol'.[1] I would add that he is a prophetic one as well. Indeed, for all us Russians there is something unquestionably prophetic in his appearing. Pushkin arrived just as we were beginning to be truly conscious of ourselves, a self-consciousness that had barely begun and that developed in our society after the whole century that followed the reforms of Peter the Great, and his appearance did so much to cast a guiding light along the shadowy path we traveled. It is in this sense that Pushkin is prophetic and revelatory. I divide the work of our great poet into three periods. I am speaking now not as a literary critic: in discussing Pushkin's creative work I wish merely to explain my idea of his prophetic significance for us and what I mean by those words. I might note in passing, however, that I see no firm boundaries between these periods of Pushkin's work. For example, it seems to me that the beginning of *Onegin* is still a part of the first period of the poet's work, but *Onegin* ends in the second period, when Pushkin had already found his ideals in his native land, had fully taken them into his loving and perceptive soul, and had come to cherish them. The accepted view is also that during the first period of his work Pushkin imitated the European poets—Parny, André Chenier and others, particularly Byron.[2] Yes, there is no doubt that the poets of Europe had a great influence

---

1 The quotation is from Gogol's essay "A Few Words about Pushkin," which appeared in his collection, *Arabesques* (1835).
2 Parny, André Chenier and others: Everiste-Désiré de Parny (1753–1814), French poet. Parny had profound influence on the verse of the young Pushkin. André de Chénier (1762–1794),

on the development of his genius and that they continued to exert an influence on him for the rest of his life. Nevertheless, even Pushkin's first narrative poems were no mere imitations, so that even they express the extraordinary independence of his genius. Imitations never contain the kind of personal suffering and depth of self-consciousness that Pushkin, displayed, for example, in "The Gypsies"—a poem I place entirely within the first period of his creative work.[3] And I am not taking into account the creative power and energy that would not have been so evident had he been merely an imitator. In the character of Aleko, the hero of "The Gypsies," one already finds a powerful, profound, and completely Russian idea, subsequently expressed in such harmonious fullness in *Onegin,* where we see almost this same Aleko, no longer as an outlandish figure but as someone palpably real and comprehensible. In Aleko, Pushkin had already found and brilliantly rendered that unhappy wanderer in his native land, that historical, suffering Russian who appeared with such historical inevitability in our educated society after it had broken away from the People. Such a character Pushkin derived not only from Byron, of course. This is a genuine and flawlessly conceived character, a type that has long become a permanent fixture in our Russian land. These homeless Russian wanderers continue their wandering even now and, it seems, are unlikely to disappear for a long time yet. And if in our day they no longer frequent the camps of the gypsies to look for universal ideals in their wild and distinctive way of life and to seek in the bosom of nature some respite from our confused and ridiculous Russian life—the life of educated society—then, still, they go running off to socialism, which did not yet exist in Aleko's time; they take their new faith to a different field and work it zealously, believing, as did Aleko, that through their bizarre labors they will achieve their goals and find happiness not only for themselves but for the whole world. For what the Russian wanderer needs is the happiness of the whole world in order to find his own peace of mind: he will not settle for less—so long as matters are confined to theory, of course. This is still the same Russian, only belonging to a different era. This person, I repeat, came into being in our educated society, detached from the People and the People's strength, just at the beginning of the second century after the great Petrine reforms. Oh, the vast

---

French poet, the greatest French lyricist of the eighteenth century. Chénier influenced Pushkin in the 1820s, in his "Byronic" period.

3   "The Gypsies," narrative poem by Pushkin. Its central figure, Aleko, is a weak but vicious character who, disgusted with civilization, flees the city to seek freedom among the "primitive" gypsies in southern Russia. He wants freedom for himself, however; eventually he murders a gypsy girl and her lover and is banished from their community.

majority of educated Russians even then, in Pushkin's day just as in our own time, served and serve peacefully as functionaries, for the state, the railways, the banks, or simply made a living by other means; some even took up scholarly work, giving lectures, and they did all these things in a regular, leisurely, peaceful fashion, receiving their salaries and playing cards, with never the slightest notion of running off to the gypsy camps or whatever their equivalent might be in our time. At most they might flirt with liberalism "with a tinge of European socialism" but with a certain Russian softheartedness about it—but this is only a question of the age, after all. What does it matter that one fellow still hasn't begun to be troubled, while another has already managed to get as far as the locked door and painfully knocked his head against it? The same thing awaits them all in due time if they do not take the road to salvation through humble communion with the People. Granted, the same fate does not await every one of them; still, it is enough if it happens merely to "the chosen few," merely to a tenth of those who began to be troubled, since through them the remaining vast majority will be deprived of their peace of mind.

Of course, Aleko still does not know how to express his anguish properly: for him it is still all some kind of abstraction; he has merely a longing for nature, a grievance against fashionable society, universal aspirations, a lament for the truth which someone, somewhere, has lost and which he simply cannot find. There is a bit of Jean-Jacques Rousseau here. Of course, he himself cannot say what this truth is, where and in what it might appear, and just when it was lost, yet he is genuinely suffering. This bizarre and impatient character still seeks salvation from external things first of all, and so he must: "The truth," he imagines, "is somewhere outside him, perhaps in some other land, in Europe, for instance, with her stable historical order and well-established social and civic life." And he will never understand that the truth is to be found, first of all, within himself; indeed, how could he understand that? He is a stranger in his own land, after all; for a whole century he has been unaccustomed to work; he has no culture; he has grown up behind solid walls like a boarding-school miss; he has carried out some odd, unaccountable duties associated with one or another of the fourteen classes into which Russian educated society is divided.[4] He is still no more than a blade of grass, torn from its stem and carried off by the wind. And he can

---

4   In 1722 Peter the Great instituted the "Table of Ranks," a hierarchy of fourteen categories of civil servants and military officers. He thus abolished, in theory at least, the previous tradition of aristocratic privilege, since henceforth all who served were expected to begin at the bottom of the hierarchy and advance by their own merit. Even one of humble birth could acquire the status of gentry by attaining a certain rank.

sense that and suffer for it, and often suffer so painfully! So what does it matter if he, who perhaps belongs to the hereditary nobility and very likely owns serfs, took advantage of the freedoms of the nobility and indulged in a little fantasy to fall in with people who live "outside the law" and lead a trained bear in a gypsy camp? One can understand that a woman, a "wild woman" as one poet has called her, would be most likely to give him hope of relieving his anguish; and so, with frivolous yet passionate faith, he throws himself at Zemfira: "Here," he says, "is my way out; here I may find happiness, in the bosom of nature, far from society, here, among people who have no laws or civilization!" And what happens? In his first encounter with this wild nature he cannot restrain himself and reddens his hands with blood. The unhappy dreamer is not only unsuited to universal harmony, he is even unsuited to the gypsies, and they drive him away—without vengeance, without malice, in a dignified, simplehearted fashion: "Depart from us, O haughty man; / Savages are we, not bound by law, / We neither punish nor chastise."[5]

This is all rather farfetched, of course, but "the haughty man" is real, and Pushkin's perception here is apt. Pushkin was the first among us to perceive him, and we must remember that. The very moment Aleko finds something not to his liking, he angrily attacks his opponent and punishes him for the offense or—what he finds even handier—he remembers that he belongs to one of the fourteen classes and may appeal (for this also happened) to the law to attack and punish; and he will resort to the law, so long as his personal grievance can be redressed. No, this is not an imitation, this is a brilliant poem! Here we already find a suggestion of the Russian solution to the question, the "accursed question," in accordance with the People's faith and truth: "Humble thyself, O haughty man; first curb thy pride. Humble thyself, O idle man; first labor on thy native soil." That is the solution in accord with the People's truth and the People's wisdom. "The truth is not outside you but within; find yourself within yourself; submit yourself to yourself; master yourself, and you shall see the truth. This truth is not to be found in things; it is not outside you or somewhere beyond the sea but is to be found first in your own work to better yourself. Conquer yourself, humble yourself, and you shall be freer than ever you imagined; you will embark on a great task and make others free, and you will find happiness, for your life will be made complete and you will at last understand your People and their sacred truth. Universal harmony is not to be found among the gypsies or anywhere else so long as you yourself are still unworthy of

---

5   At the end of the poem, an old man dismisses Aleko with these words.

it, if you are spiteful and proud and expect life as a gift, not even supposing that it must be paid for." This solution to the question is already strongly suggested in Pushkin's poem. It is still more clearly expressed in *Eugene Onegin,* a poem that is not farfetched but palpably realistic, a poem in which actual Russian life is embodied with a creative power and accomplishment such as had never been seen before Pushkin or, perhaps, after him.

Onegin arrives from St. Petersburg—it had to be from St. Petersburg; this was absolutely essential to the poem, and Pushkin could not have omitted such a major, realistic feature of his hero's biography. I repeat once more: he is the same Aleko, particularly later in the poem, when he exclaims in anguish: "Oh, why, like some poor Tula assessor / Am I not lying paralyzed?"[6]

But at the beginning of the poem he is still half a dandy and socialite and has not yet lived enough to be completely disillusioned with life. But even he begins to be visited and troubled by "The noble demon of secret ennui."[7]

Deep in the provinces, in the heartland of his native country, he naturally feels out of place and not at home. He does not know what to do and feels as if he were a guest in his own home. Subsequently, when he wanders in anguish through his native land and through foreign parts among strangers, he, as an undoubtedly intelligent and sincere man, feels even more a stranger to himself. It's true that he loves his native land, but he has no faith in it. Of course, he's also heard of the ideals of his native land, but he doesn't believe in them. He believes merely in the utter impossibility of any sort of labor on his native soil, while—then, as now—he regards those who do believe in this with sad mockery. He killed Lenskii simply out of spleen; and who knows?—his spleen may have been caused by his longing for a universal ideal; this is very much in our style, this is very probable.

Tat'iana is another matter: she is a strong character who stands solidly on her own native soil. She is deeper than Onegin and, of course, more intelligent than he. Her noble instinct alone tells her where and in what the truth is to be found, and this is expressed in the poem's ending. Pushkin might have done even better to name his poem after Tat'iana rather than Onegin, for she is unquestionably its protagonist. She is a positive, not a negative character, a type of positive beauty; she is the apotheosis of Russian womanhood, and the poet has given her the task of expressing the poem's idea in the remarkable scene of her last meeting with Onegin. One might even say that a positive type of

---

6   From *Eugene Onegin,* "The Travels of Onegin."
7   From Nekrasov's poem, "A joy to see . . ."

Russian woman of such beauty has almost never been repeated in our literature except, perhaps, in the character of Liza in Turgenev's *A Nest of Gentlefolk*. But Onegin's manner of looking down on people caused him to disregard Tat'iana entirely when he met her the first time, in a provincial backwater and in the humble image of a pure, innocent girl who was so timid in his presence. He was unable to see the accomplishment and perfection in this poor girl and perhaps really did take her for a "moral embryo."[8] She, an embryo, and this after her letter to Onegin! If there is anyone who is a moral embryo in the poem, then of course it is he, Onegin himself: there is no disputing that. Indeed, he was utterly incapable of recognizing her: what did he know of the human soul? He is a man of abstractions, he is a restless dreamer, and has been so all his life. He did not recognize her later either, as a grand lady in Petersburg, when, in the words of his letter to Tat'iana, "his soul perceived all her perfections."[9] But these are merely words: she has passed through his life unrecognized and unappreciated by him; herein lies the tragedy of their romance. Oh, had Childe Harold or, somehow, even Lord Byron himself come from England to Onegin's first meeting with her in the country, and had one of them noticed her shy, humble charm and pointed her out to him—oh, Onegin would at once have been amazed and astonished, for these people afflicted by Weltschmerz often have such servility of spirit! But this did not happen, and once the seeker after world harmony had given her a lecture and had, still, treated her honorably, he set off with his Weltschmerz, his hands stained with blood spilled in a foolish fit of anger, to wander over his native land without ever perceiving it, brimming with health and strength, exclaiming with curses: "I am young and full of life, But what awaits me? / Inner strife."[10]

Tat'iana understood this. In some of the novel's immortal stanzas the poet has shown her visiting the home of this man she finds so fascinating and mysterious. I need not speak of the artistry, the matchless beauty, and the profundity of these stanzas. We see her in his study, examining his books, his possessions, his trinkets, trying through them to comprehend his soul and solve her riddle; the "moral embryo" stops at last, deep in thought, with a strange smile on her

---

8 "Moral embryo": Belinskii, in his ninth article on Pushkin, thus describes Tat'iana. V. G. Belinskii, *Sobranie sochinenii* (Moscow: Khudozhestvennaia literatura, 1981), vol. 6, 422.

9 Paraphrase of Onegin's remarks in his letter to Tat'iana, chap. 8, stanza 32.

10 In chap. 8, stanzas 12 and 13, after Onegin has killed his friend Lenskii and been rejected by Tat'iana, he travels aimlessly through Russia. The couplet quoted is from the uncompleted "Fragments from Onegin's Travels."

face, sensing that she has solved the riddle; and she gently whispers, "Is he a parody, perchance?"[11]

Yes, she had to whisper that; she has solved the riddle. Much later, when they meet again in Petersburg, she understands him completely. Incidentally, who said that society and court life had a pernicious effect on her soul and that it was precisely her standing as a society lady and her new ideas inspired by society that were part of her reason for refusing Onegin?[12] No, that was not what happened. No, this is the same Tanya, the same country girl as before! She has not been corrupted; rather, she is depressed by this ostentatious Petersburg life; her heart aches and she suffers; she despises her position as a society lady, and anyone who sees her differently does not understand anything Pushkin was trying to say. She tells Onegin firmly: "But now I am another's wife, / And will be true to him for life."[13]

She said this specifically as a Russian woman; this is her apotheosis. She expresses the truth of the poem. Oh, I shall say not a word about her religious convictions, about her view of the sacrament of marriage—no, I shall not mention that. But still, why did she refuse to follow him even though she admitted she loved him? Was it because she, "as a Russian woman" (and not a southern woman or some Frenchwoman), was incapable of taking such a bold step, unable to break her shackles, unable to overcome her worship of honors, wealth, and social standing, to break with conventional virtue? No, the Russian woman is bold. The Russian woman will boldly follow one in whom she believes, and she has proved that. But she "is now another's wife, and will be true to him for life." To whom, then, and to what is she being true? To what obligations? To this old general,[14] whom she cannot love because she loves Onegin, and whom she married only because "in tears her mother begged, implored,"[15] while in her aggrieved and lacerated soul there was only despair and no hope, no glimmer of light? Yes, she is faithful to this general, her husband, an honorable man who loves her, respects her, and is proud of her. Her mother may have "implored

---

11 From chap. 7, stanza 24.

12 Belinskii, like Dostoevskii, regarded Tat'iana as the essence of Russian womanhood, but he said: "Tat'iana does not like society and for the sake of happiness would leave it forever to live in the country; but while she is in society, its opinion will always be her idol, and fear of its judgment will always be the basis of her morals." Belinskii, *Sobranie sochinenii*, vol. 6:423.

13 From chap. 8, stanza 47.

14 As N. O. Lerner has shown, Tat'iana's husband is probably about thirty-five, hardly an old man. See "Muzh Tat'iany" [Tat'iana's husband], *Rasskazy o Pushkine* [*Stories about Pushkin*] (Leningrad: Priboi, 1929), 215.

15 Chap. 8, stanza 47.

her," but still it was she and no one else who gave her consent; it was she, after all, who swore to be a faithful wife to him. She may have married him in despair, but now he is her husband, and betrayal would cast shame and disgrace upon him and would mean his death. And can one person found his happiness on the unhappiness of another? Happiness is found not only in the pleasures of love, but also in the higher harmony of the spirit. How can one's spirit be set at rest if in one's past there is a dishonorable, merciless, inhumane act? Is she to run off simply because the one who represents her happiness is here? But what kind of happiness can it be if it is founded on the unhappiness of another? Can you imagine that you are erecting the edifice of human destiny with the goal of making people happy in the end, of giving them peace and rest at last?[16] And now imagine as well that to do this it is essential and unavoidable to torture to death just one human creature; moreover, let that creature be not an entirely worthy one, a person some may find even ridiculous—not some Shakespeare, but simply an honorable old man, the husband of a young wife whose love he blindly believes in; even though he knows nothing of her heart, he respects her, is proud of her, happy with her, and is at peace. And so you need only to disgrace, dishonor and torment him and build your edifice on the tears of this dishonored old man! Will you consent on those terms to be the architect of such an edifice? That is the question. And can you admit, even for a moment, the idea that the people for whom you were building this edifice would them-selves agree to accept such happiness from you if its foundations rested on the suffering of, say, even one insignificant creature, but one who had been merci-lessly and unjustly tortured—and, having accepted this happiness, would they remain happy ever after? Tell me, could Tat'iana, with her noble soul and her heart that had suffered so much, have settled the matter in any other way? No; this is how a pure Russian soul settles it: "Let it be that I alone have no happi-ness; let my unhappiness be immeasurably greater than the unhappiness of this old man; finally, let no one, not even this old man, ever learn of my sacrifice and appreciate it; but I do not want to be happy after having destroyed another!"

This is the tragedy: it unfolds, and the line cannot be crossed; it is already too late, and so Tat'iana sends Onegin away. People will say that Onegin is also unhappy, after all; she has saved one and ruined another! That may well be, but that is another question, perhaps even the most important one in the poem. Incidentally, the question of why Tat'iana did not go off with Onegin has at

---

16 The ideas that follow were developed by Ivan in *Brothers Karamazov*, book 4 ("The Grand Inquisitor.")

least in our literature, a very characteristic history of its own, and so that is why I allowed myself to go on at such length about it. What is most characteristic is that for such a long time we cast doubt on the moral solution to this question. This is what I think: even if Tat'iana had become free, if her old husband had died and she had become a widow, even then she would not have gone off with Onegin. One must understand the whole essence of this character! She can see what he is, after all: the eternal wanderer has suddenly seen a woman, whom he formerly spurned in a new, dazzling, unattainable setting; and it is this setting, perhaps, that is the entire essence of the thing. This girl, whom he all but despised, is now the one to whom society pays homage—society, that this awesome authority for Onegin, despite all his universal strivings; and surely that is why he rushes blindly to her! "This is my ideal!" he exclaims, "this is my salvation, this is the solution to my anguish; I overlooked it, yet 'happiness was so possible, so near!'" And just as Aleko rushed to Zemfira, so he rushes off to Tat'iana, seeking all his solutions in some odd new fantasy. Does Tat'iana really not see this? Has she not seen through him long ago? She knows very well that in essence he loves only his new fantasy and not her, the Tat'iana who is as humble as before! She knows that he takes her for something other than what she is, that it is not even her he loves, that, perhaps, he does not love anyone and is incapable of loving anyone, despite the fact that he suffers such torment! He loves his fantasy; indeed, he himself is a fantasy. Should she follow him, he would grow disenchanted the very next day and look mockingly at his infatuation. He has no soil under his feet, this blade of grass borne by the wind. She is altogether different: in her despair and her agonized awareness that her life has been ruined, she still has something solid and unshakeable on which her soul can rely. These are her memories of childhood, her memories of her native home deep in the provinces where her humble, pure life began; it is the "cross and the shade of boughs o'er the grave of her poor nurse."[17] Oh, these memories and images from her past are what she treasures most now; these images are all she has left, but it is they which save her soul from ultimate despair. And they are no small thing; no, they mean a great deal, because they provide a complete foundation, something unshakeable and indestructible. They represent contact with her native land, her native People and their sacred values. But what does he have, and who is he? She cannot follow him out of compassion, simply in order to console him, to use her infinite loving pity to provide him, at least temporarily, with an illusion of happiness, knowing full well that the very

---

17 Chap. 8, stanza 46.

next day he would ridicule that happiness. No, there are profound and steadfast souls that cannot consciously give up their most sacred values to be defiled, even though it may be from infinite compassion. No, Tat'iana could not have followed Onegin.

And so in *Onegin*, in this immortal and unsurpassable poem, Pushkin appeared as a great Popular writer, as no one before him ever had. At one stroke, in a most apt, perceptive manner, he identified the innermost essence of the upper levels of our society that stand above the People. Having identified the type of the Russian wanderer, who continues his wandering even in our days; having been the first to divine, through his brilliant instinct, that wanderer's historical fate and his enormous significance in our future destiny; having placed beside him the type of positive, indisputable beauty of the Russian woman, Pushkin, in his other works of this period (first among Russian writers once again, of course), showed us a whole series of positively beautiful Russian types he found among the Russian People. The beauty of these types lies above all in their truth, an unquestionable and palpable truth that makes them impossible to disavow; they stand before us as if carved in stone. Let me remind you once more that I am not speaking as a literary critic and so I shall not try to explain my idea through a detailed literary analysis of these brilliant creations of our poet. One could write a whole book, for instance, about the type of Russian chronicler-monk, pointing out all the importance and significance there is for us in this majestic Russian image Pushkin found in the Russian land, brought forth and sculpted, and whose indisputable, humble, and majestic spiritual beauty has now been placed before us forever as testimony to the powerful spirit of Popular life capable of producing images of such unquestioned beauty. The type has been provided; it exists; it cannot be denied by saying it is a mere invention, merely the poet's fantasy and idealization. Think well about it and you must agree: yes, it does exist, and so, within the spirit of the People who created it the vital force of this spirit also exists; and it is great and limitless. Everywhere in Pushkin we perceive a faith in the Russian character, a faith in its spiritual power; and if there is faith, then there must be hope as well, a great hope for the Russian: "With hopes for glory and for good, / I look ahead and have no fear,"[18] said the poet himself when speaking of another subject; but these words of his can be applied directly to the whole of his creative activity drawn from his nation. And never has any Russian writer, before him or since, been so akin in spirit to his People as was Pushkin. Oh, we have many experts

---

18 The opening lines of Pushkin's "Stanzas" (1826).

on the People among our writers, ones who write with such talent, so aptly and so lovingly about the People; and yet if one compares them with Pushkin, they are, truly (with perhaps two exceptions from his latest followers), merely "gentlemen" who write about the People. The most talented of these, even these two exceptions I just mentioned, will now and then suddenly show a haughty attitude, something from another world and another way of life, something that shows a wish to raise the People to their own level and make them happy by doing so. In Pushkin there is precisely something that *truly* makes him akin to the People, something that reaches almost the level of simple hearted tenderness. Take his "Tale of the Bear" and the peasant who killed his "lady bear," or recall the verses "Brother Ivan, when you and I start drinking," and you will see what I mean.[19]

Our great poet left all these treasures of art and artistic vision as signposts for the artists who came after him and for those who would toil in the same fields as he. One can positively state that had Pushkin not existed neither would the talented people who came after him. At least they, despite their great gifts, would not have made their presence felt with such power and clarity of expression as they did later, in our time. But the point is not merely in poetry and not merely in creative work; had Pushkin not existed, it might well be that our faith in our Russian individuality, our now conscious hope in the strength of our People, and with it our faith in our future independent mission in the family of European peoples would not have been formulated with such unshakeable force (this did happen later, but was by no means universal and was felt by merely a few). This feat of Pushkin's becomes particularly evident if one studies what I call the third period of his creative work.

Once more, I repeat: these periods do not have such firm boundaries. Some of the works of even this third period could have appeared at the very beginning of our poet's career, because Pushkin was always a complete, integrated organism, so to say, an organism bearing all its beginnings within itself and not acquiring them from without. The outside world only aroused in him those things already stored in the depths of his soul. But this organism did develop, and the particular nature of each of the periods of this development actually can be shown and the gradual progression from one period to the next indicated. Thus, to the third period belongs the series of works in which

---

19 Pushkin's "Tale of the Bear" (1830), is a narrative verse, written in the style of a folktale, in which a peasant kills a bear and captures her three cubs; it ends with the lament of the bear's mate. His "Brother Ivan, when we start drinking" (1833), is a poem written in playful folk language about peasants drinking in memory of those deceased.

universal ideas shine forth most brightly, which reflect the poetic images of other nations and which incarnate their genius. Some of these works appeared only posthumously. And in this period of his career our poet stands forth as an almost miraculous and unprecedented phenomenon, never before seen anywhere else. In fact, the European literatures had creative geniuses of immense magnitude—the Shakespeares, Cervanteses, and Schillers. But show me even one of these great geniuses who possessed the capacity to respond to the whole world that our Pushkin had. And it is this capacity, the principal capacity of our nationality, that he shares with our People; and it is this, above all, that makes him a national poet. The very greatest of these European poets could never exemplify as intensely as Pushkin the genius of another people—even a people that might be near at hand—the spirit of that people, all the hidden depths of that spirit and all its longing to fulfill its destiny. On the contrary, when the European poets dealt with other nationalities they most often instilled in them their own nationality and interpreted them from their own national standpoint. Even Shakespeare's Italians, for instance, are almost to a man the same as Englishmen. Pushkin alone, of all the poets of the world, possesses the quality of embodying himself fully within another nationality. Take his "Scenes from Faust," his "Covetous Knight," his ballad "Once There Lived a Poor Knight."[20] Read "Don Juan" once more, and were it not for Pushkin's name on it you would never guess that it had not been written by a Spaniard.[21] What profound, fantastic images there are in the poem "A Feast in Time of Plague!"[22] But in these fantastic images you hear the genius of England; this marvelous song sung by the poem's hero about the plague, this song of Mary with the verses, "Once the noisy school rang out, / With the voices of our children," these English songs, this longing of the British genius, this lament, this agonizing presentiment of the future. Just recall the strange verses: "Once, wandering 'midst a valley wild . . ."[23]

---

20 "Scenes from Faust" (1825) involves characters from Goethe's *Faust*, although the remainder is Pushkin's own creation. "Once There Lived a Poor Young Knight" (1829), set in Europe during the Crusades, is in the form of a legend or ballad and describes a knight who dedicates himself to an ideal of purity.

21 Pushkin's "Stone Guest," (1830), in which he treats the Don Juan legend.

22 "A Feast in the Time of Plague" (1830), one of Pushkin's "Little Tragedies"; it is an adaptation from John Wilson's *City of the Plague*; "Mary's Song," sung by one of the characters, laments the fact that the plague has emptied the once noisy village school.

23 From Pushkin's poem "The Pilgrim" (1835), a free adaptation in verse, of motifs from Chapter 1 of John Bunyan's *Pilgrim's Progress*.

This is almost a literal reworking of the first three pages of a strange, mystical book written in prose by one ancient English religious sectarian—but is it merely a reworking? In the melancholy and rapturous music of these verses one senses the very soul of northern Protestantism, of an English heresiarch whose mysticism knows no bounds, with his dull, gloomy, and compelling strivings and with all the unchecked force of mystical visions. Reading these strange verses, you seem to sense the spirit of the age of the Reformation; you begin to understand this militant fire of incipient Protestantism; you begin to understand, finally, the history itself, and understand it not only rationally but as though you had been there yourself, had passed through the armed camp of sectarians, sung hymns with them, wept with them in their mystical ecstasies, and shared their beliefs. Incidentally, right next to this religious mysticism we find other religious stanzas from the Koran, or "Imitations of the Koran":[24] do we not find a real Moslem here? Is this not the very spirit of the Koran and its sword, the simple-hearted majesty of the faith and its awesome, bloody power? And here, too, we find the ancient world—"The Egyptian Nights";[25] here we see these earthly gods, who have been enthroned as divinities over their people, who despise the very spirit of their people and its aspirations who no longer believe in it, who have become solitary gods in truth and who have gone mad in their isolation, who in their anguish and weariness while waiting to die seek diversion in outrageous brutalities, in insectlike voluptuousness, the voluptuousness of a female spider devouring her mate. No, I will say positively that there has not been a poet so able to respond to the whole world as Pushkin; and the point is not only in this ability to respond but in its astounding depth and in his ability to infuse his spirit into the spirit of other nations, something that was almost complete and so was marvelous as well, because nowhere in any other poet anywhere in the world has such a phenomenon been repeated. This we find only in Pushkin, and his sense, I repeat, he is unprecedented and, in my view, prophetic, for it was just here that his national Russian strength was most fully expressed, that the national spirit of his poetry was expressed, the national spirit as it will develop in the future, the national spirit of our future, already concealed within our present and expressed prophetically. For what is the strength of the spirit of Russianness if not its ultimate aspirations toward universality and the universal brotherhood of peoples? Having become completely a national poet, Pushkin at once, as soon as he came in contact with the

---

24 "Imitations of the Koran" (1824), Pushkin's verses in the style of the Koran.
25 "Egyptian Nights" (1837), a fragment of a proposed novel which deals with Cleopatra.

force of the People, at once senses the great future mission of this force. Here he is a visionary; here he is a prophet.

In fact, what did Peter's reform mean for us, not only in terms of the future but even in terms of what has already happened and already is evident to all? What was the significance of this reform for us? It meant not only our adopting European clothing, customs, inventions and European science. Let us try to understand what happened and look into it more closely. Indeed, it is quite possible that Peter first began to carry out his reform in just this sense, that is to say, in an immediately utilitarian sense; but subsequently, in his further development of his idea, Peter undoubtedly followed a certain secret instinct that led him to work toward future goals that certainly were immensely broader than mere immediate utilitarianism. The Russian People as well accepted the reforms in just same spirit—not merely one of utilitarianism but having certainly sensed almost at once some further and incomparably more elevated goal than immediate utilitarianism; I must repeat, of course, that they sensed that goal unconsciously, yet also directly and at something absolutely vital. It was then that we at once began to strive toward a truly vital reunification, toward the universal brotherhood of peoples! It was not with hostility (as should have been the case, it would seem) but with friendship and complete love that we accepted the genius of other nations into our soul, all of them together, making no discriminations by race, knowing instinctively almost from our very first step where the distinctions lay, knowing how to eliminate contradictions, to excuse and reconcile differences; and in doing so we revealed the quality that had only just been made manifest—our readiness and our inclination for the general reunification of all people of all the tribes of the great Aryan race. Indeed, the mission of the Russian is unquestionably pan-European and universal. To become a real Russian to become completely Russian, perhaps, means just (in the final analysis—please bear that in mind) to become a brother to all people, a panhuman, if you like. Oh, all our Slavophilism and Westernizing is no more than one great misunderstanding between us, although it was historically necessary. To a real Russian, Europe and the lot of all the great Aryan tribe are just as dear as is Russia herself, as is the lot of our own native land, because our lot is universality, achieved not through the sword but through the strength of brotherhood and our brotherly aspirations toward the unity of people. If you care to look closely into our history after the Petrine reforms, you will already find traces and indications of this idea—this vision of mine, if you wish to call it that—in the way we dealt with the people of Europe, even in our official policy. For what was Russia doing in her policy over these whole two centuries if not serving Europe, far more, perhaps, than she was serving herself? I do not think that this happened merely though the ineptness of our politicians. Oh, the nations of Europe simply don't know how dear they are to us! And subsequently, I am certain we (I mean not we, of course, but the Russian people to come) will realize to the very last man that to become a genuine Russian will mean specifically: to strive to bring an ultimate reconciliation to Europe's contradictions, to indicate that the solution to Europe's anguish is to be found in the panhuman and all-unifying Russian soul, to enfold all our brethren within it with brotherly love, and at last, perhaps, to utter the ultimate word of great, general harmony, ultimate brotherly accord of all tribes through the law of Christ's Gospel!

I know I know full well that my words may seem ecstatic, exaggerated, and fantastic. So be it: but I do not regret having said them. This had to be said, and particularly now, at the moment of our celebration, at the moment we pay honor to our great genius who embodied this very idea in his artistic power. And, indeed, this idea has been expressed more than once; I have said nothing new. What is most important is that all this might seem conceited: "Is it for us," some may say, "for our impoverished, crude land to have such a destiny? Can it be we who are ordained to utter a new word to humanity?" But, after all, am I speaking about economic prominence, about the glory of the sword or science? I am speaking merely of the brotherhood of people and of the fact that, perhaps, the Russian heart is most plainly destined, among all the peoples, for universally human and brotherly unity; I see traces of this in our history, in our gifted people, in the artistic genius of Pushkin. Our land may be impoverished, but this impoverished land "Christ Himself, in slavish garb, traversed and gave His blessing."[26] Why can we not accommodate His ultimate word? Was He not born in a manger Himself? I repeat: at the very least we can now point to Pushkin and to the universality and panhumanness of his genius. He could accommodate the geniuses of other nations within his soul as if they were his own. In art, in his artistic work, at least, he showed beyond dispute this universal striving of the Russian spirit, and that in itself reveals something important. If my idea is a fantasy, then in Pushkin, at least, there is something on which this fantasy can be founded. Had he lived longer, perhaps, he would have shown us immortal and grand images of the Russian soul that could have been understood by our European brethren and might have attracted them to us much more and much more closely than now; he might have managed to

---

26 From F. I. Tiutchev's poem, "These Poor Villages . . ." (1855).

explain to them the whole truth of our aspirations and they would have understood us more clearly than they do now; they would have begun to divine our purpose; they would have ceased to regard us as mistrustfully and haughtily as they do now. Had Pushkin lived longer, perhaps there would be fewer misunderstandings and dispute among us than we see now. But God did not will it so. Pushkin died in the full flower of his creative development, and unquestionably he took some great secret with him to his grave. And so now we must puzzle out this secret without him.

CHAPTER 10

God

Dostoevskii grew up in a devout family; later in life, he would recall treasured memories of his nurse, Alena Frolovna, teaching him what would become one of his favorite prayers: "I place all my hope in Thee, Mother of God; preserve me under Thy protection." He recalls the impression that his first reading of the Book of Job made on him as a young man. The central issue raised in that book—how human beings can retain faith in God in the face of great suffering—arguably became the motivating question that undergirds his fiction. Although Dostoevskii did broach his own faith in his journalism, it appears that he felt that the novel was the best vehicle for exploring questions of faith and articulating his own Christian vision.

Even during the 1840s, when Dostoevskii moved in socialist circles, the brand of utopian socialism that he professed bore the imprint of Christianity. However, it was the four years in a Siberian prison camp (1850–54) following his mock execution that led to what the writer himself called "a transformation in his convictions," often referred to by critics as his "conversion." This chapter begins with an excerpt from an 1854 letter to Natal'ia Fonvizina (1803–69), a document often cited as illustrative of Dostoevskii's post-conversion views. Here, he expresses the paradoxical idea that doubt nourishes faith: he describes a "longing for faith" that grows "all the stronger for the proofs I have against it."

Of the novels, *The Idiot* in particular provides fertile ground for critics interested in exploring how Dostoevskii's engagement with faith through fiction. Dostoevskii himself described the novel as his attempt to create a "wholly good man" in the form of Prince Myshkin, yet critics have wondered why this Christlike figure seems to cause more harm than good, albeit unwittingly. A key role is played in this novel by Hans Holbein the Younger's painting *The Body of the Dead Christ in the Tomb* (1521), a copy of which is displayed in the home of one of the novel's main antagonist, Rogozhin. The painting, which shows Jesus's decaying corpse, made a significant impression on Dostoevskii when he saw the original in Basel. A passage describing the painting in *The Idiot* is reproduced here, in which Myshkin, struck by the painting, comments "that picture might make some people lose their faith." After this encounter, Myshkin and Rogozhin experience a moment of spiritual brotherhood as they exchange crosses, but Myshkin ultimately proves helpless to stop the grisly events that make up the novel's denouement.

Dostoevskii scholars include among their ranks theologians and philosophers as well as literary critics, and the debates over the place of God in his work have been particularly fierce. One critical school, represented here by the philosopher Lev Shestov (1866–1930), argues that despite Dostoevskii's professions of Christianity, his works end up contradicting the ideal Christian love that they purport to celebrate. A rather different view is given by his contemporary, Nikolai Berdiaev (1874–1948), a philosopher who began as a skeptic but who became a fierce opponent of the Russian Revolution and an adherent of Christianity. For Berdiaev, Dostoevskii "prophetically revealed all the spiritual groundings and moving principles of the Russian Revolution"; his interpretation of the "Grand Inquisitor" story in *Brothers Karamazov* is reproduced here.

Recent criticism on religion in Dostoevskii's works has diversified significantly. The bibliography is vast, and, for the purposes of this volume, we have chosen excerpts that focus on the intersection of religion and poetics. An excerpt from Nina Perlina's *Varieties of Poetic Utterances* focuses on how Dostoevskii draws on the Bible and hagiographic traditions in *Brothers Karamazov*. Diane Oenning Thompson also takes an intertextual approach, but, intriguingly, she focuses not on Christian texts, but on Dostoevskii's use of a motif from the Koran in *The Idiot* and *Brothers Karamazov*.

Can one read Dostoevskii without being a Christian? On the one hand, the answer is obviously "yes": Dostoevskii's works have retained their popularity in the post-Christian west, while also enjoying enormous success in largely non-Christian societies such as China and Japan. Some readers, regardless of their beliefs, find in Dostoevskii a powerful antidote to the secularism, philosophical materialism, and a soullessness that they perceive in the contemporary world. On the other hand, Dostoevskii's absolutist view of Christianity, as well as his insistence on tying together religion and national identity, does not sit easily with the kind of liberal relativism common in our own cultural moment. This section closes with a skeptical view from Steven Cassedy, who gives a troubling account of how Dostoevskii's religion is not simply metaphysical, but national. However, Cassedy's view should not be taken as the last word on Dostoevskii's religion, a topic that will undoubtedly go on to inspire innovative critical work in the future.

Further Reading

van den Bercken, Wil. *Christian Fiction and Religious Realism in the Novels of Dostoevsky*. London and New York: Anthem Press, 2011.

Berdyaev, Nicholas. *Dostoevsky*. Translated by Donald Attwater. New York: Meridian Books, 1964.

Blake, Elizabeth A. *Dostoevsky and The Catholic Underground*. Evanston, IL: Northwestern University Press, 2014.

Cassedy, Steven. *Dostoevsky's Religion*. Stanford, CA: Stanford University Press, 2005.

Discherl, Denis. *Dostoevsky and the Catholic Church*. Chicago, IL: Loyola University Press, 1986.

Jones, Malcolm. *Dostoevsky and the Dynamics of Religious Experience*. London: Anthem Press, 2005.

Murav, Harriet. *Holy Foolishness: Dostoevsky's Novels & the Poetics of Cultural Critique*. Stanford, CA: Stanford University Press, 1992.

Shestov, Lev. *Dostoevsky, Tolstoy and Nietzsche*. Translated by Bernard Martin and Spencer Roberts. Athens: Ohio University Press, 1969.

Pattison, George, and Diane Oenning Thompson, eds. *Dostoevsky and the Christian Tradition*. Cambridge: Cambridge University Press, 2001.

Williams, Rowan. *Dostoevsky: Language, Faith and Fiction*. London: Continuum, 2008.

A Confession of Faith
Letter to Natal'ia Fonvizina,
early March 1854*

Fedor Dostoevskii

Omsk

Beginning of March, 1854

With what delight I read your letter, dearest N. D. You write quite admirable letters, or, more precisely, your letters flow easily and naturally from your good kind heart. There are reserved and embittered natures, which only in very rare moments are expansive. I know such people. They are not necessarily bad people—quite the contrary, indeed. I don't know why, but I guess from your letter that you returned home in bad spirits. I understand it; I have sometimes thought that if ever I return home, I shall get more grief than joy from my impressions there. I have not lived your life, and much in it is unknown to me, and indeed, no one can really know exactly his fellow-mortal's life; still, human feeling is common to us all, and it seems to me that everyone who has been banished must live all his past grief over again in consciousness and memory, on his return home. It is like a balance, by which one can test the true gravity of what one has endured, gone through, and lost. God grant you a long life! I have heard from many people that you are very religious. But not because you are religious, but because I myself have learnt it and gone through it, I want to say to you that in such moments, one does, "like dry grass," thirst after faith, and that one finds it in the end, solely and simply because one sees the truth more

---

* From *Letters of Fyodor Michailovitch Dostoevsky to His Family and Friends*, trans. Ethel Colburn Mayne (New York: Macmillan, 1917), 66–69. Natali'a Fonvizina was the wife of the Decembrist Mikhail Fonvizin. Dostoevskii had met her in Tobol'sk in 1850. During his captivity, when he himself was not allowed to correspond with his brother, she was his only medium of communication with the outside world.

clearly when one is unhappy. I want to say to you, about myself, that I am a child of this age, a child of unfaith and skepticism, and probably (indeed I know it) shall remain so to the end of my life. How dreadfully has it tormented me (and torments me even now)—this longing for faith, which is all the stronger for the proofs I have against it. And yet God gives me sometimes moments of perfect peace; in such moments I love and believe that I am loved; in such moments I have formulated my creed, wherein all is clear and holy to me. This creed is extremely simple; here it is: I believe that there is nothing lovelier, deeper, more sympathetic, more rational, more manly, and more perfect than the Savior; I say to myself with jealous love that not only is there no one else like Him, but that there could be no one. I would even say more: If anyone could prove to me that Christ is outside the truth, and if the truth really did exclude Christ, I should prefer to stay with Christ and not with truth.

I would rather not say anything more about it. And yet I don't know why certain topics may never be touched on in society, and why, if anyone does introduce them, it makes the others uncomfortable. Still, enough of it. I heard that you were desirous of travelling somewhere in the South. God grant that you may succeed in obtaining permission to do so. But will you please tell me when we shall be quite free, or at any rate as free as other people? Perhaps only when we no longer need freedom? For my part, I want all or nothing. In my soldier's uniform I am the same prisoner as before. I rejoice greatly that I find there is patience in my soul for quite a long time yet, that I desire no earthly possessions, and need nothing but books, the possibility of writing, and of being daily for a few hours alone. The last troubles me most. For almost five years I have been constantly under surveillance, or with several other people, and not one hour alone with myself. To be alone is a natural need, like eating and drinking; for in that kind of concentrated communism one becomes a whole-hearted enemy of mankind. The constant companionship of others works like poison or plague; and from that unendurable martyrdom I most suffered in the last four years. There were moments in which I hated every man, whether good or evil, and regarded him as a thief who, unpunished, was robbing me of life. The most unbearable part is when one grows unjust, malignant, and evil, is aware of it, even reproves oneself, and yet has not the power to control oneself. I have experienced that. I am convinced that God will keep you from it. I believe that you, as a woman, have more power to forgive and to endure.

Myshkin and Rogozhin Exchange Crosses in *The Idiot* (1869)*

They went through the same rooms that Myshkin had passed through already; Rogozhin walked a little in front, Myshkin followed him. They went into a big room. On the walls there were several pictures, all of them portraits of bishops or landscapes in which nothing could be distinguished. Over the door leading into the next room there hung a picture of rather strange shape, about two yards in breadth and not more than a foot high. It was a painting of our Savior who had just been taken from the cross. Myshkin glanced at it as though recalling something, but he was about to pass through the door without stopping. He felt very depressed and wanted to get out of this house as soon as possible. But Rogozhin suddenly stopped before the picture.

"All these pictures here were bought for a ruble or two by my father at auctions," he said. "He liked pictures. A man who knows about paintings looked at all of them. 'They are rubbish,' he said; 'but that one, that picture over the door there, which was bought for a couple of rubles too,' he said, 'was of value.' When my father was alive one man turned up who was ready to give three hundred and fifty rubles for it; but Savel'ev, a merchant who is very fond of pictures, went up to four hundred for it, and last week he offered my brother Semen Semenovich five hundred for it. I've kept it for myself."

"Why, it . . . it's a copy of a Holbein," said Myshkin, who had by now examined the picture, "and, though I don't know much about it, I think it's a

---

* From *The Idiot*, trans. Constance Garnett (London: Heinemann, 1915), 216–20 very good copy. I saw the picture abroad and I can't forget it. But . . . what's the matter?" Rogozhin suddenly turned away from the picture and went on. No doubt his preoccupation and a peculiar, strangely irritable mood which had so suddenly shown itself in him might have explained this abruptness. Yet it seemed strange to Myshkin that the conversation, which had not been begun by him, should have been broken off so suddenly without Rogozhin's answering him.

"And by the way, Lev Nikolaevich, I've long meant to ask you, do you believe in God?" said Rogozhin suddenly, after having gone on a few steps.

"How strangely you question me and . . . look at me!" Myshkin could not help observing.

"I like looking at that picture," Rogozhin muttered after a pause, seeming again to have forgotten his question.

"At that picture!" cried Myshkin, struck by a sudden thought. "At that picture! Why, that picture might make some people lose their faith."

"That's what it is doing," Rogozhin assented unexpectedly.

They were just at the front door.

"What?" Myshkin stopped short. "What do you mean? I was almost joking, and you are so serious! And why do you ask whether I believe in God?"

"Oh, nothing. I meant to ask you before. Many people don't believe nowadays. Is it true—you've lived abroad—a man told me when he was drunk that there are more who don't believe in God among us in Russia than in all other countries? 'It's easier for us than for them,' he said, 'because we have gone further than they have.'"

Rogozhin smiled bitterly. When he had asked his question, he suddenly opened the door and, holding the handle, waited for Myshkin to go out. Myshkin was surprised, but he went out. Rogozhin followed him on to the landing and closed the door behind him. They stood facing one another, as though neither knew where they were and what they had to do next.
"Goodbye, then," said Myshkin, holding out his hand.

"Goodbye," said Rogozhin, pressing tightly though mechanically the hand that was held out to him.

Myshkin went down a step and turned round.

"As to the question of faith," he began, smiling (he evidently did not want to leave Rogozhin like that) and brightening up at a sudden reminiscence, "as to the question of faith, I had four different conversations in two days last week. I came in the morning by the new railway and talked for four hours with a man in the train; we made friends on the spot. I had heard a great deal about him beforehand and had heard he was an atheist, among other things. He really is a very learned man, and I was delighted at the prospect of talking to a really learned man. What's more, he is a most unusually well-bred man, so that he talked to me quite as if I were his equal in ideas and attainments. He doesn't believe in God. Only, one thing struck me: that he seemed not to be talking about that at all, the whole time; and it struck me just because whenever I have met unbelievers before, or read their books, it always seemed to me that they were speaking and writing in their books about something quite different, although it seemed to be about, that on the surface. I said so to him at the time, but I suppose I didn't say so clearly, or did not know how to express it, for he didn't understand. In the evening I stopped for the night at a provincial hotel, and a murder had just been committed there the night before, so that everyone was talking about it when I arrived. Two peasants, middle-aged men, friends who had known each other for a long time and were not drunk, had had tea and were meaning to go to bed in the same room. But one had noticed during those last two days that the other was wearing a silver watch on a yellow bead chain, which he seems not to have seen on him before. The man was not a thief; he was an honest man, in fact, and by a peasant's standard by no means poor. But he was so taken with that watch and so fascinated by it that at last he could not restrain himself. He took a knife, and when his friend had turned away, he approached him cautiously from behind, took aim, turned his eyes heavenwards, crossed himself, and praying fervently 'God forgive me for Christ's sake!' he cut his friend's throat at one stroke like a sheep and took his watch."

Rogozhin went off into peals of laughter; he laughed as though he were in a sort of fit. It was positively strange to see such laughter after the gloomy mood that had preceded it.

"I do like that! Yes, that beats everything!" he cried convulsively, gasping for breath. "One man doesn't believe in God at all, while the other believes in Him so thoroughly that he prays as he murders men! . . . You could never have invented that, brother! Ha-ha-ha! That beats everything."

"Next morning I went out to walk about the town," Myshkin went on, as soon as Rogozhin was quiet again, though his lips still quivered with spasmodic convulsive laughter. "I saw a drunken soldier in a terribly disorderly state staggering about the wooden pavement. He came up to me. 'Buy a silver cross, sir?' said he. 'I'll let you have it for twenty kopecks. It's silver.' I saw in his hands a cross—he must have just taken it off—on a very dirty blue ribbon; but one could see at once that it was only tin. It was a big one with eight corners, of a regular Byzantine pattern. I took out twenty kopecks and gave them to him, and at once put the cross round my neck; and I could see from his face how glad he was that he had cheated a stupid gentleman, and he went off immediately to drink what he got for it, there was no doubt about that. At that time, brother, I was quite carried away by the rush of impressions that burst upon me in Russia; I had understood nothing about Russia before. I had grown up as it were inarticulate, and my memories of my country were somehow fantastic during those five years abroad. Well, I walked on, thinking, 'Yes, I'll put off judging that man who sold his Christ. God only knows what's hidden in those weak and drunken hearts.' An hour later, when I was going back to the hotel, I came upon a peasant woman with a tiny baby in her arms. She was quite a young woman and the baby was about six weeks old. The baby smiled at her for the first time in its life. I saw her crossing herself with great devotion. 'What are you doing, my dear?' (I was always asking questions in those days.) 'God has just such gladness every time he sees from heaven that a sinner is praying to Him with all his heart, as a mother has when she sees the first smile on her baby's face.' That was what the woman said to me almost in those words, this deep, subtle and truly religious thought—a thought in which all the essence of Christianity finds expression; that is the whole conception of God as our Father and of God's gladness in man, like a father's in his own child—the fundamental idea of Christ! A simple peasant woman! It's true she was a mother . . . and who knows, very likely that woman was the wife of that soldier. Listen, Parfen. You asked me a question just now; here is my answer. The essence of religious feeling does not come under any sort of reasoning or atheism, and has nothing to do with any crimes or misdemeanors. There is something else here, and there will always be something else—something that the atheists will forever slur over; they will always be talking of something else. But the chief thing is that you will notice it more clearly and quickly in the Russian heart than anywhere else. And this is my conclusion. It's one of the chief convictions which I have gathered from our Russia. There is work to be done, Parfen! There is work to be done in our Russian world, believe me! Remember how we used to meet in Moscow and talk at one time . . . and I didn't mean to come back here now, and I thought to meet you not at all like this! Oh, well! . . . Goodbye till we meet! May God be with you!"

He turned and went down the stairs.

"Lev Nikolaevich!" Parfen shouted from above when Myshkin had reached the first half-landing. "Have you that cross you bought from that soldier on you?"

"Yes," and Myshkin stopped again.

"Show me."

Something strange again! He thought a moment, went upstairs again, and pulled out the cross to show him without taking it off his neck.

"Give it me," said Rogozhin.

"Why? Would you . . ." Myshkin did not want to part with the cross.

"I'll wear it, and give you mine for you to wear."

"You want to change crosses? Certainly, Parfen, I am delighted. We will be brothers!"

Myshkin took off his tin cross, Parfen his gold one, and they changed. Parfen did not speak. With painful surprise Myshkin noticed that the same mistrustfulness, the same bitter, almost ironical smile still lingered on the face of his adopted brother; at moments, anyway, it was plainly to be seen. In silence at last Rogozhin took Myshkin's hand and stood for some time as though unable to make up his mind. At last he suddenly drew him after him, saying in a scarcely audible voice, "Come along."

Dostoevskii's Religious Thought (1903)*

Lev Shestov

In the very same way that Raskol'nikov seeks his hopes solely in Lazarus's resurrection, so Dostoevskii sees in the Gospel not the propagation of this or that moral philosophy, but the pledge of a new life. He said: "Without a sovereign idea, neither man nor nation can exist. And there is *but one* [Dostoevskii's italics] sovereign idea in the world: namely the idea of the immortality of the human soul, for all the rest of life's 'sovereign' ideas that man can live by derive solely from it."[1] [...]

All this, of course, is not "scientific"; moreover, it is all diametrically opposed to the basic premises of modern science. And Dostoevskii knew better than anyone else how little support he could get from the latest acquisitions and achievements of the human mind. That is why he never tried to make science his ally, and, simultaneously, why he was equally wary of going into battle against it with its own weapon. He understood perfectly well that there are no longer any guarantees from Heaven. But the triumph of science, the certainty and manifestness of its incontestability do not reduce Dostoevskii to submission. After all, he told us long ago that, for him, a wall is not an insuperable obstacle, but merely an evasion, a pretext. To all scientific arguments he has one answer (Dmitrii Karamazov): "How can I live underground without God? A convict can't exist without God" (12:700). Raskol'nikov arouses violent,

---

* Excerpted from Lev Shestov, *Dostoevsky, Tolstoy and Nietzsche*, trans. Spencer Roberts (Athens: Ohio University Press, 1969), 227–39.

1 Shestov draws his citations from an earlier *Polnoe sobranie sochinenii* than most of the other writers excerpted in this volume. He uses F. M. Dostoevskii, *Polnoe sobranie sochinenii*, 12 vols. (St. Petersburg: A. F. Marks, 1894–1895), 10:424. Subsequent references to this edition appear in-text.

implacable feelings of hatred in his fellow convicts because of his scientism, his adherence to indisputable evidence, his lack of faith, which, in Dostoevskii's words, they immediately sensed in him. "'You're a pagan! You don't believe in God,' they would shout at him. 'You ought to be killed!'" (5:541). It goes without saying that all this is illogical. From the fact that the convicts regard lack of faith as the most horrible of crimes, it by no means follows that we must deny the incontestable conclusions of science. Even if all convicts and men of the underground were to perish, we must not, because of them, revise the axioms recently acquired from the work of dozens of generations of men; we must not renounce a priori judgments, which were vindicated only a hundred years ago, thanks to the great genius of the Königsberg philosopher [i.e., Kant]. Such is the clear logic of the people who live above ground as contrasted to the vague yearnings of those from the underground. It is impossible to reconcile the two inimical sides. They struggle to the point of complete exhaustion and, *à la guerre, comme à la guerre,* they are not fastidious about the means of struggle.[2] Convicts have been slandered, cursed, and dragged through the mud since the world began. Dostoevskii tries to apply the [. . .] same methods to free people as well. Why not, for example, make a vulgar lampoon of a scientist? Why not ridicule Claude Bernard?[3] Or slander and humiliate a journalist, an employee of a liberal publication, and along with him, all liberally inclined people? Dostoevskii did not stop at that. The things he fabricated about Rakitin! The most inveterate convict seems a noble knight in comparison to this future leader of the liberals, who for twenty-five rubles does not scruple to assume the role of pimp. All that is said of Rakitin is out-and-out slander of the liberals, and the slander is deliberate. Say what you will about them, there is no doubt that the best and most honest people joined their ranks. But hatred is not particular about its means. If they do not believe in God, they should be killed—this is Dostoevskii's inner impulse, this is what impels him to fabricate all sorts of cock-and-bull stories about his former liberal associates. The Pushkin Speech, in which all strata and parties of Russian society were apparently called on to unite, was in fact a declaration of unceasing struggle to the death. "Humble thyself, proud man; get to work, idle man." Surely Dostoevskii knew that these words would arouse a whole storm of indignation and resentment in the very people they were intended to reconcile. What do they mean?

---

2   EDS: The meaning of this phrase roughly equates to the English "All fair's in love and war," meaning that any methods are justified in war.

3   Claude Bernard (1813–1878), a French physiologist. [Tr.]

They summon the aboveground man to the underground, to penal servitude, to eternal darkness. Dared Dostoevskii hope for a single minute that anyone would follow him? He knew, he knew all too well, that those of his listeners who were unwilling to play the hypocrite would not accept his call. "We want to be happy here and now,"—that is what each aboveground man thinks. What does he care if Dostoevskii has not yet completed his penal servitude? It is said that everyone present at the Pushkin Celebration was deeply moved by Dostoevskii's speech. Many even wept. But what is surprising about that? After all, the speaker's words were taken by the audience as literature, and only as literature. Why not be moved, why not weep? It is a most common story.

But there also happened to be people who saw the matter in a different light and who began to object. They answered Dostoevskii by saying that they willingly accepted his noble words about love, but that this in no way prevented—it must not prevent—people from "concerning themselves with the establishment of happiness here on earth," or in other words, from having "social ideals." Had Dostoevskii allowed this, just this one limitation, he could have reconciled himself for good with the liberals. But he not only did not make concessions, he attacked Professor Gradovskii (who had undertaken the defense of the liberal cause) with such mad, with such unrestrained fury that it seemed as if Gradovskii were robbing him of his last possession. And the main thing is that Gradovskii not only was not repudiating the noble doctrine of love for man, to which Dostoevskii had devoted so many ardent pages in his *Writer's Diary*, in his novels, and in the Pushkin Speech—on the contrary, he was basing all his plans for the social order on it, and on it alone.

But this was precisely what Dostoevskii feared most of all. In Renan's Preface to *The History of Israel*, there is a curious appraisal of the significance of the Hebrew prophets: "Ils sont fanatiques de justice sociale et proclament hautement que si le monde n'est pas juste ou susceptible de le devinir, il vaut mieux qu'il soit détruit: manière de voir très fausse, mais très féconde; car comme toutes les doctrines désespérées, elle produit l'héroisme et un grand éveil des forces humaines."[4] In this very same way, Professor Gradovskii regarded Dostoevskii's ideas. He found them "essentially" false, but admitted their fruitfulness, i.e., their ability to arouse people and provide those heroes without which the progress of mankind is impossible. Actually, one could not have

---

4   EDS: Translation—"They are fanatics fighting for social justice who grandly proclaim that if the world is unjust, or incapable of being just, then it would be better to destroy it altogether. It is a very wrong view of the world, yet strangely fecund, for, like all doctrines born of desperation, it leads to heroism and a great awakening of human forces."

wished more. For a "teacher," at least, it should have sufficed. But Dostoevskii saw his condemnation in such an attitude toward himself. He had no need of "fruitfulness." He did not want to content himself with the handsome role of the old cardinal in "The Grand Inquisitor." He wanted one thing, and one thing only: to be convinced of the "truth" of his idea. And if necessary, he was ready to destroy the whole world, to doom mankind to eternal suffering—if only to guarantee victory to his idea, if only to rid it of all suspicion of being incongruous with reality. Worst of all was the fact that deep in his heart he obviously feared that right was not on his side and that his adversaries, although more superficial than he, were nearer the truth. That was what aroused such fury in him; that was what made him lose his self-control; and that is why he overstepped all the bounds of decency in his polemic against Professor Gradovskii. What if everything turns out exactly as scholars say, and his work, contrary to his will, ultimately plays into the hands of the liberals and proves to be fruitful, while the idea that guided him proves to be false, and if sooner or later, the "devilish good" actually does prevail on earth—an earth inhabited by content, joyful, and regenerated people beaming with happiness?

It goes without saying that the most sensible thing for a man with such views and sentiments to do would be to steer clear of journalism, where he would inevitably run into the practical question: what is to be done? In novels and philosophical discussions, one can, for example, assert that the Russian people like to suffer. But how can such an assertion be put into practice? By proposing the formation of a committee to protect the Russian people from happiness? Obviously, that will not do. Moreover, one cannot even express one's joy constantly over forthcoming occasions when mankind will have to suffer. One must not celebrate when sickness or famine befalls man; one must not rejoice over poverty or drunkenness. People are stoned for things like that. Mikhailovskii reports that the idea expressed in articles in *Notes of the Fatherland* for January, 1873, according to which "the people, after the Reform, and partly even in connection with it, are threatened with the misfortune of being mentally, morally, and economically fleeced," seemed "a new revelation" to Dostoevskii. Very likely, Dostoevskii understood, or, more accurately, interpreted, the articles in *Notes of the Fatherland* in exactly this way. The Reform, in which visionaries had placed so much hope, had not only not brought the "hateful happiness," it was threatening terrible misfortune. Evidently, the matter could get along even without the gentleman with the retrograde physiognomy on whom the underground dialectician had relied. It is still a long way to the Crystal Palace if the most lofty and noble undertakings bring only unhappiness instead of abundant fruit.[5] True, as a publicist, Dostoevskii did not say such things openly. His "cruelty" did not yet risk such frankness. Even more than that, he never missed a chance to castigate (and how he castigated!) all possible manifestations of cruelty. For example, he rebelled at European progress on the grounds that "rivers of blood would be shed" before the class struggle would do our Western neighbors even the slightest good. This was one of his favorite arguments, which he tirelessly repeated dozens of times. But here one can be quite certain that all *argumenta* are *argumenta ad homines*. Dostoevskii afraid of blood and horror? But he knew how to produce an effect on people, and when necessary, he drew terrifying pictures. At almost one and the same time, he was reproaching the Europeans for their struggle, which was as yet relatively bloodless, and adjuring the Russians to declare war on the Turks, although, of course, the most modest war requires more bloodshed than dozens of revolutions [. . .] One can find a great many such examples in Dostoevskii. On one page, he demands renunciation of us in the name of delivering our neighbors from suffering and on another, almost the very next, he sings the praises of this same suffering. From this, it follows that the underground man has nothing to say when he appears in the role of teacher of man. In order to keep up such a role, he must forever conceal his truth and deceive people, as the old cardinal did. And if it is no longer possible to remain silent, if the time has finally come to tell the world the secret of the Grand Inquisitor, then people must seek their priests not from among teachers as in the olden days, but from among disciples, who always perform all sorts of solemn duties willingly and in good faith. The teachers have been deprived of their last consolation: they are no longer acknowledged as the people's benefactors and healers. They have been told, and they will be told: physician, heal thyself. In other words: find your task, find your cause, not in the doctoring of our illnesses, but in looking after your own health. Look after yourself—only after yourself [. . .]

Karamazov (Ivan, of course) declares bluntly: "I do not accept the world." What do these words mean? Why is it that Karamazov, instead of hiding from dreadful, insoluble problems as everyone else, goes straight at them, charges them just as a bear charges a huntsman's spear? After all, it is not because of ursine stupidity. Oh, how well he knows what insoluble problems are and how man must beat his already clipped wings against the walls of eternity! And nevertheless, he does not give up. No *Ding an sich*, no will, no *deus sive natura* tempts

---

5   EDS: See the material relating to the Crystal Palace in Chapter 7 of the present volume.

him to reconciliation.[6] This man, forgotten by good, treats all philosophical systems with undisguised contempt and disgust. Karamazov says: "Some sniveling moralists call the thirst for life despicable." Not one of Dostoevskii's heroes who questions fate ends up a suicide, with the exception of Kirillov, who it is true does kill himself, but not to withdraw from life, but to test his strength. In this respect, they all share old Karamazov's point of view: they do not seek oblivion, no matter how difficult life may be for them. Ivan Karamazov's youthful daydreams, which he recalls in his conversation with the devil, can serve as an interesting illustration of this "point of view." A certain sinner was condemned to walk a quadrillion kilometers before the heavenly gates would be opened to him. But the sinner was stubborn. "I won't do it," he said. He lay down and refused to move from the spot. Thus he lay for a thousand years. Then he rose and started out. He walked a billion years. "And two seconds had not passed after the heavenly gates had opened to him when he exclaimed that for those two seconds, he would have walked, not only a quadrillion, but even a quadrillion quadrillion kilometers, even if it were raised to the quadrillionth power" (12:272). Such were the things Dostoevskii pondered over. Those staggering quadrillions of kilometers traversed, those billions of years of nonsense endured for the sake of two seconds of heavenly bliss for which the human tongue lacks the necessary words are merely an expression of the thirst for life about which we have been talking. Like his father, Ivan Karamazov is an egoist through and through. Not that he cannot, he does not want to try in some way or other to dissolve his personality in a noble idea, to fuse it with the "primordial," with nature, et cetera, as philosophers recommend. Although he received a very modern education, he is not afraid to make *his* demands in the face of the entire body of philosophical science. He is not even afraid that he will be confused (and at the same time rejected) with his father. He bluntly says so himself: "Fedor Pavlovich, our dad, was a swine, but he thought correctly" (12:702). And Fedor Pavlovich, the swine, who saw and knew perfectly well the opinion people had of him, "thought" that even though he had lived long enough, this life was too little for him. He also wanted immortality for himself. This is shown by the following conversation with his children:

> "Ivan, tell me, is there a God or not?"
> "No, there's no God."

---

6   EDS: *Ding an sich*, in Kant's philosophy, "the thing in itself," which cannot be perceived by human beings. *Deus sive natura*, in Spinoza's philosophy, "God or nature": the pantheistic idea that God is indistinguishable from nature.

"Alesha, is there a God?"

"There is a God."

"Ivan, is there immortality, in some form or other—well, at least a little, a tiny bit?"

"There's no immortality either."

"None?"

"None."

"You mean, there's a complete blank? But maybe there is something or other. After all, there can't just be nothing."

"Absolutely nothing."

"Alehsa, is there immortality?"

"There is."

"Both God and immortality?"

"Both God and immortality [...]"

"Hmm. More than likely, Ivan is right."

As you see, like father, like son. Dostoevskii endows even Fedor Pavlovich Karamazov with the ability to seek the "sovereign idea." After all, you must admit that the conversation is most characteristic. "More than likely, Ivan is right"—this is merely an objective conclusion which kept thrusting itself on Dostoevskii and which he feared so much. But the important thing here is the fact that Dostoevskii found it necessary to show Fedor Pavlovich in a good light. It may seem to the reader that if there is immortality, it is not, at any rate, for such vermin as Fedor Pavlovich, and that some law will certainly be found that will put an end to this disgusting being. But Dostoevskii cared little for the views of the readers. He keeps Rakitin at a mile's distance from his sovereign idea, but lets the old man Karamazov walk right up to it—he accepts him, if only partially, into the honorary society of convicts. Accordingly, all that is ugly, disgusting, difficult, and agonizing—in brief, all that is problematic in life— finds an ardent and exceptionally talented mouthpiece for itself in Dostoevskii. As if on purpose, he tramples before our eyes on talent, beauty, youth, and innocence. In his novels, there are more horrors than in reality. And how masterfully, how truthfully he describes these horrors! We haven't one artist who could describe the bitterness of insult and humiliation as Dostoevskii does [...] That is how convictions "are born" in Dostoevskii's heroes and heroines, to say nothing of Raskol'nikov, Karamazov, Kirillov, and Shatov. They were all subjected to unprecedented humiliation. How cleverly Dolgorukii (*The Adolescent*) is thrown out of the gambling casino! How the underground man is humiliated!

Dostoevskii assembled all the means at his disposal in order once again to strike a blow of unprecedented power at the reader's heart, but this time it was not to make the reader a better person or to have him magnanimously consent to call the humblest man his brother on Sundays and holidays. Now the task was different. Now it was necessary to force science, or "ethics," as Rakitin and Dmitrii Karamazov call it, to admit that the chief problem of life cannot be solved by a felicitous arrangement of things for the majority, by the future happiness of mankind, by progress, by ideas, et cetera—in brief, by all that had previously been used to justify the disgrace and destruction of the individual man. And indeed, when faced with reality as depicted by Dostoevskii, the most inveterate and convinced positivist, the very best person would be ashamed to think of his ideals. When "egoism," which everyone slanders so much, leads to tragedy, when the struggle of a solitary human being turns into unceasing torment, no one would have the impudence to use lofty words. Even believing hearts grow silent. But here we encounter not the doctrine of the positivists or idealists, not philosophical theories or scientific systems. People can be brought to reason, philosophers and moralists can be restrained in their pursuit of synthesis and the formation of systems, if they are shown the fate of tragic people. But what can be done with life? How can it be forced to reckon with the Raskol'nikovs and Karamazovs? As you know, it has neither shame nor conscience. It looks indifferently on the human comedy and the human tragedy. This question leads us from the philosophy of Dostoevskii to the philosophy of his successor, Nietzsche, the first person openly to display on his banner the terrible words: the apotheosis of cruelty.

On the Grand Inquisitor (1921)*

Nikolai Berdiaev

The Legend of the Grand Inquisitor is the high point of Dostoevskii's work and the crown of his dialectic. It is in it that his constructive views on religion must be sought; all the tangles are unraveled and the radical problem, that of human freedom, is solved. This problem is more or less openly the theme of the whole Legend, and it is noteworthy that the extremely powerful vindication of Christ (which is what the Legend is) should be put into the mouth of the atheist Ivan Karamazov. It is indeed a puzzle, and it is not clear on the face of it which side the speaker is on and which side the writer; we are left free to interpret and understand for ourselves: that which deals with liberty is addressed to the free.

Every man is offered the alternatives of the Grand Inquisitor or of Jesus Christ and he must accept one or the other, for there is no third choice: what appear to be other solutions are only passing phases, variations on one or the other theme. In the Grand Inquisitor's system self-will leads to the negation and loss of freedom of spirit, which can be found again in Christ alone. Dostoevskii's way of setting this out is most admirable. His Christ is a shadowy figure who says nothing all the time: efficacious religion does not explain itself, the principle of freedom cannot be expressed in words; but the principle of compulsion puts its case very freely indeed. In the end, truth springs from the contradictions in the ideas of the Grand Inquisitor, it stands out clearly among

---

* From Nicholas Berdyaev, *Dostoievsky: An Interpretation*, trans. Donald Attwater (London: Sheed & Ward, 1934), 188–96. Translation copyright © Sheed and Ward, an imprint of Bloomsbury Publishing Plc.

all the considerations that he marshals against it. He argues and persuades; he is a master of logic and he is single-mindedly set on the carrying-out of a definite plan: but our Lord's silence is stronger and more convincing.

Two universal principles, then, confront one another in the Legend: freedom and compulsion, belief in the meaning of life and disbelief, divine love and humanitarian pity, Christ and Antichrist. Dostoevskii makes an impressive figure of the Grand Inquisitor. He is one of the "martyrs oppressed by a great sorrow and loving mankind," an ascetic, free from any material ambition, a man of one idea. But he has a secret: he does not believe in God or in any meaning of life which alone could give sense to people's suffering in his name, and, having lost this belief, he sees that large numbers of persons have not the strength to bear the burden of freedom conferred by Christ. Not believing in God, the Grand Inquisitor also ceases to believe in man for they are two aspects of the same faith; Christianity is the religion of the God-man and therefore demands belief in both God and man. But the idea of the God-man, the uniting of the divine and human principles in one freedom, is precisely the idea that the Grand Inquisitor will not have; it is asking too much of man to saddle him with this spiritual responsibility, he must escape from Christian freedom and its burden of discriminating and choosing between good and evil. "Why distinguish these diabolical principles of good and evil when to do so is the cause of so much unhappiness?" A man can bear neither his own sufferings nor those of other people, yet without suffering there can be no liberty of choice, so we are faced with a dilemma: on the one side, freedom; on the other, contentment, well-being, rationalized organization of life; either freedom with suffering or contentment without freedom.

An overwhelming majority of people choose the last. They give up the great ideas of God and immortality and freedom and come under the spell of a fallacious love of one's neighbor in which God has no part, a false compassion which promotes a godless systematization of the world. The Grand Inquisitor sets himself against God in the name of man, in the name of the least of those individuals in whom he believes no more than he does in God. That is an important point. Those who devote themselves to the earthly welfare of mankind rarely believe that man is destined for a higher, a divine life. The Euclidean mind, full of revolt and self-limitation at the same time tries to improve on the work of God. He created a universal order that is full of suffering and imposed on man the intolerable load of freedom and responsibility; in the Euclideans' world there will be no suffering or responsibility—or freedom either. That mind necessarily leads to the Grand Inquisitor's system, the human ants' nest.

Freedom, he argues, is incompatible with happiness and should appertain only to a tiny aristocracy, and he accuses Christ of acting as if he did not love man when he imposed freedom on all. "Instead of taking away man's freedom thou didst increase it. Didst thou forget that man prefers peace and even death to freedom of choice of good or evil? Nothing is more attractive to him than freedom of conscience, but nothing causes him more suffering. And thou, instead of giving clear-cut rules that would have set man's conscience at rest once for all, thou didst put forward things that are unfamiliar, puzzling, and uncertain . . . By so doing thou didst act as if thou didst not love mankind." If man is to be happy his conscience must be lulled, and that can be most easily done by taking away his freedom of choice; those who can cope with that freedom and move towards him who "did desire man's free love" are very few.

The Grand Inquisitor says that people "look less for God than for miracles," and the words well illustrate his poor opinion of human nature and lack of faith in mankind. He reproaches our Lord accordingly: "Thou didst not come down [from the cross] because thou wouldst not coerce man by a miracle: thou didst crave for a free faith and not for one born of marvels; thou didst crave for willing love, not the obsequious raptures of slaves before the might that has overawed them. But thou didst think too highly of men: they are only slaves, even though rebellious ones [. . .] It was pitiless of thee to value [man] so highly, for thou didst require far too much from him. Hadst thou respected him less thou wouldst have asked less, and that would have been more like love, to have given him a lighter load. He is weak and despicable." The aristocratism of Christ's religion disturbs the Grand Inquisitor.

"Thou mayest well be proud of these children of freedom, of their unconstrained love, of the glorious sacrifice that they have freely made in thy name. But remember, there were only some few thousands of them, and they were as gods—what of the rest? Are all those weak ones to blame that they could not endure what the strong endured? Is a weak soul to blame if it cannot take thy terrible gifts? Is it not true that thou didst come only to the elect and for the elect?" Thus does the Grand Inquisitor take up the defense of enfeebled man and deprive him of liberty in the name of love. "Did we not love mankind in that we meekly admitted its weakness and wished lovingly to ease its yoke?" He says to Christ exactly what socialists are always saying to Christians: "Freedom and enough bread for all cannot go together, for men will never be able to share and share alike voluntarily. They will always be convinced, too, that they cannot be free, because they are weak, vicious, worthless, and rebellious. Thou didst promise them bread from Heaven, but can that compare with earthly bread in the eyes of this everlastingly sinful, thankless, and infirm human race? And if thousands and tens of thousands turn to thee for the sake of the heavenly bread, what is to become of the millions and tens of millions of those who will not have enough strength to forgo earthly bread for heavenly? Are we to believe that thou dost care only for the tens of thousands of great and strong, and that the millions of others, numerous as grains of sand on the shore, who are weak but yet worship thee, must exist only for the purposes of the great and strong? No, it is the weak that we are concerned for [. . .] The spirit of the earth will rise up against thee in the name of this same earthly bread, it will overcome thee, and all will rally to it [. . .] A new building, another and terrifying tower of Babel, will arise on the place of thy temple." Christianity has always been reproved by atheistic socialism for not having made men happy and given them rest and fed them, and by preaching the religion of earthly bread socialism has attracted millions and millions of followers. But, if Christianity has not made men happy or given them rest or fed them, it is because it has not wished to violate the freedom of the human spirit, because it appeals to human freedom and awaits therefrom the fulfilling of the word of Christ. Christianity is not to blame that mankind has not willed the accomplishment of that word and has betrayed it; the fault lies with man, not with the God-man.

This terrible problem of liberty simply does not exist for materialistic socialism; it expects to solve it and achieve the liberation of man through a materialist and planned-out organization of life; its object is to overthrow freedom and get rid of the irrational element of life in the name of happiness, sufficiency, and leisure. Men "will become free when they renounce freedom [. . .] We shall give them an unexciting modest happiness, suitable to the feeble creatures that they are. We shall persuade them at last to give up being proud, for thou didst lift them up and thereby taught them pride [. . .] Certainly we shall make them work, but in their spare time we shall organize their life like a children's game, with children's songs and cantatas and innocent dances. We shall allow them even sin, knowing that they are so weak and helpless." The Grand Inquisitor promises that people shall be saved from "the great anxiety and terrible agony they endure at present in making a free decision for themselves. And all these millions and millions of creatures will be happy [. . .]" He has "left the proud and turned to the lowly for the happiness of the lowly," and to justify himself he appeals to the "tens of millions of beings who will never have known sin." Dostoevskii often returns to the notion of Christ's pride which is voiced by the Grand Inquisitor. In The Adolescent somebody says of Versilov: "He is a very proud man, and many of these proud men believe in God, especially the most scornful ones. The reason is simple: they choose God rather than bow before men; to submit to him is less humiliating." Faith in God is a sign of high-mindedness, unbelief a symptom of superficiality. Ivan Karamazov understands the stupendous grandeur of the idea of God: "The astounding thing is that this notion of the necessity of God has been able to get a footing in the head of so wild and vicious an animal as man, so holy and moving and wise is it, and so honoring to the individual." If man has a higher nature and is called to a higher end it is because God exists, and man must believe in him; but if there be no God then neither is there a higher nature in man, and he must fall back into the social ant-heap whose principle is compulsion. A picture of this utopia can be seen in the Legend and in Shigalev's system, and everywhere else that man dreams of a future harmony for society.[1]

In the three temptations presented to Christ "the whole of the future history of mankind was foretold; they are the three forms in which all the historically insoluble contradictions of earthly human nature are reconciled." Our Lord refused them in the name of man's spiritual freedom, for it was not his will that the human spirit should be won over by bread, by an earthly kingdom, or by miracles. The Grand Inquisitor, on the contrary, welcomes them in the name of human happiness and contentment, and in welcoming them he renounces freedom. Especially does he approve the suggestion of Satan to turn stones into bread: "Thou didst reject the one banner that was offered thee that would have infallibly made all men bow down before thee alone—the banner of earthly bread; and thou didst reject it in the name of freedom and of a heavenly bread." The triumph of the three temptations will definitively mark man's attainment of content: "It was in thy power to have taught men all that they want to know on this earth, that is, to whom they must look up, to whom and how they can hand over their conscience, and how they can all join together and make a single unanimous common ant-heap of themselves, for the craving for a universal fusion is the third and last torment of man."

---

1   EDS: Shigalev is a radical visionary in Dostoevskii's *Demons* who outlines a system of social organization that divides the populace into two uneven categories in an attempt to obtain equality: one-tenth of the people will have freedom and control over the other nine-tenths, the "herd" who will lose their free will and individuality. Shigalev himself admits: "I started out with the idea of unlimited freedom but ended up with unlimited despotism" (PSS 10:311).

Hagiography in *Brothers Karamazov* (1985)*

Nina Perlina

D ostoevskii suffered from the absence of spirituality in the social life and the literature of his time. In his writing he deliberately widened the generic borders of the novel by introducing several foreign features, which originated in the didactic genres of religious literature, not in *belles-lettres*. The basic generic elements of hagiography, of the religious legend, or patristic writing and of pilgrim works are incorporated into and amalgamated with the narrative fabric of the novel, which now accommodated and absorbed these multidirected features of heterogenous non-novelistic genres. It also re-accented the central properties of the novel in order to create a new moral, ideological, and aesthetic unit. *The Brothers Karamazov* is centered not upon the life of a private person (a cardinal generic feature of a novel), but upon the *way of life of a remarkable man* (a fundamental feature of hagiography). Indeed, hagiography represents not a private life of an individual, but describes the life of a saint, an exemplary and righteous person. The subject of hagiography is not a human biography, but the life of a man of God. *The Brothers Karamazov* is not centered upon the history of one family, but transforms the secular motif of fathers and sons into the Christian theme of the Father and Son which is the essential subject of hagiography. *The Brothers Karamazov* does not depict the social circumstances that influence people's lives, as was typical of nineteenth-century novels. *The Brothers Karamazov* depicts a hero pursuing his course; both the path and the landmarks are revealed to him as miracles from heaven, for he is a chosen

---

*   Excerpts from Nina Perlina, *Varieties of Poetic Utterance: Quotation in* The Brothers Karamazov (Langham, MD: University Press of America, 1985), 70–71; 73–82. Copyright © 1985. Used by permission of Rowman & Littlefield Publishing Group. All rights reserved.

one. This concept of divine predestination is also typical of the genre of hagiography. Dostoevskii's novel does not focus on the protagonist's elaboration of his own individual world view, nor does it focus upon the main character's downfall or triumph. This novel is centered upon the revelation of a universal, all-embracing spiritual love. Thus the compositional and narrative fabric of *The Brothers Karamazov* both anticipates and prefigures the emergence of a quite different and highly specific poetic word in the novel. This anticipated word was originally conceived within the limits of various religious genres: hagiography, religious legend, and patristic writing. This type of word always appears as quotation in the novel. Since the quoted word represents its own chronotope, one may expect the emergence of a different type of time-spatial relationship in *The Brothers Karamazov*, which does, indeed, occur.

[...]

Saints' Lives are submerged in the narrative and conceptual structure of *The Brothers Karamazov*. While the commingling of the word of hagiographer with the words of the narrator or of the hero renders direct quotations invisible or indistinguishable, the influence of the hagiographic genre is still apparent. This intense influence of hagiography was clear to Dostoevskii's contemporary readers. Even the average reader of the 1870s quickly recognized borrowings from the Gospels and easily grasped their general, direct meaning. More importantly, in the 1860s and 70s interest in spiritual literature among the Russian secular public was particularly high. This attraction to ecclesiastical literature was motivated by a variety of factors.

The radicals, mostly the university students and the young free-minded intellectuals, were inspired by the emergence of Russian schismatic dissidents abroad. Groundlessly, yet insistently, the radicals politicized the religious views of schismatics. They associated religious dissent with political dissidence and worshipped the instinctive adherence of simple Russian people to the ideas of Christian Socialism. (It is not an insignificant detail therefore, that in *The Brothers Karamazov*, Ivan, an atheist and a nihilist, demonstrates a thorough knowledge of Apocrypha and other sources of Russian Schism. In his quotations from the Bible, Ivan subsequently uses the Old Church Slavic translation which circulated among the schismatics). A rather conservative group of the readers, the Slavophiles of the 1870s, still felt an attraction for Apollon Grigor'ev's organic concepts. The works of Leskov, Tolstoi, and the vigorous activity of the Slav Benevolent Society in Moscow and Petersburg were also responsible for increasing interest in Russian religious culture. Dostoevskii himself with his later novels and with his *A Writer's Diary* repeatedly brought to public attention the events of the Balkan War (the Holy War, the Christian war, the war on behalf of the triumph of Russian Christianity, in his interpretation). With his *Diary* Dostoevskii also encouraged readers' interest in the writings of Tikhon Zadonskii and in Christian ideas of early Slavophiles and Apollon Grigor'ev.[1] In addition, in this decade the works of Nikolai Tikhonravov and Vladimir Kliuchevskii appeared. These books were respected and frequently discussed in academic and university spheres.[2]

Among all the works which are responsible for widening the cultural horizon of Russian intellectuals, Kliuchevskii's 1871 study *The Lives of Russian Saints as a Historical Source* must be singled out. This study is written from a diachronic perspective; Kliuchevskii comments on and explains the ideas that have been carried in hagiography since the emergence of *The Lives*, while he simultaneously discusses the historical and factual value of hagiographic sources for a contemporary reader. Kliuchevskii notes that at the time when *The Lives* was written, many contemporary cultural concepts did not as yet exist. The concept of authorship in its modern sense was not present in hagiography either psychologically or historically. For the hagiographer, the expressions "my work," "my own view," "my own theory," etc., were irrelevant. His intention was described in terms of a revealed word, a spiritual revelation, and conceiving the word under constraint of the spirit. These ideas dominated hagiography and shaped the annalist's self-awareness and the spiritual awareness of his audience.

Kliuchevskii's *Lives of Russian Saints* and *The Brothers Karamazov*, both literary phenomena of the 1870s, reveal more than a few similar features. Kliuchevskii's work, which unites historical, psychological, aesthetic and moral approaches to the problem of spiritual literature, can easily be compared to Dostoevskii's renovation of the novelistic tradition that he achieved within *The Brothers Karamazov*. Dostoevskii augmented the genre of the family novel with traditions of Russian hagiography but did not damage the novel's mimetic nature. In his work Kliuchevskii had shown that the personality of the saint, his righteous life, his holy deeds, and his words retain an undisputed authority for all people, including the hagiographist himself. In the manner of narration, on the ideological and stylistical levels, the personality of the holy man of God and

---

1 Fyodor Dostoevsky, *The Diary of a Writer*, trans. Boris Brasol (Santa Barbara and Salt Lake City: Peregrine Smith, 1979), 202–5; 350–58.

2 N. S. Tikhonravov, *Pamiatniki otechestvennoi literatury* (Moscow: Obshchestvennaia pol'za, 1863); V. Kliuchevskii, *Drevnerusskie zhitiia svyatykh kak istoricheskii istochnik* (Moscow: Tip. Gracheva, 1871).

the authority of his true word dominate the consciousness of the scribe. From a historical and psychological point of view, Kliuchevskii demonstrated the existence of a hierarchy of moral and spiritual values embedded in the genre of *The Lives of the Saints*. One can see that in the *Lives*, the image of the saint (the object of description and in this respect, the hero) governs the consciousness of the scribe (the author of the manuscript, in this respect, the writer). In *The Brothers Karamazov*, Zosima's exhortations and conversations are all given as his own direct utterances, as his own words, which differ stylistically from those of the narrator of the novel. At the preparatory stage of his work Dostoevskii repeatedly insisted that even though his views are the same as Zosima's, the way in which the Elder utters his ideas belongs to Zosima alone. The hero and the author differ from each other in their individual manner of uttering their views, and in many instances Zosima possesses a more harmonious and perfect world view than even the author himself. While progressing in his ability to preserve all the authority and autonomy of the hero's own utterance, Dostoevskii found inspiration in reading *The Lives of the Saints*.

The Lives of the Saints incorporates the evangelic idea of resurrection. "Christ was resurrected from death having overcome death by death" is the central idea of Russian hagiography. The motif of resurrection plays a seminal role in *The Brothers Karamazov*, and in a figural way, it relates to all the leading personages of the novel.

In his work, Kliuchevskii discussed the problem of premeditated and "accidental" historicity in hagiographic sources. He argued that by the inclusion of various events from the life of the saint in the narration an appearance of historicity is given to the hagiographic genre. Conceptually, however, these biographical features convey the abstract idea of the evanescent nature of terrestrial existence—rather than contribute to the persuasiveness of the events in the saint's biography. Kliuchevskii explained that medieval Russian society was not interested in the political or psychological implications of the specific events of a saint's life on earth, but drew from these events one and only one message: a spiritual and morally edifying one. Kliuchevskii also argued that in hagiography reader's interest was centered on the general typical features, moral paradigms which constitute the concept of a Christian ideal, whose realization is not to be found in any individual life. In his book Kliuchevskii succeeded in making it clear to the readers why the Russian hagiographic tradition contains a number of Stylites, Fasters, Compassionate Saints. This plurality is religious in nature. The life of a saint is not his biography. It does not fall into a sequence of everyday episodes, each succeeding the other (as was the case in the person's real life). On the contrary, by representing several episodes as patterns and models, (sometimes depicted with scrupulous realism, sometimes in a schematic form), the Life (*zhitie*) reveals a certain didactic Christian idea and interprets it as an attribute of holiness: self-denial, mercy, humbling of the flesh, fasting, hermitism, etc. Since the saint has a life rather than a biography, his actions are not the events of daily existence, but rather acts and holy deeds that all serve the triumph of an edifying moral paradigm. Not only does the saint behave righteously, more significantly, he abides by Christian law.

In *The Brothers Karamazov*, Dostoevskii uses plurality, this generic principle of hagiography, as an obvious moral and aesthetic paragon when he models the figures of Zosima and Alesha and ascribes to these heroes the individual traits of several admirable Russian saints. Here his task is not to achieve mimetic likeness in persons, but rather to mimetically depict the general idea of holiness. To this end Dostoevskii creates in *The Brothers Karamazov* a chain of heroes who are, as it were, variations of each other's essence: the youth Markel, Zosima's elder brother; Father Zosima himself; the youth Alesha, Zosima's spiritual son; the Elder Zosima's life noted down from his own words by Alesha, his true disciple—this reciprocal chain of images is created in line with the generic principles of hagiography, because the fundamental idea of hagiography is to demonstrate the salutary power of Christian love as a spiritual virtue in various ways. This new type of connection between the archetypal spiritual model and its multiple poetic replications is established through figural interpretation of hagiographic sources in *The Brothers Karamazov*. In this novel all transformations of documentary and biographical materials originating in the poetic paradigms of *The Lives* are of the same artistic nature.

An essential step toward recognition of this aesthetic principle was taken by R. Pletnev in his article "The Wise Hearts: On Elders in Dostoevskii."[3] Pletnev investigates the significance of the religious concept of the wise-hearted Elder for Dostoevskii. Pletnev proves that the portrayal of the wise-hearted Elder in *The Brothers Karamazov* synthesizes individual features from several Russian and European religious zealots as well as the features from Dostoevskii's own previous artistic work. Dostoevskii incorporates into the lives of Zosima as a teacher and a wise elder and Alesha as his disciple the religious idea of Christian love for all living beings. In various ways this idea was similarly incorporated into the chain of holy figures who inspired Dostoevskii

---

3   R. V. Pletnev, "Serdtsem mudrye: O startsakh u Dostoevskogo," in *O Dostoevskom*, ed. A. L. Bem (Prague: Petropolis, 1933): 82.

in his work. The Russian saint Sergius of Radonezh, the Italian Francis of Assisi, and Saint Father Gerasim in *The Spiritual Meadow* by John Mosch are of equal importance as inspirational models, because in their lives Dostoevskii immediately recognized the presence of the same authoritative Biblical paragon of the wise heart. One can see again that in *The Brothers Karamazov*, the novel's structure adopts several generic features of hagiography, the major elements of plot and composition are subordinated to the concept of the divine word of the Bible, which is revealed as a quotation. Even when the elements of plot have the appearance of a biographically successive set of events, their essence is paradigmatic rather than syntagmatic. Paraphrasing Auerbach, one can say that in *The Brothers Karamazov* a biographically successive set of events, while it presents itself as an ultimate truth which possesses a single factual meaning, on the other hand claims "a constant interpretative change in its own content."[4] In Dostoevskii *figuras* and figural interpretations of authoritative texts thus reveal the polyphonic properties of his novels.

[...]

As an artistic creation of Dostoevskii, the image of Alesha Karamazov can be read as the result of figural interpretation of the Biblical formula: "the blessing wherewith Moses the Man of God blessed the children of Israel before his death" (Deut. 33:1). Figural interpretation always suggests more than one poetic implication at a time, and it easily tolerates identity in symbolic meaning with eventual disparity in depicted occurrences. Pluralistic analogies are operative on a higher interpretative level of the novel. Biographically, as a hero of a nineteenth-century novel, Alesha Karamazov behaves quite differently than his holy patron, Saint Alexei. Alesha Karamazov does not seek a hermit's life, but goes into secular life. Unlike his holy patron, he does not part from his bride after the wedding feast, but firmly intends to marry Liza Khokhlakova and to stay with her forever. He does not abandon his father's home, and Zosima, his wise teacher, encourages him to go home and to be "his brothers' keeper there." While these actions of Dostoevskii's hero seem to be deviations from the canonized hagiographic version, they are not. Through the intermediary of a Russian religious folkloric poem on Alexei, the Man of God, the novel's poetic meaning returns to the canonic hagiologic text.

In his historical treatise, Kliuchevskii discusses the problem of the medieval chronicler's relationship to the subject of his writing, i.e., to the personality

---

4   Erich Auerbach, *Mimesis: The Representation of Reality in Western Literature*, trans. W. R. Trask (Princeton: Princeton University Press, 1968), 16.

of the Saint. Indeed, if the chronicler is just a humble monk, and the Saint whose life he dares to describe is one of those chosen and bidden by God, how then can an imperfect human mind comprehend and grasp the divine wisdom of the Saint's holy life? Where will the chronicler find the words to describe the Saint's holy deeds? On the basis of Old Russian sources, Kliuchevskii reconstructs an intellectual situation, now known as the psychology of the creative process, as it relates to the personality of the medieval monastic writer. Kliuchevskii writes: "He [the hagiographer] is above any everyday observations, he is beyond any mere collecting and grouping of facts. Only the Truth excites him, and he attempts to reveal this Truth to people."[5] "This is how Kliuchevskii describes the inspirations and moral feelings of a hagiographer: from the sentiments of "a humble narrator," through the state of "an exultant meditative quietness," the religious writer ascends to the highest stage. "He adheres to the style of the lofty didacticism and invites his listeners to share spiritual food with him; he feeds them with the immortal food of spiritual exhortation." Several induce-ments live in his heart: "his unquenchable thirst to write on the Saint and his humble love for the Holy Elder inflame and excite his thoughts; a great zeal encourages and inspires him to speak and write [...] But his unworthiness and imperfection, the impurity of his passionate heart restrain him. He suffers per-plexedly, being at a loss to know whether he is among those called to the task of hagiography. How does he wax bold [in his God] to speak unto his listen-ers and to fulfill this work that is beyond his power, for great and marvelous works require a righteous tongue."[6] Sometimes a prophetic dream or a vision of the beloved Saint are sent to the hagiographer. These tokens encourage him to continue with his work. As Kliuchevskii explains, a Saint was omnipresent in the medieval author's mind. The monastic scribe felt the Saint's protective glance and he could converse with his divine patron as if the latter were alive. The hagiographer was never able to distinguish clearly between these visions and reality.

Kliuchevskii's observations find their parallels in the compositional structure of "Cana of Galilee." They also help us to understand Chapters 2 and 3 in Book VI, "A Russian Monk." Aesthetically, "Cana of Galilee" is one of the great achievements of world literature. But from the point of view of nineteenth-century psychological realism the brilliance of this chapter seems "aesthetically redundant," inexplicable and thus unconvincing. Indeed, whose

---

5   Kliuchevskii, *Drevnerusskie zhitiia*, 384.

6   Ibid., 403–4.

words are these? Who is the author of this passage? That it is not Alesha comes clearly from the third person narration. The story is not even taken down in his own words, and there is only one phrase, added later in quotation marks by Alesha himself, which is Alesha's direct utterance. Hence, "Cana of Galilee" is written by the novel's meek and resigned narrator, who always feels "somewhat at a loss," who is always afraid that his readers are still unconvinced, and constantly doubts whether "he will succeed in proving" his ideas to the reader. One cannot fail to notice that here "style is not the man himself" and that here the concept of a person's style is out of line with the concept of his character. Similarly, Chapters 2 and 3 from the book "A Russian Monk," which are taken down by Alesha Karamazov from Zosima's words, dominate Alesha's intellectual capacities. In Dostoevskii's mind and in the framework of the novel, Zosima's ideas are really "great" (*velikie*), whereas Alesha is "by no means a great man" ("*chelovek on otniud' ne velikii*," PSS 14:5), as the narrator describes him in the preface. The dominant impression Alehsa makes on all the personages of the novel and on the novel's readers as well is more emotional than intellectual. Finally, from a realistic point of view, considering a "true" sequence of events, Alesha did not have enough time to reach the level of lay-brother in the monastery, for he spent less than a year there. Nevertheless, it is Alesha as a secular person who is chosen to complete Zosima's life (*zhitie*), and it is he who is numbered among the chosen, as is indicated in the text of "Cana of Galilee."

There is no other way to explain the stylistic complexity of the narrator's pose and his figure in *The Brothers Karamazov* than by paralleling it with the role and position of a hagiographer. *The Lives of Russian Saints* is a convincing paradigm for the aesthetic and conceptual image of the narrator in *The Brothers Karamazov*. In the chapters "A Little Onion" and "Cana of Galilee" one can easily find all the elements of narration and of the chronicler's relationship to his holy patron that Kliuchevskii notes as required features of hagiography. The title of the chapter, "Notes of the Life in God of the Deceased Priest and Monk, the Elder Zosima, Taken from His own Words by Aleksei Fedorovich Karamazov. Biographical Notes [...] Conversations and Exhortations of Father Zosima," is an accurate imitation of the titles of the works of Russian hagiographers. The entire style of Zosima's life is hagiographic in nature. Alesha's renunciation of his own judgement and his complete submission to the authority of his Elder's word are also modelled on the medieval Russian scribe's self-abnegation and the latter's submission to the divine power of the Saint. Similarly, the chapter "A Little Onion" is analogous to the scribe's temptation and to a divine token or sign whose appearance usually precedes a miraculous revelation of

Truth to the annalist's mind. "A Little Onion" is followed by "Cana of Galilee," where the sacred wisdom of the other world comes to Alesha as revelation and is embedded in his soul for the rest of his life. Alesha's prophetic dream is an obvious parallel to the divine visions that came to Russian hagiographers in the crucial moments of their lives. Here "Cana of Galilee" serves as a prologue to a Life in which the future Saint feels the Holy Spirit descend upon him and speak to him for the first time in his earthly life. These visions always symbolize the momentous transformation of a humble meek creature into a Christian zealot.

On the Koranic Motif in
The Idiot and *Demons* (2012)*

Diane Oenning Thompson

Throughout his literary career Dostoevskii's interest in the Koran and the Prophet Muhammad found sporadic but significant expression in his writings. While in Siberian exile, Dostoevskii requested that the Koran be sent to him, which he read in a French translation.[1] The opening verse of chapter (*sura*) 17, called *The Night Journey*, particularly stimulated his creative imagination. He introduced a version of it into two of his great novels, *The Idiot* (1868) and *Demons* (1873). The original reads in English translation: "Glory be to him who took his servant on a night journey from the sacred place of prayer to the furthest place of prayer upon which we have sent down our blessing that we might show him some of our signs. He is the all-hearing, the all-seeing" (Sura 17:1).[2] This brief verse is known in Islam as one of the major "Ascension stories," and has been greatly elaborated over the centuries. The "sacred place of prayer" came to be identified as Mecca and the "furthest place of prayer" was interpreted as Jerusalem.[3] Dostoevskii's French version reads: "Gloire à celui qui a transporté, pendant la nuit, son serviteur du temple sacré de la Mecque au temple éloigné de Jérusalem, dont nous avons béni

* Excerpted from Diane Oenning Thompson, "On the Koranic Motif in *The Idiot* and *Demons*," in *Aspects of Dostoevskii: Art, Ethics and Faith*, ed. Robert Reid and Joe Andrew (Amsterdam: Rodopi, 2012), 115–23. Some of the footnotes have been excised. Published with permission of Brill N. V.

1 The French translation was by M. Kasimirskii, published in 1847. For more details see Michael Futrell's excellent article, "Dostoevsky and Islam (and Chokan Valikhanov)," *The Slavonic and East European Review* 57, no. 1 (1979): 19, 25. See also PSS 1:494–5.
2 Quoted from Jane Dammen McAuliffe, ed., *Encyclopedia of the Qur'ān* (Leiden: Brill, 2001), vol. 1, 176.
3 Ibid., 176–77. For a discussion of related ascension motifs in the Koran, see 178–81.

l'enceinte, pour lui faire voir nos miracles. Dieu entend et voit tout"[4] ("Glory to the one who transported during the night, his servant from the sacred temple of Mecca to the far temple of Jerusalem, whose surrounding we have blessed in order to show him our miracles. God hears and sees everything").

Later Jerusalem was identified as the Ka'ba, the heavenly dwelling of Allah. Muhammad's nocturnal journey, then, was envisaged as a horizontal flight from Mecca, followed by a vertical ascension through the heavens to the celestial Ka'ba.[5] There were further elaborations. According to Koranic tradition, one night when the archangel Gabriel woke up Muhammad to take him to paradise on a miraculous steed, he brushed his wing against a water jug beside Muhammad's bed. Before the water had time to spill, Muhammad had the time to make a complete circuit of paradise where he spoke with God, the angels and prophets before returning to earth.[6] It was Muhammad's instantaneous flight to paradise that was paramount for Dostoevskii's own conception of the Prophet and he variously attached this motif to his depictions of Myshkin in *The Idiot* and Kirillov in *Demons*.

There were compelling personal reasons why Dostoevskii was attracted to Muhammad's *Night Journey*. Whilst it is generally a risky procedure to identify an author's biography with the characters and events in his or her fiction, in this case it is particularly suggestive. Dostoevskii, as is well known, suffered from epilepsy, and he shared the belief, widespread in his time though now discredited, that Muhammad was an epileptic. It is also well known that he depicted salient features of his pre-epileptic aura in the experiences of Myshkin and Kirillov. Add to this his lifelong fascination with religious prophecy and transcendent visions which momentarily reveal a divine eternal reality, and the deep appeal of *The Night Journey* is not surprising. This emerges with dramatic clarity in a conversation of 1865 when he told some friends about his first epileptic fit which occurred after his release from the prison camp. He related how one Easter Eve, while he was languishing in lonely Siberian exile, an old friend called and they sat conversing through the night. Finally they touched

---

4   Cited in Futrell, "Dostoevsky and Islam," 25.

5   McAuliffe, *Encyclopedia of the Qur'ān*, 177.

6   The editors of the PSS have identified Washington Irving's book, *The History of Mahomet and His Successors*, translated into Russian in 1857, as an important source for Dostoevskii's conception of Muhammad (9:441–2) and (12:318). Futrell points out, though, that the later additions to the stories about Muhammad were easily accessible to Dostoevskii from Kasimirskii's footnotes. See Futrell, "Dostoevsky and Islam," 25.

on religion. A heated discussion ensued, but no agreement could be reached; his friend was an atheist, Dostoevskii a believer:

> "God exists, He does!" cried Dostoevskii at last, beside himself with excitement. At that very moment the bell of the neighboring church began to ring for Christ's radiant morning service. All the air became vibrant and full of sound. "And I felt," related Fedor Mikhailovich, "that heaven came down to earth and absorbed me. I really apprehended God and was filled with Him. 'Yes, God exists!' I cried, and I remember nothing more."[7]

Dostoevskii's passionate exclamation ("God exists"), is as if confirmed from above by the church bell, suddenly filling "all the air" with its ringing for the Easter service, and putting an end to the human dispute. Dostoevskii's ecstatic rapture is consistent with those of Christian mystics who, seeking absorption into God, testify to a spiritual union with Him that transcends human understanding. Such experiences are believed by those who have them to reflect a reality, so they must be true, otherwise, they would not occur. Thus, Dostoevskii's apprehension of Grace, of the descent of "heaven" and of being "absorbed" by the plenitude of God's presence ends with his emphatic affirmation: "Yes, God exists!"

Just here Dostoevskii draws a parallel between his theophany and Muhammad's visit to paradise:

> All you healthy people [. . .] have no idea what happiness is, that happiness which we epileptics experience a second before a fit. Muhammad declares in his Koran that he saw paradise and was in it. All clever fools are convinced that he was simply a liar and an imposter. But no! He is not lying! He really was in paradise during the fit of epilepsy, which he suffered from, as I do. I don't know whether this bliss lasts for seconds, or hours, or months, but believe me, I wouldn't exchange it for all the joys that life can give![8]

Commentators have long been divided over the issue of whether Muhammad's journey to paradise actually took place, or was a revelatory

---

7   We owe this account to S. V. Kovalevskaia who was present during this conversation. See her *Vospominaniia i pis'ma* (Moscow: Akademiia nauk SSSR, 1961), 105–6.

8   Ibid., 106.

dream. Michael Futrell cites a footnote in Dostoevskii's copy of the Koran as a likely source for his belief in its reality: "It is one of the beliefs universally received among Muslims that this ascension took place in reality"—where "in reality" chimes with Dostoevskii's "he really was in paradise."[9] In the novels, the same sequence is observed: Dostoevskii first depicts Myshkin and Kirillov in an ecstatic state symptomatic of the pre-epileptic aura followed by an allusion to Muhammad's *Night Journey*. Their experiences have some initial similarities to the one Dostoevskii describes above, but then, in response to the demands of his art and the ideas he wished to convey, they become problematic and change into something quite different.

Prince Myshkin, the epileptic hero of *The Idiot*, has often been interpreted as a Christ-like figure. One passage usually cited as evidence of his exalted spiritual insight is that which relates his moments of ecstatic joy just before a *grand mal* attack, and ends with his likening his experience to Muhammad's in *The Night Journey*. Analysis of this passage prompts a more ambiguous interpretation of Myshkin's Christological status. It is constructed as an indirect dialogue in which the narrator's attempt to convey his hero's experience during his pre-epileptic aura is interrupted by the direct speech of a physically absent but vocally present Myshkin. It is a particularly vivid example of Bakhtin's idea that speech in Dostoevskii is profoundly shaped by an acute anticipation of the other's response. The narrator begins:

> The sense of life, of self-awareness (*samosoznanie*) increased nearly tenfold [. . .] His mind, his heart were lit up by an extraordinary light; all his agitations, all his doubts, all his worries as if [. . .] resolved into a kind of sublime tranquility, full of clear harmonious joy and hope, filled with reason and ultimate cause (PSS 8:188).

Joy, light, hope, harmony, sublime tranquility: these are feelings common to spiritual testimonies through the ages. They command the narrator's sympathetic respect as shown by the complete merging of his voice with his hero's ecstatic tones. These lines could have been written in the first person without significantly changing their style, register or meaning. Liza Knapp finds that this description of Myshkin's aura "gives a momentary sensation of what is to be experienced eternally in heaven" and is thus an "emblem of the resurrection."[10] However neither Myshkin nor the narrator makes these connections.

9 Futrell, "Dostoevsky and Islam," 25.
10 Liza Knapp, *The Annihilation of Inertia: Dostoevsky and Metaphysics* (Evanston, IL: Northwestern University Press), 81–82.

For almost at once, the narrator begins to distance himself from his hero's word, introducing subtle doubts and qualifications into what develops as a complex dialogic struggle between Myshkin's affirmation of his experience, the narrator's attempts to defend his hero's subjective experience and his increasingly objective reservations as to its meaning. For a sublime illumination that occurs only with the onset of illness is problematic, as the narrator and his hero are aware. Myshkin, he says, when restored to his healthy state, would often wonder whether:

> all those flashes and gleams of a higher self-sense (*samooshchushchenie*) and self-consciousness (*samosoznanie*), and therefore of the "highest being" are nothing but an illness, a violation of the normal state, and if so, then it's not the highest being at all but, on the contrary, should be counted as the very lowest [...] (loc. cit.)

In putting Myshkin's phrase, "the highest being" into quotation marks, the narrator graphically demarcates his word from his hero's, thereby introducing a reservation. Indeed, if all those "flashes and gleams" are just physiological symptoms of epilepsy, they cannot signify any contact with the real highest being. Underlying the narrator's hesitation to attribute Myshkin's ecstasy to a transcendental source is Dostoevskii's awareness of the rapid growth of medical science in his age which ascribed all religious revelations to physiological abnormalities, and thus deprived them of any supernatural significance.[11] This dilemma, this tension between a spiritual and a medical explanation is never resolved and remains anxiously poised on that "if" between "the highest being" and "the very lowest."[12] But here Myshkin's voice interrupts the narrator's, countering these rational doubts and anxieties with an "extremely paradoxical conclusion":

> "So what if it's an illness [...] who cares that it's an abnormal strain, if the actual result, if the minute of sensation, recalled and examined in one's healthy state, turns out to be the highest degree of harmony, of beauty,

---

11 Harriet Murav offers an excellent discussion of this cultural, historical situation in her *Holy Foolishness: Dostoevsky's Novels and the Poetics of Cultural Critique* (Stanford: Stanford University Press, 1992), esp. 39–50.

12 Murav remarks that Myshkin "demystifies his mystical experience," that "he quotes himself against himself, undermining his own religious language" with "medical language": Murav, *Holy Foolishness*, 82. However, it is not Myshkin who speaks here, but the narrator whose own doubts most undermine Myshkin. Moreover, Myshkin's language is not markedly "religious."

> giving a hitherto unheard-of and unknown feeling of fullness, measure, reconciliation and an ecstatic prayerful merging with the highest synthesis of life?" (loc. cit.)

To this the narrator remarks: "These vague expressions seemed to him himself very comprehensible" (loc. cit.). In this subdued response to his hero's impassioned defense of his experience, the narrator betrays his awareness that to a normal rational mind, Myshkin's expressions may be "very comprehensible" only to himself. But he immediately vouches for his hero's sincerity: "That it really was 'beauty and prayer,' and that it was really 'the highest synthesis of life,' he could not doubt and could not admit any doubts" (loc. cit.). But the narrator does doubt. Again, the most precious highlights of Myshkin's experience are displayed in quotation marks and enclosed in his speech, indicating that the narrator is not wholeheartedly convinced. Even when he stands up for Myshkin, he phrases it as a question: "He wasn't dreaming these visions at that moment as from hashish, opium or wine which deform the reason and soul . . . was he?" Finally, the narrator settles on a definition: "Those moments were precisely only an extraordinary intensification of self-consciousness (*samosoznanie*) . . . and at the same time a self-sense (*samooshchushchenie*) in the highest degree immediate" (loc. cit.).

Here again Myshkin's voice breaks into the narrator's word: "Yes, for this moment one could give up one's whole life!" (loc. cit.) However, the narrator's doubts finally come openly to the fore when he remarks in a sober voice entirely his own, from which Myshkin's tones have been expunged, that his hero's "evaluation of this moment without doubt contained an error" (PSS 8:188). Yet, when the narrator asks: "What, in fact, was he to do with this reality?", we may hear Dostoevskii, three years after his theophany, wrestling with his own doubts about the meaning of his pre-epileptic aura. That these experiences are real, that they are precious to the hero, cannot be reasonably denied, but the question is: how are they to be interpreted? Surely it does matter whether the "highest being" reflects a divine reality or is just a subjective and wishful interpretation of a pathological state. What strikes one here is the absence of an object; a "prayer" to whom, "beauty" of what, "reconciliation" with whom? Myshkin's heightened "self-consciousness" and "self-sense" are psychic states focused entirely on the self, they are what Futrell aptly calls "private ecstasies."[13] In what are held to be authentic encounters with the divine, such as those of

---

13 Futrell, "Dostoevsky and Islam," 29.

saints, what is achieved is not "the highest degree" of "self-consciousness," but freedom from the self as one becomes filled with the consciousness of a divine presence. For an apprehension of the divine entails a relationship, a sense of some intimate contact with a personified and transcendent Other (God, Allah, angel, saint). Such a relationship for Myshkin is absent. He does not interact with, nor does he attempt to achieve communion through prayer with a higher Other. What is more, he does not evince any awareness, either during or after his aura, that such a higher Other exists, or is there to be addressed. Such terms as "highest being," "beauty," "light," "the highest synthesis of life," are not religiously marked either in Christianity or Islam. They could be invoked for a variety of rhapsodic states, artistic inspiration, wonder at the grandeur of the universe, romantic rapture, the "oceanic feeling," among others. Myshkin's fleeting exaltation, then, is not marked as an expression of Christian spirituality. As Jostein Børtnes has shown, "towards the end of the story the points of similarity between Christ and the prince are superseded by a marked emphasis on the differences between them."[14] These differences are given further emphasis in Myshkin's allusion to Muhammad's *Night Journey*.

The narrator's reflections on his hero's aura culminate with Myshkin in his direct speech drawing an analogy between his experience and that of Muhammad:

> "[A]t that moment I somehow understand the extraordinary saying that *time shall be no more*. Probably," he added smiling, "it's the same second in which the overturned jug of water of the epileptic Muhammad did not have time to spill, while he had time during that same second to survey all the dwellings of Allah" (PSS 8: 189 [Dostoevskii's emphasis]).

The key point for Myshkin is his enhanced comprehension of the mystical prophecy about the end of time (Revelation 10:6) to which his aura gives unique access. The Book of Revelation promises the sight of the glory of heaven and the restoration of Paradise. However, Myshkin's citation of this enigmatic saying, abstracted from its biblical context, is also problematic for an unambiguous Christological interpretation of his image. Many have

---

14 Jostein Børtnes, "Dostoevskij's *Idiot* or the Poetics of Emptiness," *Scando-Slavica* 40 (1994): 5–14 (12). See also my "Problems of the Biblical Word in Dostoevsky's Poetics," in *Dostoevsky and the Christian Tradition*, ed. George Pattison and Diane Oenning Thompson (Cambridge: Cambridge University Press, 2001), 69–99 (73–76); and J. Peter Stern, *On Realism* (London: Routledge and Kegan Paul, 1973), 16–19.

commented on Myshkin's preoccupation with thoughts about time, death, execution and apocalypse. As Rowan Williams points out, the phrase "there will be no more time" is also quoted by Ippolit as he prepares to commit suicide; and is thus "bound up with death."[15] (It sinisterly reappears in *Demons.*) There is no indication of what, if anything, lies beyond the extinction of time. But here Myshkin turns to the Koran for illustration, twice equating his fellow "epileptic" Muhammad's instantaneous journey to paradise with his own "second" of transcending time. But is it "the same second"? Or rather, it may be the same unit of time, but very different things happen to them in that "same second."

There are two striking points of similarity between Myshkin and Muhammad, their epilepsy and a sudden, extreme compression of earthly time. But the differences between them are much greater, and far more significant. For the problem of the absent object persists. Muhammad's is not an apocalyptic end-of-time experience, but a crossing of the boundary from the temporal to the eternal realms. His survey of "all the dwellings of Allah" is an image of fullness which designates a place—paradise—and implies the presence of dwellers, those who have been granted eternal life. It also implies a relationship between Muhammad and Allah who vouchsafed his Prophet a supreme vision.[16] Mochul'skii claims that "the prince knows world harmony by *experience* (emphasis Mochul'skii's), he really was in the dwellings of Allah, in paradise."[17] But was he? The idea of Allah reserving a place in paradise for the faithful is reminiscent of Christ's words of comfort to his disciples shortly before his Crucifixion: "In my Father's house there are many mansions [. . .] I go to prepare a place for you" (John 14.2).[18] It is a measure of Myshkin's detachment from the canonical Christian sources that he refers not to God's mansions, but Allah's dwellings. Myshkin goes nowhere during his aura, nor does he see, say or hear anything; he is radically alone, without embodiment, without temporal and spatial location. He often gives the impression of not being entirely in the world he inhabits, but somewhere else. As Williams observes, Myshkin, unlike

---

15 Rowan Williams, *Dostoevsky: Literature, Faith and Fiction* (London: Continuum, 2008), 49.

16 Muhammad's journey to paradise can be generically traced back to the stories of Enoch's ascent to heaven. See the *Encyclopedia of the Qur'ān*, 181.

17 K. Mochul'skii, *Dostoevskii: zhizn' i tvorchestvo* (Paris: YMCA Press, 1980), 305. He claims that the "higher being defeated the lower one," but in light of Myshkin's fate this view is hard to sustain.

18 Dostoevskii marked this verse in his New Testament with "N. B. Sm.," an abbreviation for *Smotri* (See). See Geir Kjetsaa, *Dostoevsky and His New Testament* (Oslo: Solum Forlag A. S., 1984), 38.

Christ, "has no 'hinterland,' no God behind him."[19] Nor, we may add, before him. He has only a sense of merging with "the highest synthesis of life," a vague, abstract sentiment that verges on pantheism.

Perhaps the oddest thing here is the narrator's sole intervention: "he added smiling." Why "smiling"? Is his a beatific smile, or one of pleasure in hitting on this analogy, of embarrassment, or does it bear a faint trace of idiocy? Would he even compare himself to Christ, let alone "smiling"?[20] We cannot know for sure. What we do know is that Islam rejects the divinity of Christ, and Dostoevskii did not. And what we can say is that Myshkin's likening his experience to that of Muhammad makes him seem strange, slightly alien, and places him at an eccentric angle to the Christian tradition, and to the Islamic one as well.[21] Projecting significant features of Muhammad's story into his own story about Myshkin, Dostoevskii emphasizes the un-Christ-like nature of his hero, but without turning him into an imitation of Muhammad.

Shortly after these ruminations, Myshkin suffers an epileptic attack. Epilepsy was traditionally seen from two opposed sides, as a sacred illness and as demonic possession. Myshkin's attempt to impart a lofty interpretation to his aura is further undermined by its demonic aspect. The momentary light, illuminating his soul during the aura is superseded by "complete darkness" and immediately followed by a "terrible scream" in which "everything human disappears [. . .] as if someone else were screaming from inside the man" (PSS 8:195). In light of this image of possession, it is perhaps not surprising that Williams discloses some telling resemblances between Myshkin and the two "demons" of Dostoevskii's next novel, Petr Verkhovenskii and Stavrogin.[22]

Much later, at the Epanchins' soirée, at the end of his "tirade," Myshkin prophesies that the Russian Christ will lead to the future renewal and resurrection of all mankind, whereupon he inadvertently knocks over the fine Chinese vase and suffers his second epileptic fit. The broken vase is a symbolic image of Myshkin, the beautiful, but fragile, broken man, and it forms a subtle contrast

---

19 Williams, *Dostoevsky*, 48.

20 Murav finds that Myshkin's smile is "self ironizing"; Murav, *Holy Foolishness*, 80. But he is not represented as one capable of self-irony, or of irony in general.

21 As Bakhtin remarks, Myshkin is altogether "at an eccentric tangent to life," "he occupies no position in life," and "lacks the *flesh of life*." See Mikhail Bakhtin, *Problems of Dostoevsky's Poetics*, ed. and trans. Caryl Emerson (Minneapolis: University of Minnesota Press, 1984), 172–73.

22 Williams argues that Petr Verkhovenskii is "almost a negative image of Myshkin," but of course Myshkin does not share his malevolence nor Stavrogin's criminal acquiescence in murder. See Williams, *Dostoevsky*, 97 and 124.

with the water jug of Muhammad who "really was in paradise"—overturned, but righted and intact.[23] And let us recall that Myshkin relates his association with Muhammad to Rogozhin, in whose house hangs the Holbein painting of the un-Christ-like Christ that so disturbs him: "one could lose one's faith looking at this picture" (PSS 8:182). Williams persuasively dubs it "a diabolic image."[24] These two figures, the non-Christian Muhammad and the de-Christianized Christ are inseparable components of Myshkin's image. For all his Christian qualities, Myshkin enacts not an *imitatio Christi*, but an imitation of the humanized, demystified Jesus advanced by nineteenth-century writers (Renan, Strauss), an image which hauntingly resonates with the Holbein painting of Christ as a broken mortal corpse. Even so, he is a figure of great pathos and as such quite different from the heroes in *Demons*, Dostoevskii's novel about political terrorism and Russian nihilism, where *The Night Journey* of Muhammad acquires a much darker accentuation.

---

23 As Robin Feuer Miller puts it, the vase is "a physical extension of Myshkin's personality": *Dostoevsky and* The Idiot: *Author, Narrator, and Reader* (Cambridge, MA: Harvard University Press, 1981), 150. The narrator's stance in this passage also supports her analysis of his gradual withdrawal from Myshkin.

24 Williams, *Dostoevsky*, 53.

From *Dostoevsky's Religion* (2005)*

Steven Cassedy

L et's say we've read every single word Dostoevskii wrote and it's time to say what he's had to tell us about religion. If we're shopping around for a religion, it seems unlikely we'll be in a position to declare ourselves "Dostoevskians" and go forth to do good works of a particular sort. Even in the eyes of the readers who feel most strongly that this author was possessed of a reasonably coherent set of religious convictions, what would a Dostoevskian do? Accept lots of suffering? Embrace poverty? Sin gravely and then seek redemption? Attempt to dissolve into a general synthesis with the all? Fight for the glory of the Russian nation? No, nothing like this seems plausible.

So what *did* he have to tell us about religion?

He had much to say about *us* and religion, or us *in* religion. For Dostoevskii, the human being seems initially to be inescapably an *animal metaphysicum*. Our perpetual position on a continuum between opposing ideal poles indicates that each of us exists in a necessary relation to a metaphysical absolute, just as for Hegel every rational being exists in a necessary relation to Absolute Spirit. We saw how characters who are polar opposites—Myshkin and Stavrogin, for example—are always condemned to live out their existence (before their inevitable destruction, of course) on *this* side of an ideal. The Stavrogins of Dostoevskii's universe, those who pursue an ideal that is oddly nonmetaphysical or antimetaphysical, cannot escape the presence of something that is positively metaphysical. Things grow confused when we get to the earth worship

---

* From Steven Cassedy, *Dostoevsky's Religion* (Stanford, CA: Stanford University Press, 1995), 174–78. Copyright © 2005 by the Board of Trustees of the Leland Stanford Jr. University. All rights reserved. Used by permission of the publisher, Stanford University Press.

of Ivan Karamazov and Father Zosima, and things grow especially confused when we get to the Slavophilism that so many of Dostoevskii's characters (and Dostoevskii himself on many occasions) professed. Perhaps it wouldn't be too paradoxical to say that the pagan earth worshiper and the Slavophile both *believe* their outlook is founded on something metaphysical, even though that something might not appear to be *Christian* in most traditional senses of the term. At the very least, we can say Dostoevskii has shown as a human characteristic that bears almost no exceptions the tendency to seek—even unwittingly, even against one's will, even in the presence of contradictory intentions—something metaphysical.

What about Christianity in particular? Take, for example, the critique of Christianity we find in Ivan's story about the Grand Inquisitor. For more than a century, readers have persisted in asking the wrong question about this amazing piece of writing. Who cares if we can identify the point of view that is Dostoevskii's? What difference should it really make if Dostoevskii can be proved to stand squarely and permanently on the side of the Inquisitor or on the side of Father Zosima? Dostoevskii had an idea. It's critical of Christianity, and we read it. So he has offered it to us.

Dostoevskii was fond of placing his most interesting ideas at two or more degrees of separation from the reader. Raskol'nikov's extraordinary-man theory appears in an article that he, Raskol'nikov, wrote. Stavrogin's theories of good and evil appear in the confession that he, Stavrogin, wrote. Ivan's critique of Christianity appears in a work of fiction that he, Ivan, composed, and it is delivered by the Inquisitor, a fictional character, that Ivan, a fictional character, invented. Dostoevskii thus seems to have gone out of his way to distance himself from these ideas. Yet there they are. Like it or not, Ivan's critical observations about Christianity are *true*, at least for any version of it that insists on the personal freedom of the individual worshiper.

We can decide as much as we want that the solution to the difficulties Ivan poses is a leap of faith or a decision that the sense of what we do when we believe is unknowable, but this doesn't make the Grand Inquisitor's observations any less true. It's not just that they're true; they're *fundamental*.

I can't help thinking, in this connection, of Dostoevskii's unwitting *alter ego* Nietzsche, himself no mean critic of Christianity. From *Beyond Good and Evil* (1886) till the end of his sane life, but especially in *The Genealogy of Morality* (1887), Nietzsche hammered home the theme of Christianity's inversion of a "natural" morality. The "slave revolt" by which a renegade group of Jews in Roman-occupied Palestine came to redefine morality, so that what was formerly strong and noble now came to be oppressive and wicked, while what was formerly weak and abject now came to be humble and virtuous, led to the lamentable set of features that characterized Christianity and in turn Western morality for almost two thousand years. The Catholic Church established its hold on the Western mind essentially by a type of emotional manipulation: the formerly weak and powerless, through a life devoted to self-denial, gained control over the formerly powerful by inspiring in them a sense of guilt and bad conscience. Hence an institution that has sought, with considerable success, "to become master [. . .] over life itself."[1] Nietzsche's condemnation of Christianity is strong stuff. In *Twilight of the Idols* (1889), he referred to the religion as "the hangman's metaphysics," because of the nasty predilection its proponents show for judging, convicting, and punishing.[2] But how much more fundamental is Dostoevskii's critique! In Nietzsche's account, Christianity arose and developed as it did merely owing to an accident of history. The Jewish priestly caste acquired its peculiar character in response to certain conditions, but there was no *necessity* to the emergence of *ressentiment* and the occurrence of the "slave revolt in morality." The priests who established their power on a foundation of bad conscience were, in Nietzsche's eyes, simply opportunists, exploiting human weaknesses in a certain historical moment. The Grand Inquisitor's condemnation, by contrast, is aimed at Christianity's inner core, at the very logic of the ideas on which it is built. If the Catholic Church seized an opportunity, it was one that would have presented itself at any time in history, provided that someone like Jesus came along, claimed divine origin, and asked people to follow him solely on the strength of their own free faith.

This brings me to another observation. Whatever Dostoevskii's attitude toward religion in general and Christianity in particular might really have been, and whatever features he might have endorsed in his moments of faith, he unquestionably made certain assumptions about the religion's basic ideas. For the moment, let's speak only of Christianity as a metaphysical system and leave to one side the more dubious nationalist Christianity Dostoevskii propounded.

1 Giorgio Colli and Mazzino Montinari, *Nietzsche Werke: Kritische Gesamtausgabe* (Berlin: Walter de Gruyter, 1969), VI, 2:381.
2 *Nietzsche Werke*, VI, 3:90.

To him, "Christianity" as a system of thought carried with it certain axiomatic propositions. Here are some of them:

1. There is a suprasensible world to which we have no direct access.

2. In that world dwell, among other things, a set of ideals (such as perfect love and perfect faith) and the secrets of God's justice.

3. The ideal of perfect love is defined as an absolute synthesis of the individual with everyone and everything, with the result that the individual ceases to exist.

4. We are given a set of commandments that we must obey, but it is beyond our power to obey them perfectly.

These propositions, of course, supply the sense of the Masha entry and of Ivan's rebellion. But they also underlie virtually every religious project Dostoevskii describes in his fiction, except for the nationalist one. Sonia Marmeladova declines to answer the question whether she would let Luzhin die or let her stepmother die, since this is a matter of God's justice and we can't know it. Prince Myshkin is a walking definition of the unattainability of perfect love and faith. Bishop Tikhon in *Demons* knows that he can't ask God to move a mountain, because this would reveal the imperfection of his own faith. Father Zosima, before he gets to his Slavophilic speech, urges us to celebrate the mystery of God's designs.

This conception of Christianity furnishes especially rich soil for Dostoevskii's ideas about the nature of belief, though those ideas could probably stand on their own. If you're inclined to think that an individual can properly hold mutually contradictory beliefs at different moments, that beliefs often come in antinomic pairs, and that they are never perfect, you'll find a hospitable reception in a system of thought in which it is axiomatic that true belief is unattainable. Dostoevskii's "theory" of belief, if it can be called that, thus has the twin qualities of being remarkable in its own right and of implicitly forming part of the critique of Christianity that surfaces so often in his writings. Christianity, conceived in the way I've just described, irresistibly leads to a type of believing that threatens the wholeness and internal continuity of the individual personality, Dostoevskii appears to say.

This conception of Christianity furnishes equally rich soil for Dostoevskii's ideas about the individual. If the Christianity that Dostoevskii conceives requires an *ideal* brotherhood, then we find ourselves once again facing an impossible commandment: to surrender our individuality to the collectivity. Just as we're condemned to strive for perfect faith without ever attaining it, we're condemned to be individuals while striving not to be. Of course, Dostoevskii muddies everything the minute he introduces religious nationalism, where a kind of tribal brotherhood stands in for the ideal one and where it is never quite clear what the relation is between the two.

It would be irresponsible to omit religious nationalism from an account of Dostoevskii's religion, dubious though its claim is to be treated as religion. The ease with which Dostoevskii's characters make the passage from a truly metaphysical Christianity to the national one suggests that the national one bears some resemblance to the metaphysical one. The chief point on which the two systems resemble one another is undoubtedly their emphasis on collectivity. No doubt a "synthesis with everything" is very different from a feeling of ethnic community with actual, living Russian peasants, but the idea of the collective is present in both. If Dostoevskii regarded humility as a virtue that would necessarily be associated with Christianity and also regarded this virtue as particularly embodied in the figures of Russian religious men who served as models for some of his characters, then it makes sense that he should regard as exemplary the sort of Christianity that (in his eyes) has been practiced in his own country.

Index

CPSIA information can be obtained
at www.ICGtesting.com
Printed in the USA
BVHW091229101218
535223BV00019B/628/P